MCMASTER UNIVERSITY
VOLUME 3, 1957–1987

JAMES G. GREENLEE

McMaster University

VOLUME 3, 1957–1987
A CHANCE FOR GREATNESS

Published for McMaster University
by
McGill-Queen's University Press
Montreal & Kingston · London · Ithaca

© McGill-Queen's University Press 2015

ISBN 978-0-7735-4492-5 (cloth)
ISBN 978-0-7735-8268-2 (ePDF)
ISBN 978-0-7735-8269-9 (ePUB)

Legal deposit second quarter 2015
Bibliothèque nationale du Québec

Printed in Canada on acid-free paper that is 100% ancient forest free
(100% post-consumer recycled), processed chlorine free

McGill-Queen's University Press acknowledges the support of the
Canada Council for the Arts for our publishing program. We also
acknowledge the financial support of the Government of Canada
through the Canada Book Fund for our publishing activities.

Library and Archives Canada Cataloguing in Publication

McMaster University.

Volume 3 published: Montreal : McGill-Queen's University Press, 2015.
Volume 3 issued in electronic format.
Includes bibliographical references and indexes.
Contents: Volume 3. A chance for greatness, 1957–1987 / James G. Greenlee.
ISBN 978-0-7735-4492-5 (v. 3 : bound). – ISBN 978-0-7735-8268-2 (v.3 : ePDF). –
ISBN 978-0-7735-8269-9 (v. 3 : ePUB)

1. McMaster University – History.

LE3.M32J64   378.713'52   C760-039577
                                    C2014-907582-0

Typeset by Jay Tee Graphics Ltd. in 10/13 Sabon

For

Dr Gary Rush Purdy
– engineer, scholar, gentle man

along with,

R.A. "Andy" Duncan and C. "Curt" Heckaman
– the Great Facilitators

Contents

Acknowledgments

To acknowledge properly all who aided in bringing this book to life would be to draft a passage longer than the volume itself. Within the compass of the possible, however, allow me to scribble inadequate words of thanks to a few among a kind and resourceful legion.

To President (Emeritus) Peter George, my thanks for inviting me home to resume charting the history my alma mater where my life-long mentor, C.M. "Chuck" Johnston, left off. Infectiously enthusiastic, always available, and ever helpful, Dr George rendered this, rather daunting, voyage of discovery far more comfortable for me than it might have been. His successor, President Patrick Deane, has been no less understanding and supportive. Gentlemen: for your patience and the gift of an engaging "retirement project," I thank you.

The true heavy lifting of month-in-month-out coordination, however, fell on the willing shoulders of two irreplaceable people. Thus, the vivacious Karen McQuigge rallied her able team at Alumni House, whenever their considerable service to the cause was required. Meanwhile, Gary Purdy rode shotgun, as chair of the project advisory committee, whose members include some of McMaster's most illustrious veterans: Melvin Preston, Richard Rempel, David Sackett, Alvin Zipursky, James A. Johnson, Anne Newbigging, and Peter George. These accomplished people gave unstintingly of their time and advice. I stand deeply indebted to them all.

Of course, the historian without an archivist is akin to the blind without a guide in unfamiliar territory. In this respect, I could have asked for no better pathfinders than those who led the way, during my years at the William Ready Division of Mills Memorial Library. Carl Spadoni was a gracious, scholarly, and always entertaining host. Rick Stapleton, Bev Bayzat, Renu Barrett, Sheila Turcon, Rob Whitfield, Nicholas Ruest, and Kim Kerr were my tireless Sherpa of the stacks and stashes. Meanwhile, the learned Ken Blackwell helped keep me awake by the example of his own relentless concentration. Hearty thanks must also be extended to Jim and Louise Barber, who give of their "free time" in retirement to catalogue McMaster's enormous photo archives. Their assistance to me was cheerfully given and unstinting.

At Gilmour Hall, my fellow historian Bruce Frank made available invaluable records held by the University Secretariat, as well as supplying keen insight into them. His colleague, Leesa MacKenzie, spared no effort unearthing this, that, or any other priceless item from the catacombs, at a moment's notice. Anne McKeage, archivist at Health Sciences, was a welcoming and open-handed host to my research assistants, as were her colleagues at the Divinity College. Nor could this work have been undertaken without expert assistance from radio wizards at CFMU and the many alumni who helped to compile a magnificent collection of recorded interviews with scores of voices from the past. To each and all, my enduring thanks.

No list of the generous would be complete without mention of the several deans and countless department heads who opened their doors and their files to me and mine, in the quest to find out what transpired "in the trenches," during the period under review. It would, in any case, be impossible to forget the sight of Dean David Wilkinson (now provost), prying open a broom closet in the engineering building, only to unveil a rich vein of high-grade historical ore, much of which found its way into this volume. Above all, I will long be grateful to the genial Ken Cruickshank and the Department of History, who took me in, gave me a home, and all the collegial succour one of Clio's vagabonds could seek. This sustenance included the indispensable assistance of Wendy Benedetti – she who personifies the term *professionalism*.

I was fortunate to have the unflagging help of three dogged research assistants: Maarten Gerritsen, Gary Pedersen, and Heather D. King. With only minimal guidance, they collectively gathered an immense amount of documentation, without which this book could not have been written. Always in good spirits and ever ready, they undertook all and more that was asked of them. The same is true of Gary D. McEwan, who gave freely of his time to photograph hundreds of articles from the *Silhouette*. My thanks, "Ace." Mention must also be made of David Moore, who supplied me with his lovingly compiled record of student organizations. The same holds true for the officers of MUFA and the MSU, who opened their files to nosey investigators, without the slightest hesitation.

Off campus, several people played cardinal roles in keeping me relatively sane, during five years of intense labour. In Hamilton, Duke and Kay O'Sullivan will never know how much their tolerance and kindness meant, daily, to an often grumpy, self-absorbed historian on the road. Sundays with John and Pat Watts were, as ever, a balm to the soul. In like manner, Chuck and Lorna Johnston continued to coddle an ageing, former student. Marcel Faulkner served as Keeper of the Gate, our favourite retreat from a too-noisy world. As for game nights with Mitch, Rocky, Slam, Bat, Xena, Juice, Weasel, Pollux, Turk, Gandalf, Dutch, Jobu, Bubbles, Maestro, Dosi, and Mazz, all I can say is: "Semper Fly"! At home, on "The Rock," eight-ball heroics with Adrian Fowler and Tom Daniels did much to ease the weekly grind. So did sweat-soaked jousts with Martin Ware on the squash court. As always, Olaf and Ellen Janzen offered sumptuous escape, while the Stewarts of St John's suffered gracefully many a harried phone call. Ultimately, of course, my faint, lingering hold on stability depended on the kindly ministrations of my caretaker, Heather Dawn King.

Sincere thanks are, also, extended to Julia Monks and the outstanding editorial team at McGill-Queen's University Press. The sharp-eyed critique and sympathetic assistance of Carol Harrison and Ryan Van Huijstee were beyond price, as they struggled to turn a rough-hewn draft into a readable work of history. May their tribe increase!

In the end, no army of words could ever scale this mountain of debt.

James G. Greenlee
Professor of History (Emeritus)
Grenfell Campus
Memorial University of Newfoundland
2 May 2014

Preface

Since history is the art of interpreting the significant past, as opposed to merely recording all that happened, it is a necessarily selective craft. In this work, the principle of selection is the effort to identify and analyze the general ethos and specific events that gave McMaster its particular personality, during the period from 1957 to 1987. Phrased differently, focus is on the definition and evolution of the whole, rather than on groups or individuals. Thus, some, perhaps many, readers will be disappointed that there is no mention of this or that unquestionably worthy person; no chapters devoted explicitly to women, or minorities, let alone each and every department. Two primary reasons informed these choices. One is the extremely uneven nature of the evidence. The departmental papers of mathematics, for example, lie (quite literally) encased in concrete: victims of mould and mildew. More decisive, however, was the desire to maintain clear thematic, interpretive, and narrative flow. Had whatever evidence exists suggested that the experience of gays, lesbians, women, First Nations people, or visa students was significantly different at McMaster than at other contemporary Canadian universities, it would have been integrated into this study of that which was particular to the university, in the age under review.

Where usage is concerned, the voice of the era has been retained, for the sake of consistency and accuracy. Thus, until very late in the period, there were no "chairpersons"; only "chairmen," regardless the gender of the office holder. In like manner, official documents regularly spoke of all faculty members as "he." The intent, here, is not to spurn today's more enlightened diction but to reflect faithfully the hour. One, for example, would never write of the "chairperson of W.E. Gladstone's cabinet committee on tariffs." If offence be taken, please be assured that none is intended.

Abbreviations

ACAP	Advisory Committee on Academic Planning
ACUA	Advisory Committee on University Affairs
AECL	Atomic Energy Canada Ltd.
AUCC	Association of Universities and Colleges of Canada
BIU	basic income unit
BSCAP	Board-Senate Committee on Academic Planning
CAAT	Colleges of Applied Arts and Technology
CAP	Committee on Academic Policy
CAUT	Canadian Association of University Teachers
COPSE	Commission on Post-Secondary Education
COU	Council of Ontario Universities
CPUO	Committee of Presidents of the Universities of Ontario
CRL	Communications Research Laboratory
CUA	Committee on University Affairs
CUS	Canadian Union of Students
FIRA	Foreign Investment Review Agency
FSU	French Student Union
GSA	Graduate Students Association
HMRI	Hamilton Medical Research Institute
IMR	Institute for Materials Research
IRC	Inter-Residence Council
LRPC	Long-Range Planning Committee
MCAT	Medical College Admission Test
MIES	McMaster Institute of Energy Studies
MNR	McMaster Nuclear Reactor
MQTWW	McMaster, Queen's, Toronto, Waterloo, and Western (Universities)

MRC   Medical Research Council of Canada
MSM   McMaster Student Movement
MSU   McMaster Students Union
MUFA   McMaster University Faculty Association
MUMC   McMaster University Medical Centre
NDG   negotiated development grant
NOMP   Northwestern Ontario Medical Program
NRC   National Research Council
NSERC   National Science and Engineering Research Council
OATRU   Organic and Associated Terrain Research Unit
OCGS   Ontario Council of Graduate Studies
OGS   Ontario Graduate Scholarships
PBAC   President's Budget Advisory Committee
PBL   problem-based learning
RBG   Royal Botanical Gardens
SDS   Students for a Democratic Society
SDU   Students for a Democratic University
SEC   Student Executive Council
SOCS   Society of Off-Campus Students
SQUAL   Subcommittee on the Quality of Academic Life
SRA   Student Representative Assembly
SSHRC   Social Science and Humanities Research Council

George P. Gilmour

Henry G. "Harry" Thode

Arthur N. "Art" Bourns

Alvin A. Lee

Howard E. "Howie" Petch

H.E. "Harry" Duckworth

Melvin A. "Mel" Preston

Daniel M. "Mike" Hedden

Edward Togo Salmon (left)
with William Ready

John W. "Jack" Hodgins

John S. "Jack" Kirkaldy

William Ready in
the Russell archives

Martin Johns

Gordon Vichert holds his
controversial report

Ed Sanders

George Grant

John R. Evans

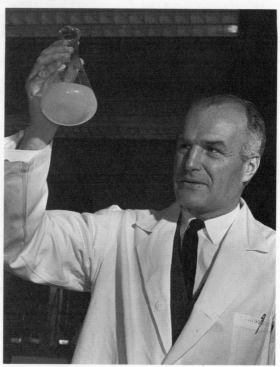

J. Fraser Mustard

C. Barber "Barb" Mueller

Eberhard Zeidler

McMaster Nuclear Reactor

Open Senate Meeting, 28 March 1974

The Great McMaster Elm, winter 1954

MCMASTER UNIVERSITY
VOLUME 3, 1957-1987

INTRODUCTION

The University as Protagonist

To author a volume in the history of one's alma mater is a singular honour. To do so, however, as successor to C.M. Johnston, is to render an already considerable challenge even more daunting. Still, it is always a luxury to follow an astute pathfinder, and, thanks to him, the way ahead is clear.

Picking up where he left off, the task is to interpret McMaster's striking metamorphosis during the period from 1957 to 1987, when not only the size, but the fundamental ethos of the university underwent dramatic change. Here, the word *interpret* is used advisedly, not casually, because this is a work of history, not a simple chronicle, or extended yearbook. Thus, an effort to understand the most basic forces that shaped modern McMaster must focus on the university as an evolving whole. Simply put, the institution, rather than its constituent parts, will be the protagonist of this story.

The reason for this is simple enough. Like people, Canadian universities share much of their "DNA" in common. How, then, might one distinguish one from another? Why bother to try? In reply, it might be said that the principal justification for penning the history of an individual university must reside in clarifying its particular personality and its relation to broader currents of the day. In McMaster's case, a central theme fairly leaps out. In less than thirty years, the university was designedly transformed from a modest confessional college into what could justifiably be termed Canada's "Little Big U." Indeed, by 1987, a still relatively compact McMaster was perfectly capable of holding its own, in select fields, among Canadian siblings of much greater size.

Approaching the university's history from this angle need not entail either an exclusively top-down vantage point or a strident triumphalism. After all, institutional redefinition proved to be the work of many hands. Meanwhile, it never went unchallenged. Nor was all sweetness, light, linear progress, and collegial concord. Such things, obviously, are foreign to any inherently dialectical institution; especially one afloat on a rushing tide of social, economic, technological, and other change. Similarly, as McMaster assumed a new sense of purpose, dead ends, lopsided emphases, and outright failures were not uncommon. Dissent, within and without its walls, was far from rare. All this must be acknowledged and given fair attention.

That said, during the period under review, there emerged at McMaster a dominant paradigm of development. This evolved out of a matrix of basic assumptions that would inform the entire post-Baptist era and leave a deep, lingering footprint. Central to this was a burning desire, not merely to grow but to transform a once unpretentious undergraduate enclave into a medium-sized powerhouse synonymous with the highest attainment in research and graduate study. J.S. "Jack" Kirkaldy captured this spirit succinctly when, in a 1967 report to the senate, he dared to declare that "McMaster has a chance for greatness."[1] The fact that he was not immediately laughed out of the chamber indicated that something deep in McMaster's collective psyche had shifted to alter its time-honoured posture of reserve.

In all this, no single individual better personified the focused ambition at work than eminent scientist Henry G. "Harry" Thode, who was university president from 1961 to 1972. It was he, above all others, who nurtured the seeds of aspiration and oversaw expansive growth in the 1960s. In truth, many of his core ideas remain pertinent on campus as the new millennium rolls on. Accordingly, it is to the rise, institutionalization, and persistence of what might be called the "Thodean ethos" that one must turn if one is to understand the animating spirit of McMaster University: this history's protagonist.

I

According to Harry

"Baptist Control Ends," declared the *Silhouette*'s banner headline on Friday 21 September 1956. Word had just come that secularization was imminent, and the student paper hastened into print. Potentially anxious readers were assured that there was no cause for alarm, since little fundamental change was expected. After all, said the *Sil*, certain deeply rooted principles already guided McMaster along lines fully compatible with most small, secular universities on the continent. Indeed, thanks to the latitude long afforded by an enlightened Baptist Convention, McMaster enjoyed a decidedly liberal ethos. Thus, early and excessive specialization were eschewed, while core requirements, spanning a broad range of general knowledge, knit the community together, rather like the "Kitten" sweaters and "Mac" jackets ubiquitous on campus.[1]

Within a week, however, "Keep It Small" became the watchword of the same undergraduate scribes. Now, rumour had it that both unprecedented numbers and (heaven forbid) professional schools were to be added to the established scene. Suddenly, there seemed to be plenty of cause for concern. Citing the law of diminishing returns, the journal argued that a rush to growth could have deleterious effects on student–faculty relations, while degrading the quality of education. "In the usual manner of accepting something better," ran editorial opinion, "this campus may not realize that its excellence is partially due to its size." Worse still, professional faculties might not integrate smoothly with existing liberal values. Instead, the likely outcome was a large group of segregated buildings dedicated to churning out those who specialized in "a well-indexed store of facts."[2] Several students' letters to the editor, such as that from Gordon Vichert, agreed, noting that McMaster had always emphasized learning in the broadest sense, rather than the production of "highly skilled units for industry."[3] This was a theme to which Vichert would later return as a professor.

An ambivalent president George Gilmour, no doubt, nodded in silent empathy as he perused these columns. Although a father of the new university, he yet remained very much a son of old McMaster. Such was readily apparent in his 1960 presidential remarks, when all manner of change was proceeding visibly apace. "This rush to the universities," he wrote, "and this crying up of the power of education has a frightening as well as an encouraging side." The president worried that people would expect mere growth automatically to herald a vaguely defined, but inevitably better, tomorrow. As well, Gilmour was concerned that burgeoning specialization might threaten cherished liberal learning. Still, he added, "To recognize the existence of this danger is to possess some power to avert it."[4] Ambivalent or not, Gilmour was committed to expansion; not that there was much choice, given the imperatives of the hour.

Prominent among these was the inescapable need to respond to public demand. From the Rowell-Sirois Commission (1940), through the Massey Report (1951), to the Royal Commission on Canada's Economic Prospects (1957), various observers had called official attention to a correlation between higher education and national well-being.[5] By the late fifties, this message filtered down to the general public, at which time it was embraced with a hitherto unimaginable fervour. The story of how unprecedented prosperity, the baby boom, soaring consumer expectations, and not a few Cold War anxieties fuelled the mania for university degrees is a twice-told tale.[6] No local phenomenon, it gathered force in all developed states, reaching a crescendo in the sixties. Specific to McMaster, however, was the cardinal fact that Hamilton stood at, or very near, the Canadian epicentre of those developments: the so-called Golden Horseshoe. Indeed, within that arc, sweeping round the head of Lake Ontario from Oshawa to Niagara Falls, the intertwined postwar booms registered a heavily concentrated impact.

Economically, an ebullient Hamilton positively roared during the smokestack era's resounding, last hurrah. From the end of war until the early seventies, the "Ambitious City" rose to be the thriving capital of Canadian heavy industry. Westinghouse, International Harvester, Otis Elevator, National Steel Car, and sundry other substantial firms offered jobs aplenty. The making of steel, however, dwarfed all other endeavours. Canada's giants in the field, Stelco and Dofasco, afforded truly mass employment. Smaller, specialty outfits, such as Burlington Steel, Slater Steel, Hamilton Bridge and Tank, and scores of spinoff companies also flourished. With the opening of the St Lawrence Seaway in 1959, the cost of imported iron ore fell, rendering steel all the more profitable. Later, the 1965 Auto Pact created an insatiable, nearby market, as sprawling branch plants of the American "Big

Three" thundered into production across southern Ontario.[7] All told, by the early seventies, Hamilton's share of Canada's steel output was in excess of 70 per cent.[8] There was, to be sure, a period of slower growth during the so-called Diefenbaker Recession (1957–61). The Steel City, however, rode this out better than many other locales, and its populace reaped the reward in the form of increased purchasing power, even for the common labourer.[9]

Inextricably linked with all this was a potent local edition of the nation-wide population explosion. Gilmour, for one, was sharply aware that, second only to Toronto, Hamilton was the fastest growing city in Canada.[10] In 1942, its population was 167,855.[11] By 1959, natural increase and rising immigration required the doubling of civic limits and the expansion of bordering suburbs, as Greater Hamilton came to embrace fully 327,831 inhabitants.[12] Two years later, it was proudly (albeit inaccurately) announced that the city had supplanted Winnipeg as Canada's fourth-largest urban centre.[13] Within months, the metropolitan Planning Board projected (erroneously) that, by 1985, Hamilton would be home to no fewer than 740,000.[14]

While the full extent of this economic and demographic explosion was only dimly perceived in 1957, it was already clear that keeping McMaster even smallish would be a chore. Later, a new factor made this all but impossible. Wholly unforeseen, a prolonged spike in the post-secondary participation rate would mark the boomers off from all earlier generations. As early as 1955, the National Conference of Canadian Universities forecast that university enrolments would double by 1965.[15] In fact, they did so within eight years, as a greater proportion of eighteen-year-olds elected the higher educational route. No mere blip, per capita participation rose even more dramatically for almost a decade thereafter. By 1969, Canada stood second only to the United States in the proportion of those eligible who opted to attend university.[16] The reasons for this were manifold, but bounding prosperity, the chance for upward mobility, and pleas for social justice, certainly helped feed the trend.

Unfailing clairvoyance was in short supply, but thinking at McMaster was informed by an at least vague glimmer of what lay ahead. In 1957, for example, it was estimated that enrolment, currently hovering around 1,000, might jump as high as 3,000 by 1965.[17] Meanwhile, there were even more novel features on the shifting scene. Not only were numbers swiftly rising; the composition of the student body was being radically altered. Thus, first-generation, blue-collar applicants were starting to outnumber those who came from families with long traditions of higher learning. Furthermore, a good many of these newcomers were children of recent immigrants from southern and central Europe.[18] On this latter score, the *Hamilton Spectator* took particular note of a powerful drive toward social mobility within the city's substantial Italian community. "There is," said the *Spec*, "enormous prestige for the people on a street off James North that boasts six professional men out of the eight boys who once played together."[19] With Quinto Martini elected to the House of Commons (1957) and Frank Cosentino quarterbacking the University of Western Ontario Mustangs to a national championship (1959), denizens of James North had living proof that a university education was well worth overtime at the mill. Accordingly, in common with longer-established locals of many social stripes, new Canadians joined the growing press of first-timers knocking at McMaster's door. In this situation, Gilmour ruminated: "McMaster faces a real problem in getting the University through its students as well as getting its students through the University."[20] Some nostalgia for accustomed homogeneity aside, the newcomers were welcomed, even by a once cautious student press.

"Keep It Small," in fact, had died a quick death in the pages of the *Silhouette*. By 1958, the paper was voicing popular anxieties that led in quite the opposite direction. First, Sputnik had "lashed a large slice from the western ego."[21] Russia, it was argued, raced ahead of the West, thanks largely to Soviet willingness to support legions of advanced students with cold, hard cash.[22] Meanwhile, as well as Canada was doing, the United States, Germany, and Japan were outstripping the Dominion both economically and educationally.[23] Given all this, student council president Don Stratton issued an academic call to arms; one in tune with myriad others resounding nationwide. Canada, he proclaimed, must produce more university graduates, lest it sink to the level of an under-developed country. The sacred trust of government, he continued, was to ensure that McMaster and her sisters had the wherewithal to expand and that every capable individual was offered support.[24] As it happened, federal and provincial governments were already in general sympathy with such arguments. From 1951 on, public spending on universities rose at a steadily increasing rate.[25] Then, in 1959, Ontario's treasurer officially committed the province to universal access for every qualified candidate.[26] The means by which this was to be achieved were left fuzzily defined, to say the very least. The basic policy, however, would remain gospel thereafter.

Within this heated context, late-fifties McMaster scrambled to meet the anticipated flood of students. At least there was time to prepare. Backed firmly by a supportive board of governors and significantly larger operating grants from government, Gilmour began the "stockpiling of staff" as early as 1957; yearly hiring more than immediately needed, against the day when the university would be unable to bid successfully for first-class faculty in an exhausted market.[27] Meanwhile, he struck a deal with the Royal Botanical Gardens for the purchase of lands adjacent to the university sufficient to accommodate the expansion of campus facilities.[28] Simultaneously, a twelve-year, two-phase construction scheme was laid out by the planning and building committee of the board, with phase one extending to 1960 and the next to 1965. Armed with this detailed plan, Gilmour approached Queen's Park with a well-reasoned plea for capital assistance.[29] He was aware, however, that it would weaken his case were he to approach government as a penniless or (seemingly) uncommitted supplicant.[30] As he later wrote, "I understand that even heaven, let alone the Province of Ontario, is willing to help those who help themselves."[31] Accordingly, the board launched an expansion campaign to raise $3 million for capital projects, with 1960 as the target date.[32]

On the whole, things went according to plan; so much so that, by 1961, alumni of yesteryear would have needed a guidebook to tour their reconfigured alma mater. An impressive engineering complex now stood near the refurbished home of physical sciences. Tucked discretely behind these was McMaster's nuclear reactor. Visually unimposing but symbolically potent, it was the first to grace a Canadian or Commonwealth campus. Across the grassy mall, a new arts and administration building stood replete with offices, classrooms, a handsome council chamber, and spacious bookstore. It was Gilmour's fondest wish that this signal building be dubbed Carey Fox Hall. After all, the selfless man in question was the longest-serving governor on any university board in Canada, with forty-seven years to his credit by 1960. Moreover, since 1954, unprompted and without publicity, he had privately shelled out more than $750,000 to bolster McMaster's endowment, most of this during the post-1957 recession.[33]

Typically, the self-effacing Fox declined the invitation, despite the unanimous endorsement of Gilmour's suggestion by enthusiastic governors.[34] Later, as fate (and no small dose of irony) would have it, Fox was on hand when Gilmour Hall was christened. Meanwhile, additional residences had sprung up, and accommodation doubled as Whidden and Moulton Halls welcomed males and females, respectively. Wentworth House, named after McMaster's home county, opened as a student centre where, it was hoped, the off-campus majority might meet and mingle informally with resident classmates, as well as the occasional faculty member, thereby fostering a sense of community. Closest to Baptist hearts, of course, stood the new Divinity College; a structure of "striking appearance" whose "inspiring chapel," Gilmour thought, might offer continuity and a different kind of focal point.[35]

Clearly, the visible face of McMaster was changing, as was that of every university in Ontario. Beneath glossy superstructure, however, lay the far deeper issue of framing, as Gilmour put it, "an adequate philosophy of education" for a mass age.[36] Several options were on offer during the first heady "rush to the universities." Initially, different institutions defined individual notions of their particular missions. Carleton and York, for example, committed early to a broad, liberal concept of higher education.[37] Waterloo, by contrast, adopted a specific emphasis on applied knowledge, with engineering as its centrepiece.[38] Toronto, as ever, loomed over all, with its claim to be the provincial university, competent at all degree levels across myriad fields.[39] As time wore on, all, to one extent or another, were to follow a similar comprehensive-cum-research path toward what Clark Kerr would call the "multiversity."[40] This was thanks to variety of powerful steering forces.

Civic pride was one such factor. No one wanted to father a truncated feeder college in an age when full, degree-granting universities were prized status symbols. Meanwhile, across a province bigger than western Europe, parents asked why their deserving children should have to bear the expense of travel to distant centres to study that which could be provided nearer home. Under these pressures, Queen's Park found it politically difficult to limit the charters of soon-to-be-numerous new universities. This would apply to both undergraduate and graduate instruction. Where the latter was concerned, calls to expand advanced work were spawned, in part, by intense competition for suddenly scarce faculty, whether foreign or domestic. Clearly, Canada would have to groom more of its own. Such would be a major conclusion of the Deutsch Commission, which, in 1962, called for a crash program to generate more Ontario-bred doctorates.[41] In any event, university leaders, on the hunt for faculty, were finding it increasingly difficult to recruit the best and the brightest without the lure of graduate supervision and research opportunity.

Successive Ontario Cabinets understood all these matters only too well. Indeed, by the late sixties, government "formula funding" was so heavily weighted toward graduate programs that every institution of higher learning was competing avidly for advanced students.[42] McMaster would be no exception, save for one crucial fact: many of the steering forces noted above were leading in the direction some key figures on campus had long been aching to go. As luck would have it, these people were rising to positions of influence at precisely the opportune moment.

As early as 1955, Gilmour's vigour had begun to flag, enough so that a concerned Carey Fox urged him to pace himself more carefully and to delegate more often.[43] The next few years, unfortunately, offered slim chance

of rest. Negotiating with the Convention, Queen's Park, the City, Hamilton College, and sundry others, the president was hip-deep in the taxing
legal and physical transformation of McMaster. Inevitably, this exacted a
heavy toll on his already dwindling personal resources. So too, one suspects,
did the evidence of rising tension on campus. It would be too simple to set
this internecine strain down to a straightforward clash featuring hidebound
traditionalists in arts versus brazen reformers in science and the professions.
While there was something to that, Gilmour perceived the conflict in more
subtle terms. The root, he thought, was "the unfortunate division of opinion
between the old college and the new university."[44]

Nothing illustrated this better than the wrangling sparked by a curriculum study that the senate launched in 1957. A committee, chaired by J.E.L.
"John" Graham, was charged with reviewing the structure and philosophy
of undergraduate education as McMaster eased into its new public role.
It was expected to report within the year.[45] In the end, the exercise proved
complex and heated, with champions of old and new academic visions scattered, in varying measure, across arts and sciences alike. As a result, the
committee's recommendations were not submitted until 1961. A younger,
more energetic Gilmour might have taken a major role in expediting this
formative academic debate. By 1958, however, he was nearing the end of
his strength. Increasingly, he was subject to bouts of sudden and extreme
fatigue. In 1960, the underlying cause of these episodes was finally diag-
nosed. Writing to historian Gerald S. Graham, the president confided, "I am
under permanent orders to watch an incurable disability, aortic stenosis, but
there is every chance that I can outlive Olympic athletes yet, provided I do
little and sleep much."[46] Scant months later, however, he was far less san-
guine. "News of myself is only fair," he told Yale scholar, Roland Bainton.[47]
Under these circumstances, Gilmour was grateful to turn the burden of
day-to-day matters over to others. D.M. "Mike" Hedden, hitherto assistant director of research, was made business administrator of the university. Meanwhile, Gilmour's dynamic vice-president, Harry Thode, was given
authority over all matters academic, as of 1 July 1960.[48] A year later, he
would succeed an exhausted Gilmour as president.

Here, it is important to note that individuals do matter. True, a nexus
of grand structural forces shapes the general nature of society and defines
the limits of the possible at any given time. Still, some measure of choice,
however constrained, remains, and people do the choosing. At a micro-
historical level, therefore, it was of supreme importance to McMaster's long-
term development that Thode came to power when he did. While Gilmour
had accepted the necessity of change, he had done so rather in the spirit of

accommodating the inevitable. He had presided over the strenuous process of secularization with courage, a silver tongue, and political finesse. In short, for that particular task, he was undoubtedly the right person, in the right place, at the right time. He was less than comfortable, however, with the times themselves, and somewhat torn as to the course the new McMaster should chart.[49]

Thus, Gilmour was cautious about any move that might tip the balance against the university's time-honoured focus on liberal education.[50] Similarly, he acknowledged that more attention to research and graduate work was needed. This would be good for staff morale, as well as McMaster's prestige, but he hastened to remind all that "the University's fundamental duty is still the education of undergraduates."[51] In like manner, he supported engineering and could even foresee the advent of a medical school on campus.[52] At the end of the day, however, no clarion call to reimagine a wholly new future for McMaster issued from Gilmour, ever the loyal son of "a Christian school of learning." By contrast, *carpe diem* might have been emblazoned on Harry Thode's office door, such was his ardour to seize opportunities of the moment and, in the process, cast the university in a new mould. As Alvin Lee would later note, "It was Thode, more than anyone else, who changed the university's character for the foreseeable future."[53] One could go further to observe that, while the paradigm he outlined for McMaster was never fully realized, the ethos Thode engendered remains very much alive in the new millennium.

Never one to equivocate, Thode made plain the animating spirit he wished to instill, shortly after being offered the presidency upon an ailing Gilmour's decision to leave office. In May 1961, he wrote to Ben Bradley, vice-president of International Harvester and a governor of the university, confessing his surprise at the sudden turn of events, but stating emphatically: "McMaster University has had a great start and it will be a challenge to make it the best university in Canada."[54] This bold declaration was no mere rhetorical flourish, tossed off by an excited neophyte anxious to impress all and sundry with bubbly enthusiasm at the outset of his tenure. Rather, it encapsulated a deep-laid sense of mission Thode had long embraced and strove to inculcate from his earliest days on campus until his last. This new, questing tone, this urgent drive to excel would worry some colleagues and inspire others, as he came to office. Few, however, would have been surprised by his message.

This is not the place to repeat at length that which has already been ably described by C.M. Johnston and Thode's biographers concerning his life prior to 1957.[55] Suffice it to say that he was what David Lloyd George had called a "man of push and go," in an earlier generation. This is not to imply that he was in any way loud, loutish, or abrasive. Quite the opposite, Thode was soft-spoken, outwardly reserved, and publicly polite; the image of a prairie gentleman from sturdy Saskatchewan stock. Beneath this mild exterior, however, stood controlled ambition harnessed to a keen mind, an iron constitution, and a genuine love of both physical and mental labour. Allied to these attributes was an almost romantic eclecticism; one that left him impatient with those who could not see beyond disciplinary walls to the more holistic vision of science he embraced. As a graduate student (Chicago) and post-doctoral fellow (Columbia), he had explored the blossoming field of atomic research, a realm that welcomed free-ranging problem-solvers from across the scientific spectrum, regardless of disciplinary pedigree.[56] The experience marked him for life.

Thus, Thode came to McMaster in 1939, as much a physicist as he was a chemist. He dove headlong into isotopic research, enthralled by its potential for myriad applications to pure and applied science alike, not to mention the factory floor or the medical office. Both prolific and seminal, his publications brought him international recognition, including induction into London's elite Royal Society (1954). By the time Gilmour retired, Thode had also been entrusted with considerable decision-making authority. Director of research since 1947, he succeeded Charles Burke as principal of Hamilton College in 1949. Six years later, he retained these offices, while assuming the mantle of vice-president of the, now secularized, university as a whole. When Gilmour stepped down, there was really no question as to who should fill his place.

Tight-knit Hamilton College was the most dynamic wing of the university. This fact, along with the fifties' craze for science, virtually ensured that the new president would come from the laboratories, rather than the stacks. Decades later, celebrated mathematician Bernard Banaschewski looked back on that time and wistfully recalled Thode strolling the halls of Hamilton College "like a king."[57] In short, the choice was obvious, except to some nervous faculty in arts. Crucially, board chairman Carey Fox threw his substantial weight behind Thode, who he thought well suited to bring regional business and industrial leaders into closer touch with McMaster.[58] For his part, Thode had no craving for high office in and for itself. He was a research hound, at home in the fraternal atmosphere of Hamilton College, which he had done so much to shape. Anxious to guard his laboratory time, he was also uncomfortable in the limelight. Signals of sincere support from other elements on campus no doubt had some influence on him. For example, had he been hewn from stone, Thode might have been unmoved by Marion Bates' words concerning his appointment. "I should like to say," wrote the dean of women, "how proud I have been of the magic name 'Dr. Harry Thode' as I have travelled – of the respect you command as a scholar and a fine person."[59] While, no doubt heartened by endorsement from one of the old guard, on balance, it was the opportunity to transfer the energy and ethos of the college to the university at large that was decisive in his mind. Gilmour and Burke had given him almost unfettered rein. He dared not risk reversal by leaving the presidency to chance.[60] With a dose of "push and go," Thode was convinced that McMaster could compete with the best, and the competitor in him duly refocused at the institutional level. Accordingly, he took the plunge. He did so, moreover, as a man with a plan, a clear idea of what a fully modern university ought to be.

Thode, although bursting with ideas and consistent in his views, was not philosophically inclined. He was no latter-day Cardinal Newman, wont to ruminate on the university as an abstract concept. Rather, Thode was a pragmatist, concerned with spelling out that which was best for McMaster in the here and now. Thus, one could plumb his sundry addresses, letters, and writings without ever discovering a stand-alone, fully articulated "mission statement," as such broad visions are now termed. Still, a coherent matrix of interwoven ideas fairly jumps into view, once his utterances and actions as president are considered as a whole. Together, they constituted something approaching a paradigm of development for the new McMaster. For clarity's sake, it might be wise to trace, in outline, the interlaced filaments of that matrix, before discussing them in detail.

As Thode saw it, McMaster had the potential to be a medium-sized, but aggressively front-rank, multi-faculty university. The secret, he believed, was focus. Indeed, he was a firm believer in "differentiation" long before the term became a Queen's Park buzzword. To that end, he believed that McMaster should not grow in all directions at once. Instead, he contended, it should seek targeted excellence in fields of established strength, or areas of carefully defined, specific promise. Wherever possible, research and graduate studies should be cultivated assiduously, for out of them grew the stature and esteem that attracted the best faculty, as well as the strongest students, be they raw freshmen or aspiring doctoral candidates. Drawing on his own experience, Thode held that work on the true frontiers of knowledge was best done in an interdisciplinary environment; again, whenever possible. In this, critical mass was essential, while uncontrolled growth was the enemy of fruitful cross-fertilization. Thus, Thode planned for a small, compact campus with disciplinary relatives in close proximity to one another. Besides, he was enough the old college man to wish to preserve that sense of community, which had long characterized the university. Finally, he believed that only a reinvigorated, research-intensive McMaster could offer the community beyond its ivy walls meaningful service in an age of big booms. Such, had he ever sat down to pull it all together, was the mission statement of Harry Thode.[61]

An exchange with University of Toronto president Claude Bissell offers a good starting point for exploring the Thodean paradigm. In 1962, the urbane Bissell was chair of the recently formed Committee of Ontario University Presidents (CPUO). Its function was to counsel the Advisory Committee on University Affairs (ACUA). The latter was a provincially appointed "buffer body," which recommended to Queen's Park (supposedly at arm's length) on matters concerning higher education.[62] With new institutions clamouring for accreditation, seemingly every week, an uneasy Bissell sought Thode's thoughts about the place and priority they should be afforded in an emerging Ontario system. How, he asked, might one fairly distinguish between a college and a full university? The subtext, of course, was a question as to who ought to have first and highest call on provincial resources. Bissell scarcely had time to blink before Thode's unequivocal reply was on his desk.

Thode isolated the right to confer doctoral degrees as the defining characteristic of a university. The Torontonian, ever gracious, thanked Thode handsomely for crystallizing thoughts on the issue, while sending along a draft of definitions intended for the edification of government. "A University," Bissell asserted, "is a multi-faculty institution of higher learning with a Faculty of Arts and Science, at least one of the major professional faculties and a graduate school that offers the Doctor's degree in a number of areas." A college, on the other hand, "is an institution of higher learning with a Faculty of Arts and Science only, and during its early stages [is] affiliated with a parent university and receiving provincial support only through the parent institution."[63] Reading this, Thode must have whispered a quiet "amen," albeit a qualified one, since he was quite prepared to go further in assigning appropriate places to new boys on the block.

Indeed, Thode was an early and staunch advocate of what was later called the "two-tier" approach to rationalizing higher education in Ontario. He hinted at this in his first presidential report (1961–62), asking how many fully developed universities (in Bissell's sense) Ontario could reasonably support.[64] Next year, he waxed far more assertive. Since 1960, he noted, there had been many new institutions, as well as older liberal arts colleges, which had indicated a desire to offer doctoral programs. Was this, in any way, realistic? Thode, most emphatically, thought not. Pointing to the patience, time, and expense required to forge a worthy graduate school, he also underlined the current shortage of first-class researchers and qualified students. Ontario, he continued, had a few, well-developed universities in a position to expand their advanced programs and blossom forth. "However," he warned, "if we insist on every institution having a graduate school and reject the American pattern of junior colleges, senior colleges and liberal arts colleges, outright, then we will surely be in trouble." Driving the point home, Thode observed that, while there were more than 2,000 homes of higher learning in the United States, only 40 were considered to be in the top echelon of research and graduate study. If Ontario hoped to compete in the first division, he avowed, its resources would have to be husbanded and concentrated.[65]

The 1962 Deutsch Report had called for an all-out push to enlarge graduate study and research in Ontario. That plea, of course, rang sweetly in Thode's ears. Less pleasing, however, was the loud scramble of every Tom, Dick, and Brand-New U to get in on the action. "Very thick in the growing university battle," Thode would hammer away at the theme of differentiation, time and again.[66] Nor was he shy in stating McMaster's claim to stand among those few institutions in the upper tier. As one contemporary candidly put it, he could be "single-minded to a fault."[67] He could also be quite blunt. Taking up the cudgel in January 1963, he fired off a missive to J.R. McCarthy, secretary to the ACUA. Echoing Deutsch, he agreed that the greatest problem of the coming decade would be to train sufficient professors to handle the swelling onslaught of undergraduates in Ontario. He vigorously rejected, however, the notion that any "crash program," such as had been developed to meet the postwar veteran bulge, would suffice, in this instance. Current growth was vastly larger in scale and likely to increase with time. Nor could he support the idea of creating graduate schools out of thin air on newborn campuses.

Instead, he argued, the great load of advanced work should be borne by those three or four Ontario universities, Toronto, Queen's, McMaster, and Western, best equipped by experience, planning, and reputation to do so. This was the high road to quality. To duplicate would be to dilute. As for new institutions, such as Brock and Trent, it was Thode's "considered judgment that the expansion of higher education in Ontario should be in the form of feeder campuses (junior colleges) for one or more of the established universities." He allowed that the day might come when such colleges would earn their university spurs, but that would take a long time. For the moment, he urged ACUA to emphasize the unique needs of those particular institutions which had already achieved critical mass in research and graduate training. "We can," he assured McCarthy, "forge ahead, if given support."[68]

Argue as he might, Thode entertained few illusions about the realities of the situation. This did not mean that he accepted them with equanimity, however. Writing to Bill Schneider of the National Research Council (NRC), he confessed to mounting frustration with his political and bureaucratic masters. Growing dependence on government largesse, he told his fellow chemist, meant reliance on the goodwill of ACUA, a body composed (until 1964) exclusively of civil servants. Unfortunately, he explained, this was not a committee of experts, but a part-time group of laymen who knew little of the actual details of university affairs. Nor did they seem much interested in acquiring hands-on knowledge. Thus, he reported that the committee had only briefly visited McMaster and Queen's not at all. Thode wrote that he and others had "tried to explain to them the difference between graduate and undergraduate students and between master's and PhD students," but to little avail.

Instead, eight universities had already signalled a desire to proceed with graduate work. Meanwhile, unlimited charters had just been issued to York, Brock, and Trent, each backed by strident "citizens' committees who want graduate schools to be established overnight." At York, he noted, President Murray Ross was bent on getting started immediately. Thode exploded: "It took McMaster seventy-five years!" As though all this were not enough, there were rumours that Oshawa, Sarnia, and Oakville were preparing to enter the great game. Academic planning, he fumed, was being trumped by political pressure and grants were being calculated on nothing more sophisticated than aggregate student numbers.

"What we need, of course," he told Schneider, "is a university Grants Commission [as in Britain] free from politics of all kinds, which could lay down a plan for Ontario and which could allocate funds to the different universities." As a start, he suggested a Royal Commission; one tasked to bring order to and define priorities amid the incessant sprawl. As ever, Thode had a model ready to hand for presentation to any such prospective inquiry. He drew on the system growing south of the border in sunny California. There, he explained, extensive doctoral work would be the province of five or six multi-faculty campuses, such as Berkeley, UCLA, and La Jolla. Each of these would be restricted in size and fed by a state-wide network of senior and junior colleges forbidden to do graduate work. This arrangement, he thought, offered the universal and local accessibility demanded in a democratic age, while preserving the essential difference between undergraduate and advanced study. Still, as he told Schneider, until something like this developed at home, "a university must have a story to tell," a tale unique to itself, if it were to carve out a special place amid the rough and tumble of Ontario's higher educational politics.[69] As things transpired, Harry could spin a rattling good yarn, when he had to. Indeed, he did so yearly in annual budget submissions to government, via ACUA and its successor, the Committee on University Affairs (CUA).

We tend to look back on the sixties as halcyon days, when money flowed torrentially downhill and the living was easy. While there is some retrospective truth in this, things seemed far less simple to Thode, the aggressive leader of a small university on the make. To be sure, the Progressive Conservative governments of Leslie Frost and John P. Robarts were firm supporters of higher education. Still, beyond established base funding, nothing further could be taken for granted by any institution in any given year. For Thode, who yearned to transform McMaster into an elite research university, there were always resources well beyond a comfortable minimum to be sought. Thus, in approaching Queen's Park, he crafted annual sales pitches that sold his university's "story" in a well-documented and thoroughly consistent fashion. The tale was always the same; only the numbers varied.[70]

The narrative line Thode constructed for bureaucrats combined something approaching historical teleology, backed by hard statistical evidence. As he took pains to note, prior to 1947 only five Canadian universities had conferred doctoral degrees. Immediately after the war, University of British Columbia, Western, and McMaster joined that exclusive group. Since the award of its first PhD, in 1951, McMaster had systematically developed its offerings until 1964; when fifteen doctoral programs were firmly in place, with several more in the offing.[71] The unmistakable message was that McMaster's claim to special status as a full university were historically prior to those of newcomers. Moreover, its progress in that direction was presented as inexorable. Drawing on figures compiled by the Dominion Bureau of Statistics, Thode illustrated that, in 1965, McMaster stood third in Ontario and eighth Canada-wide among institutions churning out PhDs. As for total graduate enrolments in the province, the university stood in second place, with Toronto and bursting Waterloo tied for first.[72] These, however, were merely raw numbers. As Thode packaged them, the key statistics were proportional, rather than absolute.

During Gilmour's last year in office, the graduate corps at McMaster stood near 7 per cent of total full-time enrolment. This ratio was almost double that found at most neighbouring universities, save Toronto, and well above the national average of 5 per cent.[73] Between 1960 and 1963, the proportion had risen steadily, from 6.9 to 12.1 per cent. As Dean Harry Duckworth calculated, this was one of the highest graduate-to-undergraduate correlations in Canada.[74] This was music to President Thode's ears. Indeed, as general enrolment grew, he twice speculated in print whether it might be best that McMaster restrict undergraduate admissions, in order to concentrate on honours programs, graduate students, and research.[75] In January 1963, Thode was telling ACUA that planning at McMaster envisaged 500 graduates alongside 3,500 undergraduates within two years. By 1970, he continued, the figures would be 1,000 and 7,000 respectively.[76] Some months later, Thode revised this estimate for the minister of education, indicating that graduate students might well constitute 25 per cent of McMaster's full-time complement, by 1975.[77] This prognostication had to be modified, as competing universities, old and new, siphoned off an increasing number of available recruits. Even so, in 1966, Thode's judicious dean of graduate studies, Melvin "Mel" Preston, correctly projected a figure of roughly 2,000 candidates for higher degrees within the next nine years. This would constitute 20 per cent of full-timers on campus.[78] Implicit in these historical recitations and proportional calculations was McMaster's claim to be different from other institutions: a purpose-built centre of graduate study and research. Altogether, the seemingly dry budget submissions Thode annually composed spun a sufficiently compelling tale that he got most of what he sought, at least before 1969. It needs to be emphasized, however, that the spinning of this yarn was not the work of Thode unaided.

By virtue of his office, Thode was the public voice of McMaster, but it was a solid cadre of colleagues on campus who helped shape, refine, and promote the paradigm he championed. Never one to plan by a show of hands, Thode relied on selective consultation and carefully chosen administrators to achieve his ends. Accordingly, it was no accident that veterans of Hamilton College were conspicuous among his intimate advisors. Thus, chemist, Arthur "Art" Bourns, followed by physicists Harry Duckworth and Mel Preston served as his increasingly powerful deans of graduate studies, during the sixties. Meanwhile, the dynamic Howard "Howie" Petch, also from physics, succeeded Thode, first as director of research and later as principal of Hamilton College in 1961 and 1963 respectively. Mike Hedden, a graduate of the latter institution, was that rarest of beings, a widely liked business administrator and number-cruncher-in-chief. Petch, Duckworth, Preston, and Bourns were each research-driven scientists of superior accomplishment and considerable personal ambition. With Thode as leader of the pack, this made for a heavy concentration of alpha-dogs in one relatively small kennel. A measure of jostling was only to be expected. Some differences notwithstanding, Bourns, Preston, Hedden, and Thode would be friends for life. However, first Duckworth (1965) and then Petch (1967) would depart. Still, in the formative early to mid-sixties, this cadre proved to be remarkably like-minded as to the course the university should chart. Moreover, the group had support in high places.

Significant here was Carey Fox, who threw his substantial influence behind Thode and company. The ageing board chairman was an iconic figure among his peers and, more importantly, remained as shrewd as ever. Indeed, it was the canny Fox who coached Thode during the new president's introduction to the Byzantine labyrinth of Queen's Park bureaucracy. This was never more apparent than in the tutelage Fox afforded following 2 January 1963, after he, Thode, and Hedden had met with the ACUA in Toronto. The committee, under the chairmanship of former premier Leslie Frost, was still groping to define policies for a mushrooming Ontario university system. As noted above in Thode's subsequent letter to Schneider, the president had left the meeting deeply demoralized by the committee's evident inability to grasp the difference between undergraduate and graduate education. The veteran Fox, on the other hand, read both body language and subtext far more astutely during that session. Thus, he wrote next day to Thode, saying that he should not be discouraged.

After all, said Fox, "something happened yesterday that was extremely vital and for which we'd been waiting." Thode must have been puzzled, until Fox reminded him that Frost had suggested, in passing, that McMaster might present a special brief clarifying its particular needs. To the sharp-eyed Fox, it was "quite obvious that Mr. Frost and the Committee was [sic] throwing up their hands and looking for help." Here, he advised Thode, was a gift from the gods, a golden opportunity to hammer home an unambiguous statement of "your educational philosophy." This, Fox underscored, would be the first brief in which "we will be able to express our own views," unclouded by simultaneous submissions from other institutions. He, therefore, urged the president to be as frank and pointed as possible.

Just to be sure that there was no misunderstanding, Fox penned his own synopsis of Thode's position. "If I am able to read correctly your views with regard to postgraduate work," he wrote, "they are rapidly developing to the point where you wish to place a great deal more emphasis on this than has been done and possibly ... more emphasis on this than on the undergraduate problem."[79] The governor read the president perfectly and supported him wholeheartedly. Until his retirement as chairman in 1965, Fox was an excellent tutor, who helped Thode craft his crucial storyline in annual budget submissions to ACUA. Encouragement, however, also came from other board heavyweights, including Hugh Hilton and Frank Sherman, chief executives of Stelco and Dofasco, respectively. In short, Thode was not alone in his quest to refashion the university.

All involved understood that careful, well-articulated planning was the *sine qua non* of shaping the particular McMaster they envisioned. As early as June 1962, Thode wrote to Bill Warrender, federal minister of labour, saying that community and Ontario government pressure to accept ever-more undergraduates was mounting and could not justifiably be resisted. Indeed, Thode ventured that anything up to 7,000 students could be expected by 1970. The university, he went on, was ready to do its reasonable part in accommodating this tide, but not at the sacrifice of its goals in research and graduate work. "We are," he asserted, "at the cross roads." Waxing rather grandiose, Thode declared, "McMaster has the opportunity to become one of the great universities of this continent." Everything, however, depended on how growth was directed. Thus, he said to Warrender, "It is clear to me and members of our board that the time has come to prepare a master plan for the future development of McMaster."[80]

Gilmour's phased campus plan, laid down in 1957, had already been rendered obsolete by the heavy influx of students. Additional space was badly needed. Accordingly, 130 more acres of land were purchased from the obliging Royal Botanical Gardens. Meanwhile, the firm of Sasaki, Walker, and Associates (Watertown, Massachusetts) was hired to design an expanded scheme; one tailored specifically to the Thodean vision. A large parcel of property west of Highway 102 (now Cootes Drive) was set aside for playing fields, parking facilities, and non-academic buildings. The remaining, prime, fifty-five acres were immediately adjacent to campus. These lands, as Thode made clear in his 1962–63 presidential comments, were to be systematically zoned, under the Sasaki plan. He desired like to stand beside like so as to "allow maximum communication and interchange between all departments and colleges." "This principle," he explained, "is in accord with the McMaster educational philosophy to encourage and foster the development of interdisciplinary teaching and research." Working plans, he continued, were already on the drawing board for a new, large arts complex, and a whole network of "interrelated, interconnected science buildings." A state-of-the-art physical education facility was also in the works.[81]

What Thode and his colleagues were offering here was the promise of "more scholar for the dollar," almost a decade before education minister John White coined the chilling phrase in 1971. McMaster could never be truly large; not on the scale of Toronto or the University of British Columbia (UBC). There was simply too little land available. In any case, Thode felt that enrolment should never exceed 10,000, if maximum efficiency were to be attained. Properly designed, however, McMaster could punch far above its weight. Here, quality and focus, rather than mere size, were key. Mel Preston, perhaps the most articulate and reflective of Thodes advisors, spelled this out repeatedly. "Obviously," he wrote, "no university can be superb in all possible activities, but there is no reason why McMaster should not achieve excellence in a wise and realistic selection [of fields]."[82] The trick, in other words, was to wring the most out of limited resources. This, it was felt, could best be achieved by pooling faculty expertise in concentrated fashion as a matter of policy, both in pedagogy and research. Of course, no department or individual could be compelled to embrace interdisciplinary work. Still, encouragement and inducements to do so were regularly proffered.

Thus, closely monitored associate memberships and cross-appointments became increasingly common during the period. These conferred prestige but also gave the individuals involved a voice in the affairs of related departments or faculties; a sense of having a stake in the broader university enterprise. In like manner, joint honours programs were nurtured and promoted, in order to bring some liberality to undergraduate specialists.

The centrepiece of this interdisciplinary paradigm, however, was the integrated research unit. To do significant work, Thode once told *Silhouette* readers, researchers interested in a common problem or area were well advised to join hands and concentrate efforts.[83] For him, cross-disciplinary work was not an end in itself. It was a vehicle for tackling major-league research with medium-scale resources. Yet, it was also something more. While he never quite spelled it out, Thode appears to have viewed cross-fertilization as means of adapting older, liberal values to a new age of necessarily intense specialization. As he stated in 1963, "It is no longer possible for a single individual to acquire all the knowledge and to master all the techniques in his own subject let alone in related or borderline fields." For this reason, he continued, "some collaboration is essential if progress is to be made," especially in that fertile Everyman's land where disciplines overlapped. At the highest levels, therefore, the integrated research unit embodied both the practical and the ideal.[84]

Such units were to be neither new departments nor free-standing institutes. Quite the opposite, as Petch explained, they were intended to counteract fragmentation, while forwarding targeted research and graduate study which fell between departmental boundaries.[85] Thode rejected the idea of establishing "institutes" with specially hired staff. For one thing, such bodies tended to become "little empires within a university, isolated from the departments."[86] Furthermore, they usually did little to enhance graduate education; yet graduate students were vital as laboratory, tutorial, and research assistants. The unit, therefore, would be staffed by faculty cross-appointed with mainstream departments and be "completely integrated

with the university teaching program."[87] On this point, Thode had taken a
cue from recent developments at Harvard and Berkeley. He did not, however, favour the ad hoc committee system these American schools employed
to encourage interdisciplinary work. Such arrangements, he thought, did
not serve to inspire a sense of long-term commitment or esprit de corps.
Instead, he preferred officially sanctioned, more-or-less permanent, collaborative entities, which performed mission-oriented research and facilitated
graduate instruction over the long, developmental haul.[88] These units, he
felt, would help McMaster wring the maximum out of standing resources,
while positioning it to bid for even more. To Thode, they symbolized the
search for that targeted excellence he so prized.

Clearly, as he nestled into Gilmour's chair, President Thode was projecting
a paradigm, which had evolved at Hamilton College, onto the university
as a whole. Its utility in the confines of a small, research-intensive school
for the senior sciences was demonstrable. Just how it might be adapted to
the more complex university was a matter for conjecture. For example, he
noted: "Whether the unit idea would be useful in certain areas in the humanities and social sciences is not certain."[89] Whatever the case, Thode, and
those around him, were committed to catapulting McMaster into the front
rank of Canadian universities, each of which was experimenting with higher
education for a mass age. Of course, if there was one thing Thode enjoyed,
above all else, it was a well-planned experiment. The question, however, was
how this would play out in the years ahead amid an ever-increasing number
of variables on and off campus.

2

Great Balls of Fire

On 24 June 1964, Hamiltonians scanning the *Globe and Mail* must have done a sharp double take. In a rare tip of its upscale bowler, that proud Toronto daily heartily applauded academic initiatives in lunch-bucket Steel Town. Indeed, in a feature story, entitled "A Powerful Push at McMaster," columnist J.B. St John went so far as to predict that the former Baptist institution now stood on the brink of becoming "one of the most impressive university sites in the province." He founded this assertion less on swelling undergraduate numbers than on a recent growth spurt in doctoral and post-doctoral studies on the Hamilton campus. As a close observer of the contemporary university scene, he thought this surge notable in itself, but what truly caught his eye was the organic way it seemed to flow from decisions taken a generation before such endeavour had become all the rage everywhere. Thus, he drew attention to the founding of Hamilton College in the late forties and its long-term, systematic coupling of scientific research with graduate study in a co-operative, interdisciplinary atmosphere. This, he concluded, was the secret behind McMaster's smooth acceleration in advanced work.[1] In emphasizing continuity, rather than change, and in identifying a particular modus operandi, St John had hit the nail squarely on its head.

For most denizens of Hamilton College, 1957 and its aftermath had occasioned little of the hand-wringing found in some other precincts on campus. On the contrary, as pure and applied scientists viewed the transition, matters were unfolding precisely as they should. A few initial misgivings were alleviated swiftly by equitable representation on the new board and the senate.[2] Thode's powerful position in the revamped central administration only added a sense of familiarity. Meanwhile, an established pattern of research and graduate supervision was steadily gaining momentum. In 1956, standing doctoral programs in chemistry, physics, and biology were augmented by new ones in pure mathematics and geochemistry. Next year, sod was turned where a nuclear reactor would soon stand, even as the first freshman class enrolled in engineering. So, what had been disturbed? Where was there cause for lamentation or insecurity? In fact, 1957 was a banner year for Hamilton College; one that signalled affirmation of purpose, rather than uncertainty in the face of change. A few years later, when President Thode called for a "powerful push" in research and graduate study, the pure and applied sciences stood ready to pick up the pace. For them, this just signalled a welcome intensification of business as usual. Thus, as the president talked the talk, the sciences walked the walk. After all, at that moment, only they had the legs to do so. By the time St John's article appeared, McMaster boasted numerous doctoral programs. Only one of them (history) was in arts. There were also almost thirty post-doctoral fellows on camps. All wore laboratory whites.[3]

. St John, therefore, correctly underscored the locus of this thrust toward research intensiveness. Even more perceptively, he identified the co-operative ethos that facilitated it. Today, we take collective, interdisciplinary effort as a one aspect of every university's normal activity. It was not, however, always thus. Consider, for example, the rather dour memoirs of Howard Clark, retired president of Dalhousie. Between 1957 and 1965, he was on the scene when UBC caught the research-intensive itch and bent to scratching it with a will. As a young chemist, Clark saw his own department grow from twenty-two to forty-five faculty members in the course of twelve short years, with physics, biology, and English following a similar trajectory.[4] Emphasis on research and graduate study escalated dramatically. Sheer scale was also prized. Thus, UBC took pride in becoming the third largest university in Canada. The atmosphere, however, was "gladiatorial," according to Clark, who recalls vicious internecine strife, the "splendid isolation" of departments, and three suicides as concomitants of unregulated expansion.[5] To be sure, this was extreme, by any measure. Even so, others have noted that a strong tendency toward disciplinary particularism was far from unique to UBC during the period.[6] By contrast, however, it was all but official doctrine at Hamilton College that disciplinary boundaries were dated fictions and, as such, outmoded barriers to higher inquiry.

"When I arrived at McMaster in 1966," engineer David Embury later recalled, "I was astonished by the close contact which existed between the group of Metallurgists and the people in Chemistry and Solid state Physics [sic]." That contact, he reminisced, encompassed uninhibited scholarly exchange, the unquestioned sharing of equipment, and a vibrant research environment. Very soon, he came to realize that this was no chance matter.

Rather, it was company policy[7] Embury's observations could be dismissed as typical of nothing more than one man's experience, were it not for the fact that similar, almost carbon-copied, reflections abound for the period 1957 through 1987. Moreover, internally generated statements of this kind were not mere products of collective self-delusion, let alone official propaganda. Instead, as will be seen, independent corroboration was consistently provided by visiting scholars, official assessors, and journalists, alike. They, too, agreed that McMaster science, pure and applied, had a particular affinity for collective enterprise.

One, of course, must be careful not to distort the picture. Thus, Thode and the faculty (sad to say) did not gather weekly to don love beads and sing in fraternal harmony. On the contrary, Hamilton College experienced its share of personal rifts and departmental huffs. Biology, for example, long felt that its interests were unduly subordinated to those of the physical sciences.[8] Thode, for his part, had more than one dust-up, particularly with Petch and Duckworth.[9] Friction, however, rarely overrode common sense, let alone enlightened self-interest. Accordingly, most accepted Thode's notion that the only way a small school of science could engage in truly significant research was for its members to focus tightly on specific, achievable goals and, when helpful, put resources to multiple or collective use. Of course, it was also simply imprudent to gainsay Thode.

On this score, one must remember that, in 1957, the entire faculty complement of McMaster could be gathered together in one fair-sized room. It mattered greatly, therefore, that, while Thode commanded genuine respect, he also held very real power and was not afraid to use it. Respect flowed from his record of personal academic achievement, during and after the war. As Duckworth later put it, Thode had "status in the world of science."[10] If nothing else, this guaranteed him at least a serious hearing in the councils of Hamilton College. Furthermore, while no orator, on a private level Thode was also quite capable of infecting others with his own fiery enthusiasm for a greater McMaster, as geographer Leslie King testified from personal experience.[11] Above all, however, his was not merely one voice in the crowd. There were plenty of scholarly knights, but no Round Table, at Hamilton College.

After his appointment as principal in 1949, Thode called all the major scientific shots. When interviewed for this volume, Arthur Bourns recalled, "What was remarkable, and not appreciated by many, is the degree to which Gilmour allowed Harry to develop things and to accept what Harry felt should be the direction to [sic] which the University should go and develop."[12] This included a virtually free hand in selecting faculty to suit his grand designs.[13] In 1955, for example, Thode received word that a brilliant, young German mathematician, Bernard Banaschewski, was looking for a post. Anxious to stimulate graduate work and research performance in a desultory mathematics department, Thode swiftly made personal contact with Banaschewski and literally created a position for him, much to McMaster's enduring benefit.[14] By 1961, Thode was president; the last one in the university's history to be appointed "without term." In short, if not quite undoubted Caesar, Thode was, nevertheless, in an exceptionally strong position. While always open to suggestions, he was wont to "make up his own mind, do a thing, and live with the fallout."[15] Some could accept this; others could not. In any case, there can be little doubt that his single-minded clarity of purpose, allied with many willing hands, contributed heavily to the forceful push St John noted in 1964. Evidence of this thrust was apparent, however, even as the new McMaster Act was being negotiated in 1957. This came in the form of two emerging initiatives: one, to acquire a nuclear reactor and the other, to found a school of engineering.

Given its potent symbolism in McMaster's drive for scientific recognition, it is curious that the precise origins of the reactor bid are unclear. Most, including Harry Duckworth and geologist Henry Schwarcz, attribute the notion to Thode.[16] As Martin Johns told the story, however, it was he and Howard Petch who first pitched the idea to Thode. Typically, the principal mulled it over, methodically weighing the pros and cons. Meanwhile, Johns, Petch, and nuclear chemist Richard "Dick" Tomlinson went south of the border scouting examples, just in case the boss signalled thumbs up. During their shopping trip, Johns related, Thode had a chance conversation with an American colleague, who, consciously or unconsciously, touched his most sensitive nerve. A reactor, the fellow said, "would be exactly what would pull a campus like McMaster together."[17] No words could have been better calculated to spur the president to action. Here, it seemed, was the ideal Thodean tool. No single department had the numbers or the strength to justify the cost, but combined, several could. With potential applications ranging from nuclear physics, to chemistry, medicine, geology, archaeology, and beyond, it could serve as a bonding agent like no other, as well as facilitating work in emerging borderline areas of great promise. Equally important, it could put the university boldly on the map, as an institution both serious and unique. Duckworth, for one, certainly recognized that "the desire to acquire something spectacular for McMaster University constituted a strong motive."[18] Thus, regardless who conceived the original idea, the quest to obtain a reactor soon became, very much, Thode's baby. The great question, of course, was how to go about it.

This was where Thode's status in the broader world of Canadian science paid off. He was, according to Johns, "the only scientist at McMaster at that time with the prestige to win this large installation for what was, even by Canadian standards, a small university."[19] A recognized player, he enjoyed the confidence of influential figures, such as Edgar "Ned" Steacie of the NRC and C.J. Mackenzie of the Atomic Energy Control Board (later, AECL), as well as key people at Ontario Hydro.[20] Indeed, such was the level of Thode's national profile that, following Steacie's sudden death in 1963, Prime Minister John Diefenbaker telephoned personally to offer him the presidency of the NRC. Thode politely declined.[21] Meanwhile, he had long cultivated close ties with executives of major Hamilton industries: people who could be sold on the manifold practical outcomes of nuclear research.[22] On campus, board chairman Fox was stood four-square behind the project.[23] Best of all, Thode had sound pitch to make. Indeed, small university or not, McMaster could actually state a believable case for this seemingly improbable venture.

Dated 3 November 1955, the NRC application was a slim fifteen pages of text; laughably shorter than most travel requests today. Canny thought, however, had gone into its careful compilation. This was apparent, even in its revealingly crafted title: "A Nuclear Reactor Program for McMaster and Canadian Industry." Throughout, emphasis was placed equally on the fight to retain Canada's economic place in the developed world, as well as on the notion of pure scientific research. Indeed, read the proposal: "the line between pure and applied research can never be accurately drawn." Seen in this light, McMaster was presented as the logical site of a nuclear facility, given its proximity to Canada's industrial heartland. "The closer the reactor to the industry," it was posited, "and the better the liaison between industry and the university the greater will be the value." As for McMaster, itself, although small, it was described as tailor-made to squeeze the last whisper of promise out of the proposed facility.

Nuclear research had begun at the university as early as 1943. Meanwhile, about a quarter of the science staff was engaged in related work and many of them made regular pilgrimages to the national shrine at Chalk River. Since 1951, it was noted, McMaster had boasted a nuclear research building, replete with a "hot lab" capable of handling curie levels of radioactivity. Seven mass spectrometers were also in place, including a ten-ton behemoth fathered by Harry Duckworth. In all, wrote the applicants, McMaster might be small in an absolute sense, but it was home to relatively large departments of chemistry and physics that normally had about twenty-five graduate students working in the nuclear field. Best of all, standing resources would minimize start-up costs, and researchers' salaries were already covered. This brief, but well-crafted, submission ultimately carried the day.[24] With a single blow, Johns later remarked, McMaster won "a place on the world scene and attracted in the next decade students from all over the world."[25]

Bureaucracy moved with surprising efficiency. Contracts were let to a local firm, Pigott Construction, and sod was duly turned in 1957. Meanwhile, a pre-emptive campaign was launched to calm the fears of jittery locals. Some envisioned great balls of fire engulfing their fair city, as egg-heads tickled the dragon. Less apocalyptically, others worried that radioactive water might find its way into the Dundas Marsh.[26] Adding a different twist, with the reactor pool not yet full, a February 1958 issue of the Silhouette opined that, in the event of a sudden power surge, "the girls in both residences would be sterilized within twenty-four hours."[27] Some ardent freshman, no doubt, saw a bright side to glow-in-the-dark co-eds.

Real or fantasized, these varied notions had to be nipped in the bud. Dick Tomlinson, in charge of safety measures, took the lead in comforting the disquieted. Tireless, he offered talks all over the Golden Horseshoe. Duckworth also pitched in, arranging a series of two-week courses for senior members of the industrial community, at which he, Thode, Johns, Petch, Preston, and Tomlinson schooled executives in the practical advantages and safe use of the reactor. The drop-out rate at such seminars, Duckworth noted, was practically zero.[28] Much was made of the care that had gone into design. The building's shell, for example, had an odd number of sides (fifteen), in order to counter the effects of any seismic shock. Barites, mined in far-off Walton, Nova Scotia, had been mixed with the concrete to increase shielding.[29] It was, however, the "swimming-pool" configuration of the reactor that afforded the highest security. The lattice of fuel elements was immersed in 105,669 gallons of water that removed heat, shielded radiation, and slowed stray neutrons for capture by control rods.

Once in place, carefully orchestrated, regular, guided tours of the McMaster Nuclear Reactor (MNR) attracted hundreds of locals, who left comforted that atomic bombs were not on the research menu and that safety actually did come first.[30] The good burghers of Hamilton, it appeared, had nothing to fear and everything to gain. Several, indeed, spoke approval with yawning wallets. J.R. White, for one, gave $20,000 as Imperial Oil's contribution to the scheme.[31] Frank Sherman pledged Dofasco to provide $15,000 a year for ten years, in order to support cancer research using radioisotopes.[32] Other business and industrial magnates, including Carey Fox, followed suit.[33] With capital costs covered largely by Ontario Hydro and NRC, the reactor was finally opened by Prime Minister Diefenbaker on 10 April

1959. In an atypically effusive gush, Gilmour told those assembled: "This day should be designated Harry Thode Day at McMaster."[34]

Up and running, the MNR soon proved its worth. Versatility would be its hallmark. With multiple neutron beam ports, numerous experiments could be performed simultaneously. Pneumatic "rabbits" whisked samples to the research building in a flash, allowing for the study of material whose half-life might be mere seconds. Increasingly, such matter found its way to ever-more-sophisticated analytical instruments. After 1962, for example, Bertram "Bert" Brockhouse brought his triple-axis spectrometer to McMaster where, as a physics professor, he carved out an illustrious career, crowned with a Nobel Prize (1994). Yet for all that the MNR was an undoubted boon to nuclear physics and chemistry, the Operational Control Committee, appointed in 1959, ensured that it catered to the needs of the many, rather than the interests of the few.[35]

Indeed, in his report for 1961–62, Director of Research Petch took pains to delineate the wide applications to which the reactor was regularly put. Thus, he noted that all but two of the science and engineering departments had made use of the MNR that year in the course of over 800 irradiations.[36] Thode struck a similar chord, whenever he had to pay court to granting agencies. Writing to J.B. Marshall of the NRC in 1965, for example, Thode explained that he had little patience with those who saw nuclear science as a narrow, rarified field. On the contrary, he expostulated, it had applications in most areas of science, engineering, and medicine, as well as several in industries, such as steel and petrochemicals. For that matter, he continued, the MNR was currently being put to greater use in solid state studies and materials science than in nuclear research itself.[37] Indeed, later in the period, health sciences would emerge as the heaviest user of this flexible facility.[38]

The MNR was also an efficient teaching device. Graduate students in nuclear studies often acquired several tangential, but highly marketable, skills. After 1959, as physicist Terry Kennett has observed, the MNR was in direct competition with better-endowed national laboratories, such as Chalk River (Ontario), Los Alamos (New Mexico), and Oak Ridge (Tennessee). "To make matters worse," he notes, "these institutions had departments or units that developed electronics, detectors, instrumentation, computer programs, and applied mathematics to provide algorithms for the scientists to handle their data." The answer at McMaster was to encourage graduate research that would help the MNR to catch up. In the end, says Kennett, this had the beneficial effect of providing students with valuable employment options at a time when digital electronics and computers systems were in the formative stage.[39] Meanwhile, as Helen Howard-Lock indicates, visiting students and scholars abounded. By 1995, she notes, virtually all the reactor engineers, nuclear chemists and physicists, trained in Canada, had spent at least some time at the MNR. The same was true of most in nuclear medicine or reactor design. The facility was open to all comers at next to no cost, and proved magnetic.[40]

While never a "unit," in the sense that Thode used the word, the MNR hosted a corps of regular users from physics, chemistry, engineering, biology, geology, and other disciplines. As Mel Preston wistfully recalled in 2011, "we were all of an age," and came to enjoy lively discussion as friends, on and off campus, concerning things as varied as theoretical physics and archaeological dating techniques.[41] Later, the medics would join in. In short, during its prime (the mid-seventies), the reactor was a hub, not only of meaningful research, but also of that "no-boundaries" exchange which fed the Thodean ethos. Altogether, in McMaster lore, the MNR stands as a symbol of the university's take-off as a research-intensive institution. However, another contemporary initiative would strongly reinforce this drive and prove to have even better legs.

McMaster had long had a preliminary year in engineering studies. Having completed it, promising students would then go elsewhere to pursue their full professional education. Queen's was the usual destination. Since the founding of Hamilton College, however, Thode and the university had come under increasing pressure from local industrialists to establish a full-fledged Faculty of Engineering on campus. Stelco and Dofasco, eager to keep technological pace with competitors, had been especially persistent that world-class metallurgy be established.[42] In this regard, as has been noted, an important strand in Thode's paradigm of a university was visible: practical service to the local community. Besides, with Bissell, he also believed that one or more professional schools marked a first-division university off from a second-tier college. However, Harry was even more heavily committed to crafting an institution recognized for its special attention to research and graduate study. Herein lay the rub.

Traditional engineering faculties had promoted technique, as opposed to inquiry. At first blush, therefore, the fit between a research-intensive McMaster and skill-oriented engineering might have appeared tenuous. It certainly seemed so to many of the older guard, including Gilmour, who felt that "training" had no place in a home of higher education.[43] It is ironic, therefore, that, by 1969, McMaster engineering would be one of the most Thodean branches of the university: research-fixated, graduate-heavy, highly interdisciplinary, and rather disdainful of mere training. Any irony in this, however, was more apparent than real. Thode saw to that.

In 1955, the first step was to lure John W. "Jack" Hodgins from his post as professor of chemical engineering at the Royal Military College, Kingston. A creative, liberal, man, Hodgins ostensibly came as director of the old engineering studies program. In fact, he was hand-picked by Thode to help plan an innovative engineering school. The two men were as one in emphasizing the word *science* in the term *applied science*. Indeed, an emphasis on fundamental science and research was the agreed premise upon which the new school was designed, so as to differentiate itself from others in Ontario.[44] Thode and Hodgins also shared the view that the technological revolution unfolding in their age was so closely interwoven as to defy disciplinary or even faculty boundaries. Indeed, Hodgins held that, in an era of hyper-technology, acquaintanceship with basic engineering ought to be as core to anybody's liberal education as classics or mathematics. Better read than Thode, he was also eager to bring the arts to bear on the education of well-rounded, truly modern, engineers. "Humanizing the scientist and simonizing the humanist," he once quipped, should be the goal of McMaster engineering.[45] In any case, as a team, the Renaissance man and the driven principal helped devise a plan that won approval from board members, senators, and industrialists alike.[46] Forty-seven candidates were admitted to first year in 1957. The Faculty of Engineering was officially approved next year. Another bold experiment was underway; now with Dean Hodgins at the helm.

Commenting on all this in September 1957, the *Globe and Mail* rhapsodized, as it lavished praise on a curriculum so designed as to lead engineers "in the direction of wisdom rather than in the mere accumulation of technical information." Behind this, the editorialist saw "an atmosphere of intellectual receptiveness" among Hamilton corporate executives, who, running counter to popular stereotype, favoured "independence and responsibility" over submissive conformism in their future employees.[47] In 1959, just prior to the new building's opening, the less florid Thode issued a more prosaic press release. In it, he stated that the project had cost a staggering $3,800,000: the largest single expenditure out of the university's entire budget. Well worth every penny, he continued, the facility would be home to Canada's most modern engineering faculty. "It is hoped," he continued, "that, unhampered by tradition, we can build an engineering school closely linked to science." Equipped to handle 500 undergraduates, it would also house significant research and, thereby, prove attractive to at least some graduate students, as well. As it happened, this latter prognostication proved to be an almost laughable understatement.

Meanwhile, Thode drew special attention to the breadth of education on offer. McMaster engineers, he emphasized, would take required courses in

English and other arts throughout their programs. In this way, they would be better equipped for adaptation to a rapidly changing workplace. In a word, they would be educated men and women; not mere technicians.[48] Although regulations changed with time, Hodgins later instituted a regular series of humanities lectures, featuring renowned guest speakers, including Arthur Hailey, Irving Layton, and Mavor Moore, to ensure that the original spirit of the program was maintained.[49] Much later, a thought-provoking course in "Engineering and Society" kept that ethos alive in altered form.

Although the building incorporated five wings, each designed eventually to house different branches of engineering, the initial plan had been to start with keystone programs in chemical and metallurgical studies. This gradualist scheme, however, went quickly by the boards, when local industries and academic logic declared that mechanical and electrical departments were essential to support the two star players.[50] Civil engineering followed shortly, thereafter. Still, at the outset and for years to come, chemical and metallurgical engineering were the pacesetters. The path followed, however, while undoubtedly pleasing to the Thodean eye, was not quite the one predicted in the mid-fifties. Indeed, it was a full decade before engineering reached its undergraduate capacity of 500. This had been expected, in some measure. Wholly unanticipated in 1957, however, was the magnitude of graduate enlistment. The scale of that influx, in fact, would be such that, by the late sixties, some departments functioned essentially as research and graduate units, with a scattering of majors appended. This was a blessing or a curse, depending on viewership.

Gilmour had understood that, starting from scratch and in the midst of recession, it would take time to fill all the undergraduate places available. Writing to the minister of education, in December 1959, he asked for patience. It would, he wrote, be at least three years before the new school could tote its own financial weight. "During that interval," the president continued, "the University must carry the Faculty of Engineering with a serious annual deficit."[51] Gilmour missed the mark, but only by a scant fifteen years! The Faculty would remain a fiscal headache for McMaster well into the seventies, until it finally and decisively turned the corner. Meanwhile, other departments, knee-deep in undergraduates, bewailed the annual transfer of revenue to engineering and bemoaned the striking difference in student-professor ratios. Senior administrators and many engineers, however, saw things differently. From their perspective, engineering showed promise as an elite unit within a research-intensive university, while also providing palpable, high-profile assistance to industry. Seen in this light, the Faculty was a pearl well worth the price.

Metallurgical polymath Jack Kirkaldy, for one, had absolutely no reservations on this score. Writing confidentially to Thode in 1963, his pen flamed as red as the hair on his head. Relations with other in-house departments, he told the president, were far from cordial at the moment. The feeling was being freely voiced that metallurgy and chemical engineering were administrative darlings, unfairly showered with resources. There was, he admitted, a small grain of truth in this. That, however, he averred, was the consequence of "superior and authoritative leadership" on the part of two departments whose members could not buy the idea that good engineers were basically different from good scientists. Warming to his subject, Kirkaldy fumed that the major engineering innovations of the century had largely gone all but unnoticed by conventional practitioners. He set the steady, continent-wide drop in engineering enrolments down to (supposed) public recognition of this fact and heaped scorn on some local faculty who clung to the "fuzzy-minded philosophy of the professional engineer." Lukewarm to graduate studies and emphasizing pedagogy over research, such people, he railed, retarded, rather than furthered, advancement of the Faculty. Henceforth, he counselled, more staff had to be recruited with doctorates in pure physics or engineering physics, if McMaster were to compete for eminence with the likes of UBC.[52] The implication was that front-line engineering, like first-class science, involved high-stakes investment, before any prizes could be reaped. Anything less meant playing penny-ante.

Kirkaldy, of course, was preaching to the choir. Indeed, as early as 1959, Thode had formed an engineering physics committee on the premise that such studies were essential for future engineers.[53] Physics happily obliged, and a long-lived, fruitful integration of pure and applied science took root. In truth, this symbiosis went back to the founding of Kirkaldy's own department. As Petch tells the story, he and Thode crossed paths, one sunny day on campus, in 1956. They paused to chat about the vexing problem of finding just the right, scientifically minded person to chair metallurgy. In the midst of this, Petch was thunderstruck when, out of the blue, Thode suggested that he (Petch) should do it. With his personal research in solid state physics starting to blossom, Petch felt both reluctant and unqualified to accept. As a collegial gesture, however, he agreed to sleep on it. He did, but only for a few storm-tossed hours.

Then, if not quite Saul on the road to Damascus, he sat bolt upright, in epiphany's grip. Thus, it came to Petch that, properly founded, metallurgy could become the core of a much broader, multidisciplinary, materials research centre, at the precise moment burgeoning new technology demanded myriad new materials. Excited now, he put the idea to Thode, with the caveat that the department would have to be "overbuilt" to accommodate an expansive tomorrow. Predictably, Thode agreed, without the slightest hesitation.[54]

In many ways, the department of metallurgy and metallurgical science ("metallurgy and materials science" after 1966) became a poster child for Thodeanism and its critics. Big steel, of course, was delighted. In 1960, Stelco happily endowed a chair in metallurgy to the tune of $20,000 per annum for ten years.[55] External funding agencies were also impressed by the flood of high-quality publication that flowed regularly from the department. By 1967, the chair could report that grants averaged just over $40,000 for each of its faculty members.[56] Adding sheen to its Thodean gloss, metallurgy had launched upon graduate work at its inception, and proved to be a magnet for aspiring candidates. In 1963, it attracted fifteen graduate students, while supporting five post-doctoral fellows.[57] Four years on, the figures were twenty-nine and ten, respectively.[58] Life was good, save for one sour note. The undergraduate program, so lovingly designed, failed to capture anything resembling a significant following. Writing confidentially to the president in 1964, chair of the department R.G. Ward alerted Thode that "next year, we'll have more graduate students than undergraduates graduating."[59] The picture would remain much the same throughout the sixties. If this disturbed Thode, however, he gave no initial indication of concern. After all, the department proved to be the seedbed of one of the most innovative and prestigious, multidisciplinary units in McMaster's history: the Institute for Materials Research (IMR). This was Thodes's dream and Petch's epiphany rendered wholly solid (pun fully intended).

The IMR was in the cards, in some form, from the moment Petch outlined his terms for accepting the chair of metallurgy. It took time to communicate the notion fully to others across campus, but the concept was a natural. By 1963, Thode publicly announced plans to seek external support for a materials research unit and a laboratory dedicated to its use.[60] Behind the scene, he launched a far-ranging campaign at the highest levels to forward the cause. A fifty-page brief, prepared by Petch, stated the case powerfully, albeit not succinctly. The basic rationale, however, was as clear as Waterford crystal. Since the war, Petch argued, technological ingenuity had leaped far ahead of the materials available for the full realization of its potential. This, he maintained, held true in fields from the exploration of space to the development of myriad industrial and consumer goods. The value of solid state technology in electronics alone had risen, since 1950, from zero to a projected $20 billion by 1970, given the demand for computers, let alone every teenager's closest companion: the transistor radio. With major laboratories springing up in Europe, Russia, and the United States, Canada faced a choice: commit to the game, or forever fall behind.

Were commitment chosen, Petch contended, McMaster was the logical site for a concentrated program, given its interdisciplinary tradition, established work in solids, and its specific graduate-cum-research atmosphere. "At McMaster," he pointed out, "the graduate program is considered of equal importance to the undergraduate program and professors are given considerable time for graduate teaching and research; as a general policy, a professor is expected to devote one-half of his time to these activities." He was, of course, speaking primarily of the sciences, whose members, he noted, received special summer stipends to stay on campus to carry out such work. McMaster, in short, stood ready.[61]

Armed with this brief, Thode dispatched it, along with carefully personalized letters, to well-placed contacts at, among others, the NRC, the Defence Research Board, and the Advanced Research Projects Agency in Washington, as well as industrial leaders at Stelco and Dofasco.[62] He drummed on the need for focused, concentrated effort, to the point of proposing that the NRC develop a wholly new type of award: a "block grant," designed to support the interdisciplinary unit, rather than any particular individuals who worked under its auspices.[63] While this novel suggestion percolated through slow-drip, bureaucratic filters, McMaster formally established the Materials Research Unit, in 1963. Comprising twenty-two charter members, it embraced representatives from chemistry, physics, geology, and three engineering departments, all under Petch's creative leadership.[64] For its part, in 1965, the university promised dedicated space for the unit in a planned senior sciences complex. The great Catch-22, however, was that the search for ultra-modern materials required ultra-modern equipment; precision instrumentation whose cost far outran ordinary university or NRC support. It was, therefore, with joy in 1967 that word came of a three-year, half-million-dollar "negotiated development grant" (NDG) from the NRC. This was the new form of block grant for which Thode had lobbied so hard. Individual members of the unit, now thirty-four in number, could continue to apply for personal awards, as ever. The NDG, however, was earmarked for the unit; in this case to provide the new laboratory with electron microscopes, microprobes, crystal growing apparatus, and copious other state-of-the-art gadgetry.[65] While non-renewable, the NDG kicked the renamed IMR into high gear. Participants responded with concerted energy. Others took note, especially annual visitors sent by the NRC to evaluate the efficacy of NDG funding.

In 1969, those visitors reported that of the three negotiated grants issued for materials research, one each to UBC, Toronto, and McMaster, the latter had produced, by far, the best return on investment. Good points were noted at Toronto, but, said assessors, the "organizational and academic structure is still vague." UBC's effort was described as scattered, while lacking both academic content and creativity. In sharp contrast, the report called attention to the "real, definite, and enthusiastically accepted" interdepartmental collaboration at McMaster, which gave rise to a tangible research atmosphere within the unit. The IMR's concentration on basic research was praised but so was its attention to "use problems." A healthy liaison had developed with local industry. Work in microelectronics was singled out as an example of this. Meanwhile, teaching functions were well-coordinated with standing departmental degree programs across science and engineering. In all, stated the enthusiastic visitors, thirty-four faculty members from eight different departments worked closely, in their own well-appointed facility, with more than a hundred graduate students and thirty-two post-doctoral fellows; all in a manner that fully validated the NDG concept.[66]

The only fly in this otherwise unctuous ointment was the sudden, less-than-cordial departure of Howard Petch. A brief memo of 7 July 1967 from Thode to members of the unit confirmed rumours that had sent a chill down spines for weeks.[67] Coming at this crucial juncture, hard on the heels of glad tidings concerning the NDG, Petch's acceptance of a senior post at Waterloo caused uncertainty and a sharp plunge in unit morale, as physicist Martin Johns made plain in a note of 30 June to Thode. What, he asked, were the precise plans for the grant? What was to be done with a ceramicist, newly hired by Petch, but without clear instructions to other members as to his duties, or even the space he might be given?[68] Herein, it might be suggested, was a partial clue as to the reasons behind Petch's leave-taking; that it was the outcome of full-bore head-butting between two bullish moose, Harry and Howard, is beyond dispute. In his interview for this volume, however, Bourns categorically dismisses as fanciful, the suggestion of Thode's biographers that Petch's criticism of the president's, perceivably inconsistent, stand on full charters for new universities had much to do with the final collision between the two men.[69] Rather, all observers, then and now, agree that both individuals were headstrong in their views and jealous guardians of their own authority. Neither could long tolerate opposition to his confirmed agenda.[70]

Serious divergence first appeared when it was announced that McMaster would be the site of Ontario's newest school of medicine; a scheme to which Harry was obsessively committed. However, Petch, in his 1965 report as principal of Hamilton College, made public his fear that this development threatened that of his own departments. "Little publicity," he wrote, "has been given to lack of financial support for university research in the basic sciences and engineering, whereas the increased support for medical research is continually before the public."[71] He later objected to the site chosen for the health sciences complex, which would entail the destruction of the Royal Botantical Gardens' storied Sunken Gardens.[72] But Johns' letter of 30 June 1967 hints at a further issue. Like Thode, Petch played his cards close to the vest and resented intrusion on his bailiwick. Hence, the IMR members' concerns as to what came next when their chairman suddenly decamped. Petch had not informed them fully. In the end, says Bourns, it all boiled down to a tragic clash of two potent personalities.

As Thode grew convinced that the IMR chair was overstepping the bounds of his mandate, he asked him to step down.[73] Petch went further: all the way to Waterloo. The IMR, however, survived. The tumult and the shouting died, as one-time mentor said sharp farewell to erstwhile protege. The unit, itself, went on to steady development under a new leader, Director James Morrison. Graduate degrees in materials science were drafted and sent for assessment to renowned experts at Harvard, Stanford, and the Massachusetts Institute of Technology (MIT). Uniform, hearty endorsements came from these independent reviewers by May 1969.[74] Housed in the Department of Metallurgy, these programs soon drew candidates from Canada and abroad.

The story of metallurgy and materials science, from 1957 to 1969, affords a fairly typical case study of engineering as a whole, with its emphasis on scientific research, focused group effort, and graduate work, along with practical service to the local community. Chemical engineering, the subject of a recent departmental history, exhibited all the same Thodean traits. Thus, graduate work began in tandem with bachelor's studies and grew steadily, drawing as many as twenty-eight candidates in 1967.[75] Aggressive research was encouraged and rewarded. Professor Albin "Ab" Johnson, for example, led a team that pioneered computer simulation of chemical plants, such as that of Canadian Industries Limited in Hamilton. Their report on the subject (1965) was the first published on digital simulation of a chemical process, and has been cited as one of the hundred most significant achievements in twentieth-century chemical engineering.[76]

Waste water treatment had also been a particular focus of cross-departmental study since the early 1960s. Perhaps few places in Canada offered more scope for such investigation than Burlington Bay, for decades the refuse pit of choice for Hamilton's heavy industry. Combining talents, scholars from chemical and civil engineering won a $500,000 grant in 1969 from the federal Department of Energy, Mines, and Resources, to launch the first concerted attack on water pollution in Canada.[77] Later, the department focused increasingly on polymer research, often availing itself of the MNR. For its part, civil engineering made special efforts in earthquake studies, utilizing the new applied dynamics laboratory, after 1968.[78] This picture was replicated throughout the Faculty of Engineering, most of whose members seem to have taken Kirkaldy's tirade about basic science and graduate work to heart by the mid-sixties. Indeed, differences of outlook must have faded as early as 1964, since Hodgins reported that "an interdisciplinary philosophy is rampant in shared labs."[79] Still, while there were laurels aplenty to be had, there was also room for concern.

By 1967, engineering almost reached its intended undergraduate capacity. It had, however, been an uphill battle. In part, this was ascribed to a continent-wide decline of interest in the field, as well as to the proliferation of facilities at other Ontario universities. Dean Hodgins, however, also felt that, given the rapid growth of technology, programs had become too crammed, too intense. He advised either lengthening the academic term, or adding a fifth year to ease the pressure on undergraduates.[80] Meanwhile, the unexpected swelling of the graduate cadre threatened to strain space, equipment, and faculty to their limits, given the greater demands such students placed on everything. In 1967, undergraduates numbered 423, while 109 graduate students constituted fully 26 per cent of total full-time enrolment.[81] Although proud of the reputation for research to which this ratio stridently testified, Hodgins feared that continued rapid growth of the graduate population would saturate facilities by 1970. He recommended expanding the building and slowing the graduate intake.[82]

Complicating matters, by the late sixties, government funding was tightly tied to per capita enrolments across the province in all disciplines. Granted, the formula was weighted heavily in favour of graduate students, but even then the board, through Thode, informed engineering that the faculty would not be viable with fewer than 1,000 undergraduates by 1978.[83] In response, the core curriculum was streamlined, extension studies were introduced, and a vigorous recruiting campaign in regional high schools was launched. As well, one of the most creative initiatives of the day came with the start, in 1969, of a five-year, combined degree in engineering and business administration. The brainchild of business professor George Torrance and colleagues in engineering, the program blended the best of both professional educations, while cheapening neither. Immensely successful, it was heavily subscribed from the outset and remains unique in Canada today. A start on a new phase of development had begun.

In 1969, Hodgins laid down his decanal mantle. He reflected that, in 1958, he had forecast that Canada would soon shift emphasis from primary to secondary industries. The transformation had taken place more slowly than anticipated, largely, he thought, because of sluggish coordination among government, industry, and universities. There were, however, signs that such synergy was finally being realized. Accordingly, Hodgins prophesied that the seventies would see unprecedented demand for the new engineer.[84] Thus, he left office confident that the targets set by the government, the board, and the university could be met. That same year, McMaster engineering adopted the dramatic "Fireball," based on a 1960 student design, as its official emblem.[85] Others, it appeared, shared Hodgins' bright outlook, some storm clouds hovering over Queen's Park notwithstanding.

Two great balls of fire, engineering's symbolic and the MNR's spectral, had been ignited as the transition of 1955 through 1961 was occurring. Neither, however, was even imaginable in the absence of solid scientific bedrock. The same, of course, was true for those branches of science that took greater wing as the sixties moved on. There was more to the legacy of Hamilton College than neutrons and transistors

3

Bedrock

The Faculty of Science, as it eventually came to be known, was the bedrock upon which the MNR, numerous research units, as well as the university's unique approach to engineering and, later, medicine stood. Above all, from the fifties through the sixties, it lay at the heart of McMaster's claim to be distinctive: a compact, research-intensive institution, heavily committed to graduate studies, with science underpinning much of the combined burden. By its nature, this foundation was expensive both to build and maintain. Moreover, its fashions and frontiers were never static. A university seeking to keep pace with scientific practice and fierce competitors, even if only in specially targeted areas, had to be light on its feet and heavy in its purse. This is why Thode was such a stubborn proponent of what was later called "differentiation." One size, he insisted, would never fit all when it came to making policy for Ontario's universities. McMaster's particular configuration, emphasizing research and graduate study in science, made it recognizably distinct and called for special consideration when funding was at issue.

To put solid flesh on skeletal generalization, some numbers (however tedious) might help. In 1958, there were 1,466 full-time students registered in all programs at McMaster. Of 1,331 undergraduates, 406, or 30.5 per cent, were enrolled in science. The graduate corps numbered 135, or 9.2 per cent of the whole student body. Among the 121 identifiable graduate students, 71.9 per cent opted for science, there being relatively few other choices.[1] By 1967–68, things had altered. At that point, there were 4,448 full-time candidates, all degree levels considered. Science registrations had slipped to 27.4 per cent of the undergraduate total. Meanwhile, the 779 graduate students, spread across campus, now comprised fully 17.5 per cent of the combined university population. Other faculties had made considerable progress at the graduate level during the decade, but science (excluding engineering) still claimed the lion's share: 52.1 per cent of all advanced students.[2] Clearly, while no longer the quasi-monopolist of 1958, science remained vigorous and preponderant in the prestigious realm of graduate studies throughout the sixties.

This fact became increasingly critical to the faculty's well-being for several reasons, some of which were notably peculiar to science. Thus, in all sectors of the university, graduate students afforded vital assistance in undergraduate instruction. Moreover, they were especially valuable sources of revenue. Before 1967, provincial grants to universities were issued on a discretionary basis. An institution with a high proportion of graduate candidates, especially in the highly prized sciences, was in a strong position to bid for a larger slice of the pie. The Deutsch Commission's 1962 call to graduate arms only reinforced this. As will be discussed in detail later, in 1967 provincial operating grants were established on the basis of formula funding. The weight fell heavily on the graduate side of the scale, with an undergraduate in general arts accorded one "basic income unit" (BIU) and a PhD candidate accounting for six.[3] As a result, master and doctoral students became even more significant generators of operating funds.

Beyond these general considerations, however, graduate students were especially important to the sciences. For one thing, they were deemed essential to research to a degree, and in a manner, that was not the case in most arts disciplines. Physicist Harry Duckworth candidly admitted that he was slow to recognize this difference, when he succeeded Bourns as dean of graduate studies in 1962. In science, he came to note, the student was expected to participate in a well-defined, ongoing, research program, be it that of a unit, a department, or a particular professor. The arts candidate, by contrast, was taught to function on his or her own, and generally defined a wholly original project. Not infrequently, that work was, at best, tangential to the core interests of an advisor.[4] Put another way, professorial research in arts could proceed with, or without, graduate students. In science, however, the latter were viewed as indispensable, integral parts of a general research effort. Furthermore, from the university's perspective, scientific research was "value-added," in that it attracted external grants out of all proportion to the size of its staff and student complement.[5] For these particular reasons, as well as more general ones noted above, both the size and quality of its graduate cadre were reckoned imperative by the Faculty of Science – McMaster's chief claim to distinctiveness.

A 1966 report from the chair of geology offers some insight into the mentality and priorities of the hour. D.M. "Dennis" Shaw informed the president that his department had a faculty establishment of ten, with an additional member expected next year. Five full-time technicians assisted staff and students. Among the latter, there were sixteen doctoral candidates and eleven working toward their MSc. On the other hand, he noted, "Undergraduates are still in painfully short supply and their calibre is not generally high." There were, in fact, only fourteen candidates spread across the last three bachelor years. This was disappointing, but, able to append an impressive list of grants and publications to his report, Shaw felt confident in declaring that "we have the best department in the country."[6] This conviction was reinforced two years later when the next chair, B.J. Burley, reported that geology now had twelve faculty members, seven technicians, and five secretaries, along with six post-doctoral fellows, twenty PhD and twenty MSc candidates. Meanwhile, it catered to (a whopping) twenty-eight undergraduate majors. Publications were, as ever, at a high level.[7] Best of all, he continued, in 1968 McMaster had produced 10 per cent of all the geology PhDs who graduated in Canada that year, despite being the smallest department in the nation to offer the degree.[8] Using Thode's yardstick, McMaster's geology department might very well have been, per capita, the best of its kind in the country. By 1969, however, it was also dangerously graduate-dependent in the light of formula funding. To a lesser degree, the same pattern held true for those two thoroughbreds that had led McMaster's charge into the sixties: chemistry and physics.

In his report for 1956–57, Principal Thode was pleased to note that, at all levels, enrolment in science was increasing slightly faster than in other sectors of the university. He suggested that this would probably continue for some time. After all, the country was desperately short of trained scientists. True, honours enrolments were down a bit, but he expected them to recover shortly, once the current recession let up. For the moment, with Gilmour's blessing, he was stockpiling faculty against the forecast onrush of boomers. Chemistry's standing establishment was small, but was already making a stamp: Thode in geochemistry, Arthur Bourns in organic, Lawrence Cragg in physical, and Richard Tomlinson in radiochemistry. Recruited from Great Britain in 1957, Gerald W. "Gerry" King, Ian D. Spenser, and Ronald J. Gillespie added research heft and diversity to physical, biochemical, and inorganic chemistry, respectively.[9] Each of the newcomers would prove prolific. King, for example, went on to author a seminal book on spectroscopy and molecular structure.[10] Spenser would be central to the development of biochemistry at McMaster. It was Gillespie, however, whom Bourns later judged to have provided "great leadership in research" throughout the sixties and seventies.[11]

The trio, as it happened, arrived just in the nick. Indeed, by 1960, three further appointments were needed to cope with "the largest undergraduate class in many years." Not all of these students were destined for chemistry degrees, but the subject was required for science freshmen, whose numbers were augmented by engineers. With 250 to 300 anticipated in year-one science by 1961–62, the pressure was palpable. More staff was urgently requested.[12] Meanwhile, morning laboratory slots were introduced to accommodate undergraduate numbers, and chemistry, along with the other major sciences, experimented with closed-circuit television (CCTV) in first year.[13] In 1963, a harried Chairman Gillespie reported to Thode that, so rapid was the growth of enrolment at all degree levels, an assistant to the chair was appointed, just to handle the volume of work. He was gratified that the department hosted nine post-doctoral fellows, but was concerned about the future of chemistry's research effort. Granted, graduate student numbers had risen, but they had not kept pace with total department needs. There had been twenty-two graduate candidates in 1959–60; by 1962–63, there were thirty-eight. This was progress, but not nearly enough, said Gillespie. All these people were fully occupied as undergraduate teaching assistants. None could be spared for research. Therefore, he told a sympathetic president; "continued and strenuous efforts must be made to attract good research students to the department."[14] Confidentially, he informed Thode that, despite increasingly diverse offerings, nuclear chemistry was the only area in which the department received more graduate applications than it had places.[15]

The shortage, it should be said, was not for want of a strong departmental profile. Indeed, its research output grew ever-more prodigious, with continued success in grant applications and the attendant ability to attract able post-doctoral fellows. Thus, between 1964 and 1969, the annual *President's Reports* regularly featured anywhere from six to eight pages of closely typed titles authored by McMaster chemists.[16] Reputation, therefore, was not an issue; nor was expression of interest. Rather, a concern for quality recruitment constituted the chief problem. Department minutes show that, in 1963, some 242 inquiries were received, with the overwhelming bulk (198) coming from overseas. Only 22 were deemed up to scratch, less than half of whom were Canadian.[17] Meanwhile, experience with candidates from non-English-speaking countries led the department to insist on a minimum standing of over 80 per cent for their admission.[18] Hungry for graduate students, or not, chemistry remained picky. Indeed, in 1964, out of 226 applicants, only 54 were given any consideration, 41 of whom were quickly rejected.[19]

By 1965, vigorous recruiting, especially in Britain, brought graduate numbers up to sixty-six, with eighty likely the next year. Still, this was fewer than necessary to support the research needs of twenty-one staff, let alone the twenty-eight expected by 1970.[20] Eventually, it dawned on department members that their programs might be just a bit too demanding; thus deterring otherwise good candidates from applying. Accordingly, course (as opposed to research) loads were streamlined and reduced.[21] This worked. In the academic year 1969–70, chemistry could boast 110 graduate students, in company with twenty-one post-doctoral fellows. This afforded strong support for the twenty-eight faculty members. Not surprisingly, research was at an all-time high. There was but one fly in the chemical ointment – a scant eighty students were registered in years two through four of the undergraduate program.[22]

As early as 1964, a dip among honours candidates prompted concern. The department's curriculum committee offered some wry advice to colleagues. "Having devised such an excellent program," the committee reported, "it may seem to some that a major revision at this time is premature." Such persons, however, were advised to think again. After all, the report went on, "Our enthusiasm to cover the required chemistry in three years has left us with virtually no students to appreciate our excellent program in Year IV."[23] Dean Ronald Graham was in a less whimsical mood. "Many students," he observed, "have no sound reason for attending university." In his view, a 25 per cent failure rate in first-year science attested stridently to this. Far too many, he continued, were admitted with high-school notions of proper study habits. "It is significant," wrote Graham, "that the admonition on the sundial of Hamilton Hall, '*aut disce aut discede*' ["either learn or leave"], has been translated by generations of McMaster students as 'cram or scram.'"[24] Whatever the case, chemistry began a review of its offerings immediately, but got bogged down in interminable debate. Meanwhile, in 1966, Gillespie advised Thode that the proportion of students opting for the four-year programs was declining "at an alarming rate." Excellent as it might be in design, the honours degree was, he thought, "unrealistically heavy," given that less than half the candidates in second year had made the grade. The situation, he warned, was becoming critical.[25]

The administration was listening – with considerable concern. In August 1967, the President's Council, Thode's "inner cabinet," took stock of the declining applications, not just to chemistry, but to all the physical sciences. McMaster science, they concluded, had gained a "bad reputation." The university was losing excellent candidates to other institutions because of the inflexibility and "severe course load" of the undergraduate curriculum, especially in honours programs. Similarly, a high rate of attrition in first-year science was doing little to attract applicants by the thronging legion. Departments, therefore, were advised to reduce the load without lessening the intellectual challenge.[26]

Chemistry, as noted, was already struggling to do just that, but failed to achieve consensus. When, in September 1968, proposals for revision were put forward, there was still division. Bourns, speaking as a fellow chemist, voiced a level of frustration that still echoes sharply in yellowed department minutes. Almost obsessive emphasis, he said, was placed on honours courses for those who would go on to graduate school. The problem was that fewer and fewer students were electing to do so. Did it not make sense, he asked, to pay more attention to preparing undergraduates for careers in industry? After all, he added, most companies much preferred to hire people with a BSc or MSc and then mould them to specific needs on the job. Some colleagues agreed, arguing that the department should adopt a philosophy of training potential leaders of industry.[27] Later that year, Bourns suggested inviting outside experts to assist in developing an industrial stream.[28] Eventually, an "honours applied chemistry" program was proposed, only to provoke more bickering. Major curriculum revision, which included adding the applied stream, was delayed by debate until 1974.[29] Even then, honours programs remained the centre of attention; despite the fact that chemistry and its sister sciences traditionally insisted that their own candidates go elsewhere for graduate training, while complaining when other universities did not follow suit.

Heartland of the Thodean paradigm, chemistry unquestionably flourished between 1957 and 1969, at least in most respects. The faculty complement had been steadily reinforced. Its members had been prolific on the research front. External grants were closing in on the $400,000 mark by 1970.[30] Chemists were key players in several cross-departmental research groups, such as the MNR and IMR. A score of post-doctoral fellows and more than a hundred graduate candidates were living evidence of the department's sterling reputation. On all these counts, Thode must have been well pleased with the progress of his first born. Still, the relative decline of undergraduate numbers, especially in the prized honours stream, offered cause for concern. So did the fact that almost 40 per cent of the graduate population was non-Canadian and, thus, ineligible for some forms of external support.[31] Given that its first-year course was compulsory for all science students, there was no immediate danger of chemistry emulating the enrolment patterns in geology. Even so, the once tidal undergraduate flood had clearly begun to ebb. This, it should be underscored, was not specific to McMaster. Instead, as

Tomlinson mused in 1969, "an international change in science fashions" was under way.[32] His colleagues in other disciplines would note the same shifting currents.

Physics, stately queen of the sciences, followed a trajectory closely paralleling that of chemistry. The department entered the post-Baptist era in a strong position. Since 1949, it had been carefully sculpted. As a matter of policy, hiring focused on two research areas: nuclear and solid state physics, with an emphasis on the former.[33] Boyd McClay specialized in spectroscopy, Martin Johns in nuclear physics, Gerald Tauber in relativity theory, and Duckworth in mass spectroscopy. So close were relations with some chemists that both Thode and Tomlinson could fairly be counted physicists, as well. Melvin Preston filled the pivotal post in nuclear theory and, in the opinion of Duckworth, "gave real credibility to the program."[34] By 1957, twenty graduate students were on hand and undergraduate numbers began to rise. To cope with this, Robert G. Summers-Gill, an experimental physicist, and Paul R. Zilsel, a quantum theorist, were added to the roster, along with Howard Petch in solid state studies. Rudolph Haering joined the tribe, shortly thereafter.

As with chemistry, business in physics was brisk. By 1961, Chairman Duckworth was lobbying the administration for more classroom and laboratory space, as registrations in the first two undergraduate years spiked 20 per cent over the 1959–60 level. Meanwhile, graduate students, most of them in the doctoral program, numbered thirty-five. This, Duckworth contended, was a heavy burden for nine staff, each of whom maintained a high research profile. Extensions of the physical sciences building had helped with space, but facilities were quickly coming under strain.[35] The cavalry, sympathetic administrators assured him, was on the way. Indeed, within three years, six new faculty members were recruited; the biggest catch being Bert Brockhouse, who had been lured from Chalk River by the opportunity to teach at a university with research facilities appropriate to his interests.

Enrolments, however, kept climbing. Thus, in 1963, there were 375 in the freshman class, with 399, 153, and 128 in years two, three, and four, respectively, while graduate candidates numbered 57.[36] Like chemistry, physics turned to CCTV for freshmen and appointed an associate chairman to oversee the undergraduate program.[37] Physics, it seemed, was hot stuff; destined to grow hotter. In the face of this, Petch ventured that the department would require thirty staff to cope with a projected 1,000 freshmen and 600 second-year students by 1970.[38]

On the research front, physicists mirrored assiduous chemists. Thode already enjoyed an international reputation. Preston's work in theory brought election to the Royal Society of Canada, in 1960. Brockhouse was doing seminal labour in triple-axis spectronomy that would lead him to Nobel laurels. For his part, Duckworth won acclaim for papers presented in Vienna (1963) and Paris (1964) that revealed the true potential of his personally designed, mass spectrometer.[39] Courted by both Toronto and Manitoba, he left McMaster late in 1964. Rumour had it that he and Thode had fallen out, but the records do not speak to the point. Feelings, however, could not have been too badly bruised, since the president made no fuss when Duckworth took his unique instrument to Manitoba. Returning the professional favour, Duckworth was later instrumental in persuading an initially reluctant NRC committee to lavish funds on McMaster for a tandem accelerator.[40]

A catalogue of physics' scholarly achievement could be drawn out ad infinitum. Suffice it to say, however, that the department put a high premium on research. Nothing demonstrated this more clearly than an incident in December 1962. Physics had been asked to contribute to the university's burgeoning extension program. Meeting to discuss this, members voiced "violent opposition," based on the distraction this would cause. One member won wide approval when he observed that "our current research and teaching are more than enough and Physics should not be put in the same category as some other departments in which professors do little or no research."[41] No doubt, several active scholars in arts would have asked to meet the physicist (and his seconds), had they been privy to this comment. Fortunately, the words were spoken privately, and no duelling dons were bloodied on the college green. Still, the comment, itself, spoke volumes about the self-image and priorities of this driven group.

The MNR, of course, was a priceless resource for many in the department, but there was much more going on. Duckworth and Petch, for example, had forged close ties with chemists, geologists, and metallurgists anxious to advance solid state studies.[42] Such links would only strengthen with the flowering of materials research. At the undergraduate level, Preston took the initiative in forming an applied mathematics unit, in 1963. The intention was to supply service courses to science and engineering students, who did not require initiation into the deeper mysteries of pure mathematics. Analysis and computation of the sort useful in laboratory or field work were emphasized. Most of the instructors were practising scientists or engineers, who spoke a tongue familiar to their youthful charges.[43] By 1966, these popular offerings led to the founding of a separate department, which acted as an arm of the growing computation centre. Typically enough, no sooner had the department been sanctioned than there was talk of instituting graduate work. This was, after all, still a Thodean universe. For the moment, staff poured out papers on analysis, computation, and other aspects of applied mathematics.[44]

Meanwhile, nuclear physics did not rest on its reactor's laurels. In 1962, Duckworth represented McMaster at a gathering with colleagues from Queen's and Toronto when the prospect of forging a tri-university consortium to acquire an "Emperor" particle accelerator was on the menu. It quickly became apparent, however, that interests differed. McMaster specialized in low-energy physics, whereas the others concentrated on high-energy inquiry. There was no natural fit. Thode, however, instructed his department to prepare a brief to government that would suit McMaster's own purposes. The pitch to the NRC rested on the need to keep up with developments abroad. At that time, the interior of the nucleus was all but *terra incognita*. Particle accelerators were capable of probing its internal structure and the elemental forces dancing at play. As European and American groups made ever greater use of the new devices, Canada could ill afford to fall behind; unless it was content to see its best young nuclear scientists emigrate, in order to keep abreast of the field. From another point of view, an accelerator was deemed vital, if physics at McMaster were not to atrophy. Looking further still, the brief's authors foresaw an institute for nuclear studies, tied closely to industry, taking shape on the shores of Lake Ontario. An accelerator at McMaster would be the first step toward that happy consummation.[45] Expense, they did not add, need not be spared.

Others felt differently. Indeed, the fourteen-person NRC committee charged with considering the proposal was less than wildly enthused, at least at the outset of deliberations. It was at this juncture that Duckworth, now vice-president at Manitoba, came to the aid of his former department. As Martin Johns told the tale, Duckworth, a member of the grant committee, stood all but alone in support of McMaster's brief. Ever determined and persuasive, over long months and numerous meetings, he swung sufficient votes around. Late in 1965, word finally came that McMaster had been awarded several million dollars to acquire, house, and staff an MP model tandem Van de Graff electrostatic particle accelerator. Dr John A. Kuehner was promptly hired away from Chalk River to plan and oversee development of the new treasure.[46] With the opening of the facility in 1969, McMaster entered the age of particle physics.

Altogether, research and graduate studies in physics reached, or exceeded, Thode's fondest hopes during the sixties. In 1966, for example, graduate candidates hit the 100 mark and lingered around that comfortable figure for the rest of the decade.[47] Better yet, there were vastly more applications for post-doctoral positions than could ever be accommodated. In 1967 alone, more than 200 sought a place, giving the department the pick of a bumper crop. The reactor, augmented by the promised accelerator, not to mention the surging materials program in engineering, seemed magnetic. Research productivity soared to new levels, and a proud chairman reminded the president that his department continued to attract the highest grants and graduate enrolment per faculty member in Canada.[48] And the beat went on.

By 1970, external funding, exclusive of the reactor and accelerator, topped $400,000. Meanwhile, Chairman Brockhouse tallied all the papers delivered at the last six meetings of the Canadian Association of Physicists and was pleased to announce that McMaster had contributed fully 122; second only to Toronto's 171 – with half the latter's faculty complement.[49] Adding lustre to all this, McMaster had been the headquarters of CAP since the end of World War II, until the organization moved permanently to Ottawa in 1968. In so many fruitful ways, physics, like chemistry and geology, had vaulted the university into first-division play, just as Thode had dreamed in 1957. There was, however, one serious cause for misgiving.

Petch's 1963 forecast of 600 second-year registrations by 1970 was proving wildly off the mark. Honours enrolments were the first to drop; small wonder, given that over half the candidates failed to maintain standing in 1963.[50] By 1966, there were only 41 spread over the last three years of the program. Even worse, students in the general and pass programs numbered a scarce 36.[51] In conclave, Dr Donald Sprung alerted colleagues to some solemn facts of life. The department was giving consideration to new areas into which it might venture. Applied and health physics seemed the most promising avenues. Sprung, however, reminded his peers that, with formula funding, resources were now largely pegged to enrolments. The development of any new fields would, therefore, necessitate the recruitment of many more students.[52] Accepting that the salad days were done, his colleagues moved on this sound advice. New brochures were published. High-school and freshman students were invited to tour the full array of wonders available to them, were they to join the department. A student-faculty committee was struck to give undergraduates a sense of having a stake in physics' affairs. In this, physics was an early innovator. At the same time, questionnaires were circulated seeking candid advice from undergraduates as to the strengths and weaknesses of the programs on offer. Responses, moreover, were closely studied and seriously considered.[53] Meanwhile, as the race to the moon heated up, a new course in astronomy and astrophysics was devised to attract the curious. "Relevance," that sixties buzzword, had resonance well beyond the arts. At the same time, nuclear physicist Terry

Kennett spearheaded a move to ensure that every undergraduate major had a personal advisor, thereby turning to an old McMaster tradition.[54] There was, in short, no lack of effort or imagination in attempts to recover a once healthy audience.

Even so, in 1968, Brockhouse noted, somewhat resignedly, "There is a tendency for physics to be falling in the estimation of incoming students."[55] As chairman, he was relieved that the department still carried its weight under the formula's terms, but he failed to mention that this had a lot to do with the high BIU value of its 100 graduate candidates and the still numerous, but undeclared, first-year students.[56] Recognizing the need to capture more of the latter, CCTV was abandoned as a teaching tool. More importantly, the large freshman class was subdivided into sections of no more than fifty to sixty each. Meanwhile, professors were furnished with handbooks featuring photographs of their youthful charges all in an endeavour to personalize the physics experience. The clearest evidence that the departmental worm had turned, however, came early in 1970. Without a single dissenting vote, without a peep of protest, physics agreed to offer degree work in extension.[57] Gone was the "violent opposition" voiced in 1962. The logic of Sprung's admonition – no new students, no new research areas – proved compelling. As he left the chair, Brockhouse rendered a sobering tally. In 1970, despite all best efforts, physics could claim only thirty-nine registrations beyond first year, as against 110 graduate students.[58] Like chemistry and geology, the department was turning into an admittedly renowned, but potentially vulnerable, research-cum-graduate sector of the university. If anything should dampen graduate enrolment, serious trouble would inevitably ensue.

Administrators certainly recognized the dangers. Bourns, as vice-president of science, surveyed the scene in 1968. At one level, he conceded, the drift away from physical science was a continent-wide and, therefore, inescapable phenomenon. There were, however, some aspects particular to McMaster that aggravated the problem. Chief among these, he opined, was the inflexibility of honours programs, which discouraged many worthy candidates because of an "unrealistically heavy load." His dean, Dennis McCalla, echoed this view, but applauded initiatives by chemistry, physics, and applied mathematics to bring more variety to first-year offerings.[59] Still, from his vice-presidential perspective, Bourns described 1968–69 as a "transition year." After a period of rapid expansion, numbers in the physical sciences were levelling off or, in some cases, declining. This, he added, was not necessarily detrimental in itself. The real problem arose with the slowing rate of annual increase assigned by Queen's Park to the BIU.[60] The latter, after all, was vitally important by decade's end, as the province had become the overwhelming fount of university income.

Initially, Ontario's universities had lobbied hard for formula, as opposed to negotiated, discretionary funding. A 1965 national-level commission under Toronto economist, Vincent Wheeler Bladen, had recommended just such a formula-based approach. After two years of dickering, Ontario chose that route. It offered block grants to universities based on weighted enrolment, without line-by-line scrutiny on the part of government.[61] Thode felt that the weights assigned to science, professional, and graduate faculties were too low, but accepted the scheme as a step toward more predictable income and better planning.[62] Both Bourns and McMaster graduate Bernard Trotter had been involved in negotiations.[63] Thode was prepared to accept their judgment that, for the moment, a reasonable deal had been struck. He could always haggle later.

Thode and others, however, were far less than happy when, in 1967, the federal government ceased direct, per capita subsidization of individual universities in favour of lump transfers to provincial coffers. Meanwhile, as early as 1966, Minister of Education William "Bill" Davis began politely to caution Ontario universities that a measure of discretion might well be needed. The sky, he warned, was definitely soaring well above the limit of government largesse.[64] In 1969, the minister of university affairs, Bill Davis, declared that "we have reached the end of the line."[65] Thode, of course, deployed his traditional gambit, arguing that no block grant could ever mesh with McMaster's particular configuration. Davis replied personally, citing the changed facts of provincial life. "It is evident to all of us," he wrote, "that we are living in a time when apparent needs can be seen in many aspects of our society and when institutional hopes and aspirations are running at an extremely high level." "At the same time," Davis continued, "it has also become very clear that available resources, while also at an all-time high, are not sufficient to meet all of these apparent needs, hopes, and aspirations."[66]

Bourns, who had helped devise the formula weights, understood quite well that Davis was a genuine friend of higher education. Equally, he recognized that the recent advent of universal health care and a bevy of new social assistance programs placed tremendous demands on government coffers; demands with which those of universities could scarcely compete in the public arena. McMaster and her sisters would not be suddenly and utterly starved, but they would need to be prudent in the years ahead.[67] This was especially true in the wake of the mid-sixties Spinks Report and its implications for the big BIU's in graduate studies.

The granting of unlimited charters to new universities had led to the proliferation of graduate programs across the province. Increasingly, these overlapped and replicated one another, just as Thode and Bissell had feared. The cost involved was considerable, especially in science and the professions. Predictably, paymasters and the press began to speak of "rationalization." In order to pre-empt unilateral government action, the CPUO bargained with the CUA to sponsor a joint inquiry into the state of graduate planning in Ontario. J.W.T. Spinks, president of the University of Saskatchewan, chaired the commission. His report, issued in 1966, sent shock waves rolling over every campus. It spoke of centralization in a "University of Ontario," backed by a strong coordinating agency with a master plan for graduate studies.

University presidents from Kingston to Thunder Bay, in a rare nanosecond of unanimity, recoiled in horror. Fortunately, for them, Bill Davis also rejected government interference in their traditional autonomy. He did, however, insist that they make greater effort at self-regulation and rationalization.[68] The Spinks Report helped pave the way to formula funding. It also led to the founding of the Ontario Council on Graduate Studies (OCGS), which, in turn, formed the Advisory Committee on Academic Planning (ACAP). The latter body would go on to develop appraisal procedures for monitoring graduate programs before they were recommended for funding. The freewheeling atmosphere of a bounteous mid-century was over.[69] In 1969, the appointment of the Commission on Post-Secondary Education in Ontario (COPSE) merely drove this home.

Against this complex backdrop, Bourns advised Thode that it "has become increasingly clear that if we are to make the most effective use of our resources, we must select within our present programs a few areas for special development, while at the same time identifying new areas of concentration for which there is student interest and a clearly defined social or economic need." On a brighter note, he added that, if the physical sciences were facing a period of slow growth, psychology, biology, and geography were positively blooming at all enrolment levels.[70]

Well before secularization, Gilmour's administration recognized psychology as a coming field of potentially wide application. In 1955, after a broad search, P. Lynn Newbigging was hired to inject fresh energy into the discipline. Radiating infectious zest, the rookie moved with alacrity to thrust McMaster psychology down a modern path. In one sense, that road would be narrow. Newbigging was an experimentalist, with little interest in clinical or social psychology. On the other hand, his insistence on strict concentration of focus, allied to a passion for research, could have been crafted by Harry, himself. In that sense, he was as Thodean as Thode. Few, in any case, would have later cause to regret the scientific modernism that underpinned all his planning.

With strong administrative support, Newbigging bent to his self-defined task with a will. First, three new experimentalists were hired, thereby signalling the direction of future development. Then, in 1958, the Department of Psychology was formally established; freed from former restraints as a branch of philosophy. Thereafter, not a horse was spared in the effort to get up and running. Thus, honours, MA, and PhD programs were all in place by 1959. Two decades on, Newbigging wryly quipped that such ambitious curricular leaps by four junior professors would hardly garner attention, let alone approval, in the eighties.[71] Be that as it may, the chairman and his colleagues, A.H. "Abe" Black, D.W. Carment, and L.J. Kamin, won swift approval for their plans, especially from Thode, ever the apostle of sharply delineated focus and graduate work. Support bred confidence and was repaid with results. Indeed, as early as 1958, Herb Armstrong, dean of arts and science, reported that student interest was high, while faculty members were bringing in external grants sufficient to cover two full salaries, with plenty left to pay research costs and assistants.[72]

Graduate- and research-oriented, by 1960 the department had sent more MA than honours students to convocation, as well as enrolling its first two doctoral candidates. Meanwhile, a gratified Newbigging informed Thode that of the total research grants awarded nationwide to faculty in experimental psychology, McMaster had won almost 20 per cent, second only to Queen's. As for awards to graduate students, fully one-third of NRC prizes had gone to McMaster candidates, leaving the university at the top of the national list.[73] Billeted in old, cramped, temporary quarters, the department had grown to seven members, by 1961. Resources were humble, but much had been achieved. With tangible achievement came political capital. By 1962, having bolted from the starting gate, the department felt the time had come to bid for a place in the Promised Land.

In February of that year, Thode received a cogent brief arguing that science, not arts, was the proper home of modern psychology. Newbigging noted that many in Hamilton College disputed this, primarily because their notions of the discipline were out of date; relics of brief acquaintance during bygone undergraduate days. Playing his ace, he emphasized decisively that the NRC felt otherwise. Pointing to that agency's recent generosity to psychology at McMaster, he outlined the department's research into learning, motivation, perception, and neuropsychology. Papers had been produced on everything from voting behaviour to psycholinguistics. All this, he underlined, was a far cry from older fixations with classical analysis or philosophical musing. Thumbing one of Thode's most sensitive buttons, Newbigging contended that psychology, as practised at McMaster, was one of the natural sciences and should be grouped with them, so as to have closer, more fruitful relations with sister disciplines.[74] Thoroughly convinced, Thode announced the transfer to Hamilton College, effective July 1962.[75] Principal Petch, who understood the space and facility needs of an experimental discipline, embraced the newcomers and helped nourish an already obsessive drive to research. Faculty grew at the rate of roughly one per year.[76] The publication level would be exponentially higher.[77]

From the perspective of the Faculty of Science as a whole, this move could not have come at a more opportune moment. Thus, while the undergraduate base of the physical sciences began to erode, psychology was becoming a home to the big battalions. Ironically, this reflected the 1960's explosion of the social sciences, many of which listed one or more psychology courses as requirements. By 1965, the pressure of numbers was such that a purpose-built psychology building was authorized. In keeping with Thode's interlaced concept of campus design, it was planned to stand adjacent to new facilities for the life sciences and medicine. That, however, was still five years in the offing. For the moment, psychology struggled to meet the needs of almost 600 first-year students, while tending to nearly a hundred candidates beyond that stage. Meanwhile, graduate admissions reached 37, and a proud chair informed the president that some of those admitted had chosen McMaster over offers from Brown, Columbia, Stanford, and (miracle of miracles) Harvard. Ten new candidates held NRC scholarships – the highest concentration of these prestigious awards of any psychology department in Canada. He was less pleased, however, to report that lack of space had forced him "to pack off all our graduate students to the recently emptied Drill Hall."[78]

Within a year, the undergraduate population boomed, yet again. Indeed, in 1966–67, seventeen instructors contended with more than a thousand freshmen, a hundred pass, and fifty honours students. The graduate corps, meanwhile, stood at fifty-one and was restricted to that level for many years thereafter.[79] This latter move, in part, reflected a concern for quality, along with the scarcity of first-class Canadian applicants. Experimental psychology was only just getting off the ground in Canada. Accordingly, the pool of outstanding, native-born candidates was shallow. At the same time, the department did not accept its own progeny, feeling it best that they broaden themselves by exposure to different mentors. As a result, the United States became a prime recruiting ground. In 1968, for example, fourteen of the twenty new graduate candidates came from south of the border.[80] Apart from these considerations, a matter of deliberate policy came into play. From the late fifties on, Newbigging and company had agreed that less was more. A relatively small but highly cohesive department with a clear-cut research mandate had been the desired goal.[81] With fewer than twenty staff, psychology did not want more graduate students than could be reasonably accommodated. The weight of undergraduate numbers, of course, also put limits on the possible.

Catering to arts as well as science, psychology was a sprawling, cross-campus enterprise at the undergraduate level. Moreover, untold hundreds of BA registrations represented precious BIU's that the Faculty of Science could ill afford to turn away. In response, for good or ill, psychology retained CCTV in year-one in order to conserve strength for majors, graduates, and research. Still, the large proportion of undergraduates hailing from social science eventually had a significant impact. By 1965, the department lacked sufficient resources to meet the rising demand for courses suited to the interests of those in the BA stream. The search for social psychologists, therefore, began in earnest. The chairman predicted the need for six out of a projected faculty of twenty-four by 1970. This, he admitted, would change the face of the department to some degree. So, too, would expected cross-appointments with clinical psychology in the emerging Faculty of Medicine. Nevertheless, he asserted, a sharp focus on research and graduate training in animal learning, physiological psychology, and human psychophysics would remain unaltered for the foreseeable future.[82]

Recognizing a good bet when they saw one, administrators put their money down, to the extent of allowing the recruitment of some senior scholars, such as A.R. Kristofferson and H.M. "Herb" Jenkins.[83] Evidence that they wagered wisely came in the form of heavy enrolments, but also via a threatening, backhanded compliment. The latter took shape in efforts by major American and Canadian universities to lure away prominent staff. This, in a sense, was the warmest praise. It was also, however, a looming danger. In 1967, for example, a distraught chairman told Thode that, while he faced pressing problems with space and numbers, no challenge was greater than beating back "voracious competition" for his strongest faculty members. The battle, he added, was not rendered easier by the fact that McMaster's salaries fell below the median for psychologists elsewhere.[84] Others complained that the promotion process was agonizingly slow, pointing out that applicants rejected by McMaster had risen swiftly in rank at nearby universities. Inevitably, there were losses, but not enough to damage the department, which took up residence in a state-of-the-art building, in 1970.

The story of psychology in this period reads like a case study in the law of unintended consequences. Traditionalists among the senior sciences had initially questioned the department's fitness as a member of the Hamilton College team. By 1969, however, like a burly, young linebacker, psychology helped to plug BIU gaps, as heavyweight veterans up front slowed, near decade's end. Meanwhile, a department that had sought to escape the confines of arts wound up teaching ever-more of the latter's offspring. Yet, amid all this, McMaster psychology retained the core identity Newbigging had fostered, as its reputation in experimental research grew apace. In broader terms, along with biology and geography, psychology was one of an increasingly muscular trio bringing fresh vigour to the Faculty of Science, as the sixties waned. University authorities took note.

Dean Dennis R. McCalla, for one, singled out the life sciences for "special comment" in his report for 1967–68. "Perhaps no other Science department," he wrote, "has such potential for growth and development as does Biology."[85] This was a far cry from administrative signals less than a decade earlier. Biology, indeed, entered the sixties with a strong sense of being neglected and undervalued.[86] To be sure, Gilmour had applauded with gusto when, in 1960–61, biology reached out creatively to the greater public, successfully offering a full-credit course via CHCH-TV. The novel experiment was a first in Canada and, better yet, had been underwritten by station owner, Ken Sobel, staunch backer and later a governor of the university.[87] Momentary applause, however, was no substitute for substantive reinforcement.

As early as 1957, biology reported that its student numbers, particularly at the graduate level, were on par with those at some of Canada's largest universities. Staff and space resources, however, were comparatively meagre. Assistance was urgently requested.[88] This plea was reiterated as the fifties rolled on. Yet, as enrolments rose and course offerings multiplied, biology's staff complement remained the same in 1962 as it had been in 1953. The department, therefore, surveyed the deployment of resources on campus and at other universities. The results provided ample ingredients for a tart brief to Thode, in 1963. Professor Norman W. Radforth, biology's larger-than-life chairman, fired the thundering broadside. Citing voluminous statistics, he noted that seven (in fact, eight) faculty at McMaster mounted a total of thirty-one courses, while McGill, with twenty-nine staff, offered only thirty-seven. Farther east, Memorial's nine instructors delivered a scant seventeen. Prodding at Thodes's competitive nerve, Radforth added that his colleagues schooled more honours students than Toronto's much larger faculty cohort. As if this were not enough, McMaster biology offered more courses than any other science department on campus. Meanwhile, biologists maintained the greenhouse, produced reputable scholarship, and participated in two of the president's beloved interdisciplinary research units. By comparison, Radforth roared, geology seemed to be a favoured son, delivering fewer courses to several hundred fewer students yet boasting the same number of staff, supported by technical assistants. Bubbling with frustration, he called on the president to re-examine "the birthright and minimum purpose of McMaster in relation to the biological sciences."[89]

Thode, in fact, had already done so; however, one suspects that he had been reluctant to reinforce a house divided, especially if it were inclined, in his opinion, to sway in the wrong direction. As Stanley T. Bayley notes in his admirable history of the department, McMaster's biologists had been slow to embrace new developments exploding, after 1953, with the description of DNA by Watson and Crick. Thus, as late as 1961, Radforth was still asking colleagues whether they preferred to emphasize classical, descriptive studies, or more recent physiological, molecular ones. Department members had been uncertain.[90] Always knowing his own mind, Thode saw little to debate. The new biology fit perfectly with the interdisciplinary matrix he sought to weave. Accordingly, he gave the department a less-than-subtle nudge. It came in the form of an end-run.

His gambit was the creation, in 1961, of the Research Unit in Molecular Biology, Biochemistry, and Biophysics, as an altogether independent entity.[91] Members would do undergraduate teaching in appropriate departments, but the research and graduate functions of the unit would be supervised by its own director.[92] Looking for new, like-minded allies, Thode imported Dr John Unrau, head of plant sciences at the University of Alberta, to lead the group. Before his untimely death in February 1962, Unrau induced two Alberta colleagues to join his eastward trek: Drs Stephen Threlkeld (genetics) and Dennis McCalla (biochemistry). These were significant additions. McCalla, in particular, would go on to play a major role in campus-wide affairs, both as scientist and administrator. Meanwhile, Threlkeld, appointed to biology, inherited the mantle intended for Unrau. Once in place, he exhibited precisely the spirit Thode hoped to instill all round. Indeed, as early as October 1961, Threlkeld wrote to Thode that compartmentalization was unhealthy in a changing day and age. Far better, he suggested, would be the integrated study of all living things in a holistic "School of Biological Sciences."[93] Thode must have chuckled, tickled by welcome advice from a strategically placed new boy.

The long-term strategy behind the molecular unit's formation was part of Thode's larger design to bring medicine to McMaster. With Gilmour, he had resisted early calls to found a medical school, arguing that such endeavour could only succeed after a modern, scientific foundation was securely in place. By the early sixties, chemistry, physics, and key elements of engineering stood ready. The reactor offered unique facilities for research, diagnostics, and, in some instances, treatment. The life sciences, however, were torn between old and new. Hence, the Thodean nudge. To Thode, it was all so clear. The whole conceptual framework of living things had been utterly revolutionized through the co-operation of chemists, physicists and biologists in recent years. McMaster had to dive into the deep end of the molecular pool. A newly minted doctoral program, lodged in the biochemistry, biophysics, and molecular biology research unit, represented the requisite plunge.[94]

In the midst of this, Radforth and company ought not to be seen as dithering rebels without a cause. On the contrary, most were respected and productive scholars. D.M. Davies, for example, was on the board of the Entomological Society of Canada. H. Kleerekoper's work in ichthyology led to regular speaking engagements as far afield as the universities of Miami, Texas, Michigan, and Cornell. J.J. Miller served as associate editor of the *Canadian Journal of Microbiology*, while P.F. Nace won substantial grants for research into diabetes.[95]

Radforth, himself, was no sworn enemy of the new. Indeed, he had stoutly supported Thode's early drive to develop doctoral programs, throughout the fifties. Meanwhile, he subscribed fully to the president's interdisciplinary paradigm. Thus, he founded the Organic and Associated Terrain Research Unit (OATRU), in 1961, with the purpose of drawing together biologists, geologists, engineers, and others interested in the potential of Canada's vast swathes of muskeg. The records present some confusion as to the status of this body. In his 1961–62 report to the president, Director of Research Petch describes it as having been "formally established."[96] However, in a 1964 memorandum, Radforth asked Thode to grant OATRU "institute status," with the power to administer its own staff, offer course remissions, and retain any income from contracts for its own use.[97] Bayley contends that the request was refused on the basis that OATRU had come to concentrate on developing all-terrain vehicles, to the neglect of its stated biological mandate.[98] However, Harry's distaste for free-standing "institutes" might have played a role in the decision, too. In any case, a disappointed Radforth would depart for the University of New Brunswick three years later. These details aside, the point remains that the department, as a whole, was not balking at research, graduate education, or growth, per se; its turn-of-the-decade hesitancy arose from other causes.

For one thing, members were simply torn as to the relative merits of classical versus newer methods. In matters such as this, hindsight can distort as easily as illuminate. Thus, Bayley notes that the full potential of a molecular-physiological approach was not convincingly established until well into the eighties.[99] It would be unfair, therefore, to dismiss classical practitioners of the early sixties as stubborn Luddites. Beyond this, a deeper concern troubled many in biology. Thode had not consulted formally with the department over the formation of the molecular unit. Of course, presidential fiats rarely sit well with all and sundry. This one, however, sparked general fear that academic biology might be subordinated to the clinical, applied interests of a forecast medical school. The chairman addressed the point in his 1963 salvo to Thode, albeit adroitly. Thus, Radforth acknowledged opportunities for fruitful intercourse with medicine, but underlined biology's determination to maintain a primary voice in shaping its own curriculum and staff. Going further, he asked the president for new appointments in invertebrate animal biology, parasitology, embryology and microbiology. This mixture of traditional and new constituted something of an olive branch. Perhaps recognizing this, or just satisfied that the molecular unit answered his most urgent needs, Thode acquiesced. Indeed, by 1966 biology could boast fourteen faculty members, rising to eighteen in 1969.

With new blood and fresh resources, the culture of the department began to change. In 1965–66, cell biology, physiology, and genetics were made compulsory for all undergraduates in the program. Radforth noted that thirty-two units of chemistry were also now required. These moves, he beamed, were "bold and imaginative but mature in the light of modern trends."[100] Students, moreover, responded in droves, eager for a future in one of the health sciences, or smitten by the new environmentalism of the age. Registrations surged to the point that, in 1968, the honours program alone included 110 students – the most of any science department at McMaster. The newly installed chair, S.T. Bayley, was pleased to inform Thode that, with its emphasis on biochemistry and cellular biology, McMaster now offered "one of the most sophisticated undergraduate programs in Canada." Aware of it or not, he closed on a classically Thode-like note, saying, "a knowledge of biology alone, without an understanding of one or more other basic sciences is no longer good enough."[101] If the wily president uttered a satisfied "amen," it was not recorded. For Thode, it was probably sufficient that biology was trawling deep in undergraduate waters, while its graduate cadre had grown from twenty-two to forty-seven, between 1964 and 1968.[102] Meanwhile, similar developments in geography added to the shifting balance in the sciences.

Despite its many affinities with arts, geography had been numbered among the sciences, ever since the founding of Hamilton College. This, initially, had little to do with any strong departmental aspirations. Instead, the move reflected the interests and foresight of Dean of Science Charles Burke, abetted by geology's influential leader, Herb Armstrong.[103] Be that as it may, the decision eventually proved highly advantageous for all concerned; some sustained, early grumbling from the "hard sciences" notwithstanding. Lloyd George Reeds, chair and principal architect of the department, certainly recognized that a home in science offered far greater access to research funds and sundry other forms of support than could ever be had in arts. Moreover, his own passion for geomorphology was decidedly scientific in spirit. He felt very much at home and fought hard, throughout the fifties, to remain there.

Indeed, in order to clarify the scientific profile of geography, Reeds went so far as to transfer anthropology and sociology courses back to arts, at a considerable cost in enrolments, which political economy was only too happy to accept.[104] This was a gamble, but one that paid handsome dividends over the long haul. Thus, while geography continued to draw most of its students from arts, during the sixties it had budget lines for field trips and equipment that social scientists could only envy.[105] In short, geography came to enjoy a competitive advantage over its close relations in University College. It should be emphasized, however, that these were fought for, rather than simply bestowed outright.

In 1962, for example, geography felt that it was being shortchanged by the administration. Harold Wood, a Latin America specialist and successor to Reeds as chair, waxed indignant at suggestions, then circulating, that his department should accept lower priority while others were being established. Targeting psychology and sociology for comparison, he trotted out statistics to make his case. Geography's total registrations, he noted, had risen from 467 in 1958 to 860 in 1962. Yet, the staff stood at five; only one more than 1954. In contrast, psychology and sociology had each grown from zero to nine and four faculty members, respectively, in the same period. To Wood, these figures indicated that geography had been held back so that others might prosper. Pointing to the research records of colleagues and the desire to expand into new areas, such as climatology, he respectfully requested new appointments and permission to launch a doctoral program in the near future. "It seems reasonable to us," he submitted, "that we be allowed at last to participate in the active growth demanded by student enrolment and the need for more advanced research in Geography."[106] In the event, administrators were easily persuaded. Surging tides in social science had the same ripple effect in geography as in psychology, with the former appealing to a strong current of humanists, as well. With considerable dispatch, a no doubt somewhat surprised chairman received all that he sought. The longed-for transfusion, moreover, had a decidedly energizing effect.

By Wood's own account, 1963–64 marked the transition of geography from a small department to a substantial one.[107] From cramped quarters in Hamilton Hall, geographers moved into spacious, specially designed ones atop the physical sciences building. With new digs came three new staff. Frank G. "Hank" Hannell was considered an especially good catch. A senior climatologist, the crusty veteran of El Alamein left the University of Bristol for McMaster, drawn primarily by opportunities to further his interest in Arctic research. For years thereafter, he and other physical geographers led fortunate students on field trips to Resolute Bay, Ellesmere and Baffin Islands.[108] At the same time, Georges Poitvin and Gerard Rushton added strength to urban geography. Within a year, Derek Ford would join the phalanx and go on to forge a brilliant career in a geomorphology. There were all manner of causes to rejoice. The bright red cherry on top, however, was the senate's authorization of a long-desired doctoral program. All in all, Wood felt that the department had reached "a new level of maturity."[109] He was, undoubtedly, correct, but this is not to say that all went without a hitch or two, henceforth.

In 1965, for example, acting chairman R.L. "Lou" Gentilcore notified Thode that geography was taking the lead in a campus-wide effort to forge an Urban Research Unit.[110] In the argot of a later day, this was a "no-brainer." As Andrew Burghardt notes, there had been a sudden recognition by governments and academics, alike, that the older urban fabric of Canada required an extensive overhaul to meet the pressures of an expansive, changing society. Planning, he observes, became "all the rage." In Hamilton, the area north of Barton Street and a neglected downtown core became the foci of concerted attention. Reeds, Wood, and Burghardt, for their part, joined various boards bent on sparking renewal. In this context, an urban studies unit could hardly help but serve both academic interests and the greater public good.[111] Leading the charge on campus, Poitvin reminded University Council of yet another consideration. "Dr. Thode," he underlined, "stated it has been the policy of this University over the years to encourage interdisciplinary programmes and ... Council might go on record as having recommended that such a Research Unit be established."[112] His proposal was duly endorsed. After all, it, too, was a natural.

Unfortunately, the Research Unit in Urban Studies achieved far less than its full potential. Indeed, by 1969, one disillusioned member forwarded his resignation from the group, alleging that the unit had been poorly coordinated, ill-formulated, and was a drain on university resources. In his view, the body lacked a clear policy-making process and tended to function on an ad hoc basis. Individuals drafted research plans that caught their interest, whereas a general, concerted strategy was required. Without contesting the potent punch of a properly constituted interdisciplinary unit, the writer argued that the "hot house" approach applied to the creation of urban studies simply would not work. Pre-existing cross-campus interest was a *sine qua non* of success. Attempts to create such enthusiasm, he continued, were doomed to failure.[113] The urban unit struggled on for a while, but the core work was eventually absorbed into geography's internal research program. This, however, was a mere blip. Tensions of a personal and professional nature would prove far more threatening to departmental well-being.

Geography faced challenges familiar to all related disciplines in the sixties: a drift toward greater specialization and the onset of the "quantitative revolution." On the whole, the department accommodated these changes with better grace than many. True, broad "regional" studies slowly yielded pride of place to methodological specialties, such as climatology. Yet general practitioners, or GPs, such as Wood (Latin America), continued to be revered. Quantifiers and describers also exhibited mutual respect. Issues of leadership, however, could fan passions to searing flame. When Hank Hannell came to the chair in 1967, embers were soon stirred to fiery life.

Having served as a major in Montgomery's Eighth Army, Hannell was accustomed to command. He also had a clear plan of campaign for the department he had inherited. Greater specialization and heavier emphasis on the scientific aspects of geography were the marching orders he issued. It was less his ideas, however, than his style that provoked opposition, even among his fellow climatologists. Not wont to consult, Hannell sought to function as a "head." This was wholly out of keeping with Hamilton College's founding tradition of limited-term chairs, whose incumbents, at a minimum, were expected to consult widely on matters of significance. In the end, Hannell was eased out of office, following a petition that he not be reappointed at the conclusion of his three-year term. Looking for an outsider to fill the post and calm the waters, the administration lured Leslie J. King from Ohio State. A rising star in the new geography, King was also an adroit leader. In careful consultation, he rallied the department round a more balanced commitment to human and physical studies, while gently forwarding quantitative methodologies.[114] Potential disaster, therefore, was averted. Geography entered the seventies with eighteen staff, close to forty graduate students, and an ever-expanding undergraduate body. As Reeds had hoped, the department was securely at home – a valued contributor amid the sciences.

In 1969, Vice-President Bourns, as noted, advised his chief that greater
selectivity and prudence would be needed as government spending priorities
shifted. This, however, was a call to sensible caution and alert adjustment,
rather than a panicked cry for retreat. Indeed, Bourns emphasized that many
recent developments in his division could be best understood as reasoned
responses to changing context and fashion. Thus, once fortified, psychology, biology, and geography had won significant undergraduate followings,
while those of the senior sciences had eroded. Division-wide, he implied,
things had balanced out. Furthermore, no one was standing pat. Biology,
having strengthened work in cell and molecular studies, had just added a
new string to its bow with the appointment of two specialists in mathematical ecology. Meanwhile, an "outstanding urban geographer" (King) had
been snatched from the United States to bring greater stability and new directions to a rising department. For its part, with fresh, new quarters in a
home of its own design, psychology was in a position to blossom.

As for the old brigade, chemistry had just won a large grant to launch
a centre for high resolution nuclear resonance spectroscopy; a powerful
stimulus for the study of complex molecules that could only draw biology
and chemistry closer. At the same time, the accelerator was getting into full
swing. Operating twenty-four hours a day, it served local physicists, while
attracting others from afar. Symbolically and practically, a new senior sciences building housed chemists, physicists, geologists, and the materials unit
together under one, purpose-built roof. The central lounge served as a con-
vivial hotbed of far-ranging interaction. Bourns underscored the spirit at
play. "One of the distinguishing features of the graduate and research activities of the Division," he exclaimed, "has been the complete disregard of
Departmental or Faculty boundaries." As firm evidence of this, he pointed to
the proliferation of associate memberships among departments, with fully
forty-four on the books at the time he wrote; nor was he shy in noting that
external grants to the division surpassed $4 million: 20 per cent more than
ever before.[115]

All things considered, Thode's paradigm for the development of pure and
applied science at McMaster had served the university well. True, some arms
had been twisted, from time to time. Similarly, navigational adjustments
were made to meet the shifting tides of scholarly fashion, student taste,
social, economic and technological change. The precise configuration of the
sciences was not what had been anticipated in 1957. Still, the model Thode
outlined in early years proved sufficiently flexible to accommodate inevitable alteration in detail. Above all, the most basic goal had been attained. By
1969, McMaster, despite its modest size, was a player on the national stage.

Moreover, it was no accident that such prestige as it enjoyed rested largely, albeit never exclusively, on the bedrock of its reputation for focused, collaborative, scientific endeavour. The "chance for greatness" Kirkaldy espied was there. Were others ready to grasp the brass ring?

4

A Voyage of Development

Like a crisp pass from quarterback Russ Jackson, McMaster science had accepted secularization without breaking stride. As noted, university reorganization was just one in a sequence of steps that reinforced an already well-established Hamilton College game plan. Across campus, however, the events of 1957 were more variously received, with ambivalence being, perhaps, the most common response. "Keep It Small," for example, had purchase in some corners of University College, just as in the pages of the *Silhouette*. Nostalgia beckoned many, as an intimate college stood on the brink of populous depersonalization. On the other hand, some welcomed fresh opportunities, but were concerned about balanced development in a future sure to be influenced, if not defined, by Harry Thode and his hustling teammates. This was not paranoia but a reasonable concern, given that the 1960 vice-president's advisory committee comprised seven members, only one of whom, Arthur Patrick, hailed from arts.[1] The fear was that few close to Thode would understand, let alone sympathize with, misgivings on arts' side of the academic street.

Physicist Harry Duckworth, however, offered more than was anticipated. Initially, as expected, he was absolutely floored by his first significant encounter with the hesitant mood of University College leaders. Succeeding Arthur Bourns, as dean of graduate studies in 1962, he assumed that colleagues in arts would rush to embrace the expansive, competitive spirit sweeping science. In his view, secularization had done much to level a, hitherto, very uneven playing field. With access to the public purse, humanists and social scientists now had the wherewithal to join lab-coated confreres in a united quest to fend off "University of Toronto imperialism" at the highest level of research and graduate work.[2] Surely, he thought, they would scurry to mount doctoral programs, posthaste.

To Duckworth's surprise, however, several senior arts professors expressed serious reservations about damning torpedoes and steaming full ahead toward a glittering Thodean horizon. Much to his credit in their eyes, the graduate dean recognized that concerns expressed by the likes of Edward Togo Salmon (history and classics) and Roy McKeen Wiles (English) could not be dismissed as curmudgeonly timidity on the part of fuzzy-minded, laggardly dons. Both were scholars of eminence; justly respected in their chosen fields. Thus, listening closely, he came to appreciate their several, and far from irrational, qualms, just as they did his willingness to hear them out.

Meaningful scholarship in arts, Duckworth was told, often required summers away from campus, in far-off archives, or in long periods of solitary contemplation. It was not, as for many (scarcely all) scientists, a matter of stepping up one's ongoing activity in a nearby laboratory. Fall and winter went to collating findings, or to time-consuming writing whose composition followed no standard, scientific template. In all this, graduate students, especially year-round doctoral candidates, loomed more as distractions than blessings. Furthermore, external support for arts research was scarce, while internal summer stipends, drawn from NRC grants, were unavailable. Meanwhile, as noted, the culture of most arts disciplines traditionally prized lone-wolf originality, rather than collective endeavour, on the part of graduate researcher and professor, alike. This, alone, could impose a crippling burden of "outside reading" on dissertation advisors.[3]

In any case, arts lacked anything resembling the MNR, or similar facilities, which made extensive graduate work in science possible on campus. Mills Library, for its part, was barely adequate for undergraduate instruction. University Librarian Marget H.C. Meikleham cautioned that the essential foundation for serious research in arts simply was not there. In 1961, she reported: "Our [library] growth has not kept pace with the academic development of the university."[4] Principal Salmon of University College was, decidedly, of the same opinion. Indeed, he advised that bolstering book and periodical holdings should have priority over everything else, including staff recruitment, if arts were to undertake large-scale graduate work.[5] In 1962–63, he estimated that the current 150,000 volumes would have to grow to at least 500,000. "A truly worth-while graduate program," Salmon ventured, "can hardly be contemplated with anything less than this."[6]

Crucially, prominent scientists in the higher administration, such as Bourns, Duckworth, Armstrong, and Petch, offered vocal sympathy and support for Salmon's point of view.[7] Addressing another concern, geologist Armstrong, fired a barbed, Parthian shot, as he left the university in 1962, having lost the presidential bid to Thode. It was, he declared, high time that summer research stipends be made available to colleagues in arts. He condemned current internal granting policies as "iniquitous." Armstrong, indeed, had belaboured the point for several years. He, therefore, added his hope that "the interests of the Arts departments will be given the hearing never accorded to me."[8] Taken together, these various circumstances led Roy Wiles, and others, to join in Salmon's cautious chorus.

It must be emphasized, however, that this was a chorus of informed prudence; not wholesale disapproval. Indeed, by 1969, there would be many an enthusiastic Thodean who called arts home. In 1962, however, science at Hamilton College had over a decade's lead on the road to development. It also lived within a different academic culture. Accordingly, it would require time and resources, not to mention modification of Thode's paradigm, for arts to match stride. There were alternatives, of course. Advanced work could be left to science, or arts could plunge headlong into haste-begotten mediocrity. Rejecting the latter options, Salmon and company counselled a modicum of patience. To be sure, there was no doubt that deeper commitment to graduate work and research was in the cards. Still, "Hurry slowly," rather than "Seize the day," was the preferred motto of leaders in the arts community, as McMaster reinvented itself. Facts were facts and not subject to nostalgia or negotiation, but they did have to be carefully weighed.

Among the various facts in play, one stood starkly paramount. Enrolment was escalating, and, increasingly, the undergraduate burden fell on arts. Science, as seen, had its own brief boom, but the explosion at University College quickly proved to be of an altogether higher order of magnitude. Gilmour and the Baptist Convention had sensed something of this; hence, the decision to go public. Few, however, imagined the actual scale of the boomer onslaught, or the degree to which it would deluge arts. Thode had noticed a relative swing away from science in the late fifties, but had dismissed this as a temporary shift. Correct in the short term, he was wrong about long-range trends. In 1960–61, the registrar drew attention to "the steep rise in student numbers entering Arts Courses," while the percentage opting for science had remained level for some time.[9] No mere blip, this trend intensified. By 1967–68, undergraduates in arts (2,223) outnumbered those in science (1,220) almost two to one, with engineering boasting only 423.[10] This, however, was but part of a much larger picture.

Counting mixed blessings in 1960, Gilmour wrote to Claude Bissell, thanking him for the results of a recent study. "It arrived at a convenient moment," he told Toronto's suave president, "and I was able to impress our Board of Governors with the fact that McMaster is doing more part-time degree education proportionately than any other Ontario university."[11]

Within an arc that stretched from Niagara Falls, along Lake Erie's strand, up through Oakville, and all the way to Kirkland Lake, imperial McMaster offered degree and non-credit extension classes to a vast hinterland. By the time Gilmour wrote Bissell, summer, evening, and off-campus registrations dwarfed full-time enrolment, with part-time degree students numbering 2,674, while non-credit courses drew a staggering 6,003.[12] In one sense, of course, this was all to the good. Extension made money for the university and fulfilled part of its promise to be of greater service to the community. On the other hand, the load imposed could be herculean, especially as it fell heavily on one sector of the university: arts.

Statistics for 1961–62 show that of the fourteen departments engaged in summer school, only three were from science. As for evening classes, twenty-three departments were involved, six of which hailed from science. In rank order, the most heavily burdened were psychology (then, still in arts), English, history, and mathematics.[13] For purposes of quality control, part-time degree studies were harmonized with day programs in 1963, and given over to administration by a new dean. Adult Education, thereafter, oversaw non-credit work. This brought greater credibility to degrees won outside regular hours, but did nothing to decrease the load on staff. By 1965, McMaster's full-time undergraduate population stood at 3,225. At the same moment, degree studies in extension included fully 3,239, while registration in certificate and non-credit courses topped 10,000.[14] Administrative niceties aside, all had to be serviced. While preferences changed and social science began to outdraw humanities, arts, as a whole, continued to bear the brunt of the extension burden. With virtually all arts departments reporting record-breaking full-time enrolments by 1962, it was no wonder that administrative calls to get doctoral wheels rolling gave some, such as Salmon, pause. Even so, there were other facts of academic life that impelled even the cautious down the research-graduate studies road.

Gilmour was alert to these considerations, at the dawn of secularization. In his 1956–57 annual report, he pointedly remarked that University College had enjoyed little support for research and graduate work. Some things were simply beyond the Convention's means. He warned, however, that this could not continue. With an expected flood of undergraduates in the offing, not only would more professors be needed, but a strong cadre of graduate assistants would be required to help with marking and to preserve something of the personal touch through small-group tutorials.[15] Gilmour, therefore, set about engaging needed staff for arts. Indeed, between 1955 and 1958, as seen, psychology was buttressed by the addition of Newbigging and others. Similarly, sociology gained true life with the appointments of F.E. "Frank"

Jones, Frank G. Vallee, and Peter Pineo. English won the services of Norman Shrive, among others, while history recruited John H. Trueman. Alexander "Sandy" McKay brought fresh energy to classics, just as Frank Thorolfson did to music. James Noxon strengthened the roster of philosophy. This list could be extended, but the cardinal point is that arts were not neglected during the "stockpiling of staff" in anticipation of a seller's market soon to come. At the time, Gilmour defended the wisdom of this on the basis that salaries would soar, once the full impact of boomer demand was felt.

As it happened, the president was only partially correct. By the early sixties, such was the market that even freshly minted PhD graduates could pick and choose from among competitors thirsting for their services. Accordingly, inducements other than cash had to be on any successful bidder's table. Among the potential sweeteners, institutional prestige and the attendant edge that it brought to grant applications ranked high. Salmon, a canny realist, grew to appreciate this new fact of recruitment life. By 1963, he was urging greater support for graduate work in arts, without which it would be hard to attract good faculty.[16] Similarly, R. Craig McIvor, chair of political economy, advised Thode: "I am convinced that in years ahead, despite market pressures, the critical factors that will let us attract and retain good staff will be not primarily financial, but considerations such as teaching loads, chances to direct graduate work, and pursue teaching and research in one's primary area of interest."[17] There was a further wrinkle in all this that Salmon underscored sharply. It entailed the lack of any viable options. As competition for faculty stiffened, he wrote, "The demands for staff will be so large and so insistent in the years immediately ahead and the prospects for getting staff from the U.K., U.S.A. or elsewhere will be so poor that Canadian universities will be obliged to develop their own graduate schools." Arts at McMaster, he intoned, would either invigorate graduate work, or be left behind; a poor sister to science and the professions.[18] This latter, grim, and wholly unpalatable prospect had haunted many of Salmon's peers, since the founding of Hamilton College in the late forties. All told, by the early sixties, the cumulative weight of post-secularization facts tipped the balance at University College in favour of following where science had led, albeit with more measured tread.

In all this, it mattered greatly that key administrators, such as Duckworth, were prepared to listen. Gilmour's understanding, of course, could be taken for granted. He was of the old blood and keenly alive to sensitivities at University College. So, too, was Carey Fox. For all that the two gave Thode considerable leeway in his fiefdom, the president and the chair of the board, while urging more balanced development, were not about to force the pace in arts. Indeed, they were on alert to dampen fears that a Thodean tide would sweep all in its path. For example, both could readily visualize the changing, late-fifties campus landscape through the eyes of observers in arts. As stone, brick, and mortar gave ever-more solid shape to scientific ambition, Fox drew attention to a powerful intangible: perception. Writing to Gilmour in May 1958, he urged that the planned order of new construction be reconsidered for the sake of morale. "I am wondering," wrote Fox, "whether we cannot shove Arts a little bit ahead of some of the tail ends of Science."[19]

Taking the point, Gilmour swiftly drafted a formal request to the governors that an extension of the south wing of the physical sciences building be deferred. Priority, he argued, should shift to completion of the new arts building, "since it is of importance to the University as a whole that money be [seen to be] spent on the arts departments after so long and so costly a program of science construction." This, he continued, was vital "because the general morale of staff and students would suffer from even a hint of delay."[20] Not surprisingly, his plea was answered, and, small though it was in comparison with the rising temples of science, the opening of what would later be dubbed Gilmour Hall was greeted warmly by many in arts as welcome recognition that their flag was still there. On the side, the president also asked Cliff Hale, McMaster's publicity agent, to tone down an endless stream of glowing rhetoric concerning the nuclear reactor. "This is good propaganda for the general public," he told Hale, "but it may react against us in certain important academic ... circles."[21] For this reason, Gilmour insisted on a high-profile, public ceremony to mark the opening of the new arts and administration building. It was a question of maintaining trust, he told Fox, "particularly as the Arts people have been waiting so many years and have seen a fuss made about reactors, engineering buildings, and science buildings generally."[22]

At the same time, without prodding the shy, Gilmour did all in his power to see that those arts departments eager to beef up MA work were in a position to do so. In this, his "stockpiling" of faculty paid early dividends. So, too, did the establishment of teaching fellowships for graduate students in arts. Instituted on a small scale, two had been awarded in 1958. By 1962, however, there were forty.[23] Tracking this progress in his 1960–61 report, Dean of Graduate Studies Bourns, described as "particularly gratifying" the growth of graduate work at University College. Five years earlier, he noted, only one full-time student had been registered for the MA. Now, he crowed, no fewer than thirty-two were on the books. "No longer," Bourns declared, "can it be said that graduate work at this University is mainly in the science fields." In his enthusiasm, the dean was undoubtedly jumping the gun, given that 141 others had opted for advanced study in science or engineering.[24] Still, palpable movement was observable in arts, and he rejoiced. In this connection, it might not be too far-fetched to suggest that judicious pump-priming played a role in the 1959 decision to approve Newbigging's bid for PhD program. Psychology, after all, was the one arts department fairly chomping at the doctoral bit. Others, perhaps, might be encouraged to follow. This could explain why a seemingly brash move by four, quite junior, staff received consideration, much to the astonishment Newbigging later admitted.[25] In any case, a precedent was set; a door was opened. Yet, no others at University College displayed any urgent desire to cross the threshold. The full implications of changing facts were still being assimilated by Salmon, Wiles, and others of their persuasion. Meanwhile, implications of the coming Thodean ascension had yet to be revealed.

Long feared as the philistine incarnate, Thode had done little in his early career to dispel this image. While devouring technical journals, it is doubtful, according to biographers, that he ever voluntarily read what others called literature. Be that as it may, he was, to be more precise, vaguely indifferent, rather than downright hostile, toward the arts. But he was an intelligent campus politician with the good sense to heed sound advice, when it was offered. Fortunately for all, his closest advisors, Bourns, Petch, Duckworth, and Preston, were scientists of broad cultivation and genuine interest in matters beyond their immediate specializations. It was they who served as a bridge between Thode and the hesitant of University College, listening to and cajoling all.

Well-tutored by such people, Thode eschewed precipitous action during his stint as acting president. Apparently, this went a long way toward changing perceptions of the heir apparent. Lawrence Cragg, a former colleague and now vice-president of the University of Alberta, certainly picked up on this, during a visit to Hamilton in the spring of 1961. Thus, he took a moment to congratulate Harry on "winning the confidence of your Arts colleagues."[26] Building on this, at his inauguration as president, Thode resoundingly denounced any notion of conflict between arts and science as "silly." Citing Albert Einstein, he averred that "all religion, arts, and sciences are branches of the same tree."[27] As olive branches went, this one was fairly verdant. Even so, it was a sober acceptance of new facts of academic life that, as much as any tenuous comfort with Thode, led the first mainstream arts department, history, to commit to doctoral studies, although with something less than unrestrained enthusiasm.

History was entering a halcyon era. From 1957 to the late sixties, the department grew rapidly in staff and student complement. In 1960–61, its chair, the redoubtable Togo Salmon, reported that his five colleagues were being swamped by large day enrolments coupled with all-but-unsupportable demands from extension students.[28] Despite this, he was pleased to inform Thode that the "burgeoning" MA program, although an added strain, was "exhilarating as well as exciting." Meanwhile, Salmon continued, all members of the staff were closely engaged in research and likely to produce works of considerable substance in the near future. Morale, he added, was high.[29] Small wonder, then, that Research Director Petch brought considerable pressure to bear on a department he considered ripe to launch doctoral studies in arts.[30]

After all, by its own admission, history was booming. Thus, Salmon's successor, Herbert W. "Bert" McCready, proudly related that, in 1961, daytime registrations hit an all-time peak at 1,156 undergraduates, leaving history with the second largest departmental enrolment in the university.[31] Most notably, at a moment when more and more students began opting for pass degrees, history was building what would soon become the biggest corps of honours students at McMaster.[32] In addition, history boasted more MA candidates than any other department of University College.[33] To Petch, among others, a move toward doctoral work appeared a logical next step. Even so, the burdens of success weighed heavily on McCready's mind. "It is," he told Thode, "the rapidity of the growth in the work to which we are already committed that gives us pause about launching a PhD program at the same time."[34] The difference between his and Newbigging's voice could not have been more striking.

Sweetening the pot, the administration granted three new appointments to history in 1962, bringing the staff up to nine. Thus, reinforced and given a hefty vote of confidence, the department submitted its proposed PhD for review that year. The initial draft was surprisingly ambitious. A total of five areas of study were outlined. Had this been ratified, the results could have proved disastrous. Fortunately, McMaster did not rely solely on its own judgment where graduate degrees were concerned. Instead, there was a long-standing policy of submitting all proposals to close scrutiny by a minimum of three outside experts – a model later adopted by ACAP in the post-Spinks era.[35] In this instance, the senate's procedure served history well. Five fields were pared down to a more realistic three, ancient Roman, British, and Canadian, which remained well-founded, staple offerings for more than a decade.[36]

Having taken the leap, departmental jitters soon evaporated. Doctoral engagement, it seemed, was not the snare once feared. Indeed, by 1964, McCready relaxed into the new reality, exuding confidence. Writing to

Thode, he noted, with satisfaction, sharp growth in the number of MA applicants, now that the PhD was fully in place. He took greatest pride, however,
in the continued rise of bachelor enrolments, which stood at 1,464. With
"by far the largest Honours enrolment in the entire Faculty of Arts and Science," he glowed, "there is considerable support in the statistics for the idea
that McMaster is becoming a History school." Accordingly, he paused to
thank Thode for the "forward-looking and generous spirit of the Administration" in fostering library acquisitions and in fending off the "raiding" of
staff by other universities through timely promotions.[37]

With gentle prodding and meaningful support, Duckworth, Petch, and
company had allowed history to draw its own conclusions from the facts
of the hour. As the department accepted its new role, some members came
to sound just a little like Thode, himself. Consider, for example, the case of
Goldwin S. "Goldie" French, who succeeded McCready as chair of history.
In May 1966, reacting to the Spinks Report, he fired off a blunt missive to
Thode. His department, he told the president, had crafted its doctoral program with a specific eye to concentrating on areas of European and North
American history that had received relatively little attention at other Canadian universities. In a word, McMaster history had "differentiated" itself.
Now, French expostulated, Spinks was suggesting that some institutions
should not develop significant PhD programs on their own but, instead,
work in concert with others on a regional basis. As a political gesture,
French held talks with historians at Brock, Guelph, and Waterloo, but with
scant delight. Privately, he notified Thode that "in light of our strong undergraduate honours tradition and significant progress at the graduate level,
we are not prepared to compromise or surrender our central position." In
words that, just as easily, could have issued from Thode's own pen, French
declared: "If there is to be one graduate program in this region, it should
be McMaster in history."[38] Thoughts of this nature came into even sharper
focus, when the prospect of declining enrolment loomed.

The early sixties had been kind to history, as they had been to all those
disciplines required by the age-old, Ontario high-school curriculum. There
were teaching positions aplenty for university graduates in these favoured
fields. By mid-decade, however, the wind of "liberalization" was blowing.
In 1965, Minister of Education Davis commissioned a twenty-one-member
panel, under Justice Emmett Hall, to inquire into the aims and objectives of
education in the province. While the Hall-Dennis Report was not released
until 1968, it was apparent, very early on, that drastic change was being
contemplated. Rote learning and a tightly structured curriculum were targeted as enemies of "child-centred learning" and personal development.

Sniffing the breeze, a concerned Department of History met, in May 1966, and found little comfort in this turn of events.[39] When it was announced that, effective September 1968, history would be rendered optional in grades eleven and twelve, university chairs across the province, including Goldie French, protested formally to Davis; to no avail. Looking down the long road, French foresaw a shrinking department. As teaching positions dried up in provincial high schools and the supply of history PhDs outran university demands nationwide, within a decade, the current enrolment of more than 2,000 undergraduates was sure to dwindle. Under these circumstances, he advised Thode, the target should be quality, rather than quantity. Indeed, he wrote, "this Department should move urgently towards our long-standing goal: to become a centre of excellence for the training of graduate and undergraduate students."[40] This was a far cry from the restrained voice that had puzzled Harry Duckworth in 1962.

If history had been tentative, English was doubly so in answering the siren call to doctoral studies. Salmon could proclaim that a "new era" had dawned with the senate's approval of history's proposal. He could prophesy all he liked about others soon to follow.[41] Roy Wiles in English, however, was not about to be rushed. "We have had," he noted in 1962, "requests for the extension of graduate work in English to the PhD level, but we do not propose to undertake this development until the library resources are very considerably strengthened."[42] In any event, catering to every freshman on campus, as well as a large corps of honours, pass, elective, and extension students, not to mention several MA candidates, his staff of nine was already bowing under the weight.[43] With thanks for the invitation, Wiles was content to wait. By 1964, however, English was raring to go. What, one might fairly ask, had changed within a scant two years?

A cynic might argue that English grew less and less prepared to cede pride of place to history at University College. The record, however, does not speak to the point. It does, however, offer strong clues as to positive developments that, no doubt, helped sway literary minds. By 1963, the university was sponsoring a series of prestigious seminars, designed to inject verve into graduate studies in arts. Money, left over from the annual Whidden Lectures, was set aside to bring world-class scholars to campus, from as far afield as Britain, Europe, and the Antipodes. During the first year alone, eleven such seminars were held, at which aspiring neophytes could mix, mingle, and debate with the great and glorious, whose works they read. Granted, this did not carry the price tag of a tandem accelerator, but it did signal that the administration was in earnest about kick-starting advanced work in arts. Salmon certainly interpreted the move in that light. "The stimulating effect of this innovation on our graduate program," he asserted, "can hardly be overstressed." He also noted that, of the eleven guests, history had hosted three, and classics two, while English had entertained but one.[44] Could this, in any way, have inspired Wiles and company to play a bigger part in the Great Game? If not, tangible evidence of significant library development most assuredly did.

Since 1957, pleas to enlarge and enrich the library had been part of a yearly mantra chanted not only by arts scholars, but by graduate deans and research directors in unison. After all, the collection was to University College what the MNR was to nuclear scientists: the *sine qua non* of significant, on-the-spot research. It was, therefore, a considerable boost to arts' morale when a large extension to Mills Memorial Library opened its doors, during the academic year 1963–64. More heartening, still, was the evident commitment to fill it with quality material, as rapidly as possible. The budget was tripled that year, with promises of more to come. Librarian Marget Meikleham noted that acquisitions were outrunning the capacity to catalogue them. She gloried, however, in "the kind of problems which any library is glad to face, for they speak of challenge rather than frustration, and movement rather than stagnation."[45] Of course, all and sundry in arts shared such sentiments, but few would have rejoiced more than Wiles and some others in English, who yearned to build a very specific, very expensive, special collection; the cornerstone of a truly unique doctoral program. In this hope, they would not be disappointed. The university, in turn, delivered on its promise to the point that Mills came to house and surpass Salmon's required 500,000 items by 1966; some of them very special, indeed.[46]

A final spur to action came in the spring of 1964. With enrolments soaring everywhere and new universities coming fast on stream, Queen's Park, reacting to the Deutsch Report, moved to ensure that Ontario could produce its own stock of professors. Inducements, however, would be needed. The sciences posed no problem, since premium candidates normally received funding out of NRC and other grants won by their instructors. It was otherwise in arts. Seeking to balance the playing field, government announced that the first Ontario Graduate Scholarships (OGS) would be available to worthy applicants in humanities and social science who intended to pursue careers in university teaching. There were hallelujahs all round, save in some higher circles at McMaster. There, Thode cried foul, telling Davis that the legislation penalized a university which excelled in science. The minister was unmoved. It, therefore, fell to Duckworth, as graduate dean, to make the best of things by scrambling to recruit as many arts candidates as he could in a few short months. Advertising across Canada and the United States, he also dispatched more than 500 letters to department heads in Great Britain, hoping to net at least a few choice recruits. In the end, Duckworth surprised himself, submitting a "more than respectable" list of nominees for the new award. As he later remarked; "graduate work in arts at McMaster was never the same again."[47]

Collectively, this concatenation of encouraging developments swung opinion in English around. By early 1964, Wiles sensed a new maturity in the department. Alvin Lee, later a noted Old-English scholar, had just been commissioned to write a book on Canadian poet James Reaney. Similarly, Norman Shrive won a substantial grant to author a tome on literary nationalist, the "warrior bard," Charles Mair. New staff had been added, and long-awaited expansion of the library was underway. OGS grants were, temptingly, in place. At the same moment, Arts I (later, Chester New Hall), the first of what would eventually be three soaring towers dedicated to humanities and social science, redefined the campus skyline.

With an entire floor of offices and seminar space, all to itself, the department felt solidly undergirded as never before. Meanwhile, Wiles noted that UBC, Alberta, Saskatchewan, Western, and the University of New Brunswick were mounting PhD programs, whereas, hitherto, only Toronto and McGill had offered higher studies in English.[48] Putting all together, he notified Thode that English was drafting its own doctoral degree that would set it apart from any other in Canada. Thus, while other streams were foreseen, McMaster English proposed concentrating on eighteenth-century literature, on the understanding that appropriate senior staff and extensive, specialized library holdings would be acquired to support it.[49]

In the end, departmental opinion swayed to a more all-encompassing, general degree. Applauded by no less than seven external appraisers from Princeton, Harvard, Columbia, Toronto, Sussex, and Leicester, it won swift approval from the senate for implementation, effective 1965.[50] True to its word, the university afforded firm support. By 1966, five new appointments were made. Simultaneously, Shrive was sent to Britain to drum up doctoral candidates, while others trawled far-off Australia and New Zealand. Furthermore, Wiles reported that generous allotments were allowing Mills to build an outstanding eighteenth-century collection.[51] In this latter undertaking, administrative generosity was augmented by the bibliophilic entrepreneurship of Dr William Cameron. The latter worked tirelessly to forge strong relations with reputable booksellers in Ithaca and Philadelphia. In turn, they hunted down scores of rare items on special order. Substantial consignments were, then, purchased in bulk, at discount. The arrangement saved thousands of dollars for further acquisitions. Sketching this out for Thode, no mean businessman himself, Wiles' excitement was palpable. If such a targeted, research acquisitions policy were widely adopted, the chairman counselled, "It is our conviction that this University can develop its work in the Humanities with as much distinction as has marked the University's striking advances in the experimental sciences, and that the Department of English can and should take the lead in that development."[52] Plainly, Wiles had taken a sip from Thode's cup. He even acquired a decided taste for interdisciplinary unit research.

In 1966, Wiles informed Salmon that McMaster now had the best eighteenth-century research collection in Canada.[53] Such treasures, he thought, fairly begged to serve as the focal point of an interdisciplinary centre; one that would attract external scholars, high-calibre students, and encourage collegial co-operation among departments on campus.[54] Setting to work, within the year he wrote to Thode on behalf of an ad hoc committee, comprising ten department heads, ready to consider collaboration in a centre for eighteenth-century studies. Given time, Wiles chimed, interdisciplinary graduate degrees might be offered. A new, specialized journal might even be founded.[55] Possibilities for the future gleamed, limitless and golden. For the moment, he advised concentrating on abundant co-operative research projects just waiting to be done; projects that embraced myriad disciplines. He envisaged boundless "cross-fertilization" that ranged over "work in the era of Rousseau, Voltaire, Samuel Johnson, and Benjamin Franklin; ... the wide spread effects of new political developments, new philosophical principals, and ... the emergence of new theories and procedures in physics, chemistry, biology, and medicine." These, he emphasized, were but a few, broad areas that could be better probed by groups, than by individuals.[56] At the very least, he argued, such work would strengthen core identity among the humanities and enhance McMaster's scholarly standing in the wider world.[57] Here was a Thodean vision for arts. Moreover, as the formal 1969 proposal noted, the centre could mollify Spinks' supporters by sponsoring structured collaboration among regional universities, with McMaster (of course) as the superintending agent.[58] Like geography's scheme for an Urban Studies unit, Eighteenth-Century Studies seemed a natural, as do so many things, at first blush.

The McMaster Association for Eighteenth-Century Studies was given formal authorization, in 1970. Yet, for all that it bore earmarks of Thode's beloved "unit" model, the body never quite took full wing. Perhaps, once-burned by the example of urban studies, the administration was now twice-shy. In any case, a small budget of a few thousand dollars put dreams of dedicated space and support for post-doctoral fellows on hold at least for the foreseeable future.[59] Still, a measure of caution was probably warranted, since some red flags had been raised, as early as 1966. For example, appropriate holdings for English might have been ample, but French reported that theirs were "thin," while those of Spanish were described as "transparent" and German's as "poor."[60] Altogether, even while arguing for the centre, English scholar Alvin Lee conceded that, before accepting students, it would be imperative to conduct a "massive buildup of materials in those disciplines currently weak in their library holdings."[61] True, the sums involved were far from titanic when compared with expenditures across the mall, but other factors might have promoted a wait-and-see attitude at Gilmour Hall.

For one thing, the association lacked the clear-cut organizational framework that marked units, such as the IMR. Instead, in 1966, it opted for a "steering committee," noting specifically that such a body "should not be as formal a structure as, for instance, [that of] the Research Unit in Biochemistry, Biophysics, and Molecular Biology."[62] Equally disturbing to one such as Thode, the group was uncertain as to how closely its mandate ought to be defined. On this score, Dr Richard Morton advised Wiles that it "might be a mistake to work out in too much detail the philosophy behind the proposal." Some scholars, he cautioned, might be put off by "too precisely explicit statements of ideals and purposes." "A smooth running Institute," he added, "need not be based on a detailed philosophy."[63] Familiar and sensible as such counsel might have been to one reared in the arts; it was alien to Thode's mind.

Moreover, the president must have been aware of tensions that, even within the English department, swirled round the scheme. Associate Professor Mary F. Martin, for one, was blunt with her chairman. Having been asked her opinion of the plan, she wrote Wiles: "I must say that I am of divided mind." Martin could see the intrinsic value of a concentrated collection of books, art, and musical scores from the eighteenth century, but she asked some tough questions. Would a degree in the area be well-received elsewhere? Did a market for its graduates exit? Was there a danger that other periods or national literatures would be unduly subordinated? Would the latter consideration lead promising people with different interests to shy away from appointments at McMaster? Clearly rhetorical, these questions led Martin to urge re-examination of the project.[64]

It was, perhaps, in response to such misgivings that the concept was broadened, in 1967, to embrace the so-called long eighteenth century, spanning the period 1660 to 1830. By covering the Restoration and Romanticism, rather than being restricted to the Enlightenment, the scheme was rendered more inclusive.[65] Whatever the case, between 1967 an 1969, the association mounted three successful seminars that attracted a goodly number of scholars from Ontario and nearby American states.[66] Thus, genuine interest could be documented. The body, therefore, received official, if somewhat lukewarm, recognition from the university. Only time would tell if it could fulfill Wiles' brighter hopes.

More generally, the department, itself, prospered. In 1968, chairman Shrive proudly appended a long list of faculty publications to his annual report.[67] The next year, he was positively buoyant. Four new appointments had been made, with another authorized for the following academic term. The staff, now sixteen-strong, was tending to more than thirty MA candidates, along with twenty doctoral hopefuls. Best of all, declared Shrive, where English studies were concerned, McMaster's reputation was on the rise, as people ceased looking to the University of Toronto "as the fountain of all things good." Here, he alluded to fallout from the Macpherson Report of 1967. Under pressure from student activists, such as future premier Bob Rae, Toronto was dismantling its long-celebrated, honours system; said to be a divisive symbol of rampant elitism. By contrast, McMaster stood fast by its frankly elitist degree. As a result, Shrive informed Thode, the chair of English at the University of Montreal had told him that he was now looking to Hamilton, rather than Toronto, as he revised his own curriculum. Warming to this theme, Shrive revealed that several highly reputable scholars at Toronto had privately expressed to him their agreement with Montreal's decision.[68] His opposite number in history, Goldie French, echoed Shrive's views in full measure.

Attacks on the honours system, said the historian, were misconceived. While it did lead to tight focus on a particular subject, honours also helped inculcate "a broad and discriminating sense of intellectual commitment." People educated in this manner, French ventured, would always be well-prepared to play flexible and important roles in society; specializations notwithstanding.[69] In any event, English, like history, made a fairly smooth transition to a new era, while remaining largely conventional in spirit. When it came to attracting national and international attention, however, a distinctly unconventional, new kid on the block would rise as a bright star in McMaster's firmament. Indeed, religious studies would demonstrate – emphatically – that arts could keep pace with anybody in pursuit of "a chance for greatness." Moreover, any perceived irony that this should be so in a post-sectarian institution was purely superficial.

Under the old dispensation, New Testament study had been a freshman requirement. So ably and with such charm did Gilmour discourse on the Synoptic Gospels that, despite exemption, even some Jewish students elected to attend.[70] In 1957, however, the status – even the continued existence – of the hallowed requisite was thrown into doubt. There was, Gilmour noted, no disposition on the part of most faculty to question the value of religious study.[71] With linguist Arthur Patrick, many felt it wise to retain it in some form, partly for historic reasons, but primarily because so many students betrayed abysmal ignorance of the bases of their own culture.[72] No doubt, the president concurred, but he also recognized that a public institution had to tread carefully. Were religion to remain in the calendar, he emphasized, instruction in it would have to be unmistakably "academic in purpose and strictly non-sectarian."[73] This was common sense in a society that insisted on the separation of church and state. It was also, however, a stark and immediate political imperative. A potentially explosive confrontation with the Right Reverend Joseph Francis Ryan, Roman Catholic bishop of Hamilton, was brewing.

Since moving to Hamilton in 1930, McMaster had been scrupulous to avoid alienating the city's large Catholic population. A growing force in civic affairs, by Gilmour's day Catholics also constituted 10 per cent of the university's enrolment: about half that of the Baptist complement. Traditionally, the Church had insisted that none but Catholics offer religious instruction to its adherents. Accommodating this, McMaster had allowed such students to do the required biblical course on an extramural basis, following the syllabus and readings, but without attending lectures. Frequently, these candidates made use of informal tutors, supplied by the diocese. As a courtesy, these tutors were often given office space, but never a university stipend, academic appointment, or any role in structuring the course. Thus, did Holy Mother Church and Baptist university achieve a tenuous modus vivendi. The advent of secularization, however, threatened to upset the balance.

Gilmour suspected (correctly) that the diocese would oppose dropping a religious requirement and, instead, press for official appointment of its tutors; perhaps even for the establishment of separate courses. There would, then, be no grounds for denying similar privilege to any denomination or faith. This, he thought, would only serve to invite a nightmare.[74] Consequently, the president stalled. He appointed a special committee to study the complexities of the matter, while citing drawn-out deliberations over general curriculum review as reason to say little and do less concerning the status of religious study. "I think we all realize," he told committee members, "that questions of public relations as well as of sound academic policy are involved." "I am," he further confided, "trying to buy time."[75]

In the end, it was Senator William McMaster who provided room to manoeuvre. A close study of the documents revealed that it had been the senate, not the senator, which had stipulated that the particular course in question be required of all students. The charter of 1887, itself, insisted only that biblical studies be part of the university's curriculum. It said nothing about the specific program of individuals.[76] What the senate could make, it could unmake. Indeed, it was in the midst of doing just that, as J.E.L. Graham's committee struggled over reform of McMaster's core requirements. With this legal trump to hand, Gilmour could honestly bide his time, while the process of curriculum review, bogged down for its own reasons, dragged on into 1961. Few doubted, however, that sweeping change was coming. It was in this complex, uncertain context that Arthur Patrick, as early as 1957, suggested that the best solution might be to create a free-standing department of religious studies.[77] Gilmour, never prone to rush a delicate decision, waited until no better option presented itself. Finally, on 12 January 1959, at the behest of Patrick, seconded by Duckworth, the senate authorized the founding of the new department. Just how utterly new it would be, few could have anticipated.

Paul R. Clifford, associate professor of homiletics and pastoral theology, was seconded from the Divinity College to serve as chair. Initially, he merely coordinated scattered, existing courses, while awaiting the outcome of Graham's deliberations. This, however, is not to say that he was passive. Instead, like Gilmour, he was acutely aware of the charged politics of religion, on and off campus. Thus, he gave careful thought to the message that a first appointment ought to send. In 1960, he concluded that an Old Testament scholar should be hired, as a balance to current emphases at McMaster. Going further, Clifford strongly recommended "all things being equal, that he should not be a Baptist." A Presbyterian, he mused, might do nicely.[78] The point, of course, was to demonstrate, conclusively, that the new department would not be a lingering Baptist infiltrator under a translucent, secular cloak.

As things transpired, Clifford scrapped his initial plans. Instead, he grabbed George Parkin Grant, while the grabbing was good. It would be a transformative decision. As the grandson of George Munro Grant, storied principal of Queen's, the candidate had some Presbyterian roots, but that was as close as he came to Clifford's original job description. Ultimately unclassifiable, Grant was as theologically eclectic as he was deeply spiritual; as much a philosopher, or political thinker, as he was a passionate student of religion. No matter, he was a great catch. Already well published and something of a public figure, he brought instant heft and profile to the new department. Surprisingly, the larger-than-life, martini-loving Grant hit it off immediately with the reserved, teetotalling Gilmour. Or, perhaps this was not so surprising, after all. Both men were devout, but tolerant, and shared a strong distaste for the rampant materialism of the age. Still, it was a rare thing for a president to gift a new recruit with his own hat! For his part, Grant returned the warmth in full measure. Charmed by Gilmour, he was impressed by the cultured outlook of his prospective dean, geologist Herb Armstrong. In any case, having recently resigned in a huff, first at Dalhousie, then at York, he was badly in need of gainful employment. The chance to lead lay students in free-flowing religious thought was far too choice to pass up.[79] Furthermore, he could certainly feel at home with Clifford, who argued, "[W]e now have the opportunity at McMaster of establishing the study of religion as an academic discipline for its own sake, and not simply as a means of professional training for ordination."[80] Indeed, the new post undoubtedly fit Grant a lot better than Gilmour's hand-me-down hat.

The year 1962 brought the senate's revision of the old university curriculum and with it, abolition of the biblical requirement. Clifford and Grant were now free to craft a new program. On that score, they were of one mind. "We hope," Clifford wrote Thode, "that McMaster will become known for research in certain specific areas and attract students from far around."[81] This emphasis on focus, the note of ambition, and the identification of a new area of promise must have been music to the president's ears. He readily assented to two fresh appointments to get the department off the ground. The first went to an American, Allen Eugene Combs, then completing his doctorate in Old Testament studies at Columbia. The second was designed to head off continuing pressure from local Catholic authorities for separate courses taught by a faculty member of their own persuasion. Here, Clifford foresaw nothing but endless problems of academic freedom for students and professors alike.[82] He, Grant, and Combs, had no objection to hiring a person who happened to be Catholic, but thought that the appointment should be in the neutral field of comparative religion. Moreover, they felt that the hour for such a move was ripe, given the ecumenical atmosphere recently engendered by Pope John XXIII at "Vatican II."[83] After much casting about, Father Anthony Aloysius Stephenson, an Oxford-trained, Irish Jesuit, brought departmental strength up to four. As a bonus, Clifford was tickled to note that the good father had recently encountered "considerable difficulties" with Jesuit censors in Britain.[84] In concert, this unlikely quartet dreamed no small dreams.

From the outset, religious studies gave primacy to graduate work. To be sure, a pass course was inaugurated in 1962, along with combined honours programs allied to history and philosophy. Relatively little enthusiasm, however, and even slimmer resources were devoted to this level of instruction. As department minutes noted in 1974, "Our undergraduate courses began very much as a minor duty." Energies, instead, were "centred on creating a substantial graduate programme."[85] To a point, perhaps, this simply acknowledged a local market reality. After all, as one faculty member observed, as late as 1972, "[A]mong the labouring class of Hamilton there is a strong resistance to allowing their children to major in such an 'esoteric' subject as religion." This, he opined, was the reason his (now celebrated) department attracted fewer majors than weaker programs elsewhere.[86] In any event, an MA was launched, virtually in tandem with the bachelor degrees. By 1964, plans for a doctoral program were being drafted. Along the way, something of an anomaly was noted. The PhD proposal had been submitted before an honours program had even been discussed![87]

This rapid plunge into advanced work flowed from a deep conviction that there existed a special mission and a once-in-a-lifetime opportunity. As the first undertaking of its kind in Canada, and one of only a few in the world, the department's two highest imperatives would be to redefine the essence of religion as a scholarly pursuit and to serve as the nursery of a wholly new cohort of the nation's professoriate. Clifford, Grant, and Combs gave collective voice to this bright vision in a memorandum, most likely generated in 1963. Targeting what would be a long-lived bugbear, they took great pains to dissociate their work from any confessional outlook or purpose. True, they conceded, Judaeo-Christian tradition was emphasized, but, they underlined, this was always "in its relation to other religions and academic inquiries." Meanwhile, they predicted, student pressure at McMaster would be heaviest at the graduate level, since there were no alternative programs in Canada. Some universities, such as UBC, Windsor, Carleton, and Alberta, were just beginning to develop BA degrees. The prevailing national pattern, however, as at McGill, Queen's, and Victoria, was for theological faculties to mount occasional service courses. McMaster, alone, offered both undergraduate and graduate work. Applications, moreover, were pouring in from Canada, the United States, Great Britain, and India.[88] As Clifford advised Thode in 1964, there was an opportunity here. McMaster could assume undisputed leadership among Canadian universities in a rising field. All that was required was a modicum of additional, targeted support.[89]

Ever ready to sponsor areas of specific promise, the administration required little convincing. In 1964–65, new appointments all but doubled the staff, which rose to seven members. Two of these, Paul Younger and John G. Arapura, brought vital credibility to a planned thrust into Indian religious thought. Important, too, was an administrative commitment to stock the library with holdings that did justice to the richness and variety of traditions in the subcontinent. Christian literature, of course, was already well represented, thanks to assiduous collection by generations of Baptist scholars. Thus bolstered, Grant played from strength when, as chair of the department, he presented a doctoral proposal to the senate, in October 1965.

McMaster, he told that august body, could be to Canada what Princeton, Duke, Columbia, and Pennsylvania currently were to the United States: a university capable of meeting the need for professors in an exploding new field. This was a heady prospect, but Grant assured the senate that it would not induce quixotic, local overreach. Instead, effort would be concentrated in three fields of established strength: Christian beginnings, Indian religions, and the philosophy of religion. To ensure breadth, students would be required to demonstrate competence in both Eastern and Western thought, regardless of their specialized interests. Let there be no mistake, Grant proclaimed, "[T]he product being trained here is the University teacher." Buttressing his case, he pointed to unalloyed endorsements from prestigious referees at Yale, Princeton, Harvard, and King's College (London).[90] In addition, there were warm tidings from Father J.M. Kelly, president of Toronto's St Michael's College. Lauding the proposed comparative approach, Kelly thought it ideally suited to a confrontational age and likely to be mimicked by the University of Toronto, once McMaster led the way.[91] Given recent local tensions, these words from the leader of a respected Catholic seat of higher learning were rather more than welcome.

Hitting his stride, Grant went on to request that the degree be called a PhD in "Religious Sciences," an unfamiliar usage originally suggested by Arapura and Combs.[92] The term, while perhaps uncommon, captured departmental intensions quite neatly. It was nomenclature, Grant explained, employed by French and German universities, which had the great merit of distinguishing a purely scholarly doctorate from conventional theological training.[93] Some thought this merely sophistical wordplay. Learned representatives of the old Baptist tradition, however, took the point and applauded roundly. Thus, Divinity College representatives hailed the exploration of non-Christian traditions. Secular department and confessional college, they asserted, could co-exist in harmony and, perhaps, even fruitful co-operation. The senate, after some debate, extended its formal benediction.[94]

The new degree, although limited to three areas, allowed for broad investigation of manifold beliefs, using myriad disciplinary tools. Even a brief glance at the faculty in the late sixties drives this home. In 1966, for example, Edward P. "Ed" Sanders arrived from the United States to stimulate comparative study of early Christian and rabbinical literature. In time, he would emerge a world-class figure. Y.H. Jan threw Buddhism and the history of Chinese religions to the mix, in 1967. Next year, Warren Lane brought psychology to bear on the study of religion. Hans Mol would inject sociological perspectives. Meanwhile, urbane southerner, John C. Robertson, and the contemplative Louis Greenspan probed philosophical and political implications in contemporary religious thought. Taken together, this was cultural and disciplinary cross-fertilization writ large. It was, also, the Thodean ethos in bustling microcosm.

Where bustle was concerned, Grant advised that, in order to establish firm credentials in the general academic community, publications of quality would have to issue in number from the staff.[95] His colleagues were more than happy to oblige, some of them in scholarly profusion. Meanwhile, Grant, himself, was becoming a full-fledged media star, following the 1965 publication of his controversial bestseller, *Lament for a Nation*. Indeed, for a time, he would be the face of McMaster in the eyes of the general public. On the premise that there is no such thing as bad publicity, perhaps his hotly debated *Lament* coincidentally helped advertise the novel program he chaired. Still, axioms can be flawed. Thus, as Greenspan later remarked, despite firm administrative support, some questioned the academic legitimacy of this high-profile, polyglot department. "There were," he observed, "those who suspected that we were a Trojan Horse of Divinity ..., while others, noting that we had a fair collection of scepticism and members of other civilizations, feared that we were a greater threat to the religious norms of our society than the offspring of Darwin."[96] He did not pause to add that, in the revisionist sixties, when old verities were joyously subjected to popular scrutiny, a program, such as his, was veritable catnip to many a thoughtful student.

Proof of this was in the registrar's pudding. In 1967, (chairman-elect) Combs reported that religious studies already had thirty-six graduate students under its care, sixteen of whom were in the doctoral program. While pleased to note that seventy-five candidates were seeking admission next year, he added that stringent culling of applicants would be necessary, and not for academic reasons alone. "We have," he told the president, "one of the largest graduate programs in Arts, but the least space." Eight to twelve students were already crammed into each of three offices. This, Combs declared, was "a blatant obstacle to our work." On the other hand, he conceded that the administration had provided substantial support in building library acquisitions commensurate with graduate study. He went on to say that $50,000 per annum would be needed during the next five years for this purpose. Sounding an imperial note, he explained: "Our department has special responsibility to establish first-class, significant, and large holdings in the field of Religious Sciences," that it might serve as a major resource for other universities in the region.[97] Thode, guided by Mel Preston, was happy to back a winner. One struggles to guess, however, what he made of whimsical cartoons Combs sketched on the cover pages of official reports! Still, even though the one for 1969 bore the too-cute caption, "Danger: Annual Report," Thode had to be pleased by news that graduate enrolment now neared sixty. Clearly, investment was paying off handsomely. So too, it seemed, was diplomacy. Thus, Combs outlined productive discussions with colleagues at Toronto who were contemplating the launch of their own PhD. The parties, happily, were amicably seeking to avoid field duplication in that post-Spinks hour.[98] Equally heartening was word from far-off California. Apparently, even vaunted Berkeley was looking at the McMaster model, as it, too, contemplated doctoral work in religious studies.[99]

Over time, the graduate program would be modified in various ways. Even so, the initial model, collectively and eclectically fashioned between 1962 and 1970, would be of considerable historical significance. As President (Emeritus) Alvin Lee remarked in 2006, the department became "a kind of imperial centre."[100] First to assume the task, it produced an exceptionally large proportion of Canada's PhDs, during the discipline's crucial formative period. This group colonized and moulded programs nationwide; from St John's to Victoria. Its members chaired departments, edited journals, and adjudicated research applications. By the eighties, there was talk of a "McMaster Mafia" in Canadian religious-studies circles.[101] In its particular realm, the model had a broad impact, comparable to that of the MNR, or the "problem-based learning" pioneered in health sciences. Such developments not only dramatically raised the profile of the university, but were McMaster's unique contributions to Canadian academe, as a whole. This was the upside of the Thodean paradigm in full bloom.

In the case of religious studies, the downside could be found at the undergraduate level. Time and again, successive department chairs commented that principal energies were being devoted to advanced students. As early as 1965–66, Grant noted that, with a small staff, introduction of the PhD would make it difficult to ensure a carefully nurtured undergraduate program.[102] On this point, he proved correct. In 1967, Combs reported that graduate supervision tended to be all-consuming. True, the department served 960 undergraduates that year;[103] however, total enrolment and majors enrolled did not necessarily equate. The registrar's report for 1967–68 cast this in bold relief. Where English and history had each graduated hundreds through their undergraduate programs since 1964, religion had produced roughly 40, all told.[104] To be fair, the latter had started from scratch. As late as 1970, however, Sanders acknowledged that, while general registrations remained adequate, relatively few candidates chose to major in religion, which might have been just as well, he implied in a confidential memo to the president. With only seven full-time staff, he wrote, "we still do not have sufficient faculty to carry on a large graduate programme and also offer a really full and satisfying undergraduate program."[105]

Priorities, in any case, had long been crystal clear. The highest imperatives voiced in 1963 still held sway a decade on, and they had little to do with immediately fostering excellence in undergraduate training. Rather, they focused on defining a new field of scholarship and generating professors to propagate it. The ethos inculcated by Thode's regime offered scope and encouragement for precisely this kind of undertaking. Religious Studies thrived in such an environment. By the early seventies, the department was well its way to branding McMaster as the gold standard in at least one branch of arts. As the 1974 ACAP report noted, it was "probably the most prestigious non-science program in the University."[106] This, however, is not to imply that others were idle or unimaginative.

Indeed, as Sandy McKay wrote in his history of the department, "If expansion was truly the watchword of the sixties, Classics at McMaster was an ardent participant."[107] In some ways, it was just as innovative, energetic, and eclectic as religious studies. For several reasons, it had to adopt a gradualist approach toward graduate work. Much attention, for example, was focused on assiduous cultivation a changing undergraduate base. There was certainly, however, no ingrained antipathy to interdisciplinary collaboration, graduate work, or high-calibre research. On the contrary, McKay recalls, somewhat wistfully, "When Henry George Thode was installed as president in 1961, the University embarked on its most dramatic voyage of development."[108] Throughout the sixties, McKay's actions and those of his colleagues indicated that classics had no intention of being left behind.

Early in 1961, Donald Shepherd told Gilmour that classics was hustling to keep up with rising undergraduate registrations by developing new offerings in conjunction with fine art and history, while trying to sponsor similar relationships with other language departments. He went so far as to propose that the latter should pool efforts in a comparative literature degree, one day. He added that a classics MA was in place, but was attracting few applicants. In Shepherd's mind, the inhibiting factor was clear enough. "Our graduate work," he wrote, "is seriously limited in the variety of courses we can offer, given the number of staff." In fact, there were but two graduate courses on the books. With Shepherd, McKay, and the occasional term appointment to carry the combined departmental weight, a truly broad range of choice at the graduate level was beyond their means.[109] Salmon could provide some assistance, but his principal commitments were in history and, later, administration. The classical spirit was willing, Shepherd underlined, but instructional flesh was skeletally weak. That, however, could be remedied.

As was their wont, Thode's close advisors were prepared to fan any spark that promised flame. Accordingly, classics received assistance to broaden its work. In 1962, the additions of Herman Lloyd Tracy and Peter Kingston doubled core staff complement. Payoff was immediate. The number and variety of classics' courses multiplied forthwith. By spring 1963, McKay bubbled as he reported increased enrolment across the board, but especially at the graduate level.[110] Granted, the tally of prospective MAS was small, when compared with that of history or English. Still, it was a start; one that encouraged further investment by an administration eager to see arts grow to maturity. Thus, in 1964–65, George M. Paul, James S.A. Cunningham, and Valerie Warrior were added to the department's roster. As it happened, they came on strength at a crucial moment.

Reformist winds that would lead to the Hall-Dennis Report were gathering momentum. Latin, long a staple of the old high-school curriculum, was coming under siege as a particular *bête noire*; the quintessential symbol of outmoded rote learning, in liberalizing eyes. Implications for university classics were clear and ominous. The welcome infusion of extra blood, however, allowed McKay and company latitude to respond creatively, before reform could destroy their undergraduate base. Instead of retreating, they multiplied and diversified bachelor offerings, as of 1965. Attention was lavished on beginners Latin, since the rudiments could no longer be assumed in freshmen. As well, there was a growing emphasis on "Classical Civilization" as a program theme. Here, the focus was on art, architecture, history, and society in the ancient world, as opposed to traditional literary analysis. The object was to open antiquity up to the curiosity of a broader undergraduate population. Throughout, the assistance of historians, such as Salmon, James A.S. "Allen" Evans, Daniel Geagan, and Edith Wightman proved invaluable in this endeavour. Similar enrichment was provided by others, especially those in fine art. Meanwhile, "Classics in Translation" made the literary heritage of the ancients accessible to many who, otherwise, might have been daunted by the linguistic challenges offered by an Ovid, Virgil, or Homer. This, wonders never ceasing, included a healthy number of engineers seeking arts electives.[111] Altogether, classics was rendered broader, and more attractive. Not surprisingly, after 1965, registrations reached all-time highs.[112] These, of course, were not the teaming multitudes that choked sociology or psychology, but they were sufficient to maintain a healthy undergraduate clientele, when it might easily have been eroded.

Encouraged by this success, McKay, Shepherd, and their colleagues also noticed that, by mid-decade, an increasing number of their MA graduates were moving on to doctoral work, and with considerable success.[113] The department, it was reasoned, must have been doing something right. Meanwhile, as PhD programs in history, English, and religious studies offered successful precedents, classics considered following suit. Altogether, the time seemed propitious to solidify classics' position in the arts community. A doctoral program would do that, quite nicely.

Thus, in 1967, a proposal was drafted that focused squarely on "Roman Studies," broadly conceived. Encompassing literature, art, archaeology, numismatics (the study of coinage), law, history, and other dimensions of the late republic and early empire, the degree was intended to set McMaster's PhD apart from others in the province. Western was concentrating on Greek studies, at the time, while Toronto leaned in a similar, if more wide-ranging, direction. Ottawa's doctoral work was in Latin.[114] Again, the Thodean notes of differentiation and clear focus were sounded. Approval was swift. By the spring of 1969, Shepherd could tell Thode that three PhD candidates were already hard at work, while eight had registered for the following term. Over the previous seven years, he reflected, the staff had grown from three to nine members, with two more coming next fall. In tandem, library holdings had risen from adequate to outstanding. Thanks to timely private donations and support by the university, Shepherd wrote, McMaster currently held one of the best collections in Canada. As was so often the case with such lofty proclamations across campus, no precise comparisons were offered to bolster the claim.[115] Even so, Shepherd was undoubtedly correct in asserting that his department had come a long way in a short time.

Classics was, and would remain, a relatively small branch of the university. The same, of course, was true of the discipline at most institutions across the continent. Still, McMaster Classics probably made the most of its potential during the sixties. This reflected the considerable scholarship of staff allied with strong, but flexible, internal leadership on the part of Shepherd and McKay. However, as the latter notes, "The departmental phoenix [also] prospered by reason of enthusiastic, confident administrative support."[116] In this connection, there is a remarkable similarity in observations made, quite independently, by McKay and Ed Sanders of religious studies, decades after the events in question. At the turn of the twenty-first century, both men identified Bourns, Preston, and other influential scientists close to Thode, as instrumental in helping to nurture their respective programs at a formative stage.[117] The regime, it appears, truly was prepared to foster a measure of balanced growth in a genuinely multi-faculty university. Moreover, it was always ready to seize opportunities of special promise, even if they arose outside the laboratory. In the general rearmament of arts, one splashy, international coup made this dramatically clear.

In 1967, Bertrand Russell was strapped for cash. True, he was comfortable enough in his small Welsh home. Comfortable, however, did not mean rich. What income he had came from an intrepid pen and an interminable round of speaking engagements. Yet, although in his mid-nineties, the renowned philosopher and Nobel laureate was still up for a brawl, and this in the expensive, heavyweight division of world opinion. Indeed, he was waging a campaign to indict the United States for war crimes in Vietnam. Uncle Sam, of course, had cavernous pockets. Lord Russell and his allies, on the other hand, could muster only personal resources. Anxious to contribute more than just a voice to the struggle, the earl announced that he was willing to sell his last, truly valuable possessions – his papers and library – in order to bankroll the cause. There would certainly be no lack of bidders; such was his fame (or notoriety); such the depth and scope of his collection.

Catching wind of this, William B. Ready pounced without hesitation. Appointed university librarian and professor of bibliography at McMaster in 1965, Ready was, as a colleague later dubbed him, a bibliophilic "buccaneer" of the first order.[118] Goals mattered. Methods could be improvised. A Thodean born, he was determined to propel McMaster's research and special collections into the front rank among Canadian universities. In this, he had firm support from influential figures in arts, such as Salmon and Wiles, as might be expected. More significantly, he quickly won the confidence of Thode, who recognized a kindred, risk-taking spirit in the gnome-like but bold librarian. Thode, as ever, warmed to anyone eager to put the university on the map. Thus, in a move that would have been risible less than a decade earlier, Ready petitioned the president to bid on Russell's collection, scant weeks after the proposed sale was announced. Thode agreed.[119] The chase was on.

There followed a breakneck campaign. Ready met with his counterparts at other Ontario universities, seeking their collective moral support for the proposed acquisition. He assured them that, should the effort succeed, the archives would be treated as a provincial treasure house, open to all, rather than as a trove jealously guarded by McMaster. Meanwhile, he and Thode beat the bushes for cash sufficient to make their bid credible amid sure-to-be-stiff competition. Ready pried $25,000 loose from multi-millionaire alumnus Cyrus Eaton.[120] The Canada Council authorized $150,000, but these sums would be nowhere near enough. Accordingly, others sources were tapped.

In January 1968, Thode approached the Laidlaw Foundation, saying, "It would be a distinct coup for Canada to acquire these papers, and it is a bit of luck that the United States is out of the market ... (the University of Texas alone would easily find $1,000,000 for them)." He was careful to add, "None of this, of course, is to be interpreted as an endorsation of Lord Russell's reasons for selling them." McMaster's interest was, literally and purely, academic.[121] In the event, Laidlaw came through, as did the Atkinson Foundation.[122] An at least respectable offer from McMaster found its way to the earl's inbox, shortly before bidding closed. For his own reasons, Russell accepted Hamilton's offer. The decision made world headlines. While many in Britain were outraged, Salmon rejoiced. "At a stroke," he exulted, the acquisition "made us an archival centre of major importance."[123]

Catching up on affairs after summer vacation, the *Silhouette* briefed students on the significance of the masterstroke. Sandwiched, appropriately enough, between an article commemorating Ché Guevara and Eugene Levy's weekly column, "The Mouse That Roars," was an item that blared, "McMaster Strikes Pay Dirt." Student scribes outlined the endless research potential of a collection that crossed all disciplinary lines. How, they asked, could it be otherwise, given that Russell was one of the most prolific letter-writers in history? His correspondents ranged from Albert Einstein to A.J. Ayer; from William James to Jean-Paul Sartre; from Ho Chi Minh to Nikita Khrushchev. Altogether, cried the author, the archive greatly enhanced McMaster's prestige.[124] Some conservative university governors felt otherwise about spending a large sum on the papers of an atheistic, anti-nuclear pacifist who entertained rather liberal views on sexuality. Thode, however, stood by Ready and carried the day.[125]

A 1969 report from the new archive revealed that the papers were being catalogued, while Ready and others travelled across Canada and the United States, studying best practice in modern documentary preservation. Large sections of the copious correspondence were microfilmed, until 110 rolls, or two miles of tape, were available. Thode was advised, in appropriate Cold War language: "One copy will be carefully packaged and cached where it will be safe from all forms of destruction, including nuclear war – which will be of some comfort to Lord Russell." At the same time, appeals were made to holders of the peer's outgoing letters, several hundred of whom donated items to the collection, free of charge. The adroit, dogged Kenneth Blackwell, Russell's assistant in recent years, was hard at work compiling a bibliography of the earl's thousands of printed and unpublished writings.

The long-term goal was to produce an authoritative, multi-volume, edition of the complete papers. That was for the future.

For the moment, it was satisfying to note that researchers were already coming from as far away as Texas and Great Britain to pour over the collection. No doubt, they also spread McMaster's good name upon returning home. After all, in that flush hour, local staff arranged their hotel accommodations and kept the archive open "to suit their limited time."[126] Halcyon days, indeed! Tour groups and distinguished visitors also passed through on a regular basis. One exhibition drew more than fifty philosophers from universities across Ontario. Ready was interviewed widely on television, radio, and by several newspapers, including the New York Times. It was all quite exhilarating, save for one puzzling anomaly. "It cannot be said," Thode was advised, "that McMaster faculty members have shown much interest."[127]

Philosophy, for example, mounted no urgent drive to exploit the new resource on its doorstep. A clue to this lack of immediate enthusiasm might lie in an earlier observation on the part of Horace A. Dulmage, head of the department in the formative early sixties. "Our ... curriculum," he reported in 1962, "provides good grounding in the History of Philosophy which is given slight treatment in many universities where the almost exclusive emphasis is on Analysis." He did add that analytical methods received careful attention.[128] Clearly, however, modern analytical philosophy, which Russell personified, was not an exclusive, or even primary, concern. Across the sixties, instead, the department was broadly eclectic, rather than narrowly focused, in its philosophical pursuits. The goal was to present a broad spectrum of offerings, to a moderate, but growing, number of undergraduate and MA candidates.[129] Logician James Noxon was a student of Hume. Sami M. Najm had special interest in Berkeley and theories of god. J.R.A. Mayer probed everything from parapsychology to religion to Esperanto. John E. Thomas was carving out a niche in medical ethics. J. Evan Simpson was keenly interested twentieth-century thought, but had just begun his career in 1965. Meanwhile, Albert Shalom wrote extensively on Wittgenstein, Collingwood, and Sartre. None were self-selected Russell scholars, just panting to plunder the new archive. Yet, why should they have been? No one could have prophesied that the earl's papers would suddenly land in McMaster's backyard. Besides, in the years 1968 through 1970, philosophy's chief preoccupation was the development of a joint doctorate with colleagues at nearby Guelph; a project that required considerable effort and bore much welcome fruit.[130]

If philosophers were preoccupied with established interests, so were others. They could not turn on a dime in the early years of honing barely hatched doctoral programs and personal research. The president, undoubtedly, was disappointed by the lack of a quick rally to the Russell holdings. Like the MNR, this unique resource had been expected to spark an immediate scramble on campus for multidisciplinary research. Still, it was early. In any case, Thode, Ready, Salmon, and others of their persuasion had to be gratified that Mills Library was now the unquestioned focal point of at least one area of international interest. If nothing else, McMaster was plainly visible on yet another square of the bigger academic map – a consideration rarely far from the forefront of Thode's competitive mind.

Bourns might have jumped the gun when he proclaimed, in 1961, that McMaster could no longer be viewed primarily as a science-driven university. By 1969, however, there was rather more truth in that claim. A number of traditional and new arts had grown significantly in terms of staff and student complement. Research activity had blossomed, too. In this regard, aggressive library acquisition had been crucial. So was the belated extension of summer stipends to non-scientists, after 1966.[131] Soon, Thode could point to "a remarkable spate of publications from the pens of Arts personnel."[132] As for graduate work, its rapid growth, especially to the doctoral level, was described by McKay as "infectious and inspirational."[133] Here, he made no reference to the modern languages, fine art, or music, which, with the exception of French, remained minor undertakings in the sixties. In 1969, moreover, he spoke only as the newly installed dean of the Faculty of Humanities, which, he effervescently proclaimed, had just come "buoyantly and confidently into existence."[134] Contemporary voices from the other major branch of arts, social science, were rather less exuberant.

5

Stepchildren

Even as McKay rhapsodized about humanities' future, in May 1969, John Melling, (acting) dean of social science, was transmitting a veritable *cri de cœur* to Thode. Excerpted verbatim from minutes of the new faculty, it read: "Let the claims of the Social Sciences be heard and heeded and may the neglect they have suffered be overcome by University action at the highest level."[1] There was, Melling counselled, palpable yearning "for a separate and distinct identity and release from a confederacy of the Arts and Science which allegedly had stifled the Social Sciences." Here, it needs be understood that Melling was speaking, not as a minor petitioner at the earliest dawn of post-Baptist growth but at a point when sprawling social science was the largest, most heavily subscribed faculty in the entire university. He was pointing to what seemed a bitter irony: the fastest growing wing of McMaster was, also, the least fully developed. Melling was not the first, nor would he be the last, to note this curious anomaly. He was, merely, among the more polite.

Indeed, justified or not, a sense of being indifferently supported afterthoughts was fairly common among senior social scientists by the late sixties. R. Craig McIvor, for one, certainly shared this feeling. As chairman of economics, he made no bones about it in a fiery 1968 missive to Thode. Speaking of a recent overhaul of the university's internal organization, he pointedly observed that all key officers were now in place, save one: a full-time dean of social science. Thus, where other faculties finally had their own machinery for truly effective planning, social science was still lumbering on, in an all-too-familiar limbo. "One may fairly argue," he emphasized, "that, in terms of McMaster's historic pattern of development and the present mushrooming of interest in the complex problems with which the social sciences must concern themselves, it is *the* Faculty within our University where the need for sound, long-term development plans has for some considerable time been most urgent." Fuming with ill-concealed frustration, he contended that "many of the social science faculty are concerned that the planning vacuum ... must lead to a relegation of their legitimate academic interests to a secondary status amid the on-going and well-planned development and growth elsewhere in the University." The appointment of a fully anointed dean, he argued, was an urgent necessity; a signal that the university placed advancement of his faculty on par with that of its more settled sisters.[2] As he hectored Thode, McIvor undoubtedly hearkened back to earlier days when the youthful star of social science seemed poised to shine.

After all, how could he forget 1957? In that crowded year, Gilmour had paused to extol, quite atypically, the potential of social science in the new McMaster. "Our civilization," the president proclaimed, "depends not on scientific discoveries alone but on the ability of university men to lead in political, social, cultural, and religious thought." No doubt, he felt that religion and the humanities were still primary in meeting this challenge. Nevertheless, he took special care to emphasize that social science was likely to be an increasingly valuable ally in the task. Thus, he noted that, "without much fanfare," both sociology and psychology had recently been strengthened at McMaster. Prepared to go farther, he recommended substantial reinforcement of political economy and the deeper cultivation of its newly added sub-field, commerce.

Although the latter endorsement might have run against his own grain, Gilmour could always separate evident necessity from personal preference. The striking need of the mid-century moment, as he saw it, was to forge thoughtful leaders for a rapidly changing urban-industrial-commercial Ontario. If invigorated social science could be of service in this new environment; so be it.[3] This is not to say that the traditionalist president had undergone a wholesale conversion experience, but he had softened his position on the sciences of society.[4] He was, in fact, opening a door, having been prompted firmly to do so.

Among those prodding Gilmour in this direction, few were more vocal than Herb Armstrong, dean of the Faculty of Arts and Science. Conscientious and well-read, Armstrong took the "and" in his job description very much to heart. Although a geologist by profession, he paid close heed to tending both estates under his combined remit. Indeed, in many ways, he was more broadly ecumenical regarding cross-campus co-operation than Thode himself. Right up to his final report of 1962, Armstrong consistently drummed on one overriding theme: the essential unity of the university. "My plea," he wrote, "is not for 'togetherness' in a sentimental ... sense, but for

that mingling which leads to unity of purpose and community of values." By
this he did not mean that all should be of one mind. He did believe, however,
that scholars of every stripe had much to offer one another, if only they took
time for more than simple chit-chat over coffee. For this dean, there was no
impermeable membrane around any organized body of thought.[5]

Thinking along these lines, Armstrong was an early advocate for the
aggressive development of social science in a systematic and holistic manner.
In 1955, he roundly applauded when Lynn Newbigging and Frank Jones
were hired to bring true expertise to psychology and sociology, respectively.
Within a year, he was advising that both areas be groomed as full departments, replete with sufficient staff and space to carry out significant research
– but not in isolation from each other. Armstrong held no particular brief
for either discipline, per se. Instead, he saw them as complementary partners in an expanding confederation of specially equipped, sister disciplines.
Thus, he pictured a large matrix of social sciences within which economic,
political, sociological, psychological, and other forms of scholarly inquiry
could serve an academically legitimate and publicly useful common cause.
That cause, he argued, entailed urgently required research into the rapidly
shifting dynamics of contemporary society. Moreover, Hamilton, with all its
flux, vigour, and diversity, offered endless scope for such integrated investigation.[6] It would have been crass, of course, to mention the obvious benefits
that would also accrue to McMaster's local image. Still, in the parlance of a
later generation, Armstrong was outlining a "win-win-win" scenario.

Viewed in perspective, there is a striking similarity between Armstrong's
vision of social science and the focused, collaborative views that informed
contemporary Hamilton College. The Thodean note is unmistakable. Moreover, it was sounded by a dean of long standing, who had at least some support from Gilmour. Given all this, why were Melling and McIvor complaining
about a "planning vacuum," "subordination," "stifling," and "relegation" in
the late sixties? The reasons as to why this was the case are complex. Indeed,
tackling the issue is akin to facing the Gordian knot – without the benefit
of Alexander's razor-edged blade. Yet, McIvor's 1968 outburst offers a clue
regarding at least one of its myriad strands: the eccentric organization of the
university in the decade after 1957. Amid its Byzantine tangles, the diffuse
social sciences lacked strategically placed, high-profile spokesmen at a time
when individual voices mattered greatly. A brief excursion into the arcane
administrative culture and structures of the day is needed to make this clear.

In 1958, Gilmour was asked for advice about lines of authority at
McMaster by A.K. Adlington, business manager of Waterloo College. He
replied, "I regret that your question is one of those to which we are seeking

an answer ourselves, and that we are at present operating with a minimum of regulations and by-laws, relying on precedents and good sense to guide us until a proper scheme of authority has been built up." There were, of course, a number of formal bodies to which he could point. Thus, Gilmour noted that a board of governors had full charge over "financial and physical matters," while an independent senate held initiative in academic affairs. In addition, there were four faculties, each with its own dean: theology (essentially Divinity), engineering, graduate studies, and combined arts and science. Responsibility for the latter was divided between University College (arts) and Hamilton College (science), both headed by a principal. He could have added that a University Council did exist. Still, it was probably easy to overlook a body that was purely deliberative, met infrequently, and had little access to significant information. Instead, he merely assured Adlington that, over time, a body of regulations and committees would, no doubt, grow.[7] Time, however, did little to define or clarify arrangements much.

Indeed, two years later, Adlington wrote from Waterloo again, asking for more precise information concerning McMaster's constitutional and organizational practices. Gilmour responded, much as he had in 1958, saying that the more such things were studied, the less he and others were inclined to reduce them to writing, since, as he observed, "written by-laws can be a nuisance in a peaceful organization and an occasion of unnecessary irritation in a divided one." Queen's, he noted, went a full century without resorting to formal bylaws. Common sense, allied with conventional checks, balances, and precedent, Gilmour averred, had served McMaster well.[8]

While all this rings somewhat archaic in the systems-attuned, twenty-first-century ear, it made perfect sense to paternalistic leaders of Gilmour's generation; people reared in the intimate, face-to-face environment of Canada's small, pre-war universities. Thus, an old administrative culture lingered at McMaster; an element of tradition in a torrent of change. One might have expected this to alter once Thode assumed the president's chair. He was, after all, the great prophet of academic modernization. As it happened, however, loosely defined lines of authority suited freewheeling Thode to an absolute tee. Vague borders, after all, offer eager pioneers substantial personal latitude.

In 1961, Justice Samuel Freedman, chancellor of the University of Manitoba, contacted Thode, asking for his thoughts on campus governance.[9] His response was revealing. He noted that a recent, four-year debate over curriculum renewal had left most staff members "fed up with faculty and committee meetings" and disinclined to broach big questions. The exercise, he said, had been most instructive. During the course of it, he had concluded that the vast majority of staff had little notion of how a university actually operated, and even less as to the detailed nature of the work involved. "It has been my experience," he continued, "that the top professors, the brilliant scholars, have the least time for committee work and are very little concerned with the prestige that comes from administrative positions or from membership on the Board of Governors." Yet, he emphasized, it was these very people "to whom I go to seek advice and counsel as a university administrator." The question of university government, he told Freedman, was delicate and required finesse.[10] Like Gilmour, if for different reasons, Thode preferred the personal touch of a traditional administrative culture.

Nowhere in this correspondence did either Gilmour or Thode comment on the ramshackle character of the actual structure over which they presided. Quite unintentionally, however, Arthur Patrick drew attention to its convoluted nature in his 1962 report as dean of arts. The McMaster Act of 1957, he pointed out, had identified four faculties. Each was administered by a dean and associate dean. On paper, it all looked so simple. In practice, things were very different. The act, he underscored, made no reference to Hamilton or University College, let alone principals of those bodies. Yet, while they had no legal status, these entities were maintained "as useful and convenient divisions of the work done in the Faculty of Arts and Science." Furthermore, Patrick observed, legislation had not defined the precise duties, terms, and powers of deans, heads, or chairs. Obviously, the same was true of college principals; yet these two officers had both considerable prestige and significant authority.

In 1962, an opportunity to clarify matters presented itself when Armstrong resigned, after ten years as dean of arts and science. Some momentary thought was given to division into separate faculties, but this was rejected in the name of preserving community and liberal education. Instead, two deans were appointed: one for arts (Patrick) and another for science (Ronald Graham), within the notionally combined faculty. Primary authority would rotate between the two on a yearly basis. As Patrick commented, this arrangement "could lead to great difficulties and misunderstandings." Fortunately, he said, he and his scientific counterpart got on well and studiously avoided wrangling. Even so, he acknowledged, everything depended "almost entirely upon the personalities of the persons appointed as deans and principals and upon their willingness to co-operate and to work constantly in mutual consultation."[11]

Within this labyrinthine, idiosyncratic framework, a given faculty or department needed a strong, consistent voice in high circles in order to prosper. In this regard, the fledgling social sciences were notably lacking.

Between 1957 and 1968, they fell under the aegis of University College, within the broader Faculty of Arts and Science. That meant dealing with Gilmour, who served as principal until 1961, and Salmon, who held the post into the late sixties. The other key figures were Dean Armstrong, up to 1962, and Arthur Patrick, dean of arts, thereafter. Ironically, of this group, the only one who showed any true enthusiasm for the development of social science was the geologist, Armstrong.[12] Yet, his star was waning in the later fifties, as Thode's rose. In the end, his voice could not compete with that of Thode, who was, at once, vice-president, principal of Hamilton College, director of research, and all but heir apparent to the ailing Gilmour. When he resigned in 1962, Armstrong remarked that his advice had gone largely unheeded for several years. With his departure, social science lost not only its most ardent administrative advocate, but also the person best placed to foster cohesive planning within the nascent faculty.

For his part, Gilmour had long harboured suspicion about "polysyllabic experts" in fields such as sociology and psychology. As noted, his views mellowed with time, but he could never be described as an ardent champion of the newer social sciences.[13] Besides, he was too broadly preoccupied to concentrate attention on them. Togo Salmon, Gilmour's successor as University College principal, expressed no particular feelings about social science as a body of learning. Yet, he came to have serious misgivings concerning the growing concentration of boomers in that area, as the first wave of a new generation flooded McMaster's halls. There was, he remarked, an unmistakable trend, both in day and extension classes, toward enlistment in three-year, social science programs. He regarded this as "an ominous development." Too much teaching power, he thought, had to be devoted to these students at a time when honours was the vital path toward nurturing an enlarged professoriate, so essential for the future.[14] The implication, here, was that social science was becoming the haven for a teeming horde of nonchalant passers-through.

Dean Patrick, on the other hand, had undisguised misgivings about social science. Indeed, as the sixties wore on, he became increasingly critical of a creeping "permissiveness" in arts generally, but particularly in political science, sociology, and anthropology. Both at the pass and honours levels, he maintained, the quality of work was slipping, as prerequisites were cut to a minimum and students cobbled degrees together in patchwork fashion. Indeed, Patrick, a scholar of romance languages, felt that there had been a growing "imbalance of talent in the student body – especially in the 'softer' social sciences," after 1963.[15] In fairness, he observed that some responsibility for this had to be laid at the door of those who perpetuated an outmoded university structure, which led to "rather little effective control over the growth of curriculum in Arts, at least." Academic policies, Patrick noted, meandered through tangled channels, only to be rubber-stamped by the senate. "Is it possible," he asked Thode in 1966, "that this abrogation of interest is the result of our illogical organization into a criss-crossing pattern of 'colleges' and 'faculties'?" Answering his own rhetorical question, the dean called for revision of university government. Clearly, not all such pleas arose simply from a mounting drive to faculty power. Whatever the case, under the unreformed system, the social sciences had no long-term, muscular paladin at the heart of what Melling later called "the confederacy of Arts and Science."

Still, while organizational muddle and alleged administrative neglect loomed large in the minds of Melling and McIvor, such things, alone, do not explain the complex history of their evolving faculty between 1957 and 1969. Indeed, one must be careful when generalizing about social science during those years. After all, this was a new, emerging faculty, whose particular identity and appropriate membership were far less clear at the outset than was the case in other sectors of the university. Birth pangs were to be expected. So were problems of identity; not to mention occasional self-inflicted wounds and all the painful sorting-out concomitant with adolescence.

Where identity was concerned, the very notion of what constituted social science was, at best, fuzzy, early on. Consider, for example, calendar regulations promulgated in 1962. According to these, three broad areas of concentration within arts and science were identified: humanities, social science, and natural science. All undergraduate candidates were required to take a total of three (unspecified) full-year courses, distributed across two areas outside that of their home specialization. To cite Salmon, "[T]he category to which a department should most appropriately belong was not always self-evident."[16] As if to prove his point, political economy, sociology, history, geography, and nursing were lumped together under the rubric of social science.

On the surface, the inclusion of history looks plausible enough. In reality, however, the epistemology, methodology, and interests of McMaster's historians were overwhelmingly, albeit not exclusively, humanistic during the fifties and sixties. Indeed, the department bolted to the Faculty of Humanities, as soon as the latter was created. Meanwhile, geography, like psychology, was striving mightily to establish its scientific credentials, and reported to the principal of Hamilton College, as did nursing. Altogether, the quirky marriage of inconvenience, concocted in 1962, rendered both identity and planning across the "social sciences" problematic. Armstrong's grand confederation never got off the drawing board. It was within this context that political economy, followed by sociology, laboured to lay the foundations of modern social science at McMaster.

Time-honoured political economy would prove to be the fruitful seedbed of substantial development. Out of it, in time, came the individual departments of economics, political science, and the school of business (now the DeGroote School). In 1957, however, it was a six-member unit that tried to do all the above on a shoestring. Small wonder, then, that the chairman, economist Jack Graham, rather liked what he (thought he) heard coming out of Armstrong's office. In fact, his departmental report for 1956–57 sounded a note that was, at least superficially, similar to the dean's holistic refrain. "The recent expansion of other somewhat newer social sciences in the University provides a necessary and increasingly valuable milieu of related disciplines [that] will contribute greatly to the development of programs in Politics, Economics and Commerce," chimed Graham.

For some time, he asserted, he had hoped political economy could expand into the field of industrial relations, but this had been set aside when the department took on heavy responsibilities in commerce, after 1954. Besides, expertise was required in areas outside strict political economy, if industrial relations were to be studied in a truly modern manner. This, he emphasized, is why his department had strongly recommended that cutting-edge psychology and sociology be fostered at McMaster. Together, they made it "realistic to consider work in industrial relations." Lest his most basic point be lost on the Armstrongs of that world, Graham hammered it home. Thus, he extended a warm welcome to new kids on the block, but voiced fervent hope that the university would, as he phrased it, "maintain balanced development of the Social Sciences – one that gives appropriate weight to the more mature of these disciplines, and particularly, at this point, to politics."[17] In short, political economy would sing in a choir of Armstrong's devising, but only as lead tenor.

There was, of course, nothing novel about departmental particularism. Newbigging and Jones, for example, had no desire to see their disciplines subordinated to the needs of a greater political economy. For his part, Graham spoke for colleagues with much on their collective plate and was loath to see precious new resources too widely dispersed. On the eve of university secularization, he was pleading for at least three new appointments to help political economy with its diverse and growing load. The economics section, although small, had a strong complement. It included Graham, a Rhodes Scholar who specialized in labour relations. McIvor, with a doctorate from Chicago, focused on Canadian banking and monetary policy, when he wasn't dazzling intramural hockey fans with his skating prowess. R.W. Thompson offered classes in statistics, economic theory, and public finance.[18] W.D.G. "Bill" Hunter rounded out the team, busy with his study of the organizational practice of industries, such as uranium mining and shipbuilding. Together, they mounted a credible undergraduate honours program, while tending to a couple of MA candidates each year. Meanwhile, they were pressed to develop special courses for non-economics majors, especially the expected tide of would-be engineers. Derry Novak was the sole political scientist, but, with assistance from colleagues, was able to sustain a degree program in theory, as well as some modest graduate tuition. Calvin C. "Cal" Potter oversaw the fledgling work in commerce.[19] All were engaged in extension work and some measure of personal research. All assisted in the delivery of commerce.[20] Clearly, with his department heavily weighted toward economics, Graham was anxious to balance its composition.

Equally, he was eager to promote graduate study. Referring to an imminent "battle of the bulge," he foresaw a looming scarcity of qualified personnel as universities everywhere braced themselves for the predictable onrush of boomers, especially in an age when social science research was sure to come to the fore. Thus, Graham lamented the ill-preparedness with which his department faced the future. Graduate work in political economy, he sighed, was sporadic, small in scale, and largely part-time. Too many students, he remarked, were forced to pursue advanced work while holding down year-round employment. This, he said, was the direct consequence of a disadvantage under which they laboured. Graduate students in science received full financial support. Those in arts, generally, did not. Political economy, therefore, put the case for graduate fellowships and assistantships in arts near the top of its shopping list. There was, Graham argued, no other way to develop a substantial corps of full-time, advanced students who could stimulate each other, not to mention whet the staff's appetite for research.[21] In time, his plea would be answered, thanks largely to the powerful advocacy of Art Bourns, who championed such annual assistantships during his tenure as dean of graduate studies.

Very soon, however, the brakes were applied to almost all development in economics and politics. Moreover, the pressure would come, quite unintentionally, from within the department itself. It took the form of an unforeseen, utterly explosive growth spurt in the area of commerce. The force in question was the meteoric rise of McMaster's MBA. By the early sixties, the latter program was either political economy's glittering box-office starlet, or its insatiable black hole, depending on the viewer's perspective. Powerfully seductive as a student lure, it also tended to suck dry all the energy nearby, at least for a time. It is, therefore, curious to note that it first took life out of, essentially, extracurricular activity.

A modest bachelor of commerce program had been added to political economy's menu in 1954, after years of lobbying by local businessmen.[22] Aspiring candidates could choose either a three-year economics and business pass degree, or a four-year BComm, in which the initial emphasis was on accounting. By 1957, however, Graham was arguing that a stream in marketing would lend greater depth and attractiveness to the program. As an aside, he put in a plug for his own particular area of interest. Thus, he suggested that industrial relations would be an excellent option to pursue – in time. For the moment, he asked only that someone be hired to mount the desired courses in marketing. He went on to project that roughly ten graduates per year could be turned out, once Potter got commerce into full gear. With a few strategic appointments across his whole province (politics, economics, and commerce), Graham thought this number manageable.

Almost as a footnote, he mentioned that political economy continued to staff six evening courses, through extension, for locals who wished to complete the first year of Toronto's graduate business program close to home. The arrangement, set in place in 1952, worked well for both universities. Over the years, Toronto benefited from enrolments it might have otherwise lost. Meanwhile, McMaster gained experience in graduate business education toward the day when it might launch its own degree. Graham noted that student calls for just such a program were mounting, but he argued that political economy would first have to expand its staff and flesh out its undergraduate curriculum, before such a step could be taken. For now, he restricted himself to requests for the reinforcement of established undertakings.[23]

Armstrong obliged, as best he could, hiring J.E. "Jack" Kersell in politics and H.C. Brian Dixon (part-time) to assist Potter. Vigorous effort to recruit a suitable economist failed, as continent-wide demand for qualified people was, to use the dean's term, "fierce." Still, as McMaster went secular, political economy could boast eight members, with the promise of a ninth in its pocket. Things were looking up, although there was some mild concern as commerce drew more and more candidates away from the traditional honours economics stream.[24] Otherwise, the department proceeded according to plan.

Kersell added the study of institutions and international affairs to politics' theoretical offerings. Dixon and Graham developed marketing and industrial relations to broaden the curriculum of commerce. Meanwhile,

Potter was off, south of the border, to investigate new methods in "simulation" (business gaming) as a means of instruction. When not assisting with BComm instruction, economists were engaged in their accustomed undergraduate duties, while helping with annual management seminars for local business executives, a public service venture that had become a departmental fixture of no small value to its civic profile. In addition, through the good offices of radio station CKOC, they delivered a twelve-week series of broadcasts on *The Canadian Economy in Review* for a listening audience agitated by the current recession.[25] All, in short, was reasonably plain sailing – until 1959.

In that year, Toronto ceased to offer or recognize evening classes in its master of commerce program. Sooner than anticipated, sooner than desired, political economy faced a crucial decision. As McIvor later recalled, the department gnawed over the pros and cons for months, before finally deciding to launch its own degree. To test the market, a survey of all who had ever registered for the evening program was conducted. The responses were overwhelmingly positive; the evidence decisive. With a steady stream of candidates all but assured, the senate's approval was swift, especially for a department far from overburdened with graduate students. In 1960, the McMaster MBA came into being as a two-year professional, rather than academic, program. Its target clientele dictated much of its form. Not aimed at neophytes, the MBA was designed for part-time, evening delivery to those who had been in the workforce roughly ten years and entertained upwardly mobile ambitions. The goal was "to fashion and develop broadly based management skills," as opposed to inculcating expertise in the specific tasks of any particular enterprise.

With this in mind, the department devised a curriculum that included familiarity with all those social science concepts deemed requisite for modern management. Accordingly, courses in psychology and sociology stood alongside those in accounting, economics, and statistics. In adopting this approach, McMaster was in line with recent developments in the United States, as were contemporary ventures at Queen's and McGill. In contrast, McIvor chuckled, Toronto was eschewing "the emphasis on behavioural insights" and would lose many a student to Hamilton, as a result.[26] Nobody, however, had any real inkling of just how magnetic the new degree would actually become.

In fact, the best guess in 1959 was that mounting the MBA would do relatively little to alter current commitments of the department. Prognosticators estimated that average enrolment would settle in at a manageable level; perhaps just above the norm for the recently defunct Toronto evening courses.

They had, however, grossly underestimated a pent-up market. The program was no sooner announced then applications doubled, from roughly forty-five per annum between 1952 and 1960, to ninety-six in 1960–61.[27] At once deliciously excited and mildly concerned, Graham informed Thode that graduate supervision had, in 1960, suddenly become political economy's "main activity." All members of the commerce and economics staff were heavily engaged, over and above their regular duties. Meanwhile, sociology and psychology graciously gave further support. As well, a large number of prominent guest speakers from industry, government, and sister universities enriched the inaugural sessions. Graham advised that a cadre of professionally trained people from local firms should be developed as casual staff, since the nature of the work entailed close liaison with industry. He appended the names of appropriate individuals at Stelco, Christie-Brown, Imperial Oil, and other companies who, with Thode's permission, would make ideal part-time instructors. Lavishing praise on Potter for outstanding management on very short notice, he then delivered the inevitable punch line: more purpose-dedicated, full-time staff were urgently needed.[28]

The administration obliged. Between 1961 and 1963, Isaiah Litvak, J.A. "Jim" Johnson, A.Z. Szendrovits, J.R. "Jack" Hanna, and R.J. Spence were hired to cope with the combined weight of the undergraduate commerce and MBA load. Still, demand outran supply, as graduate registrations in business soared past 170, in 1962–63, and showed no sign of levelling out. In his first report as chairman, Craig McIvor indicated that, even with considerable assistance from other social sciences and professionals in the Hamilton community, his colleagues were feeling the strain. "As far as the Department of Political Economy is concerned," he wrote, "the program's rapid development has created problems of organization, supervision and instruction which have all but outstripped the ability of our limited man-power to satisfy."[29] Above all, the time had come to rationalize the manifold, yet distinct, functions of a growingly crowded and far too busy house.

Accordingly, political economy sent forward two linked recommendations for Thode's consideration. One called for commerce to be hived off as an independent department, with Potter in the chair. This new body would oversee the "pre-professional" BComm and, on an interim basis, the MBA.[30] The second proposal was that a graduate school of business be authorized take direction of the latter program, as of July 1965. McIvor argued that a year's grace was necessary to study best practice at leading American schools and to consult with Western, Queen's, McGill, and Toronto, closer to home.[31] Principal Salmon expressed some concern about the costs involved, but ultimately conceded that "for public relations purposes [the school] might prove incalculable."[32] If Salmon, humanist supreme, were for this, who would stand against it? Thus, both requests were granted by the senate, just as the modest venture of 1959 was turning into an enterprise of truly major proportions.

By 1966, there were thirty-nine full-time and 295 part-time MBA students on the books. Meanwhile, 135 graced the undergraduate programs in commerce. This moved Graham to urge that commerce be merged with the school, so that its programs might be more closely geared to producing MBA candidates. Going further, he called on the university to grant full faculty status to business.[33] While the merger was approved, administrators were reluctant to meet the second request. None of the internal staff were deemed ready to assume the directorship. To his colleagues, Graham appeared the obvious choice. Salmon, however, considered him a procrastinator, unfit for a leadership role. At the same time, the principal noted growing discontent with governance by committee, as the school took shape.[34] In the end, Dr William Schlatter was enticed from his post at the University of Michigan to provide direction for the new body. By 1970, the wildest dreams of 1959 were vastly surpassed, as 470 undergraduates and 450 MBA candidates occupied twenty-three full-time staff.[35] Best of all, the operation turned a tidy profit. Indeed, a cash cow of heavy udder had been born to the McMaster herd. Meanwhile, political economy could get back to concentrating on its appropriate affairs: the academic study of politics and economics.

Commerce and the MBA, together, had been the elephant in political economy's room. Nobody said much outright, but the professional offerings undoubtedly drained both faculty energy and student numbers from the more traditional, academic wings of the department. This was particularly true of economics, as Graham and Armstrong both observed in 1961.[36] Thus, it must have been with a mixed spirit of blood brotherhood and blessed relief that the heirs of Adam Smith wished the newly independent school of business adieu, in 1964. That done; McIvor wasted no time in advising Salmon that politics and economics should also go their separate ways: not in rancour, but for mutual benefit and clarity of purpose. Only with reasonable teaching loads, increased graduate numbers, and opportunities to concentrate on specialized research could either group hope to play a significant role in a changing university environment. The competition for first-class students and professors was simply too keen to do otherwise. Exercising a measure of diplomacy, he did not add that years of caring for the elephant had left both politics and economics in a chase position, where development was concerned.[37]

Like Thode, McIvor preached disciplinary cross-pollination throughout his career, but, as he told the president, administrative separation of politics and economics had become a practical necessity.[38] Given the maelstrom soon to engulf political science, he spoke more wisely than he could have guessed. In any case, political economy, once home to the likes of Harold Innis and Kenneth Taylor, faded from the scene in 1965, when the separate departments of economics and political science took its place. Now, it was time to play catch-up with history, English, and other players on the prestigious graduate-studies stage.

Moving quickly in that direction, economics followed history and other departments in revamping its MA program to include a one-year, four-course option to the traditional thesis.[39] The latter, more time-consuming, rite of passage had made sense in an earlier age, when a master's degree had, more frequently, been terminal. Amid the hustling sixties, however, would-be doctoral candidates and instructors, alike, increasingly viewed the MA as something resembling a qualifying year: a transitory interlude shared by consenting adults en route to better things. In 1966, economics regarded a PhD program as the particular, better thing in view. It was a move deemed "essential" to attracting the best students.[40]

McIvor made his initial approach to Thode, arguing that the stage was all but set. A new undergraduate curriculum had been devised, with considerable emphasis on quantitative studies, industrial organization, and economic history. The MA had been streamlined and attracted fourteen candidates, a notable improvement over earlier years. Still, said the chairman, substantial graduate growth would not occur until a PhD was on offer. The time, moreover, was ripe. At that moment, said McIvor, only three universities in Ontario offered doctorates in economics: Toronto, Western, and Queen's. Yet, there were jobs aplenty. Indeed, best estimates had it that over sixty positions would be available shortly, at new universities and with numerous levels of government. Meanwhile, the total output of all doctoral programs across Canada was a mere thirty graduates, in 1967. Urging Thode to seize the moment, McIvor noted that his department had seventeen members on staff: "enough to do the job." In fact, between 1964 and 1967 E.H. "Ernie" Oksanen, J.R. Allan, J.R. Williams, David Winch, and C.J. Maule had all come on strength, along with Peter J. George (later to be a three-term president of the university).

As a kicker, McIvor noted that seven more would be required, so as to maintain quality in the undergraduate program. Some of the new recruits, he added, ought to be "senior people with strong credentials to strengthen our credibility." The degree, itself, would be carefully tailored so as to avoid overlap with competing institutions. He proposed, therefore, a tight focus on three areas: public finance, monetary economics, and international trade, with a good dose of theory for all candidates. A lively program of faculty research could, then, be concentrated in these fields. All that was required was sufficient university support.[41] The scheme was duly forwarded for consideration by the senate and the Ontario Council of Graduate Studies. This was, after all, the post-Spinks era.

There came a shock. Mel Preston, now a member of the OCGS, reported that external reviewers had been, at best, lukewarm in their appraisals of the proposal. One had pointed out that several other Ontario universities were clamouring to jump on the economics doctoral bandwagon and that the success of any given bid would depend heavily on relative preparedness. The reviewer in question thought that McIvor's request for several senior appointments was a dead giveaway that McMaster was not truly ready, at the moment. In like manner, a second consultant felt that the publishing record of an admittedly youngish staff had yet to mature to a point sufficient to sanction the degree. For his part, Preston found the plan well-designed and thought McMaster's facilities to be quite up to snuff. Even so, he was unimpressed by the publication record of certain key department members and recommended the delay of at least a year, until the desired senior appointments could be arranged.[42] Gone, it seemed, were the blithe days when Newbigging's fledgling four could hustle a doctorate into being, just for the asking. It was shortly after this that McIvor issued his blistering letter to Thode about the "planning vacuum" in social science.

In the event, permission to hire five new members, three of them established scholars, was forthcoming. Of these, a sterling prize was Frank Denton, later a member of the Royal Society, who served as the early workhorse among doctoral supervisors.[43] The senate, therefore, approved the new degree, and, by mid-1969, Graham reported that economics anticipated accepting up to forty-five graduate students, eight of them PhD candidates, in September of that year. He further noted that every effort was being made to associate economics with other elements of the university, such as business, political science, engineering, urban studies, and the interdepartmental committee on communist and eastern European affairs.[44] Within a year, he rejoiced to note that approximately fifty applicants, including ten doctoral aspirants, had been accepted into the graduate ranks.[45] It had been a long haul, compared to others, but economics was now firmly established as a full-service department. Best of all, it had achieved this with only a few, relatively minor teething problems along the way. In sharp contrast, its erstwhile partner, political science, passed through endless dangers, toils, and snares – most of its own devising.

In January 1967, a touch of gallows humour laced a letter to Thode from T.C. "Tom" Truman, chairman of political science. "I could only wish it were possible," he wrote, "to make an academic study of this department's affairs, because the conflict of interests and personalities is rich in data." After a mere six months in office, Truman was already teetering at wit's end. His department, less than two years old, was mired in virulent factionalism. It was also, he alleged, being undermined by the partisan interference of Principal Salmon, "a man of strong prejudices and authoritarian personality," who was a "racist" [anti-American], with a decided bias against newer approaches to the study of politics. "I have," wrote the harried chairman, "difficulties galore." Accordingly, he sought presidential advice.[46] Thode, no doubt, took some of this with a dash of salt, but he could scarcely have been wholly surprised. Instead, he must have experienced an all-too-unwelcome sense of déjà vu. After all, Truman was only at McMaster because Grant Davy, his predecessor, had recently left the chair in a huff – long before his mandate had expired.

In 1965, Davy had been attracted, from Alberta to McMaster, by the opportunity to shape a new department at a moment when the whole discipline of political science was undergoing a dramatic, if controversial, face-lift. An alumnus of Western, Davy had encountered the "behavioural" tide sweeping American thought, while doing his graduate work at Harvard. In contrast with a traditional approach that emphasized ideas, institutions, and description, the new wave focused on that which could be measured, quantified, and modelled. Champions of the latter position purported to be more scientific in the study of political phenomena than those who clung to traditional modes of inquiry. Inevitably, higher priests of the new dispensation too often claimed monopoly on insight; forgetting that there is always a faster gun, a fresh revision, just round the corner. Similarly, the self-appointed guardians of tradition too often took refuge in blast-proof shelters, secure in the comfort of established conviction. It was, of course, ever thus.

There was, in truth, nothing unique to political science in this. Indeed, most, if not all, the major disciplines were reconsidering inherited assumptions and the methods that they mandated. Jack Hodgins, for example, encountered some grumbling as he reimagined engineering studies. The arts, in short, though more prone to paradigmatic conflict, had no absolute strangle hold on intellectual flux. Nor could all be neatly ascribed to the advent of "The Sixties." The call to "relevance," to be sure, had something to do with events of that turbulent decade, but there was much of older vintage at work, too. Thus, if new tools, such as the mainframe computer, opened the door to an emphasis on quantification, the slow march toward fuller democratization, hastened by two world wars, redefined who and what was "relevant." The century-long delineation, maturation, and acceptance of the "sciences of society" also contributed mightily to the shaping of how the great questions might be tackled. So, too, did the postwar existentialism of Sartre or Camus. Meanwhile, increased borrowing across disciplinary lines could blur boundaries, but also produce tantalizing prospects, such as Fernand Braudel's concept of "total history," born out of work stretching back to the thirties.[47] Cold War ideologies, scarcely novel in 1960, added fiery spice. There was, in short, a rich stew of manifold ingredients simmering, long before the Age of Aquarius. It merely came ready to serve in the latter era.

For some, the prospect was intoxicating. For others, it was noxious. For most, things just became more interesting. Whatever the case, a potentially charged atmosphere reigned in many a department across sundry universities. Responses and outcomes varied, but leadership and personalities were always of crucial import. McMaster geography, as seen, experienced pointed debate, yet managed to avoid an all-out breakdown of collegiality. Meanwhile, "econometrics" seems to have been smoothly integrated into McIvor's department, without upsetting those who continued to focus on other interests. Political science, by contrast, lacking a Craig McIvor or a Les King, divided into warring tribes of "behaviourists" and "traditionalists." The price of this descent into factional bloodletting would be steep. Moreover, the conflict would have repercussions for social science, as a whole. Thus, it merits close investigation.

Upon arrival in 1965, Davy had hoped to instill a "progressive," behavioural ethos in his newborn department. He had not, however, inherited a tabula rasa. Instead, Derry Novak, Jack Kersell, and Peter Potichnyj were on the scene to greet him with something less than unreserved enthusiasm. Each, in fact, was a practitioner of traditional bent. Still, Davy had been appointed in time to have some influence over a spate of hiring which, by 1967, would raise the full-time complement of political science to nine. Among the newer recruits, William Lyons shared Davy's vision. So did Donald J. Grady, who, the senate was informed in May 1965, was within a month of defending his dissertation at Princeton.[48] Grady's compatriot and fellow behaviourist, Thomas M. Mongar, joined up next year, as did the far-more-conventional Klaus Hubert Pringsheim, a Canadian working on his thesis at Columbia.[49] Altogether, the cast of a tragedy, relieved by just a touch of farce, was assembled. Act one premiered in April 1966.

In that month, an angry Davy wrote testily to Principal Salmon. Having encountered obstacles to his once bright hopes, both within and without the department, he had already tendered his resignation. Still, Davy felt obliged to continue the good fight, as he saw it, over the remaining weeks of his commission. At the moment, he was concerned to alert the principal to an immediate danger, but not before venting his spleen. "I find myself," he told Salmon, "in the almost impossible position of being caught [on one hand] between the pressure of my colleagues in the Department and my colleagues in the South Western Ontario Political Science Conference for information about McMaster's intentions with regard to the future of Political Science, and [on the other] vagueness, indecision and unwillingness to make firm commitments on the part of the academic administrators at the university." Delivering this less-than-subtle barb to Salmon, Davy continued, "Unless I am given more clear and binding commitments on specific matters immediately, I must ask you to make interim arrangements for Departmental planning which exclude my participation." The foregoing tirade was, one suspects, at once purgative, satisfying, and (above all) safe for one on his way to a tenure-stream post at Alberta. The tone, certainly, was calculated to provoke little but ire in the prickly principal.

Turning to the meat of the issue, Davy reported that, within the week, he was to attend a meeting at York of political science chairmen from all universities across southwestern Ontario. The purpose of the gathering would be to draw up a general submission to the Spinks Commission regarding a five-year plan for the development of graduate work in the province. Davy cautioned that the outcome could be decisive, not just for political science, but for social science as a whole at McMaster. This flowed from his estimate that Spinks and company would recommend the initiation, continuation, or cancellation of doctoral work, not on departmental, but on Faculty-wide strength in any given university. That being likely, said Davy, it might prove disastrous for McMaster were one of its key social science departments unable to present a clear, workable, and well-supported plan. As things stood, he wrote, "I could not make a convincing case for Spinks now about Political Science at McMaster." At a minimum, he admonished Salmon, standing promises of, as yet unfulfilled, support had to made good, starting with an appointment in international politics. At stake, he reiterated, was nothing less than the future of all the social sciences.[50] As special pleading went, this was strong stuff. Still, an apocalyptic reading of Spinks and his "University of Ontario" was common enough, before the far less draconian appraisals system was finally brought into being. In any case, Davy laid blame for next-to-certain disaster squarely at Salmon's door. His successor, Tom Truman, truly an innocent from abroad, would find that matters were just a tad more complex than this.

In 1966, Truman, an Australian, had been specially recruited from his antipodean home to mediate among the explosively intemperate who staffed political science. Although favouring a behavioural approach, a liberal turn of mind left him open to an appreciation of tradition. At the level of personal relations, he appears to have preferred accommodation over confrontation. All told, he seemed ideally suited to the task at hand, so long as one assumed that something resembling a flickering ember of collegiality was anywhere alive. Alas, while there was heat aplenty, little of it was generated by campfire concord. Indeed, by January 1967, Truman was writing to Salmon in an effort to dampen a roaring factional blaze.

The principal had been informed, privately, that Lyons, Mongar, and their fellow behaviourists had openly threatened to drive all traditionalists into the sea. Truman made inquiries and reported that comments had been distorted and blown out of proportion by both sides. "I have evidence in my files," he told Salmon, "of provocative behaviour by Pringsheim and Mongar and I have had to admonish them both for childish conduct." Lyons, he assured the principal, was one of the least faction-prone members of the department. Meanwhile, he suggested that "we are taking this factional nonsense too seriously." "It should," he concluded, "be seen as childishness and treated accordingly."[51] Although diplomatic in this missive to Salmon, inwardly, Truman was seething. It was at this point that, death-row humour and all, he wrote directly to Thode, seeking advice as to how to cope with a "racist" (i.e., anti-American), interfering principal. The letter is worth close examination, since it illuminates much that followed.

Anticipating trouble, Truman had spoken with Thode on 24 January, before approaching Salmon. He had asked about the extent of his authority as chairman in dealings with the principal. Thode told him that he should consider Salmon's advice, but was not obliged to follow it. Now, Truman wrote the president to say he had rejected Salmon's recommendation that Pringsheim, rather than Lyons, be appointed assistant chairman. He went on to charge the principal with taking sides in and, thereby, encouraging factional disputes in the department. Salmon, he continued, regularly described Davy, Grady, and others of their persuasion, as "evil men," while subjecting Truman to "long tirades" against them. For his part, the chairman had no doubt that those named were sometimes "foolish and offensive," but felt that to employ the term *evil* was inflammatory and extreme. Anxious to avoid an unproductive clash with Togo, Truman asked for Thode's help in dealing with some outstanding issues.

One involved Salmon's early promise that $30,000 would be made available for library acquisitions; a figure later whittled down to $6,000. (Perhaps, this was part of what Davy had referred to earlier as undelivered support.) He then noted the principal's refusal to accept his analysis of the supposed conspiracy to oust Pringsheim and the traditionalists. Truman admitted that he had been forced to chide Grady, Mongar, Pringsheim, and others about heated remarks, but, he added, "it is foolish to take them as seriously as Salmon does." Worse still, the principal's clear bias toward Pringsheim's interpretation of events was creating the impression that Truman lacked administrative support. This, he argued, seriously damaged his ability to defuse factional strife.

It did not aid matters, he continued, that the dean of extension studies, John Melling, attended department meetings as a part-time member and tended to cast his lot with the traditional wing. Salmon, he said, frequently relied on Melling's advice in the crucial matter of recruiting faculty. Indeed, when a recent candidate of behavioural leanings was interviewed, he was grilled extensively, and later confided to Truman that "if he had had to see one more dean he would have puked." Thode was not asked to intercede. Truman merely sought counsel.[52] Whatever Thode said has been lost to time. Still, it seems clear that Truman was advised to be patient and seek accommodation with the principal.

In early February, the frayed chairman tried to explain his position to Salmon in clear, documented terms. He was at pains to outline the precise nature of behavioural studies and sent along a published paper of his own that both defined and critiqued them. He, then, surveyed the expertise of each department member, pointing out that none of them actually qualified as a full-blown behaviourist, although some came close. Meanwhile, ransacking departmental files, he traced current tensions back to a dispute over a thesis Novak had supervised. The work was deemed weak by critics, against whom the supervisor was said to harbour resentment. The message was that neither camp was wholly blameless amid the growing tumult. He went on to warn, yet again, against taking factional allegations at face value.

Tendering an olive branch, Truman expressed his complete agreement with Salmon's injunction that tolerance should be one of the foremost qualities sought in new recruits to the faculty. He did add, however, that Dean Melling should be left off any interview panel, since he was perceived, wrongly or rightly, to adhere to one of the warring factions.[53] Confidentially, he solicited another interview with Thode, asking that Salmon be bridled. "If this goes further," he cautioned, "the department will be in a shambles."[54]

Again, no presidential reply is recorded. Meanwhile, Truman's sombre prediction became bleak reality, after the events of 10 February.

On that ill-starred day, what should have been a routine departmental lunch with a job candidate signalled the end of sparring and the start of factional total war. No sooner was the table cleared than Truman was confronted in his office by Pringsheim, Novak, Potinchnyj, and Kersell, who charged Grady and Mongar with sabotaging the interview by remarking on internal dissention in the candidate's presence. As tempers flared, Pringsheim denounced the alleged wrongdoers as "scum and barbarians." He did so, moreover, with sufficient force as to reduce Truman's secretary to tears. He then threatened to take the whole, sad mess to Thode.

When asked about the episode, Grady and Mongar denied saying anything within earshot of the candidate, but did admit that they had spoken privately to the complainants in provocative terms. Truman duly admonished the duo, and then wrote to Salmon, arguing that it was past time for the principal openly to declare his neutrality and endorse the authority of the chair.[55] Sensing disaster, Salmon signed a letter, drafted by Truman, granting all the chairman's requests.[56] Thus armed, the latter wrote to Mongar and Pringsheim warning them that a grant of tenure would be contingent upon their keeping the peace.[57] Simultaneously, Grady was informed that his contract would not be renewed.[58] No explanation of the latter decision was offered. Indeed, to have done so would have been to break with near-universal practice in that pre-contractual age. One was hired, renewed, promoted, or let go with no more comment than simple notification. Formal elaboration was considered prejudicial to future decisions and external job applications. However, nothing, save common sense, inhibited professorial ripostes.

Pringsheim howled that he and his comrades stood ready "to take appropriate reaction when the time comes."[59] Grady demanded a written statement of allegations against him.[60] Mongar expressed "deep shock" at the charges and maintained that he had always carried out his duties faithfully, even though he had "serious reservations" about the chairman's capacity for leadership. He, then, reminded Truman of three "secret caucuses" the latter had called to encourage younger members to develop an empirical program that would sideline the traditionalists.[61] Was Truman playing a double game? In the absence of any other evidence, who can tell? Whatever the case, with sundry parties demanding a formal investigation, or threatening to take matters to the president, internecine civil war reached fever pitch. Two combatants sought, and were granted, temporary sanctuary in the sheltering bosom of the history department.[62] Others, meanwhile, took to the stump in an effort to rally student and public opinion behind Grady, who, by then, was symbolic of the general fray.

Over the next several months of 1967, the *Silhouette* featured a number of extraordinarily well-informed articles on the internal affairs of the department, Grady's plight, and the state of the social sciences, in general. The first such salvo was fired on 17 February. Political science major, John Ruggie, denounced the entire administrative and pedagogical culture of McMaster. "Secrecy and dishonesty," he wrote, were endemic in the higher echelons of the institution. The one clear thing, he continued, was a rapid turnover in young professors with innovative ideas, especially in social science. Archaic teaching methods and outmoded disciplines were propped up, while new methodologies and philosophical change were resisted. Indeed, wrote Ruggie, social science was "the step-child [*sic*] of the university," continually at the bottom of the pecking order. Still, what could one expect, he asked? "The fact that a chemist and an ancient historian are in positions of authority," he averred, "may have something to do with this."[63] A week later, student writers decried the suppression of modern methodology by a traditionalist cabal. The outcome of the current struggle, they proclaimed, would "determine whether McMaster is to lead other Canadian universities in the empirical and scientific study of man, or whether the so-called social sciences will wither here." Grant Davy, it was argued, had made a valiant effort to drag McMaster into the new age, but had been thwarted by the administration of University College, an administration dominated by one man who stood adamantly opposed to American-style empiricism. No wonder, said the authors, that psychology and geography had sought safe haven in the halls of science.[64] The chant rang on in a chorus of letters to the editor.

Meanwhile, Thode was treated to a "write-in" campaign. Freshman Barry J. Kay, for example, informed the president that he had intended to enrol in honours political science, but now had serious reservations. Stunningly literate, he wrote, "I have been upset to learn that the dissension surrounding that department has taken many of the decision-making powers out of its hands and has put the tenure of several members ... under a cloud of uncertainty." He expressed the highest regard for Grady and Mongar, while noting that, if this matter of academic freedom were not resolved, he would be forced to go elsewhere for his education. Was the next step, he inquired, to be the suppression of the *Silhouette*?[65] A freshman told Thode of the anguish he and his classmates shared over the harassment of certain professors. "The students of Drs. Mongar and Grady," he wrote, "are fascinated by the approach and thought of these charismatic personalities." He professed himself shocked to learn that the two men had been subjected to anonymous, threatening phone calls, without pausing to mention how he became privy to such information.[66] By March, student voices were collective.

That month, a missive, signed by twenty-five honours candidates, expressed deep concern about uncertainties in the department. The signatories, mostly third-year students, worried that the behaviourist approach was now going to be abandoned. This, they thought, would jeopardize their chances of admission to graduate school, since that paradigm was in favour at all the best universities.[67] On the same day, 27 March, two fourth-year students wrote Thode to say that they were committed to supporting "Dr. Grady who inspired us to move from Economics to the scientific study of human behaviour." "There seems," they loftily declaimed, " to be a high correlation between those students who appear to be among the most intelligent, inquisitive, and dynamic in the Political Science Department and those who have a high level of interest in the vigorous and versatile approach offered by Professors Grady, Mongar, Lyons, and Smith." Indeed, in their eyes, the "specific research proposals" of those faculty members seemed to complement the president's own efforts to promote the medical school.[68] Within a week, the executive committee of the McMaster Students Union (MSU) was contemplating "some sort of action."[69] At the same moment, concerned students in political science threatened large-scale withdrawals, should the behavioural approach be discontinued.[70] For good measure, the Student Representative Assembly and the Graduate Students Association (GSA) called for Grady to be reinstated on the grounds that proper procedure had been violated.[71]

In reply to this sustained barrage, Thode chanted a formulaic mantra, as he personally answered each student bolt. He said he was satisfied that procedure had been scrupulously followed. Grady had not been "fired," merely not renewed. The good of the students was the primary consideration in such decisions. The administration would not discriminate against behavioural instruction. It was too important to be shunned. Moreover, the professor's right to confidentiality, within and without the university, would not be violated, regardless the pressure exerted. After all, wrote Thode to the student council president, "the careers of people are at stake in these cases and selections cannot be matters for public debate or public concern."[72] As he explained, in an open letter to all faculty and students in political science, such procedure was standard throughout most of North America and was designed, principally, to protect the interests of candidates, such as Grady, who would be seeking employment elsewhere. "The matter," he underlined, "is confidential between Mr Grady and the University Administration."[73]

Never budging an inch, he might as well have borrowed from Martin Luther to proclaim, "Here I stand."

All the while, things within the department lurched from sublimely bad to ridiculously worse. Truman, increasingly isolated, tendered his resignation as chair, after an informal motion of no confidence found warring factions momentarily aligned.[74] He agreed, however, to remain in office until a replacement was named. Meanwhile, Preston, dean of graduate studies, was delegated to lead the appointments committee, a position normally reserved for the department's chair.

When Truman, near collapse, stepped down for good in late April, Thode decreed that daily functions would be handled by two committees: one for undergraduate and another graduate business. An effort was made to seat representatives of both factions on each.[75] Finding himself excluded, Mongar complained bitterly on the basis that his qualifications were better than many of those chosen.[76] Rebuffed in this and other matters, he resigned to take up at post at the Memorial University of Newfoundland, but he did not depart quietly.

On 6 June 1967, the *Globe and Mail*, along with the *Hamilton Spectator*, brought the whole affair to the public. Mongar and Grady, they alleged, were victims of character assassination and lies. More than 50 out of 175 majors were seeking admission elsewhere. Thode was said to be indifferent, as he had already committed to assuming the presidency of the NRC. Racial prejudice, said the papers, governed hiring policies in the form of virulent anti-Americanism. Meanwhile, thundered the *Globe*, Salmon presided over University College in the manner of a "Byzantine emperor."[77] Murray Ross, president of York University, took the *Globe* to task for sensationalizing one example of the kind of infighting typical at all dialectical institutions from time to time.[78] Following a blast in the same paper by Davy against his old employers, McIvor denounced the "thoroughly mendacious" assertion that the conflict had originated in a faculty struggle against an overbearing administration. Instead, he traced its roots to the intolerance of methodological ideologues within the department itself, and on both sides of the divide. "No one," he cautioned, "should ever assume to be the possessor of absolute truth in any matter."[79] Loud and raucous, the press war rolled on into the summer, only to be picked up, once more, when the *Silhouette* resumed publication in the autumn. At no point, however, was one, small but rather significant, snippet of information publicly disclosed: Grady had lied about his credentials.

When interviewed in the spring of 1965, he had told the appointments committee that he would defend his dissertation a month hence. In that hurried hour of frantic hiring, the less-than-thorough committee so assured the senate.[80] By January 1967, however, Grady was still nowhere near completion, yet had recently told Truman that the end was in sight. These falsifications, no doubt coupled with somewhat intemperate behaviour, led to the non-renewal of his contract. Moreover, all this was well known to Mongar, Davy, and others who wrote to Thode in Grady's defence. On 1 February, Davy, while confessing shock that his friend would lie about such a thing, penned a plaintive plea for clemency, accepted partial blame for Truman's plight, and expressed grave concern about what Grady might do to himself given his state of mental anguish and self-condemnation.[81] Thode, currently in the blast furnace of debate over health sciences and subject to nightly, often threatening, phone calls, understood pressure and anguish, only too well. Even so, he replied politely but firmly. He was, he said, much impressed by Davy's sincerity, but felt it in everybody's best interest that Grady move on. "Let me add," wrote Thode, "that I do not think Mr. Grady requires our 'forgiveness' since he has done the only real harm to himself."[82] This, in broad terms, was his line with all those colleagues who wrote saying that the particular pressures of a sorely dived department had led the professor, momentarily, to stumble out of character.[83]

In July, the McMaster University Faculty Association (MUFA) noted that, contrary to press reports, it had conducted no official investigation for the simple reason that none had been requested. Informally, however, its president, Goldwin French, stated categorically that, having kept a watching brief, MUFA could find no evidence of discrimination or violation of academic freedom. Indeed, he underscored that no one, in fact, had been "dismissed." Grady had merely not been renewed, while Mongar had resigned. Meanwhile, both had since secured employment elsewhere. As an active branch of the Canadian Association of University Teachers (CAUT), French continued, the association would not hesitate to act, where evidence warranted action. "To date," he concluded, "we have no such evidence."[84] This pronouncement, however, was insufficient to calm a department still rife with what was described as "morbid suspicion."[85]

July 1967 saw political science put into trusteeship. A committee of four, one each from history, sociology, and economics, along with lame-duck, acting department chairman Melling, conducted its affairs. Still, discord continued to reign. As late as March 1968, Melling informed Thode that both camps were busily recruiting support in classrooms, and that a threatened student revolt was only narrowly averted. Meanwhile, department meetings had been suspended for months in the face of persistent unruliness. His best advice was to go slowly and let the fires burn out with time. Five newly appointed members appeared uninterested in feuding, thus promising hope for the future. Unfortunately, gradualism would also entail altering the timetable for developing PhD studies. Even so, Melling thought, the slower process offered greater promise of long-term success.[86] Or, so he held, until word leaked that Salmon was considering "de-emphasizing" political science, altogether.[87] At that point, the new faculty recruits came to the fore.

Acting in concert, Robert Cunningham, George Breckenridge, Henry Jacek, Gilbert Winham, Gordon Means, and others, wrote Harry collectively to explain the urgency in appointing a permanent chairman, with full authority, as soon as possible. Thode heartily concurred, noting that, after a protracted search, a number of candidates were to be interviewed shortly.[88] By May 1968, Howard H. Lentner of Case Western Reserve University was named to the post. Playing honest broker, next year he was able to report that progress was being made, as the department "moved from uncertainty and instability to solidity." Two full professors had been induced to join the ranks, along with three new junior members. Twenty-seven graduate students were enrolled, while first-year enlistments were booming, having risen from 435 to more than 700, in one short year. Work had even begun on a doctoral program. The future, Lentner ventured, looked very promising, indeed.[89]

In 1970, the PhD proposal won the senate's approval. Early that same year, the *Silhouette*, paused to lament that Grady had just been released by the Department of Sociology at neighbouring Guelph, despite a mass outcry by students. Conflict with the local administration and repression within the department were cited as reasons for the dismissal.[90] Grady, of course, had not been the cause, so much as the catalyst of conflict at McMaster. By 1969, in truth, episodes of an even more drastic nature were commonplace across the country. In some ways, for example, the troubles at McMaster prefigured the far more volcanic "PSA Affair" (political science, sociology, and anthropology) at Simon Fraser, which erupted in 1969, led to mass dismissals, and long-term censure of that university by the CAUT.[91] Both outbursts, of course, were dwarfed by the torching of computer facilities at Sir George Williams University in Montreal. By comparison, McMaster weathered its political science squall fairly well.

Veteran Henry Jacek makes a plausible case that the injection of new faculty blood did much, at a critical juncture, to lesson friction, at least for a time.[92] Even so, the sacrifice of almost two years to internecine strife had delayed drafting of the doctoral degree. That loss of time would later prove costly, in the early seventies, when the Ontario government placed an embargo on new graduate programs. In most respects, other branches of social science would fare rather better than political science. Still, the going could be rough enough, at times. In this regard, the experience of sociology affords a prime example.

For many years, prior to the mid-fifties, occasional classes in sociology had been offered by individuals, chiefly from geography or economics, but with no degree program or long-term plan in mind.[93] This, it should be noted, was far from peculiar to McMaster. Indeed, as Peter Pineo later recalled, most Canadian universities had "between none and one sociologist" well into the late fifties.[94] Only McGill and Toronto boasted full undergraduate departments before mid-century, with the latter institution mounting the sole doctoral program, until the later sixties.[95] Sociology and its sister, anthropology, were still very much "American" preoccupations. In 1955, however, when Gilmour decided that the future demanded curricular modernization, Frank Jones, a Canadian with a McGill master's and a Harvard doctorate, was appointed to formalize sociological study at McMaster. Over the next decade and more, he would be the glue that held the department together. Initially, the addition of Jones was something of an afterthought, a bonus made possible by money left over from the Carnegie grant used to establish psychology. Armstrong, however, saw great potential in the discipline. Sociology, the dean wrote, was a necessary bridge between economics and psychology in the analysis of contemporary industrial society. As such, it needed to be thoroughly cultivated. Thus, while Jones flew solo for two years, Armstrong was convinced that a strong, independent department, with a full honours program, was a vital component of the social sciences, as he envisaged them. By 1957, he was recommending further appointments to expand sociology.[96] Needless to say, Jones could not have agreed more.

After some careful shopping, two key appointments were made. Frank G. Vallee, a social anthropologist with an MA from McGill and PhD from the University of London, was enticed to McMaster from his post as chief of the research division with the Canadian Citizenship Board. An assiduous scholar, he spent his summers among the Inuit of Keewatin and other tracts of the (then) Northwest Territories.[97] In time, he would rise to eminence among students of Arctic cultures. Meanwhile, he brought this whole aspect of their nation's experience to the attention of increasing numbers on campus. In 1959, Peter Pineo was added to the team. A Canadian with degrees from UBC, McGill, and Chicago, he was comfortable in both anthropology and sociology, and specialized in the study of the modern family. For his part, Jones focused research time on immigration and the sociological aspects of psychiatric wards. He also found time to serve on the research committee of the Canadian Corrections Association.[98] Later, he would turn to examining racial and ethnic groups. As Pineo notes, however, strict field specialization was for the summers. During the term, one had to be a generalist, in such a small group.

It was around this multi-dimensional trio that the Department of Sociology first took shape, in an affable, urbane atmosphere born, in part, of shared experience at McGill. Any campus skepticism about the new discipline might have been eased by the fact that Jones and Vallee were both middle-aged family men, with solid backgrounds of military and civil service.[99] Looking to the future, Jones wrote to Gilmour in 1959, predicting that sociology would find a solid student base in changing postwar society.[100] As it happened, he grossly underestimated the market to come. Even so, he hustled to raise the profile of the new department.

Jones and his colleagues were well aware of the rapid strides psychology was making at McMaster and yearned to follow suit. Thus, they quickly established an honours program by 1959 and an MA in 1961. As well, they co-operated eagerly across disciplinary lines. For example, the department supported the budding MBA by offering summer courses in industrial sociology.[101] Discriminating cross-pollination also figured in their attitude to scholarship. As Vallee explained, in 1962, there was considerable demand for social research in the Hamilton region, but he and his associates were not mere guns for hire. "Our department," he wrote, "undertakes only those projects which are of academic or theoretical significance, much of the research in progress being of an interdisciplinary kind involving collaboration of geographers, economists, and sociologists."[102] The research ethos in sociology, as Vallee outlined, seemed to chime nicely with that of the broader university and augur well for the future.

Meanwhile, enrolments grew faster than Jones had anticipated. In 1958, a respectable 175 were recorded.[103] By 1962–63, that number had jumped to 638, counting day and evening undergraduates, alongside ten MA candidates. Furthermore, thirty-seven applications for next year's graduate draft were sitting on the chairman's desk.[104] Within a year, it was clear that this was no mere blip, as fully 847 registered for regular or extension classes. Given this evidence of strong, mounting interest, in 1963 sociology began to plan a doctoral program. Then, the shock of "Black Week" came.

The term was coined by Salmon to describe the loss of three out of eight sociologists, including Vallee, during a bleak, seven-day period, in 1964. The trio had resigned, the principal reported, to accept higher salary offers at universities with better-stocked libraries.[105] What Salmon failed to pass on were further observations about these departures, specifically those offered by Frank Jones. The latter conceded that money had been a factor in the resignations. He added, however, that the instructors in question had also expressed deep dissatisfaction "with the rate of development of various departments in University College and over the lack of a clearly defined programme for the development of the social sciences." Unfortunately, from a historical perspective, the precise details of these complaints were not spelled out. Thus, it is unclear as to whether those who resigned were upset by perceived favouritism toward psychology, history, and the voracious MBA, or by more general concerns. In any event, the impact of their departure was plain enough. As Jones lamented, while losses in total staff complement were swiftly made good, the new draftees were simply too junior for sociology to bid for its place in the doctoral sun, at least for the moment. Altogether, he sighed, it was a "serious setback."[106]

Ever-growing undergraduate thirst, however, still had to be slaked. Thus, as registrations continued to climb, 1964 through 1966 witnessed something of a hiring binge. Ten instructors were recruited to replace others who left, or to add to the sum total, which stood at thirteen, by the latter date. Four of the new faculty, Ruth Landes, Wolfgang Weissleder, Richard Slobodin, and Ethel Nurge, joined Charles Stortroen on the anthropological side of the house.[107] Attention was now drawn further afield to include Oceania, Southeast Asia, Africa, and comparative religion, as well as North American aborigines. This altered the face of the department sufficiently for its name to be changed to sociology/anthropology, as of 1965. With this expansion and diversification, a doctoral proposal finally seemed realistic.

In drafting their scheme for a sociology PhD, planners, well versed in campus melody, strummed favourite Thodean notes. For one thing, there was self-evident need. In Ontario alone, they noted, universities hoped to make in excess of forty new appointments that year. Yet, the seven Canadian doctoral programs, then extant, had a grand total of only twenty-five candidates at different stages of preparation. Meanwhile, American institutions were so choked with PhD students that strong Canadian applicants were being turned away. Accordingly, designers anticipated that McMaster could expect to attract at least ten registrants by 1969 and twenty by 1970. In short, demand would be no problem.

As to the program, itself, emphasis would be placed on broad comparative and theoretical analysis, rather than on specialized sub-fields or the purely descriptive study of various societies. This opened the door to participation by the department's anthropologists, as well as close co-operation with related disciplines, such as history, religion, political science, philosophy, psychology, and economics. Planners went on to add that they would be careful to coordinate any offerings in consultation with neighbouring universities, presumably to avoid duplication (*pace* Spinks).[108] The draft proposal was, then, submitted for assessment by the senate and the OCGS. External adjudicators offered positive but somewhat guarded approval. One had reservations about the "unevenness" of the staff, noting that only Landes and Howard Brotz had yet published in "quality journals of high scientific standards." Meanwhile, three senior faculty members were described as well-qualified, but "non-publishing scholars." The great problem, as this referee saw it, was the constant turnover of good instructors. Too many, it was argued, had come over the years, only to leave for universities that offered better support for research. Still, high marks were awarded to the proposal, itself, in that it emphasized core sociological analysis and methods. This, the reviewer thought, contrasted sharply with so many American programs that focused on peripheral areas, such as demography, urban studies, social psychology, or the sociology of art, literature, and other specialized fields. McMaster was praised for bringing the heart of the discipline to the fore: societies, institutions, complex organizations, and analysis.

Another assessor described the proposal as "sound, if conventional." Great promise, however, was seen in recently recruited younger faculty. All referees agreed that Jones, while not a major force in contemporary sociology, had precisely the kind of common sense and leadership qualities essential to the success of any department.[109] In the end, this rigorous assessment, the first carried out at McMaster under new OCGS procedures, yielded a positive result. Sociology welcomed its first doctoral candidates in the fall of 1967. Accordingly, the popping of champagne corks resounded, at least in sociological quarters. Elsewhere, celebration seems to have been, at best, muted.

In his précis of departmental history, Jones hints vaguely at growing disquietude amid the rejoicing. "Intellectual diversity and conflicts," he writes, "were the order of the day." "Both," he continues, "spilled over into different conceptions of the department structure."[110] Some clarity can be brought to this tantalizing, if nebulous, observation, once it is viewed beside a letter to Thode, penned in December 1967, by three anthropologists. Having kept the peace during the recent assessment process, they were now ready to vent a sense of grievance. Anthropology, after all, was peripheral, rather than central, to the blossoming graduate program. Eager for a more balanced approach to development, Landes, Slobodin, and Stortroen, informed the president of their deep "consternation at the progressive attenuation of the Anthropology program at McMaster." There was, they contended, an acute need for graduate research in their discipline, but little encouragement of it. Serious work at the highest level, they continued, would require a larger and more diversified staff in anthropology. As things stood, however, "our deficiencies are woefully conspicuous in contrast with the tremendous growth ... elsewhere." While admitting that the undergraduate program at McMaster was new, they noted its rapid growth. At a minimum, they said, three more staff were needed, one each in archaeology, anthropological linguistics, and physical anthropology.[111]

Perhaps preoccupied with the contemporaneous storm in political science, Salmon advised Thode to go slowly in this matter. There was, he conceded, sufficient evidence of student interest to warrant some expansion, but added that, a couple of large classes aside, anthropologists carried a load below the norm in arts. Besides, like Thode, he preferred concentration over diversification. In this case, said Salmon, the areas in which appointments were being suggested were each potential departments unto themselves. "Maybe," he mused, "we should go in those directions, but not suddenly, or by 'drift'." He could foresee dividing sociology and anthropology into distinct departments, at some future point, but counselled gradualism in this, too.[112] No drifter, himself, the president fully concurred. Slow, steady growth became his formula for anthropology.[113] Subsequently, two additional staff members were hired in 1968. Department returns for the year 1969–70 show six students labouring toward an anthropology MA. Thus, some concessions were made, but not enough to satisfy all anthropology's immediate aspirations.

All the while, the still-combined department was catering to ever greater numbers. In 1968, undergraduate registrations vaulted with the influx of 500 newcomers, who raised the total to 1,920. This might have had something to do with the introduction of a stream in the comparative study of industrial societies, an area of inquiry sure to appeal to Hamiltonians. The price of growth, however, was steep, in that the department now boasted the highest student–faculty ratio in social science, at forty-three to one.[114] Two more sociologists, along with two anthropologists, were brought on strength, but their addition scarcely made a dent in the ratio. Indeed, reporting on the year 1969–70, Robert Blumstock pointedly informed Thode that enrolment had shot up, once again; this time by more than 1,400 to reach a staggering 3,330. Of these, he emphasized, 356 were majors of one form or another. This was more than political science and economics, combined, could claim. Yet, Blumstock underscored, he had the smallest staff of the three departments, with twelve sociologists and eight anthropologists, to economics' twenty-three, and politics' nineteen full- and two part-time members. All of which still left his colleagues with the highest teaching ratio among the social sciences. On top of this, he added, graduate registrations had risen to include thirty-two MA and twelve doctoral candidates. Inevitably, he called for further staff reinforcement.

As an aside, Blumstock noted that he and Slobodin were drafting a proposal for the amicable division of sociology and anthropology into separate entities; a feat not accomplished until 1974.[115] Here was another delay that rankled. Still, as the seventies dawned, the afterthought of 1955 had born large-scale, unintended consequences. Even in the Thodean universe, it seemed, nothing ever went strictly according to plan. Of course, entropy, itself, is a law of nature. Moreover, some developments in social science went more smoothly than those traced thus far. Social work and physical education, for example, moved to the status of schools with comparative ease.

The School of Social Work's origins date back to an exchange of letters between Claude Bissell and Gilmour.[116] In January 1961, the courteous Bissell wrote to say that proposals had been made to offer part-time instruction on McMaster's campus toward Toronto's BSW degree. Apparently, local agencies in Hamilton were eager that this be made available closer to home. Bissell, however, was reluctant to go ahead, unless formally invited to do so by McMaster. Accordingly, he sought Gilmour's thoughts on the matter.[117] Herb Armstrong was consulted, only to be caught off guard. Following some inquiry, the dean finally determined that Vice-President Thode had given the go-ahead, without consulting anyone else. Taken aback, Armstrong warned the president to be cautious about such a commitment. After all, he noted, "this is how we got involved with the MBA."[118] Thus informed, Gilmour told Bissell that this was all news to him, but that he had no objection to the use of McMaster's facilities, so long as it was clear that the arrangement remained one between the University of Toronto and the Hamilton Social Planning Council. "It should," he continued, "be clearly understood that we have no intention of setting up a School of Social Work or of giving instruction ourselves for credit in your School."[119] Bissell agreed and, on that basis, an extension program was launched under Toronto's auspices. Steering clear of direct involvement, however, proved difficult for McMaster, as the decade moved along.

The Canadian welfare state, under construction since the 1940s, reached a new level of maturity in the sixties, in step with postwar, public expectations. With the advent of the Canada Pension Plan, Medicare, and the Canada Assistance Plan, the sense of a "we-society" came to fuller flower. As never before, attention was directed to reimagining the social fabric as viewed from the perspective of groups outside the accepted mainstream. Naturally, the demand for professional guides, intermediaries, interlocutors – in short, social workers – grew apace. In June 1965, Harry L. Penny, an ordained United Church minister turned full-time social advocate, brought some facts of contemporary life to Thode's attention. Writing on behalf of the Hamilton Social Planning Council, he called on McMaster to establish its own school for the training of professionals in the field. Both need and demand, wrote Penny, were great. The nine existing schools in Canada, he noted, were swamped and had been turning away eligible and much-needed candidates for years. Yet, there were five positions for every fully qualified graduate they churned out. Furthermore, noted Penny, of the many people who served numerous agencies in the Hamilton region, only 9 per cent had anything resembling professional qualifications. In light of these considerations, Thode was asked to revisit Gilmour's pronouncements on a school of social work. For good measure, Penny added that influential figures at McMaster, such as Salmon, Melling, Frank Jones, and Jack Graham, had already expressed their support.[120] Another gentle nudge came from Philip S. Fisher, chairman of the Canadian Welfare Council, who was surveying various universities with a view to encouraging formal undergraduate education pertinent to the field of social work.[121] Duly alerted, Thode struck a committee to consider the matter.

By October, Melling, who chaired the committee, was pleased to report that progress was being made. Better yet, the University of Toronto, far from bridling at competition, offered McMaster enthusiastic encouragement to proceed, such was the pressure of demand for trained personnel.[122] As the pieces fell into place, some urgency was added when J.R. McCarthy, deputy minister of university affairs, wrote to say that several universities had shown interest, but that it was unlikely that more than one new undergraduate program would be approved in the province over the next few years.[123] Such would not prove to be the case, but this was not apparent at the time. When, in May 1966, Bill Davis announced that the government of Ontario would smile on a degree that combined a baccalaureate in social science with a BSW, Thode had all the incentive he required.[124] After all, his committee had produced just such a scheme. Even better, the plan glowingly radiated the values Thode was so eager to propagate throughout the university.

As described by Melling, a joint BA/BSW would produce versatile, professional social workers but was also a worthy educational project in itself. In it, he noted, the basic sciences, social sciences, humanities, biology, and health sciences each had a role to play. "As university resources get scarcer," he added, "all opportunities for *generic* education must be seized – and social work is a good case in point." In shaping the joint degree, he concluded, "[W]e might be best to develop Social Work education with strong connection to the life of the university as a whole."[125] This, perhaps, was larding it on a bit thick, but the committee was certainly talking Thode's language. Not all listeners, however, were thoroughly impressed.

When the proposal came before the senate on 14 June 1967, it touched some exposed nerves. McIvor, for one, had no objection to the program, per se, but he deplored the rush and lack of long-term planning involved. The senate, he argued, should make greater effort to relate the costs and harmonization of such plans with commitments already made. Another speaker picked up a theme that was gathering considerable currency in some student and faculty circles of the day: universities should fight shy of educational utilitarianism. More than money was at stake, he argued. Indeed, a university that bowed too readily to rapidly shifting public demand could easily lose sight of its broader academic goals and standards. The senate, he continued, had a duty to act as a buffer against excessive social pressures.[126] More bluntly, the *Silhouette* criticized the program as an example of the university catering to community interests, who saw the academy's only function as the production of career-oriented specialists suited to stabilizing the established order. Meanwhile, the editor continued, mainstream departments were cancelling classes for want of resources.[127] A few months later, sociology was cited as a case in point.[128]

These objections notwithstanding, the senate approved the new degree, with only one dissenting vote. Harry Penny was appointed director of the school, with Jean Jones and Karl Kinanen as its first faculty. Initially, the school reported to the dean of social science. Market predictions proved correct, and, by 1970, a novel MSW in social work administration was in the works. All in all, the school moved "from dream to gleam," to borrow Penny's words, in a scant three years. The School of Physical Education, on the other hand, was longer in gestation.

Organized sport, both intramural and intercollegiate, had long been a part of the McMaster scene. Physical education as an academic pursuit, by contrast, dates from 1956. Given Sheffield's 1955 estimate of the student-population boom to come, it was self-evident that untold scores of secondary-school teachers would soon be needed. Among them, of course, there would necessarily be athletic coaches and general instructors in physical education. As both opportunity and need presented themselves, Ivor Wynne, McMaster's irrepressible director of athletics since 1948, seized the moment. With the aid of fellow RCAF veteran, Les Prince, he spearheaded the development of a bachelor of physical education (BPE) program, designed to provide genuine instructional qualifications for would-be educators. The idea was to furnish candidates with formal accreditation and firm credentials in this "teachable" area, as an addition to their baccalaureate in one or another discipline. Such people would have a considerable edge in the search for plum positions. As such, the BPE was an intense, one-year postgraduate program.

For Wynne and his colleagues, this meant induction into the ranks of University College as a recognized academic department. The burdens attending this were considerable, given that his small staff catered to all intramural, intercollegiate, and general fitness schemes on a lively campus. Still, the new task was greeted with enthusiasm. Moreover, it proved reasonably popular. Thus, at inception in 1956, the program attracted five candidates. Within four years, that number grew to thirty, and then almost a hundred by 1966.[129] Off-campus versions were offered as far afield as Sudbury, Ottawa, Mississauga, and Windsor.[130] Inevitably, additional staff were hired to strengthen the four men and one woman who had served as full-time faculty from the outset. In part, these new recruits were needed to run the various athletic programs that grew in tandem with the university itself. Apart from overseeing intramural and intercollegiate sport, they were required to administer the numerous, compulsory physical fitness classes for a burgeoning host of first-year students across a wide range of activities. As well, they stood ready to serve as the core of a much more ambitious academic program, which Wynne had envisaged early on.

In 1959, he noted that the BPE had few links to the undergraduate life of the university and mused about the possibility of an expanded, full-degree program.[131] This, however, could be only a pious hope, until adequate facilities were available on campus. A proper gymnasium, for example, had been on Gilmour's list of building requirements from the dawn of secularization, but had low priority compared to pressing academic and administrative needs for space. Planning, however, finally got under way by 1962.[132] Meanwhile, Wynne moved into a higher gear. Writing to Thode, he requested that his department be designated a "school," lest it lose credibility in the eyes of other universities where such nomenclature was increasingly the norm.[133] This was readily agreed, and the School of Physical Education came into being in 1963. At the same time, with colleagues, Wynne began drafting a joint BA/BPE against the day when new facilities would replace the ageing Drill Hall and offer such a program true scope. In 1966, everything fell into place.

In the spring of that year, the long-awaited physical education complex was finally opened. Along with large and small gymnasia, their floors glistening in blond hardwood, it accommodated office and teaching space. A striking centrepiece was the international-standard swimming pool, in which many a future Olympian would train. As a fringe benefit, the spacious facility offered an on-campus, if unglamorous, cite for graduation ceremonies, now that stately Convocation Hall was simply too small to house such functions. For the general run of students, on the other hand, it became the infamous "Temple of Sweat," into which they were herded, en masse, come examination time.

Wynne and his associates, however, saw the complex as home to a spanking new, four-year degree, combining arts and physical education. With the advent of this program, the school was now truly ensconced in the academic mainstream, under the umbrella of social science. As one of its architects, W.H. "Bill" Fowler notes, the new program was integrative by design.[134] Candidates combined a concentration in one of the many arts with their core studies in physical education, thus graduating with two, well-grounded "teachables," as such things were called in the tortured argot of the Ministry of Education. Popular with prospective teachers from the outset, this degree stream retained its glow when, in 1968, it was decreed that only English and physical education would remain as required courses in grades twelve and thirteen.

Sadly, Wynne did not long enjoy these ripening fruits. He died in 1970 of complications arising from diabetes. *The Silhouette* paused to mourn the popular dean of students, as he had been since 1965, noting that somewhat in excess of a thousand people attended his memorial service.[135] The physical education complex was duly christened in his memory, as was the home stadium of the Hamilton Tiger-Cats, whom he championed for years as chairman of the city's Parks Board. By that time, however, late afternoons found the Ivor Wynne Centre deep in shadows cast by the soaring towers of Arts I and II (later, Chester New and Togo Salmon Halls, respectively). Arts III (Kenneth Taylor Hall), designed to house bursting social science under one, purpose-built roof, was on the drawing board. Unfortunately, grants for capital projects were slowing to a trickle. Thus, the construction of a home for that overflowing faculty was still "a matter of anguished preoccupation," as the sixties drew toward a close.[136] It would not open until the early seventies.

This delay seemed all too familiar to many social scientists, who felt that their interests had long been attenuated, compared to those of other sectors in an increasingly research-intensive university. A planning vacuum, supposedly the by-product of administrative obsolescence, complexity, indifference, or outright hostility, was most frequently cited as the root cause of this. To a point, complainants had a case. After all, Armstrong apart, no one with true authority seems to have given much sustained thought to the role of social science in the context of McMaster's overall development.

For his part, Thode was uncharacteristically quiet when it came to articulating goals for the sciences of society, although there is no evidence to suggest that he intentionally impeded development. Still, with the exception of expediting social work, he left matters largely in the hands of his lieutenants at University College, Salmon and Patrick, neither of whom evinced much love for the quantifying, theoretical social sciences. Thus, in the annals of those disciplines, one looks in vain for the kind of prodding from on high that attended the acceleration of graduate work in more "mainstream" arts, such as history or English. Moreover, when proposals for advanced work did materialize in economics, sociology, and political science, they did so in the post-Spinks environment of closer scrutiny and tighter criteria. This would slow approval processes to a seeming crawl. While unavoidable, such delay could create the impression of discrimination against the legitimate aspirations of social science.

Within this context, the prolonged debacle in political science had ramifications that ran well beyond the confines of the department, itself. Writing of that "appalling situation" and "the malaise which it spread generally among the Arts Departments as a whole," Dean Patrick drew some general lessons. Chief among these was the conviction that "we must be much more careful in future, in setting up new departments, to ensure that we have proper leadership and mature personnel ... even if this means a 'vetting' and policing of a kind we have not been used to and might seem to limit the autonomy of departments." "Departments," he went on, "must earn the right to autonomy."[137] This, of course, ignored the degree to which Salmon had helped aggravate the crisis. Yet, Patrick's caveat might well have figured in Thode's decision to go slowly in the development of anthropology, thereby reinforcing old perceptions among social scientists as a group. Indeed, the Grady affair merely heighted anxiety and suspicion in an already charged atmosphere. Even an otherwise steady old hand, such as McIvor, could fall prey to the virus, just as easily as Patrick.

In June 1967, "Mac," as he styled himself, wrote in strict confidence to his "Dear Harry" concerning fears and suspicions abroad in social science. He underlined widespread concern about the seeming lack of a plan to rehabilitate political science and emphasized the costs of delay. The committee, then running the department, he argued, could handle day-to-day affairs, but was inherently ad hoc and could not do the necessary long-term planning. With all due respect for Preston, McIvor noted, "many of your faculty members find it a perplexing anomaly that these planning functions, which are of crucial importance to the emerging Faculty of Social Science, should have been centred, however temporarily, in the hands of a physical scientist." Moving on, he addressed a hot rumour, then making the rounds. Profound disquiet among social scientists, he said, had taken hold when word was leaked that the chair of political science had been offered by administrators to a candidate without consultation with department members. Were this true, McIvor continued, "it would raise very serious questions in my mind, and in others, concerning the value attached by the Administration to the views of social scientists in their immediate affairs and concerning the amount of genuine influence over the course of its own academic evolution that the new Faculty of Social Sciences may in fact be able to achieve."[138]

Assured by Thode that the rumour was groundless, McIvor soon rushed to his president's defence in the ensuing newspaper wars. Still, the private letter spoke volumes concerning the mood and perceptions that reigned among social scientists as the sixties wound down. Thus, they pinned great hope on the end of the old administrative system and the creation a faculty they could call their own. When, however, that faculty came to life, it did so, alone among the rest, with only an acting dean at the helm. This is what led to the *cri de cœur* issued by Melling in 1969. This is what had provoked McIvor's plaint about "relegation," a year earlier. Formal status notwithstanding, the Faculty of Social Science still felt rudderless. By mid-1969, therefore, McGill political scientist Saul J. Frankel faced a considerable challenge, when he was appointed dean to the stepchildren of social science, after more than a year-long search.

6

"All or Nothing"

In 1993, Norman Tait McPhedran surveyed the history of Canadian medical schools over the preceding 200 years. Pausing to reflect on Hamilton's experience, his verdict was unequivocal. "The McMaster experiment in medical education," he wrote, "is the best known of the twentieth century."[1] "Best known," of course, is not the same as "best loved" or "unanimously applauded." Still, Thode was never one to care much about universal approbation. Audacious accomplishment was more to be prized, in his estimation. Thus, one can readily picture him, then in vigorous retirement, basking in the glow of McPhedran's emphatic observation. After all, for Thode, the McMaster University Medical Centre (MUMC) was the brightest jewel in his academy's crown. Unique in architectural, administrative, and curricular design, it bespoke all that was central to the Thodean paradigm: institutional ambition, calculated risk-taking, and interdisciplinary passion. Like a bookend to the nuclear reactor, the medical centre neatly bracketed Thode's presidency. Yet, there was a difference. Thus, while the MNR was undoubtedly daring, medicine at McMaster would be brazenly iconoclastic.

As it took conceptual and physical shape during the sixties, "Mummsy," as campus wags dubbed it, joyously sacrificed traditionally sacred cows by the overflowing stockyard. Throughout, it provoked every conceivable reaction, save neutrality. One might expect, therefore, to find some revelatory thunderclap that sparked so controversial a venture. Such, however, was far from the case. Instead, the notion of founding a medical school matured gradually in Thode's mind, from back-burner issue into grand obsession. As it did, he finessed, finagled, and occasionally bulldozed the project from first flicker to final ignition. This, after all, was to be his *chef-d'oeuvre* and summary statement as to what McMaster could and ought to be. Fashioning a front-rank medical school, especially one consecrated to heresy, was no

minor endeavour. Indeed, as Thode later confided, it was "the biggest headache any university can take on."[2] Still, the votive candle proved well worth
the cost; at least in his view and that of those young-blood confederates who
schooled him in the virtues of heterodoxy. Yet, for all his later fixity of purpose, even the venturesome Thode was markedly leery of tackling medical
education, early on.

From the moment McMaster migrated to Hamilton, local ginger groups
had sporadically urged that town and gown co-operate vigorously to help
advance medicine in the Steel City. As C.M. Johnston ably demonstrates,
however, successive university administrations, politely but consistently,
sidestepped all pressure that smacked of expensive, formal commitment. It
could scarcely have been otherwise. During the depressed thirties and war-
torn forties, it was taxing enough just to keep arts, science, and divinity up
to snuff. The very idea of plunging into anything even resembling systematic
medical training was so far beyond modest Baptist means as to be unthinkable.[3] This, of course, did not rule out a modicum of informal engagement
with health-care providers from time to time.

Starting in the mid-thirties, for example, McMaster and the Hamilton
Academy of Medicine co-sponsored a more-or-less regular series of lectures
designed to keep local practitioners abreast of the latest developments in a
variety of fields. The academy, through fees, provided the cash, while the
university lent its facilities and a cloak of academic gravitas to the project.
The arrangement was nicely symbiotic. Luminaries "of national and international reputation" were brought to a campus normally off the beaten
track. Meanwhile, these "refresher courses" benefited many a local physician delighted to brush up, at modest cost, close to familiar home and hectic
practice.[4] As a long-term bonus, McMaster cultivated a measure of goodwill
among members of the medical community. Be that as it may, pressure for
deeper engagement on the university's part grew apace.

A 1944 letter to Gilmour from Hamilton physician F.E. Coster made this
clear. The war was disrupting the work of what, in rather grandiloquent
terms, was styled the "McMaster-Academy Committee on Post-Graduate
Education." Looking down the road, Coster advised Gilmour that, while
the committee's efforts had been "of definite mutual value," he foresaw far
greater potential for scientific and medical study than that undertaken thus
far. "We of the Hamilton Academy of Medicine," he wrote, "sincerely hope
that it may be possible to work out some type of mutually acceptable programme whereby both the University and the Academy may in the years to
come contribute much to the scientific stature and fitness of those in our
community who have planned their life work in this broad and essential

field."[5] Gilmour, no doubt, winced at some Coster's deeper implications. Perhaps, this is why, next year, he snapped up a better-defined, more limited academy request simply to formalize the old "post-graduate courses" on a firm contractual basis. "I anticipate that there will be a cordial acceptance of your suggestion," he told proposers, "as it protects the University authorities against financial losses that may accrue from a venture which the University itself would scarcely feel competent to undertake."[6] In short order, arrangements were finalized, special lectures resumed, and goodwill was retained – all on a break-even basis.[7]

Providing revenue-neutral assistance to the healing arts was seemly for a Christian school of learning. Worthy in itself, this outreach to the academy was also good for public relations. In 1948, however, when rumour had it that Queen's Park might soon ask considerably more of the university, electric chills rippled down Baptist spines. Premier George Drew was hinting that a new medical school could serve Hamilton and region very nicely. Sensing that the premier had McMaster squarely in his sights, Gilmour promptly set Thode the task of preparing a barb to puncture Drew's trial balloon, before it could be inflated.[8] While Johnston has already examined Thode's memorandum on the issue, the document is worth a second glance, since it was to inform much of the future president's later thought as to what a medical school ought to be.

In drafting the brief for Gilmour, Thode drew on a recent report authored by Dr Claude E. Dolman of UBC. In it, the fundamental prerequisites for developing modern medical education on a university campus were carefully outlined. First and foremost, argued Dolman, a parent institution, fully equipped to deliver three to four years of thorough pre-medical training, was an absolute must. Furthermore, a large pool of applicants had to exist, so that only the most suitable need be accepted. In addition, initial capital financing had to be coupled with a guaranteed and adequate operating budget, since underfunding only bred mediocrity, however posh the original facilities. Then, there was the matter of staff. Only the highest calibre should be sought; collegial people, gifted both in teaching and research. Such folk, warned Dolman, were rare and unlikely to be attracted by entry-level salaries. Consequently, the search process would necessarily be painstakingly lengthy and require considerable lead time. Yet, thought Dolman, such investment was inescapably vital, since a solid corps of full-time faculty was the key to university control over its medical school. The alternative was reliance on the ever-shifting priorities of practitioners in private practice. From this, it followed that a purpose-built hospital was highly desirable. Indeed, as one Vancouver observer put it, "A Faculty of Medicine which does not have its own university hospital is as deficient as a Faculty of Agriculture without an experimental farm." A farmer by birth and avocation, Thode could appreciate this analogy.

Drawing all to mind, Thode advised Gilmour that McMaster could not even meet the first of Dolman's desiderata until Hamilton College, then still in the planning stage, was a mature school of science. Thus, he cautioned that to ignore the facts, simply to grasp a tempting plum, "would be to jeopardize the reputation of the university for a generation or more in order to satisfy a current clamour." That said, Thode did not rule out the long-term possibility of nurturing medicine at McMaster. Instead, he added his own gloss to some of Dolman's thoughts. For example, he recommended that, were pressure to become irresistible, then the university needed to insist that "the next hospital for this area should be a university hospital and be built on this campus." On this score, he counselled that thirty or forty acres be acquired from the RBG and set aside, just in case. Further, he took issue with statements seeping out of Queen's Park to the effect that medical schools should concentrate on producing physicians, rather than dabbling in research. Citing Dolman, Thode countered that all areas of medicine were increasingly dependent on basic research in fields such as chemistry, physics, and microbiology. There could be no teaching-research dichotomy in a first-class medical school. Summing up, Thode advised against moving into medicine, at that particular moment. Significant for the future, however, was his strong injunction to abjure half measures, if such a step were ever taken. Giving first voice to what would later be resounding credo, he declared, "In the case of a medical college it is either all or nothing."[9]

Gilmour, no doubt, welcomed this pointed brief. It left him well positioned to say that McMaster was currently unable to shoulder the wholesale burdens of medical education, were the premier formally to inquire. Just to be on the safe side, however, he authorized a highly confidential study of what might be needed, as he put it, "for our own information and for informed discussion with Mr Drew."[10] In any event, the premier did not press the matter. Even so, the episode was formative, particularly for Thode's later thought. As Johnston notes, however, it is maddeningly difficult to document precisely when determined avoidance turned into active pursuit of a medical school at McMaster. Long after, Thode recalled, "I don't think any comments George Drew may have made in the late 40's [sic] were taken too seriously." According to Thode, the real trigger was an early sixties clamour by Windsor and Laurentian to launch medical studies. Leslie Frost, then acting chair of the CUA, was appalled by the thought, felt McMaster far better suited to the task, and privately urged the university to

pre-empt other bids.[11] While true, to say this is, also, to downplay the cumulative momentum generated by local pressure, growing precedent, and inter-
mittent planning that preceded Frost's nudge.

However nebulous, mere rumour seems to have heightened community
expectation, as word of Drew's 1948 musings went around. It is, also, possible that Gilmour's call for a confidential study reached unintended ears.
In any case, the press began to speculate that medicine was in McMaster's
cards, somewhere down the road.[12] This prognostication could only have
been buttressed by an agreement soon reached between the Hamilton Medical Research Institute (HMRI) and the university. The institute, incorporated
in 1945, was a private body. Operating on a shoestring, its purpose was to
finance small-scale studies in local clinical wards.[13] Intrigued by the medical potential of isotopes, Thode offered his thoughts to a gathering of the
group. As chance would have it, this led him to encounter a true soulmate,
internist Charles H. "Charlie" Jaimet. A respected clinician, Jaimet was also
affable, committed to research, and fascinated by Thode's work. In short
order, the two forged a close working and personal relationship.

One of the first fruits of their collaboration crossed Gilmour's desk, on
2 May 1949. Dr Arthur Wright, president of the HMRI, wrote, asking permission "to erect a radio-isotope laboratory on University lands" for the
purpose of medical inquiry. The institute, he emphasized, would support all
capital and operating costs, while recognizing full university control over
the facility.[14] Wasting not a moment, Gilmour moved with alacrity. Within
four days, he assured Wright, "the Board is very happy about the suggestion and about the prospect of a useful piece of medical research on the
McMaster campus."[15] Confidence was born of the fact that the project was
to be financed by a grant from the Ontario Cancer Foundation, engineered
by Jaimet and Thode, and not out of the HMRI's shallow pockets.[16]

Johnston and William Spaulding have each described the pioneering work
in thyroid and heart research that flowed from this venture.[17] Suffice it, here,
to note that, with the opening of the campus reactor, such effort could be
redoubled. In 1958, Jaimet was designated (part-time) professor of nuclear
medicine – the first in Canada.[18] As Gilmour remarked in his congratulatory
letter, the appointment broke new ground in another sense. Thus, Jaimet
became the first true research professor in McMaster's history as he was
assigned no teaching responsibilities whatsoever.[19] That this should happen
in an area related to medicine was less surprising in 1958 than it would have
been a decade earlier.

By 1950, albeit with considerable misgivings, Gilmour had conceded
that prudence dictated continued quiet study of issues raised by Drew.[20] As

part of this, a survey of land requirements was made. Early in 1953, Thode wrote to say "that the site south of King Street and between University Avenue and Highway No. 102 would be the ideal location." Clearly, he had already staked out his position in what would later be the focus of tumultuous debate. For the moment, he urged "that our wishes should be made known to the Board of the Royal Botanical Gardens and given serious consideration before any other plans involving this area develop."[21] An ounce of timely pre-emption, it seemed, might be better than a pound of tangled negotiation. This was a strategy to which Thode would later return. Meanwhile, external pressure was gaining momentum.

In 1954, city fathers engaged the services of Toronto's Dr Harvey Agnew "to survey the present and future needs for medical services in the Hamilton area." Inevitably, Agnew approached Gilmour about the possibility of establishing a medical faculty at the university. Growing accustomed to such inquiries, Gilmour offered his accustomed response. So costly an undertaking, he said, would not be considered unless the province, or some other reliable body, guaranteed adequate funding. His visitor was also informed that "McMaster and Hamilton College are not eager to enter the medical field, but would do so out of a sense of duty, provided it were clear that such an action would not forfeit the goodwill of neighbouring universities." Agnew retorted that the chancellor need have no fear on the latter score. Indeed, he said, circumstances had changed so rapidly that a medical school at McMaster would have little effect on the work of others. Queen's, for example, was being swamped by the growing demands of the Kingston area. Meanwhile, he emphasized, Hamilton was one of the fastest rising urban regions in the nation, but the only one of its scale that lacked a medical college. Gilmour was invited to consider McMaster as the logical site for such an obviously needed facility. Further, he was warned that once the province decided to move, it was likely to do so quickly. A dithering city and its university could easily be bypassed.[22] Listening carefully, yet still torn, Gilmour hesitated. Finally, he called for some expert, external advice.

This counsel was provided by no less a personage than Sir Frances Fraser, director of the British postgraduate medical federation. Ostensibly on hand to deliver the annual Redman lecture in science, the distinguished Briton spent much time scanning standing resources, considering future needs, and penning a cogent, though confidential, report. Assessing population trends, Fraser was convinced that Canada would soon require many new physicians, especially in bustling Ontario. Furthermore, he deemed a new medical school at McMaster preferable to a second in Toronto, since the latter was already well served, while Hamilton boasted several substantial hospitals, but lacked a local teaching and research institution. He, then, out-lined a potential curriculum, estimated optimal enrolments, and discussed the myriad details of putting a school in place. Above all else, Fraser empha-sized the importance of appointing key administrators well in advance of admitting students. Such people, he noted, needed time not only to plan a program but to establish trust and footholds in local hospitals, private clin-ics, and civic institutions in general. While advising judicious caution, Fraser thought McMaster a credible site.[23]

A new tone coloured Gilmour's letter of thanks to his British advisor. As ever, he confessed to "a good deal of division of mind on the matter." Again, he underlined that other faculties had to be shored up, before medi-cine could be contemplated. He particularly appreciated the frankness with which Fraser enjoined that sober reflection precede final leap. "However," he added, "every school that begins has to begin, and I suppose our problem would not be essentially greater than that of any other university entering the medical field for the first time." Here, perhaps for the first time, Gilmour sounded more assertive, more self-confident than he did in his earlier dis-course concerning medicine. This was not full-scale commitment, by any measure. Even so, a definite "maybe" was creeping into his vocabulary.[24] Accordingly, in 1957, as part of his request to purchase land from the RBG to accommodate new residences and engineering, the president asked for a second parcel that would be needed, as he said, "if and when the University develops a medical school and hospital."[25] The RBG promptly obliged. Prop-erty immediately required was purchased outright, while McMaster secured options on a potential medical site.[26] In this latter business, Thode's hand is easy to detect.

Both Fraser and Agnew had thought that the Hamilton Sanatorium, located on the west mountain, might serve the university's medical purposes quite well. Methods of treating tuberculosis had slowly changed with the introduction of streptomycin, after 1946. The facility, in any case, was badly in need of refurbishment. In 1957, the Hamilton Health Association asked if McMaster was interested in the "San" as a home for the prospective med-ical complex.[27] Thode, for one, said no. His growing sense that any such development would best occur on campus had been strongly reinforced by discussions with Dr Ray Farquharson, professor of medicine at the Univer-sity of Toronto. The two had met as members of a committee struck to con-sider the San's future. Exchanging thoughts on related matters, they found themselves in full accord as to the direction McMaster might follow. In January 1958, Thode wrote to thank Farquharson for the latter's staunch support in deflecting recent suggestions concerning the mountain hospital.

"I gather from your letter," he added, "that you are not too happy about the way things are developing at the San and feel that we should seriously consider building the entire medical school on campus." He continued, "After watching things develop and after many discussions I am convinced that you are right."[28] On this score, any flickering doubts in Thode's mind must have been finally extinguished by a widely circulated address, which Dr George E. Hall delivered to university chancellors, a few months later.

Hall, dean of medicine at Western, ranged over the many issues that bedevilled universities engaged in medical education. In particular, he painted a grim picture of the difficulties any such institution faced if it relied wholly on community hospitals and private practitioners in the clinical teaching phase. Citing numerous examples of professional, financial, and political wrangles that arose under such conditions, he offered unvarnished advice to those contemplating engagement in the enterprise. "The simplest [solution], next to not having a Medical School at all," said Hall, "is to have the Medical School right in the centre of the University proper, where there could be complete integration of students and staff and facilities and research cooperation." Equally, he continued, there had to be a campus hospital, or one in close proximity, that was completely "closed," with full-time staff and ample facilities, wholly under university control. Just as vital, he contended, was "some agency, other than the university, to pick up the 'tab'." Under any other circumstances, Hall opined, universities would, eventually, "have to abandon the clinical teaching portion of that education."[29] While Thode could have scripted this himself, Hall's words, when added to Farquharson's, must have reassured him that it had been wise to secure options on RBG lands.

Over the next few years, it became almost formulaic for Thode, or Gilmour, to observe that "McMaster may be called upon to establish a Faculty of Medicine."[30] Hinting at reticence and employing the passive voice, the implication was that the university would play the role of good citizen and accept a duty thrust upon it. In reality, by 1957, the two leaders, and especially Thode, had turned a corner. A new medical school for Ontario seemed likely, and they determined, at a minimum, to present a credible bid for it. Thus, Gilmour, undoubtedly aided by Thode, penned a memorandum to government that summer. Setting out a strong case for McMaster, he emphasized population density, the availability of land, and Fraser's positive assessment, along with the university's work in nuclear medicine. This innovative research, he noted, would soon be augmented by the only reactor on any Commonwealth campus. Mention was made of a thriving School of Nursing, established in 1946, and the recent bolstering of biochemistry.

Gilmour was keen, as well, to note the many, cordial ties that had been fostered with the local medical fraternity. Bucking Thode on one point, he argued that much capital could be saved by taking over the sanatorium's facilities for clinical purposes. Summing up, Gilmour added, "So far as possible, inquiries and plans have been kept private and no publicity on the matter has emanated from McMaster University."[31] Deftly, the president was indirectly assuring the minister that no shrill public campaign would be staged to force the government's hand.

With similar diplomacy, he informed the University of Toronto of his memorandum. John MacFarlane, dean of medicine at Toronto, greatly appreciated Gilmour's fraternal gesture and replied in kind. Pledging to keep things confidential, he said that the news helped clarify planning at his own institution, whose senate had been waiting to hear from other universities, before determining how much of the looming burden it would have to undertake. That load, he underlined, was going to be substantial. Indeed, MacFarlane estimated that, "given the total number of medical graduates from all existing Ontario universities, and allowing for additional immigrant doctors, another 100 new doctors per year would be required by 1968." Thanking Gilmour for his courtesy, he wished him well; warning only that any new school had an obligation to maintain the highest standards in research, as well as teaching and clinical service.[32]

More important than the content of this correspondence, perhaps, was the goodwill it engendered. In this case, MacFarlane went on to become a trustee of the McLaughlin Foundation and chief medical advisor to the Hall Commission. The former was a major granting agency, while the latter would decisively alter Canadian life in recommending that Saskatchewan's "medicare" policy be adopted nationwide. All the while, MacFarlane offered firm support, invaluable contacts, and wise counsel, as McMaster edged toward medical commitment. A little courtesy, it seems, could return unexpectedly hefty dividends.

By 1960, cautious deliberation was giving way to a sense of urgency. Canadian emissaries, including some from McMaster, were visiting prominent schools across the continent, systematically researching all that was best, or undesirable, in contemporary medical education.[33] Reports flowed in from venues as far afield as Saskatchewan, California, New York, Kentucky, and West Virginia, to name but a few. It required little acumen to discern a bidding war in the offing. As Thode later recalled, it was then that Frost encouraged a more forceful thrust by McMaster to forestall those rising on newer, less credible campuses.[34] This backdoor hint was not quite the strident call from government Gilmour had awaited, but it was close enough.

In January 1961, he had Thode send word to Minister of Education John Robarts that McMaster stood "willing to undertake medical education as a matter of academic and public duty." For the most part, Thode simply reprised the 1957 missive to Dunlop, but two important matters were clearly broached. Thus, the San was rejected in favour of a small campus hospital. Meanwhile, the possibility of expropriating nearby residential properties was raised, should expansion be deemed necessary at some later date. He concluded by arguing that full governmental financing was essential to the development of a first-class medical school. Indeed, Thode advised the minister, "Anything less would, in our opinion, be unacceptable to the people of Ontario."[35]

Inevitably, it took time for this overture to wend its way through manifold layers of government bureaucracy. While he waited, Thode did some constructive glad-handing among local hospital authorities, with the assistance and at the suggestion of Mayor Lloyd D. Jackson.[36] During the course of this exercise, his sense of what modern medical education ought to be must have been further refined by an address that Professor K.J.R. "Kajer" Wightman gave to the Hamilton Health Association in March 1962. Physician-in-chief at Toronto General Hospital and chair of medicine at that city's university, Wightman could speak with authority born of experience. His message was a call to reform.

As he saw it, contemporary medical education was obsessively, but unwisely, riveted on scientific, learned-by-rote content. Too little attention was given to education in a broader, more humane sense. The outcome was the endless replication of body mechanics; practitioners well-equipped to treat "conditions," yet unskilled in dealing with people and ill-prepared for "life-long learning." Worse still, many a promising candidate turned away from medicine because the training was inordinately long, or the entrance requirements too scientifically narrow. Among those who did apply, too many· went the route of specialization, eschewing the needs of community medicine in favour of status and a heavy wallet. The cure for this, said Wightman, was a more holistic approach. "So," he told listeners, "if you are thinking of starting a Medical School in Hamilton all you need do is to devise some method of getting the right sort of people to enrol in it, give them an education in the true sense of the word ..., teach them the scientific method, give them an understanding and love for people, a sense of responsibility and a sense of proportion."[37] Wightman's injunctions made a deep impression on Thode, enough for him to consult MacFarlane about the ramifications involved.[38] At a minimum, his mind was opened to the possibility of embracing radical innovation, were government to heed his petition.

That month, a letter arrived from John B. Neilson of the Ontario Hospital Services Commission. As former superintendent of Hamilton General, Neilson knew Thode personally. Sympathetic to McMaster's cause, he wrote to advise Thode that he had best quickly address an issue that had arisen. Opinion at Queen's Park, he said, was leaning toward McMaster as the site for a new school of medicine, but Matthew Dymond, minister of health, saw no reason for a campus hospital, given the many facilities already available in Hamilton. Thus, discussions had stalled. Neilson urged Thode to clarify his position, as soon as possible.[39] Still easing into his many presidential duties, Thode turned the task of crafting a thoroughly documented memorandum over to his trusted lieutenant, Art Bourns.

The latter bent to his task with a will. A first draft was sent to MacFarlane, now advisor to the Royal Commission on Health Services in Canada. He, in turn, urged that certain cardinal points be emphasized, such as the all-but-inevitable advent of universal health insurance and the concomitant demand for new physicians, sure to follow.[40] Much the same advice came from Dr John F. McCreary, dean of medicine at UBC, who was gracious enough to vet the proposal. The British Columbian added that indigent, "closed wards" for teaching purposes would soon be a thing of the past. With the introduction of "fee-for-service" billing, private practitioners were unlikely to hand patients (billing units) over for medical study. More broadly, he noted, teaching institutions were failing to educate their graduates to function within the framework of a closely articulated health-care delivery team. All this, McCreary stated, had to change.[41] Assimilating all this sundry advice, Thode put the finishing touches on Bourns' draft. Then, bypassing lesser mandarins, he delivered McMaster's best pitch straight to the very top: Premier John Robarts.

While reiterating much that had been said before, Thode's submission had new tone that was both self-assured and patently aggressive. Times had changed dramatically, it read, and McMaster was ready to change with them. Twenty years had passed since the last medical school had been established in Canada. The need for doctors had grown apace, and nowhere more so than in the booming Niagara region. This, Thode argued, made Hamilton and McMaster the natural, strategic choice for any new school. The university's research assets and interdisciplinary traditions were carefully detailed for Robarts' scrutiny. So too, was its eagerness to plan "an imaginative medical curriculum in which would be incorporated many of the most important and exciting advances in medical education." A new facility, the premier was told, need not restrict itself to turning out MDs alone but could also train pharmacists, physiotherapists, laboratory, and X-ray technicians, thereby multiplying its utility. Certain things, however, were absolutely essential to such endeavour. One of these was a university hospital. Another was a core of full-time faculty in each teaching-cum-clinical department.

An on-campus hospital, he told Robarts, assured candidates ready access to clinical experience, allowed for multidisciplinary integration in training, and encouraged collegial contact among students and faculty across the whole university. Echoing Wightman's address, Thode reasoned that such conditions could only redound to the well-roundedness of all. Meanwhile, on purely practical grounds, he noted a recent report by Neilson to the effect that Hamilton would require approximately 300 additional hospital beds by 1968–70. These, he conceded, could be furnished by expansion of an existing facility. On the other hand, if government chose to fund a medical school at McMaster, the cost of a small university hospital would be no greater than refurbishing a civic one. "Since one alternative can make it possible to build a medical school of quality and the other does not," wrote a somewhat cheeky Thode, "the choice should not be a difficult one to make." The same, he felt, was true where staffing was concerned. Sounding a favourite chord, he averred that quality arose from focus, as much as from top-notch ability. Thus, he held that a cadre of first-class faculty, dedicated to full-time university service, was essential to a premium school of medicine. Furthermore, such people ought to be research-oriented teachers; role models who, by example, ingrained the importance of never-ending learning in their students.

As to the always delicate matter of money, Thode was perfectly blunt. "Under no circumstances," he underscored, "should this new undertaking, important as it is, be allowed to prejudice the $50,000,000 program to which the Board of Governors is now firmly committed." The university was already squeezing every dollar it could out of fundraising campaigns to support expansion in arts, science, and engineering. Donors were fatigued and would give no more. Equally, McMaster would never sacrifice the health of its core faculties, simply to add a new one. Thus, Thode observed that, should medicine come to McMaster, "it will be necessary that the capital funds ... be obtained entirely from Government sources." In for a penny, Thode pressed for a pound. Delay would be fatal, he cautioned, if Queen's Park wanted McMaster to graduate physicians by 1970. Outlining a schedule of development, he told Robarts that the search for a dean – just the right dean – would have to begin no later than spring of 1964.[42] Having shot his bolt, very much in an "all-or-nothing" spirit, Thode awaited word from Robarts. Still, there was excitement sufficient to fill the waiting hours.

Within a month, word of the bid had been leaked to the press. Suddenly, that which was "strictly confidential" was public knowledge. In banner print, the *Spectator* blared, "Mac Asks for Medical School." If Queen's Park smiled upon the project, the paper ventured, "it would be the realization of a dream held by Hamilton doctors and teachers since McMaster moved here." Thode was quoted as confirming the news, but had offered no detail.[43] Indeed, he was, in all likelihood, literally speechless. The last thing he wanted was for Robarts to imagine that he would raise the crowd in order to force government's hand. Nor was Thode eager for an exercise in campus damage control. Typically, he had forged ahead with the scheme, alerting only a few key advisors. Now, he had to explain all to the governors, only some of whom, such as Fox, were privy to the detailed plans. In a careful memorandum, Thode assured board members that no commitments had been made. The proposal to government, he said, had been submitted confidentially so as not to whip up public expectations that McMaster might not be able to fulfill. However, for reasons that surpassed all understanding, Frost had seen fit to release word to the media, before the matter could be brought to the next regular board meeting. Accordingly, Thode sent a copy of the complete document to all governors, asking only that the details be kept private, at least until government registered its decision.[44] After all, some proposals, such as reference to a possible diversion of King Street and neighbourhood expropriations, were bound to be controversial and need not be broached, until necessary. In the end, the board made no fuss. Members were well aware that medicine was being considered and were, undoubtedly, comforted by Thode's proviso that McMaster would reject any offer that jeopardized the growth of its established faculties. Meanwhile, as the prospect of internal tension faded, external moral support eased the tedium of waiting.

Writing on behalf of the Association of Canadian Medical Colleges, J. Wendell Macleod and McCreary passed along best wishes to Thode and offered the assistance of their organization in any way that might help. There was, they understood, more at stake here than the fate of one Ontario institution. Thinking in national terms, with momentous health-care change whispering on the wind, they set the McMaster proposal in broad context. "The way in which Canada's next medical school unfolds," they prophesied, "will undoubtedly influence greatly the direction of medical education in Canada in the next two decades."[45] Soon, MacFarlane passed on word that he had delivered a copy of Thode's brief to Royal Commissioner, Justice Emmett Hall, who, as might be expected, took "great interest in the sort of medical school that should be established in the future."[46]

Going further, in January 1964, MacFarlane prompted Carey Fox to have private words with Robarts, since it was becoming urgent that McMaster have permission to appoint a dean. His relief was palpable when Fox assured him that government was inclined to agree.[47] There was more good news in March, when Hamilton's civic hospitals officially offered their full co-operation in the enterprise.[48] Even Herb Armstrong, now president of the University of Alberta, buried an old hatchet, as he wished Thode joy of the bold venture.[49] It was all so cheering. Yet, as Thode well knew, bounteous moral support, plus the requisite twenty-five cents, would procure no more than a cup of coffee. What he needed was firm governmental commitment and cold, hard cash. On 29 October 1964, he awoke to find he had both.

Robarts announced massive grants for health care, closely paralleling recommendations in Justice Hall's national report. Four major projects were sanctioned. Facilities at the University of Toronto were to be expanded and renovated to accommodate seventy-five additional first-year candidates. Queen's was to receive a new health sciences building, along with upgrades to its standing medical establishment. Western was to house a newfound school of dentistry, while medicine got a badly needed face-lift. The weightiest benefaction, however, was bestowed on McMaster: a brand-new school of medicine coupled with an on-campus hospital. Best of all, these projects were to be financed wholly by dollar-for-dollar matching grants out of federal and provincial coffers. The broadly inclusive nature of the announcement brought a nice bonus. During the period of waiting, the only real flak Thode had encountered had come from other universities who felt their ageing medical centres should be refurbished, before any additional school was considered. Wisely concurring with this when consulted, he could rest easy in the company of fellow presidents, as 114 million initial boons were, with reasonable fairness, disbursed among all.[50] Now, all that remained was to breathe life into a new faculty.

It is a commonplace of philosophy, science, engineering, and, not least of all, popular mechanics, that form follows function. By 1964, as seen, Thode had a well-informed, layman's vision of possible futures in medical education. On one point, he was adamant. "He was not interested in setting up just another medical school, but rather something that he had pretty fond hopes would be quite new in approach."[51] While determined in this respect, from his own experience under Gilmour, he had learned the wisdom of timely delegation when it came to designing highly specialized units. Thus, he recognized that defining the precise functions and consequent form of a wholly reimagined medical enterprise was a matter for those uniquely equipped and strongly motivated to do so. Similarly, decades of personal mould-breaking taught him that, within reasonable limits, creative but cred-ible thought only flourished when given free rein and firm support.

Much, therefore, hinged on the recruitment of individuals, people for whom the challenge was the reward and who, like jazz musicians, attended to notes behind the melody. Thode always had a sharp eye for talent and a clear sense of what he sought in new faculty. In the case of medicine, two principles guided him. As J. Fraser Mustard later attested, Thode looked for people ready to stretch beyond the limits of their specialized training, but, above all, he searched for youth. Old hands, he reasoned, were simply too encumbered by tradition.[52] After much inquiry, a tip from Farquharson intrigued Thode.[53] John Robert Evans, while only thirty-five, was already a star ascendant in the University of Toronto's medical firmament. Per-haps, "glowing rogue comet" was a better description, for, along with a few others, he was bucking time-worn trends in a rather staid institution. Farquharson, however, held him in high esteem. Such advice from a close friend, who was also first president of the Medical Research Council of Canada (MRC), was good enough for Thode. In short order, to paraphrase Bob Dylan, he was "knock, knock, knocking on Evans' door."

Decades later, in 2010, Evans recalled his first meeting with Thode, as though it were only yesterday. McMaster's president, he reminisced, fairly "radiated integrity" and burning enthusiasm, as they discussed the inter-disciplinary model of a science-driven university of which medicine could be a nodal point. For Evans, the contrast with his most recent experience could not have been more striking. When the University of Toronto acquired a hundred new beds at Sunnybrook Hospital, as part of Robarts' provincial plan, Evans and like-minded colleagues had suggested breaking with trad-ition and experimenting there with non-content-driven, tutorial-style teach-ing. However, despite decanal support, the scheme died in faculty council, shredded by department heads wedded to the lecture system and jealous of their turf. Thode's openness to innovation came to Evans more like a gale than a simple breath of fresh air. In turn, Thode warmed to the reasoned heterodoxy Evans extolled, especially as it accorded closely with reform-ist advice in a recent brief from the Hamilton Academy of Medicine. Time slipped by in the comfort of the King Edward Hotel, until both men paused to chuckle that the sordid matter of salary had yet to be raised. Offered the post of dean on the spot, a rather startled Evans asked for time to consult with family and colleagues. He had expected a somewhat lesser position to be on the table. Days later, at a conference in Atlantic City, while still daunted by the prospect, he berated himself for talking a good game, yet hesitating to "put his nickel down." Drawing a deep breath, Evans signalled his readiness to take on the challenge.[54] He did so, however, with a measure of cautious acumen.

On 10 May 1965, he addressed a detailed letter to Thode, outlining the conditions he and the president had informally discussed. Thus, Evans accepted the post on the understanding that there were no existing commitments or obligations to any community hospitals or local health services. Clearly, he wanted a free hand in weaving external relations specially tailored to the needs of a new kind of medical school. He went on to stipulate that entrance requirements should be defined by a university admissions committee and that no minimum enrolment be prescribed. Marginal candidates were not to be accepted, simply to fulfill some arbitrary quota. Here, in anticipating a non-traditional student body, Evans was seeking to room for manoeuvre and quality control. In a similar vein, he insisted that the dean have an important say in the appointment of all department heads. A cohesive, collegial, and, perhaps, slightly eccentric ensemble would be vital to an off-beat, experimental orchestra.

Like a good conductor, Evans wanted to choose his first violin and counterparts without undue pressure from those with more conventional tastes. Moreover, each virtuoso would need latitude and resources to excel. Thus, wrote Evans, "[A]ctive research programs were to be supported in all departments." He was, also, careful to underline that the university would follow through on its promise of building both the medical school and hospital on campus. Equally, he was clear that provision need be made for the development of paramedical training and the expansion of nursing. This was to be a health sciences centre in the fullest sense. To forestall wrangling on another, sure-to-be sensitive issue, he outlined base salaries for full-time faculty that, while below those available to physicians in private practice, were above the stipends of regular academic staff at Hamilton and University College. Adding several other provisos, Evans, then, submitted his conditional acceptance.[55]

No doubt, Thode was impressed by this carefully worded missive. It bespoke clarity, resolve, and maturity in the youthful candidate. In any case, it raised no issue the two men had not discussed at length, during and after their first meeting. Taking the appointment to the senate, Thode was surely cheered when one member of that body volunteered from the floor that Evans was "the ablest and most all-round person I have met in my generation."[56] While some harboured reservations about the coming of medicine per se, there were no such misgivings about Evans, himself. The senate's approval was enthusiastic. Informed of the vote, the new dean of medicine, hitherto so poised, now found himself a tad weak at the knees, as he reflected on the enormity of the task ahead. Writing to a New York colleague, he apologized for rambling during a recent visit. "I was," he wrote, "still in a state of shock, as I began to realize just what I had undertaken."[57]

No egotist, Evans reached out widely for advice, as he prepared to get down to business. He took care, for example, to ask Dr R.C. Dickson, his counterpart at Dalhousie, why he (Dickson) had declined an invitation to consider the post. Was there something about the McMaster situation that had given him pause? Dickson was quick to assure him that his reasons were personal and had nothing to do with the opportunity itself. On the contrary, wrote the Haligonian, "I looked upon it as one of the most exciting developments in Canadian Medicine likely to occur in our lifetime."[58] Another correspondent, when asked for his thoughts concerning Evans' novel ideas, offered congratulations and quipped: "I should send you a bottle of holy water; it would help more than any suggestions I might have."[59] While the grace-giving vial never arrived, the enthusiasm displayed by Thode and the governors was sufficient to buoy Evans. "The support is simply fantastic," he told a friend, "and the excitement rather intense!"[60] It was, therefore, in a positive state of mind that he took on one of the most critical tasks at hand. In a seller's market, he set out to recruit those first, all-important faculty members who would translate broad conceptions into specific functions and appropriate forms.

As others later noted, Evans was not given to close, top-down management.[61] Rather, he preferred to outline general goals and let trusted colleagues thrash out detailed solutions with which they could live. In part, this reflected his democratic temperament and easy manner. It was also, however, a deliberate, strategic choice. Perhaps, his experience at hierarchically inclined Toronto taught him some lessons in leadership. If not, his travels south of the border most certainly had. "In general," he observed, "there has been a failure to involve the younger men in large departments of American Medical Schools in policy making." Too often, the price was a lack of commitment on the part of junior faculty.[62] Whatever the roots of his own decanal style, a 1967 visit to Western Reserve University convinced him that he was on the right track. Frank discussion revealed that development at the Cleveland school had stalled, until administrators had engaged systematically with faculty. Evans remarked, "The striking success of the Western Reserve programme appears to have been due to the involvement of the faculty at grass roots level."[63]

Such a process, of course, was greatly facilitated when everybody shared first principles from the outset. In that regard, Evans had been both careful and fortunate in his initial four appointees. They all knew each other from time spent at the University of Toronto. More importantly, each sought reform in medical education and viewed the McMaster experiment as a "once-in-a-lifetime opportunity." Among the original "Big Five," as their historian dubbed Evans, Mustard, William Walsh, William Spaulding, and James Anderson, free-flowing communication and wholesale commitment were givens.[64] In concert, they would establish a distinctive program and comradely modus operandi that would catapult the new school into a world-class institution.

An early faculty member later observed that many of his colleagues were "misfits."[65] This was not meant to imply that they were rebels without a cause. Instead, the speaker was describing people who were versatile to the point of defying normal professional classification. In this respect, James E. Anderson was certainly representative of the breed. As a young lecturer in anatomy at Toronto, he had nursed a growing fascination with human origins. In time, he became so absorbed in this pursuit that, by the mid-1950s, his interest embraced paleo-osteology, genetics, and anything else that helped him trace evolutionary trends in caches of Iroquoian, Nubian, and other skeletal remains, across three continents. When Evans approached him to head up McMaster's Department of Anatomy in 1966, Anderson was delighted by an exciting offer to return to his homeland. First, however, he had to resign as professor of physical anthropology at an American university![66] At ease in anatomy, anthropology, and archaeology, Anderson was a classic misfit, almost purpose-built for the kind of unorthodox medical school Evans and Thode envisaged.

James Fraser Mustard was cut from similar cloth. Although he did not rove quite so far afield as Anderson, he, too, was eclectic and difficult to categorize. Appointed in 1966 to lead pathology, Mustard was already world-renowned for his work in hematology, having demonstrated the benefits of Aspirin in warding off heart and stroke problems. Inevitably, he was drawn into cardiology, as well. Primarily a research scientist, he was, nevertheless also an outspoken critic of contemporary medical education, particularly as it showed little holistic concern with the social determinants of disease. Over the course of a long and fruitful life, Mustard would re-invent himself many times. Meanwhile, teamwork with Evans would be nothing new. After all, as undergraduates, the two had anchored the Varsity Blues' line as tight ends on the collegiate gridiron.[67]

Like Mustard and Anderson, Drs William Walsh and William Spaulding had connections with Toronto. Walsh, educated at Western, became a leading internist in the Steel City. Widely respected, he had served as chief of medicine with the Hamilton Civic Hospitals and had been president of the local academy, for a time. His appointment as assistant dean, in 1965, brought instant credibility to the venture.[68] Evans, who had interned at Toronto General when Walsh was senior resident, recognized the role that the latter could play in smoothing early relations between town and gown. "People liked him," Evans later recalled, "and knew that, if Bill was involved, it couldn't be all bad."[69]

For his part, Walsh had a keen interest in developing systematic training for family practitioners. No doubt, this helped attract him to an enterprise anxious to excel in this often-scorned, low-prestige, but ultimately vital field. McGill had considered a stream in primary care, but decided against it. Other schools offered notional tuition in the area, but felt it lacked the intellectual fibre of a full-scale department. In contrast, McMaster early concluded that, since roughly half of all medical graduates went into general practice already, the great challenge of the coming medicare age was to prepare them explicitly and methodically for integrated community health services delivery. Accordingly, the new school established the first department of family medicine in Canada.[70] The idea was catnip for Walsh. Meanwhile, it strengthened his hand as ambassador to a community partial to the concept.

Rounding out the quintet, William B. Spaulding signed on as associate dean in 1965. To a background in general medicine and psychiatry, he added a more-than-casual interest in medical history and education. As chief of outpatients at Toronto General, he had supervised both Walsh and Evans, during their internships. With a taste and touch for administration, Spaulding brought an experienced hand to a generally younger group. Experience, however, had not rendered him stale or staid. Rather, he shared his new colleagues' frustration with the rigidity of conventional medical pedagogy and the cloistered habits of mind it fostered. During his term as associate dean of medicine at the University of Toronto, "he displayed leadership in initiating inter-disciplinary teaching programs with the School of Social Work, Department of Psychiatry, and the Department of Public Health and Preventive Medicine."[71] Well-prepared and eager for the task ahead, Spaulding would chair the original education committee at McMaster.[72]

The standard educational model, against which the committee would rebel, was pronouncedly lock-step in nature. It prescribed a two-year premedical course for entry into a four-year MD program. The latter was divided into two years of formal courses in distinct disciplines, such as anatomy, physiology, and general pathology, followed by two years of clinical training, delivered in much the same discipline-oriented manner. Everything was geared toward preparation for content-based, summative exams administered by professional certifying authorities. Evans, knowing the pro-clivities of his committee members, was content to offer occasional guid-ance, but, for the most part, left his colleagues undisturbed, so that fresh ideas might be tested in the cauldron of uninhibited and often heated debate. In describing the need for renewal, he asked only that they "get away from the standard building-block structure ... away from shoving a lot of content down their [students'] throats, because they don't retain it very long any-way ... get them actively involved in the process and ... make it possible for people from a whole host of different backgrounds to enter into this, rather than strictly from the biological science model."[73]

Needless to say, translating this ambitious injunction into functional real-ity was no small order. Decades later, one faculty veteran recalled, "We had a better sense of what we didn't want than what we did."[74] There were lots of critics about, but no satisfactory, alternative model that could simply be transplanted. Instead, a template had to be conjured up anew. In the pro-cess, the merits of each detail were not blindingly and equally self-evident to all alike. Still, the essence of collegiality resides not in unanimous accord but in the mutual respect that encourages frank discourse. In just that spirit, the committee hammered out revolutionary recommendations, after long months of deliberation. Its report, submitted in January 1967, would rever-berate around the world. Some readers found it energizing. Others were skeptical. None with an interest in medical education were bored.

The core of the document was a call to promote "problem-based-learning" (PBL). At a stroke, departmental courses, formal lectures, written examinations, and numerical evaluation were consigned to history's peda-gogical dustbin. Students, traditionally regarded as empty vessels, forcibly to be crammed with facts, were now perceived as self-directing partners in their own education. Passivity was declared passé and active engagement de rigueur. The goal was to graduate highly motivated, habitual, life-long learn-ers. The key to achieving this, planners felt, was to be found in emphasizing a zest for and skill at problem-solving, both individually and collaboratively. Raw content was exploding exponentially; too much so to be adequately imparted, let alone absorbed. The trick, instead, was to examine a given series of problems and to develop proficiency at tracking down the latest that the manifold branches of medical science had to offer in diagnosing and treating them. Equally, it was vital that students learn truly to engage with patients; to "read" them closely, organically, and holistically, lest fac-tors underlying symptoms go undetected. This necessitated understand-ing "whole" persons and the communities in which they were immersed. Equally, since no one could be encyclopedically expert, judicious humility and a habit of consulting broadly had to be second nature in a physician. All told, problem-based learning in a team-oriented environment trumped rote regurgitation on all pedagogical counts, at least in the committee's mind.

As to method, Spaulding and company stood four-square behind the small-group, tutorial system. Crowded lecture halls did not allow for full, individual participation, or the extended, spontaneous exploration of alternative views. Nor did such a setting lend itself to humanization of, let alone contention with, the sage on the stage. Moreover, since standard examination was pronounced at one with the dodo, it was essential that instructors (now "tutors") be in close touch with students to monitor and credibly assess their level of personal progress. For their part, at least in theory, tutorial leaders were to facilitate, rather than lead, discussion among self-directed students who would be free to select their own particular avenues to investigating a problem. Given that this was a challenging art for some teachers to master, tutors were regularly to be evaluated by students, that they, too, be kept on their toes.

Critical to the whole process was selection of the problems, themselves, as well as the order in which they were raised at different levels of the curriculum. Granted, the program was not to be content-driven. Even so, through some logical, coherent progression, candidates had to be made comfortable with basic principles and resources in the major fields of medicine. As Mustard saw things, this presented no insuperable difficulty. "Indeed," he said, "if you select your problems properly then you will force students to cover the broad spectrum of medicine in time."[75] The question was how this might be done. This is where "matrix management" entered the frame. Evans described this complex arrangement as a "grid." Vertically, departments were organized under heads who marshalled faculty and resources. They were not, however, primarily responsible for curriculum planning or the implementation of programs. Horizontally, the faculty's teaching, research, and clinical functions fell under the purview of appropriate assistant deans or coordinators, who headed up teams. As a whole, the grid structure created an interdisciplinary mesh. Tongue in cheek, Evans nicknamed this "CHAOS": the "centralized hierarchy of administrative and organizational systems." Each year, planning committees would decide how best to deploy collective resources. On the educational front, this included devising problem packages, along with sundry published material and audio-visual aids necessary to support multiple approaches to them.[76] Inevitably, this would produce some friction over priorities, and tweaking would be a constant. As Evans put it, however, "the trick was not to lose the ability to tweak."[77]

Problem-based learning, itself, was not conjured out of the ether by Spaulding's committee; rather, it was inspired by a number of formal and informal practices already extant, which were drawn together in a coherent amalgam and systematically applied to medical education at McMaster. Both Evans and Mustard, for example, had encountered the age-old Oxbridge tradition of emphasizing small-group tutorials over, generally, non-compulsory lectures. The contrast with their undergraduate days at Toronto was refreshing, bookmarked, and remembered. In fairness to their alma mater, Mustard long recalled the stimulation derived from voluntary Saturday gatherings at the home of his physics professor. Each week, the genial Toronto don would set a problem to be puzzled out individually by keeners for lively exchange at the next session. This was all quite independent of regular course requirements, but brought the subject, and even lectures, more vividly to life for youthful physicists.[78]

PBL also had informal roots in studied truancy. As Mustard noted, medical students quickly learned to target specific lectures of true import. These were attended. Others, whose content could be absorbed through private reading, were often skipped, in favour of more time for direct involvement with patients. Why not refine and codify, he and others asked, a learning strategy that was already employed, albeit haphazardly? There were, moreover, elements of the successful case-study model, employed by the Harvard School of Business, which could be readily incorporated in a scheme for medical training.[79] When quizzed about PBL by a *Silhouette* reporter in 1967, Mustard conceded, "Some say we're crazy." He was, however, quick to add, "That's a good thing when you're trying something new."[80]

The program proposed by Spaulding's committee was novel in other respects. For instance, electives were built into the plan. More dramatically, training time was reduced from four to three years. The purpose, here, was to lower the overall tuition and living costs for students, as well as to produce more physicians faster to meet rising social demand. The academic year was to be eleven months long, thereby providing almost as much instructional time as the four-year system. "Phases," of unequal length, replaced traditional course structure. In turn, each phase was subdivided into blocks for which relevant problems were designed. Clinical clerkships would be conducted in a similar spirit, whether at the campus facility, or in one of the affiliated teaching hospitals.[81] Inherently intense, this three-year scheme was not for the faint of heart, mind, or constitution. In fact, one rationale behind it was the hope of attracting only mature self-starters, while deterring learn-by-rote devotees. Spark plugs, not sponges; young adults, not dewy-eyed post-teenagers were the target audience. So were people of genuine depth, as opposed to those who merely parroted proficiently on standard tests.

This latter consideration led to another departure from convention. Admission requirements were reinvented, so as to open the door to candidates from diverse, rather than strictly pre-medical, backgrounds. Now, anyone with a bachelor's degree, whether in arts, science, engineering, or any other recognized academic field, was welcome to apply. It was not, of course, open house. Thus, all were required to write the Medical Colleges Admissions Test (MCAT). As well, those without training in biological science had to take a short preliminary course, designed to familiarize them with the basic language and concepts of the field. On the other hand, no minimum undergraduate average was stipulated. Personal qualities, gleaned from letters and interviews, were given greater weight than simple grade-point standings.

As an aside, it might be noted that admission regulations grew more, rather than less, liberal over the next few years. For example, both the preliminary course and the MCAT were dropped, by 1973.[82] This relaxation did not reflect a crazed, desperate chase after candidates – any candidates. There were always vastly more applicants than could be accommodated. Rather, liberalization was based on surveys which showed that, at the end of three years, non-traditional students performed on par with those drawn from science backgrounds.[83] Altogether, the education committee went a long and revolutionary way toward giving precise definition to the "imaginative medical curriculum" Thode had promised Robarts.[84] It, also, cleared the path for crafting a formal statement of the Faculty's overall objectives.

This declaration was the product of long, collective deliberation, between 1967 and 1972. Early drafts were slowly pared down to a concise document. The same cardinal elements, however, can be found in each.[85] The 1969 version is the most useful for historical purposes, because it lays bare the rationale buttressing central principles. Compiled and authored by the ebullient David Sackett, it spoke (consciously or not) in the language and spirit of High Thodeanism. Four chief objectives leaped zestfully off its pages. Primary among these was the duty to educate effective, responsible, compassionate, biomedical problem-solvers who saw themselves as "bound together by their commitment to health." Lone wolves, after all, were seldom devoted primarily to promoting the public good. Meanwhile, at the level of graduate study, practicing and would-be health scientists were urged to apply fundamental research to clinical problems and to participate in the clinical phase of education. Research, it was underlined, should be conducted "on an interdisciplinary basis between the pre-clinical and clinical divisions of medicine, as well as ... with other departments of the University, such as Biology, Engineering, Physics, and Sociology." Indeed, the word *integration* recurred, echoing constantly, throughout this statement of educational purpose.

Another goal identified was that of providing effective service to the Hamilton region, broadly conceived. As part of this, McMaster was viewed as a centre of continuing education for practitioners already at work. Deemed a good in itself, this form of outreach was also tactically prudent. As early as 1966, John F. McCreary, dean of medicine at UBC, had advised Evans that quick implementation of such a program was one of the best ways a new medical school, plunked down amid an established network of general practitioners and specialists, could win the goodwill of local physicians.[86] The Spaulding committee had taken note, and Walsh had fashioned a system of continuing education that proved to be quite popular.[87] Beyond this, Sackett recommended forging close ties with Chedoke Hospital as a regional focal point for treatment of children with psychiatric disorders and for the rehabilitation of people with chronic disabilities. On a broader front, he asserted, regionalism should involve concentrating specialized clinical facilities in specific hospitals, so as to maximize educational, research, and service functions, while reducing redundancies. Although not stated here, the "region" was perceived as an arc sweeping round Lake Ontario from the Niagara through the Bruce peninsulas. Once again, integration was emphasized.

Research was a third objective underscored. Again, cross-disciplinary engagement was lauded both in fundamental and applied endeavour. While specialized "bench science" was still highly prized, research into health education and delivery was assigned new emphasis and urgency. A closely related, virtually redundant, fourth goal simply reinforced the central thrust of the prior three. Interdisciplinary approaches to education, research and service were to be fostered assiduously. Joint programs with the physical, biological, and social sciences should be cultivated. To facilitate this, sundry related sciences should be housed in close proximity to the medical centre. The latter, of course, was already in the cards, thanks to Thode's established campus plan. Still, reiteration was probably appropriate in a mission statement that, above all else, sought to endorse teamwork and the fluid exchange of ideas, up, down, across, and outside the grid.[88]

Clearly, since 1966 at the latest, considerable thought had been devoted to refining concepts of function. Early on, it dawned on Evans and company that form, too, would have to be customized to suit an institution audaciously conceived. In an organizational sense, matrix management and the tutorial system were two such structural adjustments. Still, another one, even more radical and literally concrete, seemed imperative, if the best-laid plans were not wholly to go astray. This involved nothing less than scrapping an already approved design for the health sciences complex, itself. Years later, veterans could still bring vividly to mind the soul searching that, mixed with a dash of intrigue, precipitated this decision. Of course, they could scarcely have forgotten, since this change of plans rekindled flames of discord that had only just begun to die down. To appreciate the audacity involved here, one must understand that the very thought of bringing medicine to McMaster had been a subject for heated contention, long before Evans and company arrived on the scene.

Initial views on campus had varied considerably. The *Silhouette*, unofficial voice of students, put an early positive spin on the idea. In 1963, there had been some concern when large parcels of RBG land had been conveyed to the university. Were verdant fields and stately gardens about be transformed into concrete jungles? Apparently not, reported the paper. Thode was quoted as saying that "we have agreed to do everything we can to retain the natural beauty of the area." Geoffrey MacGibbon, university information officer, went further. "I know of no plans to remove the Sunken Gardens," he told student scribes.[89] With the iconic gardens free of threat, the *Sil* even evinced a hint of pride in McMaster and the man who led it. Citing a serious, documented shortage of physicians in Canada, in November 1964, the paper applauded Premier Robarts for being quick to provide grants to upgrade and expand medical training, while noting proudly that this "owed much to Dr. Thode's prompting."[90]

Several academic departments also saw promise in the advent of a medical school. Nursing, for one, had long seen an on-campus hospital as the key to attracting larger enrolment and providing more interdisciplinary instruction to its students. If nothing else, this would solve the time-consuming business of arranging clinical training with local hospitals.[91] By 1963, Director Alma Reid was telling Thode that she had more qualified nursing applicants than could be accepted. Job opportunities for graduates with a BScN were abundant. Reid was eager, therefore, to hear from Queen's Park, "but we would like," she emphasized, "as much autonomy as possible in any medical school."[92] Similar excitement, tempered by concern for departmental interests, issued from other quarters. Radforth, for example, signalled that biology was energized by the prospect of collaboration with medicine. The opportunities were rich, given the shift of focus in his department toward cellular research. He was adamant, however, that biology, per se, be reinforced so as to continue playing a prominent role of its own, as well as aiding directly in the planning of a medical school.[93] The message from psychology was similar. In 1964, Newbigging foresaw several potential advantages, but he wanted talks with those who would develop physiology, medical engineering, and any cross-appointments "from the outset."[94] Clearly, these various life sciences welcomed the idea of medicine hanging out its shingle at McMaster, but were on guard against being subordinated to or subsumed by the newcomer.

Others, harbouring no such reservations, extended open arms. Divinity, for example, saw the health sciences as an avenue for developing wholly new forms of specialized ministry for students, who faced a traditional job market that was increasingly bleak. Training in hospital chaplaincy, geriatrics, and a host of other health-related fields was envisaged through collaboration with a medical school.[95] Meanwhile, a cross-appointed chaplain, with appropriate credentials, could help the Divinity College modernize its approach to the physical, psychological, and social problems faced by all ministers in a new age. Such, at least, was the conclusion reached by Divinity's principal, after reading Alvin Toffler's bestselling chiller, *Future Shock*.[96]

In contrast, cheerful enlightened self-interest moved Sandy McKay to hail the coming of medicine. Enrolment was bounding, he told Thode gleefully, as pre-medical students showed a distinct taste for classics in translation. Their presence, he declared, was both "welcome and salutary."[97] From his broader perspective, Mel Preston, dean of graduate studies, looked to the future with unalloyed optimism. Reporting on the year 1965–66, he noted that Evans and his team were deeply committed to basic and clinical research as part of their founding mandate. This, he thought, opened the door to cross-disciplinary work across the whole scientific spectrum – joint endeavour from which all willing hands could profit.[98] Others, however, had their doubts. Their number included Howard Petch, influential principal of Hamilton College. While not utterly opposed to a medical school, he was concerned that it might overshadow the rest of the university and, thereby, gradually retard the growth of established units that could never match its public appeal.[99]

Dean Dennis Shaw echoed this view in the senate, while also expressing disquiet about the "loss of amenities on campus," were trees and gardens to be bulldozed in sacrifice to the gods of medicine.[100] Biochemist Ian D. Spenser was of similar, if more volcanic, mind.

Decades later and almost fondly, John Evans recalled how he and Spenser fenced, bout after bout, on the bloodied floor of the senate. Two rounds, in particular, remained graven on the physician's memory. In 1966, Evans proposed that a department of clinical epidemiology and biostatistics be

founded, and that Dr David L. Sackett be appointed chairman, at the rank
of full professor. Spenser, no doubt in company with many old hands, took
umbrage. After all, the individual in question was only thirty-two years old;
a mere down-cheeked stripling. There were older post-doctoral candidates
on campus. Yet, Sackett was poised to become the youngest chairman in
McMaster's long history, while vaulting straight to the top of the professorial ladder. Spenser, determined to resist, ransacked calendars from a dozen
Canadian medical schools, but found not one department of the type Evans
was proposing. The dean shot back that that was the very point. This was
new in Canada. It was the wave of the future and Sackett was precisely the
person to fill the post, although Evans compromised by lowering the rank-
at-appointment to that of associate professor. With Thode's strong support,
the motion passed.[101] The next major slugfest came in 1970, with Spenser
leading the charge to block final approval of a curriculum that boasted
neither courses, nor formal evaluations. Evans took many a blow from an
opponent he recognized as "brilliant and sincere." In the end, Thode carried
the day, telling senators that if this was the right way, and if McMaster had
the right people, the results would be revolutionary. Again, Thode tipped the
balance. "That," Evans reminisced, "took guts."[102]

If differences of a formal nature sometimes arose between established academics and newfound medical colleagues, so did sore spots of an informal
kind. Mustard, Sackett, and others were well aware, for example, of widespread resentment against purportedly rich doctors with access to bounteous outside income. To a degree, there were understandable grounds for
this. Medical faculty were hired at market differential, with salaries generally higher than their academic equivalents. Yet, there was nothing new
about this, in principle, especially in professional faculties. One suspects that
it was heavy concentration of the practice in a discrete sector of the university that roused comment.

General lack of clear communication did not help much, either. As early
as 1966, Evans had stipulated to the governors that, while salary differential
was essential to attract good faculty, ceilings could and should be placed on
total income for medical staff. Money earned in excess of the cap, through
clinical practice or consultation, could be pooled for general use by the
school.[103] All this was understood among medical staff from the outset and
was codified by 1968.[104] In form, it bore resemblance to the tax on external
grants levied throughout science and engineering. Still, such arrangements
were largely bureaucratic, rather than matters of well-advertised, cross-
campus knowledge. As a result, physicians in tenure stream could never fully
persuade others that they, too, were living on fixed salaries.[105]

The fair-minded Sackett later conceded that some jealousies were not wholly ill-founded. Thus, he noted, "We had money coming out of our ears," by comparison with other faculties. As well, he and Evans could go straight to the minister of health to lobby for any special requests – an ease of access to decision-makers few colleagues in other disciplines enjoyed. He also granted that, by and large, his medical confreres took little interest in campus politics. Few, for example, joined the faculty association and virtually none felt solidarity with militants among that group.[106] In riposte, rank-and-file MUFA members might have argued that few of them were militant and that humanists and laboratory scientists faced often quite different problems; yet they joined together in what, after all, was not a union but an expression of mutual, collegial support.

To be fair, some in health science, such as C. Barber "Barb" Mueller, chair of surgery, and Mustard, would be deeply involved in larger university affairs. Most, however, were not. When he succeeded Evans in 1972, Mustard understood the gulf that divided medics from academics, but lacked the time and inclination to explain to all and sundry the myriad factors that worked against their smooth integration.[107] To paraphrase *Cool Hand Luke*, there seems to have been a two-way failure to communicate. Still, although mixed, campus relations were cordiality writ large, compared to the charged atmosphere that crackled between champions of the medical school and paladins of the nearby Westdale neighbourhood.

The central bone of contention was not the desirability of a health sciences centre but its location. From the moment the project had been tentatively mooted, numerous options had been considered. These included off-campus sites, such as the Sanatorium, open land on the northeast fringe of campus, and a tract across Highway 102 (Cootes Drive), among others. As noted, from 1948 onward, Thode resisted the off-campus solution with ever-increasing vigour. By 1953, he was urging that RBG property, south of King Street West and immediately adjacent the university, be purchased. There, a medical school could be placed in close proximity to scientific relatives; thus encouraging cross-fertilization. Meanwhile, a university hospital would nestle close to Main Street West, offering ease of public access. With time, Thode's stance on all these points would become intractable. In 1953, of course, all plans were strictly putative and purely in-house. However, when McMaster entered the bidding war in earnest, with early-sixties briefs to Robarts, designs had to be rendered concrete and more public. In short order, a three-way brawl erupted among fixated university authorities, irate Westdale residents, and conflicted city officials. The result was a tumultuous, four-year roller-coaster ride that left few without scars. Such, indeed, were its prolonged birth pangs that the medical school had to be delivered by Caesarean section, with Bill Davis and Mayor Vic Copps as attending physicians.

Difficulties arose as early as 1963, when McMaster presented to city council a pilot plan for developing 132 acres of land recently acquired from the RBG. Large parcels of that acreage stood south of King Street West, a major, civic cross-town thoroughfare. The area was earmarked for construction of a senior sciences building, extensions to engineering, other projected science facilities, along with the probable medical school. The plan, drafted by Sasaki, Walker, and Associates, complied fully with Thode's and the governors' vision of a compact, integrated, pedestrian campus. King Street, however, would bisect the university, represent a hazard, and eat up valuable space. The city was asked to divert the road, so as to bypass McMaster, altogether. At this juncture, Murphy's Law kicked in. Hamilton planners had just completed an expensive, city-wide traffic study that ran counter to the university's request. Much of 1964, therefore, was given over to the search for a mutually satisfactory solution.[108]

Things were still very much in doubt, as 1965 dawned. In the first week of January, Alderwoman Anne Jones presented city council with a petition from her Westdale constituents protesting the widening and twining of Main Street to handle the diverted overflow. Many residents worried about a broad, congested, high-speed corridor in an area that boasted four schools. Others, of less altruistic mind, were anxious lest property values decline. Hamilton's traffic director and its city engineer argued that the diversion simply would not work. Meanwhile, Alderman William McCullough supported Jones, adding that McMaster was being inexcusably inflexible about the location of the medical school.[109] Joining the fray next week, the *Hamilton Spectator* defended McMaster's position. This was far from surprising, in that Thomas E. Nichols, its publisher, was also a governor of the university. The *Spec* chided "a vociferous Westdale minority" for rattling all but a stolid Mayor Copps. The writer thundered on: "You could shoot a cannon down this part of King Street most hours of the day without hitting anything." Playing the "Hogtown Card," the journalist contended that to block the university's plan would be to set the city back fifty years and ensure that it remained "a lunch-pail suburb of Toronto."[110]

Amid this tumult, Thode met with city council on 19 January. He stated his case for a pedestrian campus and detailed the reasons why various sites, other than the southeast corner of campus, were unsuitable for a health sciences complex.[111] For good measure, he added a word of warning. McMaster and Hamilton, he said, might well lose the medical school to

York or another hungry bidder, unless work on the diversion and further planning went ahead soon.[112] This particular scare tactic would resurface, from time to time. A petition, signed by fully 1,800 McMaster students on a twenty-five-foot scroll, might have had a more positive impact.[113] In any case, council and the university finally agreed to a compromise solution on 29 January. King would be diverted around McMaster, but on peripheral university lands. There, matters rested – for a few quiet days. Then, on 3 February 1965, an article in the *Globe and Mail* threw something akin to fabled Greek fire on fading Hamilton embers.

Journalist Frank Adams surveyed the recent confrontation and concluded that, when the chips were down, McMaster had discarded its tweed jacket, mortarboard, and ivy-covered facade. "In their stead stood a phalanx of hard-nosed businessmen" who, said Adams, had sold Robarts on the medical school, before consulting properly with civic officials or residents. When aldermen had complained about changes to the $385,000 city traffic plan, McMaster had pointed to a clause that, in the final draft of the document, allowed for diversions in the event of university expansion. Adams claimed that the clause had been added after the main text had been approved, without city council's knowledge. The consultants, Parker, Parsons, and Brinkerhoff, who drew up the plan (and were now in McMaster's employ), acknowledged that this had been the case. Thode confirmed the story, noting that, once the engineers had been made fully aware of the university's projected growth, they "ripped the last page of the city's master traffic plan out and inserted the other part." An outraged Alderman McCullough was quoted as saying that McMaster had employed the tactics of a "shyster New York businessman." Adams, then, dropped his real bomb. Few Westdale residents, he wrote, were aware that, eighteen months earlier, a private member's bill had granted the university "full powers of expropriation" over whole neighbourhoods. McMaster, he warned, had the will, the guile, and the power to grab them.[114] Needless to say, Adams' article threw fresh wood on smouldering coals. Indeed, next month, a Westdale citizens' group demanded a thorough and open study of the university's future plans and their potential impact on surrounding neighbourhoods.[115] It was, within this context of newly rekindled, white-hot debate that thirty-five-year-old John Evans took up his post as dean of medicine, on 1 July 1965.

As he later recalled, the freshly minted dean knew something about the local discord, but had no real sense of its visceral nature, until he arrived in Hamilton. He soon found, however, that everyone he met seemed bent on informing him that newlywed Hamiltonians, by the bus-load, flocked to the Sunken Gardens for ceremonial photographs. The symbolic and emotional stakes were high, and Evans came to feel like "part of a scourge." Thode's steadiness bolstered him, as did the support of several local "heavyweights" to whom the president introduced him.[116] Among them were Ken Sobel, owner of CHCH Television and CHML radio, and Tom Nichols, publisher of the *Spectator*. Both men were governors of the university and solidly behind the health sciences project. Their influence and assistance would be crucial in days that followed.

This proved especially true when, by late 1965, Evans' team and consultants concluded that the deal struck with the city over King Street just would not work. It lopped three acres off a site already barely sufficient for current purposes, let alone a projected future.[117] Accordingly, negotiations were reopened with city hall, and battle was rejoined with Westdale residents. Feeling the heat, Thode joked darkly with a friend at the University of California, "When it is all over one way or another, perhaps I will be offering my services for a professorship, (Ha, Ha!)."[118] Nichols, however, had an idea.

As chairman of the governors' public relations committee, Nichols wrote Thode saying, "[T]he important thing is to get a letter to the Minister [of university affairs] as quickly as you can so that his reply may bring the new problems into the public orbit and give the newspaper and television a chance to elaborate and campaign." In an effort to spare Thode the trouble, Nichols (on *Spectator* letterhead) drafted missive to Bill Davis.[119] The president amended it slightly, then forwarded the letter to Queen's Park, emphasizing that "the citizens of Hamilton must be made to realize" the logic of McMaster's proposals. Urgency was underlined.[120] A few weeks later, eighty-six Westdale homeowners, whose property was marked for expropriation, were sent personal letters in which Thode outlined the rationale behind university plans. He offered to purchase their houses at current market value and, then, lease them back, until needed. This move would give those affected plenty of time to consider personal options. It was, also, made clear that the Honourable William G. Davis and sundry MLAs were privy to the offer.[121] Had an informative gesture of this nature (minus the heavy political reference) been made a year earlier, it might have eased things considerably. As things stood, in February 1966, it was too little and too late. Battle ensued, only to roar on for the best part of the year.

"The War of '66" featured what might politely be described as an ever-more frank exchange of increasingly entrenched views. Westdale activists, joined by not a few McMaster academics, became better organized. Rallies, demonstrations, and formal petitions to city hall were punctuated by occasional, but electric, meetings with university officials. On the whole, the latter gatherings were less-than-healing exercises. Indeed, following one, Jack

Moore, of the Hamilton Chamber of Commerce, wrote Evans despairingly: "I knew before Monday night's meeting that the University's Public relations were poor, but I was shocked to realize how bad they actually are." McMaster delegates had come poorly briefed to answer even such a basic question as who should be contacted, should a homeowner wish to sell his or her property to the university. Hundreds, said Moore, had left the conclave alienated, rather than soothed.[122]

For its part, the university availed itself of friendly media to get its message to the public. In February, popular columnist and radio host Gary Lautens put a folksy spin on things. Having met Evans, he described him as "a big, good-looking guy who played college football"; a witty, forthright fellow who could commune with don and labourer alike. For good measure, Lautens threw the "Hogtown" card on the table, saying Hamiltonians who failed to embrace the medical school were falling victim, once again, to an "inferiority complex" that stifled competitive instincts.[123] The *Spectator* preferred scare tactics, cautioning frequently that a "space-age health and research centre" was at risk, were dithering to continue. Plenty of other universities were said to be waiting in the wings, anxious for McMaster to default by reason of unconscionable delay.[124] No particular contenders were mentioned by name. In portraying its commitment to medicine, the university itself regularly employed what might be called the "heroic-concessive voice" (for example, "After years of giving into my natural modesty, I finally broke down and accepted the promotion, along with a hefty pay increase."). McMaster, it was proclaimed, had not sought, but had been "charged with the responsibility" of developing the province's newest medical school.[125] A sincere refrain in Gilmour's day, this was a convenient, if hollow, litany, chanted throughout 1966.

In response, the independent *Westdale Reporter* howled about "The Big Land Grab" perpetrated by McMaster.[126] In a related article, the journal alleged that the university was out to "plunder one of Hamilton's top neighbourhoods." Reference was made to "secret meetings" and the construction of an alliance among governors, newspaper, television, and radio magnates. This was, the paper charged, "a classic example of twentieth-century power politics" in which corruption had been enlisted to the detriment of the city's west end.[127] In case anyone missed the point, an editorial followed through. The writer conceded that the people behind the scheme probably acted in what they thought to be everyone's best interest. "We could forgive them," the journalist continued, "if a little stardust blinds them to the realities of the situation." What could not be forgiven was "blaming obstreperous citizens" for creating the controversy over a potential "landslide of destruction."[128]

From beginning to end, it was of signal importance Vic Copps remained squarely in the university's corner. The feisty, populist mayor personified the Steel City, with his gold hard hat and tough, but genial, manner. No stranger to controversy, his initial act, as the first Catholic in the mayoral chair, was to abolish the annual Orangeman's Day parade. Surviving a torrent of criticism, Copps went on to become, perhaps, the most popular mayor in Hamilton's history, serving from 1962 until ill health forced him to retire in 1976. It was his firm belief that the medical centre would help perk up the city's lunch-bucket image, while providing nearby access to locals eager for an education in medicine. As an ally, Copps was invaluable. When, to no little surprise, the Hamilton and District Labour Council openly endorsed McMaster's designs, the political battle was all but over.[129] City council approved modifications to the King Street diversion. All that was left was to break ground on campus, or so it seemed.

Amid the furor of 1966, Evans and his colleagues, as noted, were busily adjusting forms to suit the functions of a fully integrated health sciences centre. Matrix management, a radically new pedagogy, and other departures from standard practice were defined. As they were, it became chillingly apparent that one major, and already sanctioned, element of "form" would never be functionally appropriate. The design of the health sciences complex was anything but revolutionary. As laid down by a noted Toronto firm, the traditional eleven-storey H-shaped structure seemed more likely to inhibit, rather than facilitate, the integrative philosophy evolving among program planners. As Evans and Mustard independently recalled years later, concern over this disjuncture welled up among their colleagues to the point that, the battles of '66 notwithstanding, they felt impelled to take action, before all else went for naught.[130] It was a decision that required courage and an exercise in covert operation worthy of novelist John le Carré.

Mustard spoke to Evans confidentially. He happened to know a brilliant, unconventional architect, Eberhardt Zeidler, a creative master of moulding new forms for novel functions. One day in 1967, the two physicians slipped quietly away to consult the architect. Evans told no one, including his wife, where or why they were going.[131] Astonished, they listened with mounting enthusiasm as Zeidler outlined an idea percolating in his head. Rapidly, he explained the revolutionary concept of a "space-frame," three-to-four storey edifice that lacked interior load-bearing walls, thus allowing for an internal modular design that could accommodate precisely the kind of free-flowing access among teaching, research, and clinical facilities Evans and his planners had in mind. Better yet, since all the electrical, mechanical, and other service utilities would be housed in external support towers at the corners, modules inside could be altered at a fraction of normal costs.[132] Evans was instantly captivated. Taking a deep breath, he approached Thode with the plan. Thode, despite the trials of the previous year, did not even blink.[133] Together, they approached the executive committee of the board of governors, on 16 November 1967. With equal alacrity, the committee fired the former architects (at heavy cost) and hired Craig, Zeidler, Strong, and Associates to begin from scratch.[134] Evans was astounded that all had proceeded so expeditiously. Of course, there was bound to be some fallout, but some lessons had been learned during the struggles of 1966.

The first order of business was a press release. This time, the public would be brought up to date quickly. Issued on 12 December 1967, the statement explained that architectural horses had been switched because a vibrant, innovative program would require a flexible, first-class facility; not an outdated high-rise. Full details were unavailable, as yet, but the new design promised to put Hamilton vividly on the world map.[135] The Sunken Gardens, alas, were doomed. As a gesture of goodwill and empathy, however, the public was invited to salvage any plantings, free of charge. What followed was more akin to looting, as not only shrubbery but stonework was voraciously pillaged. Meanwhile, a last round of renegotiation with city hall ended with the signing of an agreement concerning the King Street diversion on 25 May 1968.

Wasting no time, in June, the governors ordered the expropriation and demolition of houses along Main West, so that the street could be widened to handle overflow from rerouted King. Sensitized to popular opinion, the project committee advised the governors, "As far as possible, expropriation and demolition will be positioned as the responsibility of the City of Hamilton, not the University."[136] With talk of a dramatic departure from existing campus architecture blossoming, the same committee urged the board that publicity regarding the building should be toned down, until it could be "presented with advantage." People on the streets, said the committee, "have not been as fully informed about the Health Sciences Centre and its overall design concept as perhaps they should have been."[137] For his part, Evans, too, had developed some street smarts in what had been a school of very hard knocks. Thus, he appointed Jane Drynan as Health Science's media liaison officer in 1969, and formed a neighbourhood relations committee the next year. Not all, of course, was plain sailing into golden sunsets. Howard Petch resigned, at least partly in protest over the loss of the gardens. Hard feelings lingered, on and off campus. Still, the "Zeidler Switch" had not precipitated a messy replay of 1966. Better yet, it clarified program planning and expedited faculty recruitment.

The uncertainty caused by repeated delay and controversy had seriously inhibited the enlistment of staff. By December 1966, total strength was a mere eleven: sufficient for planning, but woefully shy of a reasonable teaching complement. The unconventional program taking shape also deterred all but the most venturesome candidates. Indeed, the typical were not even approached with an offer. Instead, Evans deliberately sought out only "intelligent risk-takers."[138] This was no mean task. As he told the Hamilton *Spectator*, in the spring of 1966, "The calibre of man we're looking for isn't looking for a job."[139] The hunt was rendered even more difficult, however, by the state of central Hamilton. The decaying downtown core, he recalled, resembled London after a nocturnal tryst with the Luftwaffe. Prospective recruits lodged there seldom paid much attention during job interviews. Accordingly, Evans regularly spared them the pleasures of urban-inspired blight by having them to his own home, well removed from the centre of town. Thus insulated, the genuine risk-takers would often choose to sign on. "When you get enough of them together," Evans noted, "you create a culture."[140]

Typifying that flowering culture, E.J.M. "Moran" Campbell wrote to a friend in Britain, in March 1968. "I remain persuaded," he scribbled, "that McMaster has a reasonable chance of becoming, within the next five or ten years, the best medical school in the world." He went on to say, excitedly, that a radioactive isotope had been first administered to a human being, right there on campus. "This may not be true," he conceded, "but it does say something."[141] Campbell, surely, appreciated another intangible but potent element in the atmosphere: familial camaraderie. Long hours of intense, collaborative effort were rendered easier by good-natured ragging and deep, mutual affection. Individual joys and afflictions were collectively celebrated or shouldered, as in an extended family. Indeed, personal compatibility was appraised as closely as professional acumen, when recruiting staff.

Thus, spouses played an important, if informal, role in the faculty-selection process, which was designed to forge a genuine community, as opposed to a mere academic unit. The payoff came in the form of a sense of belonging that encouraged creative, if often blunt, debate. Meanwhile, communal ties were such that some endured for life. In the absence of a penalty box, free exchange and "no ranks in the mess" were the orders of the day. Fire and friendship were on offer, side by side.[142] Such was the culture abroad, as new recruits arrived in greater number. When it came to keeping them, the promise of a tailor-made, state-of-the-art facility was a potent ace up Evans' sleeve. A couple of timely windfalls did not go awry, either.

A 1969 gift of $500,000 from Ewart Angus of Toronto solved one enormous problem. PBL, with its emphasis on self-directed learning, necessitated a vast store of multimedia educational resources, if students were to probe problems largely on their own and from inquisitive, personal angles. Slides, videotapes, and numerous other audio-visual aids brought print sources into sharper focus. Graphic renderings, many by Lynn Johnston (later of *For Better or for Worse* fame) were invaluable.[143] The newer gadgetry, however, was inordinately expensive. Angus solved that problem. The businessman, a director of Guaranty Trust and other companies, financed a centre to house and collect the necessary material, stipulating only that it bear his name prominently.[144] At the same time, Dofasco's leading executive, Frank Sherman, endowed a chair in nuclear medicine.[145] Meanwhile, the program of study won approval from the Ontario Ministry of Health in December.[146] Altogether, 1969 was a very good year.

It was made even better by the admission of the first class. The *Spectator*, not surprisingly, took special note. Much was made of the fact that, although only 20 were admitted, 345 had applied. McMaster, the paper announced, became the first Canadian medical school to accept people from non-traditional backgrounds. Among them were graduates with degrees in anthropology, linguistics, law, engineering, and fine art. The cohort was older than average, and half their number were married. In short, these were the mature self-starters whom planners had sought.[147] With growth in faculty numbers and experience, the annual intake would slowly rise, until stabilizing around 100 per annum. Initially, teaching, both tutorial and clinical, was done off campus, while facilities were under construction at McMaster, itself.

A board of trustees was named to govern the new enterprise. Comprising faculty members, prominent physicians, and businessmen, it incorporated several university governors, as well. One of the early items on its agenda caused a minor stir. The institution needed an official name. Evans suggested that the clinical section be dubbed "The Sir William Osler Hospital of McMaster University," to distinguish it from the health sciences program.[148] Many a lead balloon, however, soared higher than this proposal. Defeated soundly in a general faculty meeting, it was tossed aside in favour of the "McMaster University Medical Centre" (MUMC). This term, in turn, aroused the ire of some, especially nurses, who felt the word *medical* detracted from the stated, interdisciplinary purpose of a supposedly different kind of undertaking.[149] This teapot tempest, however, soon blew over. Meanwhile, research had flourished from the outset and continued apace.

It would require more space and ink than available to describe the varied inquiry that engaged a bustling faculty in the late sixties. One example, nevertheless, might be noted. Ian Spenser had raised serious questions about the legitimacy of clinical epidemiology and biostatistics, when Sackett had been nominated in 1966. Perhaps this was why, in 1970, Evans took particular care to underline a major national health grant for the development of that area.[150] Hamilton's federal minister of health and welfare, John Munro, had just approved sufficient funds to establish a substantial unit in the field to train people for systematic research into the delivery of health care.[151] It was a first in Canada. Thus, the department, planned as a three-person operation in 1966, grew to involve eleven members in 1975, and twenty-three by 1985.[152] In the long term, McMaster medicine would evolve as one of the university's true research powerhouses.

The year 1972 would prove to be a clear datum point in the historical development of MUMC. The first class graduated that spring. Full accreditation was granted by American and Canadian reviewing agencies.[153] Nursing enrolment was approaching 200. Furthermore, such strides had been made on the research front that McMaster was taken off the list of "new schools," by the Medical Research Council, as its income from external grants was now equal to, or higher than, those of established institutions.[154] Most symbolically, Zeidler's sprawling complex was officially opened, on 27 May, with Davis, Copps, and other beaming dignitaries in attendance. Reactions to the edifice, which now utterly dominated campus, were decidedly sharp. In some eyes, it embodied all that might be styled "Late-Industrial Brutal." On the other hand, one old MUMC hand long recalled the warm glow that suffused him, when every day he first spied the building, during his drive to work.[155] For his part, future McMaster president Alvin Lee refused to let the book be judged by its cover. Aesthetics aside, he later observed, MUMC unquestionably saved, prolonged, and enriched lives.[156] If it saw an opening, 1972 brought an ending, too. Evans accepted the presidency of his alma mater, the University of Toronto. Mustard took command at McMaster. It remained to be seen if the centre would integrate with the university in true Thodean fashion. Time would tell. Still, Thode, who once declared that, with a medical school, it had to be "all or nothing," must have felt that a long haul had led to a good start.

7

Harried

Buoyant it might have been, but the spirit animating turn-of-the-decade MUMC was far from typical of moods campus-wide. Beyond the walls of Zeidler's Palace, anxiety was more common than optimism, and conflict as evident as camaraderie. Indeed, the period 1969 through 1972 witnessed a rather uncomfortable "second transition" in the general history of post-Baptist McMaster. These years, after all, saw the first blush of student activism and the initial thrusts of faculty self-assertion. In tandem, warm debate over university governance heated up. Simultaneously, mounting concern with the quality of undergraduate education sparked prolonged agonizing over curricular and pedagogical reform. Meanwhile, public faith in the unlimited potential of higher education, once unwavering, began to weaken. More alarmingly, so did the flow of government largesse. In differing form and degree, these interlacing difficulties afflicted every Canadian campus, from Victoria to St John's. As might be expected, this tapestry of trouble varied in warp, weft, texture, and hue, from place to place. McMaster, for one, had to deal with many a tangle in its own particular fabric. Still, the university was spared most of the extremes that tied some sister institutions in knots.

To be sure, there was substantial tension between faculty and administration on the Hamilton campus, but it paled in comparison with the 1969 PSA crisis at Simon Fraser, or the "Revolt of the Deans" that shook York and unseated its president, in 1972.[1] Similarly, McMaster had its share of student activists, but produced no catalytic leader the calibre of Toronto's Bob Rae, let alone torch-wielding firebrands, such as those at Sir George Williams' campus in Montreal. Again, like most other universities of the period, McMaster's system of governance was reshaped to render it more balanced and inclusive. Little thought, however, was given to following

Toronto down the steep path to unicameral government. Nor, amid all the tortured discussion of curricular renewal, was there serious talk of abandoning the cherished honours system, as several universities did under student pressure.[2]

Thus, viewed comparatively and in retrospect, McMaster rode out the dawning blast of academe's "Big Chill" rather more comfortably than many of her peers. Hindsight, however, should not render us insensitive to very real shivers that rippled across the Westdale enclave. To contemporaries, changing realities seemed likely to blunt that "powerful thrust," noted in the early sixties, even as its newest spearhead, MUMC, was being honed for action. For clarity's sake, the skein of change can be unravelled and its threads examined individually, so long as it is remembered that they were, in fact, tightly interwoven. As for a starting point, it is always instructive to follow the money.

In March 1969, a somewhat harried Thode wrote to his friend, Frank Sherman, president and chief executive officer of Dominion Foundries and Steel (Dofasco). Addressing a trusted confidant, Thode let his hair down and gave vent to visceral anxiety. "I'm not certain how to proceed," he scribbled, "and, therefore, write to you for advice and guidance, Frank." The question at hand was whether to launch a general or a limited fundraising campaign that year. That some kind of appeal was necessary, however, was not in doubt. Formula funding, Thode explained, left universities "extremely dependent on government." Here, he was not exaggerating, as over 80 per cent of McMaster's annual revenue was supplied by Queen's Park. The great problem, he told Sherman, was that the whole system was geared to the mean, the norm, the average. While it provided "a standardized quality of uniform mediocrity," it was not designed, he averred, to cope with the special requirements of a research-driven, graduate-heavy establishment of McMaster's ilk. Indeed, Thode's projections showed that something in the order of $14 million above current capital allowances would be needed, just to meet the minimum development targets for 1975. With only $1.7 million in its reserve accounts, McMaster would have to raise at least another $6 million from private sources to bid for matching government grants. Did Sherman, Thode asked, have any thoughts as to how this might be done?[3] In reply, his old friend pulled no punches.

A governor and long-time benefactor of the university, Sherman had McMaster's best interests close at heart, but he was not about to sugar-coat new truths, just to ease presidential jitters. "Quite frankly," he told Thode, "I don't know what the solution is." Surveying the contemporary scene, Sherman catalogued some of its more sobering highlights. The province, he noted, "must soon cut back." Taxes were already high, and all three levels of government were living beyond their means. Meanwhile, he continued; "I am pretty sure there is a growing resistance to university giving in public companies." Corporate liberality, never that impressive in the first place, was being eroded by "reaction to unrest, riots and destruction that have occurred in certain universities, and [by] the apparently inept way the problem has been handled." More ominous, he argued, was the feeling that, everywhere, campuses had been expensively overbuilt, while remaining under-utilized. "I must confess that I have some of this feeling," Sherman added. Driving the point home, he paused to reflect on a recent trip to Mexico City. There, he informed Thode, the university worked round the clock, on a three-shift rotation and without residences. In doing so, it was able to cater to more than 84,000 students on a campus much the same size as McMaster's. While recognizing that this rather industrial model would never gain acceptance in Ontario, Sherman did advise that government, business, and the community at large were unlikely to tolerate further university growth, until it was demonstrated that established facilities, staff, and programs were at maximum stretch. That, he warned, seemed far from the case, just at the moment.[4] In essence, the steel magnate was crooning a tune that would soon top the charts at Queen's Park. A hauntingly catchy little dirge, it would be entitled: "More Scholar for the Dollar." Like Sherman, Thode was already familiar with the basic melody, well before standardized lyrics were penned in the seventies.

The mid-sixties Spinks Report had served notice that boundless university expansion was not in the cards; at least, not where graduate studies were concerned. To be sure, government had quashed most of Spinks' more controversial recommendations. Even so, in his 1966 Gerstein Lectures at York, Bill Davis politely raised some awkward questions for university leaders to ponder. In truth, they were veiled words of caution from a minister genuinely friendly to the cause of higher education, but deeply concerned with evidence of carefree spending, needless duplication, and increasing competition among Ontario's universities.[5] The genial Davis, no doubt, hoped that some few words to the wise might suffice to forestall public calls for state intervention. On the other hand, neither he, nor any future government, would retreat from the policy of universal access for all qualified applicants. Similarly, Queen's Park continued to discourage fee hikes by deducting any such new income from its formula grants to offending institutions. As general enrolments continued to swell, university leaders must have sensed a lurking Catch-22. Of course, there was relatively little to fear, so long as post-secondary education remained the darling of government and public, alike. This happy situation, however, was changing as the decade wore on.

The long, postwar drift toward a welfare state became a late-sixties rush. Medicare, the Canada Pension Plan, and steady increases in unemployment insurance marked an era that produced "Trudeaumania" and the promise of a "just society." Central to all this was an effort to diminish sundry inequalities among the nation's people and regions.[6] Needless to say, this laudable ambition came with a hefty price, some of which fell on provincial shoulders, despite substantial federal contributions. On the whole, Canadians seemed content to pay for a stronger social safety net and renewed federalism. When, however, the first cold tingle of inflation was felt, Ottawa capped expenditures in its 1968 and 1969 budgets.[7] Clearly, with health, education, and welfare costs growing simultaneously, priorities would have to be closely weighed, nationally and provincially.

In this atmosphere, it did not go unremarked that public spending on Ontario universities had leaped drastically, between 1965 and 1969, from 1 per cent to fully one-tenth of the total provincial budget.[8] Meanwhile, health care was claiming an even larger share of the pie and bidding fair for more.[9] In several 1968 convocation addresses, Davis reiterated his personal faith in higher education, but noted that taxpayers were beginning to have doubts, particularly when confronted by perceived student radicalism.[10] Meanwhile, that same year, the BIU fell below levels recommended by the CUA for the first time most could recall.[11] Finally, in 1969, Davis' ministry declared that, so far as lavish increases in post-secondary spending were concerned, it had reached "the end of the line."[12] Priorities, it seemed, had been clarified.

Thode could not have been taken wholly off guard by this turn of events, save for its abruptness. After all, he had heard the undertones in Davis' 1966 Gerstein Lectures and moved immediately to separate McMaster from the pack. As always, he argued that McMaster had special needs that no simple template, designed for a Brock or a Trent, could meet.[13] Here, he intoned a mantra that his successors would chant, through to the end of our period. In the later sixties, however, it was falling on political ears increasingly attuned to a different note. Indeed, Queen's Park mandarins were giving voice to an incantation of their own devising. The latter sounded clearly in a March 1969 letter from Davis to Thode. Money was tight and university expectations were outstripping fiscal reality, said the minister. Most baleful, from Thode's perspective, was Davis' observation that graduate students were, perhaps, just a little too thick on the ground; a matter that merited "very careful study."[14] Just in case the darker notes in provincial plainsong rang less than clear, Premier Robarts followed with a resounding encore, a few months later.

Thode had written to the Ontario leader, asking for his personal assessment of the immediate future. The suave Robarts replied in polite but singularly uncompromising terms. All levels of government, he wrote, had been spending faster than the rate of real economic growth. The upshot was an alarming gap between public expenditure and tax revenue. The problem had been apparent for some time, said Robarts, but had grown in proportion with increases in medical and social assistance. "It is our hope," he continued, "that those at the operating level ..., who actually spend the money, have been convinced that money is scarce." "Unfortunately," he went on, "I have the fear that many of our largest spenders still think this is all a great bluff." Putting that fantasy to bed, the premier thundered, "Of course, it is not." Ontario, he declared, had reached the limit of its ability to finance new projects, and the government was not about to commit political suicide by suddenly raising taxes. As for the future, Robarts estimated that it would require "some years – a minimum of three – to achieve a new balance in our financial position." For their part, he concluded, universities would just have to make do and find an equitable solution.[15] Thode, of course, protested fiscal pruning, but to no avail.[16]

Far from bluffing, in 1969, the government of Ontario was calling the hand of every player at the high-stakes, post-secondary table. While Robarts and Davis had no wish to infringe unnecessarily on university autonomy, they did want to force McMaster and her sisters to sober up, after an era of (government-backed) binge spending. From the perspective of Queen's Park, there was little choice. Provincial deficits rose steadily, topping the half-billion-dollar mark in 1972.[17] Rationalization and accountability became new sacred cows, as the golden age of educational inquiries dawned. In 1969, three such undertakings held centre stage.

That year, all fourteen Ontario universities agreed to a graduate studies appraisal system. Meanwhile, a committee was formed, under the chairmanship of Philip Lapp, to look into the future of engineering across the province. Atop these loomed the more menacing Commission on Post-Secondary Education in Ontario (COPSE), chaired by the technocratic Douglas Wright. Granted, all these exercises were sanctioned by university leaders. Still, the same had been true of the Spinks Commission, whose members had raised the dread spectre of a University of Ontario. What might happen now that times were demonstrably tougher?[18]

Sniffing the prevailing wind, Thode prepared the university for a period of searching, external review. If elaborately documented rationales, bean-counting gymnastics, and studies in triplicate were on order, McMaster would be ready. Thus, in July 1969, he founded the Office of Institutional

Research – the first of its kind in any Ontario university. After a thorough search, Dr Eliot C. Higbee, of Scottsdale, Arizona, was appointed its director. His task was to bring to McMaster "the managerial revolution in higher education," growing south of the border.[19] Over the years, Higbee would churn out dozens of special reports, as he built a computerized database of manifold vital statistics. At a minimum, this helped spare McMaster wild miscalculations of the sort that cost President David W. Slater his post at York, when he grossly over-estimated enrolment projections for 1972 and hired a hundred more new staff than needed.[20] As Mike Hedden saw it, however, Higbee's immediate objective was to nail down the precise resource implications of long-term strategic options open to McMaster in the current fiscal climate.[21]

With that zest found only in the soul of an actuary born, Higbee correlated every variable he could quantify, from salaries to sabbaticals; from discipline concentrations to enrolment caps. Biasing everything in favour of grim reality, rather than wishful thinking, the best he could tell Thode was that deficits might be staved off for a little while, but were inevitable, sooner or later. Only a significant rise in the graduate proportion of the student body, or a sharp increase in BIU values could change this.[22] By the time he had Higbee's analysis to hand, Thode already understood that neither of these happy developments was likely to occur. Meanwhile, anecdotal evidence from the trenches and further tidings from Queen's Park spoke thunderously to the true meaning of "the end of the line."

In 1969, Art Bourns required no computer to see that this was a "transitional year." For him, as vice-president of science and engineering, the hour was flush with foreboding omens. Privately, he told Harry that the dramatic difference between the BIU increase requested (11 per cent) and the one granted (5.5 per cent) was having harsh effects on his flagship division. Class sizes, already too big in some disciplines, had to be enlarged as did teaching loads. Moreover, he was keeping extremely tight rein on overdue renovations, equipment purchases, and departmental expenditures in general. Much of the too-slight revenue increase had to go to salaries.[23]

In his annual public report, Bourns darkly underscored a marked "levelling off" of vital graduate numbers, especially in the basic sciences. Capital and operating grants were barely sufficient to maintain the divisional status quo. Given government attitudes, he thought this situation likely to continue for some time. There was, as yet, no reason to panic. Still, he counselled, "It has become increasingly clear that, if we are to make the most effective use of our resources, we must select within our present programmes a few areas for special development while at the same time identifying new areas of concentration for which there is student interest and a clearly-defined social or economic need."²⁴ In short, the university had to become more alert, more agile, and more discriminating in days to come. Difficult choices, of a type not faced for over a decade, were in the offing.

As he saw them, Thode spelled out the dour facts for all to read, in the March issue of *The McMaster News*. He acknowledged that government financial problems were real and likely to persist. At the same time, he underlined, university needs had never been greater. Every campus was faced with the prospect of heavier enrolments. Meanwhile, all faculty associations were pressing for salary increases, as inflation started to bite. In addition, there were demands for smaller classes, more instructors, and a less impersonal undergraduate experience. It went without saying that the thirst for graduate studies and research was unquenched. Great expectations, born of the sixties, would be difficult to sustain. Indeed, Thode warned that shortfalls in operating and capital grants meant that some programs might face cuts, while only new building projects of the highest priority could go ahead.²⁵ He was deeply troubled. A yellowing piece of undated scrap paper survives as testament to this anxiety. On that crowded sheet, he pencilled random thoughts about fiscal 1969, under the heading, "Dilemma."²⁶ As quandaries go, moreover, this one became more, not less, difficult and perplexing.

Indeed, MUMC aside, a dismal pattern marked Thode's last years in office. On one hand, it became a virtual given that government grants would fall well short of budget requests; on the other, various external agencies demanded ever-more data on university operations. In June 1970, for example, the chairman of the board put his fellow governors on high alert. They were told to prepare for a long and busy summer. Questions were pouring in from government, from Douglas Wright, from the CPUO, and others.²⁷ How much space did the university have? Was it fully utilized? Had the administration considered year-round, full-time operation? How did McMaster manage extension studies? What was the standard teaching load? What balance was struck between teaching and research?²⁸ As years rolled by, the list of queries seemed to lengthen in direct proportion to the shrinkage of income. Indeed, by 1972, Eliot Higbee might have been the one person on campus for whom this was his finest hour; such was the call for myriad calculations of manifold factors in mind-numbing, constantly shifting combinations. Others merely felt the noose of restraint begin to tighten.

Predictably, a tide of doleful plaints began to flood Thode's desk. Taking stock of 1970, Bourns lamented that, for two years, grants for operation of the reactor and accelerator had been insufficient to permit the full exploitation of these keystone facilities at the moment of their highest potential utility. There was even talk that these prestigious installations might be shut down. For the moment, every effort was being made to find other sources of funding. On this score, Bourns welcomed the appointment of Dr Alan C. Frosst, who was tasked with helping faculty prepare grant applications, outside contracts, and negotiated development arrangements. Still, he was deeply worried that something in excess of a quarter of research operating costs was falling on the university. To make matters worse, he continued, the NRC had cut its budget for university computing centres by 20 per cent, and would cease underwriting them in any fashion next year. He shuddered at the thought of the impact this would have on research in his division.[29] Already, he was turning down most requests for overseas travel, while scavenging divisional funds to the tune of $600,000 a year to prop up engineering.[30]

From his office, as chairman of chemistry, Dick Tomlinson sounded a similar note. In 1970–71, the only good news on offer was that undergraduate enrolment was up. Even so, he was sorely disturbed, both for his department and its students. A recent survey showed that only 26 out the department's last 269 honours and majors to graduate had procured jobs related to their training. Saddened, but not surprised, he added that not one of the current fourth-year candidates intended to apply for advanced work. Meanwhile, twelve had dropped out of the doctoral program, the moment job opportunities of any sort had cropped up. Rounding out a bleak picture, there was a sharp decline in graduate applications. All told, he ventured, it was "not a vintage year."[31] Nor did the next one offer better promise. Indeed, in 1972, Tomlinson noted "considerable unrest" among a still decreasing number of graduate students.[32]

Things were little better across campus. Speaking for social science, Dean Saul Frankel noticed the dampening of optimism and the rise of consternation among his colleagues. On the verge of take-off in graduate work, divisional plans were being curtailed by shifts in government policy.[33] Late in 1970, for example, Queen's Park placed an embargo on any new graduate programs, pending formal ACAP discipline assessments. This action yanked the financial carpet out from under McMaster's doctorate in political science. Delayed by the departmental implosion of the late sixties, the degree had only just been approved by the senate and students admitted. Government fiat, however, suddenly left it without provincial funding. For the next few years, the degree was supported out of McMaster's own resources, as a gesture of good faith toward students already enrolled.[34] This, however, could not continue indefinitely.

Humanities, meanwhile, was faring little better, according to Dean McKay. Graduate programs in French, German, and philosophy were suffering from the "deleterious effects" of changing economic times and political moods. In one instance, with graduate assistants thin on the ground, a bargain was struck with the government of France, whereby people liable for military service were exempted, if they took junior contractual posts in French at McMaster. Meanwhile, reported a disappointed McKay, the MA in Russian had been mothballed, all together.[35] Abrupt change, it seemed, was catching several deer in its campus-wide glare.

In 1971, on the eve of leaving McMaster to take up prestigious new duties as chairman of the OCGS, Mel Preston offered some perspective on gather-. ing woes. While he understood the imperatives behind government restraint, as dean of graduate studies he was critical of several particular policy decisions at Queen's Park. Ontario Graduate Fellowships, for example, were sharply reduced, from $5 million to $3.5 million for 1971–72. Worse still, when concerted planning was most needed, precious time and energy were being drained, just keeping up with government policy changes. In this observation, he was seconded by John Evans, who described the volume of information being requested as "appalling" in scale.[36] For his part, Preston contended that this unremitting distraction had a sharp effect on McMaster, because, more than most, the university needed to respond deftly to any changes affecting its heavy commitment to graduate work. In defence of his institution, he noted that graduate regulations at McMaster had been updated recently to make programs more attractive and to reduce completion times. He, then, penned a full historical sketch of advanced studies at the university, emphasizing orderly, planned growth and quality control.[37]

Somewhat oddly, Preston made no reference to mounting public and government pressure to reduce the number of foreign candidates in favour of Canadian graduate applicants.[38] As a member of the president's executive committee, he had certainly been at pains to criticize Douglas Wright's proposal that non-Canadian enrolment be capped at 20 per cent. After all, McMaster was especially vulnerable, since it boasted the largest proportion of foreign students of any university in the province. The heaviest concentration of these was in graduate studies. In fact, McMaster was home to fully 10 per cent of all non-Canadian graduate candidates in Ontario.[39] Moreover, the graduate corps generated roughly 40 per cent of the university's entire BIU income.[40] Still, Preston's warning that the boom had ended was right on the money – more so than he could have guessed. After three years of chipping away, the governmental axe fell, with stunning authority, in the spring of 1972.

In March of that year, the Honourable George A. Kerr, newly installed minister of colleges and universities, extended warmest fraternal greetings to President Thode, along with a brimming cup of hemlock. Without consultation, government was raising undergraduate fees, frozen since 1964, by $100. Better yet, graduate students would be charged tuition for three terms per year, rather than the accustomed two. All this, of course, would be deducted from the university's BIU income. As for student assistance, the loan portion of Ontario Student Awards was increased by $200, while the $150 Ontario Scholars entrance bursaries were eliminated. Meanwhile, the OGF fund was slashed by another half-million dollars to a scant $3 million for the province as a whole. Thus, universities would have to pick up more of the tab for graduate support. On this score, Chairman Alan Smith reported that such costs were making "frightening inroads into shrinking research funds" in civil engineering.[41] To make things even tougher, Kerr announced that scholarships and grants would now be treated as taxable income, from which Ontario Health Insurance Plan, Canada Pension Plan, and unemployment insurance premiums would be deducted. He politely concluded by wishing Thode all the best, while hinting that a capital spending freeze was just around the corner. At least, he had grace enough not invite Thode to enjoy a nice day!

Within this sombre context, Martin Johns paused to reflect on events since 1969. In 1972, the physicist plainly agonized over the state of his department. He told a tale of "belt tightening," "retrenchment," and "apprehension" as he catalogued the symptoms of recent decline and a potentially bleak future. "The reduction in employment opportunities for Ph.D.'s in science, and the often unbalanced criticism of science in the public domain, has led to a drastic reduction in the number of students wishing to embark on long, arduous Ph.D. programs," he wrote. Physics, he assured authorities, was taking all reasonable steps to streamline its hallmark degree. Even so, applications fell remorselessly. In September 1971, 106 graduates had been on the roll. By May, however, the total had fallen to 95, as dropouts multiplied. "For the first time in recent memory," Johns sighed, "there will be some faculty members without graduate students." Only five years earlier, this would have been unthinkable. Now, student morale was at low ebb, while faculty were tense. The greatest concern was that established research programs were in real danger of being starved.

Grants, he pointed out, linked enrolment and research in tandem. The problem, here, was that student interests were shifting into newer areas, such as quantum optics, while departmental strengths resided elsewhere. Complicating this was the tendency of student fancy to change quickly. Unless research and teaching were decoupled for funding purposes, Johns feared for the future of the reactor and tandem accelerator. On the other hand, he was certain that the coming ACAP assessments, along with the "growing intensity of the 'publish or perish syndrome,'" would lock McMaster into established, but now less fashionable, areas at which it so obviously excelled. Clearly, as he longed for room to manoeuvre, Johns felt the jaws of a vise tightening round him.[42] At his local level, he was merely reflecting apprehensions that had long haunted the higher administration.

As early as November 1969, Thode called for bi-weekly meetings of his inner cabinet, the president's executive committee. Hitherto, it had met ad hoc, or monthly, at best. Creeping urgency, however, brought these top policy-makers into regular session, over the next few years.[43] The committee included all vice-presidents, along with whichever deans or other advisors were felt essential to particular discussions. In concert, they dealt with everything from parking policy (always a favourite) to headier matters, such as the budget. Here was the true fulcrum of strategy at McMaster. As early as September 1970, the committee faced up to the fact that circumstances militated against realization of the full Thodean paradigm, at least for the indefinite future.

As ambitions outran resources, Bourns argued, "We must decide on our limits and then agree on the appropriate distribution involved." All constituencies could not be nourished to an equal level of excellence, as once had been dreamed. A weary Thode concurred. Much as he longed for balanced growth in research and graduate studies across the whole university, he conceded that reality dictated otherwise. Any new increases would have to be justified in terms of public and student demand. The need, he continued, was to consolidate, plan, and hold the line. Drastic cuts were not unthinkable. Enrolment caps on burgeoning social science, psychology, and geography might even be advisable. Of course, some advisors objected to this line of thought. In the end, however, even the vice-president of arts allowed that "a selective approach to excellence" was inevitable.[44] Implicit in this call to adroit navigation through troubled waters was the assumption that master pilots could retain their accustomed freedom to manoeuvre with authoritative agility. The president, aided by privy counsellors, had enjoyed just such dexterity, as long as most could remember. Such, however, was ceasing to be the case. Indeed, since the late sixties, faculty assertiveness was curtailing administrative freewheeling; every bit as much as fiscal constraint was.

In April 1969, George Grant took a moment to offer Thode some advice about preparing faculty to accept significant change. At the president's personal request, the religious scholar had served, since 1966, as McMaster's academic observer at CPUO's formal meetings. The outspoken Grant had been rather surprised by the invitation, given his reputation for frankness. Thode, however, assured him that he was chosen precisely for that quality and that nothing he said would ever be held against him. Against all bets, McMaster's "Odd Couple" got on very well. Meanwhile, Grant acquired first-hand knowledge of complex university-government relations. Thus, he felt comfortable in addressing the president on a delicate point. "One thought I had from the meeting of the CPUO yesterday," wrote Grant in March 1969, "was that the McMaster administration has an interest in seeing that our faculty members (particularly the younger ones) are clearly aware of the limitation all universities are under from the government." "I don't know how this can be done," he continued, "but I think it needs doing because the more I talk to young faculty members, the more I am aware that they are quite unrealistic about what is happening financially in the province at the moment."[45]

Thode, undoubtedly, concurred with Grant's observation about faculty naïveté and the need to communicate some home truths. He was, however, not about to surrender any more freedom of action than he had to; and especially not over anything as vital as budget deliberations. True, he did authorize T.W.D. "Tom" Farmer, director of information, to improve campus communications – to a point. Thus, the rather chatty McMaster News was replaced by the more slick Contact, early in 1970. As well, a summary of the senate proceedings and other official doings was made regularly available in the McMaster Gazette.[46] Still, both publications doled out only that which the administration thought fit to print. In practice, Thode continued to hold higher trump cards as close to his vest as he could.

Years later, Norman Rosenblood, MUFA president for 1971–72, offered a candid assessment of Harry's proclivities in this regard. Thode, he said, had an aversion to campus politicking. He liked to keep things simple, Rosenblood continued, and deplored the hairsplitting jealousies that often bogged down plans in the senate. The faculty advocate thought the president had a rather inscrutable demeanour; one that could lend several different interpretations to his words and actions. This characteristic, thought Rosenblood, stemmed from shyness in an essentially humane man, who seemed to lack any trace of bonhomie or humour.[47]

This sketch, of course, must be taken with a grain of salt. The likes of John Evans, Mel Preston, Art Bourns, and others, who shared values and closer dealings with a less Sphinx-like Thode, would never second it. In truth, the same man could be charismatically winning, face to face, yet wooden, remote, and unmovable under other circumstances. Given the less-than-revealing nature of his public and private papers, Thode the person is likely to remain an intriguing but unfinished historical puzzle. Thode the president, however, was fairly typical of his "never-complain; never-explain" generation of university leaders.

H. Blair Neatby and Donald McEown, for example, note that President A. Davidson Dunton of Carleton (1958–72) rarely delegated, had no vice-presidents, and regarded the board as titular, at best.[48] Michiel Horn underscores how President Murray Ross of York throughout the sixties, oversaw large-scale expansion with little concern for close consultation.[49] At contemporary Simon Fraser University, Chancellor Gordon Schrum ran what Johnston describes as a "one man show."[50] Yet, these men were rabid Trotskyites, compared to Dalhousie's president, Henry Hicks (1963–80). The latter, according to one successor, was an outright "dictator"; a refugee from an earlier age, replete with snuff box, cane, and bowler.[51] Of course, there were others of more collegial ilk. Toronto's Claude Bissell comes immediately to mind.

For his part, Thode appears to have been fairly typical of this generational peer group; perhaps with a tendency to lean more toward Bissell's than Hicks' end of the spectrum. He had no problem delegating to trusted subordinates. Indeed, he sought, learned from, and acted on advice from those he esteemed, as noted in the case of John Evans. Furthermore, he had little use for formalities. Thus, even in the heat of anger, most long-serving faculty addressed private letters simply to "Harry," without fear of seeming presumptuous. At the end of the day, however, Thode prized and protected the latitude to act decisively. The old administrative structure, with all its Byzantine quirks and complexities, had provided ample scope for presidential initiative. By 1970, however, some of that freedom had been bridled. In good measure, though not exclusively, this reflected the growing assertion of faculty interests.

In April 1960, Frank Jones suggested that MUFA establish a committee to formulate recommendations for the improvement of university government. In particular, he urged that instructional staff seek some representation on the board of governors. He was seconded by Harry Duckworth, who cited the recent failure of administration to consult over the timing of study week as but one example of an introverted system carelessly at work.[52] Neither Jones nor Duckworth nor the bulk of their colleagues were wild-eyed radicals; simply aching to tear up cobbles and man barricades. For the most part, MUFA was concerned with more mundane matters, such as pension and salary improvements. Like most Canadian academics of the day, however, they were rather more on guard than usual.

In 1958, the blatant absence of due process in the dismissal of Harry Crowe from United College, Winnipeg, had alerted many to the dangers inherent in loosely defined, purely paternalistic governance.[53] On the Hamilton campus, no one thought Gilmour or Thode likely to steal private letters in order to prosecute a vendetta, as college authorities had in Manitoba. Even so, MUFA's inquiry into the Crowe case concluded that a sharper definition of rights and duties, along with formal lines of communication, were required, in order to avoid undue friction at McMaster.[54] In 1960, what Jones, Duckworth, and others wanted was clarification and codification; rules and representation, not revolution.

In May 1961, Bert McCready, a former CAUT president (1956–57), recommended that MUFA establish a standing committee on university government. Its purpose was to study practice at sister institutions, while working toward the fuller participation of University Council (not MUFA) in McMaster's deliberative processes. Mention was also made of the desirability of a handbook that would spell out procedure concerning appointments, tenure, and promotion, while delineating the terms and powers of departmental chairmen.[55] The upshot was a brief that crossed Thode's desk, in October 1962. While moderate by later standards, the document called for much more than McCready had envisaged.

Indeed, MUFA asked that the McMaster Act be revised to ensure that teaching faculty be equal in number on the senate to all other constituencies combined. At the moment, even alumni held more senatorial seats (ten) than did active instructors (six). When representatives of the governors (ten) were added to a long list of ex officio administrators, the small faculty contingent was little more than a polite afterthought. This, argued authors of the brief, had to change. Furthermore, they asked that all major academic questions be referred to a better-defined University Council for recommendation, before final decisions were made.[56] Thode, predictably, said little and did less in response to the memorandum, other than to observe that University Council was far too large to serve as a significant deliberative forum.[57] Try as he might, however, he could not sidestep the issues of governance and formal process for long. The MUFA brief, after all, was no local, isolated phenomenon, peculiar to McMaster. Rather, it was one among dozens of strikingly similar calls issued by faculty, coast to coast.

Many explanations of this assertive surge have been offered. Horn makes a strong case for the impact of sheer size and speed. As universities mushroomed at high tempo, so also depersonalization grew apace. Older, informal approaches to governance, dependent on intimacy, deference, and shared values, were impossible to sustain. As he notes, by 1960, the CAUT

had already adopted the position that faculty voices should be predomin-
ant in decision-making – and the real university boom had scarcely begun.[58]
Neatby and McEown add that growing emphasis on research and graduate studies helped raise the prestige, leverage, and confidence of academics.
No longer merely "instructors," many became "grant holders," significant
attractors of external money and valued graduate students. Habits of deference eroded.[59]

No doubt, generational friction, also, came into play, as a tide of new
blood flowed into old college veins. Thus, some have noted that the sixties'
culture wars owed much to trends developing the previous decade. It was
during the latter period, of course, that the myriad young professors, who
later flooded Aquarian campuses, came to intellectual consciousness. In any
case, the many grand forces in play registered nationwide. Still, cataloging
them cannot explain the particular experiences of individual universities,
where local conditions helped to shape specific outcomes.

At McMaster, for example, it mattered greatly that even some in the
administrative cadre thought a measure of organizational streamlining was
both inevitable and desirable. In this regard, Arthur Patrick, dean of arts,
was among the most vocal. From the outset in 1962, he had regarded joint
management of combined arts and science by two colleges, two principals,
and two deans as inherently confusing, ill defined, and dangerously dependent on personalities. By 1963–64, he was arguing that this fragile house of
cards was doomed to collapse under the weight of numbers and the complexity of work. Faculty meetings could not handle the swelling volume of
committee reports. Meanwhile, ever-more responsibility was being thrust
upon departmental chairmen. The latter, he remarked, were serving "in quite
a magnificent way," but without clear guidelines, let alone sufficient support.
This muddling through, Patrick contended, could not long endure. Addressing Thode, he wrote, "I sound a warning here: the number of students predicted for us during the present decade will render our present machinery
inadequate."[60] Patrick's opposite number in science, R.P. Graham, offered a
similarly dour assessment.[61]

The following year, the two deans drew attention to deteriorating morale. As their joint faculty council ballooned, colleagues spoke to them of a
lost sense of identity and an inability effectively to voice individual opinion
on university affairs. More specifically, Patrick reported: "A small group of
Arts chairmen raised again the vexed question of the Faculty or University
Council, which they feel must be reactivated in some form to ensure better communication between Administration and teaching faculty, in order
that faculty opinion may be formulated more clearly and made known."

Citing experience elsewhere, he counselled that to ignore this discontent was to court "disruption of university life as a whole." He cautioned Thode that, unless an alternative structure was adopted soon, McMaster would likely devolve into balkanized, monolithic departments, by default. This, said Patrick, would ultimately make "discourse more difficult and a sense of community impossible." Once again, if in less detail, Graham fully supported his decanal colleague.[62]

For Thode, such consistent advice from two of his most important deans must have added weight to MUFA's polite but persistent pressure. Clearly, there was no simple faculty-administrative divide on the issue. Furthermore, much of the running critique touched on the issue of community, a central Thodean value. Few, were naive enough to imagine that the old intimacy of pre-1957 McMaster could survive the sixties rush to growth unaltered. Thode himself was not the type to dwell sentimentally on times past, in any case. However, he did view interdisciplinary co-operation as the life force behind that focused research excellence he so highly craved. To foster such endeavour, campus concord was a *sine qua non*. On this point, Thode, his deans, and many faculty agreed. Besides, the president was a realist. Like Patrick, he could survey experience elsewhere and count the cost of playing out a losing hand. He appears to have concluded that it was better to try to influence, rather than resist, change. Accordingly, in the summer of 1965, Thode appointed a presidential committee to recommend on the issues at hand. Its terms of reference, however, were carefully phrased. The group was charged "to study ways of effectively presenting faculty *opinion* in *official* discussions of the university's long-term development [author's italics]."[63] Thus, conceding nothing in particular, Thode extended an olive branch and waited upon events.

The committee, chaired by Dennis Shaw, included Art Bourns, Goldie French, George Grant, Mike Hedden, Roy Wiles, and Jack Kirkaldy. Labouring assiduously, these seasoned hands produced a unanimous report by December 1965. Their cardinal assertion, that "increasing responsibility to mould its own future should be assigned to the teaching faculty," was hardly a shocker; it could have been foretold by a deaf and cloistered mole. The real surprise, perhaps, was the moderate nature of suggestions for facilitating professorial participation. Missing, for example, was the 1962 demand that the senate be reconstituted to ensure heavy faculty representation. Instead, the committee recommended that a small advisory body to the president be formed. It was to comprise non-voting senior administrators, along with eight elected faculty members: two each from humanities, social sciences, and natural sciences; and one from both engineering and health science. Deans, who were members of the teaching corps, would be eligible for election. This body would advise the president on all things affecting university planning and development, while reporting to faculty on everything, save confidential matters.

Shaw's report, also, called for reconstitution and functional definition of the University and College Councils. As well, mention was made of the need to rethink the organizational structure of "parts of the university." Details were deliberately scant. The committee argued that structures and their more precise roles should be left to the new advisory body for close consideration.[64] It would be interesting to speculate as to what prompted the Shaw Committee to author so restrained and modest a report. How, one wonders, was unanimity attained, when at least one of the signatories was soon to lead the charge for sweeping reform? A full senate debate might have clarified much for posterity. None, however, took place. The document was presented to the senate, in June 1966 – only to be tabled without comment. In March, after all, Shaw had been utterly scooped. Indeed, the spotlight had shifted decisively to the Duff-Berdahl Report on university government in Canada.

By 1964, faculty rumbling on Canadian campuses had become so deep that the Association of Universities and Colleges of Canada (AUCC) and CAUT joined hands to delve into root causes of disturbance. Together, they sponsored a special, nationwide investigatory commission, headed by two specialists in the study of higher education. To ensure as neutral a gaze as possible, the co-chairmen hailed from outside the Dominion: Sir James F. Duff from Britain and Robert O. Berdahl from the United States. Throughout 1965, the two visited thirty-five Canadian campuses, looking into the forms and fitness of university governance. Their findings surprised few, describing, as they did, generally antiquated structures, relics of an earlier, paternalistic age. Their recommendations called for general reform, particularly in the direction of greater participation by faculty in the deliberative and legislative processes of university government.[65]

Locally, these notions were very much in line with the position sketched by MUFA, in 1962. Understandably, Shaw and company were quite content to stand down, while McMaster considered the implications of Duff-Berdahl. Indeed, Shaw advised that a joint committee, representing the board, the senate, and the faculty, be struck to undertake the task. He went further to propose, quite specifically, that the chairman be a non-administrative member of faculty, appointed by the president in consultation with governors and senators. The senate concurred, unanimously.[66] By that point, even Thode was prepared to look at matters afresh. In July, he replied to a letter from a board member, who had speculated on the changes likely to follow from the Duff-Berdahl Report.

To C.M. Harding, he confided, "[W]e haven't paid enough attention to our 'anatomy' and 'physiology', or structure and communications." Starting to feel growing heat on this score, he confessed, "The President is in the middle of the various pressure groups and continually gets squashed."[67] He did not add that, with some rather large fish on the medical frying pan, this was a good time to garner some helpful political capital. Still, the thought might well have crossed his mind. Whatever the case, Thode established the Ad Hoc Senate-Faculty Committee on University Government in September 1966.[68] The governors were invited to participate, but thought a tripartite forum too ungainly for vigorous discussion. Instead, they elected three of their number to deliberate independently. They would liaise frequently with the larger, eleven-person body.[69] At Thode's personal request, the latter committee was chaired by one whose lack of empathy with red tape, bureaucracy, and all things administrative had long been the stuff of campus legend: the incisive, uninhibited Jack Kirkaldy. Clearly, Thode had no intention of playing puppet master. Thus, the stage was set for one of the most transformative, if tangled, exercises in McMaster's post-Baptist history. If time, space, and reader tolerance permitted, an entire book could be devoted to the *Kirkaldy Report*, given the many suggestions, spinoff committees, and debates it inspired. Within the thematic compass of this volume, however, only a few of its sundry aspects need be closely examined.

To simplify the infinitely complex, the report might best be interpreted as a call to co-operative devolution. Two closely related paths to this end were sketched. One involved promoting broad sharing in the formulation of university-wide policy and planning. The other focused on rationalizing McMaster's structure in order to establish clearly defined academic units that had more control over their immediate, internal affairs. In the words of the report, what was envisaged was "not a revolution but a readjustment."[70] The adjustments recommended, nonetheless, were far from trivial. Indeed, among the most persistent subtexts of the report was a strong desire to bridle freewheeling Harry Thode. To be sure, critiquing university power structures was all the rage throughout the Western world. Targets, triggers, and tensions, however, varied from place to place.

At McMaster, the particular *cause célèbre* of the moment was Thode's extensive deployment of discretionary authority in the founding of MUMC. Overtly or allusively, the Kirkaldy Committee harped on that episode as prime justification for its panoramic institutional review. Ever since adoption of Sasaki, Walker, and Associates' campus model, it was alleged, Thode and his privy council had slowly monopolized strategic planning. Meanwhile, the senate, the board, and the faculty were increasingly sidelined, relegated to no more than ratifying or implementing virtual *faits accomplis*. For Kirkaldy and company, nothing illustrated this state of affairs better than the process whereby medicine was brought to McMaster. "In the case of the Medical Complex," said the committee, "the centre of initiative in the President and the Principal [Evans] is clear."[71] There was, it should be underlined, no hint that Thode should be censured, let alone eased out of office. Respect for his ability and achievements, as well as his sincere commitment to the best interests of the university, as he saw them, was widely shared. At question, however, was a constitutional and academic structure that left definition of those interests to the discretion of a few, rather than the collective deliberation of the many. It was an antiquated system that had to go, not a dynamic president.

The first draft of Kirkaldy's report was put to the senate on 21 December 1966.[72] Debate over its many recommendations dragged on well into 1968. Along the way, two separate ad hoc committees were spawned to examine especially contentious issues. Reduced to its essence, however, the report pivoted around the basic assertion that there should be "greater faculty participation in university Government at all levels."[73] With one major exception, matters pertaining to structural reorganization were settled by July 1967. Thus, the combined Faculty of Arts and Science was dissolved, while University and Hamilton Colleges were disestablished, along with their chief officers, the principals. These steps were taken in the name of rationalizing tangled jurisdictions and cutting away a layer of administrative fat. If such were the intention, however, only the unsharpened edge of Occam's razor was applied.

Out of keeping with growing practice elsewhere, the simple grouping of departments into faculties, headed by deans, reporting to a single vice-president (academic) was not adopted. Instead, McMaster was reordered into three "divisions": Arts, Science, and Health Sciences. Each of these major units had its own vice-president (Salmon, Bourns, and Evans, respectively). These divisions would subsume faculties, led by deans, to whom department chairmen would report. Arts included faculties of humanities, social science, and business. The faculties of science and engineering fell under the Division of Science. Health Science was to be a single faculty, although it embraced both medicine and the School of Nursing. Theology, which included (but was not coterminous with) the Divinity College, constituted a notional seventh faculty.

Some, such as Martin Johns, thought this no great improvement over the previous structure. Indeed, he worried that it might endanger the interdisciplinary exchange, hitherto encouraged by unified arts and science.[74] Medicine's William Spaulding voiced similar concern about the balkanization a divisional system might promote.[75] Meanwhile, Thode argued the case for a single vice-presidential model, on the grounds of efficiency. For the moment, however, he was content to let a trial period be the guide to future reconsideration.[76] Thus, over some objections, the divisions were born.

In the context of a report that, in most ways, emphasized streamlining and the devolution of local authority to faculties, the push for a divisional system seems rather anomalous. Championing this arrangement in debate, Kirkaldy offered a number of creative, even Jesuitical, rationales. McMaster, he said, was different from other universities, rendering comparisons moot. Besides, three vice-presidents would bring a broader, more multidisciplinary perspective to executive discussion than any one voice could. Several other considerations were trotted out. However, the sharpest note he struck was also the most revealing. It concerned the purportedly privileged position of medicine.

The principal of that school, Kirkaldy told the senate, had been delegated all but complete authority over its every facet of development. In effect, John Evans was de facto vice-president in his realm. Therefore, he argued, the divisional scheme, with chief officers of equal status and power, was necessary to balance the structure.[77] As it turned out, the arrangement was short-lived. The very fact that it was ever sanctioned, however, hints at the degree of ambivalence medicine's arrival had inspired in some quarters. At any rate, the divisional scheme seems at odds with the urge to clarify university organization and devolve local operational authority on faculties. These latter emphases were certainly clear in other recommendations by the committee.

Thus, among other things, the report led to defined term limits for deans and chairmen, albeit not without considerable debate and revision. Here, it is instructive to note that, on this and other specific matters, opinion seldom divided strictly along unyielding lines of Old Guard versus Young Turk, or administrator versus faculty member. In the case of term limits, for example, at one point Bourns and Petch, two powerful administrators, found themselves sharply at odds.[78] Within a week, however, Bourns had joined hands with Johns to hammer out a widely supported compromise.[79] This was the way of things: no one seemed prepared to risk full-scale war. Years later, Kirkaldy recalled the civility that marked even the most heated debates. There were, he remembered, "isolated cabals and personal animosities" in play, as one might expect. Overriding these, however, was a common urge among competent people to solve shared problems.[80] Indeed, most of the structural changes recommended were set in place by mid-1967. One issue, however, did bring participants close to blood sport. It arose in connection with the committee's general desire to sway power away from the centre and toward the faculties.

For all that it promoted a divisional system, the Kirkaldy Committee placed an even higher premium on strengthening the six major faculties. For instance, it recommended that, in a reformed the senate, teaching members be apportioned to faculties, not divisions.[81] Further, it stated that each faculty should have a clear-cut deliberative structure, published bylaws, and strict rules of order. Such things ought to be required by the senate. That, however, was as far as the senatorial writ should run. "It is not for the Senate," said the committee, "to specify in detail the structure of Faculties, for their requirements are often quite different."[82] In some eyes, this permissive provision seemed fraught with danger. Historian John Trueman, acting dean of arts, fired off an apprehensive missive to Thode. It was vital, Trueman wrote, that rules and regulations not diverge much across campus, lest variation provide bulk kindling for the flames of student discontent.[83] As things fell out, he prophesied better than he could have imagined. Meanwhile, Thode was concerned on another score.

For some time, he had been working with MUFA toward a statement of procedures regarding appointment, tenure, and promotion, or what was known colloquially as "The Document." The prospect that separate faculties might adopt different criteria left Thode's ever-sensitive antenna all aquiver. By 1969, he was urging strenuously that faculties avoid pitfalls by working together to develop common bylaws on this flammable matter.[84] Alas, this was not to be, and the feared potholes later became explosive tank traps. This, however, was for the future. In 1967–68, an immediately divisive, campus-wide clash erupted, when the committee proposed that authority over graduate studies be decentralized.

Since its establishment in 1958, the Faculty of Graduate Studies had been led by a succession of strong, dynamic deans: Bourns, Duckworth, and Preston. As graduate work grew in scope to become McMaster's vanguard faculty, the prestige and power of its decanal overseer followed in train. By the mid-sixties, the incumbent was viewed, by some, as second only to the president in university-wide influence; the over-mighty hammer of Thode.[85] Devout devolvers, the Kirkaldy Committee sought to change this. Initially, it recommended that the Faculty of Graduate Studies be abolished and replaced by a senate oversight board. True responsibility and initiative should increasingly be transferred to the faculties.[86] These proposals sparked a firestorm of considerable magnitude, which is unsurprising, given that they touched on McMaster's central nervous system.

Such heat was generated that the committee returned with a milder set of resolutions in July 1967. In reformulated terms, Kirkaldy proposed "that the Faculties be accorded the power to deliberate on any matter connected with Graduate Studies," while a senate graduate council, representative of those faculties, be formed to deal with broader university policy.[87] The modifications were too slight, however, to mollify opinion splintered over a broad spectrum of issues, such as quality control, the equitable distribution of resources, and the need for reform, itself. With discussion grinding to an abrasive halt in February, the senate appointed a special committee, under Dennis Shaw, to tackle these thorny matters.

The Shaw Committee deliberated throughout the winter and spring of 1968.[88] Occasionally, members surfaced for air, even as they were deluged by an ocean of briefs. No two memoranda were quite the same. Nor did views reflect simple disciplinary or faculty allegiances. Thus, geology and political science echoed one another in decrying the plight of "have-not" departments, under current conditions. History was for, but religious studies was against, Kirkaldy's recommendations. Meanwhile, the heavyweights, chemistry and physics, disagreed as to how best to proceed.[89] In the final analysis, Shaw's group fashioned an acceptable compromise.

They agreed that reform was necessary, given rapid growth since 1958 and the advent of medicine, but insisted on measured, rather than wholesale, change. Thus, Shaw recommended that the Faculty of Graduate Studies be abolished and replaced by a graduate council. The council would be answerable to the senate, which, would retain final authority over all matters pertaining to graduate work. Faculties were to have local councils with substantial day-to-day authority, but not the greater autonomy envisaged by Kirkaldy. The dean would remain and have considerable influence, as chairman of graduate council and an ex officio member of faculty-level committees. However, Shaw advised that the dean be limited to a five-year term and have no executive power over appointments or budgets. Above all, it was argued that that officer should report to divisional heads and "not have the ear of the president."[90] Under modestly revised terms of the report, the School of Graduate Studies and graduate council came into being in June 1969. After prolonged gestation and intense labour, organizational rebirth had been achieved, but not, as will be seen, without further complications and aftershocks. Meanwhile, structural change was only one aspect of the Kirkaldy exercise. Another touched on the delicate matter of power.

In striving to foster "greater faculty participation in University Government at all levels," the committee put several suggestions to the senate in
July 1967. Among these, two were of paramount import. One advocated
that, henceforth, elected faculty members should form a majority on the senate. Intimately tied to this was the prescription that the senate should have
the right to recommend "on all matters of interest to the University."[91] When
these suggestions were linked with an assertion that a senate committee on
academic policy should review all proposals, from every quarter, regarding new projects, programs, schools, faculties, or facilities "long in advance
of implementation," implications were resoundingly clear: transformative
end-runs, such as Thode had engineered regarding medicine, were to be
taboo.[92] Consciously or not, the committee was appealing to the precept of
ancient constitutional vintage: that which touches all should be approved
by all. During Canada's hour of "participatory democracy," this notion had
great purchase, even at tradition-laden McMaster. Accordingly, the committee called for "a new concept of executive leadership" – one that would
embrace the idea of "dynamic balance" among the deliberative and legislative authorities on campus.[93]

In this regard, the committee sought not to emasculate either the president or the board but to draw them into co-operative fellowship with the
senate and the faculty. The governors, for instance, were to be fewer in number and representative of broader community interests, rather than those
of big business. Yet, they were not to be stripped of final authority over the
purse, or other things that fell under their accustomed purview. They were,
however, asked to accept an exchange of six members each between the
board and the senate, so as to promote mutual understanding and integration in decision-making. It was thought that this precedent might lead to the
formation of regular, joint board-senate committees: a step that could only
stabilize and enhance the "dynamic balance." Such, in fact, proved to be the
case, and must stand as one of the most enduring, effective, and creative legacies of the *Kirkaldy Report*.[94]

For its part, the board committee supported all the reforms outlined above,
save only proposals concerning student representation. The latter issue took
less-than-wholly-collegial debate to resolve, as shall be seen. Meanwhile, the
precise powers of the president were studiously left undefined. Undoubtedly,
the committee thought that its sundry recommendations had, at the very
least, greatly circumscribed the prerogatives of that office. Indeed, they had;
just at the moment when growing fiscal constraint left Thode yearning for
maximum freedom to manoeuvre. Be that as it may, the revised McMaster
Act came into effect in 1969.

On one level, this entire exercise in restructuring testified to the all-but-inevitable fragmentation of an expansive, rapidly changing university. Thode's paradigm of a tightly interwoven and fully balanced research-driven institution was under strain. Militating against it were a number of factors, such as departmental jealousies, an explosion of disciplinary sub-specializations, and, most importantly, the advent of government parsimony at a point when graduate work and research intensity were just beginning to flower in arts. Significantly, however, central elements of the Thodean ethos were anchored by roots too deep to dislodge. Indeed, new tendrils of inter-disciplinary and collegial exchange were taking shape, even as the Kirkaldy debates went on. Foremost among these were the Faculty Club and the senior sciences' lounge.

While fragmentation was real enough, veterans of the era still wistfully recall the powerful counteraction provided by these two integrative melting pots.[95] Denizens of today's "commuter university" will be unfamiliar with the depth and range of cross-departmental ties forged therein. As early as 1961, Herb Armstrong had lobbied hard for an after-hours faculty rendezvous, as he sought to preserve something of the small-college feel.[96] Deans Mel Preston an R.P. Graham continued to press the case, as the sixties rolled on.[97] Jack Kirkaldy and numberless faculty echoed the call.[98] In this, it appears, administration and MUFA were like-minded. For a time, Wentworth House served as a temporary substitute; but as a shared facility, it lacked the privacy amid which faculty member and administrator could mingle, let their hair down, and (no ranks in the mess) speak freely of global insights or hot issues. Thode sympathized, but the problem was finding an appropriately commodious space. Finally, he and Eugene Combs brokered an arrangement whereby Alumni Hall was transformed, much to the chagrin of undergraduates who treasured their "Buttery," into a gracefully appointed faculty refuge. With more-than-adequate cuisine, an affordable "daily double," and a rafters-full "happy hour," the club blossomed.

Yet, it was so much more than a convenient watering hole. Rather, the institution served as something approaching an informal university moot. As survivors warmly recall, it was a lively place of learning, as well as relaxation. At this remove, it is impossible to say how many intellectual light bulbs flared incandescent, as philosopher held forth on scientific point, or physicist asked historian probing questions, completely but illuminatingly, outside the box. As well, one wonders how many tangled issues, left unresolved in the senate, were quietly resolved in the absence of rules of order, as administrator and faculty champion spoke at ease. Meanwhile, laboratory veterans extol the same qualities in remembrance of the senior science lounge. Strategically placed at the crossroads of departments, it served up interdisciplinary sparkle, alongside decent coffee. Many a collaborative project was hatched within its precincts, while senior students were afforded the chance to chat at length with the likes of a Brockhouse or Gillespie, international figures in their fields.[99] In their own way, both lounge and club served a higher purpose during an era of tight money, tough choices, and structural change. Still, all was not cakes and ale.

Reform robbed Thode of several prerogative cards, but he retained one trump ace, tucked tightly up his discretionary sleeve. In August 1970, speaking candidly to his executive council, Thode noted that, in a strict sense, the university had no formally constituted budget committee. To be sure, the governors had the final say on fiscal matters, but the actual formulation of financial proposals had traditionally been done by the president and a chosen few executives. Since 1968, those few had included the new divisional vice-presidents. To them, Thode made it clear that the president's executive would continue to fulfill that budgetary function for the foreseeable future.[100] He raised the point because MUFA, seeking better pension arrangements and salary increases, had put increasing pressure on him for full disclosure of university finances. In the absence complete information, the association held that it could not negotiate its annual briefs effectively.[101] As Queen's Park began to tighten purse strings, however, Thode was determined to retain sufficient executive agility to facilitate rapid response to shifting trends. Indeed, in the same August meeting, he asked his vice-presidents to frame their budget requests in such a way as to allow 4.8 per cent of the total BIU grant to be set aside for the president's discretionary fund. Hitherto, that slice had been only 1 per cent of the whole.

The suggestion provoked an immediate cabinet uproar. Evans, speaking for medicine, and William Hellmuth, Salmon's successor as vice-president of arts, objected strenuously to the proposed hike. The physician questioned the wisdom of pouring more resources into graduate studies on the grounds that a rise in MD enrolment would likely create higher BIU income. Hellmuth resented the money being drained off annually to support under-subscribed engineering, while graduate work in arts was just getting off the ground. This was a theme to which he would return frequently, during the months and years that followed.[102] For the moment, he and Evans firmly opposed any further "tax" on divisional budgets in the form of a larger presidential discretionary fund.[103] Things were heating up again, but now within the higher executive of the university. Moreover, the atmosphere grew warmer in short order.

While they were made privy to decisions regarding academic budgeting, even vice-presidents were not regularly consulted on non-academic spending. As faculty salary requests rose, only to be scaled down, Thode's lieutenants were placed in an increasingly awkward position. In March 1971, the indisputably loyal Bourns wrote forcefully to Thode. How, he asked, could he defend a large increase in non-academic expenditure to his division, when staff salary increases fell far below MUFA requests? The proliferation of administrative appointments and sharp rise in spending on sport might well be justified. Yet, how was he to explain this to colleagues in the trenches, unless he was acquainted with all budgetary figures and rationales early on? He was expecting a vote of no confidence, as soon as he met with faculty.[104] A similar missile from Hellmuth crossed Thode's desk a month later. He, too, inquired how he could be expected to defend a budget to his division, when the first glimpse of non-academic figures he got came at the governors' meeting.[105] Meanwhile, MUFA was pressing hard for full disclosure and a participatory voice in the budget process.[106] If ever a chess player needed a clever gambit at a critical moment, it was Thode. Not for the first or last time, steady Mike Hedden, vice-president (administrative), had a useful one in hand.

Having quietly observed a vise closing on his president, Hedden suggested that one jaw might tactfully be loosened. Little, he granted, could sensibly or wisely be done to fend off vice-presidential pressure, but a compromise with MUFA seemed feasible; one that yielded a little, but not too much, ground. Thus, he suggested that Thode form an advisory body, representative of several groups, to meet with the president's executive committee, at select points, during the budgetary process. "If you did this in the very near future," Hedden advised, "it might have the effect of blunting the current press on the part of the Faculty Association for direct representation on the Board's Finance Committee or other bodies."[107] Taking the hint, Thode approached the senate.

He explained that, as fiscal restraint was likely to persist, difficult choices were in the offing. "Close management," and trade-offs would be necessary to sustain excellence. Under such circumstances, he continued, broad dialogue and clear communication with all constituencies were essential. He, therefore, requested that a committee of two faculty and two student senators (one undergraduate and one graduate) be struck to join with the vice-presidents in advising his office on financial matters. The members of this body, said Thode, should also recommend on the release of budget information to the university community and, if necessary, discuss these matters with their respective constituencies. In this fashion, the President's Budget

Advisory Committee (PBAC) was born. Hedden was appointed to chair the new body, so as to avoid committing Thode to any of its recommendations.[108] If anyone, however, thought that creation of the PBAC signalled Thode's readiness to surrender all discretionary authority, they were mistaken. He had simply moved pawn to king's bishop, four.

The first meeting of the PBAC was scheduled for December 1971. A month earlier, the president's executive group walked through a preliminary draft of the next budget. As it did; some strategizing transpired. Despite provincial penny-pinching, McMaster had a revenue surplus, rather than the deficit prophesied the year before. Thode suggested that this be explained as the result of a failure to find adequate candidates to fill various planned faculty posts. There was truth in this. Still, a statement can be true without revealing all. Thus, a surviving committee minute records, "It was agreed that we should avoid the use of terms such as 'contingency' and 'reserve' in discussions with the PBAC." Further, it was deemed appropriate that "while the Vice-Presidents will defend their overall proposed staff increases before the PBAC; they will need to justify their priorities for specific positions in specific disciplines only to the President."[109] Meanwhile, in order to assuage MUFA, the association was invited to send a representative to the first and last meetings of the advisory committee, each year, so as to keep its members better informed concerning budgetary matters.[110] Under these conditions, the PBAC continued to meet for many years to come. It remained, however, a largely token, peripheral body; purely "advisory," in the most literal sense. A glance behind the fiscal veil is afforded by minutes of the 1972 president's executive committee.

In November of that year, Bourns, now president, released more than $400,000 for discretionary spending to his vice-presidents. He emphasized strongly, however, that they spend it all, "with no carry over as in previous years." This directive indicates that, government squeeze and local sackclothed hand-wringing notwithstanding, prudent management had left McMaster with cash in hand at the end of recent fiscal accountings. By design, however, these surpluses were not matters of public knowledge. As one member of the executive explained, Thode had decided not to display them, but had shunted the money into special accounts, such as the pension fund, where they were recoverable at will. The committee, then, agreed to follow precedent. The budget to be presented to the PBAC would stop at page 12. Accumulated surpluses would appear on page 13 and be for the board's eyes only. Finally, the presidential body, in camera, concluded that the advisory group should be given no indication of the tolerable salary increase limits for the year and continued, "but they will know that the final decision on this is not theirs to make."[111]

Obviously, the PBAC was not fully in the know. While faculty paladins might regard such behaviour as duplicitous, it needs be remembered that pressure from Queen's Park for financial responsibility and greater account-ability were very real. To Thode and Bourns, manoeuvring room for pro-gram and capital projects was vital to the university's long-term well-being. Thus, surpluses could not be eaten up by escalating salary demands, but had to be guarded and carefully deployed. Propriety, in such instances, resides in the eyes of beholders.

Clearly, while he might have been hobbled by Kirkaldy, Thode had no intention of being gelded. To be sure, he shared much information with vice-presidents, some with the PBAC, and a little with MUFA, but he retained significant prerogatives in the vital budget process. It is unclear how much year-to-year discretionary funding remained in the president's office. Yet, remain it did, as an irate 1973 note from science dean Dennis McCalla to (by then) President Bourns makes clear.[112] Indeed, although the reforms launched in 1966 bore much fruit, they also left loopholes through which Thode could wiggle. Meanwhile, for reasons at least partially identified by Trueman, those same reforms stirred unrest in another university constitu-ency: the students.

8

Student Moments

In their sterling volume, *Student Days,* C.M. Johnston and John Weaver admirably captured all the colour, texture, customs, and variety of student life in the years under review. From the heroics of Russ Jackson to tomato fights; from musical fashions to the theatrical sparkle of Martin Short, Eugene Levy, Dave Thomas, and "ghostbuster" Ivan Reitman, Johnston and Weaver assembled a rich collage that one ray the more could scarce improve. Clearly charted, as well, is the evolution of student clubs and government; from the fifties through the more crowded period beyond.[1] It would be both foolish and derivative to retrace, here, that which they have so ably done. Moreover, this would be out of keeping with the thematic focus of the present volume, which is on the university as an evolving whole, rather than any one of its individual constituencies.

That said, students of the late sixties occasionally sought greater power to shape the evolving university than had been enjoyed by their predecessors. To a point, their importance as a variable in the complex McMaster equation rose. This must be assessed. Still, one needs be cautious when generalizing about this element in the campus mix. Thus, a few (eminently debatable) observations seem in order, so that the attitudes, actions, and influence of turn-of-the-decade students (advisedly plural) might be better understood.

In this regard, the term *student body* offers little help in analyzing late-twentieth-century McMaster. It implies a general cohesion of identity and shared values that might have existed on Whidden's intimate campus, in terms of nationality, ethnicity, class, race, and broadly Protestant (although no longer overwhelmingly Baptist) faith. By the mid-sixties, however, these conditions no longer pertained. Secularization and the "boom" had brought legions of newcomers to campus. Many were first-in-the-family candidates, frequently representative of the prospering and ethnically diverse working and lower-middle classes. As well, an increasing proportion hailed from foreign climes, attracted by McMaster's growing reputation in science, engineering, and graduate work. Britons and Americans were most obviously in evidence, but Southeast Asians and Chinese constituted an increasingly vigorous minority. Many among the latter were drawn to the growing professional schools on campus. Growth, in short, had entailed enrichment born of diversity; but it also encouraged social, cultural, and intellectual fragmentation. Symbolic of this, the last university-wide vestige of McMaster's confessional heritage was quietly laid to rest in 1968, when formal chapel break was abolished in order to simplify daily timetabling.[2] Splintering was spurred by other factors, as well.

The rapid growth of graduate and part-time numbers added substantial groups, with markedly different identities and interests, to a traditionally undergraduate population. As noted, by the mid-sixties, off-campus and nighttime enrolment matched or exceeded that of the day-student cadre. In general, part-timers were older and more settled than the daytime peers they rarely met. The graduate corps, meanwhile, constituted a continuously rising percentage of the full-time student complement. Yet, despite occasional tensions with administration, this element shared more in the ethos of faculty than that of undergraduates.

It must also be remembered that, while new residence facilities were added, McMaster remained a predominantly commuter campus. The greatest number of students lived in or near Hamilton itself. Still others, for whom Brock was, as yet, an unproven entity, drove daily from as far away as St. Catharines, Dunnville, and sundry points of the Niagara catch basin.[3] In like manner, Bronte, Burlington, and other north-shore dwellers followed suit. For such people, home, family, and other pre-university bonds had as much or more relevance as campus life.[4] Finally, there was the sheer question of size. As the total university population ballooned, so depersonalization blossomed, not only among professors and students but among students, themselves. All told, it became ever-more appropriate to speak of distinct bodies of students, rather than *the* student body.

Under these circumstances, sixties' nostalgia notwithstanding, a broad-based, sustained, and coherent "student movement" stood less chance of taking shape at Aquarian McMaster than it had during the pre-1957 period. Students of the later era were simply too many, too diverse, and too self-consciously divided for long-term solidarity to flower. To say this, moreover, is not blithely to interpret but faithfully to replicate testimony of the hour. Consider, for example, a January 1970 *Silhouette* article. Jack Stagg, a third-year history candidate, had just been elected president of the MSU.

The paper nodded in pundit-like approval. Stagg's victory at the polls put a representative from residence in the presidential chair for the first time in six years; thus ending a long monopoly by "Wentworth House Boys." The editor thought this healthy, since a fresh perspective would be brought to bear. After all, the writer continued, the student population was clearly segregated into "quite distinct segments": Wentworth House arts activists, residence dwellers, engineer-scientists, and "jocks from the palace."[5] While too simplified, this analysis captured something of the complex fragmentation that often bedevilled those who sought to rally departmental, let alone campus-wide, student support behind this or that cause. Indeed, student divisiveness was as real and widely acknowledged as student activism. Examples of these countervailing forces abound during the period. A few will suffice by way of illustration.

Early in 1969, Eugene Levy was seeking material for his weekly *Silhouette* column, "The Mouse That Roars." When interviewed about the quality of student relationships on campus, the *Sil's* managing editor offered a frank, if elitist, response. "Stupid question," said the habitué of Wentworth House. "McMaster's social life is, of course, ridiculously terrible due to the lunch bucket pigs from Hamilton who go here." Indeed, he opined, "[t]he only way to enjoy yourself is to avoid them." That, he concluded, "leaves you about ten possible friends."[6] Evidently, there were classes and masses on the university's green and pleasant lands. The masses, however, that aforementioned brown-bag herd, were not always prepared to back the classes when the latter called for support in building a variously defined New Jerusalem. Here, an episode in the annals of the Department of History is instructive.

In October 1969, the left-leaning history society issued a stinging indictment of their home department. Leaders of the group called attention to the wall colour on the sixth floor of Arts I: a drab grey. This hue, they proclaimed, bespoke the "intellectual necrophilia" of a professoriate bent on the "lobotomization" of students. "Value, critical thought, and compassion," they railed, "have no place in the arid sterility of a historical desert separated from society by those ominous grey walls." Lavishing praise on Mel Watkins' "Waffle" critique of Canadian life, they called for demolition of a fact foundry dedicated to preserving the liberal-capitalist order.[7] In microcosm, they chanted a chorus phrased by the New Left on campuses across the nation. Like the twelve-tone, experimental music of Arnold Schoenberg and his heirs, these incantations resonated for some, while others found them garbled and inchoate. Devotees wrote off lack of enthusiasm to indifference among the untutored. Such was certainly the tendency of sixth-floor reformers who noted that, while apathy was common at McMaster, history was its operational GHQ.[8] This particular charge was a treasured rhetorical gambit of ripe vintage.

Indeed, one would be hard-pressed to read every edition of the *Silhouette*, from 1957 through 1987, and not find yearly moaning about apathy. This was one of the great constants of discourse in the student journal. Furthermore, a word count would, undoubtedly, reveal that the term was more frequently in evidence after, rather than before, the mid-sixties. Yet, the later period is remembered as the high tide of student activism. A paradox, therefore, seems to arise. The anomaly, however, is more apparent than real. Full engagement in campus, civic, provincial, or national affairs was ever the preoccupation of the few, and even they are normally of diverse opinion. Meanwhile, "apathy," itself, is often mistaken for a clash of priorities. This, at least, was the riposte offered by one history student to peers mobilizing to repaint departmental walls.

Honours history candidate Annette van Pypen was "angry with the Wentworth House Clique," according to whom campus was divided into progressive activists and the "Apathy Club." For the record, she noted that she was a member of the university choir, its tour committee, and practised with the judo club twice a week, while also getting her assignments and reading done on time. Yet, van Pypen snarled, "because I'm not worrying my ass off about campus politics, I'm apathetic." Her central concern, she continued, was the same as that of most students: completing her degree. "My suggestion to you Wentworth House habitués," she thundered, "is to look beyond the canvas covered walls of the Coffee Shop and realize that the rest of us out here are just as concerned as you are about the state of affairs, we just aren't so goddamned vocal."[9]

In more diplomatic language, historian Paul Fritz observed, "McMaster students are rather conservative, but this is an entirely different matter from being apathetic." Enlarging on this view, religion's Ed Sanders insisted that the candidates he encountered were far from indifferent about things that mattered to them, including issues of social justice. "It may be," he went on, "that students here are not so interested in campus politics as are others at other universities, but I don't think this makes them apathetic."[10] For her part, a fourth-year honours psychology major argued that the whole picture of campus was skewed by the tendency of the *Silhouette* to engage with social science and humanities types, while ignoring science students, whenever controversial issues arose.[11]

Collectively, Fritz, Sanders, and van Pypen probably best caught the spirit of the hour. McMaster students were alert to questions of the moment, but tended to be as diverse in opinion as they were in background. As well, they were broadly conservative in the sense of prizing orderly debate over all-out confrontation. This was clear in their reactions to the 1969 torching of computer facilities at Sir George Williams University. Of the many interviewed about the incident by Levy, most sympathized with Montreal peers, as far as purported racial discrimination was concerned. None, however, approved a resort to violence against property or persons. The editor of the *Silhouette* concurred. He was all for student power, but in this case, he wrote, "You take them all – all 96 of them – line them up against a wall and calmly shoot the bastards – one by one."[12] While scarcely the stuff of Fleet Street journalism, these editorial musings did, at least, have the virtue of clarity.

Backed to the wall and put to the question, the historian (gun-to-head) might venture that this Red Tory–cum–social democratic streak was widespread among McMaster students of the day. Yet, while widely variegated, often reticent, and hard to mobilize, on occasion some of them did raise their voices in sufficient number to affect the course of departmental or university history. Multi-faceted McMaster might not have produced a concerted student movement, but it did experience some significant student moments.

A clear line separates student commentary, before and after 1967. Prior to that year, in the main, substantive discussion and debate had been directed outwards: at pre-Castro Cuba, Soviet repression in Hungary, Cold War geopoliticking, cancellation of the Avro Arrow, nuclear arms testing, and the war in Vietnam. McMaster students of the 1950s and early sixties were far from taciturn, ill-informed, or unconcerned about the world beyond Cootes Paradise.[13] Insofar as broadsides were loosed inwards, they tended to be exchanged between those engaged in the annual extracurricular round and those indifferent to jazz, art, film, and council elections. Particularly heated salvoes were traded regularly over hallowed but controversial orientation rituals. After 1967, by contrast, student discourse focused increasingly on the fundamental nature of McMaster, itself. One's stance on issues related to the state of the university became the decisive litmus test whereby the "active" took measure of the "apathetic," and vice versa. Several things contributed to this shift.

In 1964, the Berkeley "Free Speech Movement" identified the contemporary university as a soulless servant of modern, technocratic society, with all its many inequalities. Ceaselessly replicating the social order it served, the academy had forfeited its vital role as disinterested critic in exchange for financial largesse doled out by the military-industrial complex. Reform of society necessitated rethinking of the purpose and governance of the university.[14] By the mid-sixties, this stream of thought found both student and faculty adherents on every North American campus. The Canadian version, however, added a tincture of growingly strident anti-Americanism. Fed in part by mounting opposition to the Vietnam War, this mood drew further fuel from talk of a "branch-plant" economic takeover and consequent cultural absorption by Uncle Sam. George Grant's bestselling *Lament for a Nation* (1965) adroitly tapped into this sentiment. Four years later, two Carleton professors, Robin Mathews and James Steele, gave more specific focus to this animus by targeting the tide of American professors that had swamped Canadian campuses.[15] Government clampdowns on higher educational funding merely added to tensions by the decade's end. Meanwhile, as numbers soared, questions as to the quality of ever-more impersonal, three-year-degree education multiplied.[16] So, too, did student demand for a voice at the centres of power.[17] This common tinder took flame at various Canadian universities, but the timing, proximate causes, and outcomes of these conflagrations differed, often considerably, from place to place.[18] At McMaster, the match was ignited by events of 1967 as the Grady affair and the *Kirkaldy Report* caught segments of student attention.

As noted, the internecine battle that exploded among political scientists, in February 1967, involved a great deal more than the release of contractual instructor, Donald J. Grady. Rather, the gentleman in question was merely symbolic of a chasm in the department, born of deep-seated ideological, pedagogical, and personal differences of the most vitriolic sort. In general, battle lines were drawn between quantifiers and descriptive scholars. This divide tended to pit younger faculty against those longer-established. For added bite, nationalism was injected into the fray, as the cry for more Canadian content and professors was raised. Almost equal in number, the feuding parties introduced the department to a fuller understanding of the word *paralysis*. Evangelists, in both camps, were wont to take their case to students.

At first, cultivation of the student constituency was restricted to classroom diatribes for or against new methodologies. In this tug of war, Grady, with the look and quiet charm of an academic Woody Allen, won a considerable student following. When his contract was not renewed, both undergraduate and graduate acolytes demanded an explanation, quick redress, and a voice in the matter. Sparks flew upward as the affair dragged on well into 1968, with all disputants seeking to mobilize student support across disciplinary boundaries. Indeed, it would be a student, not a faculty member, who declaimed that social science, as a whole, was becoming the stepchild of the university.[19] Meanwhile, the *Kirkaldy Report* inadvertently poured a goodly dose of gasoline on this localized blaze.

Duff and Berdahl had recommended greater faculty representation, but had said little about student participation in academic governance. Kirkaldy and company, by contrast, gave the latter constituency considerably more attention. Indeed, their recommendations concerning that estate prompted hotter debate, in broader quarters, for a longer period, than did any other item on their agenda. From the outset, they concluded that there "should be increasing reference to student views in university planning, and [that] their services in an advisory capacity must be sought." In its initial report, the committee held that students should be "voting members of relevant Senate committees, but [that] direct membership on the Senate was unnecessary." Kirkaldy also strongly suggested that the office of vice-president (student affairs) be created to liaise with undergraduate and graduate governing bodies and coordinate all matters affecting everything from discipline to activities and aid programs.[20] Clearly, while cognizant of the student estate, the committee's emphasis was on improving communication and holding counsel, rather than sharing real power, with perceived birds of passage. Excitable members of this avian flock were quick to reject what they regarded as little more than veiled paternalism and quicker, still, to link committee attitudes with the ongoing Grady affair.

February 1967 witnessed a spate of *Silhouette* articles from the pens of political science majors disgruntled with McMaster's conservative ways. John G. Ruggie, for example, drew a direct parallel between ideals born of the Berkeley experience and those of young faculty and progressive students who championed new methods of teaching, grading, and research – most notably in social science. Their common opponent, he declared, was an administration, cloaked in "secrecy and dishonesty" that barred younger instructors and students alike from the policy-making process. Drastic change was required, across the whole university.[21] In a variation on this theme, two of Ruggie's classmates chimed in, a week later.

With gusto, they denounced the *Kirkaldy Report*. Changing McMaster's academic configuration was all well and good, they proclaimed, but the report skirted the core issue. What was most required, in their view, was "a revamping of the power structure within the community itself." Citing the disregard of student pressure in the Grady case, they argued for significant, formal student representation, especially at the departmental level. Kirkaldy, they ventured, offered little substantive promise on that score.[22] As grumbling of this sort mounted, elected leaders of student government joined in, lest they and their organizations be sidelined.

On 8 March 1967, the senate was presented with a joint statement issued by the MSU, GSA, and the Student Representative Assembly (SRA). In spirit, it was vintage Berkeley. The associations accepted several of Kirkaldy's chief proposals on structural reform, then went leagues further. Undergraduates and graduates, along with faculty, should serve on "all universities committees." Joint faculty-student bodies should be formed at the departmental level, along the lines of a voluntary experiment already undertaken in physics, but adapted to the needs of differing units. Thereby, it was averred, many local problems could be resolved before blossoming into a campus-wide nightmare. Waxing more truly radical, signatories then declared that, henceforth, the senate should comprise one-third each of teaching faculty, administrative representatives, and students. The latter constituency would be divided equally into undergraduate and graduate members. This, it was argued, was the only route toward forging a genuine "community of scholars" and obliterating the "we-they" discourse that currently polluted campus. In the same vein, the petitioners urged that the senate abandon the idea of appointing a vice-president (student affairs). No doubt, they conceded, the notion was well-intended. Even so, it implied a "latent paternalism" in that perpetuated a concept of the student as a passive entity "to be acted upon." Far better, they suggested, that oversight be left in the hands of an appropriate senate body, since this encouraged direct exchange with students, while cutting out a potentially dictatorial middleman.[23]

Needless to say, the chamber was unusually warm, when the senate greeted student petitioners at a special session on 15 March. Donald Polsuns (GSA) and Lachlan MacLaughlan (MSU), however, acquitted themselves well in the face of sometimes barbed questioning. For example, Hedden and Dean Evans interjected that membership on the senate, with its heavy committee burden, could be the undoing of even the best degree candidate. In reply, MacLaughlan pointed out that MSU presidents had taken highly prestigious academic prizes over the last two years; in one case, the governor-general's medal. Meanwhile, Polsuns fenced with Kirkaldy. The latter, in a combative mood, was bent on defending the proposed office of vice-president (student affairs). He, therefore, submitted that, since students thought that officer likely to be autocratic and, given that vice-presidents held authority delegated by the president, it followed that they believed the president to be a dictator, too.

Unfazed, Polsuns answered that no such feelings were harboured about Dr Thode. Instead, he continued, it was those in secondary positions of power who seemed most jealous of their prerogatives. At that juncture, Goldwin French intervened, noting that, historically, Polsuns was essentially correct about governance at McMaster. It had traditionally been a "benevolent autocracy," but was now in the process of reform. Thus, immediate confrontation was defused.[24] Polsuns and MacLaughlan had persuaded few senators on every score, but they had given them pause to reconsider details of Kirkaldy's report.

This became evident on 12 April, when the senate reconvened in camera. Kirkaldy said the committee had reviewed student suggestions and, by majority vote, rejected them. The senate's minutes then synopsized what was described politely as an "active discussion." Among others, Senator H.G. Chappell, a lawyer, took sharp issue with Kirkaldy, arguing that Polsuns and MacLaughlan had presented a good brief in able fashion. Students, he declared had "every right to direct representation in university bodies." Others warned that, to create the new office of vice-president (student affairs) so abruptly might spark precisely the campus outbreak they were seeking to avoid. Deans Bourns, Melling, and Hodgins each pointed to the upheaval that could arise were the senate to authorize this office, without first securing the active support of student government. Accordingly, matters concerning students were referred back to Kirkaldy's group, once again.[25]

By May, a revised edition of the report clung to the call for a vice-president, but gave way on the matter of direct student representation in the senate. Now, it was proposed that three students, two undergraduates and one graduate, be elected. It was underscored, however, that these seats not be assigned to delegates of student government but to representatives of the new divisions. Furthermore, the committee stipulated that candidates be beyond their first year and scholars in good standing.[26] Given that student participation was one of only a few points separating the board and Kirkaldy committees, the senate decided to implement the major proposals for structural reform, as of May 1967. They were to be phased in gradually, "at the discretion of the president." The thorny issue of student representation was set aside for separate consideration.[27] This was a wise move, since such discussion proved prickly, indeed.

On 8 October 1967, electricity arced across the senate floor. Dean Preston flipped the switch by declaring, "[S]tudents had nothing to contribute as members of the Senate or the Board of Governors." Of course, their views on matters that affected them directly, such as food, could and should be heard. As a member of the board committee, however, he found their case for direct representation "inadequate," and "the proposals for student membership to be forms of appeasement to the threat of student activism." At this juncture, Kirkaldy leaped into the fray; suddenly a staunch champion of student representation. A strong-minded but reasonable man, the engineer had rethought his earlier stance, in the light of recent discussion.

To Preston, he replied that only students could present the student perspective. There was no viable substitute. Intermediaries would inevitably offer mere interpretation, rather than the authentic voice. Besides, he continued, his committee was recommending only three student seats, and those would be open solely to academically responsible candidates. To be sure, the odd troublemaker might be elected, but "trouble was not always negative." Senators Kamin, French, and Salmon agreed, noting that the senate had a brief moment to shape student representation, before capitulating to greater pressure later. In the end, there was little opposition to the admission of students senators. The sharp differences arose around qualifications for election. Thode called a straw vote. Kirkaldy's three-seat proposal was approved by a wide margin. That left questions as to eligibility and which senate, faculty, and department committees should be open to students, up in the air. Since faculties were still deliberating their individual bylaws, there was time to study these delicate issues. Thus, a special committee, with historian Harry Turner in the chair, was struck to recommend on these matters. Meanwhile, the *Kirkaldy Report* was released to the general McMaster community.[28] Some among the latter were not amused.

Indeed, leaders of student government were swift to react. The language of the *Kirkaldy Report* was clear: student members of the senate were to be representatives of the general population, not delegates of student councils. The SRA countered that, on the crucial student affairs committee, undergraduate members be appointed by and be fully responsible to the SRA. In addition, they requested student parity in membership of that body. Going further, they demanded that all senate committees be open to all members of the university. Seeking a hearing, they threatened a boycott of various committees to which students had already been appointed, should senators decline to meet with them. Simultaneously, the Graduate Student Association sent word that it desired reserved seats on the proposed graduate council. For its part, the senate was quite willing to meet with delegates of both groups. Some members, however, such as Thode and Bourns, balked at the idea open committee meetings. Such occasions, they argued, could provide copious cannon fodder for the media and faculty, even before matters came to the senate floor.[29]

Contrary to expectations, the tone of the senate's meeting with SRA and GSA delegates proved to be lively, but cordial. Undergraduate representatives went so far as to praise the Kirkaldy recommendations as a "good start" toward founding a more collegial community at McMaster. While holding firm to the quest for open meetings and delegate status for student senators, they proclaimed pride in their university and a strong desire to help reconstruct it. Graduate spokesman David Guy also sounded a conciliatory note. Graduate candidates, he declared, sought a fair say in matters that affected them. This involved significant representation on senate and presidential committees. However, when quizzed by Craig McIvor as to whether student power meant student control, Guy and his undergraduate colleagues forswore any such syndicalist intentions. All that was sought, they said, was one-third of the senate seats, a number proportionally far lower than the actual student constituency, itself. As for open meetings, Guy reasoned that people tended to accept decisions once they understood the processes and rationales that led to them. J.E.L. Graham opined that students seemed to be opting for a policy of gradualism in the reform of governance. Guy confirmed this, saying that, in the absence of any model, students were setting forth an ideal, but were willing to examine each issue on its merits. No doubt relieved by this apparent collegiality, the senate voted to refer the delegates' suggestions to the Turner Committee.[30] Such equanimity as existed, however, was soon shattered.

Reporting in May 1968, Turner authored a searching, root-and-branch analysis of current discontent at universities nationwide. The vast majority of students, he stated, were of moderate, liberal disposition and content with the status quo. On every campus, however, a small minority were bent on radical change. It was tempting, therefore, to dismiss them as unrepresentative, but to do so, Turner argued, would be a grave mistake. They were not an aberrant element, doomed to fade. Rather, they were likely to increase, as older customs and traditions steadily eroded. Rootless and alienated, they gravitated to universities, as some people did to religion, in search of a central purpose by which their lives might be ordered. In their eyes, the academy was dominated by the "Establishment," which must be fought, were society, itself, to be salvaged. Given that they represented no passing phenomenon, the university had to come to terms with them. They were not, however, all alike.

Turner and his committee colleagues distinguished between two broad activist types at McMaster. One group they dubbed the "democrats." These people, although anxious for a voice, were flexible as to how that might be had. While they believed that anybody should be eligible for election to any position, they were not fixated on numbers or ratios. Instead, said Turner, they relied on persuasion and reasoned argument, and felt that "a sense of participation was more important than precise numbers on any given body." In contrast to democrats, he continued, stood the far more militant "syndicalists," who conceived of the university as divided into three, clearly defined groups that should have equal representation on all decision-making bodies. Thinking in terms of power, rather than persuasion, syndicalist elements were the most likely to resort to force. Phrased in these terms, there was no doubt as to with which of the two radical groups the committee felt a measure of communion. In the final analysis, however, they rejected all arguments that logically ended in majority student rule. A higher good, after all, was at stake.

To define a university as an agent of social change and, then, bind it to majority rule was not, said Turner and company, "compatible with academic freedom." Such an arrangement, they posited, would leave no room for real disagreement inside the university, once an official policy was adopted on a given social issue. Freedom required power, in the sense of the ability to research and teach as individuals saw fit. Moreover, it was "intolerable" for specialists to have the content or methods of course dictated by non-experts.

The foregoing might be viewed as every bit as doctrinaire as the radical critique, however, Turner conceded that militants did have a point. "Few, if any, members of the university community," the committee noted, "can be entirely satisfied with the quality of education offered in a modern university." Change was not only in order; it was necessary, and students should be heard. Accordingly, the committee offered a series of recommendations. Any individual, they counselled, should have the right to a hearing before any committee of the university. Similarly, all members of the academy should be allowed to request information concerning questions before any committee. The nature, function, and composition of all such bodies ought to be made public knowledge. To ensure broad communication, summaries of the senate meetings and those of presidential committees needed to be published, preferably in the *Silhouette*. Naturally, confidential matters must be respected, but it was vital to dispel students' sense that all was manipulated secretively by faceless tenders of a machine.

As for representation, Turner's committee thought three seats on the senate sufficient to remind the chamber of student perspectives. Meanwhile, any student, they argued, ought to be eligible for service on all committees, save those "from which they must reasonably be excluded." The latter included the president's council, the facilities and planning board, the awards, and promotion and tenure committees. The same, said Turner, ought to apply at the faculty and department levels. Indeed, he and his colleagues strongly advised that, in formulating their bylaws, faculties should develop uniform practices, as far as was possible. Calls to parity, however, were firmly rejected, as were ideas that students serve as bound delegates, subject to recall. Pleas for fully open meetings were, also, denounced as likely to inhibit free discussion or to encourage playing to the gallery. Turner did acknowledge, of course, that any committee could declare all or part of its proceedings open, at its discretion. These matters of principle and practice having been unanimously agreed, Turner, then, released his report on behalf of fellow members, Jack Kirkaldy, Les Prince, H.G. Chappell, and Ivor Wynne.[31]

In essence, Turner had offered little more than Kirkaldy had to radical students. Predictably, the MSU replied in high dudgeon. However, when accorded a hearing by the senate in September, their representatives offered no brief on the subject. Instead, an open meeting was demanded on the Turner Report. Senators, Thode in particular, were unimpressed. Students had had the report in their hands for over two months, yet claimed they had no time to prepare a proper response. Grant queried Turner about the sincerity of these delegates. The historian ventured that an open gathering was "at best a gamble." He added that he did think the students had a case to make, but that he was rather disillusioned by their remarks about having been rushed. Lengthy discussion, then, ensued.

Throughout this debate, Grant emphasized the need to keep up dialogue with the students, since any delay could play into the hands of militants yearning for confrontation. As yet, he underlined, there appeared to be no consensus among students on matters of governance. Thus, he argued, it would be foolhardy to refuse an open meeting and, thereby, create a rallying point for radicals. As will be seen, there was enough student muttering abroad over sundry issues to make Grant's point credible. Accordingly, nerves taut, the senate called the first open meeting in its long history to convene on 27 November 1968.[32] Heightening tensions during October, there was a heated exchange in the campus newspaper between Turner and sociologist Sam Lanfranco over the justice done to students in the report.[33] Additional, if mixed, student contributions merely added to anticipation of a public showdown.[34]

Grant had been wise to urge that the senate be seen to listen, especially to elected representatives of student government. As unpalatable as the governance position of the MSU and GSU might have been, it was important that they retain credibility in the eyes of their constituents. There were, after all, far more radical elements abroad. As yet, they were small in number, but it was vital that they be given no opportunity to usurp leadership on campus. The danger, here, was all too real. The MSU, for example, had already been derided by activists and moderates alike, as a coffee-house, clique-ridden body.[35] The executive was charged, by some, with inappropriate spending, notably on the film board.[36] Others complained that it was all but impossible to participate in some officially sponsored groups, such as the board of student broadcasting, unless one was a member of the in-crowd.[37] One irate letter to the *Silhouette* went so far as to blame supposed student apathy on campus politicos, who made little effort to talk to the people whom they represented, let alone present well-articulated platforms.[38] Perhaps, this was why elected student leaders adopted an increasingly hard line on representation. After all, they faced the prospect of marginalization as unofficial groups proliferated and bid for attention.

Some of this agitation was spawned at the department level. The Grady-Mongar affair contributed heavily to lingering student unrest in political science well into 1968. Calls for a strong student voice in department affairs redoubled, as graduate students staged a two-day boycott of assistantship duties in November of that year.[39] Meanwhile, for some time, undergraduates in French had been hurling biting criticism at a curriculum that left too many of their number far from fluent in the language they studied. By 1968, promised change had yet to materialize, thus prompting formation of a French Student Reform Committee. Of 300 questionnaires sent to majors, 259 replies were received. The latter all sought "some degree of influence in the direction of their department." Meeting with the chairman, student committee leaders were convinced of his sincerity concerning reform, but less than happy when informed that most professors thought academic freedom included the right to dictate the language of instruction.[40] Inattention to these tremors would, later, precipitate an earthquake. Grumbling on the part of the History Society has already been noted. Although it faded quickly, that fate was not self-evident in mid-1968.

Amply obvious, however, was the dramatic decision of forty first-year mathematics students to march out of class in protest, just five days before the open senate meeting. Sending delegates to the dean and a letter to Thode, they complained of both the form and content of instruction. The majority of complainants were science or engineering students, who thought that pure mathematics, to which they were being introduced, bore no relevance to the programs in which they had enlisted.[41] The matter was swiftly patched up, and student apologies tendered. The walk-out, however, was ominously symbolic of wildcat assertion by students at the department level. Meanwhile, organized protest, also outside the ambit of student government, was taking shape.

Students for a Democratic University (SDU) was McMaster's edition of US Students for a Democratic Society (SDS). Its members had, of course, been prominent in anti–Vietnam War demonstrations (and met by counter-protests), but had never truly captured centre stage. The group enjoyed some success, in October 1968, when it held a memorial for the martyred Ernesto "Che" Guevara. Some 400 students and faculty attended, as SDU speakers linked Guevara's struggle with that of students who sought a larger say in university governance, while staggering under the growing weight of loans. Participants told *Silhouette* reporters that a showdown with administration was nigh. While some listeners found this quite bracing, others warned against hero-worship and turning to revolution as a first resort.[42] For its part, the SDU might have been satisfied simply to make the front page of the campus paper. After all, Che was unlikely to mobilize the McMaster masses. Food, however, proved to be a different matter.

McMaster claimed to strive for excellence in numerous fields. Haute cuisine, however, was not one of them. Still, there was acceptable and, then, there was poor fare. For several years, Versa Foods had provided catering service that challenged even the least discriminating undergraduate palates. As well, cleanliness and godliness might not have stood as closely related in the mid-sixties student mind as they had in a previous era, but inadequately washed silverware could still raise eyebrows. After much complaint, the university awarded Beaver Foods a contract to replace Versa, in September 1968.[43] The new purveyor of bulk nutrition, however, had barely ignited deep fryers, when the SDU cried, "Boycott."

Russ Brown, a former student, proposed the measure at a Wentworth House meeting in October. An employee, he alleged, been wrongfully dismissed. Meanwhile, Beaver had not rehired several senior people, who had been shop stewards during Versa's tenure. This was a step toward union busting, said Brown. He obtained the requisite fifty-three signatures to petition for an emergency session of the SRA. Redress of grievances and discussion of a student takeover of food services were on the menu.[44] Responding immediately, both Beaver and the Building Service Employees Union invited the SDU and SRA to butt out. This, they said, was a labour-management issue, governed by standard practice, in which students had no part.[45] Unlike the hamburgers on offer, however, this was too juicy a morsel for the SDU to let go. Instead, it swung into full activist mode.

Terry Campbell, another former student (1966), harangued an audience of the committed and the bemused from atop the steps of Wentworth House. Bull horn in hand, he broadened the debate, denouncing McMaster as "an academic dunghill." Apathetic students and conniving administrators alike were chastised for failure to reform an institution that bolstered "society's authoritarian bureaucracy." The impassioned Campbell then called on all right-thinking members of the university to embrace "the politics of confrontation." The *Silhouette*, in obvious sympathy, gave front-page coverage to Campbell, while simultaneously running other articles related to furor stirred by the Turner Report.[46]

Meanwhile, thought the SDU, if an army marches on its stomach, so might a revolution. Thus, by November, it was distributing free victuals to dissuade students from patronizing Beaver. At the same time, the group called for protest against unfair labour practice, high prices, and poor quality. Once again, it urged students to seize control of their food services. Some observers found the conflation of ground beef, union matters, and the university's role in modern society just a tad strained. "If You Don't Like It, You Can Always Leave," wrote one undergraduate in a *Silhouette* letter to the editor. The author, John Francis, described the SDU as non-representative malcontents who had "hijacked" the issue, simply to drum up discord.[47] Commenting on the attempt to link Beaver to Turner, another student critic penned a lengthy critique of Canadian protesters who strove ardently to ape their American counterparts, but without the same direct and urgent stake in truly great matters, such as civil rights and Vietnam. While deeply critical of Canadian society and McMaster's administration, she noted that apples were not oranges, and denounced confrontation as a measure of first resort.[48] In the end, the whole food uproar fizzled, when an MSU investigation of labour practices at Beaver concluded that the SDU's allegations were unfounded.[49] Still, the episode added to cumulative tensions, at the time of the open meeting.

"Historic Meeting Exposes McMaster Problems," wrote the *Silhouette*'s Lawrence Martin. In his extensive coverage of the event, he underlined the number and intensity of those engaged. More than 200 people crowded into an engineering lecture theatre that November day. Another 1,000 avidly followed proceedings via CCTV across campus. The floor was thrown open to any member of the McMaster community on the proviso that no motions would be entertained. Representatives of undergraduate government were quick off the mark. Unlike September, they now presented a full brief, hotly condemning the Turner Report. Students, they argued should have eight members on the senate, sit on any committee, including presidential ones, and be represented on all divisional, faculty and departmental bodies. Furthermore, these delegates should be appointed by the SRA and subject to recall. As well, all senate and presidential committees ought to be open. Having set the agenda, MSU speakers yielded the floor to representatives of the GSU. Graduates wasted no time in turning up the thermostat.

While their statements read like photocopies of those presented by undergraduate colleagues, the chief distinction was the venom with which they were delivered. Indeed, so scathing were their opening remarks that Turner, visibly fuming, stormed out of the hall. Unperturbed, graduates forged on, berating an increasingly rigid curriculum, along with "bureaucratic pressure" that sped candidates through programs. One speaker offered an inflammatory tirade on the secrecy of a university afraid "to air its dirty linen" in open meetings. Speakers rumbled on. During question period, Thode reminded the audience of the many avenues open to students who wished to voice grievances. A less restrained Kirkaldy meticulously outlined his personal scholarly qualifications then shouted, "No student can come and tell me what he thinks he should learn in Metallurgy!" Such was the tenor of the proceedings. Once the smoke had cleared, Martin interviewed various combatants. Surprisingly, all proclaimed the meeting a success, in that views had been fully and publicly aired.[50] A little steam had been released from an overheated pressure cooker. Indeed, one MSU member, who had been rather more than voluble on 27 November, later wrote formally to tender apologies to the senate.[51] Accommodation seemed possible.

The senate finally decided to admit six elected student members.[52] Academic qualifications for election, however, were keenly debated. Initially, they were intended to be stringent. In the end, they were whittled down to a bare minimum. To be eligible, undergraduate candidates were required only to be registered full-time, have completed first year, and not failed the year prior to election.[53] Meanwhile, under steady pressure to increase transparency, in December 1968 Thode and Kirkaldy urged "[t]hat subject to the limitations of space, good conduct, and confidentiality, future meetings of Senate should be 'open' to any member of the community." A motion to that effect carried unanimously. As the senate chamber was small, it could only hold about thirty observers at any given session. To compensate for this limited access, a summary of the senate minutes was, henceforth, posted in the library and other public places.[54] Altogether, from their perspective, the senate and the administration had made significant concessions to student demands for openness and representation. Now, all could only wait to see how individual faculties and departments would adapt to change in framing their internal bylaws concerning student participation.

These local decisions, it was understood, would be crucial to campus harmony, since, as Saul Frankel later observed, students generally showed a natural tendency to focus on matters closest to their immediate interests. In short, they reserved their greatest fervour for participation in departmental councils, as opposed to higher-level conclaves.[55] As if to prove Frankel's point, two student senate seats stood vacant for want of candidates, following elections in 1970.[56] Many of the "active," it seems, had shifted to pressuring departments, as faculties debated their new bylaws, including those pertaining to student representation on committees. By and large, science, engineering, and medicine, the "value-free" (quantitative) faculties, reached early accommodation with students. Far greater heat was generated in the "value-laden" (interpretive) arts where, not surprisingly, ideological voltage was often higher. Agitation in history, French, and political science has already been noted. Tension developed in religious studies, sociology/anthropology, and other departments. Detailed issues and degrees of intensity varied from one discipline to another. So did outcomes, as students pressed for a substantial role in department decision-making.

In the early seventies, for example, the activist-dominated History Society moved from lampooning grey-walled liberalism to seeking recognition as the "sole agent" for official liaison between students and faculty. In addition, the society sought the right to send three "delegates" to department meetings. These notions, however, were flatly rebuffed by the department, whose members recognized that the petitioners lacked popular backing among the majority of majors.[57] This was not an expression of head-in-the-sand indifference to student opinion. Nor was it case that majors and graduates were mired in supine conservatism. Rather, since 1967, potentially broad confrontations had been headed off by graduate and undergraduate advisory committees. These small bodies brought elected students regularly in touch with faculty representatives. In concert, they thrashed out questions of the day as they arose; before rumour or miscommunication could fog mutual understanding. Complete concord was rare, but channels remained open.[58] This gambit enabled history to stand by its 1968 resolution that "there should be no students present at department meetings."[59] It could do so because faculty was not riven by faction, while radicals were an isolated minority among students. The department enjoyed another advantage that bolstered its position. When the reorganization of 1968 had occurred, history had elected to move from social science to the Faculty of Humanities.

In its zeal to promote devolution, the *Kirkaldy Report* had emphasized that each faculty have the right to prescribe the kind and level of student participation appropriate to itself. On 30 July 1969, the senate was taken aback when the Faculty of Social Science promulgated its provisional bylaws. These, unlike the ones submitted earlier by business and science, proposed that students have a voice in the faculty-wide tenure process. An elected student advisory commission, chaired by the dean, would review tenure recommendations from departments and submit written opinions. The commission's collective appraisal would count as one vote on the faculty committee.[60] This novel proposition grated on already raw ganglia. A joint presidential-MUFA committee on procedures and criteria for appointment, tenure, and promotion was due to report that December. It was no secret that most (not all) parties on both sides favoured excluding students from formal deliberation on these matters.[61] Thus, when John Melling, (acting) dean of social science, put his Faculty's bylaws before the senate, he prodded a hornet's nest.

The chamber was torn on the question. Again and again, the draft document was referred back for consideration, as faculty champions of student involvement, such as Paul Younger, argued their case.[62] In the end, a compromise was reached. "The Document," as the MUFA-administration agreement was popularly called, set out a standard administrative-staff structure for all faculty-level tenure committees, but allowed that each faculty could, within that framework, pass additional bylaws. It was also stipulated (rather vaguely) that "a department shall seek and give appropriate weight to student opinion as one factor in determining a candidate's effectiveness ... and ensure that such opinion is sought."[63] Ratified by the board, in September 1970, these provisions virtually guaranteed that practices would vary from faculty to faculty. Thus, when humanities voted against student membership on faculty council, history, for example, was in a strong constitutional position to deflect calls for direct student participation in decision-making.[64] On the other hand, given their faculty bylaws, social science departments were not. The upshot was a series of tremors, great and small, in disciplines, such as politics, sociology, and religious studies.

In political science, strife over the Grady affair had barely subsided when, in 1970, wrangling rose once more. Chairman Howard Lentner described a "general malaise" that all but paralyzed the department.[65] Fierce professorial infighting concerning the influence of Americans over curriculum and hiring had exploded again. Furthermore, debate raged as to authority over graduate supervision, the role of the chair, and the participation of students in department committees. In many ways, the tangled situation resembled a replay of 1967–68. Once again, political scientists were almost evenly divided into two warring camps. As before, faculty flames stoked student fires; even as the embargoed doctoral program was being weighed by the OCGS.

Things came to a head in February–March 1971. The department had advertised a position in Canadian foreign policy, but failed to find a suitable candidate. It, therefore, redefined the post as one in international relations. Some, including many students riding a nationalist wave, objected. In February, a series of rallies linked Canadianization with demands for a student presence on hiring committees.[66] Tempers were amplified, when Pringsheim penned a letter to the editor of the *Spectator* entitled, "The Canadian as Nigger." Adapting arguments from Mathews and Steele, he called for more Canadian staff and course content in political science.[67] Rhetoric of this sort had traction with many students. In 1970, for example, the *Silhouette* had protested loudly when an American, Diane Morris, was hired as McMaster's advisor to degree candidates from overseas. Bewailing influence from south of the border, the editor warned, "Let us beware, if it is not already too late."[68] To an extent, therefore, Pringsheim was preaching to, at least, part of the student choir.

On 23 February 1971, Ralph Bertram, president of the student political science society, wrote to Thode complaining of the frustration that had gathered force among his peers. They had lobbied for a voice in appointments for almost three years, said Bertram, but in vain. Indeed, he underlined, students in medicine and physical education had been playing a role in decision-making for some time; yet his colleagues enjoyed no more than observer status in department affairs.[69] Walking softly on hot coals, Thode replied, saying that he recognized the importance of consulting with students, but noted, "the University does not require all departments or faculties to follow the same pattern." His hands were tied. The matter was for the department to decide.[70]

Already sunk in turmoil, political scientists were deadlocked on the issue of student participation, especially where staffing was concerned. When a vote was taken on this matter, the result was a nine-to-nine tie, with no prospect of movement. At that point, students staged an extended boycott of classes in March. A media feeding frenzy ensued and dragged on for the better part of the month. Eventually, an uneasy compromise was reached, whereby students were given voting rights on the curriculum committee, while a joint faculty-student body was struck to consider wider issues of department governance.[71] This, however, got bogged down by unrelated faculty disputes, which led to a vote of no confidence in Lentner and his resignation as chairman the next year. The question of student participation remained unresolved, for the moment. Meanwhile, other social sciences coped with pressures on the same front.

Sociology-anthropology staff divided on the issue of student participation, if not so vehemently as did political scientists. When proposed bylaws came up for discussion, in 1969, Frank Jones and Peter Pineo registered concern with the idea of a student advisory commission on faculty-level tenure decisions. They noted that, to date, students had expressed no interest in the matter. Further to the point, Jones raised questions about competence and tokenism. Nonetheless, a majority of members present endorsed the faculty proposal, while, also, acknowledging the need to develop a policy regarding student involvement in department affairs.[72] However, if they thought they had time to do so in a gradual, deliberate fashion, they were mistaken. In fact, within two months, MA and PhD candidates were demanding parity on the graduate curriculum policy committee. Moreover, they wanted decisions to be made consensually, rather than by vote.

The petitioners were in a strong position. Undergraduate numbers in sociology were skyrocketing, and the department was desperately short of teaching assistants. Graduate requests could not be shelved for future consideration. Still, parity and consensual procedure, once accepted, if only by one committee, would set a precedent of which others were sure to take advantage. Department members, therefore, trod carefully. Some saw no problem with equal representation, so long as there was no voting. Jones felt differently. There was, he argued, no basis for parity in decisions that would shape the long-term fate of the department. Faculty, alone, had the experience and responsibility to make such determinations. He accepted that there was a place for student participation, but not as equals. Accordingly, he proposed that graduates be admitted to the committee at a ratio of two faculty members to each student, and that decisions be made by majority vote. The motion passed, with some dissent.[73] For a time, all was relatively quiet on the sociological front. However, problems, uncannily similar to those in political science, were developing. Questions as to the very nature of sociology increasingly pitted older versus younger faculty. The more active students gravitated toward the newer breed.[74] By the early seventies, graduates demanded and won seats on all committees.[75] In 1974, undergraduate and graduate representatives were accorded parity with faculty and full voting rights on the plenary committee of the department.[76] This, moreover, was just the beginning of troubles that would long plague sociology. By comparison, relations in religious studies were positively sedate.

At Younger's suggestion, the department had held regular, informal meetings with graduate students since 1965.[77] This early recognition of the need to promote dialogue with its primary clientele would later pay premium dividends. Flexibility and compromise became ingrained departmental habits. In 1967, for example, students asked that their representatives be admitted to meetings at which graduate matters, especially evaluations, were being discussed. Assessment, which involved ranking for awards as well as gauging individual progress, was considered by faculty to require expertise born of long experience. Besides, issues of confidentiality and conflict of interest could easily arise. Accordingly, the student overture was politely turned aside. The request, however, was not simply rebuffed. Instead, elected candidates were offered two places on a five-person graduate policy committee, so that their peers might feel enfranchised in department affairs.[78] By 1968, these graduate representatives were given access to minutes of full faculty meetings, with the usual pledge of confidentiality.[79] Gradual, if cautious, acceptance of a student voice served religious studies well, especially after it chose to join the Faculty of Social Science following the *Kirkaldy Report*.

When that faculty's bylaws were mooted, in 1969, religious studies' graduate candidates were quick to lobby for more effective representation. A "Committee of Eight" presented Chairman Sanders with a plea for voting rights on "all faculty meetings."[80] Department members were not prepared to grant access to every form of deliberation, but they went eagerly to bat for their most prized constituency in another way. Thus, Sanders had noted that the proposed faculty bylaws mentioned only undergraduates in outlining a student advisory commission on tenure for social science. On behalf of his colleagues, therefore, he drew this anomaly to the dean's attention, arguing that graduate candidates should have greater influence than undergraduates on such a body. Religious studies, he added, preferred that students have a consultative role, rather than a vote, on matters of tenure and promotion at the department level.[81] Meanwhile, two students, with voting rights, were warmly welcomed to general department meetings, in November 1969.[82]

This was an adroit, albeit indirect, message to its graduates that the department recognized they had some valid interests. Decades later, after the turn of the new millennium, numerous doyens recalled that a modus vivendi had been established without rancour or confrontation. From early on, they explained, the department had shown that it valued students (especially graduate students) as junior partners in a contagiously exciting new enterprise. As Younger put it, there was a "comfortable feeling" during that period.[83]

Clearly, the issue of student participation in decision-making evoked different reactions from faculty to faculty and department to department. On the whole, medicine, the sciences, physical education, business, and engineering phased a student voice into their affairs with relative ease. The humanities, experienced some turbulence, but escaped outright confrontation; at least during Thode's term. In social science, on the other hand, tensions over the matter escalated, first in political science; then in sociology, only to gain even greater force in the seventies.[84] Everywhere, much depended on the nature of particular disciplines and the inclinations of students they attracted. Degrees of consensus among faculty in any given department were just as crucial. Of course, it is also possible that much squabbling might have been avoided, had the senate not ratified Kirkaldy's recommendation that each faculty have considerable leeway where internal student participation was concerned. As noted, Trueman had worried about the effect that any discrepancies among such provisions might have. For his part, Grant had counselled the senate to maintain dialogue with student government lest splinter groups gain a following. One wonders, therefore, what the two men made of growing murmurs about "course unions" replacing a centralized MSU as the sixties closed.[85]

Amid the accumulating noise, Thode concurred fully with Grant. Writing to a nervous faculty member in September 1968, he argued that "an ongoing and positive effort" must be made to communicate with and listen to students. This, he continued, was the only way to avert the disruptive confrontations that had occurred elsewhere.[86] Thode, of course, was not about to give in to each and every demand, simply to keep the peace. In 1967, for instance, he made it plain that the McMaster Committee on Vietnam, which included faculty, staff and students, was at liberty to stage an orderly protest against visitors from Dow Chemicals, producers of napalm. He emphasized, however, that he would not hesitate to call the police, should demonstrators overstep the bounds of lawful behaviour.[87] In short, Thode was prepared to live with measured dissent, but thought all parties on campus must learn to do the same. Under the new structure, there was little that he could do about arguments concerning student representation in individual departments. As president, however, he did try his hand at some diplomatic bridging over troubled university waters.

Working closely with student government, Thode organized a special two-day presidential seminar, for mid-October 1969. The whole McMaster community was invited. The topic for general discussion was "The Role of the University in Modern Society: Its Function and Purpose." He entertained high hopes that the gathering would help focus recent attempts to bring students, faculty, and administration into closer, more productive exchange.[88] Every effort was made to ensure that the dice were not loaded in favour of a particular point of view and that the intellectual fare on offer would be spicy. An all-star cast was assembled. The panels included Kenneth Hare, former president of UBC, known for his scathing criticism of contemporary undergraduate education as "a rat race for a useless degree." A.J.R. Smith, chairman of the Economic Council of Canada, was on hand to urge that wholly new concepts of higher education were required, if universities were to retain their relevance in modern society. Douglas Wright represented the CUA and the newly formed COPSE commission. (After all, every good public forum needs at least one punching bag.) The real show-stopper, however, was to be Martin Loney. Fresh from the headline-grabbing PSA affair at his Simon Fraser campus, Loney was president of the radical Canadian Union of Students (CUS) and a bona fide New Left rock star. Sparks were certain to fly, fast and furious.[89]

With a sure-fire box-office hit on tap, Thode cancelled all classes. The gym was crammed with every chair maintenance staff could scrounge. All was in readiness. Came the day, speakers poured forth impassioned views – in a cavernous echo chamber. Less than 1 per cent of the campus population had elected to attend. Keeping up a bold front, Thode joked that it was, probably, the extraordinarily fine weather that had drawn people outdoors. The depths of his personal disappointment, however, can only be imagined. Thode had thrown a lavish party at, what appeared to be, just the right time, yet no one had come. The *Silhouette* paused to praise the president and chide the McMaster community. Thode, it said, had offered an opportunity to debate the hottest issues, only to be ignored by students and faculty, alike. Documenting this, a photograph of the nearly empty gym spoke much louder than any frustrated words the editor or president could muster.[90]

In retrospect, however, perhaps this thin turnout at an official function should have occasioned less surprise than it did. After all, activist students were focusing their greatest attention on department struggles, by this time. Less and less faith was invested in formal university-wide bodies to effect change. Elected student associations, for example, were having difficulties summoning a quorum for meetings, even when significant issues, such as incorporation of the SRA, were at stake.[91] Similarly, after a five-year battle, the crusade for open senate meetings was no sooner won than the gallery stood empty.[92] While worried by the declining influence of student government, Thode and his advisors could, at least, take solace that, in 1969, the most extreme, independent radical group on campus, the self-proclaimed McMaster Student Movement (MSM), was also languishing in the doldrums.

Taking up the mantle of the defunct SDU, the MSM began as a fringe Marxist-Leninist-Maoist study group in the summer of 1969. Not surprisingly, this small cadre included students with ties to political science. One of these, Ken Stone, had recently made a momentary splash by ceremoniously tearing up his diploma at convocation in Toronto. Coming to McMaster to continue his general education, he would be the MSM's "theorist."[93] Stone and his would-be revolutionaries made their public debut in September 1969, picketing the unfinished psychology building "in solidarity with the carpenters' union, local 18."[94] A hoped-for student outburst failed to erupt. Undaunted, MSM representatives next greeted students at registration, in an effort to raise funds for beleaguered Stelco workers enduring a long and heated strike. After a few hours of lonely vigil, they left, having wrung scarcely a nickel from the huddled masses yearning to be free (of interminable course line-ups). A "Smash the Bosses" rally, during which McMaster was denounced as a class-ridden institution, went equally under-subscribed.[95]

Recognizing the need to educate the untutored concerning their own enslavement, the MSM turned to the columns of the *Silhouette*, outlining "The Meaning of Radicalism" as a thrust at the root causes of imperialism, capitalism, and the repression of class consciousness.[96] By the time this piece was authored, however, extreme New Left rhetoric had worn thin with most McMaster readers. Indeed, they, along with peers on campuses across the country, were in the process of dissociating themselves from the increasingly radicalized and crumbling CUS.[97] In short order, dissension also reared its divisive head amid MSM ranks. Two prominent members announced their intention to withdraw, citing Stone's "workers-students-alliance" credo as too doctrinaire and perversely "elitist." As if to confirm their allegations, Stone replied: "To be a Marxist you assume that there is only one best analysis."[98] Solidarity had seen better times. Radicalism had, also, had better reviews.

Thus, an angry geography major took to print, railing against Stone and the MSM as hypocrites who failed to subject those they admired, Mao, Castro, and Guevara, to the same close examination they deployed against Canadian society. The author called on fellow so-called conservatives, not to be used as pawns in the MSM game.[99] Fighting back, Stone and company called for a large-scale anti–Vietnam War rally, banking on still-fresh memories of the Tet bloodbath (January 1968). However, of the 5,000 students on campus, a paltry 167 attended. The *Silhouette* scoffed at what it termed a "dismal failure" and offered that hard-core Marxists would never learn: reform at home would always stir more people than "rigid theory applied to faraway places."[100] As it happened, the journal proved to be both right and wrong. The MSM, in fact, did learn. Licking its wounds, over the winter, the next foray by the group was pointedly aimed at matters of popular interest, close to home.

Martin, later a distinguished journalist with the *Globe and Mail*, analyzed this tactical shift, in his role as a feature writer for the *Silhouette*. With a keen eye for campus politics, he noted that, "mouthy, long-haired" MSM speakers, spouting incomprehensible jargon, were widely regarded by listeners as little more than "supercilious yo-yos," trying to convince others that revolution was somehow "cool." By December 1969, they seemed destined to join the SDU and the dodo in the curio shop of extinction. Then, with an unexpected flash of insight, they changed strategy. Targeting campus food and the maltreatment of those who served it, they took up an issue that affected every student and forged a potent (if temporary) alliance with better established groups, such as the MSU, SRA, and the Inter-residence Council (IRC). In the process, the MSM stepped from the perceived lunatic fringe into the glaring limelight.[101] The first move came, on a small scale, in the spring of 1970.

On 19 March, MSM representatives, calling themselves the "Committee of 75," occupied the office of the unit manager of Beaver Foods. A grievance, signed by the union steward, was presented on behalf of an employee, who had been assigned split shifts, even as her weekly hours had been cut. This was in clear breach of contract. With Thode on six-month leave, the matter was referred to Art Bourns, as acting president, who acted promptly to rectify the situation. The aggrieved party was granted regular hours and retroactive pay for the time spent lingering about between shifts. Elated, the MSM issued a mimeographed broadsheet, proclaiming victory for students and workers alike, while adding that more remained to be done about the indigestible comestibles Beaver served up. Students were called to rally round the cause.[102]

About 200 gathered, on 24 March, to present a list of demands to Beaver and the university concerning the quality of food and the treatment of workers. Reporting to Bourns, management officials said that talks had gone well and that an agreement had been reached.[103] When, however, Beaver was slow to post fixed prices, as had been promised, the Committee of 75 presented several new demands, backed by a petition with more than a thousand student signatures appended.[104] The MSM had struck pay dirt. There had been grumbling about Beaver's fare since the day it took over from Versa. Moreover, the workers, whom the MSM championed, were not faceless symbols from a carpenters' union, but daily familiars of hungry students. This matter was immediate and personal on several levels. Bourns was willing to deal with most of the new issues, but others were union matters beyond his jurisdiction.[105] Striking, while the iron was hot, delegates of the 75 addressed a hastily assembled meeting of the SRA, on Friday 3 April. MSM representatives proposed direct action in the form of a "sit-in." After all, the tactic had worked to good effect at Toronto, Laurentian, and Ryerson, mere weeks previously.[106] Was the SRA not up to it?

Student officials were in an awkward position. Clearly, there was widespread dissatisfaction with Beaver; too much to ignore. On the other hand, events at Simon Fraser and Sir George Williams, just months earlier, spoke to the darker side of campus confrontation. Fighting shy of Scylla and Charybdis, the SRA sought to chart a middle course. The Committee of 75 was empowered to speak for students in all matters pertaining to Beaver, but a sit-in was voted down.[107] Undeterred, adrenaline-charged leaders of the

75 gambled that they, rather than the SRA, had caught the mood of campus. Accordingly, they marched from the meeting to occupy the president's office forthwith. Upon arrival, they encountered a bespectacled gentleman, who seemed neither flustered nor surprised. Bourns had seen it coming.

Anticipating just such a move, the acting president had huddled with Ivor Wynne (dean of students), Les Prince (dean of men), and Manny Zack (assistant to the president) for most of the previous afternoon. With no university policy regarding this kind of crisis, the quartet had to pull one together in a tearing hurry. As a point of honour, Thode was not contacted for advice. He had earned his rest in California, and Bourns had accepted full responsibility in the president's absence. He was not about to shirk that burden, just because some extra weight had been added.[108] After consulting with the head of security, the four men laid down a plan for coping with a sit-in. Their strategy was based on isolating the radicals from the main body of students and the media, as much as possible. Telephone lines to any office affected would be disconnected. Security would cordon off the area to general traffic. Police would be called only if violence broke out or seemed imminent. The university would listen to and state terms, but it would not negotiate while under occupation. Meanwhile, sensitive files were gathered up and locked away in a basement vault. In short, a policy of restraint and containment was adopted.[109]

Bourns was at his desk, when protesters arrived with sleeping bags, transistor radios, and other essentials. A calm, almost casual, atmosphere reigned. Occupiers set about discussing how best to proceed. Dope and liquor were immediately declared taboo. Why give hostages to fortune? When the matter of food came up, Bourns interjected, asking for a moment to speak. The 75 expected to encounter Thode and had, hitherto, ignored the lanky, clerkish gent in the room. After a few minutes, Bourns identified himself and was besieged by students looking to negotiate matters there and then. He replied that he would not do so in an occupied office. As he left the room, one demonstrator asked him what he was going to do "to alleviate the students." Noting nearby washrooms, Bourns quipped: "They can alleviate themselves, if they like."[110] No doubt, some availed themselves of this generous offer, over the next few days. Others concentrated on churning out posters denouncing the university as a "boss," exploiting the labour of secretaries, maids, cafeteria workers, and others.[111]

On the whole, Friday and Saturday passed peacefully. An attempt by IRC members to oust the occupiers was foiled quietly by security guards at Gilmour Hall. Bourns had left strict instructions that no provocation be offered, without his sanction. Tactically, his goal was to induce student government to assert control, so that any bargaining could be conducted through normal, constitutionally recognized channels. In this spirit, he wrote to the SRA. He invited that body to designate a small group to act on its behalf, while promising to meet as soon as his office was vacated. The purpose, he emphasized, would be to ensure the immediate improvement of food services. He then drew attention to, in his mind, a larger issue. "The existing situation," wrote Bourns, "calls for positive action by the SRA." "I am convinced," he continued, "that the relationship between student government and the University Administration must be maintained and strengthened." Indeed, he cautioned, "The entire future of student government is now at stake."[112] This closing statement was not intended as a threat. Instead, Bourns' was trying to indicate that, by delegating their authority to an independent group, the MSU and SRA were abdicating their responsibility and, thereby, jeopardizing their own effectiveness as elected student leaders. Still, while clear enough to him, Bourns' words were differently interpreted by recipients of the letter.

To Stagg and other SRA officials, the missive sounded like an ultimatum. Meeting on Sunday, 5 April, the assembly reaffirmed its support for demands issued in its name by the 75. Going further, it reversed its stand on the sit-in, voting to endorse it – this time with the backing of an equally miffed IRC.[113] Politely outlining this in a reply to Bourns, the SRA underscored a deeper concern of its own. "We add that we are supporting this," they wrote, "not so much for the basic problem of food that must in any case be resolved, but because of the larger issue that is involved, namely the widespread dissatisfaction with the committees and the chronic bureaucracy that strangles the university and effectively ensures that little is effectively done."[114] In brief, the SRA was arguing that regular channels were regularly clogged. The university, it was implied, had brought the sit-in on itself. For public consumption, an MSU *Special Edition* was published. Stagg took a moderate line, describing the sit-in as a "learning experience" for students and administrators alike. More radical MSM writers painted McMaster as a "bureaucratic octopus." "Representative committees that report to deities," they scribbled, "are a farce and hypocrisy."[115] Perhaps, this latter remark helped student officials grasp what Bourns had tried to convey about ceding authority to non-elected bodies. Whatever the case, the atmosphere was decidedly different Monday morning.

Bourns was gearing up to evict the occupiers, when the telephone rang in his senior sciences office. It was the SRA on the line, inviting him to a meeting at Gilmour Hall. Refusing to enter the occupied area or to negotiate, he agreed to address students in the foyer. At the appointed hour, in an overflowing lobby, he stated calmly that the university acknowledged deficiencies in food quality and service, sketched some improvements he had in mind, and concluded by offering to meet with an SRA committee, the moment occupation ended. Later in the day, Bourns and a small group of students quietly hammered out a mutually acceptable agreement. The sit-in was over.[116] The fallout, however, was not.

Throughout the three-day period, and for a time after, regional media had feasted on these juicy tidbits. The *Globe and Mail* slammed Bourns for "caving in." Appeasement, it argued, only whetted the appetite of those who craved another Sir George Williams episode. The *Spectator* voiced much the same opinion. Letters to editors poured in, for and against the occupation.[117] The *Silhouette,* on the other hand, had no reservations. It trumpeted a supposedly clear-cut student victory. In a retrospective glance, campus scribes spoke of bureaucratic walls toppling. The sit-in, they declared, had demonstrated decisively how to move a, hitherto, sluggish administrative machine. One wag wondered whether Thode would ever dare take a sabbatical again. The antique notion that the university could stand *in loco parentis* was dead; killed by an energized student body. Barricades had crumbled. Appended to celebratory articles, a photograph showed a student searching the president's (empty) desk, during the occupation.[118] Bourns would have reason to recall that snapshot, four years later, but, at the time, he was absorbed in a personal assessment his own performance.

Yellowed by age, notes in Bourns' hand survive to document his agonized effort to analyze what had transpired. They reveal a deeply earnest man labouring hard to learn from troubling experience. While allowing that the MSM had been itching to engineer confrontation and that Beaver had opened the door, the self-critical scientist, also, freely admitted his own mistakes. For example, upon reflection, Bourns recognized that his letter calling on student government to assume control, had been open to misinterpretation and had "boomeranged." The lesson he drew from this was to "remain cool, maintain communications and involve the President [i.e., himself] more directly – I should have appeared in person before the SRA." Personal, rather than written, exchange would have clarified what he meant when saying that the future of student government was in the balance. Here, he faulted himself.

At a systemic level, Bourns accepted that the students had some legitimate complaints to which a more alert and responsive institution would have attended, well before a crisis arose. It was necessary, he concluded, vastly to improve communication with the general student body and develop far more expeditious decision-making processes. Complaints could not be allowed to fester in a welter of manifold subcommittees. This, however, ran both ways. The SRA, Bourns scrawled, had to understand that recent events reflected their own, as well as the university's, failure to stay in close touch with the broad community of students.

On a different score, he asked himself why McMaster had absolutely no guidelines for dealing with campus disturbances. Of course, everything is unthinkable until it happens. Still, student disobedience was common fare elsewhere. Why had McMaster presumed exemption? Why was there no code of student conduct defining the line between acceptable and intolerable expressions of dissent? In the absence of such policies, Bourns had had to play by ear. This necessitated several spur-of-the-moment judgment calls, such as putting off eviction of the occupiers until Monday after the SRA's offer to talk. That led to resolution but also to cries that he had caved in. In this decision, Bourns had acted alone against the advice of his counsellors. He reasoned, however, that, since the SRA and IRC had endorsed the sit-in on Sunday, and had set up a committee to deal with him, students in general would consider it a breach of faith were he not to accept an olive branch proffered by their elected government. Thus, he spoke in the lobby of Gilmour Hall. Ice was broken. An agreement was signed. Yet, it had been a near-run thing. A carefully designed policy was needed for an uncertain future.[119]

Mercilessly self-critical and subject to extensive public second-guessing, Bourns might have derived some comfort from numerous letters penned by students and colleagues. At the height of the crisis, several graduate and undergraduate candidates wrote privately to the beleaguered president, commending his stand and urging him to hold his ground against an unrepresentative minority. Many of them, also, commented sharply on the fact that the SRA had allowed itself to be co-opted by the 75.[120] Even better, from the Department of Psychology came a unanimous vote of appreciation for the "skill and tact" with which the affair had been handled.[121] In like manner, Tom Truman, no stranger to campus combat, applauded Bourns' "statesmanlike" approach to the sit-in, while passing on word that Jack Kirkaldy was praising "just the right balance between firmness and flexibility." Naming no names, Truman added: "I am glad that you were strong enough to hold off the hawks." Speaking of which, he closed by noting that US vice-president Spiro Agnew had only that morning advised all university leaders to leave dissenting students to the tender mercies of police.[122] Touched by this and similar displays of support, Bourns, wrote to Alvin Lee of the boost they provided to his sagging morale.[123] He was, perhaps, even more pleased to hear that Lentner intended, at the earliest possible moment, to propose that the senate form a special committee to set out clear guidelines concerning procedures for conflict resolution and the acceptable limits of protest.[124] After much discussion, the senate eventually promulgated such policies in 1972.[125] Still, for all that many expressed confidence in him, Bourns was deeply scarred by the events of April.[126]

On the other side of the fence, with the *Silhouette* declaring victory, the MSM was gearing up to ride a presumed populist wave. The first good opportunity of the fall term came with the FLQ crisis, in October 1970. In response to the kidnapping of British diplomat James Cross and the murder of Quebec cabinet minister Pierre Laporte, Prime Minister Pierre Trudeau had invoked the sweeping War Measures Act. While few sympathized with the Front de Libération du Québec (FLQ), Canadian opinion divided on this suspension of civil liberties. Here, surely, was a cause around which to rally the McMaster masses.

Surging to the fore, the MSM beckoned all to a demonstration outside Gilmour Hall. More than a thousand attended. However, as the *Silhouette* reported, when MSM speakers tried to put a Marxist spin on the affair, the crowd rapidly shifted moods. Heckling grew in volume. Tomatoes were hurled at Stone and his colleagues. At one point, someone called for a moment of silence in memory of Laporte. Stone, in an appalling lapse of judgment, declared it wrong to single him out as martyr. Almost as one, those assembled turned their backs to the MSM and sang "O Canada." Assessing the event, the *Silhouette* editorialized that it encapsulated the very essence of "uselessness." Engineers on hand had heckled, as though at a football game. Meanwhile, the MSM was described as behaving no better, "with their overflowing rhetoric, lack of consistency, inaccurate facts, and obscenities."[127] Clearly, Stone and company had not read the mood of their desired constituency.

Unwilling to say die, the MSM next denounced participation in departmental committees as shallow tokenism. Student representatives, especially in political science, were urged to boycott such meetings.[128] Perhaps a few did, but the right to a voice in department affairs had been so hard-won that the call to withdraw went largely unheeded. New Left extremists fared no better in November, when they plastered campus walls with posters linking the War Measures Act with capitalist imperialism, while simultaneously hailing the virtues of Maoist thought. Passersby ridiculed these declarations. When one observer asked a radical stalwart if he was happy, listeners burst into laughter, as the Maoist declared that he was objectively unhappy, even if he was subjectively contented. Meanwhile, a black student asked that posters depicting the "negro struggle" be taken down, saying the MSM had not the faintest notion of what he thought or felt.[129] By this juncture, Stone's cadre was likely feeling little better than Bourns. In truth, of course, one fraudulent hour of sunny hope aside, the MSM stood on the fringe, rather than at the centre, of student interest. Kirkaldy had noted this, during the sit-in.

On the evening of 3 April, in considerable dudgeon, Kirkaldy had traipsed over to Gilmour Hall to offer agitators a piece of his affronted mind. To his surprise, he found himself "charmed by the idealism and compassion of most participants and the fine sense of community and co-operation in the group." At that moment, moderates were asserting more influence over the demonstration, and he heard none of the MSM's florid rhetoric. Listening closely, he came to understand that food had been a smart tactical choice on the part of radicals, but was not the students' most abiding concern. The deeper issue, he garnered, was the quality, not of hamburger, but of current university education, as a whole. For the moment, this broader theme had been relegated to the status of a leitmotif, because the problems were so many, so tangled, and so diffuse. Thus, pent-up frustrations had found an outlet in organized protest over a narrowly defined target. Pointedly, he cautioned, "This may not always be the case."[130] In this realization, the engineer was not alone.

As the sixties drew to a close, the need to answer intensifying criticism of undergraduate education was becoming ever-more apparent. Government wanted more scholars for the dollar, and it was no longer talking about PhDs. Closer to home, from French to French fries, calls for instructional reform had featured in virtually every murmur of student discontent. Complaints increasingly targeted the impersonal nature of mass lectures, the rigidity of requirements, and an emphasis on formal examinations; as well as grading schemes, and purported professorial indifference toward the great unwashed in three-year programs. Of course, these and related plaints, such as the ever-shifting plea for "relevance," were far from unique to McMaster. On the contrary, they resounded on every bursting North American campus. Whether founded in reasoned pedagogical theory, utopian musing, agonized nostalgia, or well-founded fact, this many-faceted critique had to be seen to be addressed. As Kirkaldy suggested, it simply offered too much bone-dry kindling to be ignored.

As early as 1965, the senate committee on student affairs had been tasked to recommend measures for combating the depersonalization concomitant with growth. Among other things, it advised limiting enrolments and providing a substantial, purpose-built student centre. The first option ran against the grain of government policy. The second would be realized only decades later. The committee, also, ruminated on the viability of a collegiate grouping of students into bodies of no greater than 1,000 members, each with its own master, instructors, and tutors. This thought was stillborn, as it flew in the face of established campus plans. In the end, the little came of the committee's advice, apart from its early suggestion that students be represented on deliberative bodies.[131]

Meanwhile, student government tried a different tack. In 1966, the SRA opened a vent for growing dissatisfaction by launching its own system of student-run evaluations. At first, only select courses were subjected to scrutiny. By 1968, however, all campus offerings were being rated, in an effort to help candidates make informed choices.[132] At another level, individual departments began rethinking their programs. Chemistry, for example, reduced the honours load, in 1966, and began serious reassessment of its year-one offerings.[133] At the same time, physics abandoned televised teaching and began planning more attractive courses for non-specialists. It also led the way in pioneering formal liaison committees with students, well before the general cry to do so was raised.[134] Other disciplines went through similar self-assessments. In some areas, however, the flood of candidates was so unremitting that minor adjustments could have little effect. Thode once described any class numbering more than 300 as no better than "a mob."[135] Yet, by the late sixties, there were some on the go that made 300 look like a cozy seminar.

"Mega-Classes are the Standard: Classes Jammed Up," groaned the *Silhouette*, in September 1970. Citing first-year psychology and sociology as prime examples, the journal noted that enrolments were more than 2,000 and 1,300 in those courses, respectively.[136] In this context, the 823 anthropology and 897 philosophy freshmen went unremarked, at least by the *Sil.*[137] Others, however, had been taking careful note of the incessant drift into pass degrees, especially in arts. In May 1969, for example, Dean Melling rejoiced at the unprecedented surge in social science enrolment, but could not shake the fear that this might prejudice standards.[138] His humanities counterpart, Sandy McKay, reported growing and legitimate undergraduate ferment over impersonally large classes, particularly in literature and language courses which required close tuition.[139]

Determined to analyze these trends and the student unease they provoked, the senate established an ad hoc committee on undergraduate education, in February 1969. With considerable publicity, twenty-one people, drawn from all six faculties, were appointed to the group. Care was taken to include student representatives. In the chair was Dr Gordon S. Vichert, associate professor of English, prominent member of the New Democratic Party (NDP), and outspoken champion of educational reform.[140] McMaster, it seemed, had an ear to the ground and was open to the idea of significant change. Once up and running, the Vichert Committee was literally deluged with suggestions from every constituency on campus. If testimony were required as to the depth of concern about undergraduate education at the university, the committee was soon able to supply it, by the truck load.

. Students greeted the opportunity to vent their opinions with zest. The *Silhouette* featured numerous letters to the editor remarking on a widespread desire for more discussion and less memorization. Predictably, the impersonal mass lecture system came in for particularly hard knocks. The basic requirements of 1962 were characterized as a "straightjacket." All-or-nothing examinations were decried as impediments to true learning. The litany of complaint was sonorous and long.[141] Nor did faculty hold fire. Psychologist Abe Black blasted both right- and left-wing critics, when interviewed by the campus paper. The university, he held, should serve primarily neither to destroy a supposedly sick contemporary society, nor to render it more technically efficient. Instead, he offered, its task was to foster learning and scholarship. That said, Black recognized that students came to university for many different reasons. Thus, no cookie-cutter approach to curricular reform would suffice. Rather, he concluded, a wider range of programs, perhaps drastically different from current ones, was needed.[142] Echoing Black, sociologist Frank Jones told *Silhouette* readers that a large number of students, who brought no vocational goals to their university studies, might be better accommodated in less structured programs that led to a BPhil.[143] Later, when both Jones and Black were appointed to the committee, many followers of the campus press, no doubt, concluded that a major curricular overhaul was looking more and more likely.

Private submissions to the committee were plentiful and blunt. A collective brief from the deans of studies painted a doleful picture. Much, it read, was spoken about academic freedom and the rights of professors; far less was heard concerning their obligations. Broadly speaking, they continued, faculty taught fewer hours a week than had been the case ten years earlier. "Yet," rumbled the deans, "there is evidence that the individual student receives not more, but less attention than formerly." Just as damning were the observations of Reuven Kitai, professor of electrical engineering. "Faculty in University these days," he wrote, "when free to discuss loosely the things that are paramount in their minds, show themselves all too often to be concerned first and foremost with the size of their research grants and with the number of their publications, secondly with the stock exchange, and lastly with the parking problem." Broaching another issue, anthropologist Richard Slobodin slammed a system that left both teacher and student so fixated on final examinations that it was a labour of Hercules to wean them from these "excrescences." More whimsically, a senior physics major made a different but related point. "The human being," he told the committee, "is not an egg to be graded A, B, or C but an individual searching for his place in the world." By contrast, experience with eggs had left philosopher David Hitchcock hard-boiled. "The typical undergraduate," he lamented, "attends university merely as a means to financial advancement and social status."[144] All together, if in different ways, briefs flowing to the committee moved Vichert to jump the gun. Indeed, he made his own views public, in February 1970, before reporting officially to the senate.

Forcefully delineating McMaster's shortcomings, Vichert likened the condition of undergraduates to that of Marx's alienated proletariat. Such, he told *Spectator* readers, was the effect of assembly-line education at their local university. "It is in the best interests of everyone," he argued, "to pretend that something is happening during the three or four years of a university education, despite the melancholy evidence to the contrary presented by an average graduating class." The stark truth, however, was that no one could talk to students for long "without sensing a deep unhappiness." Radicals blamed the board. Faculty blamed the government. Everybody blamed "that amorphous body called the administration." By Vichert's reckoning, all were culpable by-products of a society that worshipped success measured in size, numbers, and status. The great danger, he warned, was that, one day, the alienated would simply stop coming to an institution that served only the interests of faculty and graduate students.[145] That Vichert saw fit to publish this acidic piece prior to reporting was, in all likelihood, a measure of his frustration with proceedings in the committee.

Physicist Martin Johns had been happy to join the committee, in 1969. He was of the opinion that a large segment of the student population was "not well served" and that the university had to take heed of their views.[146] By the time Vichert penned his *Spectator* article, however, Johns was losing heart. The committee, he sighed, had struggled all autumn; yet had failed even to approach a consensus. Indeed, it had begun to meet as three separate groups. The great divide, he said, was not between students and faculty, so much as among faculties. Each was so different from the others that agreement on a general curricular policy seemed doomed. This had already led, in 1969, to abolition of the old basic university requirements. By February 1970, it seemed unlikely that more acceptable ones would arise from current deliberation.[147] Johns' sour forecast proved all too accurate.

When finally presented to the senate, in January 1971, the Vichert Report was described by its author as "a tentative and uncertain document." Its purple cover, he quipped, was emblematic of the ideological dispositions of the committee's membership: "a combination of Tory blue and radical red."[148] In fact, it was not one, but three distinct reports. The majority edition, from Vichert's hand, lauded recent, scattered experiments in problem-based learning, as inspired by medicine's example, but insisted that these had to be systematized and generalized, were undergraduate education to be rejuvenated at McMaster.[149] Twenty-five recommendations as to how this could be achieved were outlined. Several, such as lowering the student-teacher ratio, were motherhood matters to which no one objected, at least in principle. Others, however, spawned tectonic divides.

Vichert, for example, advised that two-fifths of each freshman program comprise non-prescribed "supervised study," undertaken independently, or in groups no larger than fifteen. The remaining three-fifths should allow for great flexibility and imagination and be offered at the divisional, rather than faculty level.[150] Broadening this theme, it was recommended that a new faculty of independent studies be created, replete with its own building on campus. Criteria other than mere grades would be applied to those seeking admission to this three-year program.[151] Central to these, and related recommendations, was the premise that personal engagement in the process of discovery was the high road to a true education. Students, said the majority report, must be guided, not taught, and guidance was possible only in a personalized setting. Under these circumstances, formal examinations would be unnecessary.[152] It all sounded so simple. Still, true-blue Tories on the committee registered their strong sharp dissent.

G.S. French, M.W. Johns, and A.S. Gladwin proffered a scathing minority evaluation of Vichert's proposals. To be sure, they commended the majority for identifying several real problems, but argued that such difficulties would be best handled by each faculty. The propositions for reform, they continued, should be regarded as food for thought, rather than as the senate prescriptions. Moreover, they noted that some recommendations, particularly those pertaining to year-one, came with a wholly unrealistic price tag. Meanwhile, special venom was reserved for the "do-your-own-thing" approach. Too many freshmen, they argued, lacked adequate training to engage usefully in individual studies. Worse, left to their own devices, students would always resist rigorous evaluation and gravitate to courses characterized by aimless dialogue, rather than substance. The key, said French and company, was to raise admission standards, monitor program quality, and use suggestions in the majority report as a starting point by faculties for discussing the revitalization of baccalaureate education. Only at that local level, they concluded, could an informed judgment be made as to how to balance the distribution of scarce professorial resources between graduate and undergraduate instruction.[153]

A second minority statement, authored by two idealistic students, took the notion of a community of scholars to its logical extreme. "We are aware," they wrote, "that our recommendations are somewhat strong but we do not think that aspirin and gargling are sufficient cures for leprosy." Rejecting the "nihilistic tendencies of student radicals and the 'score-keeping' of contemporary university practice," they laid out detailed plans for a university commune. Built entirely by volunteer student labour, it would be strictly holistic and wholly in tune with nature. No building would be more than two stories high. Only natural materials, such as wood and stone, would be employed. Ceilings would be a minimum of twelve feet. Artificial heating and air conditioning would be banned, as would all applied disciplines. Gymnastics and musical training, however, would be compulsory. Formal grading, of course, would be banished. This, they prophesied, would be a true home for critical thought – a "secular intellectual monastery."[154] Revenue flows, oddly enough, escaped close analysis.

The Vichert Report was debated by the senate, only to be set aside for later consideration. More bluntly, it was shelved. Clear guidelines had been sought. Instead, an indigestible stew of ill-matched ingredients had been served up. In the end, while rather drawn to the spirit, if not the particulars, of Vichert's position, the senate adopted a stance closer to that sketched by French, Johns and Gladwin. Historian Ezio Cappadocia captured the central dilemma quite neatly. No one, he observed, could possibly deny the virtues of small-group problem-solving as an ideal, but the financial implications of implementing it were daunting, especially during that stern fiscal hour.[155] Others noted that freedom of course selection was all well and good in theory, but could not be applied universally in practice. After all, learning in science, engineering, languages, and some other fields was necessarily sequential and cumulative. Random selection in such areas would be crippling, not helpful. Furthermore, the allocation of resources to year-one sufficient to achieve Vichert's scheme would reduce offerings at higher levels; thereby paving the road to inevitable mediocrity.

The senate generally agreed that the committee had done yeoman work in isolating, clarifying, and defining the sources of student and (some) faculty discontent with current undergraduate education. It had not, however, set forth alternatives applicable to the university as a whole.[156] As Dean McKay put it, the committee had generated "more heat than illumination."[157] Thus, no sweeping "Vichert Reform" was systematically undertaken. Still, it is possible to glimpse something of a "Vichert Effect" at work, as faculties and departments strove to heed the call to change, each in its own way.

The most common response was to abandon mass first-year offerings in favour of smaller sections staffed by more senior teachers. History and biology, for example, chose to drop their old general courses and offer a variety of introductory classes.[158] For their part, English and economics moved to humanize the freshman experience by mounting their traditional course in multiple time slots, until virtually all their staff members were engaged in some year-one teaching.[159] Anticipating the spirit of the Vichert Report, social science developed an experimental first-year program in 1969. It was problem-based, interdisciplinary, and team-taught. Of necessity, enrolment was restricted to fifty candidates, which was but a drop in the faculty's overfull bucket. Still, an effort was being made to accommodate the broadly curious.[160] More generally, all departments were subdividing first-year offerings into several smaller sections.[161]

In science, novel combined honours programs were devised to increase the range of options open to students, such as that which embraced geography and geology. Meanwhile, a new honours general science degree offered third- and fourth-year candidates the opportunity to design their own course of study, within limits. Mathematics began pre-testing freshmen, so as to direct them into the appropriate courses.[162] Drop-in centres were set up for students in chemistry, mathematics, and other departments. The first-year science load was reduced from six to five courses.[163] At the same time, engineering was reconsidering the entire undergraduate curriculum.[164] Amid all this refurbishment, the senate decreed that every university course would be subject to formal student evaluations.[165] When to this were added seats in the senate and growing participation in department councils, undergraduates had acquired at least some influence on the shaping of their own education.

True, their voice was not a decisive one. Similarly, the sundry curricular modifications adopted across campus did not add up to the coordinated, universal liberalization some had envisaged. Cumulatively, however, they did signal the willingness of a self-consciously research- and graduate-geared university to pay closer heed to its growingly assertive undergraduate base. Indeed, during a 1971 meeting of Thode's executive committee, Bourns speculated that McMaster might require not one but several kinds of "faculty citizens," in the future. Some, he argued, would concentrate primarily on research and graduate supervision. Others, however, might be hired exclusively for their gifts as undergraduate and extension teachers. Picking up this thread, one colleague gave it a typically Thodean twist.

Thus, he ventured that, were this done, "there will likely develop a cult of excellence in teaching, just as there is now in research."[166] This, of course, was little more than a pious hope, so long as the rewards system remained heavily weighted in favour of hefty publication – as it did. Still, the fact that the idea was broached at the highest levels of university discourse was proof that occasionally tumultuous student moments had left an imprint on the Thodean agenda. The university had acknowledged problems and had begun to address them. It had yet, however, truly to solve them. There would, in consequence, be more episodes, as the seventies unfolded.

9

The Art of Bourns

In July 1972, an empathetic colleague sent wryly ambivalent best wishes to Art Bourns. "Congratulations, felicitations, sympathy or whatever you feel most appropriate on your appointment as President," wrote Carleton chemist J.M. Holmes.[1] After more than two decades of high-velocity leadership, Thode had announced his intention to "retire" into full-time scholarship, late in 1971. Never one to advertise personal feelings, Thode offered no explanation for this decision. Still, one can speculate that a sense of rounded accomplishment must have played some role. From the founding of Hamilton College through to the official opening of MUMC, Thode had reimagined McMaster, charted its course, and seen most of his principal objectives achieved. On the other hand, even his considerable personal reserves must have been severely drained by the turmoil over health science and the nitpicking grind of administrative restructuring. In any case, a brief 1970 sabbatical at Cal Tech reminded him that immersion in science held considerably more allure than wading through budget reports. Best of all, Thode was one of the very few in Canada with moon-rock samples sitting in his laboratory, just begging for close analysis. The stars, it appeared, were propitiously aligned. It was time to turn the page. If Thode had any misgivings about leaving the bridge as McMaster entered rough waters, they were quickly assuaged. An initially reluctant Art Bourns, his fellow chemist, friend, and protege, had been persuaded by the persistent board-senate search committee to take the helm.[2]

It was later remarked that, for all his native acumen and unflagging effort, Bourns was unable to put his own stamp on McMaster in the way Thode had.[3] In one sense, this is true enough; in another, it is misleading. To be sure, conditions in the seventies militated strongly against the kind of dramatic, large-scale initiatives that marked the previous era. Indeed, circumstances

were such as to make merely holding the established line a significant challenge. At the same time, a continent-wide drift toward the codification of
faculty-student-administration relations put paid to presidential swashbuckling of the Thodean variety. Thus, Bourns' imprint was bound to be less
obvious than Thode's – until glimpsed through the glass of history's muse.

When viewed under Clio's lens, the art of Bourns is much more readily
apparent. At its core was an exceptional gift for creative, adaptive management. There are, it is said, horses for courses. In that vein, it might be argued
that Thode ran best when given his head on a dry track. The sunny sixties
had suited his bolting, hell-for-leather stride. Bourns, on the other hand,
excelled when glutinous mud choked the ground and patient determination carried the day. In the soggy seventies, there was little room for flashy
élan, but great call for consistent, firmly anchored leadership. The latter,
of course, seldom evokes thunderous huzzahs from contemporaries or rapt
attention from posterity. Its importance in the life of any institution, however, is impossible to deny. Thus, in his own, low-key way, Bourns would
leave a lasting impress on McMaster by fighting doggedly to maintain the
Thodean values he not only shared but had helped shape. What Harry set
in place, Art cemented. Put another way, if Bourns did not fashion a new
philosophy or direction for the university, it was because he entertained no
such desire. Rather, his most ardent wish was to stay the course during an
era of extreme duress. The challenges would prove formidable. It was in the
way that he met them that Bourns would leave his own particular, if subtle,
stamp upon McMaster.

The tongue-in-cheek sympathy Holmes extended to the newly presidential
Bourns was proffered only partly in jest. After all, by 1972, everybody understood that both big hair and bigger deficits were likely to persist for some
period. Indeed, late-sixties economic sniffles merely prefaced seventies-long
pneumonia. Symptomatic of this, between 1972 and 1975, Canada's gross
domestic product sagged from 7.7 to 2.6 per cent. Nationwide unemployment grew steadily, until it stood near one-in-ten, by 1979. The early decade
energy crisis did nothing to encourage swift recovery. More deeply, however, a relentless shift toward de-industrialization left many groping for elusive solutions. Simultaneously, a chilling neologism was necessarily coined.
Stagflation described an especially debilitating element of the sombre new
reality, as unemployment and inflation rose in disturbing synchrony. At mid-
decade, Ottawa sought to break the cycle by instituting an anti-inflation
board, along with price and wage controls. Federal and provincial economic
stimuli, however, offered little more than band-aid solutions to deepening
problems that were global at root.[4] Older Canadians – hardened veterans of

World War and the Depression – were probably better equipped to meet this downturn than were boomer compatriots unfamiliar with limited horizons. Ultimately, however, time-honoured institutions faced intensifying pressure from an increasingly frustrated public at large.

In this anxious environment, universities fell under particularly intense fire. Once the fair-haired children of social aspiration, they came widely to be viewed as pampered, self-indulgent offspring. A late-sixties backlash against real and perceived campus radicalism had helped to spawn this attitudinal shift.[5] Growing economic angst gave it a sharper edge. By 1970, Claude Bissell could speak of a "crisis of confidence," as the public reassessed its investment in higher education. There was, he said, a widening gap "between what society expects of the university and what the university thinks of itself."[6] That gulf only broadened as doctorates, let alone baccalaureates, ceased to guarantee self-selected, gainful employment. Unable to offer any panacea for contemporary woes, the academy's stock began to dip; at first slowly, then precipitously. In 1971, for example, the Economic Council of Canada, once a perky cheerleader, pronounced that higher education was outrunning its cost effectiveness. Others, across the continent, echoed this gloomy, actuarial refrain.[7]

While Ontario fared better than many Canadian regions, the province's resources were stretching thin. By 1970, higher education was swallowing fully 10 per cent of the provincial budget.[8] Government, as noted, had already made it abundantly clear that it wanted the most for its money. Late-sixties calls for accountability, however, paled in comparison with what John Deutsch termed the "shrill cry" of the seventies.[9] Thus, when the Lapp Report on engineering (1971) and the Wright Report on post-secondary education (1972) were finally tabled, each sent electric chills down many an academic spine, with talk of rationalization, restraint, and system oversight.[10] Meanwhile, ACAP's graduate program assessments, legacies of the Spinks Commission, loomed on the horizon. The halcyon days of "macro-indicators" were dawning.[11]

Had the baby boom not peaked and had enrolments continued to rise, there might have been less concern about close performance measurement. In 1972, however, full-time university enlistment dropped nationwide for the first time in twenty years.[12] True, there was a large, one-year resurgence in 1975. This bulge, however helpful, was temporary. Year-one intake soon reverted close to 1972 levels for the remainder of the decade.[13] On the other hand, the vocationally oriented Colleges of Applied Arts and Technology (CAATS) were flowering. In Hamilton, for example, Mohawk College was inundated by more than 11,000 applications for 2,600 openings, in 1979;

figures roughly comparable to McMaster's.[14] Universities, in short, faced serious competition for the post-secondary dollar, as the seventies wore on. More ominously, not only was that precious monetary unit closely monitored by Queen's Park, its absolute value was being gutted by the remorseless cancer of inflation. In 1974, the BIU sank to 87 per cent of its 1970 worth.[15] The situation only deteriorated. By 1979, government grants had been running well behind inflation for five years.[16] These basic facts of life were much the same for all Ontario universities. Some of those institutions, however, faced particular difficulties.

From McMaster's vantage point, "more scholar for the dollar" had especially disturbing implications. Queen's Park, Bourns observed, was pushing universities to cut back on graduate work and research, so as to become more efficient undergraduate mills.[17] McMaster, however, was unusually dependent on BIU-weighty graduate candidates to meet its heavy research commitments. Indeed, among Ontario universities, McMaster and Toronto were regularly all but tied for the lead in the proportion of their graduate-to-undergraduate populations.[18] Unfortunately, post-baccalaureate candidates grew thinner and thinner on the ground, during the shaky seventies. Moreover, the ratio of doctoral to master's enrolments tilted heavily in favour of the latter, as academic jobs dried up. Some slowing of graduate enlistment had been foreseen. However, few would have guessed that the full-time graduate cadre at McMaster in 1980 would number no more than 1,073, when it already stood at 1,063, in 1969.[19]

Complicating the picture, granting agencies began to place more and more emphasis on applied research, as opposed to the pure variety toward which McMaster was geared. In 1972, for example, Queen's Park phased out its grants-in-aid to individual scholars in favour of group projects meant to have "immediate and practical application."[20] National agencies were moving in the same direction. All told, a major sea change was gathering momentum, just as Bourns assumed office. On him would fall prime responsibility for interpreting and maintaining, at McMaster, what Dr Reva Gerstein would call the "delicate balance" between accountability and institutional identity.[21]

While no seer, Bourns understood the task ahead, without illusion. A seasoned local administrator, he was also well versed in broader affairs. The native of Petitcodiac, New Brunswick, had been educated at Acadia and McGill and had taught at Saskatoon, before coming to McMaster. In short, he had a living sense of the national whole. Excelling in his chosen field, physical organic chemistry, he was a widely respected fellow of the Royal Society of Canada (1964) and chairman of the NRC's grants committee

(1969–75), at the time he stepped into Thode's shoes. For Bourns, it was the habit of a lifetime to keep a close eye on national developments and shifting international trends. Few things would catch him wholly off guard or unprepared. The same, of course, had been true of Thode. The easterner, however, brought an intangible quality to office that his prairie predecessor lacked: openness.

Indeed, Bourns self-consciously placed an exceptionally high premium on what might be termed "informed collegiality."[22] In a way foreign to Thode, he understood that singularly difficult decisions were far more readily accepted when information was widely disseminated and rationales were laid utterly bare whenever possible. Deeply introspective and given to bouts of merciless self-examination, he was genuinely interested in hearing alternative views. A strong president, he was quite capable of decisive action. Yet, as one notably feisty MUFA head later recalled, "Art Bourns would choose the truth over covering an administrative error."[23] In return, he garnered a good deal of political capital and spent it carefully. Altogether, Bourns was the appropriate horse for the rugged seventies' course. At a minimum, he was certainly poised and ready, when the starting gate opened.

From the outset, it was clear that Bourns' leadership style would differ from Thode's. In September 1972, for example, the traditional, pre-session general faculty meeting was cancelled. Sheer numbers had rendered it impersonal, and attendance had predictably declined. Accordingly, Bourns hosted a series of focused receptions for smaller groups in the well-oiled atmosphere of the Faculty Club.[24] The new president had no glad tidings to impart, but he did have significant changes in mind and desired close discussion with people in the trenches. In a similar spirit, he noted that Thode had relied heavily on his executive committee. The president's council, in contrast, had not met for some years. This left deans out of policy discussions and without a collective forum for airing their views on cardinal matters. Thus, he reactivated that body, shortly after taking office.[25] Meanwhile, in broad strokes, he outlined his plan of campaign on the floor of the senate, in the columns of campus publications, and in his inaugural address to fall convocation.

Lamentably, the best rallying cries, about blood, sweat, toil, and tears, not to mention the last full measure of devotion, had already been snapped up by practiced wordsmiths in even more precarious times. In any case, the plainspoken Bourns was not given to rhetorical flourish. Instead, quite simply, he told listeners at his formal installation, "The honeymoon between the University and the general community is over." He pledged, however, that McMaster would maintain its traditionally high commitment to basic research and graduate study, government insistence to the contrary notwithstanding.[26] From his first to last moments in office, Bourns never wavered on this keystone tenet. Even when the unexpected freshman "bulge" hit in 1975, he told his inner council, "We should strongly encourage our faculty to ... research despite public pressures for greater engagement in undergraduate teaching." Moreover, he continued, there should be no apologies offered. Deans, said Bourns, "should encourage their faculty in scholarly work and in no way screen from public view their commitment to this activity."[27] His style might have differed from Thode's, but his core values did not.

Over the first months of his presidency, Bourns sketched a design for trimming, pruning, and streamlining McMaster to meet the "considerable stress and uncertainty" ahead.[28] Everything, he underlined, was up for review, in order that specific priorities might be identified and established strengths maintained. At the head of his list was a hard look at the administrative structure. The divisional system, he suggested, was a clumsy framework within which to coordinate university-wide policy. In its place, Bourns recommended that a single vice-president (academic) be appointed and that the remit of deans be clarified. In the same spirit, he called for a close re-evaluation of the senate's functioning. The Kirkaldy reforms, he noted, had been necessary, but shortcomings were apparent in the unclear and overlapping terms of reference of several senate bodies. As an example, he pointed to the Committee on Academic Policy (CAP). Theoretically, it was responsible for long-term planning. In practice, as the senate executive, it got bogged down in an ever-growing morass of routine detail. Strategic thinking, however, had never been more vital than at that straightened hour. Accordingly, the president advised that definition, clarity and focus be brought to a more efficient administration and senate. Were this to require a new McMaster Act, so be it. Senators concurred and set to work on the details.[29] Meanwhile, Bourns went about wringing every ounce of value from each deflated dollar at the university's disposal. This, of course, was only fiscal common sense, but the president understood that much more was at stake. Individual faculty members felt the bite of inflation every bit as much as the institution they served. In order to retain their support, he knew that major and observable retrenchment had to come in the non-academic sector, since salary needs, let alone hopes, could never fully be satisfied.[30]

Some economizing was merely symbolic in nature. In October 1972, for example, the president withdrew university support for traditional honours dinners and Christmas parties.[31] These, of course, were unlikely to break even the weakest bank, but the message was clear: frills were out. More substantially, a program of energy conservation was launched. Initially, this involved little more than flicking off lights in empty classrooms. With time, however, it developed into a systematic policy that saved the university $240,000 during fiscal 1974–75 alone.[32] On one occasion, it even allowed for the killing of two annoying birds with one presidential stone. High-rolling MUMC was consuming energy the way a veteran alcoholic guzzled muscatel. Repeated requests from Mike Hedden to stem the binge went largely ignored; much to the displeasure of Gilmour Hall. That would change, however, in 1975.

Westdale residents, still smarting after their late-sixties donnybrook with McMaster, sent up new howls about the noise generated by Zeidler's sprawling complex. When nothing was done to muffle the sleep-shattering drone, which cranked up promptly at five thirty each morning, citizens petitioned the Ministry of Environment and city hall.[33] The university was threatened with legal action. An apoplectic Bourns told Hedden to "light a fire" under those responsible for this dangerous breech with the public in delicate times. "I feel," he wrote, "that MUMC have a great tendency to do anything they can get away with and let the University take the flak."[34] When a month rolled by, with still no response from health sciences, the president scrawled a terse note to Hedden. "This," he wrote, "is a priority item that we simply cannot delay facing any longer."[35] Eventually, MUMC came on board, as effective baffles were installed to dampen the ventilated roar. Better yet, in 1976, health sciences could report $594,000 in energy savings, after central control was placed on light, heat, and air conditioning.[36] Thus, not only was a public relations nightmare set to rest, but McMaster went on to win the Conservation Award for 1977, having cut back on energy consumption more than any university in the province.[37]

While scarcely the stuff to inspire bards to lyric flight, such penny-pinching helped; but only a little and never enough.

By October 1974, the executive committee contemplated a budget shortfall of $900,000. Bourns noted that government was giving universities lower priority than hospitals, secondary schools, and the CAATS. McMaster, he declared, was now facing "the crunch." While he held a series of meetings with MUFA leaders to keep them apprised of the deteriorating situation, the president authorized even more non-academic cuts.[38] Travel requests were subjected to rigorous scrutiny. Expenditure on telephone calls was closely monitored. Equipment budgets were slashed. Invitations to graduands were to be typed, rather than set by printers. The price of photocopying was raised from five to ten cents per page. At the same time, faculty were sternly reminded to prepare syllabi and examinations promptly, so as to avoid overtime in the secretarial pool. Meanwhile, the once-hefty president's report was slimmed down to a few perfunctory pages, until this valuable historical source was discontinued altogether. More painfully, fully sixty-two support staff received pink slips in 1975.[39]

Gloomily symbolic of the hour, the soaring Great McMaster Elm was felled by disease, after surviving over 325 years and countless bullet wounds inflicted by pistol-packing vandals. One section of its mighty trunk was ceremoniously fashioned into a high-gloss table for the Faculty Club.[40] Furniture, however, was the last thing on Bourns' mind. In November 1974, reflecting on the ever-falling value of the BIU, he advised that it was unrealistic to assume that non-academic retrenchment would long suffice to stave off disastrous deficits that might leave McMaster budgets open to line-by-line government oversight. In the privacy of his inner cabinet, he reluctantly conceded that some weaker doctoral programs might have to be phased out to placate Queen's Park.[41] Indeed, he had already put the axe to one treasured academic perquisite.

By 1972, McMaster was the only university in Ontario still offering summer research stipends. These internal grants were financed out of general revenue through a presidential contingency fund. Useful in science, they had been crucial in stimulating significant scholarship in arts, during the later sixties. Thus, a thousand dollars, or so, was a spit in the ocean to many a physicist, but a massive injection for the budding economist, historian, or anthropologist.[42] Even so, from a strategic point of view, Bourns argued that these grants had to go. The stipends, he contended, sent entirely the wrong message to outsiders.[43] As he explained to the head of MUFA, summer grants were inconsistent with the objective of ensuring that both government and the public understood that a professor's work was not confined to the classroom or the academic year. Those stubbornly resistant constituencies, he continued, had to be convinced that research was integral to year-round academic engagement and merited regular funding, apart from ordinary BIU grants. Summer stipends, however, especially when drawn from operating reserves, smacked of "extras."[44]

In keeping with his inclination toward informed collegiality, Bourns chose not to proceed via presidential fiat in this matter. Instead, he turned to what would become his vehicle of choice in sensitive affairs: a joint committee. The "FAIR Committee" included presidential and MUFA representatives, who studied the issue in concert. By November 1973, the group produced a report, which, in broad outline, supported Bourns' position. Unsurprisingly, the faculty association's general membership voted it down solidly.[45] Negotiations continued, but in a polite atmosphere. When MUFA leaders finally signalled that members were prepared to entertain a compromise, the president responded quickly in kind.[46] In the end, all agreed to fold an amount equal to the stipend fund into annual merit pay calculations.[47] Bourns, it seems, was mastering his craft. Meanwhile, his spirits received an invaluable boost.

As Bourns suggested during his inaugural address, a board-senate committee was struck to study academic and administrative structures, late in 1972. Under Allan "Buck" Leal's chairmanship, the ad hoc group worked swiftly to identify means of streamlining the Kirkaldy mechanisms. By March 1973, the senate was debating the proposed revisions. Speaking for his colleagues, Leal reported that the case for restructuring was powerful; most obviously because the divisional system had left the university "over-governed." Three vice-presidents, he argued, constituted an awkward administrative stratum that could be excised to the great benefit of campus-wide coordination, were they replaced by a single vice-president (academic). Institutional costs, he added, would also be reduced. Some bridled when it was suggested that the head of health sciences be styled "associate vice-president." Leal, however, explained that this was a unique case, given that MUMC's leader drew funding from several sources, not just the Ministry of Education, and had important external links with a variety of institutions beyond the academic realm. In any event, the officer in question would still report to the vice-president (academic). This issue was set aside for further consideration.

More interest was sparked by the question as to how representative the new arrangement might be. Economist David Winch was of the firm opinion that, since the president was a scientist, the vice-president should be drawn from arts. Leal retorted that his committee had considered this idea, but felt it better to select the best person available, rather than be hamstrung by rules of disciplinary eligibility. Geologist Henry Schwarcz agreed, adding that to insist that the two chief officials come from different faculties was to go back to the divisiveness implicit in a divisional system. Alvin Lee, dean of graduate studies, concurred. Both offices, he reasoned, were university-wide in nature. Thus, the key was to choose the best people; not the right faculties. When Martin Johns gave his prestigious support to Lee and Schwarcz, the notion of reserved seating in high office died on the order paper.[48]

April saw continued discussion of the report, during which Bourns' collegial values came into sharp focus. Leal suggested (surely at Bourns' urging) that the president's advisory council and PBAC, henceforth, be appointed by and from the senate, rather than at the discretion of Gilmour Hall. Granted, these bodies had no decision-making functions, but they were important forums for high-level discussion. Winch queried the notion, at which point Bourns clarified that he wanted to ensure that he received direct, regular advice from the senate, whether he liked what he might hear or not. He added that the president's council should be small; otherwise there would be a tendency to fall back on his more informal executive committee "to an extent greater than would be desirable."[49] The executive group would continue to function, but only for short-term emergency purposes. The bulk of its work would be transferred to the new senate body.[50] If there were any doubt that Bourns' approach would differ markedly from Thode's, it was further removed by Leal's tenth recommendation "that every effort be made to retain and expand the use of joint ... committees." Clearly, the new president meant to consult widely.[51]

At the same time, Leal advised against concentrating too much power in the hands of deans. Instead, he recommended that greater authority and responsibility be devolved upon departmental chairs, whose positions were more precisely defined. For his part, Bourns had once championed the idea that chairmen should enjoy unlimited stints in office. Now, he conceded that, regardless the merit of incumbents, no head of a department should serve more than two consecutive three-year terms. Fresh blood and the promise of a return to scholarship within a reasonable period outweighed the benefits of chaining the best and brightest to administrative drudgery. Moreover, said the president, it was wise to inhibit the development of fiefdoms, such as had developed in the past. None of this, however, was meant to emasculate the deans. On the contrary, the intent was to lighten their daily load in an era of paper-pushing accountability. In this connection, Leal moved that deans of studies be elevated to the rank of decanal associates, tasked with broader duties than the counselling of students. To knit all together, he further recommended that regular meetings of deans and chairmen be formally mandated by the senate, so as to bring departments more systematically into the making of faculty policy.[52]

Kirkaldy had begun the process of cleansing McMaster's Augean stable, crammed as it had been with outdated organizational relics. Some ungainly detritus, however, remained. Leal, with Bourns' imprimatur, swept it up. A more modern academic-administrative regime was the result. One of its key building blocks was set in place when the first vice-president (academic) was named. Bourns, while disputing Winch's logic, saw the wisdom in appointing someone from arts. After all, by 1973, social science and humanities, together, claimed over 54 per cent of undergraduate and 34 per cent of graduate enrolments at the university.[53] Here was a constituency too large to go unrepresented in the corridors of higher office. Moreover, it was home to several highly capable candidates. One, however, stood out with special clarity in Bourns' mind. Always preferring the personal touch, the president, therefore, drove out to "Stormont," the picturesque West Flamborough home of graduate dean, Alvin Archie Lee, for a chat.

The latter, a rising Old-English expert, who would later gain international recognition for his work on *Beowulf*, was duly flattered but deeply hesitant. In early life, he had trained for the ministry, only (with the inspiration of Northrop Frye) to find his life's true vocation in scholarship. A career in administration was the farthest thing from his mind. True, Lee was proving to be an able successor to Mel Preston, but he regarded his decanal stint as something akin to the dues-paying owed by every good academic citizen; not as a defining change of course. Bourns, however, was persistent and persuasive; enough so as to give the reluctant dean pause. When the president agreed to defer the appointment for a year, so that Lee could refresh himself in archives abroad, the two reached an accord.[54] After consulting with faculty, as well as with MSU, GSU, and alumni leaders, the senate unanimously approved Lee's appointment to the new office (today, that of "provost"), effective 1 July 1974.[55]

At first glance, Lee and Bourns must have seemed an odd pairing. The president had an informal air, a gangly frame, and a devout aversion to all things athletic. Lee, by contrast, radiated a natural austerity; born, perhaps, of a background in divinity, honed by a runner's self-discipline, and enhanced by a sonorous basso profundo. Superficialities aside, the two men also differed, at times substantially, as to where emphasis should be placed in the quest to adapt McMaster to a Spartan hour. Bourns favoured shoring up and rejuvenating established areas of proven strength, be they in fields as diverse, but firmly rooted, as materials research or religious studies. At times, he felt that Lee pressed the case for newer fields too far.[56] For his part, Lee thought that there was untapped potential in several spheres and that McMaster "should stress these strengths to O.C.U.A to indicate that we are more than Canada's M.I.T."[57]

Still, in his own way, Lee agreed with the general strategy of encouraging focused excellence, rather than across-the-board development. "The challenge [of the seventies]," he later wrote, "was to build on our strengths, even if this meant letting our less distinguished or less developed activities suffer in a period of tightening financial pressures."[58] Priority funding, as he saw it, was "a way of making sure that some very fine things emerged." Thus, he recalled: "As long as there was enough money to build up a good library and get a first-rate program in History or Philosophy or English and so on, I didn't fight it too much."[59]

Clearly, there was some (healthy) tension between the two chief administrators, but not so much as to impede good working relations. Indeed, having chosen a vice-president, Bourns was punctilious about not interfering in Lee's oversight of day-to-day academic affairs or appointments.[60] At a minimum, moreover, they most likely agreed on one cardinal point, which Lee captured nicely in a 2008 memoir concerning his vice-presidential days. "My overall goal," he wrote, "was to assist in every way possible in having McMaster be (and be known as) the academically strongest university of medium size in Canada."[61] Bourns might have rephrased this statement slightly, by adding the words: "in specific fields." The president, however, was unlikely to dissent from the spirit at the heart of Lee's assertion. After all, Bourns prized McMaster's reputation for excellence every bit as much as his lieutenant did. On that score, even late in retirement, he could wistfully recall a 1978 meeting of the newly established National Science and Engineering Research Council (NSERC). A table, ranking universities according to per capita grants and the success rates of applicants, was presented to the group. Time after time, results showed that McMaster led in its fields of special concentration. "I took tremendous pride in this," Bourns reminisced.[62] In any event, some differences notwithstanding, the two men would forge a solid modus vivendi.

Lee's initial hesitancy about accepting the new post was understandable on several grounds, not least of all because the president needed someone with steel enough to play a decidedly hard-nosed role. From his first hours in office, Bourns made it clear that, for the indefinite future, financial stringency ruled out enlarging the overall faculty. The flexibility to recruit at will was a luxury of the past, as were profuse and invigorating infusions of new blood. He did soothe some immediate fears by promising that no tenured instructor would be released on the grounds of financial exigency. This, however, meant that a largely middle-aged faculty complement would be frozen in place. Little, therefore, could be done to relieve pressure on some departments that were becoming grimly understaffed, as student preferences shifted.

Indirectly, Bourns was referring particularly to the plight of social science. When appointments ground to a halt across the university, that beleaguered faculty was ministering to as many undergraduates as science, engineering, and business, combined.[63] Such imbalance had to be endured, said the president, at least for the foreseeable future. He did not, of course, mention what Lee later called an "open secret." Enrolment caps or higher admission standards for social science were not entertained, because BIU income generated by that faculty's thronging hordes was being funnelled into science and engineering to offset research overhead costs.[64] What Bourns did emphasize was that grants of tenure would be fewer and fewer in years to come. Short-term contractual and post-doctoral appointments would have to provide improvement, flexibility, and variety in staffing, until times changed for the better.[65] That happy hour, however, moved farther and farther into an uncertain future, as time went on.

Indeed, by November 1974, Bourns was alerting colleagues that the immediate horizon loomed positively black. All signs for 1975 pointed to a sudden increase in enrolment, after several years of stagnation. In fact, the one-time "bulge," as much a curse as it was a blessing, totalled fully 18 per cent. Early discussion with government, however, indicated that operating grants would not even keep pace with inflation, let alone allow for fresh faculty appointments. The results, Bourns warned, could prove "disastrous" for McMaster.[66] Much of that winter and spring, therefore, went to formulating appeals for a new funding model; one that recognized the indirect costs of research, in addition to simple enrolments. After all external grants, from NRC or similar agencies, covered only direct expenses, for things such as equipment or travel. Overhead, for light, heat, maintenance, and dozens of other daily necessities, was provided by the university out of ordinary operating revenue.

By the early seventies, every research dollar won externally required roughly ninety cents of additional internal support. For a research-intensive university, such as McMaster, this constituted a considerable drain on its BIU revenue. In light of this, Bourns asked whether government wanted universities to surrender their research functions, altogether.[67] Such, of course, was not the case. Even so, Queen's Park had its own fiscal nightmare with which to contend and was not about to cave into pressure from Ontario's university leaders. Thus, in February 1975, James Auld, minister of colleges and universities, wrote personally and emphatically to Bourns. "We must impress upon you," said Auld, "that the constraints faced by government are real and we must live within them if the stability of the Province is to be preserved."[68] Having tossed a Hail Mary pass into a gang of swarming defenders, Bourns, then, went about rallying his McMaster teammates behind a new game plan.

In the direct manner that was becoming his hallmark, the president visited each of the faculties that spring. He was aware that the majority of staff knew little of the BIU system and less about the full implications of government policy. With bad news to break, Bourns wanted to deliver it personally and answer any questions that might arise. Thus, he outlined the basic facts, emphasizing that a spending reduction of approximately $2.5 million per annum would be necessary for the next few years, if McMaster were to avoid running significant deficits. When asked what was wrong with deficit financing, he pointed to the example of the University of Manitoba. That institution, Bourns noted, had adopted such a strategy, only to wind up "under the thumb of government for line-by-line budget accountability." This, he argued, was a fate that McMaster would avoid, like the plague, itself. Instead, he proposed instituting a system of "zero-based budgeting." The days of rolling over established budgets were gone. Henceforth, said Bourns, every unit would have to start from scratch, each year. The PBAC would strike eight task forces to develop "decision components" then rank units in order of priority. Those elements with the lowest priority might be discontinued. In all likelihood, he continued, some staff reduction was inevitable. These, Bourns admitted, were stern measures. The payoff, however, was that McMaster would keep what it valued most: top-quality faculty and first-class research capacity.[69] Enter, Alvin Lee.

As he later described it, the new vice-president's toughest task was to conduct a drawn-out "mopping up operation." The challenge was to economize at every hand, while simultaneously enhancing the university's academic stature. No simple chore under optimal conditions, this charge was rendered heavier, given that McMaster was weakest precisely where shifting student tides demanded fresh strength. During the later sixties, exploding enrolments had pitted all Canadian universities in a cutthroat scramble for instructors in the social sciences and business. As Lee recalls, McMaster found itself at a disadvantage in this rough-and-tumble scrum, having been slow to develop these areas. "The exceptions," he notes, "were Economics and Religious Studies which were well along in becoming two of the few best departments in their disciplines in Canada." Anthropology, too, had made quick strides, but other departments lacked the reputation consistently to attract premium applicants. By the time he came to office, notes Lee, the upshot was a backlog of candidates who were under-qualified for reappointment or tenure.[70] Inevitably, pruning shears were applied, as financial skies grew ever darker.

Senate minutes from the seventies are littered with appeals against negative decisions on tenure or renewal by that body's appointments committee.[71] Almost invariably, these cases arose because a departmentally recommended candidate was rebuffed at higher levels of the approvals process. In most instances, people were turned back because they had yet to complete their doctorates or had under-developed research programs. Occasionally, it was a question of shifting instructional strength to areas most in need. Considerations of faculty and disciplinary renewal, no doubt, also came into play. Winnowing and shuffling of this sort had begun during the last days of Thode's tenure, but increased sharply, after 1972. For his part, Bourns generally chose not to involve himself closely in matters of appointment. To do so would be to second-guess his vice-president.[72] Thus, in the Darwinian process of preserving faculty quality on very short commons, the heavy lifting fell to Lee.[73]

When it came to pruning, many candidates could see the writing on the wall and quietly accepted the inevitable. Some, however, chose to plead their case. At times, especially early on, extended battles ensued, since McMaster had yet to work out an adequate appeals process. Occasionally, appellants looked to students and sympathetic colleagues, people outside the hazily defined "system," for support. Those who hailed from already politicized departments had little difficulty in recruiting such aid. When cases of this nature coincided with widespread uneasiness wrought by hard times, lingering questions about student representation, and the failure of the Vichert Report to deliver readily observable change, all was in place for the most percussive hour of Bourns' presidency.

"Give Me Librium or Give Me Meth!"[74] By 22 March 1974, the *Silhouette's* tongue-in-cheek invitation to pharmaceutical escape might well have tempted even the most conservative among warring parties on a fractured McMaster campus. From protester to president, a good many hungered for any relief from stress after weeks of escalating tension, punctuated by instances of potentially explosive confrontation. For a time, indeed, it seemed that student "moments" of the late sixties might finally be transformed into a fully fledged movement capable of drawing legions to the banner of activism. Spray-paint vandalism and poster-board invective added dashes of brazen colour to a many-sided debate. "Senate Follies," "Bourned Again," "Butcher a Pig for National Police Week," and other (unprintable) slogans proliferated faster than they could be removed.[75] The MSU, ordinarily challenged to raise a quorum, had difficulty accommodating crowds jostling for elbow space at raucous meetings. MUFA, meanwhile, vigilantly on guard against student intervention in appointment, tenure, and promotion hearings. It was all so reminiscent of the 1970 food protest, but at a much higher order of magnitude. In full-flower, the affair served as a lightning rod for myriad discontents, until the original *casus belli* was all but obscured. The immediate trigger, however, was a long-simmering wrangle over matters pedagogical in the Department of Romance Languages.

More specifically, furor engulfed the French section of that department. Early rumblings were heard in 1967, when disgruntled senior students aired pedagogical concerns in the *Silhouette*. Disappointed majors were critical of a program that failed to encourage "oral fluency." Much lecturing was in English, while language laboratories were geared to the rote learning of taped phrases, rather than to honing conversational skill. Students were feeling badly shortchanged.[76] When their initial complaints went unheeded, a French Student Reform Committee was struck to document and articulate undergraduate concerns. In February 1968, the group reported on a questionnaire it had circulated to all undergraduates in French. Three hundred replies had poured in. The overwhelming majority of respondents supported the fundamental principle that French, not English, should be the primary language of instruction and examination. In addition, well over two-thirds thought that majors should have at least some voice in the process of curricular reform. Results of the survey were respectfully submitted to the department for attention.[77]

Within a week, committee leaders were cautiously optimistic. The department chairman seemed genuinely sympathetic to their call for constructive change. Still, any rejoicing was guarded, at best. After all, one professor was on record as holding that academic freedom extended to choosing the language of instruction. Furthermore, the chairman had noted that most instructors thought students lacked the grounding in vocabulary and grammar to write all papers and examinations exclusively in French.[78] Attitudes, such as this, drove some fellow academics, let alone students, to distraction. Thus, German scholar and McMaster graduate Gerry Chapple had thought twice, before accepting a post at his alma mater. In 1966, with a freshly minted doctorate from Harvard, he was not short of job offers. Still, the pull of home was strong, save for one consideration. In an era of dawning bilingualism, the fate of language departments tended to be tied closely to the health and prestige of offerings in French. Thus, Chapple hesitated, since that key discipline had had a weak reputation at McMaster, as far back as his own undergraduate days, in the fifties. Curriculum and pedagogy, he observed, were old-fashioned. Worse still, said Chapple, only one francophone had been granted tenure during the last thirteen years. Meanwhile, he had misgivings about the scholarly attainment of several established faculty members. All told, he attested, the rising student critique was not a case of mere troublemaking.[79]

In fairness, it should be noted that senior French instructors were not insensitive to student desires. As early as 1952, Arthur Patrick had initiated a policy of bringing "a more authentic language experience" to undergraduates. Accordingly, one or two young French-speaking assistants were hired annually, on short-term contracts, in order to encourage fluency. Most of these birds of passage came from France, but a few hailed from Switzerland or Quebec. Such posts were advertised and selection was competitive, with full dossiers and references required. Later, a series of exchanges brought francophone conversational assistants to Hamilton, while some local students spent invaluable time at universities in France. Then, in 1966, McMaster greeted its first "military co-operant." New cultural arrangements between France and Canada allowed qualified citizens of the republic to spend two years teaching full loads at universities in the Dominion, in lieu of military service at home. The great attraction, from McMaster's vantage point, was that the scheme facilitated a native-French presence in the department, at relatively low cost. By international agreement, salaries were capped below the rank of lecturer for the first sixteen months of what were envisaged as strictly short-term appointments. The opportunity to enlarge the faculty complement, while enhancing the French tone of the program, was too good to pass up, or so it seemed.[80]

Almost immediately, students hungry for the "authentic voice," gravitated to these youthful co-operants. Very soon, they were insisting that the best of them be retained, rather than replaced after short stays.[81] In November 1972, therefore, 200 students signed a petition to university authorities, urging that co-operant Guy Ducornet not be "fired." Signatories went on to ask that the department recognize a student representative committee and accept its advice on matters of curriculum and appointment.[82] Before long, however, rumours circulated that two other popular co-operants were on the chopping block. Accordingly, a call to direct action was raised.[83]

In March 1973, 300 concerned undergraduates proposed a boycott of classes, unless they were granted significant representation on key committees. Genteel talks with the chairman were described as pointless. The department, said rally leaders, was in thrall to a clique of British-born, senior professors who approached French as though it were a "dead language." Lectures and texts emphasized grammar and usage more appropriate to the nineteenth than the twentieth century. Furthermore, it was alleged, department "oligarchs" exhibited an obvious bias against French nationals and French Canadians.[84] A sit-in was scheduled for late March, to prompt professors to take student demands seriously. Reference was also made to the formation a French Student Union (FSU).[85] At the last moment, a compromise was reached. Two students were admitted to department meetings as voting members. As well, henceforth, all committees were to be made up of three faculty and two student representatives. The sole exception was the personnel committee, whose composition was set aside for further discussion. Both sides, then, adopted a wait-and-see stance.[86] During this uneasy truce, the FSU drafted its constitution and organized for 1974. By February of that year, it had over 180 "card-carrying" members.[87]

Meanwhile, sniping fire was kept up in the columns of the *Silhouette* and the *Radish*, an "alternative" student publication. These broadsheet salvoes, moreover, were often far from desultory. Indeed, one inflammatory January 1974 article finally elicited a sledgehammer response. Penned by a self-styled "French 1b6 Deserter," it was aimed at "anyone interested in learning how not to speak French."[88] For some faculty, targeted by sharpshooters in the campus press, this was the last straw. Banding together, they threatened legal action, if the journals in question continued their one-sided barrage.[89] FSU leaders disavowed the "Deserter's" sarcastic, personal attack. Instead, they emphasized a desire to work with the faculty to improve education in French. To that end, they asked for parity on all committees, challenged the whole concept of tenure, alleging little weight was accorded to teaching, and went on to suggest that admission standards be raised so as to keep ill-equipped candidates out of the program.[90] At the same time, the MSU president wrote Bourns asking how sincere the university was in its highly trumpeted calls for dialogue with students, when criticism in print elicited such a heavy-handed, legal response.[91] The president agreed that quick recourse to law was always unwise, but pointed out that the offending article seemed more eager to embarrass an individual professor than to forward the cause of constructive exchange. Even so, he confessed that he, too, was "most disturbed" by the professors' actions.[92]

Behind the scenes, there was more at play than anger with the student press. French instructors were rapidly dividing into two hostile camps. In the main, older members were pitted against younger colleagues, with the latter sympathetic to the SFU. Conflict came to a head over appointments. In January 1974, seven tenured faculty members wrote lividly to university authorities expressing their "total lack of confidence" in the personnel committee, asking that its hiring recommendations be nullified.[93] One of them, Brian Pocknell, spelled out the group's objections at considerable length for Alwyn Berland, recent successor to Sandy McKay as dean of humanities. A number of irregularities were highlighted for the dean's edification.

Pocknell denied that he and his colleagues were oblivious to the shortcomings of the program and the desirability of change. Indeed, he underscored, "This is the time to upgrade the language teaching in French; it is the chance to establish a well-organized and harmonious teaching body." Rejuvenation, he emphasized, meant recruiting more francophones to the permanent staff. This included hiring an expert director to coordinate long-term development of laboratory facilities. Therefore, he rejoiced that numerous, well-qualified, native French speakers had made application for these vital posts. For the first time in a long while, he said, it would be unnecessary to accept, at random, less qualified candidates through the military-cultural arrangement.

Unfortunately, he continued, collusion and self-interest seemed likely to block the path to true renewal. The current appointments committee, he alleged, was stacked with friends of the present co-operants and bent on their appointment. "All three internal candidates," wrote Pocknell, "have, with the blessing of the committee, been excused from submitting names of referees, even though their applications refer to work undertaken towards advanced degrees for which no documentation has ever been filed." No other applicants were granted this exemption. Indeed, few others were given consideration. To add to this dark picture, said Pocknell, terms of the university's appointment document had been violated in several respects. Thus, the department chairman, Antonio Alessio of the Italian section, was not head of the committee. Instead, that task had been left to a known ally of the internal aspirants. Furthermore, a short list had been sent to the dean without colleagues in the department first being consulted. Pocknell went on to detail numerous other examples of bad practice, some of which had unfortunate consequences for staffing in the smaller Spanish and Italian sections of romance languages.[94]

As a counterstroke, he and David Williams submitted their own shortlist for consideration.[95] Surveying various dossiers, the humanities appointments committee offered a one-year contract to Patrick Imbert, a French-born, landed immigrant nearing completion of his doctorate.[96] Recommendations concerning the remaining posts were reserved, for the moment. Amid growing rancour and distrust, word of this decision somehow failed to filter down to the department rank and file. A stiff price would soon be exacted for this oversight.

Tensions were amplified by forays in yellow journalism. In a January edition of the *Radish*, unsigned articles reported, in depth, on heated debates at departmental meetings. For good measure, student scribes injected shots of pure vitriol, proclaiming, for example, that the research of certain faculty had little more intellectual merit than the telephone book.[97] Outraged, Dean Berland condemned such "irresponsible and anonymous slander, name-calling and cheap invective," in a white-hot letter to the editor. Hitting back, the dean added, "Surely serious questions about the desirability of student representation in department meetings are inevitably raised when such irresponsible reporting of the deliberations ... is the result."[98]

A few days later, Alessio advised the SFU executive that seventeen faculty members were refusing to attend any department meetings until a formal apology was issued and students undertook to refrain from personal attacks.

Pointedly, he added that even professors sympathetic to the general student cause found this specific incident distasteful. Had SFU leaders lost control of their members? Alessio thought it likely, since one particularly offensive article was signed by "The French Students Committee"; yet he knew that the majority of the executive were unaware of the piece, until it appeared in print. In any case, he advised the executive that they had best set their house in order. Along with Berland, he questioned the maturity and professional ethics of student representatives on the department's committees.[99]

Far from backing off, however, the *Radish* pumped up the volume. Disaffected faculty members chimed in. One fiery associate professor, Everett Knight, declared that the SFU was merely prosecuting a cultural struggle that engaged the whole Western academic community. Clearly an avid reader of Michel Foucault, he pictured students as challenging the outdated concept of objectivity. Truth, he argued, was merely a function of time, social location, and power. Locally, the SFU was combating "institutionalized violence," as wielded by the university, backed by the police. Continental francophones, he continued, understood this and taught from that perspective; hence, they were hounded by the establishment at McMaster. "Now," he proclaimed, "it is up to the students; they will either be content to remain victims of the horrifying provincialism of English-speaking culture, or they will insist upon finding out about what is going on elsewhere." Amazingly, he did not add, "*Allons, enfants!*" Still, plenty were ready to storm the barricades, and not all were candidates in French. Thus, in the same edition of the *Radish*, sociology students issued a firm declaration of solidarity with the SFU. "Faculty stooges and lackeys with reactionary viewpoints," they fulminated, "will not be tolerated."[100]

In reply to this charged rhetoric, an irate Dr Brian Blakey wrote heatedly to Bourns and Berland. The administration, he blared, was grossly underestimating the role of raw political machination at work. Knight, he alleged, along with five of the six most recent co-operants, were devout Marxists, intent on swaying the department by catering to the FSU, while harassing fellow faculty members. They curried student favour by doling out inflated grades, on the premise that all formal evaluation was a form of "bourgeois" social control. At the moment, they were over-represented on the personnel committee and were "cynically manipulating student opinion by presenting a false choice: retention of the three internal Francophones or the hiring of new Anglophones, whilst omitting from their short list better qualified French-speakers."[101] Clearly, fault lines were turning into fractures, and fractures into chasms. Meanwhile, an in-house dispute was rapidly broadening out; enough so as to set MUFA's sensitive antenna quivering. Thus,

Gerry King, head of the faculty association, privately urged Bourns to establish a formal inquiry into the problems of romance languages, before the CAUT was called in – something nobody wanted.[102] The president, however, chose to wait. As things transpired, he waited just a little too long.

On 7 March 1974, a high-voltage meeting of the department turned biting words into disruptive action. Chairman Alessio announced that Bourns had finally invoked the mediation process adopted by the senate in 1972. Under its terms, Dr Barber Mueller, professor of surgery, was appointed as mediator among the belligerent parties. The idea, of course, was to buy time for tempers to cool and common ground to be found. Before the meeting adjourned, however, Paul Paboeuf, a co-operant, moved that students be granted outright parity, with full voting rights on all committees. By then, all present knew that the FSU was publicly committed to boycotting classes should parity not be ceded. Indeed, student leaders had threatened to advertise the sundry inadequacies of French studies at McMaster to high schools throughout the region, unless their demands were met.[103] Predictably, volcanic debate erupted. A motion to table Paboeuf's proposal passed only when a nine-all tie was broken by the chair's casting vote.[104] This triggered an immediate student riposte. Accordingly, at 11:00 a.m. on Friday, 8 March, the French strike began. In short order, it held centre stage in a campus-wide melodrama; one that would, eventually and quite literally, include a DeMille-like cast of thousands.

Like a snowball plummeting downhill, the French affair gathered weight and momentum, the longer it rolled along. In highlighting the issue of student representation, the SFU quickly became a *cause célèbre* (or *bête noire*) for many beyond the French section. Student senator Ted McMeekin, for example, grasped hold of its coattails eagerly. A candidate in social work, he hailed from a program in which student parity was taken for granted. As an elected senator, he found it hard to accept that undergraduates, by far the largest constituency on campus, had only limited representation on the university's deliberative bodies. An opportunity to address this seeming anomaly arose when the senate established the Winch and Leal committees. While the latter laboured to streamline administrative and academic organization, the former worked to revamp the structure and membership of the senate. Given this opening, McMeekin lobbied hard to expand and extend student participation, right into the sanctum of the board of governors. By September 1973, he was chiding Bourns for rambling on about "balanced representation," when students constituted only 8.6 per cent of the sixty-nine senators.[105] True, he neglected to mention that it was currently difficult to find sufficient volunteers to fill just six senate seats. Perhaps, however, the future provincial cabinet minister reasoned that there would be candidates aplenty, once representation was proportional. Whatever the case, the roiling French dispute would provide an ideal platform for McMeekin to promulgate his wider cause. Meanwhile, others gravitated to the strike, for their own reasons.

The MSU and GSU executives tendered immediate support. Several French instructors joined in, cancelling classes for the duration, while offering to stand picket and explain complex issues to the perplexed. The most ardent endorsement, however, came from sociology majors. Just recently, they had overwhelmingly voted to back McMeekin's call for student parity on the senate.[106] Now, they saw strong parallels between FSU demands and their own concerns. At that moment, they had four seats at general department meetings, but no representatives at informal caucuses of the faculty. Unconfirmed rumour had it that the next chairman was about to be selected by the caucus without student input. In addition, they shared the FSU's dislike of the increasing resort to short-term contracts and the supposed leash kept on young instructors, who had to conform or face non-renewal. Thus, they were quick off the mark to inform classmates of the stake they had in the strike.[107]

Social work candidates echoed their sociological colleagues.[108] For their part, some graduate students still harboured ill feelings over a strike by teaching assistants in the last days of Thode's tenure. The affair had been short-lived, once it was understood that it was Queen's Park that was cutting into graduate incomes, not the university. Still, the graduate mood remained anxious. Meanwhile, the MSU, while far from radical, felt obliged to support one of its recognized affiliates, so long as protest remained within accepted bounds. Altogether, the FSU enjoyed substantial moral support, as it set up picket lines on Friday morning.

It is unclear whether or not FSU leaders approached the strike with a fully defined strategy. Friday was given over mostly to establishing headquarters in the lobby of Arts II (Togo Salmon Hall), assigning various duties, and picketing those classes not cancelled. The weekend, of course, was inevitably quiet, with the majority of students and professors off campus. Behind the scenes, however, talks continued with mediator Barb Mueller, who had begun his formal inquiry just days before the strike. Judicious, widely respected, and fair-minded, he took great pains to maintain the stance of a detached, honest broker. True, he was firmly on record as favouring an enhanced role for students in university governance, but he had no axe to grind in this particular dispute.[109] Thus, his appointment had been quickly endorsed by FSU leaders and the department alike. Anxious to hear all sides of the story, Mueller readily accepted an invitation to meet informally with strike leaders, on Saturday, 9 March.

Over the course of a three-hour discussion, students restated their basic case, while adding some candid thoughts about individual instructors. In general, they emphasized a preference for younger professors, because they kept abreast of current scholarship, were on campus all day, and maintained on open-door policy. Students described parity as essential, because the department regularly divided nine-to-nine on every cardinal issue. This paralysis, they argued, had to be overcome. In his personal notes, "A Chronicle of Mediation," Mueller concluded that these students truly did seem to focus primarily on pedagogical issues. He scribbled his concern that factional fighting and the lack of procedural rules kept the department from addressing educational points at stake. Noticeably absent from Mueller's daily journal was any hint that serious escalation of the strike was being contemplated on Saturday.[110] Like many others, he was taken by surprise, when the FSU's tactics abruptly changed.

On Monday, 11 March, strikers occupied Dean Berland's office. Two days later, others invaded that of President Bourns, declaring their intent to stay indefinitely. When queried by *Silhouette* reporters as to why they had raised the ante so suddenly, FSU leaders replied that, having received no reaction from the department over the weekend, they thought it necessary to bring pressure directly on the higher administration. "We weren't getting any action," said one striker, "just talk, talk, talk." Another, somewhat snidely, offered that, since Berland's office lacked space for all who wanted to sit-in, they had occupied Bourns' as well. Whatever the motives behind this rapid escalation, the administration refused to be provoked. Indeed, Les Prince, dean of students, went so far as to provide cushions and blankets for the strikers, while ensuring that doors to Gilmour Hall were left unlocked, allowing students to come and go at will. The occupation force settled in and railed against the "tenured tyranny" of an "Anglophone clique."[111]

Meanwhile, campus reporters noted that sociology, social work, and other students were, now, members of the central strike committee. On a related front, a petition, circulated by McMeekin and friends, found strong support for student parity on the board and the senate, albeit among a small sample group.[112] Then, on Friday, 15 March, sociology students won equal representation at departmental meetings. Immediately, they swung the full weight of their department behind the FSU, general parity, and an end to one-year contracts.[113] At the same juncture, disgruntled candidates in political science were voted money by the SRA to produce a counter-calendar.[114] Things were heating up quickly: too quickly, for MUFA's liking.

Accordingly, Gerry King, president of the faculty association, fired off a barbed missive to Mueller. The executive, he said, had met, on 8 March, and was firmly opposed to student parity. This position, King noted, was not born of elitism. Instead, he argued, it reflected the commonsense experience of those men and women who peopled the nation's lecture halls, and was in accord with policy statements of the CAUT. Students, he declared, had an obvious right to a voice in some specific matters, such as curriculum, but not in complex, long-resonating decisions concerning appointment, tenure, or promotion. He underlined that student interest in university government rose and fell unpredictably. At the moment, King observed, it was difficult to fill senate, faculty, and department seats allotted to them. Who, then, would even consider granting students parity in the $40-million enterprise called McMaster University? The best method for acquiring student input, he submitted, was through informal channels.[115]

For his part, Bourns avoided all public comment. Instead, he relied on the mediation process, as the senate prescribed. On that front, things seemed promising. With great diplomacy, Mueller had won agreement from romance languages and the FSU for small groups representing each party to work with him toward a binding resolution. The department, rather surprisingly, committed itself to be bound by the outcome of these task-force talks.[116] A pinprick of light seemed to wink at the end of an otherwise black tunnel. It was, however, only flickering. Thus, Mueller was disturbed when he went to meet with FSU executives at Bourns' office the next day, Friday, 15 March. To his surprise, the room was jammed with sociology candidates, who tried to monopolize the conversation. The surgeon attempted to stick to issues particular to the FSU, but found that impossible. He soon left.

That evening, a mood of deep concern coloured a gathering at Bourns' residence. There were reports flooding in that picketers were harassing other students and systematically disrupting the few French classes still being offered. A dozen complained to Harley Steubing, newly elected MSU president, while others spoke to the *Silhouette,* of being subjected to intimidation. Steubing and the SRA put strikers on notice that council support was not unconditional.[117] Anxious to calm the waters, Bourns issued a public statement, the following day.

During mediation, Mueller had endeavoured to decouple the question of parity from pedagogical and staffing matters. Bourns followed suit. As was widely known, he told readers, a new chairman had been recruited to help refresh the atmosphere in the department. Dr César Rouben, a francophone educated in France, with a PhD from McGill and several years' teaching experience at Loyola, would be at the helm as of 1 July 1974. Since student representation at the level of departments was a matter for those bodies to decide, Bourns advised setting aside the parity issue, until the romance languages' faculty complement for the following year was clarified. On that latter score, however, he was prepared to extend a heavily laden olive branch.

Originally, four appointments had been authorized for romance languages: one in Spanish, one laboratory director, and two in French. In keeping with stated university policy, all were intended to be one-year posts. Bourns, then, noted that the Faculty of Humanities had recommended Patrick Imbert for one of these contractually limited positions, given that he was French, his doctorate was near completion, and he specialized in language, linguistics, and French-Canadian literature. Thus, the appointment was made. However, he continued, both the French section and the mediator had subsequently advised that francophone presence in the department needed further shoring up. Accordingly, the president agreed to offer three-year contracts to two of the co-operants, Françoise Pfirrmann and Paul Paboeuf, as well as to the lab director. In total, this would add a member to the French section. Furthermore, Bourns promised that the exchange agreement, whereby three advanced students were brought from France to aid in conversational programs, would be continued.[118]

All told, these were major concessions, both to the department and the FSU. It was, also, quite as far as Bourns was willing to go in bending appointment policy, especially since enrolment was steadily declining in humanities. Privately, he instructed Mueller to tell all parties, "These decisions are final and action has already been taken on them."[119] At the same time, he wrote personally to Janice Paquette, leader of the FSU, assuring her that he and Dean Berland would tolerate no academic penalties or discrimination against strikers, so long as matters were concluded peacefully by 18 March.[120]

It fell to Mueller to convey the president's message to students occupying Bourns' office, on 16 March. As a courtesy, he did so before the statement was made public. Again, he found a smattering of FSU executives amid a larger group of sociology majors. Rather than addressing the offer at hand, those assembled focused on the surprise news of Imbert's hiring. Much criticism was levelled at supposed breeches of procedure in the appointments process. When the matter of parity was raised, discussion disintegrated into shouting. Mueller departed discouraged. "I left," he confided to his journal, "with the feeling that I had used up all my points with that group." The riveting on procedural issues, he continued, "suggests to me that they are now searching for an issue ... that will generate enthusiasm to continue the strike." Under the growing influence of sociology majors, Mueller concluded, parity had assumed priority over pedagogical matters among leaders of the FSU.

His assistant, student senator Steve Fuller, noted the especially keen anger concerning Imbert. Clearly, the presidential olive branch was drooping.

Meanwhile, MUFA president Gerry King telephoned Mueller that night, to say that "the entire process had been a capitulation to the students." The association's position on student parity hardened, as the strike dragged on. Objections were based on considerations of maturity and experience but also on conflict of interest. A junior professor standing for tenure, King noted, would be grading students who might have a crucial say in his or her future employment.[121] Frank Jones, caught in the sociology maelstrom, told Mueller that trouble would continue in the absence of a university-wide policy concerning student representation on departmental bodies.[122] James D. Brasch (English) made a similar point. On 15 March, the day sociology granted full parity to students, he wrote, "It seems to me that some of the present difficulty has arisen from the tendency of some departments to pass legislation regarding representation without regard for the entire context of a parliamentary system and without considering the final effect of such legislation on the entire system." The result, he claimed, was a patchwork of inequity, with no central principal to serve as a guideline.[123] The nightmare John Trueman had foretold in 1968 was unfolding.

By Monday, 18 March, a delicate impasse was sliding toward dangerous confrontation. Tension on the picket lines was wound tight as a drum. As part of the mediation process, a separate office had been set aside for Dr Edwin B. Heaven, of religious studies, to speak privately with any student. Many who sought him out, or wrote letters, spoke of being "annoyed, confused, and discouraged." One French major protested against sociology students "coming in and ordering me around."[124] Bourns felt moved to warn both strikers and their opponents that his first duty was to guarantee the rights and safety of all on campus.[125] Meanwhile, vitriolic placards and broadsheets proliferated. This, in itself, was nothing new, but one circular, in particular, finally tipped the precarious balance.

A roughly produced handout, entitled "Berland's Bullshit: Lies, Lies, More Lies," made the rounds that Monday. Its authors were clearly privy to far more sensitive information than could be had through any jungle telegraph. Indeed, the FSU explicitly stated that it was in possession of correspondence concerning the pending appointment of Imbert, as well as candidates in business, economics, and history. Salary levels, ranks, and other confidential contractual terms were precisely delineated. All were shown to be considerably superior to the lectureships offered to Pfirrmann and Paboeuf. It was alleged that Imbert had been hired with the sole intent of getting rid of the third co-operant, Paul Jacopin. The blistering FSU document, therefore, insisted on full three-year contracts for the candidates it championed. In bold print, the circular demanded: "REHIRE JACOPIN."[126] To protesters, the case was obvious. From Bourns' perspective, however, the Rubicon had been brazenly crossed.

Mike Hedden vividly recalled a charged emergency meeting at the president's home that night. In addition to Bourns' key advisors, Harley Steubing was summoned to represent the MSU. Discussion swirled around the question of how the FSU had got hold of such carefully stored, classified information. Asking about the Imbert case, Steubing produced a sheaf of papers. They were photocopied letters of appointment, clearly emblazoned with the president's incoming date-stamp. Steubing would not reveal how they had come into his possession, nor was he pressed to do so. It was not necessary. The protocols for handling this material were formal and strictly observed. As Hedden remarked, the copies "could only have been made from correspondence retained in Presidential files."[127] Just to be certain, Manny Zack telephoned Sadie Ludlow, long-time chief secretary to both Thode and Bourns. She confirmed that established procedure had been followed. She had cleared her desk, personally filed the appointment letters, locked the cabinet, and returned the only key to her purse.[128] Next morning, Bourns called on city police to clear his and Berland's offices. Most occupants decamped quietly, but seven refused and were arrested for petty trespass, a deliberately light charge. The occupation was over. The strike, most certainly, was not.

A crowd exeeding 600 gathered on the arts quadrangle, as news of "the bust" spread. Deafening chants of "pig, pig, pig" rocked the towered square. Seizing the moment, Ted McMeekin addressed those assembled, drawing attention to the larger cause of senate-board parity. From the throng, someone called for a march on Bourns' office. The host surged, en masse, toward Gilmour Hall. Finding the president's office locked, students occupied the registrar's quarters, instead. Almost immediately, police were on the scene, but took no action. Bourns flatly refused a demand that he appear in person to negotiate on the spot. Rather, he invited leaders of the FSU to closet with him elsewhere, in order to focus on original issues. As those talks went on, hour after hour, protesters in Gilmour Hall began to divide into two camps. Some riveted on the particular complaints of the FSU. Others were for insisting on nothing less than across-the-board parity in all departments, as well as with the senate and governors. The crowd eventually dispersed, when FSU executives announced that an offer of settlement was on the table. There was an uneasy pause, as the memorandum of understanding was taken to a general meeting of the FSU for final consideration.[129]

The memorandum promised much or little, depending on the reader. Pfirrmann and Paboeuf were offered three-year contracts as lecturers, at salaries comparable to others at that rank in humanities. Strikers were guaranteed protection from academic retribution. All charges against those arrested would be dropped. In addition, students were granted eleven seats at romance-language department meetings.[130] A week earlier, this deal might have sufficed. Now, however, student blood was up over the intervention by police, as well as knowledge of the Imbert appointment and the terms offered to candidates in other departments. The settlement was voted down, with renewed cries to hire all three co-operants as assistant professors. The SRA was asked to intervene.[131]

Thursday, 21 March, began with a rally on the steps of Gilmour Hall. A thousand voices called on the hesitant MSU to act. The SRA moved into emergency session, with more than 3,000 people filling bleachers in the gymnasium. Talks began with reference to FSU affairs. Soon, however, the floor was co-opted by McMeekin, who rose to denounce the senate, the Winch committee, and MUFA for their resistance to campus-wide parity at all levels of governance. With overwhelming approval, he moved that the senate hold a special, open meeting to settle the question of parity, issues in French, and matters concerning the campus security force.[132] At this point, many left, thinking business was concluded. It was not. A further motion called for a general strike, should the senate refuse McMeekin's summons. Assent was given by secret ballot (1,020 to 647), but several witnesses complained of vote-stuffing and other irregularities. Meanwhile, Steubing escaped impeachment, for perceived hesitancy, thanks only to the support of his more activist vice-president.[133] As matters threatened to spiral out of control, Bourns convinced the senate committee on academic policy to place MSU business first on the order paper of its scheduled 28 March meeting. Very near the end of his personal tether, however, the president sternly cautioned all, "A Senate meeting is not a Roman circus."[134]

An anxious, but generally quiet, weekend passed, only to see tempers flare again on Monday. A broadsheet, entitled MSU *Special Edition* ignited smouldering passions and bid fair to disrupt plans for the open senate conclave. Bourns and Berland were accused of lying. Private correspondence concerning appointments had not been stolen from locked cabinets, said the writers; it had been "planted" in an open drawer as bait, intended to lure protesters and justify police action. The FSU was now being told to wait and trust in the good faith of the senate. In reply, would-be journalists charged that Bourns and company responded only to force. "We accept the challenge," they roared. "We know now," they trumpeted, "that the only language the university administration understands is pressure, our power to disrupt their smooth functioning." "Our struggle," they concluded, "will continue until the three are rehired unconditionally."[135] As if to show that business was meant, the office of Berland's dean of studies was subjected to brief occupation.

Livid, Bourns issued a proclamation to the whole university. In the name of the senate, he demanded that MSU executives publicly disavow the special edition and undertake to guarantee good conduct at Thursday's open meeting. The alternative would be cancellation of the session.[136] Between hammer and anvil, Steubing issued a four-page letter dissociating the MSU from the inflammatory articles and from any further actions not supported by a clear majority of the student body.[137] Official student government, however, was quickly becoming a purely reactive bit player in the unfolding drama. Meanwhile, neatly rounding off Bourns' day, MUFA leader Gerry King wrote to say that the functioning of the university was being threatened by demands that challenged the senate's authority. "I would remind you," he told the president, "that there are some five or six thousand McMaster students who did *not* disrupt classes, who did *not* sit-in offices, and who did *not* vote for strike action." The very viability of the university, he contended, was now at stake.[138] If Bourns replied to thank the writer for this insight, the note is not on record.

At the appointed hour, the senate convened in open session, on 28 March. More than 3,000 students and faculty packed gymnasium bleachers. Although the gathering ran well over five and a half hours, few left early and none complained of boredom. Bourns led off with a brief but pointed statement. He emphasized that French had been significantly bolstered, despite pressing needs in other departments. This was done, he said, because the special bilingual and bicultural nature of Canada required that all universities make extra effort in that area. "I believe my decision was right," said the president, "and I stand by it." As to the occupation of administrative offices, he recognized that there were differing opinions concerning his willingness to tolerate it for six days. Again, he assumed personal responsibility. The same was true when it came to calling the police. Bourns flatly denied, however, that confidential papers were left unsecured or had been "planted." He refused further comment, saying that the matter would be formally investigated by legal authorities. He, then, laid down rules of order for the rest of the meeting. Only senators would speak during the official part of the meeting, and there would be no discussion of individual appointments in an open forum. A four-hour question period would ensue, with former MSU president Michael Coward in the chair.[139]

Janice Paquette, in a calm and measured statement, put the case for the
FSU. With frequent reference to Mueller's interim report, she rehearsed
the difficulties students had faced for years, when working toward change
through "normal channels." Paquette swore that correspondence relating
to hiring had been found in an open drawer, not pried from a locked cabinet. Above all, she emphasized how (purported) irregularities in Imbert's
appointment had damaged FSU trust in the system. Less restrained, her colleague, Hilda Vanneste, railed against inequitable contracts offered to the
co-operants, as well as supposed efforts to muzzle the present discussion by
means of loaded rules of order. The result, she declared was "nothing but
verbal diarrhea."[140] McMeekin, then, engaged David Winch in a running
debate over university-wide parity. Some time was given, as well, to matters
touching on the future of campus security, but on this, as everything else,
no motions were entertained. After five tense hours, the session adjourned
without incident. Some complained that all had been smoke, mirrors, and
no action. Others, including Winch, declared that a lot had been learned, as
all concerned heard many things for the first time.[141] For his part, Bourns
was gratified by the relative civility of participants, noted that senate committees were already working on security and representational reform, and
declared that a new, better-informed dialogue had begun.[142] Such, at any
rate, was his fervent hope. Alas, passions roused by the whole affair did not
fade quickly.

Reactions to management of the hopelessly tangled debacle varied markedly across campus. From MUMC, Dave Sackett wrote to Bourns, "Your
integrity and patience stand out boldly in these difficult times."[143] Political
scientists Henry Jacek and Tom Truman echoed this sentiment, as did Les
Shemilt of engineering.[144] A number of French majors, also, confided their
support privately to the beleaguered president.[145] Eleven of their graduate-
student colleagues, including one former FSU executive, added to this
chorus.[146] Winch, however, chided Bourns for bending to radicals by altering budget allotments to suit them. The dispute, he boiled, had been badly
mishandled and had brought discredit on the University. Fair mindedly, he
added, "I sincerely hope that my feelings represent a gross injustice based on
ignorance and misinterpretation."[147] His fellow economist, Ernest Oksanen,
however, pulled no punches in a series of white-hot missives to Bourns.

At the height of the crisis, in March, Oksanen observed, "Whatever the
justice of the strikers' case, I view with the gravest apprehension the thought
that the Administration will cave in on the issue of parity." He noted that
much of the most radical agitation was being spurred by a group of students
and faculty from sociology. Their attitudes, he said, were "indistinguishable

from those of the SDS." Scientist-administrators, he continued, were isolated from the ranting of such people and did not understand how they would bring all true intellectual activity to a halt, once granted free rein. Bourns, he alleged, had unwittingly capitulated the moment he appointed a mediator; especially one who was far from neutral. Meanwhile, hiring the two co-operants was tantamount to surrender to ideologues who viewed economists, or any mainstream academics, as fascists ripe for purging. "I would like to know," he asked the president, "what justice there is in our department being subordinated to departments such as Sociology."

Oksanen, however, doubted that the university really cared. The arts, he raged, were treated as "expendable"; a home for hordes of "preposterously weak" students in "intellectually weak courses." After all, a throng of even marginal candidates brought "provincial financial support without which it would be impossible to operate those Divisions in which the Administration actually does have interest."[148] Obviously, the French affair had wide ramifications and stirred more than one nest of angry hornets. Nor would it simply go away.

True, the strike ended. As well, all the appointments proposed by Bourns were approved by the senate. Even so, bitterness lingered. Thus, a spray-paint rampage on the evening of 10 April triggered an appeal to Bourns from non-striking French majors. They dissociated themselves from such wanton vandalism and asked that something be done to ensure more responsible student representation on next year's departmental committees.[149] At the same time, other students carried out threats to indict the French program in letters to Hamilton and district high schools. Somehow, they procured a large stock of McMaster letterhead, along with extensive mailing lists. For once, Bourns tore a strip off Hedden. Access procedures sloppy enough to allow this to happen, said the president, were "inexcusably bad."[150] As these events transpired, the Department of Romance Languages itself was placed under the trusteeship of a five-person task force, pending the arrival of a new chair. The arrangement was part of the mediation agreement. Few lessons in co-operation, however, had been learned in the roiling cauldron of recent experience.

Indeed, the first post-strike department meeting was an exquisite exercise in anti-collegial excellence. Attending as observers, Gerry King, Dennis Shaw, and Barb Mueller left, outraged by what they witnessed. The task force made no effort to bridle an acting chairman who permitted mere observers to vote, entertained motions that were out of order, and tolerated venomous invective. When a proposal that only FSU members should be eligible for election to department committees passed, one of the first principles of the mediation document was blatantly violated. King told Bourns, "Any impression in my mind that certain faculty and students are honestly seeking to improve the quality of their education and are working honestly towards a better Departmental organization have now completely disappeared."[151] Mueller was hurt and indicated his sad displeasure to Owen Morgan, who had chaired the harmful session. "I trust and hope that all has not been in vain, and that we can salvage something from this extensive agony," wrote the surgeon to a friend.[152] Berland simply and decisively annulled all resolutions of the dysfunctional meeting, emphasizing that the FSU could not monopolize student representation.[153]

Somehow capturing the spirit of the dizzy hour, one disillusioned French major wrote to her member of provincial parliament (MPP), asking his assistance, under the "Canadian Bill of Rights," in reclaiming her tuition fees for classes cancelled or disrupted.[154] Of the Silhouette, she asked, "What is a Farce?" Answering her own rhetorical question, she wrote that it was sociology and political science students "striking" to rehire three French instructors they had never met. It was demands by three young staff members for assistant professorships, when all they had were credentials equivalent to graduate students. It was, above all, being shouted down and hassled by a student organization that proclaimed itself the enemy of tyranny.[155] It was, indeed, almost funny; until Bourns received a directive from the minister of colleges and universities to look into the matter and answer the young woman directly.[156] Given the scholar-dollar message emanating from Queen's Park, farce lost its comic appeal. Understandably, therefore, not even the faintest hint of humour coloured a concurrent exchange between Dr Everett Knight and Les King, dean of graduate studies.

In May, King scanned the results from Knight's graduate French course and noted that the instructor had awarded across the board As to all fourteen students, including one who had dropped out. He wrote to inquire how this could happen. Knight replied that he had not even bothered to look at the names, but had given firsts to all; even those who clearly did not merit the distinction. After all, he quipped, mocking the mediation agreement, "I had no wish to appear to be persecuting students whose attitude during the strike I considered to be contemptible." He did allow, however, that there was a close correlation between activism and intelligence, as well as passivity and stupidity. Crossing farther over the collegial line, Knight advised that McMaster could avoid a repetition of the year's disturbances by discouraging particularly able students from enrolling in French. Indeed, he added, a powerful step in just that direction had already been taken, when the university dismissed his bright young colleagues, Ducornet and Jacopin.

Needless to say, King was not amused.[157] He might, however, have reflected on a variously attributed aphorism that correlated academic bitterness and small stakes. Clearly, it did not apply when a professor was willing to put the credibility of an entire graduate program (and, perhaps, school) at risk, in order to vent some spleen.

Formal investigations, regarding vandalism and theft, dragged on through spring and into autumn. Final reports were inconclusive. Seven people, all strike participants, were seen in areas where spray painting had occurred. Witnesses, however, refused to testify, stating that they feared retaliation. Accordingly, no charges were laid.[158] Meanwhile, administrators and their assistants, when deposed, unanimously stated that standard protocols had been followed in securing confidential files. In like manner, strike leaders swore that cabinets had not been violated and that the sensitive material was planted in an open drawer as a trap. None, however, could say who had found or copied the letters. Ronald Peterson, chief of security, noted that, at the time strikers were evicted from Bourns' office, one cabinet stood unlocked. Still, he had no clear proof as to who might have removed the documents. Nor would he assert that the lock had been opened by key or force, since he demonstrated that the latter was easily accomplished without leaving the slightest trace of damage. Ultimately, he observed, it did not matter, as theft was involved the moment the correspondence was handled or copied without authorization.[159]

In the end, no action was recommended or taken. After all, the public media had enjoyed a field day over the French strike. Queen's Park was clamping down on all universities in the name of economy and accountability. Meanwhile, campus temper was still far from cool. What good, it might be asked, could have been served by offering up more cannon fodder under these circumstances? Lacking solid evidence, Bourns was content to let hungry dogs lie. Besides, he was second-guessing his own decision to call in the police. Upon reflection, he thought it just possible that students might have vacated his office, had he marched over in person to confront them directly concerning the purloined letters.[160] This face-to-face tactic, although risky, had worked during the food sit-in. Perhaps, it might have served on the evening of 18 March. One can never know. In any case, the French strike haunted Bourns for decades. "If you asked me about tough times as president," he observed in 2009, "that would head the list."[161]

The French affair had aftershocks extending well beyond the travails of one department and well into the future. Among other things, it pointed to gaps in the appointments and rewards system, most notably a clearly defined appeals process. Furthermore, it inspired the search for more effective means of containing and resolving group conflict. As well, it gave urgency to ongoing discussion concerning the composition, role, and powers of the campus security force. Most obviously, of course, the tribulations of 1974 made it imperative to settle the matter of student participation in university governance. The French strike, on its own, had not generated this hefty load of pressing tasks. It had, however, acted as a powerful catalyst to get the university community cracking on sundry desiderata. The affair, in short, had lasting effects, not all of them bad.

A canonically sanctioned appeals process might not have forestalled the French crisis. After all, in championing pedagogical prowess as a primary in tenure decisions, students thought that they were challenging the research-loaded values of those who would hear such a petition. Still, a clear definition of due process would not have gone amiss. This became ever-more apparent as the "mopping up operation" of the seventies went on. Best evidence, here, was provided by the case of sociologist Barry Thompson, which followed hard on the heels of the French crisis, in November 1974. The candidate's contract was up for renewal. A departmental committee composed of junior instructors and students, gave him a ringing endorsement. "Getting Barry rehired was one of our top priorities this year," one student representative informed the *Silhouette*.[162] However, the Faculty of Social Sciences appointments committee, which included two senior sociologists, begged to differ.[163] A long, rancorous, and very public appeal ensued, as an ad hoc senate committee heard the case. Rules of evidence and procedure were conspicuously unclear. All told, the proceedings were reduced to what some observers termed "a circus."[164]

Organized pressure from students on Thompson's behalf was vocal and persistent. In the end, the candidate, who had made little progress on his doctoral dissertation, was not renewed. Again, however, the media had feasted on an internally disruptive episode at McMaster. Eventually, the press was banned from hearings altogether.[165] Throughout, as though exacerbated by klieg lights, personal and ideological rivalries sharpened in an already troubled department.[166] The upshot was a formal senate inquiry into the problems of sociology, which resulted in a less-than-flattering report.[167] Perhaps, the one positive thrust to emerge from the fiasco was a determined effort to ensure that a standard appeals process was developed. With the French debacle and the Thompson case spurring them on, a joint MUFA-administration committee went to work. Together, Les King, Alvin Lee, Frank Jones, and Harold Guite fashioned procedures for handling cases over which tenure and promotions committees, at various levels, differed. Finally ratified by the senate in 1977, the process would serve for years to come.[168] A gaping hole in "The Document" was closed. At the same time, the French strike, also, led directly to reconsideration of measures for resolving large-group conflict.

The food sit-in of 1970 had prompted the senate to institutionalize methods for coping with similar disturbances in the future. In 1972, a board of student appeals was approved for dealing with individual cases. Group disputes, however, would be handled be a mediator, whose recommendations would be non-binding, unless there was prior agreement by all parties concerned.[169] The precise details of the mediation procedure were left hazy. True, some questions were raised, but the plan was approved without dissent. After all, there was "no group tension evident at the moment that could result in a crisis," according to the senator who brought the notion to the floor.[170] Less than two years later, the French strike was raging in earnest. Mueller did his level best to make the new mechanism work, but it (not he) proved inadequate to contain the ferment. Thus, in May 1974, even as he brushed still settling dust from his jacket, Winch rose to address the senate on the complex issue of campus discipline.

The strike, he offered, had illuminated the flaws in a currently ambiguous system of guaranteeing good order. The senate, of course, held final statutory authority. In practice, however, it had delegated much of this power to various groups (faculties and departments) and individuals (chairs, deans, mediators, and presidents). The result, he averred, was a disturbing lack of clarity, when widespread push came to ill-coordinated shove. As a bulwark against future confusion, the economist moved that the senate reaffirm, categorically, its ultimate sway over disciplinary matters. Further, he urged that a set of guidelines concerning acceptable conduct be spelled out. These, he emphasized, should underline that disruption of the daily business of the university was not a tolerable form of free expression.[171] There followed the same protracted debate that attended a discussion of codes of conduct at most universities across the country.

For months, senators and others wrangled over everything from the difficulty of drawing distinct lines, to questions touching on the desirability of regular department reviews. A presidential committee noted that, whatever was done, the student horizon differed significantly from that of the university. Thus, grievance mechanisms had not only to be better advertised, but also had to be seen to work more promptly than in the past.[172] All could agree on this point, but division reigned when it came to the role of departments in any conceivable process. With Mueller, most recognized that potentially major disputes could often best be nipped in the bud by adroit management at the departmental level. Some, however, contended that, in the absence of universal bylaws, individual units could easily side-step mere guidelines. Inevitably, the thorny questions of faculty and department uniqueness, as well as student representation, came into play. As a means around these delicate issues, some suggested that one individual should be identified as the person to whom any member of the university could turn for definitive information and advice. The possibility of appointing an ombudsman was mooted, but proved too divisive. At one point, philosopher David Hitchcock, tongue in cheek, offered that a select committee on protests, comprising representatives of the board, senate, administration, faculty, students, and security, be established to schedule and coordinate demonstrations. In the final analysis, the senate secretary was designated as the person to whom all could turn for counsel.[173]

Some rather more significant decisions were taken. Most of these tended in the direction of monitoring departments more closely. Many of these measures had been employed ad hoc, in the past. Now, they became official policy. The senate, for example, empowered deans to take temporary control over units in emergency situations. This included the authority, with presidential and faculty council approval, to appoint a three-person committee to manage any department in disarray. As well, the mediation procedure was reaffirmed, despite MUFA's concern that it could be abused to force, rather than negotiate, decisions. Meanwhile, no formal code of conduct was set forth. Rather, like most other universities, McMaster deemed the law of the land sufficient to protect both freedom of speech and assembly, as well as the safety of persons and property.[174] The most controversial innovation came when the senate resolved that each department be reviewed at the time a chairman was selected or renewed: in effect, every three years. Winch, Mustard, and others objected strenuously to this purported interference, by non-experts, in the choice of department leaders. The senate, nevertheless, ratified the idea.[175] Ultimately, no clear-cut process for diffusing group conflict emerged from these lengthy deliberations. Instead, it remained received wisdom that better communication would reduce inevitable conflict to tolerable proportions.[176] As a step toward this, a review of the campus security force, already underway before March 1974, was kicked into high gear by fallout from the French melee.

In September 1974, the SRA, prompted by the IRC, unanimously resolved that Ronald Peterson, chief of the McMaster University Security Police Force, be fired and that the entire service he had founded, in 1967, be revamped. No one questioned the need for the twenty-four special constables on duty. Indeed, student leaders urged that they retain full powers of arrest, if only to keep Hamilton police off campus in all but extreme circumstances. The real issue, they contended, involved attitude. Peterson, a former RCMP officer, was said to be over zealous and out of place in a university environment. It was alleged that he employed paid informers, electronic eavesdropping, and other means of keeping extensive dossiers on individual students. More generally, the SRA charged that he had instilled a mentality of deterrence, rather than assistance, in his subordinates. The result was an unhealthy, mutual, self-reinforcing distrust between constables and the community they served. The French strike had only brought this alienation into clearer relief. The answer, said the SRA, was new leadership and reform, starting with a name change from "Security Police" to "Security Service." For good measure, it was recommended that a standing presidential committee be established to provide long-term oversight of the service.[177]

This was, no doubt, a one-sided view of affairs. Neither the motion, nor subsequent *Silhouette* editorials, for example, mentioned the provocative class disruptions, the episodes of wanton vandalism, or the fashionable and bitingly porcine epithets that marred the French protest. Still, there was a marked similarity between the resolutions of the SRA and those tendered to Bourns by a concerned campus ministries council, in 1973. The latter had led the president to launch an inquiry into the police force, prior to problems with the FSU. The strike merely gave vivid urgency to that committee's deliberations. With the writing deeply graven on the wall, Peterson resigned, just before the initial report was handed down, in November 1974.

Taking a cue from students and chaplains alike, the committee placed heavy emphasis on the service, rather than policing, functions of campus security. Indeed, majority members thought it "repugnant" that officers should have powers of arrest, at all. In dissent, Les Prince, the avuncular dean of students, authored a minority report. He noted that student government, the chief of the Hamilton-Wentworth regional police, and Sheila Scott, dean of women, all recommended that security officers retain full powers of arrest. University patrolmen, he argued, had far better local knowledge than outsiders and, properly led, were more likely to take campus culture and precedent into account, when exercising authority. Without a mandate to conduct criminal investigations, campus security would decline to little more than a glorified lost-and-found department. While not obliged to, Bourns submitted the two reports to the senate for advice, in keeping with his consultative style. When that body seemed torn on the matter, the president set it aside for future consideration.[178] Meanwhile, other developments paved the road to consensus. In this process, no one played a more crucial role than Peterson's interim successor, Donald Garrett. Individuals, quite frequently, can make all the difference.

Garrett, like Peterson, was a seasoned peace officer, having served with the Metropolitan Toronto Police Force and the Ontario Provincial Police, before accepting the post of sergeant at McMaster. Professionalism, however, was the only thing the two men had in common. Thus, no sooner was he appointed interim chief than Garrett made clear his subscription to the service ethic. His first action was to meet directly with MSU leaders to work out satisfactory arrangements for a demonstration, scheduled by sociology students anxious to support Barry Thompson. Next, he met with the Student Executive Council (SEC), simply to get acquainted face to face, and assure them that he was looking forward to "getting rid of tensions" by turning security into a genuine partner with student government.

The new tone did not go unremarked, nor did tangible threats to life and limb.[179] On 20 December 1974, Wentworth House was set afire, while a grenade-like explosive device was found in a toilet at the senior sciences complex. Both incidents were quickly contained. They were serious enough, however, to convert many to Prince's views on powers of arrest. Indeed, MSU president Steubing, who had had reservations concerning the SRA's motions, now swung round and called for student volunteers to assist campus patrolmen on their rounds.[180] The senate was similarly moved.

The welcome tone set by Garrett, coupled with the lavatory bomb, opened the door for Prince to press his case home on the senate floor. Student senators heartily endorsed his position, noting that the atmosphere on campus had changed dramatically under the new chief. An independent committee to monitor the security force, they argued, would ensure quality performance. With minor opposition, the recommendations made by Prince, the campus chaplains, and the SRA were approved.[181] A new "security service" came into being. So, too, did a presidential advisory body, comprising students, faculty, and staff, in rough balance.[182] After a year of modifying procedures and changing personnel, Garrett was rewarded with appointment as director of security services in October 1975. The decision was loudly applauded by all concerned, from Les Prince to Peter Cameron, the new MSU president.[183]

Of course, no security force is ever popular in the strict sense of the term. Still, it is worthy of note that, in 1979, Ann Blackwood, first female president of the MSU, announced that her office had hired four students to assist constables on weekend rounds. Decked out in bright yellow jackets, they held no official power, but, Blackwood averred, they offered fast, young legs, during peak hours of drink-inspired vandalism.[184] Thus, a measure of accommodation concerning security was achieved with relative ease. The question of student representation, alas, proved rather more complicated.

The Winch committee was already at work on plans to restructure the senate, when the French strike gave fresh impetus to calls for universal student parity. Myriad debates that attended lengthy discussion of the committee's several recommendations could be detailed ad infinitum, ad nauseam, and with little profit. Suffice it to say that, along with Leal's report, they led to a new McMaster Act, which received royal assent, in June 1976. Most of the central proposals won wide approval, in that they met the obvious need to clear up organizational anomalies left over from 1968. In this regard, a prime example came with the dissolution of the CAP. It was replaced by a day-to-day executive and a separate, board-senate body, the Long-Range Planning Committee (LRPC), which would play a dynamic role in years to come.

Meanwhile there was some disagreement concerning the precise the size of the senate. Bourns' advocated that the institution be made more broadly representative of interests on campus. However, proposals to achieve this worthy end left senators approving an ungainly body numbering eighty-four members. Babel could be predicted by all, save the hardest of hearing. Sober second thought, on the part of student representative John J. McGurran, saved the day. At his motion, the senate reversed its earlier decision and reduced membership to a reasonable sixty-six.[185] For those present, the moment must have fairly dripped irony. After all, on his own, a student had solved a significant senate problem, yet it was the issue of student representation that produced the most heated and prolonged wrangling, before and after passage of the Winch Report.

At the height of the French uproar, the SRA voted unanimously to support Ted McMeekin's call for student parity on the senate, the board, and all committees. A snapshot poll indicated that roughly 73 per cent of the MSU's constituents agreed.[186] Yet, for all the flame and ardour of the moment, student parity on the senate, let alone the board, was never truly in the cards. As philosopher David Hitchcock pointed out, McMaster was neither a civil society nor a democracy. Moreover, even if it were, he noted, the simple argument for parity between students and faculty would collapse, given the need to accommodate support staff, maintenance workers, alumni, and numerous other stakeholders. In the event, he concluded, universities were unique institutions in which the ordinary case for democracy did not apply.[187] Most senators and MUFA members accepted this position. Indeed, so did many students, as their dismal turnouts at senatorial elections increasingly showed.[188]

By 1974, no one, Hitchcock least of all, disputed the desirability of a student voice in university affairs. The real questions swirled around how great a voice and at which tables. On these latter issues, division was especially acute over proposals to reserve student seats on the senate-appointments committee and LRPC.[189] After interminable debate, stretching over two years, one undergraduate and two graduate senators were granted places on the seventeen-person planning body, in 1975.[190] Meanwhile, the board agreed to admit six senators to its membership: three elected by and from faculty and three, without restriction on eligibility, by and from the senate.[191] In principle, at least, students would be welcome on the board under the new McMaster Act. By that juncture, however, table stakes were highest over departmental representation; especially in the social sciences.

In 1975, with echoes of the Thompson appeal still resounding, the senate looked afresh at the question of student representation on department committees. The *Kirkaldy Report* had left great discretion at the local level, and practice varied wildly across campus. CAP sought to bring some consistency by instituting general guidelines, but it fought shy of laying down firm rules. As a compromise, Bourns moved that each discipline arrange for the election of students to all committees deemed appropriate, "but not at least for the time being" those that dealt with tenure and promotion. The proposal passed, but still took the form of a mere guideline.[192] Hesitancy was spawned, in part, by current arrangements in sociology, social work, and political science whose students already enjoyed a strong say in matters of appointment. As well, departments jealously guarded traditional authority over their internal affairs. A similar discussion, in January 1976, led to the same outcome.[193] Early next year, during revision of "The Document," it was noted that there was still nothing to prevent students from participating in such departmental conclaves.[194] That, however, soon changed.

When the senate finally ratified revisions to "The Document" in June 1977, a clause was inserted that gratified MUFA, while raising some student hackles. In substance, it banned students from department tenure and promotion committees, unless express exception was granted by the appropriate faculty-level council.[195] Reaction was immediate on the part of candidates in political science, sociology, and social work. Resistance was promised.[196] The counterstroke was a motion in the senate to delete the offending clause. Predictably, it went down to defeat, with senators arguing that students were not literally excluded, and, in any event, had input in the form of increasingly standardized teaching evaluations.[197] *Silhouette* editorialists snapped back that tenure deliberations hinged ever more and more on an unhealthy "publish or perish" yardstick, with teaching a minor consideration.[198] The fight, they vowed, was not over.

A rearguard action by student associations kept their representatives on the contentious committees for the better part of a year. Finally, however,

Dean McIvor decided it was time to bring his faculty's practice into line with that of others on campus. Accordingly, in October 1978, students were removed from direct deliberation regarding tenure and promotion. Speaking to the issue, MSU president Roger Trull called this an unmitigated "slap in the face" and threatened to withdraw student involvement in a long-planned, social-science open house.[199] Following lengthy consultation with Bourns, however, Trull and others relented, on the basis that the word *normally* did not, in fact, legally exclude students from tenure bodies, while all other departmental committees were open to those willing to serve.[200] Ultimately, both men understood that nobody desired a replay of the exhausting confrontations of the immediate past – at least, not yet. Each, as chief executives of multi-million-dollar organizations, had much larger fish to fry, as the age of austerity matured.

Clearly, there was a worst-of-times side to the fiscally beggared, fractious seventies. The French strike, broadly defined, had roused or resurrected latent student passions on several counts. Meanwhile, ideological, generational, personal, and other tensions had, also, set instructor against instructor, department against department, and, to some degree, faculty against faculty. Mishandled, the crisis had the potential to spin off into conflagration or paralysis, as had happened at Sir George Williams and Simon Fraser. This is what critics missed in Bourns' management of the complex affair. He might well have gone too far for some, or not far enough for others, but he did provide flexible, responsive leadership at a moment when an experienced, delicate touch made all the difference. In the end, destructive wrangling was turned into a springboard for refining student representation, reforming campus security, and developing formal appeals procedures. To be sure, there would be squabbling and protest, in days to come. Yet, by and large, McMaster escaped its last major shockwave of sixties-style activism relatively unscathed. In no small part, was thanks to the finesse of Bourns.

Of course, there was little that he, or anyone else on campus, could do to whisk away the blackest cloud: provincial fiscal restraint. Like an intense low-pressure system that simply refused to budge, it darkened the atmosphere throughout the seventies. Moreover, it had the long-term capacity to be even more corrosive of morale than any incandescent, but short-lived, dogfight with and over students. Shortage necessitated rationing and hard choices for those who had come to view growth as an entitlement. It has been remarked that, under these conditions, "no president could be popular when expectations, nourished by a decade of affluence, were being frustrated by years of relative poverty."[201] Elsewhere, in fact, fiscal constraint, creeping anxiety, and the lack of adroit leadership frequently led to the

institutionalization of a "we-they" mentality, as a wave of faculty unionization washed over universities, coast to coast.[202] Meanwhile, at York,
an isolated and friendless President David Slater was unceremoniously
bounced from office, in 1972; the victim of a deans' revolt over budget
miscalculations.[203]

It speaks volumes for the true art of Bourns, therefore, that he ran a tight
ship; yet, within the McMaster community, enjoyed even greater confidence
at the end of his presidency than at its outset. True, there would be problems
aplenty. Most notably, difficult circumstances necessitated belt-tightening,
clarification of priorities, and creative adaptation on the part of president
and colleagues alike. Within the context of tackling these larger challenges,
the multi-faceted French affair was a dangerous episode that could have
induced paralysis. Bourns ensured that it did not. Thus, the decks were kept
clear for action on greater issues at hand. Reshaping the McMaster Act was
just one of them.

As the decade wore on, the university did not grow substantially, nor did
it achieve an elegant symmetry. With effort, however, it did adapt to con-
striction. Indeed, McMaster's core sense of purpose, as sketched by Thode,
was retained, refined, and, in 1978, decisively restated in a formal plan. Perhaps more remarkably, collegial relations between faculty and administration grew stronger, rather than weaker, despite the need to restrain some
academic, career, or remunerative expectations. Of course, all generaliza-
tions founder, to some degree, on the reefs of lived diversity. Thus, as a
nuts-and-bolts survey of the university will show, there was no singular,
no universally shared "seventies experience." Instead, while harrowing for
some, the decade would be the best of times for others. Bourns, therefore,
had to contend with myriad perspectives and shifting trends, as he sought to
chart course for the university.

Crazy Quilt

Throughout the period, Bourns made his highest institutional goal clear to government, deans, and all on campus: McMaster was and should remain a research- and graduate-intensive university, unashamedly striving to be first in select fields.[1] Economist Peter George (now president emeritus), certainly got the message. Reflecting on the seventies, he later observed, "If you wanted to have any weight around here, you had to have a doctoral program."[2] He might have added that one's PhD offering had better be right up to snuff – have true academic gravitas – if one wished to be fully nourished. This is not to say that Bourns presided over McMaster in the spirit of a dogmatic, single-minded actuary. Nothing could have been more foreign to his scholarly, collegial nature. Lean times, however, grew progressively leaner. Gilmour Hall, accordingly, had little choice except to be increasingly choosey as to where and how to invest slender resources. Forced to prioritize, on the whole, its officers tended to bolster excellence, at the expense of balanced development. This policy, of course, was in keeping with precepts established by Thode and served as a strong thread of continuity with a better-favoured past. It was, in any case, unavoidable. The university that Bourns inherited was a half-finished crazy quilt; a monument to the uneven development of the previous era. It was, therefore, with a discriminating eye that Bourns surveyed, as the historian must, the varied potential and shifting patterns across McMaster's highly chequered, 1970s landscape.

In this regard, the first ACAP reports, which filtered in even as the French crisis gathered steam, offered some external guidance. Although never regarded as definitive, they helped to confirm local notions of where the university's particular strengths did and did not reside. Unloved spawn of Spinks' 1965 commission, ACAP appraisals were a first formal attempt at exerting some quasi-voluntary control over the rapid proliferation of graduate work throughout the province. Assessing the feasibility, desirability, and quality of both standing and projected programs, they were intended to discourage expensive duplication and wasteful mediocrity in the headlong race for prestige. Initially, they were viewed by critics principally as harbingers of creeping centralization – instruments forwarding a prospective University of Ontario. By the early seventies, however, they could be imagined as a real and present danger; a threat to the survival of any marginal or nascent program. This was only natural in the wake of the Wright and Lapp Reports, not to mention Queen's Park's stated demand for the "rationalization" of graduate studies. Hence, the appraisals garnered close attention on campuses across the province. Not unexpectedly, McMaster's time-honoured flagship programs passed inspection, colours brightly snapping in the breeze. Other banners of more recent devising spanked proudly enough, too. A few, however, merely fluttered, while others sagged, altogether limply, on their staffs. Full recapitulation of the manifold reports would tax the most faithful reader's attention. Instead, a few illustrations will suffice to catch the range and flavour of these assessments.

On 9 October 1974, the senate was gratified to hear that, out of the fifteen disciplinary assessments completed thus far, ten of McMaster's programs were ranked in the prestigious "general" (comprehensive) category, rather than the "limited" (specialized) range. Only the University of Toronto boasted a better outcome.[3] To no one's surprise, the sciences and engineering saw their reputations powerfully confirmed. The province-wide report on chemistry, for example, was thorough and hard-hitting. Carleton, Guelph, Queen's, Waterloo, Windsor, and York were advised either to discontinue their doctoral programs, or to admit new candidates only after revamping their offerings. McMaster and Toronto, on the other hand, were deemed comprehensively strong and capable of delivering high-quality PhDs across the discipline's full spectrum.[4] Physics fared equally well, being judged best in the province, alongside Toronto.[5]

Meanwhile, once-troubled geography had obviously found renewed vigour, under the steady leadership of Les King. Thus, he could advise Bourns that ACAP had described his department as "internationally recognized" and, with Toronto, well ahead of provincial competitors.[6] Similarly, consultants in earth sciences praised geology at McMaster as "the outstanding centre of geomorphology" in Ontario. They went on to remark approvingly: "The total style of the solid earth sciences at McMaster is dominated by the interdisciplinary character of the entire university."[7] If they happened to note this observation, Thode and Bourns must have smiled contentedly. Indeed, across the whole spectrum of the sciences, ACAP identified only one real cause for concern. Ironically enough, that was in mathematics; the very foundation stone of science itself.

In their 1975 report, ACAP assessors described pure mathematics at McMaster as sound, but not particularly distinguished. They applauded "a large highly expert group in algebra, especially universal algebra, where a measure of international reputation has been achieved." Led by the redoubtable Bernhard Banaschewski, this cadre undeniably excelled. However, consultants contended that specialists in other areas, such as topological vector spaces and combinatorics, "while acceptable," were far less prolific and of considerably lower academic stature. Meanwhile, theses produced under the department's banner were described as "acceptable, but not outstanding." Truly biting criticism, however, was reserved for applied mathematics. "Probability and statistics at McMaster," it was noted, "are regrettably fragmented among the Departments of Mathematics, Applied mathematics, and Clinical Epidemiology and Biostatistics." The lack of clear-cut program leadership produced an amorphous approach to this broad area of inquiry, according to assessors. Personality clashes and differing disciplinary emphases only clouded the picture. ACAP, therefore, urged the reorganization and reassessment of applied mathematics by 1977, before any more graduate candidates were enlisted.[8]

Understandably, McMaster mathematicians, both pure and applied, were unhappy with and took exception to the report. To their credit, however, they responded constructively. Banaschewski, for example, co-authored a joint graduate offering with philosophy, which made imaginative use of the Bertrand Russell collection.[9] In time, an effective coordination of resources was achieved with the merger of pure and applied practitioners in a single department of mathematical sciences in 1979.[10] All told, ACAP had stung but had also encouraged the heirs of Euclid and Pythagoras toward positive change. Meanwhile, their cousins in engineering were all smiles.

The recently published Lapp Report had called for the scaling down of graduate engineering, across Ontario. Outstanding ACAP assessments, however, sparked credible hope that McMaster's programs would be spared significant trimming. After all, department after department scored highly in consultants' eyes. Mechanical engineering, for instance, was described as superbly equipped, well supported, and exceptionally proficient in the areas of design and manufacturing.[11] Other departments kept pace. Still, in the final analysis, materials science and engineering remained the brilliant comet in the faculty's galaxy. After close comparison with programs continent-wide, it was praised for the excellence of its facilities, the prowess of its staff, and the multidisciplinary sweep of its collective endeavour.

Without hesitation, assessors hailed it as "the best program of its kind in Ontario and probably Canada." From afar, Howard Petch must have taken quiet satisfaction in the success of his erstwhile project, the IMR, which served as the vibrant core for materials research.

Only one problem was noted in engineering's otherwise strong progress. The Faculty, as a whole, was heavily populated by visa students in an age when the latter were increasingly out of favour with government and public opinion.[12] This concern would soon ripen, as the seventies' push for "Canadianization" flowered. For the moment, however, engineers could take heart. They might be pulling BIU income from other faculties, but they could demonstrate, emphatically, that the pearl was increasingly worth the price. Not all the rejoicing, however, took place west of the Mall. Social science, for instance, had two rising stars in its own local firmament.

ACAP declared religious studies to be the most prestigious arts program at science-driven McMaster. Chairman Paul Younger was well pleased, and paused to add a glossary note of his own. Of the twelve doctorates awarded in his discipline across the province in 1973, he remarked, seven had been conferred on the Hamilton campus. Moreover, he continued, the one gap identified by consultants had just been addressed, with an appointment in Sanskrit. Graduate intake, he served notice, would slowly be curtailed, as the job market contracted. More attention would be directed to undergraduate needs. The goal, now, said Younger, was to consolidate.[13] At the same time, Saul Frankel, dean of social science, took unalloyed pleasure in noting that another department under his charge, economics, had been ranked among the top four in Ontario.[14]

Untouched by the ideological and personal feuding that plagued sociology and politics, economics had quietly transformed itself, during the sixties, seamlessly blending new methodologies and perspectives with older ones. The fruit was steady progress toward a diverse curriculum within a peaceable, growing kingdom.[15] Research output was, as Chairman David Winch noted, "very satisfying."[16] So were graduate enrolments. Indeed, by 1975, economics was home to more advanced candidates than any other single discipline on campus.[17] Such things, moreover, did not go unremarked. Thus, Gilmour Hall increasing turned to economists, when administrative leaders were needed.[18] In this regard, Craig McIvor and Peter George come quickly to mind. They would be dean of social science and associate dean of graduate studies, respectively. Some erstwhile "stepchildren," it seemed, were coming of age.

Anthropologists, certainly, kept pace. Separating amicably from sociology, in 1974, anthropology continued to forge a tight, well-subscribed graduate program around specializations in Canadian (especially First Nations) and Oceanic ethnography. Moreover, its advanced degrees quickly prospered. Thus, smaller anthropology slowly closed the once yawning gap between its graduate enrolment and that of (declining) sociology, from a difference of thirty-eight, in 1974, to a handful of five, four years later.[19] Meanwhile, scholarly engagement was heavy. Indeed, as early as 1975 anthropology boasted the second-highest per capita grant support in the social sciences.[20] Small wonder, then, that ACAP heartily endorsed a five-year renewal of the department's PhD, in 1978.[21] By that time, however, kudos or critiques issuing from that advisory body were ceasing to carry the weight that they had in 1973.

As Vice-President Lee told the senate, in 1976, ACAP was losing credibility as a tool for promoting rationalization and differentiation. A number of things, he said, had combined to undermine its effectiveness. For example, like parties anticipating hard bargaining in salary negotiations, universities had often presented government with wildly inflated "shopping lists," rather than realistic graduate plans. Meanwhile, Lee contended, ACAP appraisers had not always been carefully selected and had varied in their insight, objectivity, and thoroughness. Thus, the quality of many assessments was brought into question. Furthermore, the Council of Ontario Universities (COU) had proven too willing to permit reassessments, or to alter ACAP recommendations, when unhappy universities had complained. The unfortunate upshot, Lee argued, was ministerial disillusionment with the process and a hardening of Queen's Park's attitude toward financing graduate work.[22]

In short, although well intentioned, the ACAP exercise was sufficiently flawed as to satisfy neither the academy nor the government. After 1981, it gave way to more rigorously designed six-year reviews under the aegis of the OCGS. Still, the generally strong showing of McMaster's premier programs had bolstered the university's self-image and, at least for some, provided a sunny moment at an increasingly dark financial hour. Nevertheless, even some of those who were most heartily praised recognized that they could not rest on their laurels, if they were to maintain their standing in days to come. Few, for instance, understood this better than practitioners of the physical sciences. Thus, they could nod in sober agreement, as Nobel laureate Sir Peter Medawar held forth on "the public's anti-science mood," during the course of his 1972 Redman lectures.[23] Bourns undoubtedly whispered a heartfelt "amen," as he calculated mounting problems with research overhead and falling graduate student numbers. For his part, Martin Johns was moved to ruminate particularly on the state of physics.

In some ways, Johns noted, all seemed well enough, in 1973. Bert Brockhouse had just been awarded the Tory Medal, the Royal Society of Canada's highest honour. Similarly, McMaster physicists were well ahead of their nearest rivals at Toronto in terms of external grants per capita. The same held true when it came to citations in scientific journals. As chair of the ACAP disciplinary group, Johns already knew that the soon-to-be-published appraisal would rank his department in the top tier, alongside Toronto. He could, also, report that undergraduate numbers were slowly on the upswing, after the late-sixties dip. All this good news notwithstanding, the learned chairman was deeply concerned. Graduate enrolments, so central to the prized research effort, were slumping precipitously. In 1968, they had stood at 122. Johns, however, (almost exactly) projected that they would fall to an alarming 67, by 1974. To some degree, he observed, this mirrored continent-wide experience. In his view, however, some of McMaster's recruitment problems were, with cruel irony, directly related to the fabric of its success.

Indeed, Johns acknowledged that his department's reputation rested primarily on concentrated excellence in nuclear and solid state physics, "neither of which," he admitted, "[were] regarded as glamorous fields in the 1970s." More and more, those who chose to go on to graduate work were not only fewer in number but were flocking to environmental studies and astronomy; areas in which McMaster had a presence, but not deep strength. In consequence, his department had suffered a graduate enlistment drop "considerably higher than the national average." It would be necessary, he advised Bourns, to be more aggressive in recruiting graduate candidates, even if that meant "buying" them. Meanwhile, like it or not, the department would have to adapt to shifting interests, as well as find new methods for supporting teaching and research. The alternative – a life of comfortable mediocrity – was unthinkable.[24]

With the advice of colleagues, Johns penned a five-year plan for adaptation and renewal. In thoroughgoing Thodean fashion, however, he emphasized that there should be no half-baked effort to be all things to all people. Instead, new areas of excellence should be systematically cultivated through "orderly change." Given the nature of formula funding, large infusions of new resources were unlikely, especially since no sudden upswing of graduate intake could be expected. "Under these conditions," wrote Johns, "our plans for the future must be based on the development of the quality of our graduate program, rather than on its quantity." That said, he identified opportunities in medical and astrophysics that might meld nicely with and reinforce established strengths.[25] The remainder of the decade was given over to just such revitalization.

In this vein, an early start was made with the introduction of an under-graduate program in health and radiation physics. Canada was importing foreign-trained personnel in this expanding field, since no domestic degrees were available. With the reactor and a research-oriented medical school on campus, McMaster was ideally poised to initiate such work. MUMC was enthused, as were a number of prospective BSc candidates.[26] Atomic Energy Canada and innumerable hospitals were eager to accept Canadian gradu-ates. Bourns was supportive. Duly launched, in 1975, the degree enjoyed sufficient subscription to warrant approval of a graduate stream, five years later.[27] The great, department-altering departure, however, came with a deci-sion taken, after much lively debate, in 1976.

In January of that year, Johns advised colleagues that they stood at a crossroads. Administrators had hinted that two limited-term appointments might just be possible, were a credible case made. The issue, therefore, was whether to bid for support of established fields, or to step boldly into another area, with the hope that success would translate contractual into regular positions.[28] Winter and much of spring saw options arrayed and assessed. Opinion was divided. Amid the soul searching, Johns offered gentle but increasingly persuasive leadership. By March, he cautioned fellow physicists that the dean was unlikely to approve more than one position, unless a clear effort was made to broaden the department's base. On this score, he had no reservations in recommending that a significant move into astronomy and astrophysics seemed timely.[29] Next month, he played his trump card.

"I talked to Harry Thode on Monday," he informed the department. The former president, while strongly in favour of shoring up historic strengths, ultimately held that the best candidates should be hired, regardless of their expertise. For good measure, Thode added that truly creative scholars should be expected to change directions, over the course of their careers, as promising opportunities beckoned.[30] Although atypically Delphic, the prophet had spoken with enough clarity that a straw vote, held on 23 April, leaned decidedly toward a full-scale plunge into astrophysics. Accordingly, Drs William Harris and Peter Sutherland began as contractual appointees in 1976. Outstanding additions, within two years they were placed on tenure track. In co-operation with relativity experts in mathematics and theoreti-cians in their home department, they soon established McMaster as a sig-nificant player in astronomy and astrophysics. Sutherland, in fact, was one of only four scholars in Canada to be awarded a prestigious Sloan Fellow-ship in 1977.[31] Meanwhile, medicine was finding new uses for the reactor, as were hospitals and industry. Thus, without abandoning traditional ground, physics was in the process of adaptive change.

As Johns predicted, this retooling did not result in an immediate resurgence of graduate numbers. Indeed, the latter peaked at eighty-four, in 1975–76, only to decline to forty, by decade's end.[32] It was necessary, therefore, to find other ways of supporting high-level research. Post-doctoral fellows represented the obvious solution. However, they, too, grew thinner on the ground, as the market for permanent university positions continued to weaken. Accordingly, the department poured ever greater effort into luring visiting scholars on sabbatical leave to it facilities. In 1976, Johns could report that more than thirty research fellows had brought both their experience and their grants to McMaster from as far afield as Norway, Japan, France, Hungary, and other locales.[33] This was a welcome and regular infusion, but it did not solve the problem of staffing undergraduate laboratories and tutorials.

Thus, as post-doctoral candidates became "an endangered species," physics came to rely more and more heavily on full-time, "high-grade technicians."[34] While classed as staff, many of these people, in fact, held qualifications that, in a better hour, would have made them eligible for faculty posts. As a consequence, the department slowly developed a solid cadre of demonstrators who could more than hold their own in the research laboratory, as well. By 1978, eight of these invaluable people allowed physics to keep its year-one sections to a manageable fifty, while the department maintained its traditionally strong research profile.[35] Granted, it no doubt galled some physicists that, by the late seventies, their once-mighty graduate corps was, now, smaller than that of economics, religious studies, or medicine. Indeed, they were all but tied by English and only just ahead of history and philosophy.[36] Still, their vaunted grant and publication record had been sustained. The highest mandate was fulfilled.

The experience of chemistry so closely mirrored that of physics that it need not be recounted in the same illustrative detail. As graduate numbers dropped from 104 in 1969 to 56 ten years later, chemists, like physicists, rolled with the punch.[37] For example, new graduate and undergraduate programs were developed in clinical chemistry to feed the demand of hospitals for analysts.[38] Meanwhile, as doctoral candidates became scarce, increasing resort was had to skilled technicians (and even exemplary undergraduates) as research and tutorial assistants.[39] By 1978, chemistry was prepared to break with time-honoured tradition, as it contemplated recruiting advanced students among its own majors. While this was in line with the practice of Ontario competitors, the gambit was disliked, since it was considered to foster parochialism. Yet, necessity dictated compromising old principles, if the research program were to proceed at its accustomed level.[40] Qualms, moreover, were easier to abide when healthy grants continued to flow in. By 1980, indeed, significant solace could be found in the $1,161,000 of research funding from all external sources combined.[41] To be sure, the truly halcyon days of physical science were gone with the sixties. Even so, had he been available for comment, Darwin would surely have applauded the creative adaptation of physics and chemistry in their struggle to stand among the fit, during the hostile age described by Medawar.

If the two, once-mighty, flagship departments required substantial refitting, other sciences adapted more smoothly to the challenges of the seventies. Biology, for example, had experienced a spate of senior retirements, in the late sixties, and was already revamping its interests and offerings before the new decade began. Moving into molecular, genetic, ecological, and environmental studies, it anticipated changing tastes and tides. Light on its feet, the department sensed still newer trends, in the mid-seventies, and swiftly added animal physiology, population studies, and developmental biology to its repertoire.[42] If biologists could not evolve, who could? Their reward was a substantial increase in undergraduate enrolment, between 1970 and 1976. Indeed, at one point, Dennis McCalla expressed concern that the life sciences were becoming over-subscribed, to the detriment of other fields.[43]

For their part, biologists often felt under-appreciated by an administration that traditionally placed its highest premium on research and graduate study in physical science. With its large undergraduate program, the department occasionally voiced displeasure at being regarded as little more than a cash cow for chemistry and physics.[44] Members felt particularly slighted, in 1976, when appointments in biochemistry were made without biology being consulted. In addition, they complained that they were shortchanged in the distribution of teaching fellows.[45] By 1978, Stephen Threlkeld was moved to write, politely but pointedly, to Bourns that his department resented relegation to middle-weight status. Remarking that his staff of twenty-two won external support at least equal to any similar department in Canada, he went further to declare that biology would soon be the great crossroads of science itself. As such, wrote Threlkeld, it was imperative that the life sciences have a stronger voice in the councils of the university.[46] Fair or not, these sundry complaints bespoke a degree of self-confidence absent in the discourse of senior science during the seventies. A similar tone echoed in the corridors of psychology and geography.

Indeed, as Lynn Newbigging later noted, development in psychology went pretty well according to plan, the pressures of the seventies notwithstanding. After all, from the outset, he had envisaged the deliberately gradual growth of a compact department devoted to particular areas of experimental work.

Like Thode, he valued concentrated focus and teamwork. Newbigging, however, was in no rush; nor did he entertain notions of growth to the level of physics or chemistry. Thus, by the early eighties, he was reasonably satisfied with the "fortunate conspiracy of circumstance" that left his department requiring little expansion when further resources were, in any event, scarce. As planned, the new psychology building, opened in 1970, housed a little more than twenty close-knit faculty members by decade's end.[47] Meanwhile, the graduate program was kept robust but manageable, rising slowly from thirty-seven to forty-seven candidates, between 1969 and 1980.[48] If there was one serious concern, it involved the ever-swelling influx of undergraduates.

Offering BA and BSc streams, psychology attracted legions, especially youthful social scientists seeking required or elective courses. By 1977, the department, at least numerically, carried the highest workload per staff member in the university. This number included some 4,569 part-timers taught on weekends or in the evening. The beleaguered chairman managed to win two new appointments to help cope with this, but noted that any move into new fields would have to be indefinitely delayed.[49] One might sympathize more deeply with inundated psychology were it not for the fact that the department had never allowed swollen junior classes to divert its energies from higher pursuits.

For over a decade, it had employed CCTV to minister to groups in excess of a thousand. In the late seventies, improved delivery came with the bundling of students into clusters of roughly forty and the use of video-taped lectures, which could be paused, as in-class tutors answered questions.[50] Although far from ideal, this expedient did help reduce depersonalization, while allowing psychology to foster lively honours, graduate, and research programs with a medium-sized staff.[51] All told, as far as Newbigging was concerned, the period was certainly no golden age, but the department had remained more or less on track. Concurrently, geographers were positively upbeat.

Indeed, Andrew Burghardt argues that geography grew to maturity, as the seventies wore on.[52] Like psychology, the department was officially lodged in science, but it studiously maintained close ties with colleagues in arts. This included strong representation on the council of the social sciences; the faculty from which so many of its students hailed. In addition to its core programs, geography offered a number of joint honours degrees; the largest in conjunction with prospering economics. Taken together, these various streams left the department with the largest honours corps on campus, by 1974.[53] As well, ACAP's resounding endorsement gave further momentum to already healthy graduate enlistment. Thus, geography graduated more PhDs between 1973 and 1983 than at any other point in its history, up to 1991 (forty-four out of seventy-nine).[54] In part, this might have reflected growing public and student concern with the environment and its conservation. Department research certainly leaned in this direction.

Climatologists and hydrologists on staff were noted for studies of air and water pollution. Human geographers were deeply involved in investigations of the impact of regional and urban planning on the delivery of hydroelectric, transportation, and hospital services. Meanwhile, Derek Ford, along with others in geomorphology, was recognized as a world leader in his field to whom national and provincial parks services frequently turned for advice concerning the origins and preservation of caves, beaches, and other landforms, from southern Ontario to the Arctic.[55] Later in the decade, McMaster geographers lavished considerable attention on various kinds of noise pollution.[56] There was momentary concern, in 1974, when Les King moved on to decanal responsibilities, while four other faculty members were either "lost or released." Five fresh appointments, however, soon ensured that the department's sterling reputation in analytic geography was sustained.[57] Early on, King had recognized that conditions in the seventies would put a limit to growth.[58] Even so, Burghardt was undoubtedly right to assert that geography attained stability and maturity, during the period. The decade, moreover, witnessed at least one major development that warmed all scientific hearts.

In June 1975, the governors approved funds to study the design and construction of a dedicated science and engineering library.[59] At the moment, the great cache of books and journals was scattered, with the bulk held atop the Burke Science Building: an area less than ideal for their preservation and use. As University Librarian William Ready put it, taken as a whole, the collection was "the best of its kind in the province, if not Canada, housed in the worst surroundings."[60] In this (perhaps singular) case, scientists were at a disadvantage, compared to colleagues in arts for whom Mills Memorial was a purpose-built and well-ordered treasure house. Accordingly, there was both surprise and rejoicing, when the board authorized construction of the new facility. After all, capital expenditure on this scale had all but ceased, since the medical, life sciences, and psychology buildings were completed, in the early seventies.

There was general uproar, however, when it was announced that the edifice would sit directly in front of the engineering complex; thus, encroaching on the Mall, the last open green space on an increasingly crowded campus. Chemists denounced this as "visual pollution."[61] More potently, more

than 3,500 students put their names to an angry petition damning the dese-
cration.[62] The senate responded quickly, enshrining an "open Mall" policy.
Finally, on 10 November 1978, the appropriately christened Thode Library
stood ready, at a site overlooking Cootes Drive on the western edge of campus. A boon to all users, its opening was especially well timed from the perspective of engineers, whose hour had finally come.

During the early seventies, although roundly applauded by ACAP, engineering was still a drain on general university revenues and, as such, the brunt
of much concern or resentment. In 1970, for example, William Hellmuth,
vice-president of arts, took sharp exception to the close scrutiny of his
budget requests, while deficits across the Mall were treated as a matter of
course.[63] Stung by this, Bourns, then Hellmuth's opposite number in science
and engineering, retorted that he was cutting infrastructure and expenses to
the bone, as he fought to deal with inflated overhead costs that were foreign
to arts, simply to keep his programs afloat.[64] Exchanges of this nature would
remain the common coin of interfaculty bickering for some considerable
time. By 1973, even Dennis McCalla, dean of science, was questioning "the
financial and academic viability of our Faculty of Engineering." After all, he
pointed out, that faculty was siphoning off more than $1 million annually
in BIU income from other units, including his hard-pressed sciences. "We
should," he advised President Bourns, "expect Engineering to accept steps
that will reduce the subsidy involved."[65]

Conceding the point, the president, nevertheless, observed that little could
be done. The heaviest burden, he pointed out, took the form of salaries
to staff, among whom a high percentage held tenure. Having long since
pledged not to dismiss regular faculty for financial cause, Bourns had scant
room to manoeuvre. In any case, he told McCalla, "we wish to maintain a
high quality Faculty and, with the kind of enrolment we have, this will be
expensive."[66] For Bourns, as for Thode, subsidizing engineering was merely
a long-term investment from which it would be foolish to expect immediate returns. By 1975, however, there was a glimmer of hope that dividends
might soon be reaped.

In his budget brief to OCUA that year, Bourns was quite frank. Engineering, he acknowledged, had been a problem for some time. Despite the capacity to cater to a thousand, the faculty's enrolment had lingered around the
650 mark: until 1975. The mid-decade undergraduate "bulge" had, finally,
brought engineering up to its planned capacity. That was the good news.
On the other hand, the faculty was still drawing approximately $900,000
from its sisters in order to cover research overhead. Business, in particular, had been milked for BIUs, while its own staff appointments had been

frozen. The only sensible alternative, said Bourns, was for government to fund research and enrolment separately, if "principles of excellence" were to be maintained. This was, perhaps, the one recommendation of the Wright Report with which all those involved in university affairs, save Queen's Park, agreed.[67] Much time would pass, however, before this wish was fulfilled. Meanwhile, there came a pleasant surprise, at least from the viewpoint of engineers.

By 1977, the general surge in undergraduate enrolment was over. Estimates were that year-one drafts would decline, by at least 3 per cent, each of the next four years. Running strongly against that current, however, the enlistment of prospective engineers continued to grow, as it did in other professional faculties. Given the higher BIU accorded its students, engineering suddenly stood on the plus-side of the university balance sheet. Indeed, as Bourns phrased it, once burdensome engineers were now helping to "pick up the slack." Thus, where the administration had forecast a 3 per cent fall in enrolment-based income for 1978, engineering (and business) reduced that to a more manageable 1.9 per cent. The "Ring of Iron" was ceasing to be a millstone, especially as subscriptions at McMaster were rising proportionately faster than elsewhere in the province.[68] This latter fact, one suspects, had something to do with the mounting prestige of the faculty as a bustling centre of research and innovation. On that score, the template for development was sketched, early in the decade, by Dean Leslie Shemilt and the ever-engaged J.S. Kirkaldy.

The Lapp Report, formally issued in 1971, had recommended significant reductions in engineering education throughout Ontario, especially at the graduate level. Laurentian University was advised to close its program. York was urged to stick to applied science. Trent and Brock were told to scrap plans altogether, since no new engineering program would be required before 1980. Other institutions were counselled to restrict intake to specified ceilings. Lapp further recommended that graduate recruitment be cut back by 17 per cent over the next few years.[69]

Shemilt was not amused. McMaster engineering, he insisted, should not be lumped with others in some fictive, aggregate whole. In an animated missive to Bourns, the dean spelled out, at length, the "special role" his faculty had assumed as a centre of "high-calibre, research-oriented PhD studies" – different from the usual run of "professional" schools.[70] He was, of course, preaching to a fervently devout choirmaster. Like all McMaster presidents from 1961 to 1987, Bourns wholeheartedly championed the concept of differentiation, along with a reformed funding regime that truly encouraged and rewarded it. Most likely, therefore, Shemilt was thinking out loud in his letter to Gilmour Hall. Those informal thoughts, however, gave rise to a clear statement of purpose, the following year.

In "Directions to Horizons" (1973), Shemilt and Kirkaldy co-authored what later generations would call a "mission statement" for engineering. Uncompromising in tone, it was unapologetically Thodean in philosophy. From the outset, the authors forcefully asserted, McMaster engineering had committed itself to the twinning of cutting-edge research with front-rank graduate study, all in an intensely interdisciplinary environment. Indeed, they pointed out, staff members were regularly hired primarily on the basis of their research interests. Successive administrations, moreover, had given this special emphasis steadfast support. In return, the faculty had won international recognition, and annually garnered fully 50 per cent more in external grants per capita than its closet Ontario competitor. Even so, said the authors, all was not quite as it could or should be.

Thus, Shemilt and Kirkaldy called for fuller commitment to collaborative research among engineers, themselves, or with allies in other faculties. From the vantage point of granting agencies, they observed, collective work was "in," at the moment, and likely to be the high road to external funding, in the future. Such income, they argued, would allow for expansion of the research profile, even if enrolments should decline. That being the case, they concluded that, in an increasingly competitive environment, "it will be essential that we present an image of the highest individual and group research capabilities."[71] The rather didactic tone of "Directions," no doubt, put some colleagues off. At least one complained that it implied limitation on the freedom of inquiry by individuals.[72] In any case, the statement was not unanimously endorsed. Still, it did correctly anticipate the growing bias toward collaborative research adopted by granting agencies, during the decade – a trend the faculty increasingly followed. In that connection, engineer Gary Purdy later recalled the blurred nature of faculty boundaries, the shared use of equipment, and the widespread associate memberships that pervaded the pure and applied sciences of that day.[73]

By 1979, engineering played host to, or was a major player in, numerous collective research enterprises. The IMR had extended its earlier work to embrace new efforts in ceramics and microelectronics. In 1979, a collective application brought a truly major equipment grant to engineering in the form of a scanning transmission electron microscope. Pricey, by the standards of the hour, the versatile new tool had multiple applications in basic science, as well as demonstrable applied functions in, for example, the testing of automobile parts. It was one of few in the world, and the only such instrument in Canada.[74] At the same time, the Communications Research

Laboratory (CRL), founded in 1971, had four major programs. Led by Simon Haykin, this research cadre explored signal processing, digital communication, optics, and acoustics. In short order, the CRL became a magnet for leading scholars in these respective fields. Another group, in which John MacGregor played a central role, focused on the simulation, optimization, and control of industrial processes.

Biomedical engineering, meanwhile, was maturing as a model of cross-disciplinary endeavour. Within its ranks, surgeons, pathologists, physicists, and engineers of many stripes laboured over things as diverse as platelet adhesion and artificial finger joints. Indeed, John Brash would emerge as a leading figure in blood compatibility studies. As though to keep in step, Kirkaldy launched the McMaster Institute for Energy Studies (MIES) in 1979. Drawing together researchers from as far afield as chemistry and electrical engineering to the social sciences, the body was intended to coordinate research in this critical area. The hope was to co-operate with governments, industry, and public interest groups in a wide range of projects. In the end, MIES never really got off the ground, for want of contracts. Still, it certainly gave clear expression to a, by then, firmly rooted ethos.[75] Moreover, the failure of MIES to ignite could not eclipse the fact that, by the early eighties, McMaster engineering could boast double the per capita research income of any sister faculty in the nation.[76]

Simultaneously, pedagogical innovation and collaboration, as in the launch of Canada's first degrees in nuclear (1977) and computer engineering (1978), helped the faculty to shoulder its own BIU weight. So did the unique engineering-management stream, which now embraced all the undergraduate programs and drew record numbers; enough to fill an entire section of year-one economics. In 1979, even the oft-times jeering *Silhouette* tipped its hat to those who donned the fireball. Enrolments had just jumped a whopping 10 per cent, fully twice the increase to grace any engineering school in the province. A flustered dean expressed both pride and alarm at the prospect of overcrowding. The burdens of success began to loom.[77] A decade earlier, engineering candidates formed 9 per cent of the undergraduate and 14 per cent of the graduate populations. By 1980, those figures were 15.3 and 12.8, respectively.[78] All things considered, directions in engineering pointed toward promising horizons. All the while, across the street, scarcely a flimsy cloud marred the view from Zeidler's mansion.

If, for some faculties and departments, conditions in the seventies presented something akin to a traffic barrier, for health sciences they offered no more than annoying speed bumps. True, from 1975 on, Queen's Park did flash the odd amber light, cautioning about undue spending and system rationalization. Even so, McMaster medicine continued to cruise along; if easing up, ever so slightly, on the gas. Thus, while tighter budgets and tiresome inquiries caused some concern, there was nothing of the alarm expressed by the physical sciences or the sense of gloom that hovered over humanities, during the decade. Instead, the master themes in health science were growth, maturation, and recognition.

In 1974, following the Leal Report, health science was transformed from a division, with its own vice-president, into a faculty, under a dean (Fraser Mustard), answerable to Vice-President (Academic) Alvin Lee. If this administrative change ruffled any sensitive feathers, they were surely smoothed as the new faculty was expanded to include the bustling School of Nursing, hitherto affiliated with science.[79] Founded in 1946, McMaster nursing had long been a relatively small, if respected, enterprise. In 1964, a staff of roughly ten instructed a total of 75 prospective nurses across three years of the BScN program.[80] However, with the advent of medicare and increased demand, the school blossomed until, in 1971, it housed twenty-one faculty members and 195 students.[81] By the mid-seventies, it grew to include twenty-seven full-time and ten part-time staff, along with 266 candidates in a revised four-year undergraduate program. Meanwhile, eighteen graduate nurses toiled toward a master of health sciences.

In terms of outreach, the school offered a "post-professional" diploma in primary-care nursing education, which was aimed principally at keeping colleagues in remote areas up to date. Best of all, the market for McMaster-trained nurses was keen. Thus, even as the economic climate worsened, a 1979 survey indicated that, by November, 90 per cent of that year's graduating class had already found employment.[82] At the same time, under the energetic direction of Dr Dorothy Kergin, McMaster nursing was engaged in vigorous research, most notably in developing the nurse-practitioner, who could play an expanded role in primary care.[83] In short, the school was a vibrant and welcome addition to the buzzing health sciences, where all indicators were up.

Throughout the seventies, medicine flowered to an extent unimaginable in any other faculty of the university. This relative bounty reflected changing public priorities and government's honouring of implicit commitments made prior to the fiscal crunch of 1972. Health care was "in" to a degree even engineering and business could only envy. This, of course, was the way of things nationwide. Unlike the academy in general, medical faculties everywhere enjoyed enhanced, rather than diminished, popular support. Moreover, they were not solely BIU-dependent for operating revenue. Instead, they, also, drew on the deep pockets of federal and provincial ministries of health. As for research and special projects, where science relied overwhelmingly on the NRC and arts on the Canada Council (later NSERC and the Social Science and Humanities Research Council, or SSHRC), health sciences could call on those bodies but, also, on the MRC, as well as myriad, purpose-specific foundations. All told, it would have been shocking had McMaster medicine not grown. There was, however, nothing in the exogenous conditions to guarantee that the Hamilton school would, in many ways, outpace many of its older, sister institutions. Yet, it did. The proof, as Spaulding put it, was "in the pudding." Between 1977 and 1987, McMaster received more applications for admission than any other medical school in Canada.[84] Evans' brainchild was putting on weight.

Although raw numbers cannot speak to principles or quality, they can attest to sheer growth. On that score, it is worth noting a few telling figures. In 1967, for example, the first full faculty meeting included just over twenty people. By 1975, however, a seventy-nine-page document was necessary simply to list and identify the roughly 600 faculty members in health science.[85] Granted, many of these were part-timers: clinical instructors chiefly employed at hospitals or in private practice. Still, their membership, in itself, was strident testimony to the success of those, such as Bill Walsh, Moran Campbell, Barb Mueller, Alvin Zipursky, and others, who laboured to forge co-operative ties with local professionals, some of whom had initially been quite wary.[86] Meanwhile, enrolment, also, testified to the absolute and relative growth of health science at McMaster.

The first class, admitted in 1969, was only twenty-strong and constituted a miniscule 0.4 per cent of the university's undergraduate population. In addition, there were a mere nine post-graduates on the rolls.[87] By the mid-seventies, the targeted quota of a hundred annual year-one admissions was regularly filled from thousands of applications.[88] In proportional terms, this meant that, in 1979, health sciences' 383 candidates accounted for 6.6 per cent of McMaster's undergraduate cohort. At the same moment, the faculty's 113 post-MD students contributed a welcome 10 per cent to the otherwise static, university-wide graduate corps.[89] Concurrently, every department reported expansion of its clinical, academic, and service offerings, well into the decade.[90]

There were, of course, limits. Thus, in 1975, the chairman of family medicine voiced concern that resources were becoming strained, as development rushed apace.[91] One wonders, however, as to the degree to which his counterparts in history or physics might have condoled. Altogether, in strictly quantitative terms, the seventies placed no abrupt brake on plans laid down for health sciences during the previous decade. Nor did they witness any immediate alteration of ethos or method. If anything, most late-sixties statements of purpose, outlined by Spaulding, Sackett, and others, were successfully translated into lived practice, over the next ten years.

Problem-based and self-directed learning, for example, while constantly refreshed by experience and new teaching aids, remained pedagogical hallmarks of the faculty, as did the small-group tutorial. Similarly, although the role of the tutor, as premier assessor, was increasingly questioned, evaluative methods continued to eschew formal examinations and student ranking. In short, the ideal of co-operative, collaborative learning in a team-building, multidisciplinary environment moved from pious hope to refined custom.[92] In like manner, as noted, the founders' emphasis on applicants' general acuity and personal qualities, rather than stereotypical preparation, took clearer expression in the further liberalization of admission criteria, to the point that MCAT requirements were dropped.[93] Meanwhile, the early premium set on community service and outreach took better-defined shape.

Most obviously, deeper community engagement followed in the wake of closer integration with the emerging regional health-care system. Teaching clinics, residencies, and research units were strategically expanded to embrace numerous hospitals, each with its own particular clinical and research emphases, while the Faculty of Health Sciences served as a coordinating educational centre.[94] To cite a 1976 overview: "This means that there is not in the traditional sense a specific University Hospital for the Faculty academic programs but rather a community health network in which participating institutions, community physicians, nurses, social workers and other health personnel constitute the resource for the clinical education of health sciences students."[95] Altogether, roughly 70 per cent of the acute-care beds in Hamilton were involved in the teaching of McMaster medical candidates. As well, each participating hospital had, or was developing, ambulatory facilities for primary care, where students encountered the public, face to face. More intimately, prospective physicians, nurses, and others could be found in the offices of private practitioners, geriatric facilities, and other agencies spread across the region. The goal behind this elaborate network was to realize the founders' dream of breeding in students a lived understanding of the outside community and commitment to its broader, interlacing service.[96] From the beginning, this involved outreach.

Typical, in this regard, was the development of the Northwestern Ontario Medical Program (NOMP). Launched in 1971, the scheme was designed to improve delivery of service, while raising McMaster's profile, in that region. Qualified locals were encouraged to apply for admission to health sciences in the hope that they would return home to practise after graduation. For that matter, opportunities for medical and nursing trainees at McMaster to work in isolated locales were made available to all interested students, as part of their training.[97] In 1974, more than fifty established practitioners in the NOMP region gathered at Atikokan to assess progress and decide how best to broaden the program.[98]

Outreach also took the form of regular, short refresher courses for local physicians, and a 1974 television series, *Health Care Today*, which Mustard described as "a useful and ongoing educational resource for all health care professionals, as well as ... good public relations." The programs were enthusiastically received, enough so that other medical schools quickly asked to purchase broadcast rights. This foray into television was significant in an additional respect. It was undertaken in collaboration with Hamilton's fast-rising CAAT: Mohawk College.[99]

In 2004, E.J. Monahan, long-time executive secretary of the COU, lamented that truly strong working ties had yet to be forged between Ontario's universities and its colleges of applied arts and technology.[100] He must have overlooked McMaster's experience. From the beginning, Thode and, even more assiduously, Bourns cultivated close relations with Samuel "Sam" Mitminger, Mohawk College's genial president. In time, good feeling led to formal collaboration between science and engineering at the two institutions. The same proved true in other fields. In 1979, for instance, the senate approved two joint degree-diploma programs: one in broadcast journalism and the other in commerce.[101] By far the closest bonds, however, were forged in the training of various health-care professionals.

Under the umbrella of continuing education, a Mohawk-McMaster Health Sciences Liaison Committee was struck in the early seventies.[102] This active group fostered close co-operation in fields as diverse as physiotherapy, medical laboratory technology, and radiography.[103] In 1980, the senate approved two new joint diploma-degree offerings. Thus, Mohawk graduates were afforded the opportunity to take an additional fourth year at McMaster to earn a BHSc in either occupational or physiotherapy.[104] There were, it seems, no barriers between health sciences and its innovative, cross-town cousin. The faculty, quite evidently, was meeting its goals in teaching, service and outreach. The same was true in the realm of research.

Coordinated by the Committee on Scientific Development (CSD), medical research had a distinctly Thodean character at McMaster. As underscored in a number of contemporary overviews, a strong cue had been taken from science and engineering in this branch of endeavour.[105] From its inception, proclaimed a 1976 brief, the faculty "decided to concentrate its research in a few selected areas so as to achieve sufficient strength to establish good programs in a limited number of areas that relate to major health problems."[106] With slight modification, these words could have been uttered at Hamilton Hall in the early 1960s. Five principal fields were selected for special focus: cardiovascular disease, host resistance, reproductive biology, smooth muscle function, and educational development. Within these broad domains, there was ample room for interdisciplinary investigation, as well as individual effort. Moreover, there was incentive. Alongside teaching and service, research was deemed a central duty of the faculty.[107] During the seventies, it gained both momentum and recognition.

To mention but a few highlights, in 1970, the Department of Clinical Epidemiology and Biostatistics won a special grant from the federal Department of Health and Welfare to train health-care researchers.[108] The award was one factor sparking the meteoric rise of this unique unit. It was pathology's turn, in 1972, when the MRC doled out $301,800 for the study of platelets and coagulation.[109] Three years later, pediatrics took its place on the international map when McMaster's department was awarded funds by the United States National Institutes of Health for work on neonatal respiratory problems. Only five of these prestigious grants had been distributed continent-wide. McMaster was the sole Canadian recipient.[110]

As the faculty churned out more and more learned studies, dollars rolled in. By 1976, Dr John Bienenstock, speaking for the CSD, proudly informed Bourns that McMaster's was the only medical faculty in the country whose MRC grants had increased, that year, while the national decrease had averaged 19 per cent.[111] Nor did the funding tide ebb. Doing some informal calculations, in 1981, Kirkaldy reckoned that grants per capita at McMaster health sciences were double that of any other medical faculty in Canada.[112] Yet, even if the engineer's figures were well off the mark, it would still be true that the seventies held few terrors for Mustard's tribe. The experience of medicine, however, was far from typical. Business, for example, grew numerically, but did not truly flower.

In 1971, Dean William Schlatter made clear his displeasure with the relegation of business to the status of university milch cow – heavily tapped for BIUs, but never groomed sufficiently to fulfill its promise. As points of comparison, he looked to McMaster engineering and business schools at other Canadian universities. In each instance, he could demonstrate that his faculty catered to comparable or far greater numbers with considerably fewer staff. How, he asked, were he and his colleagues expected to thrive under such conditions?[113] Part of the answer to Schlatter's question was the reluctance of Gilmour Hall to curry an unproven horse, when financial restraints made speculative investment unwise. Thode, for his part, had been taken aback by complaints from the Toronto-Dominion Bank that McMaster MBA graduates seemed ill-prepared for job interviews and rather "naive" about the realities of business.[114] Bourns, meanwhile, long recalled his personal misgivings about the faculty's readiness for advancement, during the seventies.[115]

Business, to be sure, was trying to move forward. The introduction of a joint management stream with engineering was pioneering and eminently successful. As well, in 1973, the faculty introduced the first student co-op program in the province. Nor was outreach neglected. Thus, a business advisory council was formed which brought sixty-four prominent local executives together to help forge closer ties between the nascent faculty and the regional community.[116] Meanwhile, enrolment surged steadily upward. In 1971, business hosted 470 undergraduates, along with 415 full- and part-time MBA candidates.[117] By decade's end, those numbers were a hefty 1348 and 497, respectively.[118] These were all promising signs. However, there were disquieting signals, as well.

One cause for concern was a tendency toward internal wrangling. Illustrative of this was the blunt 1973 report of a committee to study revision of the MBA core. A proposal to add an additional course to standing requirements had resulted in prolonged debate among faculty. The committee had been struck in order to evaluate the merits of the specific offering in question. It came to the disturbing conclusion, however, that the course itself was not the most basic issue. Far more fundamental, said the committee, was "the *character* of the negotiations, not the conclusions derived from them." Positions became so entrenched that "*there simply was no way that the ... proposal could be considered on its merits.*" In light of this state of affairs, the committee made no recommendation on the specific course. Instead, it concentrated on formulating ways of making curricular decisions that would obviate such dangerous impasses in the future.[119] While business never indulged in the same level of bitter tussling as political science, hints of intramural discord were likely sufficient to deter Bourns from throwing lavish cash its way. Even more off-putting, however, was the faculty's inability to frame a feasible doctoral program.

As Schlatter indicated in 1972, his colleagues were working hard toward fashioning a PhD proposal for the senate's consideration. One of the primary obstacles in this endeavour, however, was the relative youth of the staff. Many faculty members, in fact, were still labouring to complete their own dissertations. Needless to say, this made it surpassing difficult to present a credible advanced degree. The comparatively slender, faculty-wide list of publications, appended to the dean's annual reports, only emphasized this problem.[120] When a draft degree was forthcoming, in 1974, it was, to say the least, ambitious. Fully four major fields were identified in the proposal: accounting, management science, marketing, and labour relations/human resources administration.[121] Under criticism, the plan was slowly scaled down. Later, when the accounting option was deleted, a number of leading instructors in the field decamped on the so-called (University of) Waterloo Express.

By the time the senate approval was won for a revised program, government had further tightened the financial noose, in 1978, as it sought to balance the budget within two years. In response, ACAP and OCUA recommended against funding new doctoral programs in business, since the best candidates tended to go straight into employment after completing an MBA. The only option left was for McMaster to finance the degree out of its own coffers.[122] The doctorate, therefore, was stillborn with resurrection indefinitely postponed. Thus, the Faculty of Business grew in absolute size but not in the kind of "weight" that Peter George later defined. In contrast, the arts had long enjoyed considerable prestige at McMaster. Even a rich inheritance, however, would prove to be no guarantee of continued prosperity, during the seventies.

By mid-decade, most arts departments had graduate programs. Several of these offered doctoral studies. A few, such as economics, boasted subscriptions that outstripped those of physics and chemistry.[123] Similarly, many were homes of productive scholarship. Historian Alan Cassels, for example, had won international recognition for his work on fascism.[124] Chuck Johnston had emerged as a substantial authority on regional history. In English, W.J.B "Jack" Owen, was already a member of the Royal Society of Canada and would later win a Guggenheim fellowship for his studies of Wordsworth.[125] His colleague, Chauncey Wood, was an established authority on Chaucer.[126] George Grant, meanwhile, was merely the public face of a widely published religious studies department. In economics, William Scammell and David Winch were noted for books concerning international trade and analytical welfare economics, respectively.[127] The list could be extended; however, the point is that humanities and social science were far from sleepy hollows in which sustained publication was the preoccupation of a few. Instead, there was plenty of good, solid muscle on their scholarly frames. However, unlike the sciences and engineering, in-depth strength was less evenly arrayed across the arts. Small or unstable departments were vulnerable, during the cash-tight seventies. The humanities, in particular, suffered a pounding from exogenous forces, such as flagging market demand and changes to the high-school curriculum.

"The spectre of declining enrolment in Humanities continues to haunt many of us." With these chilling words, Sandy McKay convened the June 1972 meeting of his faculty's council. Deigning to employ the dreaded R-word, he went on to wax defiantly Churchillian. "Our relevance," he declared, "has been challenged; our research, and its significance, has been questioned; our current degrees and degree programmes have been open to criticism and seemingly outrageous inquiry." While he made no reference to beaches or landing grounds, McKay did advise that surrender was far from imminent. Humanists could brace themselves by adopting new methods of promoting the broad, liberal, and humane teachings they so treasured.[128] Seven years on, however, his successor sounded a more sombre note. Returning from sabbatical, in September 1979, Alwyn Berland observed, "Since coming back from leave, I have been struck by the gloom hanging over campus, and by the particularly black cloud hovering over the three arts towers." He continued: "It seems to me that the Faculty [of Humanities] is dangerously demoralized and frightened, and tending toward defeatism."[129] Plainly, this was no humanistic golden age. Numbers tell part of the tale.

In 1969, with 2,046 registrants, humanities embraced just over 20 per cent of the full-time undergraduate population at McMaster. The 153 advanced candidates on the faculty's roll constituted roughly 14 per cent of the university's graduate students.[130] By 1980, those proportions had slipped to 11.2 and 11.7, respectively.[131] A slow decline had gathered momentum. Thus, in 1979, Berland reported that, despite signs of recovery in university-wide enlistment, humanities' enrolments had dropped by close to 30 per cent over the previous four years.[132] Attempts to account for this long plunge varied. At the outset of the decade, McKay thought that the seeds of decay had been planted with revisions of the traditional high-school curriculum. Languages, both ancient and modern, he argued, had suffered heavily. Latin, Greek, Spanish, Italian, and German, he contended, were "*in extremis*," throughout Ontario. Complementary university programs were following suit. Meanwhile, he contended, the abolition of provincial examinations gnawed away at standards and literacy levels. Scientists, of course, would have interjected that numeracy fared no better. In any event, McKay enjoined his colleagues to reach out to secondary teachers and students, in order to remind them of the humanist's place in this world.[133]

The chairman of history, Ezio Cappadocia, saw similar causes at the root of sliding enrolment in his department. In 1970, 2,055 undergraduates had enlisted in history courses. By 1973, that number fell to 1,633.[134] Two years later, the ordinarily effervescent Cappadocia wrote dispiritedly to Bourns. Where once history had boasted twenty regular and two part-time staff, the department looked toward a bleak 1975–76 academic year, during which only one of four members on leave was to be replaced. Having heard the president's zero-based budget presentation, he wrote, "We appreciate that the financial situation dictates a number of unpleasant choices, but the cancelling of all the classes given by G. Grinell, C.M. Johnston and D. Gagan does leave us with a very uncomfortable feeling."[135] Nor did things improve with time. Thus, in 1978, humanities' enrolments continued to dip, but history's were described as "particularly bad."[136] Chairman John P. Campbell informed Bourns that his colleagues were "stretched to the limit" to maintain the quality and variety of offerings, given that, once again, four people on sabbatical were not replaced. How the mighty had fallen! For those who could remember, it must have seemed another age since Bert McCready had predicted, in the early sixties, that McMaster might one day be known primarily as a bastion of history. Now, Campbell dourly reflected, the department was "rather small" compared to others across the province.[137]

None too subtly, Campbell was hinting that history was ensnared in a particularly crippling Catch-22. Without a full slate of diverse offerings, the department could not attract more students. Without leave replacements, let alone net reinforcement, it was hard to deliver the variety needed to entice high enrolments. An effort was made to regain "relevance" in student eyes by mounting a stream in Canadian studies. This initiative, however, fell flat because candidates were deterred by departmental insistence that some of the program include work in French. Meanwhile, David Gagan introduced a quantitative dimension to departmental fare, but this probably held more allure for graduate students than their juniors. Indeed, as the number of honours and majors candidates steadily dropped, history began, more and more, to assume the role of a "service department," as Cappadocia had earlier feared.[138]

Like those other, once-prominent, stand-bys, physics and chemistry, history simply was not "in," during the seventies. It fought a rearguard action against what Berland termed the "New Utilitarianism," which saw undergraduates flocking to vocationally oriented education.[139] Thus, Berland echoed basic scientists' concern with the rising vogue for applied studies. In any case, the one bright light for history was that graduate numbers held constant throughout the decade, hovering respectably between thirty-five and forty.[140] Accordingly, the department retained at least a modicum of "weight."

Of the larger humanities disciplines, history took the worst seventies knocks. For its part, philosophy suffered an early decade undergraduate slump, but responded with new and attractive courses of topical interest, such as "Social and Political Ideas," team-taught with politics and sociology.[141] Later, offerings in moral issues, business ethics, and critical thinking became core or service staples that drew well.[142] By 1977, Chairman S.M. Najm could report an 18 per cent rise in day-class subscriptions, although he counted this a mixed blessing. Statistics were fine, he noted, but student performance was increasingly mediocre, while resources for keeping up with service and evening classes were often inadequate in the absence of regular sabbatical replacements.[143] Still, philosophy was gaining substance, throughout the decade, thanks to the steady progress of its joint doctoral program with peers at Guelph.

Spearheaded by James Noxon, the philosophy PhD came close to foundering in the early stages. McMaster bore the brunt of the enrolment burden for a considerable period. This placed a strain on its philosophers, until enlistment at Guelph picked up. There was also some tension between the two departments over comprehensive fields and other matters, but Bourns stepped in deftly to achieve a compromise through talks with his presidential counterpart at the former agricultural college.[144] When graduate recruitment slipped, late in the decade, philosophers on both campuses explored the potential of streams in medical and bioethics.[145] The venture would pay off handsomely, in years to come.

English, the largest of the humanities, fared quite well, during the decade. In part, this reflected the relaxation some of its traditionally severe honours, major, and pass requirements. Thus, foreign-language prerequisites were reduced, or social science electives were accepted in their stead.[146] Of course, meeting ministry BIU targets was never a problem, since service to other departments more than filled established quotas, quite apart from the abundance provided by the discipline's own healthy programs. Indeed, by 1975, Douglas Duncan told Bourns that, given its wide commitments, English could shoulder the current burden, but only just. Were the load increased, he cautioned, the department would "soon either cut back offerings or lapse into the condition of unscholarly teaching drudges, which our political masters seem to wish upon us."

In this regard, he noted that an enormous amount of time was consumed supervising graduate theses and reading courses, for which duties no undergraduate teaching remission was possible in the department, unless the staff were significantly reinforced. Duncan worried about faculty morale. To date, he said, instructors had met sundry demands with "good grace." He wondered, however, how long this mood might persist, now that summer stipends had been discontinued, while few found time away from teaching to claim the three months of research time to which they were entitled.[147]

By 1976, Duncan feared that, as enrolment continued to rise, "quite a lot of students opting for English as an elective must be turned away."[148] No one seems to have mentioned the trimming burgeoning graduate offerings as an alternative.

Since its inception in 1965, the English doctoral program was the only comprehensive PhD offered in humanities. All others were specialized. Initially, an eighteenth-century emphasis had been urged by Wiles, but this soon went by the boards. Instead, throughout the sixties (and later) appointments were carefully made to balance strength across all the major fields of English literature, from medieval to modern, from British to North American.[149] The fare on offer proved attractive to graduate candidates, whose number lingered in the high fifties, most years of the decade. Completion rates were high, principally because the department insisted that applicants present a first-class standing for admission. Of course, it also helped that McMaster was one of the few universities in Canada to ensure that all arts graduates received year-round funding, as a result of which students were not faced with the need to find part-time jobs, but could concentrate on their programs.[150] This was a policy Bourns, Duckworth, and Preston had strongly fostered, when arts began serious expansion of graduate work, in the early sixties. For their part, English faculty might have voiced strain at ministering to a collectively large clientele, but were unlikely to complain about the size of the advanced cadre in a graduate-centred university. Most certainly, they would not have traded places with confreres in modern languages, art, and music.

Among the latter, French was by far the most heavily subscribed. As noted, however, its development was seriously impeded by the myriad forces that precipitated the strike of 1974. Bourns did what he could to minimize the damage. This included bestowing more appointments on the section than had been envisaged. Even so, by the late seventies, French was top-heavy with contractual instructors, had only a handful of MA students, and was in no position to consider leaping into doctoral work.[151] Meanwhile, Italian, Spanish, German, and Russian each had solid undergraduate programs, but small staffs and stagnant or declining enrolments.[152] With regret, even the humanist Lee could not see his way clear to recommending that scarce resources be directed toward their further development. The same was true of art and music, both of which were close to his heart, but seemed unlikely to emerge as centres of excellence.[153] To be sure, an MA in music criticism was launched, in 1978. It was a first in Canada. However, accepting ten or fewer students for the first several years, it was still in its infancy at the end of the seventies.[154]

As early as his 1973 inaugural meeting with faculty council, Berland had advised fellow humanists that the way forward might be found in "the development of a greater sense of mutuality and common concern which ... has flourished rather better in science in recent years than in humanities."[155] In this regard, great hopes were invested in eighteenth-century studies. After all, McMaster had accumulated substantial library and other holdings in the area. As well, scholars focusing on the age could be found in most humanities departments. Significant recognition came, in 1973, when the American Association for Eighteenth-Century Studies held its first meeting outside the United States on the Hamilton campus.[156] Even so, no formal program emerged; indeed, by the late seventies, there was little to encourage such a development, as humanities, in the main, endured stasis or outright decline, during a decade obsessed with direct, observable "manpower" outcomes. Perhaps the one truly brilliant light on the faculty's horizon was the continued growth of its great "laboratory": the library.

Will Ready presided over the extraordinary development of Mills' collection in a tight-fisted age. Beneath his deceptively gnome-like exterior, there burned a swashbuckling urge bent on sustaining momentum, gathered in the sixties, toward shaping a front-rank research library, even during a decade of general want. Of course, his ambitions would have remained little more than smouldering embers had he not enjoyed the enthusiastic support of a strategically placed ally: Alvin Lee. Fortunately for Ready, however, the vice-president shared his vision for Mills, and the two regularly made sure that a cogent brief for library acquisition was thoroughly mapped out, well before each year's round of budget talks began. As a result, these ardent bibliophiles ensured that aggressive collection continued, long after things got rough.[157] In time, library holdings rose from 200,000 volumes, when Ready came on the scene in 1966, to well over a million at his retirement, thirteen years later.[158] This bounty enriched all faculties, to one degree or another, but the greatest treasures cast at least some reflected sparkle on the beleaguered humanities.

In this regard, the Russell papers and the eighteenth-century collection had been a good start. After 1970, the shrewd Ready constructed a genuine centre of excellence by bolstering these two pillars, while expanding the range of high-profile special holdings of literary, philosophical, and historical interest. Thus, the papers of renowned Irish playwright Samuel Beckett were snapped up. To these, those of contemporary Canadian authors, including Pierre Burton, Margaret Attwood, and Farley Mowat, were soon added to what would later become a long, distinguished list. In 1974, several hundred letters of nineteenth-century British historian-essayist Thomas

B. Carlyle enlivened the archives. As accessions accumulated in volume and quality, international recognition followed in train. Thus, McMaster was named a member of the prestigious Association of Research Libraries in 1976. Joining the ranks of Harvard, Yale, Columbia, and other predominantly American bodies in the group, Mills Memorial was one of only five university libraries in Canada to attain the distinction.[159] Still, Ready was not done.

Voluminous material from publishers MacMillan (Canada) and McClelland & Stewart gave more weight to McMaster as a centre for the study of Canadian literary history. Meanwhile, in 1977, something of a capstone was set in place when Mills bought up Lord Russell's personal library of more than 5,000 books to complement his papers. This accession undoubtedly smoothed the way to a $1.5-million Canada Council grant to launch the Russell Project, an ambitious scheme to publish the philosopher's many different writings in carefully edited, annotated form.[160] Clearly, it was not for want of raw source material that the humanities languished. Rather, it was the cry for "relevance" and "applicability" that gnawed at the faculty's vitals. On those scores, the social sciences seemed to have rather more to offer. Still, even their experience of the seventies was, at best, mixed.

Writing to Bourns, in 1974, Dean Saul Frankel sketched an uneven picture of the social sciences. On one hand, he foresaw little possibility of "great new initiatives," given that austerity seemed likely to prevail for some time to come. On the other, he took heart that economics was emerging as one of the better departments in the province and that religion was solidifying its international reputation. As well, he happily noted that anthropology was receiving numerous excellent applications to its doctoral program. Furthermore, he saw a bright, long-term future for the recently launched MA in social welfare policy. Frankel, however, was deeply concerned about sociology and political science. Both were given to internal division, and both had taken a battering at the hands of ACAP. Such problems, he noted, "do not lend themselves to easy resolution." "Much," he prophesied, "will depend less on plans than on a spirit of co-operation among members."[161] From the vantage point of Gilmour Hall, neither department was achieving its full potential, as they struggled, throughout the decade, to put their graduate programs and querulous houses in order. Until they did, they could not expect to be objects of targeted development.[162]

For its part, political science paid the piper for years of internecine strife. In 1974, ACAP consultants concluded that, of the six Ontario universities offering doctorates and twelve with MA degrees, McMaster had one of the weakest departments in the province.[163] Therefore, they recommended that the PhD program, already under embargo, accept no more candidates until it was restructured and reassessed.[164] As Henry Jacek later recalled, the original degree had been far too ambitiously comprehensive; the result of satisfying competing interests, rather than reflecting depth of expertise.[165] The negative ACAP assessment was a heavy blow to a unit struggling to gain equilibrium. Yet, as the new chairman, Adam Bromke, conceded, most of his colleagues agreed that the evaluation had been fair. Thus, they acknowledged the need to restore rigour to the MA, tailor the PhD to the true abilities of the faculty, and "give more attention to research and writing."[166]

Recovery, however, proved to be painful and protracted. True, the university supported the department's doctoral program out of internal funds, for a few years, in order to allow candidates already in-course to complete their studies. Continued wrangling, however, stood in the way of a reformulated scheme. So, too, did a collectively low level of publication. There were, to be sure, outstanding individual performers, such as Gordon Means. A mid-to-late-seventies review, however, noted that, with only about half the staff engaged, "the research record of the Department has not been a good one."[167] As Jacek explains, those who did publish tended, like Lentner, to move on to less troubled climes, leaving the department with a high turnover of junior faculty who were just finding their scholarly legs.[168] In any case, the political science doctorate lapsed, and graduate enrolment fell from thirty-two (sixteen MAs and sixteen PhDs), in 1974, to a mere sixteen MA candidates, four years later.[169] Doctoral work would not resume before the late eighties. In tandem, the faculty complement dropped. In 1974, the department comprised twenty-one members. Next year, it lost two, who were not replaced.[170] For a short period, the number declined to eighteen. Prestige plummeted even faster.

On the bright side, something of a corner was turned, in the late seventies. Political science cared for far too many undergraduates to be left shorthanded for long. Although not lavished with fresh resources, it was modestly reinforced. Shortly, both Derry Novak and Alvin Lee independently remarked on the salutary effect that the appointment of promising new scholars, notably Michael Stein and William Coleman, was having on the department.[171] Bromke, moreover, was made of sterner stuff than his predecessors, Truman and Lentner. Serving two terms as chairman, he played a crucial role in bringing stability to a long-fractured department, until handing the post off to Stein, in the early eighties.[172] However, from the Grady affair, through ACAP's rebuff, and well into the troubled seventies, political science, at best, stood still. Perhaps, Bromke and company took minor consolation in the fact that they were not alone. Indeed, ACAP had advised confreres at Ottawa not to reintroduce a doctoral proposal for at least five years, while political science at Western had received a sharp rap across its knuckles.[173] Closer to home, of course, political scientists could always condole with McMaster's sociologists.

In 1974, ACAP assessors were less than impressed with the quality of sociology in Ontario, as a whole. There was, they insisted, no truly first-class doctoral program anywhere in the province. Two departments held out hope of higher development, but McMaster's was not deemed one of them.[174] In particular, the latter was said to lack sufficient senior staff to sustain credible, comprehensive doctoral studies. As well, the department's offerings in quantitative methods were accounted slim. In any case, the COU was determined to limit multiple, free-standing sociology doctorates in favour of joint efforts among neighbouring universities. Accordingly, it recommended that McMaster, Waterloo, Toronto, and York explore opportunities to pool their resources. Should this prove unworkable, these individual programs were required to submit revised, "limited," specialized proposals for assessment, no later than the fall of 1976.[175] This injunction, disheartening in itself, was all the more troubling since it came just as the divisive conflict over student parity was particularly acute. Dean Frankel grew ever-more concerned.[176]

As might have been easily predicted, talks with sister institutions yielded nothing more than vague agreements to "cooperate," as occasion arose.[177] Thus, much time was diverted to drafting a limited, rather than general, doctoral degree; one that reflected the particular research specializations of department members. After much wrangling, a program emphasizing critical social theory won the approval of the senate and the OCUA.[178] On the whole, the exercise was successful. By 1977, a respectable thirty-eight doctoral candidates were on sociology's roll.[179] Still, as late as 1979, the dean of graduate studies had serious misgivings about the department's program, given that so many of its faculty were young and, in his opinion, not ready to supervise theses.[180] A few years on, the same administrator chided sociology for allowing doctoral candidates to lag as long as four years before so much as even beginning to identify a thesis topic.[181]

In fairness, sociologists had to cope with ever-swelling numbers; to the point that, by 1979, they were serving almost half of McMaster's undergraduate population.[182] Vice-President Lee acknowledged that the department's student-faculty ratio was "deplorable" and offered assistance in the form of four (rare) contractual appointments, in 1976.[183] This infusion helped, but only to keep pace with the flood of elective-seekers. Meanwhile, the department remained torn over the persistent issue of student representation. It required all the patience of senior faculty, such as Peter Pineo,

Howard Brotz, and Frank Jones – not to mention Dean Craig McIvor – to keep the situation in hand.[184] Evidently, while the ACAP experience helped to refine its sense of direction, sociology had yet to mature as a node of genuine strength. Meanwhile, even some solid departments were voicing concern by mid-decade.

In terms of prestige, religious studies enjoyed unquestioned pride of place among the arts at McMaster. It came, therefore, as a shock to the department when it felt the sting of the fiscal lash, in 1974. Resounding ACAP approval notwithstanding, the university had refused to replace a member who had recently resigned. The effect of this, wrote Chairman Ben Meyer, was "corrosive on morale" among his colleagues. The department, he argued, was only one, final hiring round away from ensuring its worldwide stature. Why call a halt at this last, crucial juncture, he asked? In penning this cry from the heart, however, he seems not to have reflected on the rationale that his own report offered for the administrative decision. Thus, he outlined that ACAP had recommended scaling down the graduate program, in the face of poor job prospects. Similarly, he drew attention to a sharp decline of undergraduate enrolment from 1,136 in 1973 to 880 the next year, alongside a dip in part-time participation.[185] While staunch supporters of the program, neither Bourns nor Lee could have ignored this evidence, especially at the precise moment zero-based budgeting was being introduced. There was, however, always more than one way to skin the academic cat.

Early in 1976, it was announced that a team, led by Ed Sanders and Ben Meyer, had been awarded a substantial, five-year Canada Council program grant to support comparative work on Judaism and Christianity in the Greco-Roman period. In one sense, this was an unalloyed boon to religious studies. The grant brought the department not only great prestige but also the capacity to hire some contractual professors and research assistants. The university topped this up by replacing all members on leave and authorizing a hiring in Buddhism. Meyer beamed: "these appointments bring to the department promise ranging from high to brilliant."[186] Sanders and company went on to produce authoritative volumes on their subject; to the applause of most, but not quite all. Indeed, the award served to widen a breech that had been broadening for some time in the department.

George Grant, revered as one of the fathers of religious studies at McMaster, was not at all pleased. From his perspective, the purpose of the program had ever been to encourage contemplative engagement with religious thought, not the objectification of it. He held the latter approach to be concomitant with the remorseless Americanization of Canadian academe. To Grant, the hour of the "multiversity" and the elevation of technical research over reflective scholarship seemed at hand. He maintained, however, that the ineffable could never be probed in the spirit of a scientific experiment. Inevitably, he took epistemological and methodological issue with those who sought to historicize the study of religion.[187] Indeed, when Sanders first submitted his idea to Alan Frosst, McMaster's director of research, Grant· immediately helped author a counterproposal to the Canada Council. Paul Younger, who appreciated the merits of a various approaches to religion, tried to help Grant and his friends formulate their bid. He did, however, find it "hilarious to watch four of Canada's best philosophers" come to grips with what an appropriate project application might look like. "There was," he said, "something incongruous about the attempt from the beginning."[188] In the event, Bourns' executive committee concluded that it could only sponsor one of the two and backed Sanders, but took note of "the intense feeling within the department."[189]

Apart from this growing divide, in 1978, the chairman noted rising anxiety among his colleagues regarding low undergraduate participation (716 day students), poor employment prospects for a declining number of doctoral candidates, and an imbalance in the staffing of the department's fields. Further, he observed, department members felt hurt, when term appointments were given to other units, while requests from religious studies went unanswered. Morale, he concluded, was fragile.[190] It might be questioned, of course, whether the president's sense of well-being was any higher, given that he was under simultaneous pressure from another high performer in social science: economics.

In June 1976, David Winch wrote heatedly to Bourns of a threat he saw to the future of economics at McMaster. For the moment, he observed, morale and productivity remained as high as ever, but both might soon be sapped. Every year, he cautioned, valuable young professors and promising doctoral candidates were siphoned off by the civil service and business, who offered 50 to 100 per cent better remuneration than the university. "It is not exceptional," he informed the president, "for a student at the early stage of formulating his thesis proposal to secure a higher salary than his supervisor's." These circumstances were even more galling, said Winch, when Gilmour Hall regularly authorized loftier stipends to professors of business than it did to economists, given that the latter generally held higher academic qualifications. To be sure, he understood the concept of market differential, but argued that his colleagues deserved the same consideration, in light of government and private sector demand for their services. Winch, therefore, rejected a recent statement in which Bourns had declared that economists were no different from "other 'academics', as in Humanities." Thus, he alerted the president: "I may not be able to hold this department together much longer without serious losses."[191]

Next year, Winch brought other "disquieting trends" to Bourns' attention. There were, he contended, excessive numbers of weak students streaming into undergraduate courses in economics. "This is attributable," he argued, "to the maintenance in the Faculty of Social Sciences of lower minimum admission standards than prevail in some other faculties." Consciously or not, he went on to imply that an ironic parody of Gresham's law, whereby bad money drove out good, was taking shape. Classes grew larger, while the average quality of candidates sank lower, wrote Winch. As a consequence, he continued, truly gifted students received neither the peer stimulation nor the personal attention that they required in order to excel. The result was an inexorable erosion of the number applying for honours studies. The best were going elsewhere, while pass enrolments boomed. Complicating matters, there was serious difficulty in attracting high-calibre faculty and first-rate graduate students, because of rising pressure to recruit Canadians, of whom there were precious few to go around.[192]

In 1978, Winch's successor, Jim Johnson, would darkly underscore these various concerns. It was, he said, virtually impossible to hire strong faculty to mere contractual posts, when higher-paying jobs with greater hope for advancement were on offer, not only by government and industry but by competing universities in British Columbia, Alberta, and Quebec. Meanwhile, restrictions on immigration were producing a mad scramble for adequately qualified Canadian instructors and graduate students. Johnson feared that economics might soon have to endure stasis.[193] Few of these observations, of course, came as startling revelations to the president.

Indeed, charged with overseeing the crazy quilt of faculties, departments, units, and institutes outlined above, Bourns was daily bombarded with detailed and often conflicting advice as to the university's problems and interests. Amid this babel, the president was disinclined to heed special pleading, or to indulge in micromanagement. His remit, after all, was to concentrate on the commonweal. There were, in any case, more than enough issues of general import to keep him thoroughly occupied. Still, he must have nodded in solemn recognition as Winch and Johnson touched on some interlacing matters with which he had wrestled for years: intensifying dearth, faculty-administration relations, and the difficulties attending Canadianization. To these, Bourns would have added another overarching concern: the increasingly urgent need to define, with emphatic clarity, McMaster's institutional priorities. By 1978, just as Johnson's missive crossed his desk, all these matters were coming to a head.

11

The Thodean Commitment

Questions regarding Canadian identity and independence, although familiar enough in the late sixties, were becoming more urgent, during the economically strained seventies. Thus, recession, inflation, and unemployment gave economic and cultural nationalism a keener edge. The influx and influence of all things foreign came under closer review. Symbolic of the hour, the Foreign Investment Review Agency (FIRA) was established, in 1973, to exert greater domestic control over the fabric of Canada's economy.[1] In like manner, immigration regulations were progressively tightened in order to reserve dwindling jobs and expensive social assistance for Canadian nationals.[2] Inevitably, this new "Canada First" impulse had cultural implications, too. Indeed, sixties publicists, such as George Grant, Robin Mathews, and James Steele, won fresh support for their view of a Canada under intellectual occupation by foreign (chiefly American) colonizers.[3] One response to this perceived threat was a push to Canadianize the educational system, top to bottom. At the university level, this crusade took aim at lessening foreign influence in the professoriate, student population, and program content.

During the sixties, intellectual free trade had been a majority article of faith. There had, in any case, been little choice. With the demand for instructors growing faster than the supply of Canadian-minted PhDs, considerable staff had to be recruited abroad. In turn, it was hard to lure good professorial prospects in the absence of a thriving graduate school. By 1970, a Dominion Bureau of Statics survey showed that Ontario universities employed approximately 8,000 full-time instructors, some 5,000 of whom had been recruited during the hiring scramble of 1964 to 1969. Canadians comprised 61 per cent of the total complement. The rest hailed from the United States (15 per cent), Great Britain (12 per cent), and other countries.

A similar study revealed that 21 per cent of graduate students held neither Canadian citizenship nor landed-immigrant status.[4] During the previous decade, such figures had generally been greeted as signs of bounding abundance in a healthily cosmopolitan age. By the early seventies, however, academic protectionism was in vogue. It went hand in hand with a public backlash against higher education, the stereotype of underemployed, cab-driving PhDs, and a general call for retrenchment. Governments, both federal and provincial, were moved to act.

Late in 1972, Ottawa promulgated new regulations that made it far more difficult to obtain landed-immigrant status and all but impossible for visa students to find part-time or summer work. The same legislation barred non-Canadians from a range of academic awards.[5] These measures affected all Ontario universities, but McMaster was especially vulnerable, since foreign candidates constituted an unusually high proportion of its population in engineering, science, and business. On this score, *Silhouette* columnists noted that, of the last seventy-nine people to receive doctorates at McMaster, forty-nine were visa students.[6] In company with other university leaders, Bourns lobbied Ottawa to exempt students from the legislation, but to no avail. Indeed, having urged the whole McMaster community to sign a petition against the regulations, he succeeded only in drawing the ire of Robert Andras, federal minister of manpower and immigration.[7] This particular episode, moreover, was just the beginning.

In January 1973, Bourns informed the senate that the Ontario legislature's Select Committee on Economic and Cultural Nationalism had requested details concerning the citizenship of faculty. Appalled by this seeming intrusion on university autonomy, he and fellow presidents had sidestepped similar queries from the CUA for a couple of years.[8] Now, however, he advised that a brief be prepared.[9] No fool, Bourns could see that a gathering wind was about to blow a gale. The AUCC, for example, had only recently launched a Commission on Canadian Studies, chaired by Thomas H.B. Symons, founding president of Trent University. Moreover, Bourns had received a snappish letter, incorrectly addressed to Thode, from the Canadian Sociology and Anthropology Association, just prior to the January senate meeting. In that missive, the CSAA roundly protested the supposed stranglehold that a foreign-born, old-boy network had on appointments and, therefore, on perspectives in the burgeoning social sciences. Accordingly, a memorandum proposed that 75 per cent of new posts, along with all departmental headships and higher administrative positions, be reserved exclusively for Canadians.[10]

No doubt, Bourns was aware that some influential figures at McMaster shared similar views. If he imagined otherwise, a delegation of eleven professors, led by Grant, made this plain, in April. It outlined plans similar to those of the CSAA, but with greater concern for ensuring a (non-tenured) cosmopolitan presence on campus.[11] In any case, Bourns and the senate, along with other Ontario universities, submitted the information – but grudgingly and only in aggregate terms. Individuals were not named. To have singled out persons, said one McMaster senator, would have been "tantamount to abetting a witch-hunt."[12] Government, the media, and the public took a different view. To them, universities appeared to be stalling; to be evading the issue at every turn.

Tired of negotiating the matter, in 1975 the Committee on Economic and Cultural Nationalism recommended to Queen's Park that hiring quotas be implemented.[13] There was, as yet, no ultimatum. Thus, the COU and its affiliate universities continued to lobby for all the manoeuvring room they could get. Bourns, however, was soon in an awkward position. The McMaster Act, so vital to the university's reimagined organization and governance, was ready for submission to the legislature by March 1976. Its framers, however, resolutely refused to limit eligibility for board and senate seats to Canadians. Minister of Colleges and Universities Harry Parrott, on the other hand, was equally adamant that such provision be included. For all that he was a McMaster alumnus, who lived next door to his alma mater, the minister was under tremendous political pressure. He dared not give an inch.

Accordingly, Bourns turned to another McMaster graduate, Liberal MPP Robert Nixon, who introduced the undiluted measure as a private member's bill. After fierce wrangling in legislative committee, Nixon informed the senate that some kind of citizenship requirement would have to be conceded, or the draft would die on the order paper. As a compromise, McMaster proposed that all board members be Canadian citizens, save those who might be elected from the senate. Parrott, however, would not be moved. The bill was duly amended to suit the government's wishes. Even so, the minister was not utterly unbending. Thus, he spoke effectively against an NDP motion that all senators be Canadian citizens.[14] Still, it is quite possible that this early round of head-butting merely helped confirm Parrott's sense that, if left to themselves, Ontario's universities would do nothing substantial to further the cause of general Canadianization. Whatever the case, the minister soon turned up the heat on Bourns and his fellow presidents, even as the McMaster bill wended its way toward final reading.

On 26 April 1976, Parrott rose to address the Ontario legislature. He informed his colleagues that his ministry had been monitoring the citizenship of new and tenured faculty in Ontario, through data provided by Statistics Canada. The results, he said, were discouraging. Gentle persuasion, railed Parrott, had been met with truculent avoidance. Thus, figures for 1974–75 showed that only 66.5 per cent of Ontario faculty were Canadian citizens. In passing, he noted that, of the fifteen universities listed, McMaster (at 63.2 per cent) had the third-lowest number of Canadians on staff. In fairness, Parrott highlighted a system-wide improvement for the current year, as more and more foreign-born professors, who had come in the sixties, took up citizenship. He hoped that this trend would continue, but was not about to trust solely to individual initiative, especially as universities were still hiring foreign nationals at a high rate. Accordingly, he told the house of a new set of appointment procedures that he had worked out with the COU.

Henceforth, said Parrott, each faculty opening would be properly advertised. All Canadian applicants would be given "fair consideration." Qualifications for university positions would be "clearly identified." Moreover, it was stipulated: "each president will be personally responsible for the implementation of this agreement." The minister concluded by emphasizing that "strict adherence" to these regulations was expected, and that presidents must do their utmost to ensure that Canadianization of the faculty moved briskly apace.[15] During question period, Parrott assured all that he meant business. Either the universities moved swiftly to improve conditions, he said, or a variety of sanctions would be deployed.[16]

Disliking cattle-prod politics, Bourns took polite umbrage with Parrott's veiled threats.[17] He was, however, in no position to ignore them. After all, in tune with public opinion, Ottawa, too, was leaning toward restricting immigration, as the recession deepened. Moreover, Parliament, for once, was consulting officially with the provinces on this matter and paying heed to the protectionist views of the two most affected: Ontario and Quebec. To anyone conversant with the daily papers, it was clear that it was only a matter of time before the Trudeau government would act.[18] Nor could one ignore early drafts of the Symons Report, *To Know Ourselves*, with its calls for the vigorous promotion of Canadian studies. In these circumstances, Bourns played for as much elbow room as could be won.

Writing to the *Spectator*, in May 1976, Bourns acknowledged the cause of "reasonable nationalism" and pledged McMaster scrupulously to adhere to the agreement Parrott had sketched. Even so, he continued, there were unavoidable impediments to filling each and every position with a Canadian. Foremost among these was the demonstrable fact that, in some key fields, there were too few qualified Canadians on the market. Economics, statistics, and business, for example, were attracting ever-more undergraduates, but the nation's graduate schools had yet to produce sufficient doctorates to keep pace with demand. Worse still, wrote Bourns, governments and private firms regularly offered such people far higher salaries and benefits than any university could hope to match. Clearly, he had listened to Winch and Johnson. In any case, the president assured readers that McMaster would do all in its power to hire Canadians, but asked them to understand that this was not always possible, if he were to maintain unimpaired "the university's fundamental commitment to intellectual excellence."[19] Minister Parrott took note of this hedging. Over the next few months, he and Bourns had words about niceties raised by the term *qualified*.

In October, Parrott challenged some recent appointments at McMaster. He pointed out that only 20 per cent of Canadian doctoral recipients had obtained positions in Ontario that year, whereas roughly half of their American peers found employment in the United States. Bourns was asked if he found this discrepancy defensible. In reply, the president offered an answer that Thode would have countersigned happily. Everything, he wrote, came down to quality. Where differences were minimal, Canadians would always receive preference. "It must be emphasized, however, that differences in quality are often not marginal, even in the case of young scholars," said Bourns. All PhDs were not, ipso facto, equal. Indeed, he continued, there was "a world of difference between the truly outstanding scholar and a person who is merely competent." The former, he averred, was always to be preferred, citizenship notwithstanding. Sounding a familiar note, Bourns wrote, "This is critical to the maintenance of excellence in a university such as McMaster which has established for itself a special role in graduate study and research." He utterly dismissed comparisons with American examples. There, liberal arts colleges proliferated to absorb candidates who would not receive so much as a hearing at a research-oriented university. Illustrating his point, Bourns noted that, recently, the sole Canadian candidate for the strategic post of Russell Scholar came poorly recommended and did not even approach the promise of "world stature" demonstrated by Nicholas Griffin, a young, but well-published, foreigner. What, the president asked, would the minister have done, if confronted by such a choice?[20]

In adroit riposte, Parrott answered that, since only one in every 10,000 Ontarians received a doctorate, it should be assumed that this group constituted the intellectual elite of the province. "If this is not the case," wrote Parrott, "then serious doubts will be cast upon the entrance standards and quality of Ontario doctoral programs." Moreover, he challenged Bourns' assertion that only the top 5 to 10 per cent of Canadian PhD holders should be considered for faculty positions. While universities skimmed off the cream, Parrott inquired, what was to happen to the remaining 90 per cent in which so much time and so many resources had been invested? For his part, the minister had nagging fears that Ontario's graduate schools were "creating a boneyard [sic] of shattered aspirations – reasonable aspirations." Further, he thought it ironic that foreign excellence should be imported, if the best it could guarantee was 90 per cent domestic mediocrity.[21]

Sparring of this kind went on for some time after, with both sides clinging to their positions. In essence, they spoke at cross purposes. Parrott, and other government leaders, emphasized the undergraduate functions of the professoriate, for which general qualifications were normally sufficient. Bourns, in company with many university heads, focused more on the professor as an expert, with specialized research and graduate obligations beyond the reach of the generalist. As well, there was the simple question of supply – even of undergraduate instructors.

Writing to Donald F. Dawson, president of the University of Guelph, Bourns noted that, in 1977, only three of forty posts at McMaster, scattered across arts, science and engineering, had gone to non-Canadians. "Not even [the NDP's] Eli Martel should complain about that," he observed. However, all six openings in business had been filled by foreign applicants. Year after year, he explained, efforts had been made to find satisfactory Canadians; but the number on offer was tiny compared to the demand. As a result, said Bourns, often half the available positions in business had been left vacant. This led to insufferable understaffing. Still, he told his colleague, it would be better to close the faculty down than to short-change students by appointing the under-qualified.[22] In the long run, of course, Bourns swam against the tide. Eventually, government mandated the preferential hiring of Canadians. Nor did he disagree with the policy, when domestic candidates were, in his estimation, truly qualified. Yet, he remained ready to dispute that which should be weighed in the balance. On the whole, officials were willing to concede that exceptions were inevitable, at least for the time being.[23] They were far less accommodating, however, when it came to questions regarding foreign students.

It was no secret that various levels of government wanted to reduce the number of foreign-born students on their educational rolls. The 1972 visa regulations were clear enough testimony on that point. There was evidence of the same sentiment on the local front, as well. Thus, in 1973, McMaster biologist George Sorger helped to lead unsuccessful protest against a fee hike for out-of-province students attending Hamilton high schools.[24] Anticipating a post-secondary crackdown by Queen's Park, McMaster voluntarily imposed an overall 5 per cent limit on its intake of first-year visa students, in February 1976. Other Ontario universities did much the same, following UBC's early example. Meanwhile, McMaster further stipulated that, in all courses subject to limited enrolment, preference would be given to Ontario residents.[25] However, these measures proved insufficient to satisfy a cash-starved government. Indeed, even as he laid down the law for universities concerning off-shore faculty, Minister Parrott was preparing a policy statement regarding visa-student fees.

On Tuesday, 4 May 1976, he announced that fees for foreign candidates at Ontario universities would triple as of the coming September. This step, Parrott emphasized, was in line with growing international practice and in no way unique to the province. If anything, he argued, Canada lagged behind jurisdictions in Britain, Europe, and the United States, where surcharges on visa students were the norm. The legislature, noted Parrott, had been under mounting public pressure. Ontario taxpayers demanded relief from subsidizing the higher education of non-citizens whose governments did not reciprocate such largesse. Tuition fees, he noted, covered only a small portion of the heavy cost each student imposed on the province. Even tripled, they would not recover all the revenue involved. The hike, however, would take some of the burden off Ontario, while levelling the international playing field. In fairness, the new rates would apply only to students entering the system after September 1976. Those already enrolled would continue to pay the old fee, so long as they did not change programs. By 1980, the new tuition structure would be in full effect.[26] Most Ontario universities objected, to some degree, but bent to the new policy. There were two exceptions: Trent and McMaster.

Two weeks after Parrott's proclamation, undergraduate council unanimously recommended that the senate reject the sudden fee increase. While some differential might be acceptable, a tripling of fees was said to discriminate against all but the rich. Bourns clarified that government was not directly challenging university autonomy. McMaster was perfectly free to take in as many foreign candidates as it wished. Queen's Park, however, would deduct BIUs from annual grants in proportion to the number of international students registered. The university could pass the shortfall on to the latter, or not, as it chose. Personally, Bourns registered his strong objection to the policy, but cautioned that McMaster stood virtually isolated and, therefore, vulnerable on this issue. The only solution, he advised, was to explore ways of providing visa students with scholarships, or some other form of assistance, out of non-formula funds raised specifically for that purpose. A motion to defer the fee until 1978, so that an alternative might be found, passed without dissent. Still, one senator did urge colleagues to call a spade a spade. Thus, mathematician Carl Riehm noted that institutional self-interest mingled with internationalist altruism, in the sense that keenness to maintain a viable graduate program in certain departments melded nicely with humane concerns.[27]

The senate's stand on this matter won enthusiastic support from idealistic MSU officials, who backed Bourns' call for a funding drive on campus. Faculty, staff, and students were asked to dig deep in aid of the cause.[28] A somewhat bemused Parrott simply noted that they were at complete liberty to search for the estimated $200,000, but that the province had no intention of bailing anybody out.[29] For its part, the *Silhouette* applauded the senate's grand gesture, yet warned that the sum in question was almost certainly beyond reach. Faculty was praised for donating $17,000, but this was a mere drop in an almost bottomless bucket. Meanwhile, wrote the scribe, average students were just scraping by and were in no position to make up the difference, even if, by some miracle, all on campus proved to be likeminded.[30] As it happened, they were not.

By January 1978, the senate was forced to concede defeat. Dejectedly, Bourns reported that the appeal had failed to fire anything like allconsuming ardour among the McMaster community. Students, in particular, he said, had made their views clear. Only 109 of them had contributed to the drive. A student senator interjected to explain that his Canadian peers seemed ready to help fund special bursaries for truly needy international classmates, but were unwilling to subsidize all and sundry, some of whom were far better off than they. Whatever the case, Bourns contended, the crystalline facts stood out in razor-sharp relief. Pledges fell some $150,000 short of the mark. General enrolment was sliding downhill. Ordinary revenues were being ravaged by inflation. Government would not bend. Accordingly, the president advised that McMaster disengage from the fray and levy the full fee on incoming visa students, effective 1 July 1978. The senate concurred, only a few votes dissenting.[31] The board gave its approval, early next month. Anticipating the obvious, overseas enrolments dropped by 25 per cent, well before these decisions were made final.[32]

While the fate of foreign professors and students was being debated, thought was also given to Canadianization of the curriculum. On this score, irresistible pressure came from within the university, as well as from without, which was common on campuses across the nation. Although stating the extreme case, Grant was not the only person to lament the possible development of a branch-plant intellectual life, given the influx of foreign media, corporations, and scholars, after the Second World War. Indeed, one could trace the urge to national cultural self-assertion back to the Massey Commission of the 1950s, and to its great monument, the Canada Council. At McMaster, battles royal over Canadian content in political science had been just the tip of a substantial iceberg, throughout the later sixties. In 1973, the issue threatened to bubble over, when the delegation of eleven professors approached Bourns on this matter, as well as on the question of hiring preference for Canadians. Since he had no objection in principle to careful curricular modification, Bourns obliged the group by requesting the senate establish an ad hoc committee on Canadian studies.[33]

While the committee surveyed general dimensions of the question, individual disciplines were at work beefing up their Canadian offerings. History, for example, mounted an honours program in the field. English strengthened a thriving stream in Canadian literature. Anthropology was already noted for its special attention to the indigenous aboriginal experience. Similar expressions of interest in things Canadian were apparent in other disciplines, from economics to geography, as the seventies progressed. It was not until 1979, however, that a more sweeping plan was laid before the senate. In January of that year, a proposal was put to found a general honours program in Canadian studies that combined the manifold resources of humanities and social science. Quite unexpectedly, it met with some stiff criticism.

No sooner had the proposal reached the senate floor than consternation was voiced over the lack of significant requirements in French. Amazed, scientist Dennis Shaw opined that to ask only for a single, introductory course in one of the nation's two official languages seemed paltry. This shallow nod toward biculturalism, he thought, deeply undermined the credibility of a supposed Canadian studies honours stream. Were the program to go forward without stiffer demands, he ventured, it would be "pilloried in any French language publication." In retort, champions of the program noted that the Department of History's earlier solo venture in the area had foundered on the rocks of student resistance to working in French. They, also, pointed out that many McMaster graduates who majored in that language lacked fluency, even after three or four years of study. To require higher proficiency from Canadian studies candidates seemed, to program proponents, both unfair and unrealistic. Encouragement in that direction, they argued, was probably the most that could reasonably be asked for, if the degree were to enrol sufficient candidates to be viable.

Student senators confirmed this reasoning. Grade-thirteen French was no longer required for entrance to university, they noted. Accordingly, several interested students would be deterred from taking up the combined program, were language demands sterner. Shaw, again, vented his displeasure, but the proposition was passed, in principle. The senate did, however, register its intention to review the whole matter, three years hence.[34] On this ambiguous note, the long struggle over Canadianization came to a pause. Indeed, by the late seventies, it was already a back-burner issue, as attention was increasingly preoccupied with what was menacingly called the "new reality."

Of course, there was nothing altogether novel about the new reality. It was the garden-variety seventies edition – with sharper thorns. In 1977, Ontario treasurer Darcy McKeough announced that the province would seek to balance its budget by 1980. Few, in university circles, had any illusions about the implications of this policy decision. After all, that same year, Ottawa had withdrawn from direct funding of post-secondary education, save through its research councils. Instead, taxation points were transferred to provinces for use at their discretion. In an era prior to large-scale private sector involvement, this move left universities under the fiscal thumb of one provincial master, and, in Ontario, that overseer was crying penury in the face of inflation, industrial difficulties, and the soaring costs of various health and social assistance programs.

Even before the funding change became official, Bourns had warned the senate that the consequences could be dire, especially for graduate programs and research; neither of which stood high on Queen's Park agenda. He had hoped that the ACAP exercise would promote clear differentiation among universities and that this would lead to appropriate tailoring of their financing. This long-sought change, however, had not come to pass largely because ACAP, said Bourns, had been a "less than truly rigorous process." In blunt terms, therefore, he advised the senate, "High quality can be found in each of the Faculties that offer doctoral work and these must receive support to assure continued development." In other areas, he warned, it might be necessary to confine efforts to the undergraduate and master's levels. The province, he indicated, was unlikely to be any more sympathetic to McMaster's particular needs in the future than it had been in the past.[35] Ruminating gloomily, in February 1978, on McKeough's statement, Bourns pencilled a disconsolate note for his own reference. Ontario universities, he scribbled, had long yearned to have a clear financial picture that extended beyond a one-year horizon. "For the first time," he continued, "we appear to know the situation for at least and more likely 4 or 5 years and I rather wish I did not know."[36]

After prolonged analysis of income and expenditures, Bourns outlined the bleak situation in a late-1978 brief to the whole McMaster community. True, the federal Anti-Inflation Board was being phased out, but Bette Stephenson, Ontario's minister of education, had warned universities to show continued restraint.[37] Bourns estimated, therefore, that operating increases were likely to hover around 5 per cent for the foreseeable future, while inflation ran well ahead.[38] Meanwhile, there was no indication that

Queen's Park would allow tuition to be raised without deducting corresponding sums from annual grants. In depressing tandem, year-one enrolment, dipping since 1976, was predicted to fall by 3 or 4 per cent each year, well into the eighties. The same drop was expected in graduate numbers. The latter was especially bad news.

In 1976, government graduate funding had been frozen at current levels. At the time, this had been a backhanded boon to McMaster, as enlistments there had declined more sharply than throughout the rest of Ontario. By late 1978, however, Bourns had word that the freeze would soon be lifted. He feared a return to some form of enrolment-based funding scheme. His institution, he understood, would suffer more than most, given that some phantom BIUs would disappear. When pent-up salary demands of faculty and support staff were thrown into the mix, said Bourns, the university deficit was projected to top $6 million by 1981–82. With an accumulated reserve of just under $2 million, as of April 1978, and interest on loans running at 10 per cent, there was little alternative, save to undertake another round of in-house retrenchment.

As a start, Bourns announced that fifteen faculty posts would be left entirely fallow, during 1978–79, while thirteen retiring professors would be replaced by junior people on contract. Furthermore, McMaster would convert from expensive oil to cheaper natural gas heating. In addition, he urged that the whole university follow the lead of psychology and engineering in using word processing as much as possible, in order to cut clerical costs. In conclusion, Bourns called for calm. There was, he assured readers, no need for panic, so long as all on campus performed "with clear heads and in a spirit of restraint."[39] He was asking for patience, co-operation, and trust. This plea for collegiality in the face of financial distress became even more earnest the following year.

In March 1979, Vice-President Lee informed the university that, recent economizing notwithstanding, McMaster would be forced to reduce its faculty complement by sixty-five members, over the following three years. The governors were about to approve a budget deficit of $745,000.[40] Tenured instructors, Lee said, were not imperilled, but numerous contractual posts would be left unfilled, as would some vacated by retirees. Humanities could expect the hardest hit, but science and social science would suffer, too. Enrolment was in free fall, across the province. McMaster, however, was especially vulnerable, since Hamilton-region high schools reported lower registration than the already declining provincial average. The threat of staggering under an $11-million deficit by 1982 meant that academic cutbacks were not a choice but a necessity.[41]

Since 1977, Bourns had been encouraging any and all means of squeezing the last ounce out of standing resources. He had implored the senate to suggest ways to combine purchasing measures and integrated programming. "Project 80" was devised to reduce costs by computerizing all services.[42] The merging of humanities and social science had even been considered, albeit briefly.[43] A large-scale fundraising campaign, the first in a decade, was in the planning stage, but could not be launched before 1980 or 1981, at the earliest. Local steel magnates, enduring a downturn, had advised Bourns to wait until better conditions prevailed.[44] For the moment, the president could only call for collective forbearance. In the main, and perhaps to his surprise, he received this in good measure. Indeed, as dark as they were in so many ways, Bourns' last few years in office, in other respects, would prove to be among his finest hours.

There was, for example, no torrent of outrage against Gilmour Hall in the student press, when academic cutbacks were announced. True, the *Silhouette* kept up its steady barrage against tenure, which was said to sacrifice fresh, invigorating blood to protect all-too-seasoned wood.[45] Editors, however, did not lay blame at local doors for the reduction in contractual positions. Rather, they fired broadsides at a purportedly short-sighted Queen's Park. Indeed, the senate was roundly applauded, when it formally supported a student demonstration on the steps of the Ontario legislature. Those from McMaster who attended the 16 March 1978 protest in Toronto felt that they had been transported back to the sixties, as they stood, shoulder to shoulder, with peers from across the province, alongside representatives of the Ontario Federation of Labour, as well as opposition NDP and Liberal leaders.[46] The exercise was purgative and uplifting. It was gratifyingly nostalgic. It was, also, absolutely to no avail.

Student journalists, however, were clear that Bourns and the governors had done all they could to stave off the academic effects of government parsimony, until the last moment possible. Rehearsing the many creative efforts at economizing over the last few years, the *Silhouette* stated emphatically that McMaster and its leadership were not at fault.[47] If Bourns found this ringing student endorsement a boost to his spirits, he must have been even more buoyed by the general tenor of faculty response. He should not have been surprised, however, for he merely reaped as he had so carefully sown.

Mark Levinson, reflecting on his years as a leading member of the faculty association, later wrote, "Everything depended on trust between individuals." No sentimentalist, he adopted a strictly *realpolitik* stance in dealings with the administration. Still, after many hard-fought bouts with Bourns over various discrete matters, Levinson came to trust in the essential collegiality of the president, when it came to policies affecting the general well-being of the university community. In the end, he was given to reminisce: "It would be hard not to remember such a man with some affection."[48] If this were a singular observation, it could be dismissed as idiosyncratic. When, however, every past-president of MUFA, to a man or woman, echoed the same opinion in print, Levinson's view must stand definitive. Thus, for all that he presided over McMaster during a period when grim news was daily fare, Bourns won far greater trust and general confidence among faculty than his more renowned predecessor.[49] This was no mean feat, given that he stepped into a hornet's nest of trouble, upon assuming the presidency in 1972.

In March 1969, a white-hot missive from the volcanic Jack Kirkaldy sat steaming on Harry Thode's desk. Fuming over presidential statements concerning possible trade-offs between programs and salaries, the engineer fulminated, "It is now clear to me, as it never was before, that the detailed and up-to-date budget of the university must be made the property of the faculty through the Faculty Association."[50] In penning this note, Kirkaldy put his finger on what, during the next decade, would be the keystone issue in faculty relations with Gilmour Hall. For the moment, as months drifted by, the association stepped up pressure for greater access to university accounts. By 1971, the executive was contemplating an appeal to the CAUT. At MUFA's request, Norman Rosenblood and William Hunter had written Thode, asking for discussion of formal procedures whereby faculty could co-operate in the budgetary process. As Rosenblood tells the tale, Thode summoned him "immediately" to his office and, forsaking pleasantries, asked, "What do you want?" When informed that the association sought representation in budget talks, Thode inquired, "Why?" Eventually, saying he would think about it, the president bid the association member a polite good day. Rosenblood was left to reflect that faculty-administration relations at McMaster were swiftly becoming "the worst in Ontario."[51]

As noted, Thode momentarily doused potential conflagration by forming the PBAC. In reality, of course, that body was little more than a timely placebo, in that MUFA was not granted direct representation on a committee which, in any event, received only sanitized information. Thus, matters of a structural nature were not really settled. Meanwhile, the association's annual brief for 1971–72 noted that average salaries at McMaster were below those at nearby Guelph and closer to remuneration at new universities, such as Laurentian. These figures, said MUFA leaders, presented "a dismal picture, at variance with the image of this university as a strong, progressive and competitive institution with high standing in the Province."

Furthermore, sharp exception was taken to the considerable gap separating the salaries of medical and traditional academic faculty on campus.[52] Meanwhile, to enliven matters, beneath these issues there lurked a wide range of long-lived, non-monetary concerns.

Among other things, there was increasing pressure to offer classes outside normal working hours as part of regular teaching loads. Here, several factors were at work. For one thing, Queen's Park was disinclined to regard research as integral to professorial duty. To ministry mandarins, it was a "free-time," voluntary activity and subsidiary to the prime directive: accommodating universal access at the undergraduate level. Hence, formula funding recognized only the ratio of posteriors to podiums. Meanwhile, as extension studies boomed in the sixties, most universities took steps to ensure that part-time degree programs truly were equivalent, both in structure and quality, with their daytime counterparts. At McMaster, the two degree streams were integrated under the aegis of faculties.

When, however, general enrolment declined or shifted during the next decade, instructors in lightly subscribed programs could find themselves required to undertake extension teaching, with no extra stipend, in order to meet BIU formula demands. Naturally, this raised a host of questions, such as who was to make such decisions and what shape proper criteria might take.[53] In like manner, issues of Byzantine complexity involving the finer points of parking, not to mention tenure, promotion, pensions, sabbaticals, and appointments, were still up for consideration, when Bourns succeeded Thode. Yet, if these matters carried over from one regime to the next, the manner and the mood in which they were addressed did not.

One could get lost in the rabbit warren of faculty-administrative relations during the seventies – and to no edifying purpose. After all, the questions, noted above, informed commonplace discourse on every campus in the country. The true historical task, here, is to explain how and why McMaster successfully developed an atypical, non-adversarial model for dealing with those very issues which, at so many other universities, led to deadlock and faculty unionization. McMaster, of course, would be no stranger to strife. Moreover, the option of collective bargaining was certainly discussed, from time to time. It was never, however, widely or fervently pursued. Instead, faculty-administration collaboration waxed stronger rather than weaker at McMaster, the worse constraints became. It is this seeming paradox that commands historical attention; not the particular details of sundry negotiations.

Among the cardinal factors in play, Bourns' innate political savvy was certainly of paramount importance. Like a chess master, he could see long-term implications in even in the most minor move. Allied with this was a genuine willingness to look sympathetically at issues from another's point of view. For faculty-association paladins, Bourns was a refreshing change from the respected, but, as one colleague described him, "almost chillingly professional" Thode.[54] Still, it takes two to play.

Thus, Les King surely identified a significant point when he observed that MUFA was historically well-disposed toward sensible administrative olive branches. Throughout its history, he notes, seasoned academics regularly supplied the solid core of faculty association leadership, holding hair-triggered Young Turks respectfully in check.[55] This fortunate coincidence of tempered, institutionally centred thought, on both sides of the administrative-faculty line, served to facilitate creative and often unique solutions to potentially explosive problems, even as the fiscal cinch was pulled ever tighter. The principal instrument of adaptive collaboration would be the joint faculty-administration committee. An ad hoc device in Thode's day, it became an institutional fixture during the seventies and an enduring legacy for the McMaster that followed. Bourns came to understand its utility the hard way: through trial and error.

During the first months of his presidency, for example, he encountered considerable friction over the question of teaching loads. An agreement had been reached on the subject by a joint committee, only the year before. The terms, however, were vague and designed for normal times of sustained growth. In essence, it was merely stipulated that some junior appointees would be specifically exempt from obligatory extension duties, while others would not. These guidelines were designed to be revisited, after some experience was had.[56] Then suddenly, in the fall of 1972, enrolment dipped at the moment Queen's Park was clamping down on university expenditures and cracking the statistical whip, in order to ensure that it got more scholar for the dollar.

Alert to the dire possibilities of reporting apparent excess teaching capacity to accountability-obsessed ministry wallahs, Bourns quickly inserted load-teaching clauses in all letters of appointment and tenure. Overnight, the amount of extension instruction done on load rose from 10 (1971) to 25 per cent (1972) of total teaching commitments.[57] Unsurprisingly, MUFA issued a stinging response, complaining of this unilateral modification of the original agreement.[58] Reporting this to his inner cabinet, Bourns admitted that the association had a point, but he was equally certain that he could not recant his position without forfeiting his credibility as a responsible president. Here, he was supported by the redoubtable Mike Hedden, who advised that government would feel fully justified in further cuts, did the university not show that all its current teaching power was required. Absorbing some overload stipends into regular duties allowed McMaster to keep faculty numbers up to respectable strength, while mollifying Queen's Park. As for MUFA, Bourns accepted that he would just have to take some flak for the moment and play the rest "by ear."[59]

Meeting the senate on 8 November 1972, the president moved quickly to put his case. "What is important to the university and to its faculty," he emphasized, "is that only if a substantial number ... are committed to load teaching, including summer school, will it be possible to retain most of our very good faculty currently on term appointment." He hoped that volunteers would come forward in sufficient number so as to obviate the necessity of large-scale compulsion. Blumstock (sociology) expressed concern that social science, which had a high proportion of junior instructors, might bear an unfair share of load assignments. Bourns adroitly conceded that different faculties would be differently affected, simply because of shifting enrolment patterns; yet sociology, for example, need have little fear. Indeed, said Bourns, it was load teaching across the university that would allow understaffed departments, such as sociology, to receive new appointments in the future. When queried about his recent unilateral decision concerning letters of appointment, Bourns swallowed a sliver of humble pie, allowing that some consultation should have preceded it. Even so, he continued, that was one of those moments when a difficult choice had to be made expeditiously. He assured listeners that he had acted in the long-term interest of the community as a whole, since it would have been irresponsible to count on unpredictable volunteerism in the face of implacable Queen's Park accountancy.[60] The blustery meeting went on for some time, but the new president left with his credibility intact and, no doubt, some lessons learned. Meanwhile, he was engaged in formulating a "gentleman's agreement" on matters pertaining to load with economist Bill Hunter, president of MUFA.[61]

As Hunter looked back on his year in office, he was more than pleased with Bourns' appreciation of association sensitivities. After reviewing MUFA's objections to unilateralism in load and summer stipend decisions, he underscored that the president was quick to take a hint. Thus, four joint faculty-administration committees came into being in December 1972. These dealt with issues of core interest, such as staffing policy, the phasing out of summer stipends, and the issue of tenure for part-time faculty. Better yet, said Hunter, reports of such bodies had to be approved by the general membership, as would any changes suggested by the senate. By April 1973, Hunter could inform the annual general meeting that Bourns had demonstrated a sincere interest in co-operating with MUFA. Indeed, he told members,

"[O]ur aid and advice is being sought over a whole range of matters that, only a short while ago, were never referred to us at all." In token of the new relationship, Bourns found office space for association headquarters and even footed half the bill.[62]

The significance of this episode resides not in its details but in the cast of mind and manner it reveals. Both Bourns and MUFA leaders regarded faculty, not as employees, but as partners in the enterprise that was McMaster University.[63] The proliferation of joint committees, during the seventies, was the most tangible expression of commitment to this outlook, as well as the principal vehicle for translating it into concrete action on matters as diverse as a polished tenure document, an authoritative faculty handbook, and a clear statement concerning teaching loads.[64] This is not to imply that the partnership always enjoyed full concord. On the contrary, sharp exchanges and tough negotiation were common enough. In 1976, for example, throbbing veins bulged on MUFA temples, when governors switched firms managing the pension fund – without consultation. As the association president of the day acknowledged, however, Bourns was "shrewd enough not to bring matters to the boiling point." In this case, he merely fell back on a, by then, well-tried gambit by striking a joint committee with faculty to oversee the fund thereafter.[65] Altogether, by the late seventies, Bourns had earned substantial political capital among senior leaders of the association. The new reality would force him to draw heavily upon that stock. Not surprisingly, the greatest test of collegial partnership arose over the always ticklish issue of faculty salaries.

From his earliest days in office, Bourns held that, ideally, the president should have the final word in formulating salary recommendations to the board. In part, this stance was a holdover from established routine. Gilmour Hall, as Hedden noted in 1973, had never negotiated settlements with the association. MUFA drafted annual briefs for presidential consideration. In time, the PBAC added its advice. Traditionally, however, the president, assisted by his executive committee, crafted a definitive document for submission to the governors. As shortage increasingly afflicted the university, moreover, Bourns was convinced that only the president, with his global overview, was in a position to make informed and often difficult decisions concerning across-the-board increases and merit pay. To him, it was a delicate, intricate exercise in both gauging and preserving the harmony of a complex community.[66]

On this score, however, he thought it essential that MUFA be more fully consulted than in the past. As he told his executive committee, in 1975, "Human concerns will have to be very carefully approached so that morale at the University may be maintained." Accordingly, he insisted that the faculty association should have access to all data available to the executive, so that it might draft better informed briefs.[67] Nevertheless, he wished to reserve final judgment in salary matters to his office. Philosopher kings, alas, were distinctly out of vogue, their best intensions notwithstanding. Inevitably, Bourns would face pressure to negotiate in this age of much-trumpeted participatory democracy. It was merely a matter of time. The fact that academic incomes were taking a pasting at the hand of inflation, while falling well behind the earnings of other professionals, simply hastened that moment. The decisive hour came in 1978.

Administration talks with MUFA delegates produced verbal salary agreements in 1976, 1977, and 1978; only to have those proposals rejected by the association's annual general meeting each year.[68] Since 1975, there had been desultory mention of alternative approaches, including collective bargaining.[69] The latter option, however, held little general appeal. Meanwhile, moderates on the association executive, privy to the general financial state of affairs, had reminded members that BIU increases were regularly below university needs and that the Anti-Inflation Board stood in the way of truly satisfactory pay hikes.[70] For a time, the lid was kept on creeping faculty dissatisfaction. However, in March 1978, pent-up steam finally boiled over, when it was learned that Toronto had offered 1.5 per cent more than McMaster proposed as an across-the-board raise. The annual general meeting (AGM) echoed with calls for more budgetary information, questions about the size of the university surplus, and a resounding rejection of Bourns' offer. Going further, members moved for adoption of the "Toronto model," whereby parties at impasse left the choice between proposals to an external mediator.

In an effort to slow things down, and pay due respect to a collegially minded president, Tom Truman urged that Bourns be given a chance to address the membership, before any vote was taken. In the end, the motion to approach the governors regarding the Toronto scheme won approval; but Bourns was invited to speak at a special meeting.[71] The president, who had vowed to impose a settlement were the current one rejected, wisely accepted the invitation with alacrity. The upshot was a conclave that would shape collegial relations for decades to come.

On 27 June 1978, Bourns addressed MUFA's executive committee. After diplomatically thanking members for the courtesy of a hearing, he launched into an unvarnished description of the immediate context as he saw it. The dimensions of the problems facing universities, he maintained, were readily predictable "within fairly narrow limits of uncertainty." The great variables –

government fiscal policy, economic sluggishness, and falling participation rates – were known, at least to those who paid attention to broader trends. Thus, the annual margin for guesswork or manoeuvre was actually much smaller than many people imagined. In fact, said Bourns, current conditions assured a yearly deficit of roughly $2 million over the next several years, the cumulative weight of which would be intolerable. These basic elements, he underscored, were not in dispute. The issue at hand was how best to cope with them. This observation brought him to the heart of things.

"I have," he declared, "one guiding principle in attempting to 'manage' the University (if I may dare to use the word 'manage'): that has been to avoid crisis situations and precipitous responses to financial problems." On these grounds, Bourns continued, he had adopted a consistent strategy to handle fiscal difficulties in any particular year. That policy, he said, was to buy time for "orderly adjustment." Accordingly, in the crises of 1974–76, he had refused to sink the entire university surplus into futile attempts to maintain the status quo. Instead, he had drawn upon two crucial reserves. One was a portion of the surplus. The other, he underlined, was "my credibility with the Board of Governors," which swayed them to accept a manageable budget deficit for one year. The result was that sufficient time was bought to reduce expenditures in such a way as to do minimal damage to the educational enterprise. In time, the small surplus was restored.

Now, he noted, some were saying "throw all caution to the wind, 'go for broke and let government bail you out'." Bourns cautioned, however, that no government would rescue any university, until it declared bankruptcy. In that case, he argued, Queen's Park would simply assume direct control and make the cuts it saw fit. For that reason, he asserted, he was not prepared to change strategy, merely to settle a momentary difference over salaries. Nor would he accept sole responsibility for the present impasse. Indeed, he reminded his audience that, three years in succession, he had dealt in good faith with their fully informed delegates, only to have agreed proposals scrapped by the AGM. If blame was being apportioned, he said, it had to be shouldered by all parties concerned. That said, he shifted seamlessly from the authoritative voice of "President Bourns" to the more familiar one of "Art."

He expressed strong sympathy with desires to improve the approach to salary determinations. In statesmanlike fashion, he went further to acknowledge errors of omission on his part. Full budgetary information, he admitted, did not always reach the general membership, because he had relied, too complacently, on word-of-mouth exchange with delegates. As a consequence, much was frequently lost in transmission. Going further, he confessed to projecting a somewhat paternalistic attitude, from time to time. For these things, Bourns sincerely apologized. He was adamant, however, that there had never been an intentional effort to conceal vital financial data. Having broken a little ice, he then asked what was to be done.

As he outlined them, four models of procedure seemed available. One was the path of collective bargaining. He cautioned, however, that such a step could not be restricted solely to salary negotiations. Instead, it would eventually come to embrace all faculty activity in an industrial framework. The Toronto scheme, he continued, was just unionization in fancy dress, since it was predicated on adversarial bargaining, with final appeal to an external arbitrator. Waterloo's practice offered a third potential avenue. Under that scheme, arbitration was left to the board of governors. While attracted to this design, because it kept ultimate decision-making in-house, Bourns outlined improvements to the existing "Queen's-McMaster Model" as his preferred format.

On this score, the president suggested several proposals for strengthening collegiality in the context of the existing system. Thus, he offered to provide MUFA with far more detailed and written financial information, the moment it became available. To that end, he advised that salary and fiscal discussions should be frequent, rather than reserved for one fixed point of the year. Ready to stand accountable, Bourns offered to meet with the general membership annually and answer any queries from the floor. Finally, he advised that the PBAC, henceforth, report to the senate which, in turn, might make final budget recommendations to the board. Admitting that he had yet to think all these ideas through, Bourns concluded by inviting association executives to consider and flesh out with him these, and other, collegial solutions to their common problem.[72]

It was as though a glowering thunderhead temporarily evaporated. In refraining from imposing an immediate settlement, while offering the hope of collectively authored reform, Bourns won the ear of an audience willing at least to discuss his suggestions. For its part, the association voted to hold a direct approach to the board in abeyance, until the ramifications of a refined Queen's-McMaster Model were explored. Opinion within MUFA was divided, but informal talks went on, throughout the summer. Finally, on 19 September, MUFA representatives Marianne (Walters) Kristofferson, Harold Guite, Mark Levinson, and Tom Truman met with Bourns, Lee, and Hedden. During what all parties agreed was a cordial encounter, the framework of a landmark structure was sketched.[73] After intense debate, the November AGM voted to accept the new procedure, albeit far from unanimously. Balloting revealed eighty-two in favour and sixty-four opposed, with four abstaining.[74] A great deal, therefore, would hang on how well the reformed arrangements functioned.

Such were the origins of the Joint Administrative-Faculty Committee on University Finance and Remuneration, linear ancestor of today's broader Tripartite Committee. Under terms agreed to in 1978, the body comprised three faculty delegates, along with three senior administrators. The chair was elected by the six assembled and rotated annually between administrative and association members. Yearly deliberations were broken down into three distinct phases. In the first round, the committee received all the necessary budget information, considered general university spending priorities, and offered advice to the president on these. With this broad contextual overview established, salaries were then addressed. If an agreement were not reached, contending positions were to be put to the AGM. Should the administrative proposal be accepted by that body, it would go directly to the governors as "agreed." In the event that differences arose, further negotiation was to ensue. If consensus remained elusive, separate proposals would be placed before the board, where a final determination (not selection) would be made.[75]

The scheme was not perfect, but it worked. Indeed, the joint committee never failed to reach agreement, during Bourns final years in office. On this score, all acknowledged the large role played by Hedden, who went to great lengths to ensure that full and reliable financial information was made readily available.[76] Genial and trusted by all, his part in refurbishing faculty-administration relations is hard to exaggerate. He would be sorely missed, when points of friction resurfaced in the eighties. For the moment, association leaders hailed Bourns and his colleagues for giving collegiality more concrete form. Indeed, a new enthusiasm is clearly detectable in MUFA records of the hour. There was a sense of greater enfranchisement abroad. This translated into constructive co-engagement in trying to manage the new reality.

In 1979, for example, the university looked favourably on an association scheme to retain as many contractual instructors as possible at a moment of financial exigency. Thus, a pre-retirement workload scheme was planned, whereby senior faculty, aged sixty or older, could lower their commitments by as much as 50 per cent, while retaining full pension credits and benefits. The idea stalled out, entangled in silken webs that only the Department of National Revenue could weave. Even so, the effort spoke volumes. MUFA signalled its recognition that oft-touted "tough choices" were, in fact, quite difficult. The proposal also made clear MUFA's readiness to collaborate with Gilmour Hall in confronting them. Accordingly, much joint thought was given to early retirement schemes, flexible teaching loads, and how best to employ surplus pension funds. For its part, the university reciprocated. Thus, it absorbed the full cost of medical insurance premiums and aided association studies of pension and benefit adjustments, designed to maximize after-tax incomes.[77]

Not all these endeavours bore immediate fruit. Even so, the tone of the moment was every bit as significant as the substance of particular undertakings. Teamwork, of course, had always been part of the Thodean credo, but in expanding on and institutionalizing the concept of partnership Bourns put his particular stamp on the university. The McMaster Act had emphasized the inter-related functions and shared membership of the board and the senate. Now, the joint committee offered a similar framework for relations between the administration and faculty association. The board, the senate, MUFA, and Gilmour Hall, if not always in cheerful agreement, at least acknowledged that they were interwoven threads of a common fabric. This was just as well. After all, scarcity and enlightened self-interest decreed that, henceforth, far more careful planning be put into weaving the McMaster quilt. Bourns, of course, recognized this, early on. As the seventies unfolded, evident necessity brought others round to this view. The outcome was institutional commitment to the (unmistakably Thodean) *Plan for McMaster*.

In September 1970, a meeting of the president's executive committee found Vice-President (Arts) William Hellmuth in a disconsolate mood. Having uttered a few pieties about the just claims of his division, he conceded that truly balanced development, however desirable, was simply not in the contemporary fiscal cards. Reluctantly, he agreed that, henceforth, there should be "a selective approach to excellence." Seconding this point, his counterpart in science, Art Bourns, argued that achieving literal balance was, in any event, both highly unlikely and not truly desirable. All universities, he asserted, ought not to be cookie-cut and alike. The core issue for the seventies, he continued, would be "to decide on our limits and then agree on the appropriate distribution involved." In a word, the task was one of differentiation. Hedden interjected that, hitherto, it had been a question of "grow or die." He doubted that this outlook could be sustained, given unstable economic currents and shifting public opinion. Encapsulating the gist of discussion, Thode put things bluntly: it was time to "consolidate and plan."[78] Throughout his own hours in office, Bourns would sound this same note, time and again – only with ever-increasing urgency.

Indeed, a summons to this effect knit together the many threads of his first presidential address to the senate in September 1972. To one degree or another, the desire to facilitate priority-planning underpinned his appeals to restructure both senate and the old divisional system, install a single vice-president (academic), and begin the detailed cost analysis of teaching and research. It was time, Bourns emphasized, "to take a hard look" at long-range planning and decide what kind of university McMaster should become.[79] Later on, even when engrossed in the French strike, dwelling on Canadianization, attending to faculty relations, or polishing elements of the McMaster Act, his mind was constantly attuned to the central question of institutional self-definition. In this preoccupation he was not alone.

Alvin Lee, dean of graduate studies in 1972, surveyed the contemporary landscape and concluded that an end to the sixties' boom was of less concern than "the crudity and non-reflectivity of the way expansion is being halted." Queen's Park, in his estimation, was taking a broad brush to the task of rationalizing post-secondary education, whereas a refined pointillism was more in order. In any event, Lee foresaw an extended period during which tough choices would be the stuff of daily routine. That being the case, he argued, close examination of basic assumptions would first be required. He noted, however, that division over fundamental principles was already heating up. Oversimplified terms, such as *conservative* and *innovative*, were being hurled about. Debate, of course, was both healthy and necessary. What disturbed Lee was "how quickly people got locked into fixed positions so that it made difficult, if not impossible, any real meeting of minds as to what McMaster is and should be."[80] While first principles were foremost in Lee's mind, others were increasingly worried about efficiencies.

Writing to Bourns, following a 1973 meeting of the PBAC, Hedden observed, "Consideration of academic budgets is still very superficial and I do not believe we have developed effective guidelines that can be used in assessing academic priorities." It was, he admitted, exceedingly difficult to set out the goals and objectives of a university, but advised that McMaster had better do so in order that scarce resources, henceforth, be allocated on clearly articulated, well-understood grounds. Here, he pointed to a recent study at Cornell, which advocated "better, more systematic, thorough and professional planning as a high-level function involving a co-ordinated approach." In Hedden's estimation, this boiled down to better reporting, accountability, and effectiveness in spending.[81]

A year later, thinking in even broader terms, Barney Jackson (English) lamented, "There appears to be no forum within the University in which to discuss what the goals of the University might be in ten or twenty years' time." At that moment, he was speaking in the senate on behalf of a motion that a specific body be formed to fill this dangerous void. In the new spirit that emphasized the inextricably overlapping functions of McMaster's two governing bodies, David Winch moved that the proposed committee be a joint endeavour of the board and the senate. When both chambers approved this venture, the fateful LRPC was born.[82] Like the Leal and Winch committees before it, the LRPC would leave its own lingering imprint on the university.[83]

The committee began official deliberations in September 1975, with distinguished chemist Ronald Gillespie in the chair. Over thirty-strong, its core membership was broadly representative of the diverse McMaster community and included Chancellor Lawrence Pennell, along with a cross-section of administrators, governors, senators, faculty, and students. Ambitious in conception, its thirteen task forces and subcommittees were authorized to conduct an exhaustive study of the university's strengths, weaknesses, and potential, with a view to defining priorities for future development. To ensure that all was done thoroughly and with maximum consultation, Gillespie was given fully three years to inquire and report. Bending to his duty with a will, the earnest chemist, quite literally, wore himself out by February 1978. Engineer Mark Levinson, then, stepped into the breach pro tem, until historian Charles "Chuck" Jago was appointed to the chair. The fruit of all this collective toil was the comprehensive, *Plan for McMaster*, ratified in June 1978.

Although long in gestation, the overriding thrust of the eventual report was crystal clear from the moment of its first iteration. Offering an early draft to the senate in November 1976, Gillespie was unambiguous about bedrock principles that guided the LRPC. Differentiation, he declared, was the ultimate goal. McMaster had to define its specific place in the context of the Ontario university system. It was necessary, therefore, to clarify the roles it currently played and identify others that it might reasonably assume. One thing, however, was blatantly obvious. "It is clear," he told the senate, "from the number and high quality of McMaster's graduate programmes and from McMaster's record as a research institution that the University already does have a special role in the Ontario system." There were, he acknowledged, areas of weakness that had to be addressed. This raised the difficult question as to whether some programs should be strengthened or phased out. The committee, said Gillespie, was currently wrestling with this (sure-to-be contentious) issue. The overarching plan, however, was to ensure that McMaster retained "international stature ... in carefully chosen areas."[84] Now, when had this been heard before, and how often? Clearly, the LRPC was not intent on changing McMaster's fundamental game plan, but on modifying its well-established playbook for particularly challenging seasons ahead.

After interminable consultation with individuals, departments, faculties, and student government, a final draft of the plan was submitted for the senate's consideration on 18 May 1977. Divided into five major sections, the report dealt with: the context and criteria that informed recommendations, issues of a university-wide nature, priorities concerning faculties and departments, matters relating to adult education, and the general state of physical facilities. Too sweeping to be debated at one session, the compendious document would be parsed in laborious detail over the next several months. For the moment, Bourns moved to calm the nervous by emphasizing that planning would be dynamic and flexible, not graven in stone. Recommendations regarding specific units were intended as guidelines, he said, rather than as binding, once-and-for-all prescriptions. Gillespie reinforced this, while outlining the central assumptions upon which the committee had based its findings.

Much, he said, was predicated on the easily predicted, if none too comforting, enrolment vectors ahead. A brief rise in the late seventies would preface a levelling off, followed by significant decline during the mid-eighties. Throughout, the period, he continued, university income would shrink in terms of buying power. This unfortunate nexus, said Gillespie, put paid to any notion that net additions to the faculty complement would be feasible for several years to come. There would, of course, be new faces on campus as a result of retirements, lapsed contracts, and so forth. On this score, however, the committee was adamant that all instructional positions belonged to the university generally, not to specific units, departments, or faculties. Inevitably, some vacated posts would be re-allocated. Thus, all departments were being closely assessed in order to establish priority ranking for replacement and, in a few cases, additional faculty members. In short, a fixed number of cards would be shuffled, and the deck would be stacked to favour hands with the greatest potential. At the cutthroat table of high-stakes funding, McMaster was going after strategic pots.

The key, Gillespie underscored, was to resist an across-the-board approach to resource allocation. Such a policy, he said, would only lead to a general levelling down to uniform mediocrity. This could be avoided, he argued, only if all elements of the McMaster community stood four-square behind a common plan; one that preserved the current level of research and graduate study, while paying due heed to the quality of undergraduate education. In the latter connection, Gillespie noted that the committee was reviewing a proposal for an exciting new general baccalaureate that would set McMaster apart from the common university herd. After sketching other elements of the report, he called for questions. They welled up in profusion.[85]

Philosopher David Hitchcock wondered whether the committee was being completely realistic. For example, he pointed out, the report urged that strong research, graduate, and honours programs be maintained, while also recommending that pass degrees be improved and smaller year-one classes become the norm: all with no additional faculty. Furthermore, expanded graduate enrolment was encouraged for some departments, along with the maintenance of high admission standards. How, asked Hitchcock, did the committee propose that all these goals be met without major dilution through inevitable trade-offs? Gillespie vaguely replied that the report sought not to dictate matters best decided at the departmental level but only to offer an ideal to which the university might aspire.

Seizing on the matter of ideals, Dennis Shaw criticized the report as an essentially "empirical document" that lacked any clear philosophical underpinnings. He compared the university to a ship on a voyage. The committee, he argued, merely showed the best route to a stated destination without questioning the fundamental purpose of the sojourn itself. Some thought, he suggested, needed to be given to the institution's function within the context of modern society. For example, he queried the extent to which professional education should continue to proliferate on campus. Was it the task of the university to train people for specific roles, or for other, broader purposes? Indeed, he asked if the committee had given any thought to setting forth a general statement of its underlying educational goals.

Gillespie responded, saying that Shaw was correct. The report was designedly empirical in nature for one simple reason: had the LRPC debated primary assumptions, in the spirit of a Cardinal Newman or a Thorstein Veblen, it would likely have done so ad infinitum. Besides, said the chemist, McMaster had long since launched upon a particular voyage to which substantial resources were already committed. So well-charted a course, he averred, could not be altered easily in the short term. Bourns and Levinson were quick to echo this view, while noting that, if "axioms" were not explicitly stated in the report, they were clearly evident in its foremost recommendations.[86]

This assertion led another senator to observe that the draft was little more than a description of the status quo, upon which the committee had simply placed its seal of approval. He was particularly concerned that the document said nothing about mechanisms for faculty contribution to future planning. Bourns and Gillespie countered that, should the senate so desire, the LRPC could be constituted as a permanent body, disseminating information to and receiving advice from faculty at large. Then, truly broad thinking about the very long term could be a co-operative, ongoing undertaking.

For the moment, the president stated, the committee had restricted itself to a more practical approach, because several things required immediate attention in light of the McKeough budget statement.[87] Still, in the privacy of his own mind, Bourns must have thanked the anxious senator for opening this door to the establishment of a standing joint committee dedicated exclusively to planning. He might, however, have been rather surprised by a question from Fraser Mustard.

Why, asked the dean of medicine, was so much emphasis being placed on increasing the number of graduate students? Was this just a formula-funding consideration? The unspoken answer, of course, was "yes," at least in part. Gillespie, however, pointed out that graduate studies were essential to differentiation and to the health of research programs, especially in science. As an example, Levinson noted that engineering could handle many more doctoral candidates without strain, and that such people, as teaching assistants, could greatly enhance the quality of undergraduate instruction. Besides, he observed, it would be a waste to have what was, perhaps, the best research-oriented engineering faculty in the country providing less graduate training than it readily could.

Alert to other sensibilities in his audience, Bourns deftly drew attention to the committee's call for a substantial increase of doctoral students in the Department of English. This recommendation, he underlined, had nothing to do with any need for research workers but reflected recognition of growing scholarly strength in the department. The subtext, of course, was that the committee did not envisage a purely scientific-cum-professional future, but was cognizant of the just claims of arts, as well.[88] On that note, first discussion of the plan came to a close. Debate, however, was far from over; indeed, it would rattle on for the better part of a year.

In November 1977, matters touching on the potentially flammable issue of department autonomy arose. Here, the committee identified a serious, university-wide problem. As Guite described it, there was a wasteful lack of co-operation and coordination regarding admission policies and course planning, among and within departments. The Calendar, he said, was littered with a large array of seemingly overlapping and redundant courses. This situation, he mused, reflected the traditional freedom of departments and individuals to teach what and how they saw fit, along with an urge to develop ever-more specialized offerings. While professionally understandable, Guite wondered whether such uncontrolled curricular wildcatting was affordable or wise, in that money was tight and enrolment was predicted to decline. Bourns pitched in, adding that every effort had to be made to ensure that all courses could be justified to government. Gillespie bolstered the point by reminding listeners that, on 24 April 1975, the senate had called on all departments and faculties to exercise greater economy and more co-operative effort in streamlining curricular development. Guite acknowledged that surrendering old freewheeling ways would require a significant change of attitude on the part of faculty, but saw no viable alternative, if McMaster were to devise programs that were, at once, cost-effective and likely to attract high-calibre candidates.

Somewhat surprisingly, this entreaty met with little resistance, at least on the senate floor. Earlier, it might have prompted outcries about infringement on academic freedoms. This, however, was the late seventies. The ferociously real new reality led many, including MUFA leaders, such as Levinson and Guite, to accept the closer monitoring and greater rationalization of resources. The senate, accordingly, endorsed a series of LRPC recommendations that promoted increased cross-pollination within and among faculties in the form of joint appointments, associate memberships, and shared courses. Duplication of offerings was to be avoided, and the calendar was to be stripped of accumulated detritus. Meanwhile, curriculum submissions were to be subjected to more demanding scrutiny, at all levels of approval, in relation to the number of courses, faculty, and students on any given department's books. In short, as Bourns put it, scarce resources would be guarded and apportioned with far greater care than in the past. Under obviously straightened circumstances, few openly disagreed with the concept of rationalization, per se.[89] The devil, of course, is in the details. Thus, concern soon arose when general ideas were applied to particular cases. Debate on this level could grow very warm, indeed. On this score, discussions regarding the fate of humanities offer an illustrative example.

Some feathers were certainly ruffled, when that faculty came up for review. Departments with established doctoral programs fared well enough. Thus, English, history, philosophy, and classics were merely urged to be more aggressive in trawling for students; especially the graduate species. Several other disciplines, however, were informed that their priority for new or replacement appointments would be low. For want of space, the art and art history program was advised to restrict studio enrolment and concentrate on academic functions. Music was told that its priority would be dependent on the fate of a proposed MA in criticism. Meanwhile, dramatic arts and film was directed to phase out its professional theatre courses in favour of an emphasis on theoretical and literary study. Taken aback, historian David Russo asked whether, given the lively theatrical tradition on campus, the recommendation was tied solely to considerations of space. Seizing this opening, an irate Dean Berland informed the senate that it was "shameful that McMaster had the worst theatre facilities of any university in Ontario." Robinson Memorial Theatre, he remarked, was a converted lecture hall with no backstage or dressing rooms, yet astonishing use had been made of it. In the end, Berland's words notwithstanding, relatively small enrolment and the exorbitant cost of a purpose-built theatre swayed the senate toward the LRPC's point of view.[90] True heat, however, flared over modern languages.

The Department of German, for example, was sorely affronted by an LRPC recommendation that its long-standing master's program be formally appraised by graduate council. Berland objected vociferously to the blunt wording of the proposal, describing it as "invidious," based on insufficient consultation, and likely to do grave damage to the department's reputation. Lee, speaking from the committee's perspective, conceded that the recommendation might have been unduly brief and baldly put, but it was not ill conceived. He noted that German excelled at innovative undergraduate instruction. Indeed, McMaster's department was the only one in the province whose enrolment had increased in recent years. This, said the vice-president, was a major achievement at the baccalaureate level. On the other hand, he noted that the master's program was increasingly offered on a course-only basis, with no comprehensive examination or thesis required. In short, it was deemed to lack academic gravitas. The same, he inferred, was true of the faculty who, in the committee's opinion, paid too little attention to scholarly endeavour. Incensed, Berland retorted (accurately) that many other programs at the university were similarly structured, and that to single out one for review was blatantly unfair. Taking the point, Lee moved to refer the matter back to the committee.[91] In its final draft, the LRPC deleted the call for a formal review, but underlined that "the Department should place more emphasis on the scholarly work and publications of its members."[92]

As for other modern languages, the message was much the same: none were to be significantly nurtured. Apart from introductory French, undergraduate demand was low. Moreover, the prospects of developing first-class PhD programs seemed remote. In the LRPC's opinion, scholarly attainment in the romance languages was too uneven to sustain credible doctoral work.[93] The four-person Russian department, on the other hand, while home to scholars of great distinction, was simply too small to handle more than its current load of pass and combined-honours courses.[94] Putting all this in context for the senate, Lee explained the LRPC's thinking. Unlike studio courses in theatre, none of the smaller language programs were to be phased out. They were, however, to be treated as enriching elements for which the Faculty of Humanities must share the cost. "This," he said, "might mean that some of the larger departments might not be able to develop to the extent they would have otherwise."[95] For a passionate humanist of Lee's ilk, this must have been a galling message to deliver. Still, he was only voicing, if indirectly, the foremost among those unspoken "axioms" to which Bourns had alluded: effective differentiation necessitated bolstering established strengths.[96]

When finally approved, bound, and published, in June 1978, the *Plan for McMaster* ran to 187 pages of much-revised description, oft-modified recommendations, and numerous appendices. Amid this welter of fact, assessment, and advice, one injunction appears to have been the fulcrum upon which much else pivoted. Thus, McMaster was enjoined to "give highest priority to maintaining and further developing a university of high international standing."[97] Distilled down, all other recommendations were means to this superintending end. The merely good would be subordinated to fostering the proven or potentially excellent. Excellence, moreover, was defined primarily in terms of research intensity, publication, grant income, and graduate studies. There were, of course, some pious incantations about improving undergraduate education, but, said the report, thoroughgoing differentiation could not arise there, since all Canadian universities acknowledged a common commitment in that regard.[98] Besides, superior instruction was declared (not documented) to be inextricably linked with demonstrated scholarship "*at all levels of instruction*" (author's italics).[99] Given that scholarly achievement was readily weighed on the basis of peer-adjudicated papers and funding, in the committee's mind it followed that it was relatively easy to identify particular nodes of strength.[100] Since all disciplines could not be freely nourished out of shrinking revenue, each had to be assigned priority for preferment. Such were the major underlying assumptions of the report. The application of these to humanities has already been noted. No faculty, department, or unit, however, was exempt from close scrutiny.

Determined to protect specific academic strengths and selectively promote new ones, the LRPC instituted a three-tiered ranking system. Every department was assigned either: a low priority for replacement appointments; a high one for replacement, but low one for net faculty additions; or high precedence for both.[101] In the main, there were few surprises. A longstanding, informal pecking order was largely confirmed. Thus, the research-intensive sciences and engineering were, on the whole, accorded high priority for replacements. A few eyebrows might have been raised when under-subscribed chemistry, with twenty-six faculty members, was cleared for two net additions. This, however, was made contingent on the department's willingness and ability to recruit specialists in the emerging field of biological chemistry, for which there seemed to be significant student demand. In contrast, geology, although described as excellent by any standard, was not even sanctioned for replacements, given its very low enrolment. The same was true of mathematics, although for a different reason. Here, the LRPC pressed for consummation of the long-delayed merger of pure and applied branches of the discipline, before any adjustments to the faculty complement were entertained.[102] The union, less than universally popular among mathematicians, was completed only in 1979.

As for engineering, it was kudos all round, save for chemical engineering, whose undergraduate enlistment had sagged. Like physics and chemistry, the applied sciences were urged to increase their graduate numbers to facilitate research and ease the burden of undergraduate instruction. On the other hand, and again in tandem with the sciences, engineering was advised to eliminate part-time baccalaureate studies in the face of sparse enrolments and the need to conserve professorial energies, as the ratio of teaching assistants to BEng candidates worsened.[103] Furthermore, engineers were applauded for the depth and variety of their programming. With most other faculties, however, they were enjoined to reduce the range of electives and develop more common core courses, so that teaching power might be better focused at all levels of the curriculum.[104] At base, the LRPC envisioned growth in engineering and was trying to clear decks to accommodate it – but without significant additions to staff. By comparison, recommendations for other faculties were far more complex.

Business, for example, housed only one department, commerce, which was subdivided into five "areas." The LRPC commended the faculty on its comparatively high student-teacher ratio and on the diversity of its offerings. Indeed, said the report; "Among university schools of business in Ontario, that at McMaster offers the greatest variety of undergraduate commerce and M.B.A. program options." As well, it boasted a unique and attractive co-op MBA stream. These, and many other features, were all to the good. The committee, however, noted some causes for concern. Thus, it found pockets of strong scholarship, but not overall consistency. In particular, production and management science had developed a more uniform and enviable research profile than any other area. With several net additions to business already approved, the committee urged the utmost care in hiring decisions, lest a single sector come to dominate all the others. For the moment, it recommended that any prospective doctoral program be limited to business administration, as devised by the production and management section, rather than being a faculty-wide offering. Still, an undertone of anxiety about creeping imbalance was palpable in the report.

This concern might have influenced the committee's call on business to draft, within university guidelines, custom-tailored promotion and tenure criteria. These rubrics, it said, should acknowledge "the varying commitments by individual faculty members to teaching, research, and professional services activities." In so recommending, perhaps the committee sought to create greater flexibility and a more level playing field within this emerging, non-traditional faculty. One can only speculate. However, business instructors were notoriously hard to recruit and retain. Moreover, their professional activities were often difficult to categorize. Thus, curbing the upward mobility of scarce staff by narrowly defining research was likely considered unwise when trying to build a stable, balanced faculty.[105]

Balance figured in advice to health sciences, as well. Given their professional nature, complex external ties, and general lack of integration with other university programs, most individual departments were not directly assessed. Research and graduate study, however, were subjected to a searching critique.[106] The LRPC had nothing but praise for the volume and quality of a faculty-wide research effort that garnered fully $7.3 million of external funding in 1977–78. It did, however, have a related and extremely sharp' bone to pick. Indeed, the committee criticized the nature of the graduate program and its apparent lack of coordination with research undertakings. In essence, the LRPC argued that health sciences had strayed from its original mandate in this vital realm.

The founders had intended that graduate work would mirror the holistic, interdisciplinary ethos of the faculty's general educational philosophy. The focus of master's and doctoral study was to be human biology, broadly conceived. Over time, however, forces external and internal had militated against this closely integrated approach. ACAP, for example, had stalled the development of some the program's key components. At the same time, a planned interdisciplinary graduate committee, with representatives from other faculties, failed to materialize. In its place, a faculty-graduate curriculum body was established, but was never given a clearly defined mandate. Moreover, unlike the scientific development committee, which oversaw research, the graduate chairman had no seat on the central faculty executive. The result was that graduate studies had a relatively low profile in the councils of health science. Complicating matters, there were constant wrangles as to who, among the myriad clinical appointees, was qualified to supervise advanced students.

Altogether, said the LRPC, medical graduate work had not been systematically cultivated. The rigour and coherence of some core courses seemed suspect. Worse still, three rather distinct doctoral programs, rather than one, broadly interdisciplinary stream, had taken shape. Most alarming, in committee eyes, graduate programs and faculty research were not as effectively integrated as they were in science and engineering. Health sciences had just begun a sweeping review of its arrangements. The LRPC applauded this initiative, but vigorously counselled the faculty to bring its practice back into line with the holistic intentions of its fathers.[107] In effect, John Evans' heirs were offered a dose of their own medicine. Even so, this was a spoonful of sugar, compared to the stronger physic meted out to social science.

Comprising seven academic departments and two professional schools (social work and physical education), social science was said to be "not as tidy a logical structure as ... the other Faculties of the University." Adding to this jumble, several hundred of the faculty's undergraduates were enrolled in psychology and geography, whose chairmen reported to the dean of science. All told, said the LRPC, "the integration of these different administrative units into a cohesive and strong faculty has been a challenging task." Perhaps deliberately, any mention of who might ultimately have been responsible for this unwieldy agglomeration was sidestepped. Instead, the committee emphasized continuing "signs of immaturity" among these variegated stepchildren, with political science standing as the prime example. Strong scholarship was noted in economics, religious studies, and anthropology. Elsewhere, research was described as uneven, or, as in social work and physical education, difficult to categorize. The foremost problem identified by the LRPC was oversubscription, especially by students of dubious quality. Thus, the faculty was urged to cap enrolment and raise entrance standards, as a step toward general improvement. Strangely, no advice was tendered concerning administrative rationalization, apart from noting that the senate was currently reviewing physical education's affiliation with the social sciences. On the whole, the LRPC gave middling priority to the bulk of programs in this still young faculty.[108]

As with humanities, all final recommendations in the Plan for McMaster were outcomes of extended debate, widespread consultation, and some sprained feelings. Inevitably, many of its proposals met with mixed reactions. The MSU, for example, was quick to denounce what it saw as the committee's obsession with research and skimpy attention to teaching.[109] Meanwhile, as he stepped down from the chair in June 1978, Levinson paused to lash out against those who claimed that the LRPC had done little more than rubber-stamp established administrative priorities. On the contrary, he declared, the sundry recommendations reflected the considered views of a representative body, as well as the counsel of many who advised it. Going further, he added that the LRPC should stay in being and commence a regular five-year planning cycle, using the report as a guideline.[110] He might have added that there had been no minority report.

Experienced hands, such as Gillespie, Levinson, and Bourns, undoubtedly understood from the outset that universal applause would not be forthcoming. Given the panoramic remit of the committee, imperfection and controversy could be assumed. What truly mattered was that a documented baseline for future planning was laid down. On this score, Levinson's parting shot hit its target squarely. Thus, a later board-senate committee on academic policy (BSCAP) would long conduct cyclical reviews and course approvals using the *Plan* as its yardstick to measure progress, regression, and promise.

Moreover, just as significant as the report's recommendations was the manner in which they were conceived. They came not as a fiat from on high but as the product of a deliberately eclectic, broadly collaborative effort. Once again, Bourns' collegial penchant, embodied in a joint committee, took time but paid large and lasting dividends. This stood in sharp contrast with the fate of York's 1977 *Red Book*. Crafted by a presidential commission, York's planning document went down to defeat, partly because it proposed radical change but also, one suspects, because it lacked the cachet of collective authority behind the LRPC report.[111] Offering few, if any, real surprises, the *Plan for McMaster* was essentially a reaffirmation of Thodean values – adjusted to a rigorous hour. Some on campus might have been disappointed, but few were shocked. Thus, no cobbles were upended; no barricades were manned. For that matter, many could agree that at least one spinoff of the exercise was altogether novel and, maybe, worthwhile.

Since the early sixties, countless voices had expressed displeasure with various aspects of undergraduate education at McMaster. True, the university's honours programs were generally held to be of sterling calibre. However, obliging the non-specialist with an equally rewarding experience was a nagging conundrum. Following the 1962 Graham Report, the time-honoured general degree had been replaced by multiple three-year "pass" programs, Many of these, however, came to lack breadth, depth, and structure; satisfying few – other than a nonchalant contingent of academic passersby. As a result, disillusionment with such "education" was a leitmotif of virtually all student protest during the period. The Vichert Committee had tried to come to grips with root issues of purpose and pedagogy at the baccalaureate level, but only produced more questions than answers. Cognizant of smouldering concern, Bourns struck a presidential committee on teaching and learning. The senate, in turn, sanctioned the founding of a centre for instructional development, designed to help interested faculty and teaching assistants share and hone their classroom skills. Within this evolving context, the LRPC made its own not-so-modest proposal for change.

As Alvin Lee tells the story, he and Levinson were indulging in some nocturnal brainstorming when they hit upon an idea rich in potential. Energized, they drew up a preliminary sketch for colleagues on the LRPC.[112] Duly impressed, the committee agreed to recommend the scheme to the senate. Thus, on 24 November 1977, Gillespie moved that a special committee examine the possibility of fashioning a distinctive undergraduate degree program; one that would irresistibly intrigue gifted non-specialists who, in its absence, might be lured to other universities. Lee clarified that this it would be no warmed-over liberal arts program but a wholly unique baccalaureate in arts and science. Levinson elaborated that it should not be simply a "cheap program to attract students." Instead, he said, it ought to be an innovative, pace-setting degree that would challenge students to confront major questions across the broad spectrum of manifold academic cultures. Graduates from such a program, he said, would be superbly equipped for more specialized education later. While cautious, the senate was willing to listen. Thus, an ad hoc body of undergraduate council was struck to study the proposal.[113] There followed almost two years of broad consultation and often pointed debate.

In June 1979, verbal rapiers flashed unsheathed. Senators did battle over a motion to sanction development of the new program and appoint its first director. Economist Peter George voiced personal enthusiasm for the project. He noted, however, that this inherently elite and, therefore, small program as yet lacked any specific detail concerning curriculum and resources. Picking up on these observations Chuck Jago spoke for the LRPC. The undertaking, he argued, would be worthwhile only if it were done well. Success would require enthusiastic commitment not only on the part of the best faculty but also by a regular flow of highly able students. Altogether, he said, the LRPC had some reservations, since costs were so difficult to calculate at that moment. If Jago was merely probing to test administrative resolve, he was successful. Indeed, Lee was quick to retort that, short commons notwithstanding, every effort would be made to underwrite the program properly. For some in attendance, however, other matters were at stake.

MSU representatives, for example, voiced serious concern on several counts. How, they asked, was a designedly elite program going to reinvigorate the general undergraduate experience? Furthermore, they queried, why invest in experimental liberal education at a time when professional training was in far higher demand? They also wondered who was going to offer the courses, given that the supposedly "best professors" were normally intensely specialized and, therefore, ill equipped or little inclined to teach such a program. Finally, they noted that graduate schools might look askance at such scattered preparation for focused, higher studies. Reinforcing some of these points, philosopher David Hitchcock offered that it might be wiser to introduce a little more general education in all programs. He was certainly unimpressed by the modest depth requirements of the arts-and-science proposal, as it currently stood.

In reply to these varied misgivings, economist Melvin Kliman issued a spirited riposte. Tellingly, he noted that none of the current degrees in arts or science were vocational in form or content. As for the availability of instructors, he intoned a familiar theme: the best scholars understood that the boundaries between disciplines were not graven in stone and would welcome the chance to teach across them. Meanwhile, he maintained, students of high calibre would have no difficulty gaining admission to graduate schools, especially in that enrolment-starved hour. Kliman went on to say that details of the curriculum had been left vague deliberately. Such fine-tuning was for a director and select colleagues to calibrate, before a final proposal was put to the senate. Persuasive and determined, Kliman won the day.[114] Psychologist Herb Jenkins was appointed first director of the arts and science program that September. Now, all that remained was to define a credible degree.

Jenkins and an eclectic, five-person planning council took up the challenge.[115] Enthusiastically assisted by Vice-President Lee and his successor, Les King, they devoted a year's labour to translating a nice idea into a concrete proposal. As Jenkins explained to the senate, in May 1980, the degree had three principal features. The first was a balanced commitment to serious work in both arts and science. The second involved explicit attention to specific and transferable intellectual skills. The third emphasized inquiry into the complex issues facing evolving modern society. While core courses in quantitative reasoning, logic and writing were required, an important cue was taken from medicine.

Thus, a strong dose of self-directed, problem-based learning was injected into the pedagogical philosophy of the program, especially in its senior years. There need be no fear about enrolment, said Jenkins. Here, he pointed to a version of the degree at Concordia, which, although considerably watered down, never lacked a goodly number of first-class candidates. By comparison, he contended, the stronger, rounder McMaster degree should attract able candidates aplenty. In all candour, said Jenkins, this was a "high-risk" program. The danger of failure was real. The rewards, however, were potentially great. Was the senate, he inquired, prepared to take the plunge? "Yes," said the conclave, remarkably without dissent.

Crucial in this respect was wholehearted endorsement by the LRCP. Chuck Jago and his colleagues had had their initial doubts. However, concerns about financial feasibility had been allayed by Lee and King. Meanwhile, deeper fears that science would eclipse arts also dissolved, once the program matrix was spelled out. Jago reminded the senate of the LRPC's call to cultivate at least a measure of differentiation at the undergraduate level. One wonders, of course, how an elite program, aimed at roughly fifty to sixty candidates, was supposed to answer broader student discontent with the university's sprawling pass degrees. Still, on a number of counts, the LRPC found the arts and science proposal squarely in line with the *Plan for McMaster* and bestowed its imprimatur.[116] In any event, the degree won approval. First offered in September 1981, it remains one of the distinctive features of McMaster and its penchant for what William Hellmuth had dubbed "selective excellence." At the moment of its adoption, however, news about the program was overshadowed by two headline-grabbing events. One was a bombshell that captured national attention. The other was a windfall of staggering proportion. Together, they capped Bourns' last months in office.

Fireworks crackled, in the spring of 1980, when luminary George Grant dramatically announced his resignation. His decision, he said, was "an act of impatience with what the Arts Faculty has become at McMaster."[117] Whether promulgation of the *Plan* had any role in this is uncertain. If it did, it was only as a final straw. In fact, Grant had long felt uncomfortable with the direction in which both the university and his own department seemed headed. A Christian humanist of increasingly mystical proclivities, he might have flourished in the neo-platonic atmosphere of early Renaissance Italy. Late twentieth-century McMaster, however, had little in common with Marsilio Ficino's Florentine Academy. Instead, in his mind, the former was rapidly becoming that which he most despised: a soulless, Americanized "multiversity," wherein a positivist, value-free, objectivist, scientific (call it what you will) paradigm of knowledge reigned supreme. This epistemological model, he contended, had its useful, even noble, purposes, but it could never grapple with questions pertaining to justice, beauty, love, or the final purpose of being. He cringed, therefore, as quantitative methods, "modelling," linguistic gymnastics, and other techniques aping the sciences seeped inexorably into mainstream arts; including his beloved religious studies. Mechanical "research" into an objectified past, said Grant, was displacing active engagement with and reverent contemplation of inherited wisdom.[118]

One of the sadder by-products of this process, he told the press, was that the rewards system had become so skewed in favour of publication that the essentially "erotic art" of teaching counted for little. The highest goal, he lamented, was "to sparkle at a meeting in Chicago," rather than tend to the educational needs of the young Canadians.[119] Indeed, he told one reporter, "McMaster hasn't cared for Hamilton and Canada as much as it has cared for an international reputation." "And by that," he emphasized, "they mean the United States."[120] Tendering his goodbyes in such terms, Grant inevitably touched off a media firestorm.

Sympathizers and critics traded barbed exchanges in the columns of the *Dundas Star Journal*, the *Hamilton Spectator*, the *Globe and Mail*, and their syndicated affiliates. For the better part of two months, McMaster was caught in the uncomfortable glare of a public spotlight. Columnists and letter-writers, of varied erudition, expounded on the relationship of teaching to research, the ultimate purpose of universities, the question of national self-realization, and a variety of other heady themes. Amid the uproar, student opinion was divided. MSU president Ann Blackwood lambasted McMaster for ignoring the needs of her constituents in favour of graduate studies and research dollars.[121] Some of Grant's students sought to clarify subtle points their mentor had raised in his summary press statement of 28 April.[122] At least one of their peers, however, was "puzzled and saddened" by Grant's remarks. Thus, Anne E. Yarwood, of Ancaster, wrote endearingly of her former professor, but found her personal experience at odds with his assertions. Her most effective instructors, she submitted, were those most passionate about research. As for national origins, she rejoiced that "eminent scholar-teachers from abroad" found McMaster "an excellent environment in which to seek the good, the true and the beautiful."[123] Meanwhile, if students, such as Yarwood, joined in the media scrum, so did a wide range of Grant's professional colleagues.

Bourns, for one, leaped to his university's defence. Backed by MUFA president Marianne Kristofferson, he penned a stinging op-ed for the *Globe and Mail*, denouncing the alleged divide between teaching and research as a false dichotomy. The best professor, he argued, was a life-long learner who, through active engagement, demonstrated to students "the need constantly to challenge or seek new understanding of existing knowledge." Ironically, Bourns added, few better exemplified this wholesome nexus than the well-published Grant, himself.[124] Less generously, some critics contended that the religious scholar was hurling boulders at others from within the fragile confines a glass house. Preferring to teach graduate students, he kept (at best) irregular office hours, while no name plate adorned his door as a ready welcome to younger folk on campus.[125]

A far more common reaction, however, mingled disappointment with regret. Long-time friends and colleagues of Grant, such as Eugene Combs and John Robertson, expressed dejection with the growing simplification of inherently complex issues regarding teaching, research, epistemology, and nationality.[126] On the other hand, some, such as English professor A.G. Bishop, welcomed a debate over the divergent philosophies that, according to Grant, differentiated Oxbridge from Germanic-American models of higher education.[127] Meanwhile, from his literary desk at York, Professor Ernest Griffin attacked all such efforts to reduce the teaching-research issue to an either-or proposition. Having personal experience of the German, American, and Canadian traditions, he questioned whether the distinctions among them were anywhere near as sharp as Grant portrayed them. Indeed, he ventured that "either-or" was increasingly becoming "both," as contemporary scholars rose above such a "tired old battle."[128]

Yet, tired though the supposed conflict might have been, there was obviously enough spark left to ignite contention aplenty. Thus, Grant departed McMaster for Dalhousie with controversy trailing in his wake. Given contemporaneous innovation on the Hamilton campus, it was surely a wry twist of fate that found him appointed "professor of arts and science" in Halifax. No doubt, the whole sad episode cast something of a pall over Bourns' last months as president. Still, he could always take at least a measure of comfort in an equally dramatic and altogether more pleasant surprise.

In February 1980, it was announced that the recently deceased Dr Henry Lyman "Harry" Hooker had left the (then) staggering sum of $25 million as a bequest to McMaster. At a stroke, the university's reserves skyrocketed from $5 million to more than $30 million.[129] The one-time Baptist backwater suddenly stood, it was reckoned, as the best-endowed seat of higher learning in Canada.[130] What, many asked, had occasioned this prodigious windfall; and who, for that matter, was the generous Dr Hooker? As details were forthcoming, a made-in-Hollywood tale unfolded. Born on a train in Buffalo to Canadian parents, Harry Hooker spent his youth in Hamilton. At maturity, he was a teacher in the city's schools. Pursuing a dream, in 1900 he left to study medicine at Columbia University. Following graduation, he established a practice in New York City. Throughout, however, he stayed in touch with friends in Hamilton. When the Great War erupted, the Canadian in Hooker led him to volunteer as a physician with the British Army and the Royal Flying Corps. At war's end, he returned to New York, where he practised surgery and taught anaesthesia at Bellevue Hospital for the next several decades. Thus far, Hooker had followed his dream down a rewarding and productive, if not abnormally lucrative, career path. He was a fortunate soul. Then, in middle age, things took a sharp turn for the even better.

In 1942, Hooker was appointed resident physician and medical director at the Waldorf-Astoria, New York's sumptuous home away from home for the rich, famous, and influential. Politicians and potentates, along with stars of stage, screen, and Wall Street, filled his waiting room. For the next seventeen years, Hooker was made privy to all manner of intriguing information, some of which could be put to direct and very profitable use. Canny in his own right, he listened carefully when one patient, Thomas Watson, advised him to buy shares in the company of which he was chief executive officer. In due course, Hooker became the holder of significant stocks in IBM. By the time he retired, in 1959, his thousands invested had become millions in the bank.

Always interested in the affairs of his old home town, Hooker kept up ties with friends in Hamilton. During one visit to the Steel City, Harry Thode took him on a private tour of the new reactor. Impressed by the energy on campus, the physician joined the McMaster Board of Friends, a small group of expatriate alumni resident in New York. Thereafter, both Thode and Bourns maintained cordial relations with the ageing internist, who they visited whenever chance allowed. In the late seventies, Jack Moore, director of alumni affairs, made a point of meeting privately with Hooker four times a year, prior to more formal gatherings of the Friends in New York. Clearly, the good doctor was quietly but carefully courted. Still, even those in the know must have been dazzled by the size of Hooker's bequest when he died at the ripe old age of a 102. There had been nothing to match it in Canadian university history.

Inevitably, suggestions as to how best to employ the welcome trove streamed giddily across Bourns' desk. In the end, the money was invested as part of the university's general endowment, rather than ploughed into salaries or any specific project. As Bourns noted, the annual interest, even on this hefty sum, only came to 3 per cent of McMaster's yearly budget. With shortfalls in BIU revenue and rising inflation forecast for the next several years, the Hooker fund would help ease, but not erase, the university's financial deficit. Ever prudent, Bourns chose unglamorous compound interest over a splashy, one-time spending spree.[131] There were, however, some immediate and demonstrable benefits. Thus, as Alvin Lee notes, the prized arts and science degree was rendered feasible, thanks in great part to the Hooker legacy.[132]

In June 1980, Bourns hung up the presidential spurs he had so ably won over eight years of unrelieved toil. That he did so, before his second five-year mandate was up, was a matter of personal choice. In that regard, he had made his intentions clear at the time of his renewal, in 1976.[133] Having served in a variety of high administrative posts since the late fifties, he was hungry for a return to the energizing sanctum of the laboratory. There were, however, too many complex matters requiring an experienced hand for him simply to walk away, in 1977. Thus, he remained to provide prudent management of the New Reality, collegiality in reshaping relations with the faculty association, and, above all, continuity in the initial stage of long-range planning. While Thode left some highly visible monuments behind him, Bourns' impress upon McMaster was more subtle, but no less deep. One of its highest expressions was the sense of co-engagement, born of the McMaster Act, the joint-committee network, and other vehicles that brought the board, the senate, the administration, and the faculty, however imperfectly, into a uniquely dove-tailed and ever-evolving working relationship. The arrangement would, of course, would be strained more than once. Yet, a significant descendant endures today in the shape of the tripartite committee. Nor should one overlook the long-lived influence of the *Plan for McMaster*, which stood as something more than a mere shadow of the Thodean project. In these and many other ways, Bourns had proven to be the appropriate horse for the seventies' course.

12

"An Adequate Balance"

Cabbage Patch Kids and Reaganomics, a Shamrock Summit and the Meech Lake (almost-but-not-quite) Accord, glasnost, perestroika, and "star wars": the eighties would be anything but dull. Thus, the "Great Communicator" and the "Iron Lady" bestrode the West, arm in arm, even as the Eastern bloc ambled toward messy dissolution. While velvet revolutions unfolded, anti-apartheid sentiment bubbled out of South Africa. Yet, colourful though it might have been, the decade also offered an ample fund of mundane drudg-ery, especially for those who sought to balance the ledger of either a cap-italist or command economy; not to mention that of a mere province, city, or workaday family. Indeed, as the paradoxical stability of the Cold War waned, the great post-industrial shift was in full cry; that which might fol-low was, at best, uncertain. Swings to the right marked much of a Western world craving stability and some comforting measure of continuity. If not the best of times, this would, at least, be a most interesting era, as Alvin Archie Lee was about to discover.

Revelling in a well-earned research leave, Lee was cheerfully plumbing the fathomless depths of *Beowulf*, when an unexpected summons interrupted his literary reverie, late in the autumn of 1979. Having advertised nation-wide, the board-senate committee searching for a new president sought his personal advice. Could he, they inquired, meet with them at the Royal Con-naught Hotel to discuss the qualities most desirable in any successor to the all-but-irreplaceable Bourns? While only too happy to be out of the loop, after years of demanding administrative service, Lee could hardly refuse. Accordingly, he passed the better part of a lively day with the governors, senators, faculty, students, and alumni who, together, comprised the ten-person selection committee. Ever cogent, Lee was perhaps doubly so on this occasion. After all, he was perfectly at ease. Not having applied for the post, he could address matters confronting the university fully, frankly, and without concern for personal gain or consequence. Once all was said, Lee prepared to leave – only to be floored, as the committee invited him to stand as a candidate. Momentarily stunned, he rebounded to thank them all, but declared, with polite emphasis, that he entertained absolutely no presidential ambitions. *Beowulf*, family, and the classroom beckoned.

A few months later, therefore, it was "with some dismay" that Lee found John Panabaker, chairman of the committee, rapping at his West Flamborough door; asking him to reconsider. Bending just an inch, Lee requested ten days to think things over. He, then, proceeded to torment himself, his family, and his friends with the counter-balancing pros and cons in play. Collegial confidants were all for the move. His wife, Hope, however, advised against it, knowing that he longed to return to full-time study and, in any case, found limelight rather garish. All in all, there was no obvious answer, no luminous signpost pointing straight ahead. Decades after the fact, Lee could still vividly recall the tortured indecision that haunted those long days of rigorous self-examination. In the end, finding only selfish reasons to refuse collegial responsibility, he phoned Panabaker to accept. Having finally rolled the dice, he could only hope that they would not come up snake eyes.[1]

Once the decision was made, Lee was soon chomping at the bit. In a *Silhouette* exclusive, he confessed to being more than slightly nervous and "a bit daunted at the enormity of the task." Even in the best of times, he reckoned, Arthur Bourns would be "a hard act to follow." Still, once committed, he cast aside second thoughts and began eagerly to anticipate the bright side of the job. For him, this was the opportunity to continue the most vibrantly liberal of educations. Inevitable tribulations notwithstanding, he noted, his years as graduate dean and vice-president had been rewarding, primarily because they had required him to glimpse the university as a whole and appreciate its many paths to learning. Enriching in itself, the experience also left Lee on a first-name basis with approximately two-thirds of the faculty and well-apprised of their myriad scholarly interests. Along the way, his sense of the university's strengths and weaknesses had been sharply honed, as well. McMaster, he told his interviewer, was "one of the strongest universities in Canada," well in the forefront of scientific, engineering, and medical research. In time, he averred, the arts could pull even, although quality in their endeavour had to be measured in publication and teaching; not merely by tallying grants. All told, Lee observed, he had inherited a strong hand. There was, he conceded, always room for improvement. In this regard, nothing struck him as more in need of repair than the condition of undergraduate life at McMaster. If nothing else, Lee told the *Silhouette*, he intended to set that right.[2] These, of course, were initial musings. At his formal installation, in November 1980, the new president was both more lyrical and more emphatic in identifying specific goals.

Straight out of the gate, Lee subtly set to rest any fears that a man of letters might be at odds with his immediate, scientific predecessors. Thus, with crystalline eloquence, he extolled the virtues of an objective, phenomenological approach to knowledge; one characteristic not only of science, but increasingly of social science and the more advanced species of humanities. It was, he told convocation, both a scholarly and moral imperative that "every discipline ... be as rational and scientifically objective as its subject matter permits." Having, thus, reassured listeners than no abrupt paradigm shift was in the offing, Lee, then, paused to sound a cautionary note. Every virtue, he intoned, had its attendant vice. Objectivity was no exception. Invaluable in the laboratory or archive, it was invidious when carried over into the arena of human relations where, at least seemingly, it could took the form of a cold, aloof indifference toward students in particular and society at large. Research-intensive McMaster, he hinted, was becoming insensitive to this lurking snare. Planting this thought, Lee moved to outline his three principal goals as president: maintaining and extending McMaster's traditional research thrust, sparking a "renaissance in undergraduate education," and fostering more thoroughgoing engagement with communities beyond the ivy walls.

That these objectives were inextricably intertwined, the president had no doubt. Where vigorous scholarship faltered, he argued, so did refreshment of knowledge. In turn, learning gone stale offered no education at all. Likewise, when the academy paid no heed to an ever-shifting social context, Lee observed, "we neglect the obligation to show that our teaching and research have human relevance." In this latter regard, he did not counsel the abandonment of pure scholarship for the pursuit of every changing public fancy. He did, however, advise that, if McMaster were to realize and demonstrate its full potential as a genuine seat of higher learning – one set in the context of a living society – it had to reach out to "ever-widening spheres."[3]

Like every inaugural address, before and after, much of what the president said no doubt sailed, unabsorbed, past the quasi-somnolent majority in attendance: another exercise in motherhood rhetorically adulated. Careful listeners, on the other hand, would have noted that the new boy was deeply steeped in McMaster's research tradition, but sincerely committed to extending similar excellence into the undergraduate arena. Some might have applauded unreservedly, while others withheld judgment. Indeed, as Lee's first term got under way, many must have wondered less about the president's goals than whether the status quo could be maintained.

The banner headline "400-Metre Track and Stadium: McMaster Builds $30 Million Velodrome" graced the 29 March 1983 edition of the *Courier*, the university's in-house newsletter. Loud hosannas were intoned, as the broadsheet detailed plans to construct a domed cycling venue, replete with seating for untold thousands of rabid fans. Readers, of course, were later informed that these gladsome tidings were intended as an April fool's joke.[4] Few, one suspects, were hoodwinked, given that a worldwide recession, the worst since the 1930s, had taken hold, scant months after Lee's installation.

Oil prices doubled, as turbulence in the Middle East presaged the outbreak of the near decade-long Iran-Iraq War. Inflation, bane of the seventies, rose to be the scourge of the eighties, hitting almost 11 per cent by 1982. Unemployment in Canada soared close to 12 per cent the next year, putting rising pressure for social assistance on already strained federal, provincial, and municipal coffers.[5] Deficit financing spun out of control to the point that Ottawa was spending more on interest payments than on health and welfare combined.[6] Clearly, university velodromes were not on the agenda – least of all in sledge-hammered Hamilton.

"Our City Is Shrinking," moaned the *Spectator* in August 1986. At the height of a postwar growth spurt, Hamilton laid claim to the title of fourth-largest urban centre in Canada. By the mid-eighties, it had slid to ninth place, with planners estimating no more than a 1 per cent population increase over the next twenty years.[7] In large part, this dour prognostication was predicated on the all-too-obvious decline of the city's industrial base. Rampant inflation precipitated a bitter 125-day strike, as local 1005 of the United Steelworkers battled over wages with Stelco in 1981. A pyrrhic victory for the union led only to lowered production and layoffs in the context of a viciously competitive, slumping steel market. By April 1982, more than 1,300 members of local 1005 were out of work.[8] In October, it was projected that the number would soon climb to 3,000.[9] Meanwhile, in the cash-strapped public sector, the mayor of Stoney Creek was urging staff layoffs to cut the cost of education.[10] Adding true profundity to the pervasive gloom, Hamilton's only professional sports franchise, the once-vaunted Tiger-Cats, had not won a Grey Cup since 1972. Truly, the salad days seemed to be over. Speaking as early as November 1981, Lee remarked that, were this so, there might be nothing to look forward to, save "night blindness and scurvy."[11] The president, of course, was ruminating about McMaster's future, not civic gridiron woes. On that score, he would not be far off the mark, especially during his first term in office.

Enrolment was no longer a problem, at least not at the undergraduate level. Quite the contrary; as the recession hit, people flocked to higher education in record numbers. Some were merely postponing entry into a dreary job market. Others were seeking a competitive edge. Whatever the case, participation rates among eighteen- to twenty-four-year-olds unexpectedly skyrocketed after 1980. This included a new wave of foreign students. As so-called Tiger Economies in Southeast Asia underbid and out produced struggling world rivals, their rising entrepreneurial classes sought higher education for their offspring. With limited opportunities at home, many saw Ontario universities as an affordable option, even at triple the domestic fee.[12] Altogether, demand, whether foreign or homegrown, was exceedingly strong. For instance, by September 1983, McMaster, alone, was flooded with 15,000 applications for 3,300 spots.[13] This should have been good news. In reality, it was highly problematic. After all, Queen's Park had its own financial difficulties, and funding higher education was low on its list of priorities.

In February 1982, these facts were driven home with a will. During a closed session with Premier Davis and his tough-minded minister of education, Bette Stephenson, university presidents were told that their annual grants had deliberately been kept low the last few years in order to encourage fiscal responsibility. Still, the minister bristled; some institutions had elected deficit financing, rather than true rationalization. Were this to continue, she warned, government might feel obliged to step in with legislation requiring prior ministerial approval of deficits, as was the case in six other provinces.[14] In unison, university leaders pointed to the manifold cutbacks they had undertaken. Such howling, however, was to no avail – partly, one imagines, because the presidents were united in little else.

As much competitors as allies, Ontario's universities were locked in what McMaster registrar Alexander "Sandy" Darling dubbed a fierce "tug-of-war." The struggle, he maintained, was one of principle, between those who championed quality control and others who emphasized maximum accessibility.[15] In truth, of course, self-interest and self-identity also figured in the tussle. With thousands clamouring for admission, older, established universities, such as McMaster, tended to raise entrance standards and place ceilings on enrolment. In this, their objectives were to guard against overcrowding and the progressive dilution of their undergraduate cadres in the wake of successive changes to grade-thirteen requirements and notorious high-school grade inflation. As well, there was a strong desire to not to sacrifice research capacity to heavier teaching commitment. Newer institutions, such as Brock, Trent, and Laurentian, pulled in the opposite direction.

Anxious to grow, the latter accepted an ever-higher number of applicants, citing a social obligation to do so. As York president Ian Macdonald argued, in 1983, to shut the door to qualified hopefuls was to condone an ivory-tower elitism inherited from the past.[16] This was, perhaps, a noble sentiment, but it came at a price. The once quite simple BIU formula had been heavily amended, since the mid-sixties. By the early eighties, for example, the unusually low, average enrolments of 1974 through 1977 were used as a base for calculating operating grants. New admissions beyond the mean level were discounted, sometimes as much as 50 per cent. The upshot was that additional numbers did not translate into neatly proportionate increases in annual revenue from government. Thus, as Darling explained, if steady-state universities had difficulty balancing their books, growth-oriented institutions inevitably ran into even greater difficulty.[17] Not surprisingly, the two camps also differed substantially as to how best formula funding might be reformed.[18] Amid all this infighting, Queen's Park cracked the whip with vigour.

In December 1982, Stephenson reiterated threats to purportedly free-spending university presidents. Those whose projected shortfalls came to more than 2 per cent of their annual budget allocations would face a take-over of their financial reins by government "advisors" with authority to make spending decisions.[19] The minister went so far as to frame legislation to this effect, but the minority Tory government was unable to rally sufficient votes for Bill 42, in the face of Liberal and NDP opposition.[20] Stephenson, however, did insist that all new undergraduate programming be submitted for review, in order to ensure prudential expenditure. As bureaucratic hoops were added to red-tape hurdles, academic patience waned. Lee, normally politic in public pronouncements, gave vent to pent-up steam in the campus press. "Given the rigorous pruning and cutting that we have been doing here at McMaster every recent year," he fulminated, "I find it irritating in the extreme to be urged yet again by the minister to manage our resources 'in a fiscally responsible manner'."[21] This outburst aside, Lee knew that Stephenson was no inveterate foe of higher education. She was, he recognized, under extreme pressure from Cabinet colleagues and a public who did not grasp "that university faculty are fully occupied in teaching and research; that sabbatical leaves are not paid holidays, and that tenure does not protect incompetence and maintain undue inflexibility in academic staffing."[22] All this, Lee understood. Still, it could be most exasperating, and events in 1983 would only add to this discomfiture.

With the recession deepening and loyal opponents nipping daily at minority-government heels, the Conservatives had to be seen to be financially prudent. As ever, universities offered targets of opportunity. Accordingly, despite recent tuition hikes and continued heavy enrolment, Ontario Student Assistance Program levels for 1983–84 were pegged well below the level of inflation. When a new provincial sales tax was thrown into the mix, students found it increasingly difficult to make ends meet; especially as well-paid summer jobs became rare. Meanwhile, in response to the public xenophobia that so often accompanied hard times, visa-student fees were raised by a staggering 40 per cent. This fiat was rendered all the more unpalatable at McMaster because the university had neglected to warn foreign candidates of the impending change.

Stephenson had informed the board well in advance and had made it clear that no one in the system would be grandfathered. In turn, the university had formally protested. Assuming that the much-discussed issue was common knowledge, administrators forgot to notify students, until very late in the day. Embarrassed, the registrar, Sandy Darling, then scrambled to explain this oversight in the columns of the Silhouette.[23] Over the next two years, there was an overall 23 per cent drop in visa-student enrolment across Canada.[24] At McMaster, engineering would feel the blow especially keenly.

Gathering angst intensified in June 1983, when it was clear that operating grants would, once again, lag behind spiralling inflation. This sad old tune was becoming monotonously depressing; an added note made it positively dour. Thus, the Inflation Restraint Act, restricting salary increases in the public sector to 5 per cent, blackened moods among MUFA members anxious to restore their purchasing power to 1971 levels. Altogether, few observers were surprised by a 1983 COU survey that showed Ontario tenth out of ten provinces, when it came to per capita funding of higher education, and fully 25 per cent below the national average.[25] This would remain a solemn fact of life, throughout the decade.

If the external context within which Lee sought to realize his goals was challenging, the McMaster scene was no shimmering oasis of tranquility. Indeed, to borrow from British parliamentarian John Bright, the Angel of Disquiet was so frequently abroad on campus that one could almost hear the beating of its wings. Some unrest, while decidedly keen-edged, was of the garden variety and took the form of in course, student protest over immediate matters. Concurrently, however, at a more disturbing level, long-festering discontent with the whole quality of undergraduate life at McMaster was bubbling to the surface. Here, the normally quiescent alumni association assumed a spirited role in stirring a long-simmering pot. Occasionally, student complaints meshed with and reinforced lingering alumni concerns. Sometimes, they just added to the accustomed noise. Lee, in any event, took careful note of all this rumbling unease. He could scarcely have done otherwise, as alumni began lobbing blistering salvoes at their alma mater. These blasts, at least in part, help to explain Lee's call for a renaissance, not just in the classroom but in the fabric of undergraduate life as a whole. What, however, explained the fusillades themselves?

In later years, when asked about any shortcomings he might have had as president, Bourns candidly allowed that he had done little to cultivate alumni support.[26] He did not add that, in this, he differed little from Thode. Indeed, for both men, the alumni association often seemed more a burden than an asset, given that the cost of maintaining its campus office usually exceeded revenue raised by the organization.[27] By 1978, Bourns was both puzzled and frustrated. Writing to Jack Moore, director of alumni affairs, he wondered how "to solve the McMaster problem of complete [alumni] apathy with respect to financial support for the University." Effective change, he suggested, might yet be sparked by a select core of dedicated persons. On the other hand, mused the president, maybe it was simply time to acknowledge defeat. "Perhaps," wrote Bourns, "after two decades of failure, this is the only reasonable course." Closing the alumni office was a distasteful but potential option under consideration. For the moment, he posed the question foremost in his mind. "What," he asked Moore, "is unique about the McMaster situation which results in our Alumni fund raising efforts, for as long as I can remember, being the least productive in the country?"[28] This was no idle question.

In 1978, a survey of twenty-six Canadian universities showed that McMaster was in the bottom tier, when it came to alumni giving. At neighbouring Guelph, for example, 20 per cent of graduates responded to a plea for aid, that year, by donating $175,000. Contemporaneously, only $37,000 came from the mere 9 per cent of McMaster alumni who bothered to reply to a similar call.[29] Even more disconcerting was the fact that smaller Acadia regularly outperformed its erstwhile Baptist cousin by a considerable margin.[30] At the time, Bourns ascribed this sorry state primarily to the lack of clear understanding and dynamic leadership on the part of association leaders.[31] There was, however, rather more to the story. Indeed, even the most cursory stroll through its records reveals an alumni association that, from the mid-sixties onward, frequently felt forgotten, ignored, and marginalized as a piece of the McMaster equation. Sparse pecuniary support registered not only hard times and outmoded organization but also growing estrangement between a rapidly changing university and its increasingly disillusioned graduates.

Bourns had no sooner assumed office, in July 1972, than he was presented with a frank brief from Dennis Carson, director of alumni affairs. "The

Alumni," wrote Carson, "represent a body which is larger than all the other constituencies of the University – students, faculty, and staff – combined." Numbering in excess of 20,700 members, it was a great reserve of potential strength, especially as the threat of government interference loomed large. However, he cautioned the president, "it cannot be ignored as it sometimes has been." In passing, Carson noted that roughly 40 per cent of alumni had graduated in the last ten years.[32] Consciously or not, he was making a telling point. Alumni membership was approaching equilibrium between those nurtured in the intimate atmosphere of a small, Baptist institution and those who had experienced the rush to growth of a budding multiversity bent on winning a reputation for excellence in research and graduate studies. By Lee's time, the scales had dipped even further in the direction of the latter group, among whom some, when undergraduates, had taken active issue with Thodean emphases. At the moment of writing to Bourns, however, Carson was reacting to a 1971 association report that foreshadowed much of what was to come.

Winnowed down to its core, that long, rambling document highlighted the importance of making graduates feel more fully enfranchised in the shaping of an evolving McMaster. In the past, the report noted, the association had functioned largely as a social and fundraising body. Those purposes, however, were no longer enough to sustain the interest of Aquarians, some of whom called for more significant engagement. One contributor to the study, for example, urged that alumni be employed as honest brokers amid the growing hubbub of student-university disputes. The association, he said, "may get its feet wet and may get its hands dirty," but such was the price of retaining relevance in a changing age.[33] As things currently stood, however, ventured another observer, "most alumni do not consider themselves to be extensions of the university community, and are in fact quite cynical toward much of the public image which the University and its agencies encourage."[34]

There was certainly considerable resentment among active members that alumni had not been invited to participate in the search to replace Thode.[35] Equally, there was a sense that association magazine, *The McMaster News*, was being fed "puff pieces about faculty," rather than being encouraged to tackle major issues, "warts and all."[36] All told, authors of the report were eager "to contribute in as many ways as possible to the welfare, prestige, and excellence of the University," but gave notice that interest might wane, unless their important constituency were properly cultivated.[37]

To be sure, some halting efforts were made in that direction. Thus, Bourns continued to fund the alumni office, albeit necessarily on a shoestring. As well, the traditional Alumni Fund, suspended in 1963 to make way for a broader capital drive, was revived in the early seventies. Still, the pitch to graduates had to be low-key, since, as Carson explained, "the immediate need of the University was the establishment of good relations with alumni after a period when neglect was evident."[38] The results, as noted, were disappointing. So, too, was continued wrangling over where initiative in such funding drives should reside and how the sums raised should be allocated.[39] By 1978, association morale was at low ebb. That May, Mimmo Lostracco, the body's dejected president, noted a sharp decline in the number of five-year reunions. In fact, there were no such gatherings scheduled for the classes of 1958, 1963, 1968, or 1973. Given this evidence of lassitude, he remarked, "No wonder we don't have a greater voice in the University's affairs."[40] Lostracco and his fellow executives were determined to rectify this by revivifying the association and transforming administrative attitudes to it. Fireworks would result.

On 30 April 1979, alumni leaders presented a strongly worded brief to the board-senate LRPC. Pulling no punches, the report's authors stated, "We do not feel that the University administration has utilized the services of the Alumni association as effectively as possible." It was alleged that offers of assistance, other than monetary ones, too often went unanswered. Meanwhile, major projects, such as the 1978 open house, were undertaken with no association input. To many graduates, the brief asserted, Gilmour Hall seemed to view the alumni solely as a source of revenue. Disappointing results in annual fund drives were described, in the brief, as "a response to the lack of consideration of the Alumni Association's role by the University Administration." Underlying this dreary cycle, the authors continued, were fundamental problems in the undergraduate environment at McMaster – problems that produced alumni indifference.

The university, they wrote, had to play a more dynamic part in cultivating campus esprit de corps, "from initial registration, on." Only in this way could a truly enthusiastic alumni association be developed. In this regard, all members of faculty, not just a minority, had to commit to improving the daily student experience. The recent report of the senate Subcommittee on the Quality of Academic Life (SQUAL) was applauded. However, to ensure that its recommendations were carried into effect and expanded, the association proposed a two-day retreat to examine the multitude of inter-related issues involved.[41] The LRPC was impressed by this summons to fashion a new alumni-university relationship in the context of holistically reviewing the quality of undergraduate life. For his part, however, McMaster's president was livid.

"The shortest distance between the Alumni and myself is the direct one," wrote an outraged Bourns to Moore. Officially and personally affronted by the brief, the president chided the director of alumni affairs for permitting this end-run around Gilmour Hall to the LRPC. Responsibility for alumni and all external relations rested with the president who, Bourns underlined, should be informed personally, when difficulties arose in such areas. "I would have welcomed a strong representation by the Alumni directly to me," he told Moore. His complaint was not with the critique, per se. Indeed, wrote Bourns, "I am the first to admit that there is a substantial basis for concern about relations between the Alumni and the administration." What he objected to was the selection of the LRPC as the forum for airing grievances, some of which were thinly veiled criticisms of a president whose door, he emphasized, was always open.[42]

Bourns' outburst was occasioned by a prior letter from Moore, in which the latter had expressed surprise at the president's sharp reaction to the alumni document. "Quite frankly," Moore had written Bourns, "I am at a loss to understand why you would take offense at this brief." It was, in his eyes, "a fair and honest reflection of alumni beliefs at this time." Moreover, Moore claimed to have sent Bourns a draft copy, well in advance of its presentation to the LRPC. In any case, he observed, "The whole long term future of the relationship between the University and the Alumni is at stake at the present time." Thus, to him, a retreat at which the myriad problems of the university could be openly and freely discussed seemed highly desirable.[43] After venting some spleen about established protocol and common courtesy, Bourns concurred. "Let us," he concluded, "together find ways for closer consultation and communication regarding our common goal."[44] In the event, that task fell to his successor: Alvin Lee.

The alumni-sponsored retreat was held in Scarborough, late in August 1980. For two days, approximately forty people, from the ranks of faculty, staff, students, alumni, and administration, examined the broad question of sagging school spirit. Knowledgeable representatives from sister universities were invited, so that assessments might not be made in a vacuum. Points of comparison were unflattering. Queen's and Western, for example, were subject to many of the same pressures as McMaster, but their campus and alumni morale seemed far higher. The essential factor, visitors advised, was that a university unmistakeably be seen to care about its students. The point resounded in President-Designate Lee's already receptive ear.

Addressing the retreat, he was incisively frank. McMaster, he said, lacked adequate balance. On one hand, he noted, the university had encouraged superb scholarship, along with outstanding honours programs. On the other, he continued, there was "a lack of provision for those students who have no thought of becoming scholars but need to get a good education so that they can become richly informed and intelligent citizens."[45] These, no doubt, were welcome words. Indeed, as proceedings drew to a close, organizers must have felt that some clarity had been given to what Bourns had vaguely described as "our common goal." In earnest of this, Lee appointed a presidential task force to study university-alumni relations, just weeks later. In that respect, the retreat proved to be a landmark in the history of the modern alumni association. More immediately, the task force served powerfully to reinforce the president's inaugural call for a comprehensive renaissance in undergraduate education.

To describe the eventual report of the task force as blunt and sweeping would be to understate its tone and scope. Presented on 16 April 1981, it was the outcome of more than twenty meetings with different constituencies and two open forums. In the end, the seven-member committee penned a stinging critique of life at contemporary McMaster. Taking a cue from the 1979 alumni brief, the panel worked on the assumption that it was the comparatively brief student experience that determined life-long attitudes of graduates toward their alma mater. A vibrant, committed alumni association, they asserted, was the by-product of each individual's sense of three or four early years well-spent. Accordingly, the vast majority of the report's copious recommendations focused chiefly on undergraduate life, rather than on formal arrangements between the alumni and the university.

To some extent, the committee's findings read not unlike a catalogue of student assessments in the sixties. In many ways, of course, that was precisely the point. As the authors noted, much of what they advised was already on record, notably in the SQUAL Report (1979). As yet, however, several clearly identified problems had been only partially addressed. To avoid another well-intentioned but fruitless exercise in spouting truisms, the committee counselled that implementation of its various recommendations be assigned to specific groups, rather than merely stated as generally desirable goals. This plea stemmed from the conclusion that most of the key factors influencing school spirit were interpersonal in nature, which, in turn, rendered custom-tailored leadership in each of the university's subcommunities crucial.[46] The great thing, wrote the committee, was "to dispel the aura of negativism, rigidity, self-doubt, and conservatism that seems to have become the University's over-riding hallmark."[47] The manifold recommendations were grouped under five major rubrics: communications, orientation, interpersonal relationships, academic matters, and the case for a student centre.

Communication, said the task force, needed to be far more candid and comprehensive than was currently the case. Bad news, for example, had to be shared, alongside best tidings, if informed and constructive campus-wide dialogue were to be had. Equally, greater attention had to be drawn to the history, traditions, and achievements of the university and its graduates. Above all, McMaster had to project a clear image of itself to all its many audiences. Here, special note was made of Princeton's recent statement of institutional goals. More specifically, the report advised replacing the campus newsletter, *Contact*, with a "publication at the highest levels of objective journalism." In broader terms, the wholesale professionalization of public relations was emphasized, along with energetic outreach. Meanwhile, the committee enjoined all to remember that first and personal impressions tended to be the most lasting.

On that score, the task force urged Gilmour Hall to assist the MSU and the IRC in their efforts to reform orientation week. A strong steering committee "with teeth" would be needed to transform the often chaotic, roughhouse of time-honoured tomato fights and similar sophomoric hijinks into an integrative, welcoming experience that targeted the majority day students, as well as residence dwellers. In broader terms, the university had to be more aware of and actively involved in energizing the rather lacklustre extracurricular life on campus, which currently centred too much on student pubs and residence rowdiness. The key here, argued the committee, was for faculty and administration, from the top down, to present themselves as available to and approachable by students and staff alike. "The president of a university," for example, "should be highly visible on campus, accessible to all, and in day-to-day contact with as many campus members as possible." Meanwhile, hitherto marginalized groups, such as the alumni and part-time students, should be drafted into the active life of the university.

In promoting all these desirable ends, a purpose-built student centre, replete with office space for organizations, dining facilities, and a theatre to house symphonic and dramatic performances, would work wonders. In order to finance this, the committee recommended selling off dozens of expropriated Westdale homes, no longer required for the expansion of health sciences since their integration with the Chedoke hospitals. All in all, the task force advised, shy McMaster had to promote "undisguised boosterism" unapologetically on campus and in the wider community at large, if it were to counterbalance the soul-destroying funk induced by long-term financial restraints. Toward that end, a long list of specific recommendations was offered.[48]

As for academic matters, the report echoed a generation of student demand for a better balance in faculty commitment to teaching and research.

The rewards system, involving tenure, promotion, and merit pay, had to be geared to encourage this systematically. Equally, if strong research and good instruction were truly inseparable, it followed that the top professors in every field should play their fair part in pivotal year-one offerings, where youthful imaginations were often either fired or extinguished. Similarly, said the task force, the lead some departments had taken in reviving a tradition of personal academic counselling should be copied university-wide. Moreover, it asserted, every faculty member ought to assume this duty as part of his or her normal load, and be made aware of all the professional services available to troubled students.[49]

Altogether, the task force presented Lee with an ambitious plan of campaign. Of course, it might well have shared the long, dust-encrusted shelf lives of similar documents, from the Vichert Report on, save for the crucial fact that its many injunctions meshed neatly with the initial agenda of a new administration. Writing to Lee, Vice-President Les King, a member of the task force, heartily endorsed its recommendations, with the sole exception of the committee's plea for a dedicated student centre. As a member of Lee's inner cabinet, he was aware of the pressing need for academic space, especially in overcrowded engineering. Apart from that, he stood ready to assist in implementing all other suggestions in the report.[50] Lee, himself, required little persuasion. Having already committed to an undergraduate renaissance, he was undoubtedly pleased to have an affirmative, detailed manifesto. This was one document, it appeared, that was not about to sink into archival oblivion.

As his convening of the task force signified, Lee was already sprinting into action, before the committee's reported. The 1980 retreat had merely encouraged him down a path that he sincerely wanted to travel. He was, however, no blithe neophyte, aflame with bold vision, yet blind to stark realities. Indeed, as he advised the senate in 1981, transforming the social and academic quality of student life, broadly conceived, was bound to be "a considerable challenge."[51] This observation, as things transpired, proved to be all too prophetic. Truth to tell, few could have predicted the level of tension that steps toward a renaissance would engender on campus. Timing, interpretation, and context proved to be crucial. Thus, that which seemed logical and beneficent to reformers often met with resistance from those who saw only infringements on old prerogatives and purported bureaucratic aggrandizement. As well, attempts to bring the manifesto of 1981 to life became entangled in a new wave of intertwined "student moments." Meanwhile, inertia, habit, and specific university responses to government-commissioned reports offered ample cannon fodder for those who argued that "renaissance-speak" was mere patter, compared with the enduring voice of research as usual. Inevitably, continuing fiscal drought also placed limits on the possible. Even so, some important change was wrought, albeit not always on the hoped-for scale. For clarity's sake, an analysis of Lee's attempted renaissance might best be conducted by separate examination of its two overarching but simultaneous thrusts: rejuvenating the general quality of campus life and upgrading the undergraduate academic experience.

When it came to revamping university spirit, few of Lee's ventures paid higher dividends than his determined effort to bring alumni into closer communion with their alma mater. In this regard, a simple willingness to consult went a long way. From 1980 on, the president met monthly with representatives of the association and the director of alumni affairs. News and views were exchanged in scheduled, face-to-face sessions, as a working partnership was systematically forged.[52] Smaller gestures helped facilitate closer bonds, as well. In 1981, for example, limited membership was made available to alumni in that, hitherto, most exclusive sanctum sanctorum: the Faculty Club.[53] The results of outreach to graduates registered, almost immediately, and in tangible form.

As part of a general, $12-million campaign, launched in October 1980, alumni leaders assumed the burden of raising $1 million as their contribution to the five-year drive. This was ambitious, to say the least, given the alumni track record. At that point, the most the association had ever wrung from its members in any given year was a grand total of $56,000. It was, therefore, with elation that organizers reported pledges exceeding $250,000 by former students, after only four months of canvassing. Suddenly, five years seemed more than ample time within which to reach their target. In part, this turn of events was ascribed to better organization and more professional methods. In greater measure, however, observers credited "a new attitude in both the alumni and the administration" for renewed vigour. Particular note was taken of the 1980 retreat and Lee's readiness to accept constructive advice; even when it stung.

Proof of the pudding came when hundreds volunteered to commit time to updating contact lists, intensive "phone-a-thons," and mail-out campaigns. For their part, front-line workers remarked on the receptiveness of graduates, when approached personally and told how their donations would be spent, as well as being assured that they still had a real voice in university affairs.[54] As the campaign gathered steam, so did alumni giving. Indeed, between 1980 and 1985, it averaged over $300,000 per annum.[55] In the latter year, the association established a permanent fundraising committee, in order to retain the savvy and momentum acquired during the drive.[56] A corner, it seemed, had been turned.

Over the remainder of the decade, the peripatetic Lee punctiliously included personal sessions with local alumni branches as integral elements of his many global sojourns on general university business. Thode and Bourns, of course, had done the same, but haphazardly. For Lee, such effort was routine and systematic. In the end, he, his assistants in the development office, and a succession of highly able graduate leaders emerged as the true parents of a thriving, modernized McMaster alumni association. Thus, despite occasional minor problems, one plank in the renaissance platform was slotted snuggly into place. Another fell into line as Lee responded to alumni calls for greater presidential visibility in and responsiveness to the broader community. In doing so, he would redefine the nature of the presidency.

If the alumni recommended a higher presidential profile beyond McMaster's walls, objective circumstance absolutely demand it. After all, as fiscal times got tougher, those who would tough things out had to get going. In practical terms, this meant that Lee, to a far greater degree than his predecessors, had to master the fine arts of public and private persuasion. The alternative was to wait passively upon dwindling government largesse for this, that, or the other worthy project to take flight. Recognizing that any university worth its salt would always have more energy than money, Lee took to the road. Untutored in glad-handing and not a little intimidated by the prospect, he took an early cue from Sir Edmund "Ted" Leather. Over lunch at the Hamilton Club, the former governor of Bermuda advised him: "[B]elieve in the cause, be fairly personable, and ... be utterly shameless." The fledgling president had no difficulty with the first two desiderata. In time, he learned to cultivate the third. Indeed, with much practice, he came to understand that "movers and shakers, who are accustomed to doing things on their own, like to be asked." "And," he would later add, "you don't insult them by asking for too little."[57]

Another prerequisite was the ability to recognize and seize the moment, as Lee discovered one early morning, during his daily jog through Crooks Hollow. Happening on Michael "Mike" DeGroote, a wealthy local businessman of philanthropic bent, the president fairly flew home on winged heel. De Groote, in the course of friendly chat, had offered more than $3 million to kick start funding of a new home for the business school, which now bears his name. In later years, the gentleman would contribute in excess of $130 million to McMaster, primarily in support of health sciences.[58] As will be seen, this was not the only occasion on which Lee was pleasantly taken aback by a shaker. Still, most of the $100 million added to McMaster's endowment, during his years in office, came as the result of relentless personal networking and the efforts of development staff, such as Marnie Spears and Roger Trull.[59] Inevitably, for Lee, such endeavour meant time away from Gilmour Hall.

One consequence of this was a sharper division of, hitherto, shared administrative labour. As Les King later put it, the vice-president became "Mr Inside," while the president evolved into "Mr Outside."[60] For days, sometimes weeks, Lee was off campus, raising the university's profile at home and abroad, as well as soliciting cash. King, meanwhile, held the academic fort on a day-to-day basis. Since the two were on the same policy wavelength, their partnership worked smoothly. Lee, however, would later face difficulties, as, per force, he became more the roving CEO and less the close-at-hand college head. Inevitably, he lost that close, daily touch which had aided Thode and Bourns in reading shifting campus moods. At times, as will be seen, this growing distance would sharpen confrontations with MUFA. On the other hand, his peregrinations brought McMaster to the attention of bankers and corporate heads, as well as civic, national, and international bodies too numerous to mention. Thus, along with helping to energize the alumni, he successfully undertook another chore that the 1981 task force had thought essential to any renaissance. Others, however, would prove to be far more troublesome.

Improvements to residence life and orientation week had been identified as top priorities by those who sought to refurbish the undergraduate experience at McMaster. Just as he moved swiftly to foster closer ties with alumni, so also Lee wasted little time moving on these other fronts. The going, however, proved inordinately heavy, as reform initiatives collided with jealously guarded traditions, while simultaneously becoming enmeshed in heated controversies of the moment. At the tangled heart of all debate was an enduring issue: the relative status of the student voice. Thus, the IRC had long enjoyed a higher degree of self-government than was common at Ontario universities. Similarly, the MSU had ever been the principal driving force behind frosh week. Both branches of student government acknowledged that some measure of renewal might be beneficial. Neither, however, was eager to surrender historic claims to a major role in its own bailiwick. As chance would have it, this natural inclination was powerfully reinforced by three separate, but concurrent, clashes between students and university authority. From February 1981 until the following January, contretemps involving sociology, the LRPC, and business served only to complicate and cloud renaissance designs. The precise details of each fracas are less important, here, than the conclusions many students and faculty, rightly or wrongly, drew from them, when lumped together.

Serious trouble erupted first in sociology. Since 1974, students had enjoyed parity on all department committees, including that which dealt with appointments, tenure, and promotion. In 1977, the senate had decreed that, henceforth, only tenured faculty should participate in the latter form of deliberation. It had, however, allowed that any given department could grant voting privileges to students, so long as the more senior, faculty-level appointments body approved. For several years, the Faculty of Social Science allowed sociology to use this notwithstanding clause in order to accommodate students (and many professors) wedded to the idea of full co-management. Over time, squabbles accumulated concerning individual cases and the department's unorthodox use of secret ballots in making recommendations. Eventually, an explosion was set off, in February 1981, when the department faculty caucus opted to end student participation in appointments decisions by the slimmest of majorities: one vote. Crying foul, students lobbied administrators, while conducting a vigorous campaign to mobilize campus-wide peers. On 19 March, frustrated by deadlock, a dozen of their number threw up barricades, as they seized control of the chairman's sixth-floor office in Kenneth Taylor Hall.

At first, Dean Peter George was prepared to tolerate orderly protest. As the day wore on, however, and sociology majors blocked access to all elevators in the building, he felt duty-bound to act. Many individuals, afflicted with sundry handicaps, could not use the stairs yet had every right to go about their daily academic affairs. Protesters had crossed a line. In return, casting velvet gloves aside, George delivered a solid and decisive right-cross. Campus security and city police were summoned. With little immediate fuss and no arrests, demonstrators were ushered from the building. Predictably, student outrage ensued. The *Silhouette* pointedly reprinted headlines from the 1974 French debacle, including photos of bumper-to-bumper police cars and baying crowds. For good measure, speakers at a boisterous rally provocatively likened the eviction of sociology students to recent raids on gay bathhouses in Toronto. Mimicking the spirit of '74, the SRA contemplated a one-day general strike in solidarity with sociologists. Meanwhile, the latter took control of the vice-president's office on Monday, 23 March. Playing things softly, King made no move to oust the occupiers. Instead, he brokered a truce, four days later, to allow for further negotiation of the representation issue.

As the matter dragged on in a sorely divided department, Dean George finally assumed the vacant chair, in September 1981. Disinclined to countenance further sparring between conservatives and dissidents, he imposed a moratorium on all hiring and graduate admissions. Threatening potential closure of the doctoral program, George prodded warring parties to frame a constitution in line with university-wide practice. They did so, in short order.[61] Thereafter, sociology slowly relaxed into an era of productive calm. This drawn-out episode might merit little more than a footnote, had it not coincided with other, roughly similar, disruptions on campus, to form part of a seemingly larger whole.

"Students Lose Stake in Future of Mac," cried a November 1981 *Silhouette* editorial. The article referred not to the sociology wrangle but to a senate decision to remove students from the LRPC.[62] The latter was being transformed into the BSCAP, a body invested with greater authority and a far broader mandate than its predecessor.[63] Because it would have access to confidential salary information and demand a breadth of experience that even few junior professors had, many senators (by no means all) concluded that students ought not to be members. Lee and King set forth the rationale for this decision, asking those excluded to take no personal affront, where none was intended.[64] They asked, not surprisingly, in vain.

Instead, the senate was deluged with briefs and petitions from groups as varied as the McMaster Association of Part-Time Students, the alumni association, the MSU, the Union of Graduate Students (formerly the GSA), and others – each of which expressed sentiments similar to those sketched by the *Silhouette*. Disenfranchisement was the resounding note. One disillusioned student boldly informed the senate that decisions, such as this one, were far from isolated and stood in sharp contrast to the ideals outlined by Lee in his inaugural address.[65] Meanwhile, the SRA voted to censure Vice-President King.[66] After much heated debate, and with concession only on the matter of alumni representation, the senate endorsed BSCAP, in January 1982. Elsewhere, the beat went on.

Concurrent with the BSCAP and sociology disputes, seething student discontent was threatening to erupt in the normally quiescent precincts of business. Once again, specific complaints were linked with general concern over the future of the student voice. In December 1981, plans to overhaul the traditional BComm program sparked widespread student and some professorial resistance. Among other revisions, the accustomed right (not requirement) to specialize intensively was being abolished, in favour of an emphasis on better-rounded, more liberal education. While in line with renaissance objectives, this change would have a particularly significant effect on candidates destined for careers in accountancy.

Hitherto, they had been able to complete all courses necessary for eligibility to write the certified chartered accountants examination, after a few years of employment. Proposed liberalization would make this smooth transition to professional accreditation next to impossible. Given that roughly 40 per cent of fourth-year students tended to be would-be accountants, this was no minor matter. Moreover, students were not the only group upset. Indeed, wrangling over this issue, as well as the future role of accountancy in any proposed PhD program, had led several leading faculty to depart on the Waterloo Express already.[67] When the senate endorsed the program change, on 13 January 1982, it became clear that business could not be conducted as usual.[68] Students mobilized.

Quite apart from program specifics, their chief complaint was that neither in-course nor incoming candidates had been properly consulted, let alone duly informed, concerning these fundamental changes. Accordingly, almost 500 members of the normally buttoned-down commerce society organized to gather evidence and pressure the senate.[69] In the end, they successfully demonstrated that effective notice had not been given. Taking the point, in mid-February 1982, the senate voted to delay implementation of the new program, while "grandfathering" those currently enrolled.[70] Even so, if justice was eventually served, significant collateral damage was done along the way. The student press and MSU made this patently clear, late in 1981.

On 3 December of that year, the *Silhouette* endeavoured to put the many symptoms of contemporary student unrest into broad perspective. Tremors generated in sociology, business, and the LRPC, it proclaimed, had much in common with simultaneous rumblings concerning residence policy and orientation. Indeed, they were all of a piece. Most notably, said journalists, each matter demonstrated university willingness to disregard or override student opinion (the business affair had only just arisen, at that point). In this connection, one editorial writer sounded a warning. "The importance of the alumni looms larger, as the financial forecast grows dimmer," he scribbled. If McMaster wanted to build a generous alumni, he cautioned, it had best stop disregarding the views of prospective members.[71] Related articles drummed loudly on this theme.

Much, for example, was made of proposals for a merit-based residence admissions policy, the principles of which were formulated by a committee of deans, who had not consulted fully with the IRC. Condemning ivory-tower elitism and administrative end-runs, MSU President Alex Daschko railed, "the bottom line is that students are not being respected." Similarly, he sided with student representatives who were refusing to sign the report of a presidential committee on orientation. Their advice, Daschko claimed, had been ignored. Worse still, they had been forbidden to discuss specific proposals outside the committee – even with elected student leaders. Surveying the whole scene, Alison Bell, the president of Brandon Hall, lamented, "Whatever we say doesn't matter." In her eyes, the creeping ten-drils of administrative control were clawing relentlessly forward.[72] Such was the view of many student leaders, as much-heralded change in their quality of life took shape. There was, however, an altogether different perspective on the contemporary landscape.

For many senators, especially MUFA members, the sociology affair was just the glaring tip of an unwholesome iceberg. No sooner had King per-suaded students to vacate his office, than he was raked over the coals in the senate, on 8 April, for being too soft on troublemakers. His attention was drawn to a faculty-association letter that linked the sit-ins with a pattern of increasing disorder in residences and during orientation week. "The image of McMaster has been thoroughly tarnished by unacceptable behaviour," read the missive. Permissiveness was breeding contempt. Note was made of recent vandalism at the Faculty Club, and King was reminded that, during the occupations, beer bottles and obscenities had rained down on passersby near Edwards Hall.

What steps, he was asked, had been taken to curb this "barbarous behav-iour"? Where were the police on these occasions? Why were those who had interfered with the normal conduct of academic business at Taylor Hall not charged with trespass? Why, in more general terms, were residence leaders not cracking down on those whose rowdiness made serious study all but impossible in the dormitories? Caught in the vise of student anger and fac-ulty outrage, King replied that he had merely followed guidelines governing group conflict, set out in 1974. Senate critics replied that clearer regula-tions concerning non-academic offences were in order. The upshot was the striking of a senate committee to recommend on matters pertaining to stu-dent conduct and behaviour.[73] This reaction, coupled with student percep-tions sharpened during the sociology, LRPC and business disputes, ensured that the reforms Lee hoped to carry out co-operatively would proceed in a charged atmosphere.

That electricity was obvious, the following January, when the president's orientation steering committee, established in May 1981, brought its report to the senate for discussion. Lee did his best to sound a conciliatory note. Universities, he said, were complex institutions, subject to all manner of fragmenting tendencies, none of which served anybody's best interests. Alluding to ongoing tensions over residence and orientation reform, Lee remarked that the IRC had recently voiced its concerns emphatically. That, he declared, was a good thing. Debate, after all, was the very lifeblood of a university, and no one wanted to live in an authoritarian environment. What was ultimately most desirable, he submitted, was a healthy dialogue between the senate and all who were concerned with the university's welfare. Having shot his diplomatic bolt, he opened the floor to comment.

Speaking for the committee, mathematician Evelyn Nelson said that its chief goals were to add academic elements to orientation, more closely involve day students, and put an end to the often humiliating initiation rites inflicted on newcomers. She noted that progress had been made in the first two areas, particularly with the formation of the Society of Off-Campus Students. As well, the IRC had distributed guidelines for residence initiation, which showed improvement over previous years. Still, she contended, much of the hazing that went on remained unacceptable. The university, Nelson advised, should move toward true orientation and away from fraternity-like initiation. Taking keen exception to Nelson's views, Murray Hassard, one of the five students on the nine-person steering committee, submitted his own minority report.

Co-signed by numerous residence leaders, the document offered a different notion of orientation's purposes. Three goals were identified: the promotion of solidarity and cohesion among hall members, the introduction of frosh to the social structure of residence, and the provision of facts about campus, services, and courses. Peter George immediately underlined a fundamental difference between the IRC and committee. The former, he said, almost wholly neglected the three-quarters of students who lived off campus, whereas the latter sought to integrate all newcomers in common. Other senators took issue with the authoritarian note in Hassard's report. "Solidarity and cohesion," remarked Alwyn Berland, were worthy military goals, but university was not a boot camp. Alex Daschko retorted that suppression of tradition might cost McMaster the future loyalty of its residence cadre. In the end, the majority recommendations won strong senate approval.[74]

Thereafter, gradual alterations to orientation were implemented by an expanded steering committee, with the (sometimes reluctant) assistance of the IRC and MSU. Thus, change forged by negotiation made some headway. Indeed, by late 1983, Lee voiced considerable pride in the improvements he detected.[75] Yet, as late 1987, reformers and student leaders continued to do noisy battle over incidents arising during frosh week.[76] Finally, in 1988, the senate shortened the induction period to two days explicitly designed to guide and welcome those fresh to campus. Student organizations continued to play an important role in orientation, but the university assumed increasing responsibility and initiative in these proceedings. Residence restructuring, meanwhile, went forward in tandem with orientation reform and in much the same direction.

In February 1982, a proposed merit system of residence admission was introduced to the senate, with the hope of improving the sometimes raucous atmosphere of McMaster's live-in halls.[77] Coming hard on the heels of Nelson's orientation report, this proposition roused some students to immediate fury. Indeed, even the MSU was surprised, when, for the first time in five years, a true quorum turned out for its general meeting that month. The 300 attending roared mass disapproval, when Dr Larry Kurtz, dean of student affairs, explained that there had been no requirement to consult the IRC, since the recommendations were made by a group of deans at the request of a senate committee.[78] Banners aloft, student leaders protested. The senate, however, was not about to budge. In March, it refused even to receive an MSU petition to reconsider the matter.[79] Instead, it forged ahead, bringing McMaster in line with practice at most other universities.

In May 1982, the offices of director of residence life and manager of administration were approved.[80] The elected IRC continued, but with a remit circumscribed by closer university supervision. Adjustment to the new arrangements was not always smooth. Thus, the SRA was still up in arms over preferred admissions to varsity athletes and club leaders, in 1984. Significantly, however, it had come to accept that strong academic performance was a reasonable criterion for sorting applications for rooms.[81] Slowly, some broadly acceptable change was negotiated. In 1985, for example, arrangements were made to clarify lines of authority, give student-hall masters systematic training, improve cleaning services, revise the meal plan, and generally make residences more habitable.[82] Conflicts, essentially personal at root, led to the abrupt resignation of the first director in 1987. Gilmour Hall took careful note and astutely replaced him with the student-centred, energetic, Ronald Coyne.[83]

Efforts to ameliorate orientation practice and residence life were high-profile elements in Lee's campaign to improve the quality of undergraduate experience at McMaster. Inevitably, they provoked resistance from specific student elements long-accustomed to relatively free sway in those domains. The degree to which that backlash reflected general undergraduate opinion is difficult to determine. Quite possibly, daytime candidates – fully three-quarters of the student body – took only passing interest in these matters, if any. Perhaps, they felt the influence of other initiatives more directly. These included the better training of campus security officers, a presidential committee on access for the disabled, the establishment of a senate committee on student affairs, a clarified code of student conduct, and scholarships for part-time candidates, among many other things.[84] At a minimum, Lee made an honest start at addressing the major items outlined by the 1981 task force, save one: a modern, purpose-built student centre. Throughout the eighties, such a facility was touted, time and again, as the true key to revivifying campus life. Invariably, however, financial exigency and academic space requirements stood in the way. Indeed, a 1986 report of the planning and building committee saw no point even in reopening discussion on the issue until the mid-nineties, at the earliest.[85]

Standing back from the welter of detail, can one say that various efforts, after 1980, actually engendered something approaching a renaissance in the daily fabric of student life? Perhaps the best answer is that, if they began one, it was far from complete by the end of our period. The 1987 MSU brief "The Quality of Student Life at McMaster: An Oxymoron," made this clear. More balanced than its provocative title would suggest, it was closely argued, moderate in tone, and included the views of faculty members, such as Stephen Threlkeld, who could scarcely be described as wild-eyed radicals. Lee's sincerity, for instance, was never in question. On the contrary, the authors had only praise for a president who was readily approachable and had done much to ease communication with student leaders. Equally, they applauded the way he practised that which he preached to senior professors, by continuing to teach, despite the strains of high office. That said, there was harsh criticism of faculty and administrators who failed to follow the president's example.

Directives, it was noted, were not always implemented by people on the ground. Residences, allegedly, stood in dire need of better maintenance. Hall masters were not always thoroughly trained, senate injunctions notwithstanding. Counselling, especially of foreign students, was haphazard. Meanwhile, across the university as a whole, lounge and study space was woefully inadequate. The litany of complaint, along with offers of collaborative assistance, filled more than ninety pages. All told, the brief bore an uncanny resemblance to that of the 1981 task force.

Ultimately, the MSU report concluded that the lack of significant progress was attributable to a variety of factors. Sustained, debilitating underfunding was the most obvious of these. The want of full engagement on the part of some individuals was cited as another. Beyond these problems, however, a deeper, paradigmatic influence was said to be at work. McMaster, the report declared, had a distinct predilection to elevate research and graduate studies above all other considerations, including undergraduate interests.[86] This analysis, of course, cannot be taken at face value, given that the MSU spoke from its own, particular perspective. Perhaps, a look at academic aspects of the renaissance project might help to clarify the general picture. On that score, some achievements notwithstanding, adding meaty flesh to the undergraduate bone proved difficult, especially when the spirit of general commitment was, at best, rather ambiguous.

Fiscal restraint, government red tape, established degree programs, and limited numbers of staff imposed objective limits on change. As will be seen, so did bred-in-the-marrow assumptions underpinning the *Plan for McMaster*. Still, efforts to invigorate undergraduate academic life were made. In this regard, the innovative arts and science degree sparkled as McMaster's unchallenged, glimmering crown jewel. However, a small, avowedly elitist program could not, on its own, a renaissance make. Thus, in order to offer spice, variety, and focus to those not attracted down single-major paths, numerous interdisciplinary "studies" degrees were authorized. Some of these, such as labour studies and gerontology prospered mightily. Others fared less well.

Labour studies had begun life as a non-degree, trial offering by business in extension, aimed primarily at would-be union executives. By 1980, it was drawing day students into its orbit, as it assumed more formal academic shape. A year later, the senate translated it into a full-degree program, under the aegis of social science, adding an honours stream in 1986.[87] It was the first of its kind in Canada. The same was true of gerontology studies (1986), which quickly led to external funding of a multimillion-dollar geriatric centre in 1987.[88] Meanwhile, a number of other options were developed, such as peace studies, Canadian studies, and an interdisciplinary degree in humanities. Unfortunately, the latter two programs withered on the vine, primarily for want of student interest.[89] Nevertheless, efforts were clearly made to open some new avenues to erstwhile undergraduate vagabonds. In a similar spirit, suggestions for enriching the experience of part-time students were made.

In 1981, the LRPC offered the senate a plethora of recommendations concerning new initiatives in continuing education. Given the rising addiction to catchy acronyms, this particular brief was irresistibly dubbed the "NICE Report." It detailed myriad innovations in part-time studies adopted by universities across Canada and the United States. These changes included new techniques for delivering distance courses, novel programs aimed specifically at adults, and fresh methods of fostering independent study, to name only a few. McMaster, said the committee, lagged behind best practice in catering to the unique needs of a potentially large, off-campus constituency. It was time to catch up. Lee and King were enthusiastic. Others applauded in principle, but voiced serious reservations on practical grounds. Chief among the latter were faculty deans and MUFA leaders. How would this affect agreements concerning load-teaching, asked David Winch? Deans inquired where the resources to expand continuing education might be found, given that they were barely adequate for the delivery of current day programs. Berland thought that the whole scheme was out of line with the *Plan for McMaster*. In the end, the report was passed, with mild amendment, but remained a consummation devoutly to be wished, rather than a wholesale plan of action.[90] Meanwhile, and much more vigorously, various measures of general academic quality control were examined.

Ever since relaxation of the traditional grade-thirteen curriculum, concern had mounted regarding the preparedness of candidates entering university. Indeed, a blistering attack on the corrosive effect of sixties-inspired "progressive education" marked Lee's first remarks as president to the senate.[91] To be sure, all faculties had gradually raised de facto admission standards.[92] Yet, it was not clear that even these were keeping pace with high-school grade inflation. As Peter George grimly observed, hordes of first-year candidates with outstanding secondary-school marks were regularly "slaughtered," when faced with university demands. Accordingly, he voted with the senate to study the possibility of instituting entrance examinations.[93] Meanwhile, carrots, as well as whips, were on offer. Thus, the Hooker fund was tapped to increase the number of entrance and in-course scholarships open to high-achieving undergraduates.[94]

At the same time, BSCAP began regular, searching departmental reviews. Unlike ACAP assessments, these scrutinized undergraduate as well as advanced studies and research. Nor were they perfunctory. Instead, the template devised in the *Plan for McMaster* was applied to the ranking of departments for replacement or additional positions.[95] BSCAP recommendations were never slavishly rubber-stamped by the senate, yet all understood that they could not be blithely ignored. Panicky, late-eighties rumours concerning the possible closure of art history indicated just how seriously negative reviews were taken.[96] The most obvious and controversial move toward quality control, however, involved the adoption of a compulsory literacy test.

Alarmed by anecdotal evidence of widespread student unfamiliarity with the basics of English grammar and composition, the senate authorized an experiment in 1985. That September, a forty-minute test was administered to 1,042 first-year candidates in psychology. More than half of those examined were registered in social science or business. Another third hailed from humanities and the sciences. The result was an abysmal mean score of 38 per cent. Appalled, the senate instituted the "McMaster Test of Writing Competence," in order, as Dean David Gagan of humanities put it, "to prevent illiterate students from continuing." Tests were to be administered three times a year. Candidates could sit the exam as often as necessary. Remedial assistance was offered by the centre for continuing education, albeit at the stiff price of $115.[97]

Introduced in 1986, the scheme was greeted with strident student catcalls. It was deemed unfair, because it was multiple-choice in form and purportedly pedantic in content. *Silhouette* commentators doubted that half the faculty knew sufficient grammatical minutiae to pass.[98] Perhaps they were right, given that the senate would soon reject an official health sciences document on the basis that it was painfully "convoluted and poorly written"![99] Meanwhile, an error, written into the first test by examiners themselves did little to enhance student confidence in the process, whose overseers were said to "look like dorks."[100]

At the same time, school boards and the public press cast doubt on the nature of the test, in light of astonishingly high, early failure rates. With time and refinement, the system improved. By 1987, Frank Jones could report that 80 per cent regularly passed successive exams. True, some, such as historian John Trueman, regretted the wholly objective form of the test, as well as the "public relations disaster" it had initially precipitated.[101] Still, for all its shortcomings, the requirement did, at least, forcibly raise the literacy level of most who graduated. As such, it stands as further evidence that there was substance underpinning talk of a desired academic renaissance in undergraduate education. Such musing, moreover, can only be fully understood when viewed against a wider backdrop. Indeed, Lee's hopes were closely related to the emergence of an informal alliance among Ontario's premier universities.

Like Thode and Bourns before him, Lee thought that the key to Ontario-wide excellence, at every level of academic endeavour, was thorough-going, tough-minded differentiation. Throughout the eighties, in concert with a small, "self-selected entente," which included like-minded leaders from Queen's, Toronto, Western, and Waterloo, he worked assiduously toward achieving that happy outcome.[102] The so-called MQTWW group (pronounced: "McToo") had its origins in an informal panel discussion hosted by McMaster in March 1980. Alarmed by the erosion of support for university-based research and development, the assembled presidents recognized the need for a major "selling job," as Bourns termed their task. All agreed that Ottawa, Queen's Park, and the general public had to be convinced to adopt imaginative, new approaches to post-secondary funding, lest Ontario universities decline to the level of intellectual "hewers of wood and drawers of water."[103] Upon assuming office, Lee was initially hopeful that change of this nature was imminent.

The Fisher Report (1981), commissioned by Queen's Park and authored by Bette Stephenson's own deputy minister, offered almost everything that MQTWW most desired. The primary recommendation was that excellence be promoted, either by significant increases in grants to universities, or by cutting some institutions off from the provincial purse, altogether. The alternative, a slide into collective mediocrity, was, in Fisher's view, unacceptable. If this meant reducing accessibility, so be it. University autonomy should be respected, the report continued, but it was high time that government direct each institution to state its chief objectives, so that funding could be determined appropriately.[104] For fiscal and political reasons, Stephenson quickly shelved the report. MQTWW, however, was stimulated to press its own, crystallizing agenda.

At Lee's invitation, members of the group met at McMaster, on 27 November 1982, to mull over a discussion paper. The landscape, as described in the document, was starkly lunar.[105] With the recession and underfunding continuing, several universities were literally on the brink of insolvency. Academic quality and morale were sinking. Meanwhile, there was no indication that government was considering any major policy change. Instead, Queen's Park insisted on treating often strikingly different universities as interchangeable parts of a single Ontario "system." Worse still, the COU, "immobilized and deeply divided" by internal squabbling among its disparate members, offered little in the way of coherent leadership. Moreover, it was pointless to count on any significant increase in overall revenues from the province. With this grim synopsis of current reality in mind, the MQTWW caucus warmed to a radical, new suggestion. In a pencilled sidebar, Lee described this as "an act of leadership far beyond the immediate context of what we're doing." Others, who championed COU solidarity, would call it an act of betrayal on the part of rogue "McTwit."[106]

The proposal was to author a mission statement that would identify MQTWW as a separate tier in a formal hierarchy of Ontario universities. After all, the group argued, this would only ratify reality. These five institutions were all highly diversified in undergraduate, graduate, and professional studies. Together, they accounted for 68 per cent of provincial doctoral enrolment. Most of Ontario's major health sciences programs were in their collective domain. All members had capped enrolments. All had higher entrance standards than most other universities. Each was also heavily committed to significant research, collectively garnering over 74 per cent of all external grants won in the province. In short, the five presidents thought that, given all this common ground, MQTWW had a mission distinct from its less fully developed provincial sisters and should be funded accordingly.[107] This idea was refined, the following month, when MQTWW sketched a rough plan for a multitier university system in which clear differentiation by function would be the key to excellence in each echelon – including undergraduate work.[108] Impetus to clearer definition of this vision was soon supplied by Queen's Park.

In December 1983, Minister Stephenson announced the formation of the Bovey Commission. Among other things, she asked its members to recommend potential changes to the method of distributing university operating grants. There was even a hint that true differentiation might be recognized in a revised formula. "The universities of tomorrow," she said, "should have more clearly defined, different and distinctive roles." Each and every academic haven, said Stephenson, ought not to aspire to do all things. Instead, they should identify and build on their own established strengths. There would be no large infusion of new money, but the current pot could, she thought, be more rationally divided.[109] With these guidelines in mind, Bovey asked each university to define its own nature and objectives, as well as its position on system modification. Lee was quick off the mark, with a reply straight out of the MQTWW playbook. In so doing, he (inadvertently) clarified how the McMaster research paradigm might be reconciled with his thoughts about an undergraduate renaissance.

There should be, he argued, four types of universities, distinguished by function. The sprawling University of Toronto could be deemed uniquely "comprehensive." Next, McMaster, Queen's, Western, and Waterloo, with their wide range of programs at all degree levels, would be described as "full-service" institutions. Veterinary-oriented Guelph and bilingual Ottawa would be designated as "specialized." Meanwhile, a number of regional universities, such as Brock and Trent, would flourish primarily as homes to "undergraduate" studies. Ideally, more revenue would be made available. Failing that, however, any rational allotment of grants, based on function, should cover the cost of research overheads. In that case, said Lee, McMaster could retain its scholarly intensive character, while much cash was freed up for undergraduate education.[110]

On the latter point, with quiet elitism, he emphasized quality over quantity. Indeed, as he told the commission, he foresaw McMaster accepting a somewhat smaller but much higher calibre undergraduate enrolment, in the future. Ordinary pass degrees, of course, would be retained, but slowly de-emphasized in favour of a broader range of honours and specially tailored interdisciplinary studies – programs better suited to the interests of McMaster's research-minded faculty and a more rigorously selected freshman intake.[111] When quizzed by the *Spectator* about going after only "the cream of the [student] crop," Lee just smiled broadly, but he never denied the idea.[112]

When released, in January 1985, the sixty-five-page Bovey Report came close to encapsulating MQTWW's fondest hopes. It called for a funding formula geared to a competitive system. Individual universities would be rewarded for the quality with which they fulfilled their specific functions.[113] Yet, if Lee and others of his persuasion found this pleasing, faculty associations, student groups, teacher federations, and members of the general public raised objections too numerous to detail. Most notably, there was a backlash against proposed tuition hikes and recommendations that might restrict or redefine accessibility. For the moment, the registrar, Sandy Darling, cautioned everyone to wait and see what Queen's Park had to say, before wasting a lot of energy on potentially pointless angst.[114] As things transpired, this was excellent advice.

The shaky minority government of Premier Frank Miller, Bill Davis' Tory successor, was ill-placed to handle such a hot iron. Thus, like so many before it, the Bovey Report was consigned to the darkest limbo of the ministry's cavernous catacombs.[115] There it lies at rest: the last serious attempt to differentiate among Ontario's universities to date. Yet, officially interred though it might have been, its spirit lived on in MQTWW. Indeed, Lee underlined his unswerving commitment to realizing the essence of the report in a mission statement he penned, as late as 1989.[116] To him, movement in Bovey's direction was the *sine qua non* of achieving a true undergraduate renaissance that extended Thodean values to the baccalaureate level, without doing violence to the commanding research imperative.

In 1988, Ken Post, Lee's personal assistant, tried to clarify this complex notion for a student bewildered by the reverberating exhortations to better teaching coupled with ever-more emphasis on research. The president, Post wrote, was trying hard to enhance student life and education. He underscored, for example, the introduction of teaching awards by the university, among many other initiatives. He added that "None of these efforts, however, were intended to diminish the centrality to University life of academic endeavour and the focus on determining what is not known."[117] There was, he implied, no inherent tension between the renaissance ideal and McMaster's research-intensive mission. Some faculty, however, reserved judgment on the point.

Looking back on the period, thirty years later, Peter George recalled Lee's many injunctions to invigorate all things undergraduate. As he remembered, however, those rousing pleas encountered a good deal of skepticism among faculties, departments, and individuals captivated by the research-graduate studies paradigm.[118] True, teaching prowess had being extolled with great earnestness by Gilmour Hall. In 1981, for example, Vice-President King went so far as to pen an open letter in which he made clear his reluctance to recommend merit pay for any professor who did not engage actively and effectively in undergraduate instruction.[119] It is unclear, however, that he followed through on the threat. In any event, as George recalled, external grants, prestige publication, and doctoral supervision continued to trump all in what he referred to as "the priority loop."[120]

BSCAP reviews from the period suggest that he was not alone in entertaining this perception. Thus, with remarkable similarity, assessments of English, philosophy, and sociology, for example, noted a distinct trend on the part of many (by no means all) department mandarins to fob off undergraduate duties on others, while they concentrated on graduate students and replenished their research portfolios.[121] True, many established professors answered Lee's call. Senior philosopher John Thomas, to mention but one, took his research interests directly to the undergraduate multitude, offering a course in biomedical ethics that drew enrolments topping 800.[122] On the whole, however, the safest route into "the loop," for an individual or department, was via publication and doctoral supervision. As Sami Najm, chairman of philosophy, pointed out, immersion in undergraduate teaching could leave instructors in a bind, when promotion was on the line.[123] Historian David Gagan understood the loop and its implications, only too well.

As dean of humanities during the eighties, Gagan was acutely conscious that the Plan for McMaster and later strategic statements had a powerful "branding" influence at the university. In his view, distinctions were drawn between undergraduate-teaching departments and those with higher functions. Generally, he contended, heavier entitlements were reserved for the latter. Humanities housed several small units, such as music, art, and sundry foreign languages, which lacked the necessary mass or scholarly output to mount doctoral programs. Gagan, accordingly, found himself hard-pressed simply to maintain stasis. Well-rounded growth was out of the question. Meanwhile, colleagues who sought promotion or tenure primarily on the grounds of teaching excellence were frequently told to think again. "That [argument]," Gagan observed, "wasn't going to pass muster anywhere in the university." In response, some humanists retreated into bruised passivity, pining for a return to the values of an earlier McMaster. Others, vibrant research scholars but locked into small departments with scant opportunity to engage in graduate supervision, were deeply frustrated. All told, said Gagan, a defensive "bunker mentality" characterized even the larger, doctoral departments, whose members felt like poor cousins at the university table.[124]

Of course, some very good things happened. At times, however, they came at a cost. In the mid-eighties, for example, the elderly Herman Levy tottered shakily into Lee's office, one afternoon. The wealthy bachelor, however, immediately stunned the president by donating his collection of 185 French Impressionist and post-Impressionist paintings to McMaster. Lee recognized the financial implications of proper housing and curatorship for assorted masterpieces by Monet, Pissarro, and other luminaries. He also knew that he had to act quickly, since many prominent galleries lusted after these treasures, estimated to be worth more than $25 million. Accordingly, he accepted the magnificent windfall. In time, an old wing of Mills Library was refashioned to accommodate the university's increasingly world-class holdings.[125]

At a stroke, the Department of Art History was lavishly bolstered. Naturally, as dean of the faculty affected, Gagan approved the decision. Even so, he was deeply saddened that, with no new funds available, this lustrous addition entailed a heavy trade-off: the death of the McMaster symphony orchestra.[126] Gagan, it should be noted, never cast blame for this, or humanities' other troubles, on Lee or King. They supported his (generally unsuccessful) efforts to coax small departments into larger, more dynamic coalitions, such as a unified department of fine arts. Larger units, thought Gagan, would be better equipped to compete for a place in the loop. In turn, as a dynamic scholar himself, he accepted what the administration was trying to accomplish across the university as a whole. Thus, he could only regret that, "when push came to shove ... there was that research-intensive, graduate-training model," and the humanities, labouring under a bunker mentality, "weren't at the top of the list."[127] Instead, that lofty perch was still occupied by the usual suspects, whose numerous achievements were, as ever, loudly trumpeted. Meanwhile, what can be safely said about the "renaissance"?

Ultimately, the president's call to rejuvenate undergraduate life lingered as an ideal toward which to strive, rather than materializing in full-flower. Even so, no matter how imperfectly realized, it merits close historical attention, if only because, in complex fashion, Lee's most fundamental notions concerning the would-be renaissance powerfully affirmed the continuity of established values at McMaster. To be clear, though beating the drum of undergraduate rejuvenation, Alvin Lee came not to bury Harry Thode's concept of the university but to burnish, expand, and add a new dimension to it. Thus, like his scientific predecessor, this humanist president never wavered in his conviction that research and scholarship were, as he put it, "the basis of everything we do, including teaching."[128] Moreover, and very much like Thode, he was determined that there should be sharp distinctions among

Ontario universities, with research-intensive institutions, such as McMaster, seated among the more favoured echelons. All that he longed for was that "adequate balance" he found missing, in 1980.

Thus, Lee's call for a renaissance was perfectly sincere, but it was never simple or unconditional. Instead, it was utterly contingent on progress in his simultaneous campaigns to sell the idea on campus and to have government underwrite the true cost of research. In neither case did he enjoy unalloyed success. Even so, the effort was far from in vain. Precious bonds with alumni were carefully woven. Innovative programs, such as the arts and science degree, were sponsored, when possible. Orientation was gradually transformed, and residence ceased to resemble *Animal House* in ethos. Public outreach and greater professionalization in fundraising were given serious attention. All told, a good deal of the mandate sketched by the task force of 1981 was realized. In the end, however, a true renaissance was probably unachievable, under contemporary circumstances. By 1987, McMaster had yet to achieve truly "adequate balance."

Centennial

The many-faceted campaign to promote a renaissance in undergraduate education touched on and was touched by several developments on the McMaster scene. At best, however, it was a provocative leitmotif embellishing the central theme of an opus composed by Thode. Thus, from his inaugural address through to his mission statement of 1989, the truly dominant chord struck by Lee was in close harmony with that which had resounded at Gilmour Hall, since the late fifties: McMaster was and would remain a virtuoso among Canada's research-intensive universities. If, in addition, it could be forged into a premier undergraduate school, then some striking grace notes might polish an evolving institutional score. Melodic continuity, however, was still the prime directive. Accordingly, Lee's many forays into outreach were undertaken at least as much to broadcast a tried-and-true concert piece, as to voice any renaissance rendition of it. This was never more in evidence than in 1987, McMaster's centennial year, when the university orchestrated the largest gathering of the Canadian learned societies, to date. There were, however, a few sharply discordant notes heard on campus, prior to that happy hour.

That Lee was an energetic and accomplished impresario on the public circuit is beyond dispute. Surging alumni support and a swelling endowment were merely the most tangible proofs of this. On home ground, progress was also made, during his first term, toward achieving most of the objectives he had outlined, in 1980. Therefore, a 1984 board-senate committee, struck to consider his renewal, recommended unanimously in his favour, albeit in somewhat muted tones. "In reviewing Dr. Lee's performance," wrote the committee, "it was clear that, with one important exception, Dr. Lee has performed exceedingly well."[1] Evidently, there had been a near-fatal collision, during the president's first tour in office. He survived it, learned from it, and went on to enjoy centennial fruits; but not before passing through fire.

Universities across Canada set aside the period 24 to 31 March 1982 to mark a "Week of Concern" over their deepening financial woes. Every effort was made, not a horse spared, as senates, boards, students, and faculty rallied in what amounted to a nationwide, public teach-in regarding the dangers of continued underfunding. At McMaster, a special edition of the *Courier* drew attention to the many ways in which inflation, recession, and cutbacks had eroded the foundations of higher education, during a decade of constraint. Lest all this groaning be construed as special pleading by pampered dons, isolated from harsh experience of the "real world," Dr Alan Kay of metallurgy underlined the dollars-and-cents reality of professorial life. Already low by the standard of comparable professions, faculty salaries, he noted, had been systematically restrained by government and lethally gutted by inflation. Indeed, said Kay, faculty purchasing power had declined by fully 20 per cent, between 1978 and 1981. At that moment, the author focused blame for this state of affairs on underfunding by government. He did, however, concede that, had salaries actually kept pace with inflation, universities would have been bankrupt, long ago.[2] In short, the pecuniary plight of faculty was systemic, rather than local, in origin. Thus, complaint, he reasoned, should be forwarded to Queen's Park, not Gilmour Hall. Yet, even as Kay typed, this interpretation was under revision on the Hamilton campus.

As early as 1981, there were rumblings in MUFA ranks that the days of transparent collegiality at McMaster were over. The savvy but flexible Bourns had retired. So had Mike Hedden, everybody's trusted go-between, who was stricken by an illness that would shortly claim his life. Meanwhile, it was alleged that President Lee was rendering the inherently difficult salary-negotiation process tougher than it needed to be. Faculty association leaders charged that, two years in a row (1981 and 1982), they had accepted lower-than-requested settlements in the face of prophesied deficits, only to find the university in surplus, long after signing off. Worse still, from their point of view, Gilmour Hall had unilaterally assigned those leftover funds to purposes other than salary adjustment, without so much as consulting the joint committee on remuneration.[3] During a tense special meeting of MUFA, on 7 May 1982, Lee tried to explain the necessary caution that had informed his framing of an intentionally pessimistic budget for 1982–83.

Thus, he reminded his 125 intent listeners of Minister Stephenson's deadly earnest threat to place under trusteeship any university that showed more than a 2 per cent deficit. Furthermore, he asked that the association take note of the strenuous lobbying that he, along with other university heads in concert with the CAUT, had conducted in order to persuade Queen's Park to loosen its purse strings. Lee allowed that McMaster's salary determination mechanisms could stand some improvement, and declared that he stood ready to assist the association in such endeavour. He refused, however, to discuss potential retroactive salary adjustments, as the surplus had already been spent on graduate-student stipend increases, improvements to the library, and other items of benefit to the university as a whole. Unmoved, his audience maintained that the surplus had been entirely foreseeable, and that the president was being less than fully collegial. In the end, the salary dispute was referred to the board for adjudication, as prescribed under the 1978 agreement on impasse procedure.[4] Governors found in favour of Lee, but a grim battle had only just begun.

In 1983, skirmishing over pay increases was rendered moot. Government imposed a 5 per cent ceiling on wage hikes in the public sector, under terms of an inflation restraint act. Still, there was plenty of steam generated at MUFA's AGM. Thought, for example, was given to scrapping the joint committee in favour of Toronto's external mediation model. This notion was rejected, but some argued that next year's proceedings should be the last chance for McMaster's joint-committee approach to prove its worth. Meanwhile, association members placed more and more emphasis on refining procedures and gaining early access to full budget information. On the latter score, indignation was formally expressed that, yet again, a forecast deficit had materialized as a significant surplus, the proceeds of which were disbursed without reference to the joint committee. Taking the podium, Lee replied that no offence was intended; no effort had been made deliberately to deceive. "Unusually large uncertainties," he said, demanded conservative budget estimates. Further, he pointed out that there was no reason to refer discussion of the surplus to the remuneration committee, since the legislated 5 per cent maximum had already capped salaries, independently of any preference he might entertain.

By this juncture, however, MUFA was changing tack. Increasingly, members were asking for a greater role in defining the broader financial priorities of the university as part of the annual remuneration process. As Harold Guite put it, the joint committee might be in no position to adjust current salaries, but it could share in the determination of "other things to which it might assign higher priority [than did the administration]."[5] For the moment, everything hung in tense abeyance, so long as the inflation restraint act was in effect. Festivities, reminiscent of those at the "O.K. Corral," were reserved for 1984. The great difference between the Tombstone shootout and the McMaster showdown, however, was that the latter was ultimately informed by a historically deep undercurrent of collegiality: some noisy fusillades notwithstanding.

As Lee recalls, in the spring of 1984, MUFA president-elect, economist Don Dawson, "breezed unannounced into my office, told me of his election, and stated that his top priority for his year as head of the Association was to make sure that I was not appointed to a second term as President of McMaster."[6] This brusque intrusion was Dawson's response to yet another failure of the joint committee to reach salary consensus. Many on campus had expected that, with the expiration of legislative restraints, 1984 negotiations would result in significant pay adjustments. However, in his capacity as chair of the COU, Lee had earlier been present at Queen's Park, when Ontario treasurer Larry Grossman made it menacingly clear that any raises in excess of 5 per cent would still be subject to the most stringent review. Indeed, the minister had flatly threatened "more violent means of control" for those universities exceeding the guideline.

Just what those means might have been was left to the vivid, if morbid, imaginations of his audience. There was, among other dire conjecture, muttering about line-by-line oversight of institutional budgets, such as was common in some jurisdictions outside Ontario. The threat seemed far from fanciful, at least as Lee read the treasurer's mood and body language. Accordingly, he interpreted his own refusal to entertain MUFA requests for remuneration above the "suggested" limit as an evil necessarily embraced, in order to preserve McMaster's autonomy.[7] For their part, some disgruntled MUFA members derided Lee as little more than a government lackey too frequently away from campus to understand the temper of the moment.[8] Throughout that molten spring, the McMaster caldera bubbled toward Pompeian eruption.

A series of MUFA assemblies witnessed a wide range of reactions to the volcanic situation. During one such session, Lee and fellow administrators tried to drive home the reality of Grossman's threat and all that it implied. Les King and Peter George invited the membership to view professorial salary increases as a delicate public-relations issue, when seen against the broader social and economic context of general unease, widespread unemployment, and palpable want. It was, George later recalled, the only time he was ever booed off a stage.[9] Fired by faculty association president David Inman and MUFA representatives on the joint committee, faculty riveted on monetary reward as a symbol of the worth that the university placed on their service. As well, it was argued that Gilmour Hall habitually delayed the transmission of vital budget information. Some expressed resentment that the

Hooker fund was declared off-limits as a source of rewarding excellence in teaching and research.[10] Other parties, trigger fingers itchy, seemed ready simply to slap leather.

On 12 April, at a sparsely attended MUFA AGM, it was moved that the governors be asked to implement a system of binding arbitration as a means of resolving future deadlocks. Upping the ante, another motion called for a vote of no confidence in Lee's ability to make the joint committee function properly. At this point, faculty fissures began to open. Harold Guite, Herb Jenkins, and others objected to both motions on two grounds. The matters, they said, were too serious for the mere eighty-five members on hand to decide. Beyond this, they wished the no-confidence motion reworded so as not to imperil the tenure of a president who, in all other respects, had done stellar work for the university. There were also misgivings about employing an external arbitrator, when university matters were always best decided in-house. The motions were duly tabled for discussion at a better-advertised gathering.[11] Meanwhile, a vigorous campaign to recruit broad faculty support was waged in the pages of the association magazine, *Ta Panta*, and its less formal *Newsletter*.

On Thursday, 25 April, faculty turned out in better numbers for a special meeting to decide the two fateful questions. Again, there was confusing debate over the proper wording and appropriate objectives of the motions. There was no question that members were frustrated and desired change. Far less clear, however, was whether Lee or the joint committee system should be targeted for censure. In the end, although far from unanimously, MUFA voted no confidence in the president, while asking the board to accept binding arbitration, or face certification. The latter was not considered truly desirable. Instead, it was a gambit designed to pressure the board, rather than an outcome positively sought, even by the most militant of members.[12] Still, explosion seemed imminent.

There followed a hot summer of discontent as MUFA and Gilmour Hall exchanged broadsides, some of which left deep and lasting scars on all most directly involved. The board, however, proved its worth as a chamber of sober, second thought. Listening to all parties to the scuffle, it bought precious time for tempers to revert from boil to simmer. Meanwhile, Chairman Douglas "Doug" Marrs drew Lee and Dawson into a series of informal talks. Eventually, all agreed to examine one last option for preserving collegial process. That September, a six-person tripartite committee, with equal representation from the board, administration, and faculty, was struck to consider a new approach to impasse resolution. To the utter amazement of the skeptical many, the outcome was, as David Winch described it, "a massive step forward." In announcing the good news to his constituents, even the feisty Dawson paused to acknowledge that administrative representatives, Deans Peter George and Ron Childs, had been even-handed, reasonable, and open-minded during the talks, as had board members. Indeed, while it might have stuck in his throat, he went on to hail Lee for a "very fair speech in support of the recommendations."[13] Thus, "final offer selection" was born in December 1984: an early Christmas gift to a troubled McMaster community.

Under terms of the swiftly ratified tripartite agreement, two matters, which had long gnawed at the vitals of campus accord, were set to rest. The president's budget advisory committee was redefined to include balanced representation of faculty and Gilmour Hall. Furthermore, MUFA was, henceforth, formally to be consulted on proposed faculty nominees, one of whom would serve as chair of that body. The reconstituted PBAC was to have full access to all financial information and rights of final approval over budgets submitted by the president to the board. All told, the call to share power among partners in a collegial enterprise, first raised in the sixties, was nearer fruition. Whether that would aid or inhibit rational planning (or expedite "tough decisions") remained to be seen.

As for that recurrent rite of spring, salary negotiation, the joint committee processes were retained, but with a dramatically new twist. Henceforth, should all else fail, the last offers of MUFA and the administration would go to an external arbiter, chosen by lot from a pre-agreed list, for final selection. That choice, furthermore, would be binding on all parties, including the board. While a few balked at this arrangement, most agreed with Gerry King, who argued that the process would inevitably drive all participants toward moderate, middle ground. With any luck, and a modicum of goodwill, annual bloodletting would be translated into a more amiable, more predictable exercise.[14] In large measure, King's prognostication proved to be correct.

While these various arrangements were thrashed out, Lee was being assessed for appointment to a second term by a ten-person panel of governors, alumni, faculty, and students. The committee members were acutely aware that due diligence was a high priority at that delicate hour. Accordingly, the process was scrupulously painstaking. Calling for input from all sectors of the university community, the committee received more than sixty, often lengthy, briefs. When all was weighed in the balance, the panel was unanimous in recommending that Lee be invited to accept reappointment. This, in itself, was no small thing. Nearby Toronto, for example, would have no fewer than three different presidents (John Evans, James Ham, and George Connell) over the full span of Lee's decade in office. Furthermore, it should be stressed that the latter's confirmation was not grudgingly bestowed. Instead, Lee was wholeheartedly lauded for his unswerving application to fulfilling numerous goals, even by panelists who vocally criticized his handling of budget disputes.

Thus, the committee cited, with enthusiasm, his successful invigoration of alumni ties, his tireless efforts to increase McMaster's involvement in pivotal regional affairs, and his sterling performance as a fundraiser. Equally, it applauded the president's ongoing effort to reform both orientation and residence policy. In like manner, his support for higher admission standards, innovative undergraduate programs, and general academic quality control won sincere plaudits. Furthermore, Lee was praised for adroit diplomacy in maintaining open channels with student leaders; thereby ensuring that controversial changes did not precipitate unmanageable "causes." This, of course, was exquisitely ironic, in that the committee's sole reservation concerned Lee's alleged inability to forge strong collegial bonds with faculty – his erstwhile peers.

At considerable length, the committee reviewed administrative-faculty relations over the previous four years, and concluded that the president stood in need of some advice. Professorial morale, it noted, had plummeted, during Lee's first term. Some of this, the committee recognized, could be laid at the door of a parsimonious government. However, the panel, also, apportioned responsibility to the ever-peripatetic, widely engaged Lee. "It is easy," said the committee, "for an overworked administration to begin to lose contact with the members of the various constituencies comprising the University." This caveat was a reference to growing complaints about Lee's frequent absences in service to fundraising, or to the many civic, provincial, national, and international bodies of which he was a member. More worrisome, however, was the way in which these absences seemed to detract from his ability to read, understand, and collegially deal with those in McMaster's trenches. In a number of frank discussions, centring specifically on these points, the committee conveyed its very real concern to Lee.

In reply, the president allowed that his off-campus commitments had resulted in his losing effective contact with faculty and staff members. He, also, publicly recognized that times had changed and that older administrative practices had to be re-examined. Satisfied with his sincerity, and understanding that, in any case, the tripartite agreement had established a viable system of checks and balances, the board unanimously endorsed the committee's recommendation that Lee be offered another term.[15] Having listened carefully, and accepting constructive advice, he signed on for five more years. As it happened, they were to be far better years, on balance, for most involved in the McMaster enterprise.

A life-long learner and introspective self-critic, Lee was both singed and edified by the experiences of 1984. In later life, he reflected that his greatest regret was having failed to keep a finger on the pulse of his constituents and adequately to inform them at all times. Indeed, he would point to the example of Peter George, president from 1995 to 2010, who, under the same pressure for off-campus service, always took care to explain the rationale behind his extramural activity, in an endless stream of communiqués to faculty, staff, and students.[16] Still, just as he attended to Sir Edmund Leather's advice concerning the fundamentals of fundraising, so also Lee made efforts to heed the committee's words regarding faculty relations. He certainly got off on the right foot, engineering a grand alliance of all administrative, faculty, staff, and student groups in October 1986, to wage a concerted public campaign for increased government funding and support for research. Faculty Association president Gerry King, for one, was deeply impressed by the high sense of purpose and commitment displayed by all parties to the venture, which contrasted sharply with the mood that prevailed scarcely a year earlier.[17]

Not surprisingly, tensions occasionally resurfaced and opinion concerning Lee's leadership style varied. Even so, a scan MUFA records for 1985–90 reveals nothing like the harsh vituperation than had coloured administrative-faculty dealings during the preceding five years. Given the thinness of hard evidence from the period, it is impossible impartially to decide who had the better case in each of the various spats that cropped up.[18] Nor can or should relative presidential popularity be greatly weighed. Even if such were possible, few would have stood a chance in any contest with Lee's immediate predecessors, given Bourns' folksy charm and Thode's almost monarchical aura. Far more demonstrable and vastly more significant is the point that, many hands contributing, a sense of stability returned, after 1984. Moreover, it did so as the university approached its centennial, well poised to reap the advantages of a change of government and of official mind which greatly facilitated McMaster's most enduring impulse: to, in the spirit of Thode, excel in the realm of research.

For all its flux and ferment, Lee's era witnessed no great shift in core drives that had been familiar in the days of Petch, Duckworth, Preston, and others who had subscribed to Thode's creed since its earliest articulation. While fashions and emphases inevitably came and went, research, scholarship, publication, and standing remained the high road to what Kirkaldy had termed "a chance for greatness." Thus, keeping up with the classes and ahead of the masses was as much a preoccupation of the eighties as it had been when St John first noted "a powerful push at McMaster." Enshrining this ethic, a clause had been inserted into "The Document," in 1977, to the effect that no candidate would be promoted to the rank of associate professor in the absence of refereed scholarly work, albeit much to the chagrin of some, including the well-published David Winch.[19] Meanwhile, for his part, Lee never missed an opportunity to differentiate McMaster from the common herd by reason of its research-intensive tradition. In short, despite all the anxieties of the decade, the university clung to and polished its accustomed self-image.

In 1983, relatively small McMaster stood fifth among the nation's universities, in terms of total research funding received, and much closer to the top on a per capita basis. On campus, traditionally well-supported areas continued to thrive. Thus, the MNR and accelerator were still employed by various groups, from physics and chemistry to medicine and materials science. They were, however, no longer the brightest stars in McMaster's galaxy. Increasingly, pride of place was falling to medicine. Indeed, health science became the university's top grant-earner by a considerable margin and has remained so, ever since. Along with five major, ongoing programs, each with several strings to its bow, the faculty housed numerous independent or small-group projects. A new positron emission tomography scanner was the first on a Canadian campus, and greatly enhanced cutting-edge work in neuroscience. Equally, McMaster was earning particular renown as a centre for neonatal and cardiac inquiry. Meanwhile, clinical epidemiology and biostatistics, which had been scoffed at, had now become the global focal point for a series of worldwide, randomized studies that helped advance the proper treatment for strokes. In this capacity, it coordinated endeavour throughout North America, Europe, and Japan that did much to debunk antiquated myths and promote more effective measures of intervention and rehabilitation.

To mention these specific undertakings, moreover, is to touch only on a few cogs in a mushrooming research machine which, by 1985, was bringing more than $25 million in grants (and attendant prestige) to the university. At mid-decade, although medium in absolute size, McMaster's faculty ranked fifth in external research funding among medical schools in Canada.[20] Meanwhile, if publicity counted for anything, it was surely a stellar boon when McMaster neuroscientist Dr Roberta Bondar was selected by NASA to be Canada's first female astronaut. While a glamorous leading lady, however, health science was not the university's only star ascendant. Engineering, for example, had a brilliant turn or two upon the stage, too.

Indeed, the house that Hodgins built was bustling. Apart from a wide range of individual projects, it was home to four major research institutes. The IMR continued its pace-setting work on solids, contributing, for example, to the development of ceramic heat shields for the space shuttle.[21] After 1986, a $200,000 grant from the Department of National Defence kept ceramicists occupied in developing improved, lightweight armour for infantry, tanks, and other military uses. Meanwhile, they continued to break new ground in civilian applications of their science to industrial and communications purposes.[22] On the international front, in company with President Lee, Gary Purdy was abroad advising Chinese steel manufacturers, as the country began its painful recovery from Mao's Cultural Revolution.[23] For its part, the CRL was hopping, with major projects in radar, digital, and satellite innovation. One of its many undertakings entailed nationally vital work concerning Arctic search and rescue. While already healthy, the CRL received a significant booster shot, in 1985, in the form of a $500,000 injection from NSERC.[24] Adding to the overall faculty bustle, a large 1982 strategic grant assisted the launch of engineering's Institute of Polymer Research. At the same time, the recently founded energy institute was probing reactor systems and solar power, as well as improvements to conventional carbon-based fuels.[25] It was a busy time. Still, there was no arrow-straight path to hope and glory for all concerned.

Thus, the Centre for Applied Research and Engineering Design (CARED, pronounced "Care-Ed") was falling on hard times. Launched by Hodgins as a form of community outreach and contract research, it had done reasonably well matching faculty expertise with local industrial needs, during the seventies. Hard times and confusion of purpose, however, led to its decline in the next decade. Even more precipitous was the fall of the Canadian Institute of Metalworking (CIM). Forged along lines similar to CARED, it suffered a similar fate, ending life as a humble shed on Ancaster's fairgrounds, several million dollars in debt.[26] These resounding flops aside, engineering remained a prime magnet for research income and eager students, enough so that Queen's Park saw fit to contribute $8.4 million, or two-thirds the capital cost, toward enlarging its facilities, in 1987.[27] Though taking longer to mature than first imagined, the 1957 vision of a vibrant, scholarly engineering faculty was established fact by the late eighties. Meanwhile, across the Mall, research in the arts displayed a new aggressiveness.

Amid the social sciences, the Judaism and Christianity project, centred in religious studies, had yielded several notable publications by 1983. At the same moment, Project TASO (Technology Assessment for Sub-Arctic Ontario) brought together McMaster economists, anthropologists, sociologists, and scientists in a joint, long-term study of the ramifications of hydroelectric development in the Moose River basin. Backed by $500,000 from SSHRC, the team investigated the social, economic, and environmental impact of that massive enterprise in power generation. Closer to home, social scientists co-operated with Hamilton's chapter of the Kiwanis Club in a systematic study of decaying urban housing.[28]

In humanistic quarters, the most high-profile undertaking was the Russell Project. Funded to the tune of $1.8 million by SSHRC, this fifteen-year venture was intended to produce an estimated twenty-eight volume, fully annotated edition of *The Collected Papers of Bertrand Russell*. An editorial board, which included scholars from English, history, and philosophy, was slow to get off the ground. No one had been appointed editor-in-chief. The result was an oft-times endless round of angels dancing on pinheads, during debates over the very finest of fine points. A more satisfactory and productive arrangement was not devised until the late eighties.[29] On the broader scene, in keeping with the nature of the disciplines, much of the stepped-up research in humanities and social science was individually pursued and too diverse to be catalogued here. The central point is that, recession or no, McMaster research remained at a high pitch, even in the darkest hours of the early decade. In this connection, moreover, 1985 would see a turning point for the very much better.

In October 1985, David Peterson's Liberal Party won a convincing electoral victory at Ontario polls. After a string of shaky Conservative minority governments, the simple prospect of near-range stability at Queen's Park raised popular spirits. For university leaders, the transition was a particularly welcome one. Like his penultimate Tory predecessor, Bill Davis, Peterson was a vocal friend of higher education. Better yet, in contrast to Davis' last years, he held a majority in the legislature and need not walk on eggshells. Convinced of the cardinal role of research and development for the province's economic recovery, he was open to suggestions. Alvin Lee, as it happened, had just such a proposal in mind. Painting it in broad strokes for colleagues at COU, he soon found himself delegated, with engineer Lynn Watt of Waterloo, to draw up a more formal plan.

The outcome was an ambitious project to found various centres of excellence that would combine and coordinate the cumulative research power of leading Ontario universities, with an emphasis on direct application to the economic and social challenges confronting the province. Given COU's imprimatur, Lee was tasked with presenting this blockbuster notion to the premier's council. Reasonably confident of success, he was treated to a warmer reception than anticipated. Peterson was in – and with considerably more than spare pocket change.[30] Indeed, the 1986 speech from the throne featured the mention of a $1-billion technology fund. By March 1987, $200 million was earmarked for the centres of excellence to encourage joint research and technology transfer. These centres were not conceived as places but as consortia among those best suited to carry out focused tasks. The scramble for pieces of the action was immediate.

Quick off the mark, McMaster submitted its bid for a role in materials research, telecommunications, integrated manufacturing, protein engineering, and mineral exploration. There was even a long-shot nod toward the arts, when the university proposed a centre for natural-language computing.[31] Like Thode before him, Lee refused to think of McMaster as a small or bashful institution. A realist, however, he was delighted when the university was designated as a major player in three of the seven centres identified by the province: materials research, integrated manufacturing, and telecommunications. Among other things, this paved the way for a new ceramics processing laboratory, up-to-date equipment for optoelectric and polymer studies, and the hiring of a number of badly needed junior faculty members.[32] For some, this bounty was cause to rejoice; others, however, harboured misgivings.

As early as May 1986, Peter George informed the senate that a number of Ontario academics were gravely concerned about the potential steering effects of government largesse. There was worry, he noted, that Queen's Park was looking only to the short term and expecting immediate, practical payoffs. Furthermore, nothing was said about the needs of existing nodes of concentrated research endeavour. Broader perspective, he said, was in order.[33] By November 1987, the senate was urged to study, very closely, the implications of participation in the centres as they bore upon the whole sweep and balance of university activity, from programming to hiring, and from promotion criteria to undergraduate teaching. Lee and King assured the chamber that the new scheme would be compatible with McMaster's emphasis on basic research. They agreed, however, that BSCAP should scrutinize the arrangements carefully to avoid undue skewing toward the applied side. The senate voted to go ahead with the study, which is hardly surprising, given that the same meeting witnessed the deletion of a large number of courses in humanities and social science for want of teaching resources.[34] To the frustrated dean of humanities, David Gagan, the centres represented little more than confirmation of the "branding" he found in the pages of the *Plan for McMaster*.[35] On that point, at least, Lee was in full agreement. The centres, he noted, were wholly in line with McMaster's tradition of concentrating energy on "areas of existing strength."[36]

Despite another bad-news general operating budget, the mood on campus was infectiously upbeat, as McMaster paused to mark its centennial in 1987. Celebrations were orchestrated by a small group, with the ferociously energetic Dr John Weaver in the chair. Unfortunately, colourful banners, hung from light posts, lintels, and other places, had to be taken down, in the face of rampant vandalism.[37] Little else, however, went awry. More than sixty special events, great and small, were staged. Three special publications were lovingly produced: one documenting McMaster's art treasures, another examining the university's long relationship with the Steel City, and a third chronicling a century of student life. In a similar vein, twenty-two conferences, hosted by individual departments and research groups, provided a hefty dose of academic gravitas and infectious good cheer to the year's proceedings. Among these gatherings, the most luminous by far was the meeting of Canada's sundry learned societies, under co-operatively brilliant (sometimes blazingly hot) weather conditions. Meanwhile, the 1987 edition of, hitherto, often lightly attended Homecoming set an all-time record, drawing hundreds of graduates to campus.[38] Months later, a lone visitor, historian William Morley Kilbourn, took a moment to reflect on McMaster, as he found it, after several years' absence.

Writing for *Saturday Night*, Kilbourn took note both of change and continuity on the Hamilton campus, since his departure for Toronto's York University, in the early sixties. Two stunning additions captured his undisguised approval immediately. Thus, he rhapsodized about the rapid rise to prominence of Mills Memorial Library as a centre of research collections, second only to those of the University of Toronto. Russell, of course, held centre stage in that regard, but depth, he wrote, was provided by rich holdings in Canadian and eighteenth-century literary treasures beyond count. On this score, he might have paused to acknowledge Alvin Lee's efforts. Throughout the hungry eighties, the president had laboured hard to ensure that the library acquisitions budget had received every penny that the university could reasonably afford. Kilbourn, of course, was in no position to know this. Instead, he riveted attention on another new feature that inescapably caught his eye: the medical school.

Diplomatically, he offered no comment on the architecture of Zeidler's palace, but he waxed eloquent about the daring vision it embodied. During his own day, Kilbourn recalled, engineering, religious studies, and psychology were already making their stamp. Still, in his eyes, McMaster medicine, with its problem-based learning, was the university's "crowning achievement." Looking more closely, he had high praise for innovative programming in music criticism, the sparkling arts and science degree, and other evidence of cogent planning linked to abundant energy. Putting all into perspective, he observed, "Such signs of life stand in bold relief against the general malaise of today's universities."

No starry-eyed romantic or academic dilettante, Kilbourn was savvy enough to see that McMaster faced and suffered from many of the same problems that plagued all universities of the era: underfunding, crowding, and sometimes poorly prepared high-school drafts. Nor did he argue that every quarter of the university was as polished and well-stocked as one might wish. Still, he sensed a mood, a culture, a spirit of "curiosity, energy, and commitment in several areas at McMaster" that he had rarely seen elsewhere. What, he asked as an outsider looking in, had generated this unusual ethos? In part, he thought, an answer could be found in the university's distant past. Baptists, he opined, were rebels by nature and unafraid to embrace free enquiry, whether in science or theology. Still, as he reminisced, McMaster was a place of "plain living and good learning," when he came on staff in 1951 – a solid, comfortable college, but with no outsized ambitions. It was Harry Thode, he contended, who, more than anyone or anything, changed all that. Visiting that living icon, still in his office near the reactor, Kilbourn described the ageing Thode as a study in "Canadian gothic": lean, square, and direct, just as he had been in his prime. "Harry Thode," he ventured, "was probably the last important university president in Canada to inherit a position of great personal power and scope – and use it."[39]

To Kilbourn's thoughts, the historian might add that, great as Thode's contributions were in setting a tone and defining a sense of purpose for McMaster, one should not overlook the vital fact of continuity in leadership. From 1957 to 1987, all the presidents (save Gilmour), vice-presidents, and graduate deans were groomed in the ethos that Thode cultivated. Each, as objective circumstance or personal proclivity dictated, tinkered with the research-intensive paradigm he described; one ray the more, one shade the less. None, however, seriously questioned its core propositions. Indeed, Alvin Lee was surely correct when, in February 1987, he noted that thirty years earlier some pivotal planning decisions were made and, then, adaptively adhered to. To the casual eye, many still seem operative today. Whether this was for good or ill depends solely on the perspective of the viewer. That a Thodean ethos pervaded McMaster during the period under review, however, seems less open to dispute.

Notes

INTRODUCTION

1 Kirkaldy, *Report on Government*, 15.

CHAPTER ONE

1 George Gilmour, "Last in Ontario to Sever Links," *Silhouette*, 21 September 1956, 1–3.
2 "Keep It Small," *Silhouette*, 28 September 1956, 2.
3 Gordon Vichert, "Another 'Nay,'" *Silhouette*, 5 October, 1956, 2.
4 Gilmour, *President's Report,* 1959–60, 2.
5 Macleod, *All True Things*, 189.
6 Norrie, Owram, and Emery, *Canadian Economy*, 377–87; Owram, *Born at the Right Time*, 3–31; Axelrod, *Scholars*, 14–33.
7 Norrie, Owram, and Emery, *Canadian Economy*, 377.
8 Dear, Drake, and Reeds, *Steel City*, 202.
9 Francis, Jones, and Smith, *Destinies*, 358.
10 Gilmour, *President's Report*, 1958–9, 13.
11 "Increase to Date," *Spectator*, 17 August 1942.
12 "City Growth," *Spectator*, 22 May 1959.
13 "City Moves Up," *Spectator*, 16 September 1961.
14 "Metro Hamilton 740,000 in 1985," *Spectator*, 18 March 1962.
15 Sheffield, et al., *Systems*, 12.
16 Ibid., 6.
17 Gilmour, *President's Report*, 1957–8, 1.
18 Ibid., *1959–60*, 3.
19 "Education, Careers Sought for Children," *Spectator*, 18 July 1961.

20 Gilmour, *President's Report*, 1959–60, 3.

21 "Where Ignorant Armies," *Silhouette*, 31 January 1958, 2.

22 J.B. St. John, "Universities Race against Father Time." *Silhouette*, 14 February 1958, 2–3.

23 Ibid.; see also Johnston, *Radical Campus*, 17.

24 Don Stratton, "Aim Is for More Grads," *Silhouette*, 14 February 1958, 4.

25 Norrie, Owram, and Emery, *Canadian Economy*, 380; Monahan, *Collective Autonomy*, 5.

26 Monahan, *Collective Autonomy*, 17.

27 Gilmour, Comment on the budget, 12 April 1957, McP, box 61.

28 Gilmour to the Trustees of the RBG, 28 October 1957, McP, box 61.

29 Gilmour to Dana Porter, treasurer of Ontario, 31 October 1957, McP, box 61.

30 Gilmour to George Gathercole, 18 November 1959, McP, box 82.

31 Gilmour to James Allen, treasurer of Ontario, 18 November 1959, McP, box 82.

32 Gilmour, *Review and Prospects on McMaster's Fund Raising Program*, 6 August 1957, McP, box 75.

33 Gilmour to Board of Governors, 10 June 1960, McP, box 32.

34 Gilmour to Board of Governors, 4 April 1960. McP, box 32.

35 Gilmour, *President's Report*, 1960–1, 5.

36 Ibid., 1959–60, 1.

37 Neatby and McEown, *Carleton*, 114; Horn, *York*, 19.

38 Duckworth, *One Version*, 14.

39 Friedland, *University of Toronto*, passim.

40 Kerr, *Uses of a University*, 1.

41 Monahan, *Collective Autonomy*, 20.

42 For a fuller understanding of this concatenation of steering forces (1955–65) see Monahan, *Collective Autonomy*, 15–38; Owram, *Born at the Right Time*, 180–1; Axelrod, *Scholars Dollars*, 22–34.

43 Johnston, *McMaster*, vol. 2, 240.

44 Gilmour to W.E. Gwatkin, 4 October 1960, McP, box 53.

45 Gilmour, *President's Report*, 1957–8, 5.

46 Gilmour to Gerald S. Graham, 14 October 1960, McP, box 53.

47 Gilmour to Roland Bainton, 18 January 1961, McP, box 53.

48 Gilmour, *President's Report*, 1959–60, 10.

49 Johnston, *McMaster*, vol. 2, 265–6.

50 *Spectator*, 12 April 1957.

51 Gilmour, *President's Report*, 1956–7, 3.

52 Gilmour to Porter, treasurer of Ontario, 31 October 1957, McP, box 81.

53 Zack, Martin, and Lee, *Thode*, iii.

54 Thode to R.B. Bradley, 15 May 1961, McP, box 54.

55 Johnston, *McMaster*, vol. 2, 63–4; Zack, Martin, and Lee, *Thode*, 1–82.

56 Zack, Martin, and Lee, *Thode*, chapter 2.

57 Banaschewski, interview with author, August 2011.

58 Zack, Martin, and Lee, *Thode*, 119.

59 Bates to Thode, 20 April 1961, McP, box 54.

60 Zack, Martin, and Lee, *Thode*, 79.

61 The closest thing to a full statement of these views can be found in his "President's Comments," Thode, *President's Report*, 1962–3, 5–12.

62 Monahan, *Collective Autonomy*, 1–17.

63 Bissell to Thode, 13 December 1962, McP, box 68.

64 Thode, *President's Report*, 1961–2, 1.

65 Ibid., 1962–3, 9–10.

66 Thode to W.G. Schneider, 18 February 1963, McP, box 37.

67 J.S. Kirkaldy, in Jackson, MUFA's *First 50 Years*, 31.

68 Thode to J.R. McCarthy, 18 January, 1963, McP, box 81.

69 Thode to W.G. Schneider, 18 February 1963, McP, box 37.

70 For a full run of Thode's budget submissions, see McP, boxes 81–2.

71 Budget Submission for fiscal 1965–6, November 1964, McP, box 81.

72 Ibid., December 1966, McP box 82.

73 Gilmour to John P. Robarts, minister of education, 15 November 1960, McP, box 81.

74 Harry Duckworth to Thode, 13 October 1964, McP, box 19.

75 Thode, *President's Report*, 1963–4, vi–x; *1965–6*, vii.

76 Thode to J.R. McCarthy, 18 January 1963, McP, box 81.

77 Thode to Wm. Davis, November 1963, McP, box 81.

78 Mel Preston to Thode, 24 August 1966, McP, box 20.

79 Carey Fox to Thode, 3 January 1963, McP, box 73.

80 Thode to Bill Warrender, 1 June 1962, McP, box 55.

81 Thode, *President's Report*, 1962–3, 5.

82 Preston, *Graduate Studies Report to the President*, 1970, McP, box 23. Preston voiced similar views in earlier reports. See boxes 20–1.

83 "An Interview with the President," *Silhouette*, 16 October 1970, 7.

84 Thode, *President's Report*, 1962–3, 10.

85 Howard Petch to G.E. Hall, president of the University of Western Ontario, 9 March 1966, McP, box 66.

86 Thode, *President's Report*, 1962–3, 11.

87 Thode to Wm. Schneider, 18 February 1963, McP, box 37.

88 Thode, *President's Report*, 1962–3, 11; Petch to Hall, 9 March 1966 McP, box 66.

89   Thode, *President's Report*, 1962–3, 12.

CHAPTER TWO

1   J.B. St. John, "A Powerful Push at McMaster," *Globe and Mail*, 24 June 1964.
2   Johnston, *McMaster*, vol. 2, 258–9.
3   Thode, *President's Report*, 1963–4, 12.
4   Clark, *Growth and Governance*, 28–30.
5   Ibid., 30–46.
6   For examples, see Neatby and McEown, *Creating Carleton*, 151; and Friedland, *University of Toronto*, 479.
7   Kirkaldy, Morrison, and Brown, *Howard Petch Compendium*, unpaginated.
8   Bayley, *Biology at McMaster University*, 6.
9   Mel Preston, interview by author, August 2010.
10   Duckworth, *One Version*, 5.
11   L. King, interview with G. Purdy and R. Rempel 2008, 2.
12   Arthur Bourns, interview by M. Preston and G. Purdy, transcript, 22 April 2009, 10.
13   Melvin Preston, interview by G. Pedersen, transcript, August 2010, 2.
14   B. Banaschewski, interview by author, 28 July 2011.
15   J.S. Kirkaldy interview by author and C.M. Johnston, 9 December 2009.
16   Duckworth, *One Version*, 146; Schwarcz, "Harry Thode" (typescript of a paper delivered at a symposium marking the hundredth anniversary of Thode's birth, McMaster, Hamilton, ON, September 2010). ·
17   M. Johns interview by M. Zack, transcript, 2 October 1995, 15–16.
18   Duckworth, *One Version*, 146.
19   Johns, "Talk on Harry Thode" (typescript copy courtesy of Helen Howard-Lock, Alumni Day, McMaster, Hamilton, ON, 1983), 8.
20   Preston and Howard-Lock, "Emergence of Physics," 160.
21   Bourns interview, 14.
22   Duckworth, *One Version*, 120.
23   Fox to Gilmour, 29 May 1959, McP, box73.
24   Thode, "A Nuclear Reactor Program," copy courtesy of M.A. Preston, 3 November 1955.
25   Johns, "Talk on Harry Thode," 8.
26   Duckworth, *One Version*, 147.
27   "$500,000 Error: Girls in Trouble," *Silhouette*, 28 February 1958, 1.
28   Duckworth, *One Version*, 147.

29 Howard-Lock, "50th Anniversary of Nuclear Work at McMaster," 5, typescript in Thode Papers, box 6.

30 Nuclear Group, interview by author, transcript, 28 February 2011, 6.

31 Gilmour to F.A. Sherman, 3 December 1957, McP, box 32.

32 Sherman to Gilmour, 21 December 1959, McP, box 32.

33 Fox to Gilmour, 29 May 1959, McP, box 73.

34 Gilmour, "Prime Minister Opens Reactor," *McMaster Alumni News*, 22 June 1959.

35 Committee members are listed in a document dated 27 April 1959, McP, box 73.

36 Petch, report of the director of research: 1961–2, McP, box 18.

37 Thode to J.B. Marshall, 16 November 1965, Thode Papers, box 2.

38 Nuclear Group interview, 18–19.

39 T. Kennett, email message to author, 19 August 2010.

40 Howard-Lock, "50th Anniversary," 5.

41 Preston interview by Gary Haarding-Pedersen, 2011.

42 Howard Petch, DVD Message on the Fortieth Anniversary of the IMR, Summer 2007, in *Petch Compendium*.

43 Crowe, et al., *Chemical Engineering*, 1.

44 Shemilt, "Engineering at McMaster," in Disher and Smith, *By Design*, 176.

45 "Kellock Confers First Engineering Degree," *Silhouette*, 30 October 1959, 2.

46 Gilmour, *President's Report*, 1956–7, 10.

47 "New Engineering Degree at Mac," *Globe and Mail*, 6 September 1957, 22.

48 Thode, untitled, press release, September 1959, McP, box 36.

49 Hodgins to Thode, 4 August 1964, McP., box 19.

50 Gilmour, *President's Report*, 1956–7, 72.

51 Gilmour to W.J. Dunlop, 2 December 1959, McP, box 81.

52 Kirkaldy to Thode, 24 May 1963, McP, box 18.

53 Thode to Duckworth, 9 January 1959, McP, box 36.

54 Petch, DVD.

55 Gilmour to C.W. Hale and W.N. Paterson, 11 April 1960, McP, box 61.

56 Purdy, *Report to the President*, 1967–8, McP, box 12.

57 Kirkaldy to Thode, 24 May 1963, McP, box 18.

58 Purdy, *Report to the President*, 1967–8. McP, box 12.

59 Ward to Thode, 29 May 1964, McP, box 19.

60 Thode, *President's Report*, 1962–3, 11.

61 Petch, "An Interdisciplinary Materials Research Laboratory for McMaster University," brief, January 1963, McP, box 37.

62   B.G. Ballard (NRC) to Thode, 25 February 1963; chairman of the Defence
      Research Board to Thode, 22 February 1963; Thode to C.F. Yost (director of
      ARPA), 21 January 1963; Thode to F. Sherman (Dofasco), 31 January 1963;
      Thode to V.W. Scully (Stelco), 31 January 1963, McP, box 37.
63   Thode to G. Ballard (acting-president, NRC), 21 January 1963, McP, box 37.
64   Thode, *President's Report*, 1964–5, 11.
65   *Bulletin, McMaster University News*, 14 March 1967, McP, box 37.
66   "Summary of Report of the NRC Review Committee on Support of Materi-
      als Research Centres through Negotiated Development Grants," January/
      February 1969, McP, box 37.
67   Thode to members of the Materials Research Unit, 7 July 1967, McP, box 37.
68   Johns to Thode, 30 June 1967, McP, box 37.
69   Bourns interview by M.A. Preston and G. Purdy, transcript, 38.
70   See interviews of Bourns, Kirkaldy, and Preston.
71   Petch, *Report to the President*, 1964–5, McP, box 19.
72   Kirkaldy, preface to *Howard Petch Compendium*, 1.
73   Hedden to Thode, 30 June 1967, McP, box 37.
74   Preston to Thode, 13 May 1969, McP, box 37.
75   Thode, *President's Report*, 1967–8, 195.
76   Crowe et al., *Chemical Engineering*, 8–9.
77   "Pollution Grant," press release, 30 December 1969, McP, box 36.
78   Oravas to Thode, 6 June 1968, McP, box 12.
79   Hodgins to Thode, 4 August 1964, McP, box 19.
80   Hodgins to Thode, 12 July 1963, McP, box 18.
81   To be specific, there were 423 undergraduates and 109 graduate students on
      the roll in 1967–8. Thode, *President's Report*, 1967–8, 195.
82   Hodgins, *Annual Report to the President*, 1967–8, McP, box 12.
83   Ibid.
84   Hodgins, *Annual Report to the President*, 1968–9, McP, box 22.
85   Shemilt, "Engineering at McMaster," 177.

CHAPTER THREE

1   Gilmour, *President's Report*, 1959–60, 53. Fourteen of the 135 graduates
     were "Class-B" candidates whose affiliations are not listed. Eighty-seven of
     121 are identified as science graduate students.
2   Ibid., 1967–8, 194. The figure is 406 out of 779 full-time graduate students.
3   For a good overview, see Monahan, *Collective Autonomy*, 36–8. For greater
     detail, see *A Formula for Operating Grants to Provincially Assisted Univer-
     sities in Ontario*, a report of the Subcommittee on Finance of the Committee

on University Affairs, (copy) D.T. Wright to Bourns, 25 July 1966, McP, box
82.

4   Duckworth, *One Version*, 163.
5   Thode, *President's Report*, 1962–3, 51.
6   D.M. Shaw to Thode, 31 May 1966, McP, box 20.
7   For a list, see Thode, *President's Report*, 1967–8, 168–71.
8   B.J. Burley to Thode, 10 June 1969, McP, box 21.
9   Gilmour, *President's Report*, 1956–7, 13; 67.
10 King, *Spectroscopy*, 1964.
11 Bourns, interview, 44.
12 Gillespie to Thode, *Report of the Department of Chemistry*, 1960–1, McP,
box 18.
13 Thode, *President's Report*, 1964–5, 10; 1965–6, 17.
14 Ibid., 1962–3, 57–8.
15 Gillespie to Thode, *Report of the Department of Chemistry*, 1962–3, McP,
box 18.
16 See, for example, Thode, *President's Report*, 1964–5, 77–82; and ibid.,
1967–8, 157–64.
17 Minutes of the Department of Chemistry, 10 April 1963. Currently, I hold
these ring-bound notes. They will be deposited with the McMaster Archives
upon completion of the book.
18 Ibid., 14 February 1964.
19 Ibid., 31 January 1964.
20 Gillespie, *Report of the Department of Chemistry*, 1965–6, McP, box 20.
21 Minutes of the Department of Chemistry, May 1966 and 4 July 1967, McP,
box 20.
22 Gillespie, *Report of Department of Chemistry*, 1969–70, McP, box 22.
23 Minutes of the Department of Chemistry, 23 October 1964.
24 Graham to Thode, 6 August 1964, McP, box 19.
25 Gillespie, *Report of the Department of Chemistry*, 1965–6, McP, box 20.
26 Minutes of the President's Council, 25 August 1967, McP, box 22.
27 Minutes of the Department of Chemistry, 20 September 1968.
28 Ibid, 10 December and 13 December 1968.
29 Ibid, 10 October 1974.
30 Gillespie, *Report of the Department of Chemistry*, August 1969, McP, box
21.
31 Ibid. In 1969, out of ninety-eight graduate students, seventy were Canadian.
32 Ibid.
33 Minutes of the Department of Physics, 2 December 1965.
34 Duckworth, *One Version*, 121.

35   Duckworth to Thode, 12 July 1961, McP, box 18.

36   Ibid, McP, box 19.

37   Minutes of the Department of Physics, 3 April 1963.

38   Ibid, 10 September 1963.

39   Duckworth, *One Version*, 132.

40   Martin Johns, interview by M. Zack, transcript, 2 October 1995, 19–20.

41   Minutes of the Department of Physics, 7 December 1962.

42   Duckworth to Thode, 12 July 1961, McP, box 18.

43   Preston to Thode, 30 June 1963, McP, box 18.

44   Preston to Thode, *Annual Report of Applied Mathematics*, 1966–7, McP, box 20.

45   Duckworth, "A Program for Nuclear Science at McMaster," May 1963, McP, box 36.

46   Minutes of the Department of Physics, 8 September 1966.

47   Johns, *Report of the Department of Physics*, 1966–7, McP, box 20.

48   Ibid., 1967–68, McP, box 21.

49   Minutes of the Department of Physics, 16 June 1970.

50   Ibid., 25 October 1963.

51   Johns, *Report of the Department of Physics*, 1966–7, McP, box 20.

52   Minutes of the Department of Physics, 19 December 1967.

53   Ibid., 27 October 1966; 16 April 1968.

54   Ibid., 25 September 1969.

55   Ibid., 16 April 1968.

56   Ibid., 6 September 1968.

57   Ibid., 11 February 1970.

58   Ibid., 16 June 1970.

59   Thode, *President's Report*, 1967–8, 18; 25–6.

60   Bourns to Thode, 31 October 1969, McP, box 22.

61   A copy of the final report can be found in McP, box 82.

62   Thode, "Statement on Provincial Grants," *McMaster University News*, 13 March 1968, copy in McP, box 82.

63   Bernard Trotter to the Presidents of Ontario Universities, 2 August 1966, McP, box 82.

64   Axelrod, *Scholars and Dollars*, 96; 145–6.

65   Monahan, *Collective Autonomy*, 59.

66   Wm. Davis to Thode, 4 March 1969, McP, box 84.

67   Bourns to Thode, 31 October 1969, McP, box 22.

68   Axelrod, *Scholars and Dollars*, 96–8.

69   For details on the commission, see Monahan, *Collective Autonomy*, 28–34.

70   Bourns to Thode, 31 October 1969, McP, box 22.

71   Newbigging, "Psychology at McMaster," in Wright and Myers, *History of Academic Psychology*, 135.

72   Gilmour, *President's Report*, 1957–8, 10.

73   Newbigging to Thode, McP, box 18.

74   Newbigging to Thode, 10 February 1962, McP, box 33.

75   Thode to all faculty, 11 May 1962, McP, box 33.

76   Newbigging, "Psychology at McMaster," 135.

77   For a sample of psychology's productivity, see Thode, *President's Report*, 1966–7, 136–7.

78   Newbigging, *Report of the Department of Psychology*, 1965–6, McP, box 20.

79   Ibid., 30 June 1967.

80   Ibid.

81   Newbigging, "Psychology at McMaster," 135.

82   Newbigging, *Report of the Department of Psychology*, 1965–6, McP, box 20.

83   Newbigging, "Psychology at McMaster," 139.

84   Newbigging, *Report of the Department of Psychology*, 30 June 1967, McP, box 20.

85   Thode, *President's Report*, 1967–8, 25

86   For a detailed history of the department, see Bayley, *Biology at McMaster University*, passim.

87   Gilmour, *President's Report*, 1960–1, 4.

88   Ibid., 1956–7, 65–6.

89   Radforth to Thode, 3 June 1963, McP, box 18.

90   Bayley, *Biology at McMaster University*, 59–60.

91   Gilmour, *President's Report*, 1960–1, 18.

92   Ibid., 60.

93   Threlkeld to Thode, 12 October 1961, McP, box 35.

94   Thode and Fox to the minister of university affairs, 4 November 1964, McP, box 81.

95   Gilmour, *President's Report*, 1960–1, 22–5.

96   Thode, *President's Report*, 1961–2, 48.

97   Radforth to Thode, 23 May 1964, McP, box 35.

98   Bayley, *Biology at McMaster University*, 73.

99   Ibid., 58.

100 Radforth to Thode, 31 May 1966, McP, box 20.

101 Bayley to Thode, 17 June 1968, McP, box 21.

102 Thode, *President's Report*, 1967–8, 195.

103 Burghardt, *Geography*, 5.

104 Ibid., 8–10.

105 Leslie King, interview by G. Purdy and R. Rempel, transcript, 2008, 2.

106   Harold Wood, brief submitted to the president, McP box 32.

107   Wood, *Report to the President*, 1963–4, McP, box 19.

108   Burghardt, *Geography*, 16–17.

109   Wood, *Report to the President*, 1963–4, McP, box 19.

110   Gentilcore, *Report to the President*, 1964–5, McP, box 19.

111   Burghardt, *Geography*, 18.

112   Minutes of University Council, 22 March 1966, McP, box 32.

113   Samuel Lanfranco to Thode, 3 February 1969, McP, box 32.

114   The story of Hannell's troubled leadership is well told by Burghardt in *Geography*, 18–23; and in King, interview, 2.

115   Bourns to Thode, 31 October 1969, McP, box 22.

CHAPTER FOUR

1   Minutes of the Vice-President's Advisory Committee, 10 June 1960, McP, box 24.

2   Duckworth, *One Version*, 165.

3   Ibid., 163.

4   Gilmour, *President's Report*, 1960–1, 57.

5   Thode, *President's Report*, 1961–2, 36.

6   Ibid., 1962–3, 37.

7   Gilmour, *President's Report*, 1959–60, 30; 1960–1, 37; 1961–2, 44.

8   Armstrong to Thode, *Annual Report of the Dean of Arts and Science*, 1961–2, McP, box 18.

9   Thode, *President's Report*, 1962–3, 77.

10   Ibid., 1967–8, 194.

11   Gilmour to Bissell, 18 November 1960, McP, box 16.

12   Gilmour, *President's Report*, 1960–1, 7.

13   Thode, *President's Report*, 1961–2, 71–3.

14   Ibid., 1965–6, 130–4.

15   Gilmour, *President's Report*, 1956–7, 5.

16   Salmon to Thode, 30 June 1963, McP, box 18.

17   McIvor to Thode, 16 June 1964, McP, box 19.

18   Thode, *President's Report*, 1961–2, 37.

19   Fox to Gilmour, 12 May 1958, McP, box 73.

20   Gilmour, memorandum to the Executive Committee of the Board of Governors, 10 July 1958, McP, box 61.

21   Gilmour to Hale, 13 July 1960, McP, box 73.

22   Gilmour to Fox, 3 January 1961, McP, box 72.

23   Thode, *President's Report*, 1962–3, 50.

24 Ibid., 1960–1, 43–4.

25 Newbigging, "Psychology at McMaster," 135.

26 Cragg to Thode, 28 April 1961, McP, box 54.

27 "Thode Gives Challenge in Inaugural Address," *Silhouette*, 3 November 1961, 1.

28 Gilmour, *President's Report*, 1960–1, 49.

29 Salmon, *Report to the President*, 1960–1, McP box 18.

30 This pressure was noted in the department's PhD proposal of 1962. See, History Department File, McP, box 30.

31 Thode, *President's Report*, 1961–2, 54.

32 Salmon to Thode, 15 July 1964, McP, box 19.

33 PhD proposal, Department of History, 1962, McP, box 30.

34 Thode, *President's Report*, 1961–2, 54.

35 This point was clarified by M.A. Preston at a senate meeting. See, Minutes of Senate, 19 May 1967, 99. These minutes are held in the university archives in microfilm copies and bound form.

36 PhD proposal, Department of History, 1962, McP, box 30.

37 McCready to Thode, 28 May 1964, McP, box 19.

38 French to Thode, 31 May 1966, McP, box 20.

39 Minutes of the Department of History, 23 May 1966.

40 French to Thode, 31 May 1968, McP, box 21.

41 Thode, *President's Report*, 1962–3, 36.

42 Ibid., 1961–2, 52.

43 For a complete list of department staff, see ibid., 1962–3, 63–4.

44 Ibid., 1962–3, 36.

45 Ibid., 1963–4, 13–14.

46 Ibid., 1967–8, 30.

47 Duckworth, *One Version*, 164–5.

48 Wiles, proposal to establish PhD studies in English, 1964, McP, box 30.

49 Wiles to Thode, May 1964, McP, box 19.

50 Minutes of Senate, 1 February 1964, 172.

51 Wiles to Thode, 31 May 1966, McP, box 20.

52 Wiles to Thode, 12 June 1965, McP, box 19.

53 Wiles to Salmon, 1 June 1967, McP, box 20.

54 Wiles to Thode, 31 May 1966, McP, box 20.

55 Wiles to Thode, 21 February 1967, McP, box 30.

56 Wiles to Wm. J. Cameron, 24 January 1967, McP, box 1.

57 Wiles to Thode, 21 February 1967, McP, box 30.

58 Wiles, "Proposal to Establish at McMaster University an Association for Eighteenth-Century Studies in the Humanities," December 1969, McP, box 1.

59   Williams to Helmuth, 8 November 1971, McP, box 1.

60   Lee, report of a meeting held in the Rare Books Room, 22 November 1966, McP, box 1.

61   Lee, "A Graduate Centre for Eighteenth-Century Studies," 1966, McP, box 1.

62   Minutes of a meeting in the Rare Books Room, 29 November 1966, McP, box 1.

63   Morton to Wiles, 28 October 1966, McP, box 1.

64   Martin to Wiles, 11 November 1966, McP, box 1.

65   Wiles to Cameron, 24 January 1967, McP, box 1.

66   Wiles proposal to establish the association, December 1969, McP, box 1.

67   Shrive to Thode, 30 May 1968, McP, box 20.

68   Shrive to Thode, 31 May 1969, McP, box 21. For details concerning the McPherson Report and its impact on the University of Toronto, see Friedland, *University of Toronto*, 531–3.

69   French to Acting-President Bourns, 11 June 1970, McP, box 22.

70   Duckworth, *One Version*, 15.

71   Gilmour to C.W.H. Linton, et al., 13 November 1957, McP, box 34.

72   Patrick to Gilmour, 22 November 1957, McP, box 34.

73   Gilmour to Linton, et al., 13 November 1957, McP, box 34.

74   Ibid.

75   Gilmour to the Committee on Religious Studies, 20 March 1958, McP, box 34.

76   Gilmour to Linton, et al., 13 November 1957, McP, box 34.

77   Patrick to Gilmour, 22 November 1957, McP, box 34.

78   Clifford, memorandum on Department of Religion, 1960, McP, box 34.

79   Much of this paragraph is drawn, with thanks, from Christian's *George Grant*, 199–210.

80   Clifford, *Annual Report*, 1962–3, McP, box 18.

81   Ibid.

82   Clifford to Thode, 23 January 1963, McP, box 34.

83   Clifford to Salmon, 9 October 1962, McP, box 34.

84   Clifford to Thode, 24 May 1963, McP, box 34.

85   Minutes of the Department of Religious Studies, 10 October 1974.

86   Younger to Bourns, 15 June 1972, McP, box 24.

87   Minutes of the Department of Religious Studies, 9 September 1965.

88   Paul Clifford, George Grant, and Eugene Combs, "Why a Department of Religion at McMaster," ibid.

89   Clifford to Thode, 1 May 1964, McP, box 19.

90   John E. Smith (Yale) to Duckworth, 12 January 1965; Paul Ramsey (Princeton) to Duckworth, 28 June 1965; Wilfred C. Smith (Harvard)

to Duckworth, 3 July 1965; H.D. Lewis (King's College, London) to Duckworth, 13 September 1965, McP, box 34.

91 Kelly to Duckworth, 24 June 1965, McP, box 34.

92 For first mention of the term, see Minutes of the Department of Religious Studies, 9 September 1965.

93 This was spelled out most clearly in a letter to the new dean of graduate studies. See Grant to Preston, 20 September 1965, McP, box 18.

94 For the full text of the proposal, see a copy in McP, box 34. Grant's presentation to the senate can be found in the Minutes of Senate, 22 October 1965, 31.

95 Grant to Thode, 30 May 1967, McP, box 20.

96 Greenspan, "In the Beginning," in Coward et al., "Addresses," 1.

97 Combs, addendum to Grant's report, 30 May 1967, McP, box 20.

98 Combs to Thode, June 1969, McP, box 21.

99 Ted E. Thomas, Oakland, California, to Thode, 2 April 1968, McP, box 18.

100 Lee, remarks in in Coward et al., "Addresses."

101 Coward, "Contributions of McMaster's Graduate Program," in Coward et al., "Addresses," 11–16; 20.

102 Grant, Annual Report, 1965–66, McP, box 20.

103 Combs, addendum to Grant, Annual Report, 30 May 1970, McP, box 20.

104 Thode, President's Report, 1967–8, 206–8.

105 Sanders, confidential memo to the president, 1971, McP, box 22.

106 M.E. Duckworth, Y.A. Harvey, and H. Smart, Report of Religious Studies Consultants to ACAP, March 1974, section 2.32 of Minutes of the Department of Religious Studies.

107 McKay, Classics at McMaster, 49–50.

108 Ibid., 41.

109 Shepherd to Gilmour, 26 May 1961, McP, box 18.

110 McKay to Thode, May 1963, McP, box 18.

111 McKay to Thode, 6 May 1968, McP, box 20.

112 For full discussion of these curricular changes, see McKay, Classics at McMaster, 44–7.

113 Ibid., 45.

114 Ibid.

115 Shepherd to Thode, 26 May 1969, McP, box 21.

116 McKay, Classics at McMaster, 40.

117 Sanders, "Religion at McMaster," in in Coward et al., "Addresses," 3.

118 Personal recollection of Richard Rempel, professor (emeritus) McMaster, March 2011.

119 Zack, Martin, and Lee, Thode, 117–18.

120 Ibid.

121   Thode to Trustees of the Laidlaw Foundation, 28 January 1968, McP, box 55.
122   Undated list of donors to the Russell purchase, McP, box 55.
123   Salmon to Thode, 24 June 1968, McP, box 21.
124   "McMaster Strikes Paydirt," *Silhouette*, 11 October 1968, 7.
125   Zack, Martin, and Lee, *Thode*, 118.
126   Russell Archives to Thode, August 1969, McP, box 22.
127   Ibid.
128   Thode, *President's Report*, 1961–2, 57.
129   For a glance at philosophy's enrolments from 1963 through 1968, see ibid., 1967–8, 195; 206.
130   J.E. Thomas to Thode, 2 June 1969, McP, box 21. See also, 5 May 1970, McP, box 22.
131   Thode, *President's Report*, 1966–7, 9.
132   Ibid., 1967–8, 8.
133   McKay to Thode, spring 1969, McP, box 21.
134   Ibid.

CHAPTER FIVE

1   Melling to Thode, 26 May 1969, McP, box 22.
2   McIvor to Thode, 31 July 1968, McP, box 21.
3   Gilmour, *President's Report*, 1956–7, 5–6.
4   Johnston, *McMaster*, vol. 2, 222.
5   Thode, *President's Report*, 1961–2, 38–9.
6   Gilmour, *President's Report*, 1956–7, 21–3.
7   Gilmour to A.K. Adlington, 21 January 1958, McP, box 89.
8   Gilmour to H.M. Axford (Waterloo University College), 21 October 1960, McP, box 89.
9   Freedman to Thode, 18 December 1961, McP, box 89.
10   Thode to Freedman, 9 February 1962, McP, box 89.
11   Thode, *President's Report*, 1962–3, 38–9.
12   Johnston, *McMaster*, vol. 2, 222.
13   Ibid., 222–3.
14   Salmon to Thode, 15 July 1964, McP, box 19.
15   Patrick to Thode, 6 October 1966 and November 1967, McP, box 20.
16   Thode, *President's Report*, 1961–2, 35.
17   Ibid., 1956–7, 47–50.
18   For a profile of the economics section, see "Economics Ho!" *Silhouette*, 22 February 1957, 3.
19   Gilmour, *President's Report*, 1956–7, 46.

20   Ibid., 48.

21   Ibid., 49.

22   Johnston, *McMaster*, vol. 2, 227.

23   Gilmour, *President's Report*, 1956–7, 47.

24   Ibid., 1957–9, 33; 52.

25   Ibid., 52.

26   McIvor to Thode, 30 December 1963, McP, box 35.

27   Ibid.

28   Graham to Thode, 1960–61 Report, McP, box 18.

29   Thode, *President's Report*, 1962–3, 82.

30   McIvor to Thode, 31 December 1963, McP, box 35.

31   Ibid., 30 December 1963.

32   Salmon to Thode, 30 June 1963, McP, box 18.

33   Graham to Thode, 15 June 1966, McP, box 20.

34   Salmon to Thode, 23 August 1966, McP, box 20.

35   Schlatter to Wm. F Hellmuth, 22 February 1971, McP, box 20.

36   Gilmour, *President's Report*, 1960–1, 37; 51.

37   McIvor to Salmon, 16 June 1964, McP, box 19.

38   McIvor to Thode, 1 June 1966, McP, box 20.

39   McIvor to Salmon, 30 June 1965, McP, box 19.

40   McIvor to Thode, 1 June 1966, McP, box 20.

41   McIvor to Thode, 20 July 1967, McP, box 20.

42   Preston to Thode, 1 April 1968, McP, box 32.

43   Personal recollection of J.A. Johnson in conversation with author.

44   Graham to Thode, 10 July 1969, McP, box 21.

45   Graham to Thode, 25 June 1970, McP, box 22.

46   Truman to Thode, 31 January 1967, McP, box 33.

47   For example, see Braudel, *On History*, passim.

48   Minutes of Senate, 27 May 1965.

49   Ibid., 26 May 1966.

50   Davy to Salmon, 12 April 1966, McP, box 33.

51   Truman to Salmon, 30 January 1967, McP, box 33.

52   Truman to Thode, 31 January 1967, McP, box 33.

53   Truman to Salmon, 2 February 1967, McP, box 33.

54   Truman to Thode, 3 February 1967, McP, box 33.

55   Truman to Salmon 13 February 1967, McP, box 33.

56   Truman and Salmon to all members of the Political Science Department, 13 February 1967, McP, box 33.

57   Truman to Mongar, 15 February 1967, McP, box 33; Truman to Pringsheim, n.d., box 33.

416 Notes to pages 115–20

58 Truman to Grady, McP, box 33.

59 Pringsheim to Salmon, 16 February 1967, McP, box 33.

60 Grady to Truman, 20 February 1967, McP, box 33.

61 Mongar to Truman, 21 February 1967, McP, box 33.

62 Personal communication from C.M. Johnston to author.

63 John Ruggie, "The Educational Revolution," *Silhouette*, 17 February 1967, 5.

64 Ruggie, "The Educational Revolution ... a Moral Choice for Mac," *Silhouette*, 24 February 1967, 5.

65 Kay to Thode, 27 March 1967, McP, box 33.

66 Sloan to Thode, 3 April 1967, McP, box 33.

67 Shimizu, Thrasher, et al. to Thode, 27 March 1967, McP, box 33.

68 Gullett and Tomlin to Thode, McP, box 33.

69 Minutes of the SEC, 4 April 1967, McP, box 33.

70 Ingram et al. to Thode, 5 April 1967, McP, box 33.

71 Cairns, MSU president, to Thode, 19 April 1967; Polsuns, GSA president to Thode, 14 April 1967, McP, box 33.

72 Thode to Cairns, 21 April 1967, McP, box 33. For a selection of Thode's replies to student missives, see this box.

73 Thode to all faculty and students in Political Science, 4 April 1967, McP, box 33.

74 Truman to Thode 6 March 1967 and Thode to members of the Political Science Department, 17 March 1967, McP, box 33.

75 Thode and Salmon to all members of the Department of Political Science, 21 April 1967, McP, box 33.

76 Mongar to Preston, 25 April 1967, McP, box 33.

77 Warren Gerard, "Discord Rips Department at McMaster," *Globe and Mail*, Tuesday, 6 June 1967; "Faculty to Study Charges," *Spectator*, 6 June 1967, 8, clippings, McP, box 33.

78 Ross, letter to the editor, *Globe and Mail*, 9 June 1967, clipping, McP, box 33.

79 R.C. McIvor, typescript of letter to the editor, *Globe and Mail*, 12 June 1967, McP, box 33.

80 Minutes of Senate, 27 May 1965, 272.

81 Davy to Thode, 1 February 1967, McP, box 33.

82 Thode to Davy, 23 February 1967, McP, box 33.

83 For example, see Thode to T.A. Smith, 4 April 1967, McP, box 33.

84 French to Thode, 20 July 1967, McP, box 33.

85 Melling to Thode, confidential report, June 1968, McP, box 21.

86 Melling to Thode, 4 March 1968, McP, box 33.

87   Melling to Thode, 15 March 1968, McP, box 33.

88   Thode to Breckenridge, et al., 20 March 1968, McP, box 33.

89   Lentner to Thode, 30 June 1969, McP, box 21.

90   "Grady Fired from Mac … Now Guelph," *Silhouette*, Friday, 23 January 1970, 3.

91   Johnston, *Radical Campus*, 293–314.

92   Interviewed by author for this volume on 15 April 2011, veteran political scientist Henry Jacek argued that it was the influx of several new staff members that defused tensions inside the department, over time.

93   "Three New Departments Started," *Silhouette*, Friday, 8 February 1958, 1.

94   Pineo, questionnaire, 22 April 2007.

95   Jones, *Historical Background*, 1.

96   Gilmour, *President's Report*, 1956–7, 23.

97   Ibid., 1959–60, 25.

98   Ibid., 23.

99   Pineo, questionnaire, 22 April 2007.

100   Jones to Gilmour, 26 May 1959, McP, box 34.

101   Jones to Gilmour, report, 1960–61, McP, box 18.

102   Thode, *President's Report*, 1961–2, 62.

103   Gilmour, *President's Report*, 1957–9, 56.

104   Jones to Salmon and Thode, 31 May 1963, McP, box 18.

105   Salmon to Thode, 15 July 1964, McP, box 19.

106   Jones to Salmon, 29 May 1964, McP, box 19.

107   Thode, *President's Report*, 1964–5, 28; and 1965–6, 27.

108   Sociology PhD Proposal, December 1966, McP, box 34.

109   The letters of assessment can be found in a packet from Preston to Thode, received 10 May 1967, McP, box 34.

110   Jones, *Historical Background*, 1.

111   Landes, Slobodin, and Stortroen to Thode, 18 December 1967, McP, box 34.

112   Salmon to Thode, 3 January 1968, McP, box 34.

113   Thode to Salmon, 16 January 1968, McP, box 34.

114   Sociology/Anthropology annual report, 1968–9, McP, box 21.

115   Blumstock to Thode, June 1970, McP, box 22.

116   For a detailed history of the school, see Penny, *From Dream to Gleam*, passim.

117   Bissell to Gilmour, 6 January 1961, McP, box 16.

118   Armstrong to Gilmour, 13 January 1961, McP, box 16.

119   Gilmour to Bissell, 18 January 1961, McP, box 16.

120   Penny to Thode, 11 June 1965, McP, box 34.

121   Fisher to Thode, 20 July 1965, McP, box 34.

122   Melling to Thode, 27 October 1965, McP, box 34.
123   McCarthy to Melling, 6 December 1965, McP, box 34.
124   McCarthy to Thode, 30 May 1966, McP, box 34.
125   Melling, notes on social welfare education, December 1966, McP, box 34.
126   Minutes of Senate, 14 June 1967, 10–11.
127   Penny, *From Dream to Gleam*, 39.
128   "Sociology Department Troubled," *Silhouette*, 29 September 1967, 3.
129   Gilmour, *President's Report*, 1960–1, 51 and Thode, *President's Report*, 1966–7, 97.
130   Wm. Fowler, interview by M. Gerritsen, transcript, Fall 2009, McMaster Archives.
131   Gilmour, *President's Report*, 1957–9, 33.
132   Thode, *President's Report*, 1961–2, 38.
133   Wynne to Thode, 7 May 1962, McP, box 18.
134   Fowler interview, 2009.
135   "McMaster Loses Ivor Wynne – a Leader and Builder," *Silhouette*, 6 November 1970, 1.
136   Thode, *President's Report*, 1967–8, 9.
137   Patrick to Thode, November 1967, McP, box 20.
138   McIvor to Thode, 22 June 1967, McP, box 33.

CHAPTER SIX

1   McPhedran, *Canadian Medical Schools*, 215.
2   Thode to Charles M. Johnston, 8 March 1976, Thode Papers, box 26.
3   Johnston, *McMaster*, vol. 2, 189–91.
4   *Report of the McMaster-Academy Committee to Organize and Administer Post-Graduate Refresher Courses*, January 1945, McP, box 39.
5   Coster, secretary, Hamilton Academy of Medicine, to Gilmour, 1 December 1944, McP, box 39.
6   Gilmour to Warren, 28 March 1945, McP, box 39.
7   Gilmour to Warren, April 1945, McP, box 39.
8   Johnston, *McMaster*, vol. 2, 189–91.
9   Thode, Memorandum to Chancellor Gilmour concerning the establishment of a Medical College at McMaster University, March 1948, McP, box 39.
10   Johnston, *McMaster*, vol. 2, 190.
11   Thode to C.M. Johnston, Thode Papers, box 26.
12   Johnston, *McMaster*, vol. 2, 191.
13   See bylaws of the HMRI, 22 November 1945, McP, box 39.
14   Wright to Gilmour, 2 May 1949, McP, box 39.

15   Gilmour to Wright, 6 May 1949, McP, box 39.

16   Jaimet to Dr W.O. Stevenson, president of the HMRI, 5 June 1952, McP, box 39.

17   Johnston, *McMaster*, vol. 2, 191; Spaulding, *Revitalizing Medical Education*, 16.

18   Gilmour, *President's Report*, 1957–9, 8.

19   Gilmour to Jaimet, 21 May 1958, McP, box 2.

20   Johnston, *McMaster*, vol. 2, 191.

21   Thode to Gilmour, 30 January 1953, McP, box 39.

22   Gilmour, Memorandum on Medical School Possibilities, 27 July 1954, McP, box 39.

23   Fraser Report, 14 March 1956, McP, box 39.

24   Gilmour to Fraser, 22 March 1956, McP, box 39.

25   Gilmour to the Board of the RBG, 28 October 1957, McP, box 61.

26   Gilmour to Ambrose, 29 October 1957, McP, box 61.

27   Rice to Bradley, Thode, et al., 23 December 1957, McP, box 61.

28   Thode to Farquharson, 8 January 1958, McP, box 39.

29   Hall, *The Place of the Medical School in the University*, 29 August 1958, McP, box 39.

30   For example, see Thode, *President's Report*, 1961–2, 2.

31   Gilmour to W.J. Dunlop, Ontario minister of education, 31 July, 1957, McP, box 39.

32   MacFarlane to Jean Montgomery, secretary to the president, McMaster, 2 October 1957, McP, box 39.

33   Many such reports can be found in a file labelled, "Reports of Visits to Other Medical Centres: 1960–62," McP, box 39.

34   Thode to C.M. Johnston, 8 March 1976, Thode Papers, box 26.

35   Gilmour, pencil notes, 13 January 1961 and Thode to Robarts, January 1961, McP, box 39.

36   Jackson to Thode, 23 January 1962, McP, box 39.

37   K.J.R. Wightman, Address to the Hamilton Health Association, 26 March 1962, McP, box 39.

38   MacFarlane to Thode, 5 April 1962, McP, box 39.

39   Neilson to Thode, 16 March 1962, McP, box 39.

40   MacFarlane to Thode, 6 August 1963, McP, box 39.

41   McCreary to Thode, June 1963, McP, box 39.

42   Thode to Premier John P. Robarts, 26 September 1963, McP, box 39.

43   "Mac Asks for Medical School," *Spectator*, 2 October 1963, 1.

44   Thode to the Board of Governors, 3 October 1963, McP, box 39.

45   J.W. Macleod to Thode, 21 October 1963, McP, box 39.

46   MacFarlane to Hall, 28 October 1963 (copy), McP, box 39.

47   MacFarlane to Thode, 14 January 1964, McP, box 39.

48   Board of Governors, Hamilton Civic Hospitals, to Thode, 9 March 1964, McP, box 39.

49   Armstrong to Thode, 19 October 1964, McP, box 39.

50   Thode to C.M. Johnston, 8 March 1976, Thode Papers, box 26.

51   Dr Ken Ingham, quoted in Spaulding, *Revitalizing Medical Education*, 23.

52   Fraser Mustard, interview by author, D. Sackett, A. Zipursky, and H. King, transcript, 26 March 2010, McMaster Archives

53   Thode to Ray Farquharson, 22 June 1965, McP, box 54.

54   J.R. Evans, interview by author, D. Sackett, A. Zipursky, and H. King, transcript, 26 March 2010, McMaster Archives. Concerning the brief from the Hamilton Academy of Medicine, see Spaulding, *Revitalizing Medical Education*, 24. Regarding the rebuff of reform plans at Toronto, see Friedland, *University of Toronto*, 512–13.

55   Evans to Thode, 10 May 1965, Evans Papers, box 1, 141.1.

56   Minutes of Senate, 27 May 1965, 264, McMaster Archives.

57   Evans to Dr J. Thomas August, Albert Einstein College of Medicine, 7 June 1965, Evans Papers, box 1, 141.1.

58   R.C Dickson to Evans, 29 June 1965, Evans Papers, box 1, 141.1.

59   August to Evans, 15 July 1965, Evans Papers, box 1, 141.1.

60   Evans to McGregor, Western Reserve University, 22 June 1965, Evans Papers, box 1, 141.1.

61   Spaulding, *Revitalizing Medical Education*, 27; transcript, Mustard, interview, n.p.

62   Evans, comments on a visit to Western Reserve School of Medicine, May 1967, Evans Papers, box 47, 146.2.

63   Ibid.

64   Spaulding, *Revitalizing Medical Education*, 27.

65   Dr Alvin Zipursky, aside in transcript, Mustard interview, 6.

66   Jerkic, "Influence of James E. Anderson."

67   Spaulding, *Revitalizing Medical Education*, 27.

68   Ibid.

69   Evans interview, 16.

70   Ibid., 22.

71   Thode, *President's Report*, 1965–6, x.

72   Spaulding, *Revitalizing Medical Education*, 27.

73   Ibid., 28.

74   The comment issued from Dr David Sackett as an aside in the transcript, J.R. Evans interview, 13.

75 Mustard as quoted in Spaulding, *Revitalizing Medical Education*, 59.
76 Accreditation, ACMA-LCME Visit Survey Report, 29 May 1972, Evans Papers, box 30, 144.3.
77 Evans interview, 13.
78 See Mustard interview, 1.
79 Spaulding, *Revitalizing Medical Education*, 59.
80 "Pathologist Raps Doctors' Ignorance," *Silhouette*, 17 February 1967, 4.
81 Spaulding, *Revitalizing Medical Education*, 41.
82 Unsigned brief to Evans, "Evolution of Basic Requirements for Admission," 22 June 1977, Evans Papers box 44, 145.8.
83 Zipursky, aside transcribed during the Evans interview, 23.
84 While Spaulding spells out the education scheme nicely in *Revitalizating Medical Education*, the original planning document is more concise and easier to follow. See "The Undergraduate Medical Curriculum," 31 October 1968, Evans Papers, box 44, 145.8.
85 Compare "Principal Objectives of the Faculty of Medicine, 1967" and "Objectives of the Faculty of Medicine," January 1969, with "Revised Statement of General Goals," 12 July 1972, Evans Papers, box 44, 145.8.
86 McCreary to Evans, 29 December 1966, McP, box 39.
87 Spaulding, *Revitalizing Medical Education*, 27.
88 Sackett, "Objectives of the Faculty of Medicine," January 1969, Evans Papers, box 44, 145.8
89 "We're Twice as Big, Now," *Silhouette*, 8 November 1963, 1.
90 "Ontario Acted First," *Silhouette*, 3 November 1964, 2.
91 Alma Reid, director of nursing, to Thode, 1 June 1961, McP, box 18.
92 Reid to Thode, 5 June 1963, McP, box 18.
93 Radforth to Thode, 3 June 1963 and 27 May 1965, McP, boxes 18 and 19.
94 Newbigging to Thode, psychology report: 1964–65, McP, box 19.
95 Principal of the Divinity College to Thode, June 1968, McP, box 21.
96 Nathaniel Parker to Thode, *Divinity College Report*, 1971–2, McP, box 24.
97 McKay to Thode, 6 May 1968, McP, box 21.
98 Preston to Thode, 24 August 1966, McP, box 20.
99 Principal of Hamilton College, Report to the President, 1964–5, McP, box 19.
100 Minutes of Senate, 18 February 1966, 130.
101 Evans interview, 5.
102 Ibid., 6.
103 Evans to the Board of Governors, 28 October 1966, Evans Papers, box 2, 141.2.
104 Evans to Thode, 12 May 1968, McP box 41.

105   Mustard interview.

106   Sackett as recorded in transcript, Mustard interview, 13.

107   Mustard interview, 13.

108   For a detailed chronology of these events, see George Yost (Sasaki, Walker, et al.) to Thode, 3 January 1966, Evans Papers, box 15, 142.6.

109   "King Stays Open – for Now," *Silhouette*, 8 January 1965, 1, 13.

110   "Copps Stands Firm," *Spectator*, 15 January 1965, clipping, McP, box 39.

111   Thode, statement to City Council, 19 January 1965, McP, box 40.

112   "Thode Tells City Council King Street Closing Imperative," *Silhouette*, Friday, 22 January 1965, 1.

113   King Street Debate Ends," *Silhouette*, 29 January 1965, 1.

114   Frank Adams, "A Growing McMaster Strains More than Its Boundaries,"*Globe and Mail*, 3 February 1965, 7.

115   "Group to Study McMaster Growth," *Spectator*, clipping, 29 March 1965.

116   Evans interview, 3.

117   For details, see Meeting of Consultants Regarding Site of the Medical School: (Confidential), 11 January 1966, McP, box 40.

118   Thode to Peter D. Smith, assistant to the chancellor, University of California, Santa Cruz, 25 January 1966, McP , box 55.

119   Nichols to Thode, 31 January 1966, McP, box 40.

120   Thode to Davis, 1 February 1966, McP, box 40.

121   Thode to homeowners, 17 February 1966, McP, box 40.

122   Moore to Evans, 1 March 1966, McP, box 40.

123   Gary Lautens, CHML radio, transcript, 17 February 1966, McP, box 40.

124   "McMaster and Hamilton," clipping, ibid. 6 April 1966, McP, box 40.

125   "McMaster to Teach Medicine," *Niagara Falls Review*, clipping, 22 February 1962; Owen Sound *Sun-Times*, clipping, 22 February 1962, McP, box 41; "McMaster and Hamilton," clipping, 6 April 1966, ibid. box, 40.

126   "The Big Land Grab," *Westdale Reporter*, clipping, November 1966, 1, McP, box 40.

127   Ibid., 1–2.

128   Ibid., 3.

129   Hamilton and District Labour Council, open letter, 6 May 1966, McP, box 40.

130   Evans, interview, 9.

131   Mustard, interview, 8.

132   For a full description of the architecture design, see "New Design Concept Approved for Health Sciences Center,"*McMaster* News, 27 June 1968, 1; and Spaulding, *Revitalizing Medical Education*, 135–46.

133   Evans, interview, 10.

134 Minutes of the Board of Governors Executive Committee, 16 November 1967, Evans Papers, box 2, 141.2.

135 Untitled, press release, 12 December 1967, Evans Papers, box 2, 141.2.

136 Minutes of the Board of Governors, 25 June 1968, Evans Papers, box 3, 141.3.

137 Ibid., 20 January 1969.

138 Evans, interview, 7.

139 "John Evans Starts a Medical School," clipping, *Spectator*, 23 March 1967, Evans Papers, box 145.8.

140 Evans, interview 10–11.

141 Campbell to Dr E. Williams, Middlesex Hospital, London, 20 March 1968, Evans Papers, box 32, 145.7.

142 Personal communication, Sackett to the author, 2013.

143 Spaulding, *Revitalizing Medical Education*, 64.

144 Concerning the Ewart Angus Centre, see correspondence related to the gift 18 December 1969 to 28 October 1970 in McP, box 41.

145 Thode, *President's Report*, 1969–70, 19.

146 K.C. Charron, deputy minister of health, to Evans, 10 December 1969, McP, box 41.

147 "Mac Accepts First Med. Students," *Spectator*, 5 July 1969, 8.

148 Evans to Thode, 19 August 1969, McP, box 41.

149 For example, see Dorothy Pringle to Evans, 30 June 1970, McP, box 41.

150 Evans to Thode, Division of Health Sciences Report: 1970–71, McP, box 23.

151 Evans to Munro, 30 July 1970, McP, box 41.

152 Spaulding, *Revitalizing Medical Education*, 160.

153 T.W. Fyles, et al., accreditation report, 29 March 1972, Evans Papers, box 30, 144.3.

154 F. Mustard, *Division of Health Sciences Report*, 1972–3, McP, box 25.

155 Sackett, email to author, 23 January 2011.

156 Personal communication, Lee to author, 13 December 2010.

CHAPTER SEVEN

1 Johnston, *Radical Campus*, 293–314; Horn, *York University*, 144–54.

2 For a discussion of Rae, the development of unicameral government and the end of the honours system, see Friedland, *University of Toronto*, 520–47; Owram, *Born at the Right Time*, 292.

3 Thode to Sherman, 5 March 1969, McP, box 54.

4 Sherman to Thode, 9 April 1969, McP, box 54.

5 For a detailed analysis of Davis' Gerstein Lectures, see Horn, *York University*, 112.

6   Norrie, Owram, and Emery, *History of the Canadian Economy*, 387–98.
7   Ibid., 385.
8   Axelrod, *Scholars and Dollars*, 141; Friedland, *University of Toronto*, 561; Neatby and McEown, *Creating Carleton*, 186.
9   Norrie, Owram, and Emery, *History of the Canadian Economy*, 397.
10 Axelrod, *Scholars and Dollars*, 145.
11 Ibid., 158.
12 Friedland, *University of Toronto*, 561; Neatby and McEown, *Creating Carleton*, 186.
13 Thode, Budget Submission, December 1966, McP, box 82.
14 Davis to Thode, 4 March 1969, McP, box 84.
15 Robarts to Thode, 19 February 1969, McP, box 84.
16 Thode, "Statement by Dr. Thode on Budget Speech," *McMaster News*, 5 March 1969, 1.
17 Kerr, minister of colleges and universities, to Thode, 29 March 1972, McP, box 85.
18 For a full discussion of these committees and commissions, see Monahan, *Collective Autonomy*, 32 and chapter 2.
19 Higbee, Proposal for Implementing Institutional Research at McMaster, June 1970, McP box 44.
20 Horn, *York University*, 140–8.
21 Hedden to Thode, 21 July 1969, McP, box 44.
22 Higbee, *Financial Implications of Steady-State Enrolment*, 5 March 1971, McP, box 44; Higbee to Thode, 9 July 1971, McP, box 24.
23 Bourns to Thode, 30 June 1969, McP, 68.
24 Bourns to Thode, 31 October 1969, McP, box 22.
25 Thode, "Statement by Dr. Thode on Budget Speech," *McMaster News*, 5 March 1969, clipping, McP, box 84.
26 "Dilemma," scratch notes in Thode's hand, undated, but clearly from mid-1969, McP, box 84.
27 Taylor to all members of the Board, 11 June 1970, McP, box 84.
28 For a sample of the questions and questioners, see McP, box 84, folder 8.
29 Bourns to Thode, January 1971, McP, box 23.
30 Minutes of the President's Executive Committee (PEC), 1 April 1970, McP, box 7.
31 Tomlinson to Thode, Report for 1970–71, McP, box 7.
32 Ibid., July 1972, McP, box 24.
33 Frankel to Thode, July 1971, McP, box 23.
34 Wm. Hellmuth to Thode, Report: Vice-President of Arts: January 1972, McP, box 23.

35 McKay to Thode, July 1971, McP, box 23.

36 Minutes of the PEC, 12 June 1970, McP, box 7.

37 Preston, *Annual Report*, 1970–71, McP, box 23.

38 D.T. Wright to Thode, 25 November 1970; Davis to Thode, 29 January 1971, McP, box 84.

39 Minutes of PEC, 9 December 1970, McP, box 7.

40 Ibid., 18 August 1970.

41 Smith to Thode, June 1972, McP, box 24.

42 Johns, *Annual Report*, 1971–72, McP, box 24.

43 Minutes of PEC, 16 November 1969, McP, box 7.

44 Ibid., 12 September 1970.

45 Grant to Thode, 11 April 1969, McP, box 68.

46 Farmer to Thode, 8 June 1970, McP, box 23.

47 Rosenblood, as cited in Jackson, *MUFA's First 50 Years*, 48.

48 Neatby and McEown, *Creating Carleton*, 117.

49 Horn, *York University*, 43–5.

50 Johnston, *Radical Campus*, 10.

51 Clark, *Growth and Governance*, 22.

52 Jackson, *MUFA's First 50 Years*, 19.

53 For full details on the still-controversial Crowe case, see Horn, *Academic Freedom in Canada*, 223–9.

54 Jackson, *MUFA's First 50 Years*, 15.

55 Ibid., 20.

56 J.E. Kersell and R.W. Thompson, faculty association brief on university government, 2 October 1962, McP, box 2. For the composition of the senate, see the McMaster Act (1957), articles 11, 12, and 14.

57 Minutes of the President's Advisory Committee, 15 October 1962, McP, box 2.

58 Horn, *Academic Freedom in Canada*, 253–8.

59 Neatby and McEown, *Creating Carleton*, 148–9.

60 Patrick to Thode, 31 July 1964, McP, box 19.

61 Graham to Thode, 6 August 1964, McP, box 19.

62 Patrick to Thode, 31 July 1965 and Graham to Thode, 30 July 1965, McP, box 19.

63 Thode to all faculty, 31 January 1966, McP, box 9.

64 Shaw Report, 22 December 1965, McP, box 9.

65 For full details, see Duff and Berdahl, *University Government*, 1966.

66 Minutes of Senate, 23 June 1966, 206.

67 Thode to Harding, 13 July 1966, McP, box 54.

68 Minutes of Senate, 19 September 1966, 215.

69   Members of the committee included J.S. Kirkaldy (chairman), A. Brown (alumni), G.S. French (History), D.M. Hedden (vice-president, administration), B.W. Jackson (English), L.J. Kamin (Psychology), C.D. Kent (London Public Library), J.M. Laycock (Sociology/Anthropology), I.A. Litvak (Commerce), H.E. Petch (principal, Hamilton College), and P.N. Smith (Engineering). Thode and J.P. Evans (registrar) were ex officio, non-voting members. See *Kirkaldy Report*, May 1967, iii.

70   Ibid., i.

71   Ibid., 17.

72   Minutes of Senate, 21 December 1966, appendix D, 231–3.

73   J.S. Kirkaldy, et al. *Report of the Senate Committee on University Government* (hereafter: *Kirkaldy Report*), May 1967, i, University Secretariat.

74   Minutes of Senate, 31 January 1967, 17.

75   Ibid., 8 February 1967, 22.

76   Ibid., 24.

77   Ibid., 22.

78   Ibid., 25 January 1967, 9.

79   Ibid., 31 January 1967, 14.

80   Jackson, MUFA's *First 50 Years*, 32.

81   Kirkaldy, *Kirkaldy Report*, 5.

82   Ibid., 11.

83   Trueman to Thode, 12 July 1968, McP, box 21.

84   Minutes of Senate, 8 October 1969, 34.

85   For one clear expression of this view, see T. Husain, "Mathematics Brief on the Faculty of Graduate Studies," Minutes of Senate, 11 December 1968, appendix A-3, 12.

86   D. Shaw, *Report of the Senate Committee on Graduate Studies* (Shaw Report), Minutes of Senate, August 1968, 7–8.

87   Kirkaldy, *Kirkaldy Report*, 12.

88   The Shaw Committee consisted of Shaw (chair), A.N. Bourns, D.R. McCalla, J.W. Hodgins, J.F. Mustard, M.A. Preston, W.J. Schlatter, F.N. Shrive, D.M. Winch, and P. Younger.

89   For all briefs to the Shaw Committee, see *Report of the Senate Committee on Graduate Studies,* appendix A-iii.

90   Shaw, *Shaw Report*, 12–32.

91   Kirkaldy, *Kirkaldy Report*, v.

92   Ibid., 17.

93   Ibid., 15.

94   Ibid., 16.

95 For warm testimony to the significance of the two meeting places, see, transcripts of interviews with, Les King, Bob McNutt, Art Bourns, Mel Preston, Peter George, Helen Howard-Locke, and others.

96 Armstrong to Gilmour, 31 July 1961, McP, box 18.

97 Graham to Thode, 30 July 1965, McP, box 19.

98 Kirkaldy, MUFA brief to Thode, August 1966, McP, box 20.

99 Bob McNutt, interview by R. Rempel, transcript, 2012.

100 Minutes of the PEC, 18 August, 1970, McP, box 7.

101 Jackson, MUFA's *First 50 Years*, 21–3.

102 For example, see Hellmuth to Thode, 1 October 1970, McP, box 3.

103 Minutes of the PEC, 18 August 1970, McP, box 7.

104 Bourns to Thode, 29 March 1971, McP, box 2.

105 Hellmuth to Thode, 6 April 1971, McP, box 2.

106 Lanfranco to Thode, 2 April 1970, McP, box 2; Minutes of the PEC, 9 June 1971, McP, box 7; Jackson, MUFA's *First 50 Years*, 21–6.

107 Hedden to Thode, 18 May 1971, McP, box 3.

108 Minutes of the PEC, 16 September 1971, McP, box 7.

109 Ibid., 27 November 1971.

110 Thode to N. Rosenblood, MUFA president, November 1971, McP, box 74.

111 Minutes of the PEC, 10 November 1972, McP, box 7.

112 McCalla to Bourns, 12 February 1973, McP, box 3.

CHAPTER EIGHT

1 Johnston and Weaver, *Student Days*, passim.

2 Minutes of the Senate, 24 January 1968, 93.

3 Personal recollections of Prof. Olaf U. Janzen, in conversation with author, 12 November 2013

4 Johnston and Weaver, *Student Days*, 99.

5 "Stagg New President, Captures 50% of Vote," *Silhouette*, 30 January 1970, 4.

6 Eugene Levy, "The Mouse That Roars," *Silhouette*, 21 February 1969, 3.

7 Bob Fraser, "The History Department: No Place for Critical Thought," *Silhouette*, 31 October 1969, 9.

8 Ibid.

9 Annette van Pypen, "Wentworth Cliques," *Silhouette*, 31 October 1969, 9.

10 Fritz and Sanders as quoted in "University Forum," *Silhouette*, 24 October 1969, 5.

11 D. Kinch, "Closed Society," *Silhouette*, 31 October 1969, 4.

12   Levy, "The Mouse That Roars," *Silhouette*, 14 February 1969, 3.
13   For student discussion of Batista's Cuba, see several articles, *Silhouette*, 7
     November 1958. On the Arrow, see "Criticize Arrow Policy with Letter to
     John D.," *Silhouette*, 6 March 1959, 2. On the Hungarian revolt, see "Peti-
     tion to Khrushchev," *Silhouette*, 6 November 1959. On atomic weapons and
     Cold War politics, see Mike Walton, "Arms and Men," *Silhouette*, 3 Septem-
     ber 1960, 1; "Council's CUCND Decision Supported," *Silhouette*, 13 October
     1961, 1; and "Cuba," *Silhouette*, 26 October 1962, 4. On Vietnam, see "Stu-
     dent Militancy in US," *Silhouette*, 30 September 1966, 5; "Propose 11 Nov-
     ember Protest," *Silhouette*, 28 October 1966, 1; and "Anti-Vietnam Group
     Formed," *Silhouette*, 11 November 1966, 1.
14   "Berkeley and Free Speech," *Silhouette*, December 1964, 5.
15   Mathews and Steele, *Struggle for Canadian Universities*, passim.
16   Friedland, *University of Toronto*, 540; Neatby and McEown, *Creating
     Carleton*, 155–8, 193; Johnston, *Radical Campus*, 109.
17   For an overview, see Clark, *Growth and Governance*, 13–15; Owram, *Born
     at the Right Time*, 12–15.
18   Compare, for example, the exceptionally mild response at Carleton, with the
     near dysfunction wrought at Simon Fraser. See Neatby and McEown, *Creat-
     ing Carleton*, 164–84; Johnston, *Radical Campus*, 117–34, 293–301.
19   Ruggie, "The Educational Revolution," *Silhouette*, 17 February 1967, 5.
20   Kirkaldy, *Kirkaldy Report*, 1–2, 7, citing its initial recommendations of Octo-
     ber 1966.
21   Ruggie, "The Educational Revolution."
22   Wm. Gullett and Brian Tomlin, "The Educational Revolution ... a Moral
     Choice for Mac," *Silhouette*, 24 February 1967, 5.
23   Minutes of the Senate, appendix A, 8 March 1967, no. 23.
24   Ibid., 15 March 1967, 59–66.
25   Ibid., 12 April 1967, 77–9.
26   Kirkaldy, *Kirkaldy Report* 9–10.
27   Minutes of the Senate, 19 May 1967, 104–8.
28   Ibid., 10 October 1967, 11–18.
29   Ibid., 15 November 1967, 34–41.
30   Ibid., 13 December 1967, 64–72.
31   "Turner Report," Minutes of the Senate, 24 May 1968, appendix J, 1–31.
32   Minutes of the Senate, 9 October, 1968, 29–31, and 21 October 1968,
     52–7.
33   "Turner Defines, Defends Report's Limits," *Silhouette*, 4 October 1968, 4;
     "*Silhouette* Interviews Liberal Lanfranco about Learning," *Silhouette*, 11
     October 1968, 5.

34 "Terry Campbell Accuses, [Mac] an Academic Dunghill," *Silhouette*, 29 October 1968, 1; John Francis, "If You Don't Like It, You Can Always Go Home," ibid., 5–6.

35 Louis Ladouceur, "Student Politics," *Silhouette*, 24 November 1967, 4.

36 Ray Guy, "An Open Letter," *Silhouette*, 19 January 1968 1; Ivan Reitman, "Film Board Must Attract," ibid., 23 February 1968, 5.

37 "Writers Claim BSB Enemy of Student Body," *Silhouette*, 2 February 1968, 4.

38 Ray Barker, "Politicians are the Biggest Contributors to Student Apathy," *Silhouette*, 16 February 1968, 5.

39 "Grad Students Stage Two-Day Boycott," *Silhouette*, 29 November 1968, 1.

40 "Spoken French Neglected at Mac," *Silhouette*, 16 February 1968, 7; "Committee Pleased: French Reform Continues," *Silhouette*, 23 February 1968, 9.

41 "Math Students Walk out in Protest," *Silhouette*, 22 November 1968, 1.

42 Lawrence Martin, "Guevara Memorial Attracts 400," *Silhouette*, 11 October 1968, 1; "Berets, Flags, Guevara Suggest SDU is Dead," *Silhouette*, 18 October 1968, 5.

43 Johnston and Weaver, *Student Days*, 101.

44 John Spencer, "Boycott Beaver," *Silhouette*, 29 October 1968, 1.

45 "Stay Away from Food Issue: Leave to Company and Union," *Silhouette*, 29 October 1968, 1.

46 "Campbell Accuses 'an Academic Dunghill,'" *Silhouette*, 29 October 1968, 1.

47 John Francis, "If You Don't Like It, You Can Always Leave," *Silhouette*, 1 November 1968, 1, 5.

48 Sheila Walton, "Fat Cat Gets the Dung. Why?" *Silhouette*, 15 November 1968, 5.

49 "SRA Gets Food Report," *Silhouette*, 15 November 1968, 1.

50 Lawrence Martin, "Historic Senate Meeting Exposes Problems," *Silhouette*, 29 November 1968, 1, 8.

51 Minutes of Senate, 2 December 1968, 91.

52 Ibid, 12 November 1969, 56. Four undergraduate and two graduate senators took their seats.

53 Ibid., 11 March 1970, 172.

54 Ibid., 11 December 1968, 81–3.

55 Frankel, *Report of the Faculty of Social Science*, 1970–1, McP, box 23.

56 Minutes of the Senate, 14 October 1970, 30.

57 Minutes of the Department of History, 17 October 1972.

58 Ibid., 7 November 1967; 27 November 1970. See, also, Cappadocia to Thode, 16 June 1971, McP, box 23. For student opinion regarding the effectiveness of these groups, see Gerry Killan, later president of King's College

(UWO), in his response to a questionnaire circulated to alumni in researching this volume.

59   Minutes of the Department of History, 17 October 1968.

60   Minutes of the Senate, 30 July 1969, 4.

61   Initially, the joint committee recommended that only academic "peers" participate in faculty-level proceedings regarding appointments, tenure and promotion. See Minutes of the Senate, 22 December 1969, 100–1.

62   Minutes of the Senate, 11 February 1970, 150.

63   Ibid., 30 March 1970, 183–8.

64   Minutes of the Faculty of Humanities, 23 October 1969.

65   Lentner to Thode, Spring 1971, McP, box 23.

66   Ibid.

67   K. Pringsheim, "The Canadian as Nigger," *Spectator*, clipping, 8 February 1971.

68   "Tip of the Iceberg," *Silhouette*, 18 September 1970, 4.

69   Bertram to Thode, 23 February 1971, McP, box 33.

70   Thode to Bertram, 26 February 1971, McP, box 33.

71   Lentner to Thode, Spring 1971, McP, box 23.

72   Minutes of the Department of Sociology-Anthropology, Thursday, 25 September 1969, 1–2.

73   Ibid., 6 November 1969, 3.

74   For a retrospective analysis of long-standing trouble in sociology and political science, see "Two Departments Troubled," *Silhouette*, 15 November 1974, 1.

75   "Compromise Plan Diminishes Threat of Sit-In," *Silhouette*, 23 March 1973, 1.

76   P. Sherriff clarified the departmental constitution, ratified in September 1974, at a meeting of the department on 10 February 1975. See Minutes of the Department of Sociology, 10 February 1975.

77   Minutes of the Department of Religious Studies, 9 September 1965.

78   Ibid., 13 November 1967.

79   Ibid., 4 March 1968.

80   Ibid., 23 September 1969.

81   Ibid., 9 November 1969.

82   Ibid., 13 November 1969.

83   Collective interview of Religious Studies retired members by author, transcript, March 2010, n.p. Office of Alumni Affairs and McMaster Archives.

84   On the different experiences of phasing in student representatives, see E. Marseglia (Fine Arts) to Thode, June 1969; K. Denner (German) to Thode, 30 May, 1969; J.E. Thomas (philosophy) to Thode, 2 June 1969, McP, box

21; J.W. Hodgins (engineering) to Thode, June 1969; D. McCalla (dean of science) to Thode, 4 July 1969; J. Melling (dean of social science) to Thode, 26 May 1969, and A.G. McKay (dean of humanities), to Thode, spring 1969, McP, box 22.

85 "About Course Unions," *Silhouette*, 30 October 1970, 4.

86 Thode to Chauncey Wood, 24 September 1968, McP, box 62.

87 Statement by Thode, 1 December 1967, McP, box 54.

88 Thode to Macdonald (CPUO) 16 June 1969, McP, box 68.

89 "Seminar Poses Problems in Dismal Turnout," *Silhouette*, 17 October 1969, 1.

90 "The Students' Failure," *Silhouette*, 4; "The President's Seminar," *Silhouette*, 17 October 1969, 7.

91 "No Quorum – No Meeting: SRA," *Silhouette*, 12 December 1969, 1.

92 "Open Senate Meets Today: Nobody Shows," *Silhouette*, Friday 16 January 1970, 1.

93 Summary of Events Leading to Sit-In, 10 April 1970, McP, box 71. Stone's role as "theorist" was noted by M. Quigley, "MSM: The Meaning of Radicalism," *Silhouette*, 3 October 1969, 9.

94 MSM to Thode, Zack, and Hedden, 8 September 1969, McP box 71.

95 Summary of Events Leading to Sit-In, 10 April 1970, McP, box 71.

96 Quigley, "MSM: The Meaning of Radicalism."

97 "CUS Loses Vote at Carleton," *Silhouette*, 24 October 1969, 9; "CUS Dead after Loss at Toronto," *Silhouette*, 31 October 1969, 1; Friedland, *University of Toronto*, 164–84; Johnston, *Radical Campus*, 158.

98 "Split in MSM Could Lead to Dissolution," *Silhouette*, 31 October 1969, 1.

99 Phillip Martin, "Misguided Desires for Their Own Satisfaction – MSM," *Silhouette*, 31 October 1969, 10.

100 Lawrence Martin, "Hard Core Marxists," *Silhouette*, 21 November 1969, 4.

101 Lawrence Martin, "The Barricade Crumbled," *Silhouette*, 18 September 1970, 9.

102 Anonymous, "Workers – Students Win First Round," mimeographed poster, McP, box 71.

103 Bourns, "Statement," *McMaster Gazette*, 10 April 1970, 1.

104 "The Sit-In," *Silhouette*, 18 September 1970, 1.

105 Reply to demands of the 75, 3 April 1970, McP, box 71.

106 "This Way Anarchy," *Globe and Mail*, clipping, 11 April 1970, McP, box 71.

107 "The Sit-In."

108 Bourns, "Statement to Senate," 10 April 1970, McP box 71.

109 Summary of Events Leading to Sit-In, 10 April 1970, McP, box 71, 4–5.

110 "Mac Sit-In Peaceful – but Determined," *Spectator*, clipping, 4 April 1970, 7, McP, box 71.

111 Anonymous, "The University as Boss," poster, McP, box 71.

112 Bourns to the SRA, 5 April 1970, McP, box 71.

113 "The Sit-In."

114 SRA to Bourns, 6 April 1969, McP, box 71.

115 *MSU Special Edition*, 7 April 1970, 1–4, McP, box 71.

116 For the terms, see, Bourns, "Statement by Acting President Arthur N. Bourns to the Senate," *McMaster Gazette*, clipping, 10 April 1970, 1, McP, box 71.

117 For a selection of newspaper items, consult the clippings file, McP box 71.

118 Photograph, *Silhouette*, 18 September 1970, 9.

119 Bourns, undated pencil notes, McP, box 71.

120 See letters of support from Dale S. Cooper, G. Fuchs, Peter Gillespie, W.J. Jenkins, Ruth Smith, Charlotte Swick, and Brian Anderson to Bourns, 5–6 April 1970, McP, box 71.

121 A.H. Black to Bourns, 6 May 1970, McP, box 71.

122 Truman to Bourns, 29 April 1970, McP, box 71.

123 Bourns to Lee, 15 April 1970, McP, box 71.

124 Lentner to Frankel, 13 April 1970, McP, box 71.

125 Minutes of the Senate, 24 November 1971, 83–7; 12 April 1972, 182–90.

126 Bourns admitted to the scars left by the sit-in, when interviewed later. "Bourns Talks with News Editor," *Silhouette*, 15 September 1972, 5.

127 "No Thought at All", *Silhouette*, 23 October 1970, 4.

128 "Representation said to be Tokenism in Politics Dept.," *Silhouette*, 30 October 1970, 1.

129 "Maoists Ridiculed by Students," *Silhouette*, 13 November 1970, 3.

130 Jackson, *MUFA's First 50 Years*, 43.

131 Minutes of the Senate, 23 June 1966, 211–14.

132 "Complete Course Evaluations This Year," *Silhouette*, 5 December 1968, 1.

133 R. Gillespie, *Report of the Department of Chemistry*, 1966–7, McP, box 20.

134 M. Johns, *Reports of the Department of Physics*, 1966–7, 1967–8, McP, boxes 20, 21.

135 "An Interview with President Thode," *Silhouette*, 16 October 1970, 7.

136 "Mega-Classes are the Standard: Classes Jammed Up," *Silhouette*, 25 September 1970, 3.

137 *Spectator*, clipping, 28 September 1970, 8.

138 Melling to Thode, 26 May 1969, McP, box 22.

139 McKay to Thode, May 1969, McP, box 22.

140 For a complete list of members and their affiliations, see the *Vichert Report*, January 1971, vii.

141 "Letters to the Vichert Committee," *Silhouette*, 6 September 1969, 5, 11.

142 A. Black, "Black Responds to Invitation," *Silhouette*, 14 February 1969, 5.

143 "Jones' Proposals Accepted," *Silhouette*, 21 February 1969, 5.

144 For these excerpts from various briefs, see *Report of the Senate Ad Hoc Committee on Undergraduate Education*, January 1971 (hereafter, *Vichert Report*), 11–13.

145 "Students Deeply Unhappy, says Vichert," *Spectator*, clipping, 28 February 1970, McP, box 17.

146 Minutes of the Department of Physics, 12 September 1969.

147 Ibid., 5 February 1970.

148 Minutes of the Senate, 13 January 1971, 73.

149 The impact of MUMC's pedagogical model can be clearly seen in the *Vichert Report*, 4, 6, 22, 28, 38–40.

150 Ibid., recommendation number 8, 21.

151 Ibid., recommendation number 14, 22.

152 Ibid., 38.

153 Ibid., Minority Statement, 68–88.

154 Ibid., 89–137.

155 Minutes of the Senate, 27 January 1971, 84; 24 February 1971, 107.

156 For a summary of debate concerning Vichert see, Minutes of the Senate, 27 January 1971, 78–84; 24 February 1971, 105–7.

157 McKay to Thode, July 1971, McP, box 23.

158 Cappadocia to Hellmuth, 20 June, 1972, McP, box 24; unsigned, *Biology: Annual Report*, 1970–71, McP, box 23.

159 Shrive to Thode, spring 1970, McP, box 22; Graham to Thode, 8 July 1971, McP, box 23.

160 Frankel to Thode, July 1971, McP, box 23.

161 Frankel to Bourns, August 1972, McP, box 24.

162 McCalla to Bourns, June 1971, McP, box 23.

163 McCalla to Bourns, July 1972, McP, box 24.

164 Shemilt to Bourns, February 1972, McP, box 23.

165 McKay, *Humanities Annual Report*, July 1971, McP, box 23.

166 Minutes of the PEC, 14 August 1971, McP, box 24.

CHAPTER NINE

1 J.M. Holmes, (chairman of chemistry, Carleton) to Bourns, 21 July 1972, McP, box 56.

2 "A.N. Bourns," *Silhouette*, 15 September 1972, 5.

3 Leslie King, interview by Office of Alumni Affairs, transcript copy, 6, McMaster Archives.

4   Norrie and Owram, *History of the Canadian Economy*, 402–4.
5   Clark, *Growth and Governance*, 23; Monahan, *Collective Autonomy*, 19; Neatby and McEown, *Creating Carleton*, 188; Horn, *York University*, 147; Axelrod, *Scholars and Dollars*, 141.
6   "University-society gap seen widening," *Contact*, 24 April 1970, 1.
7   Axelrod, *Scholars and Dollars*, 145.
8   Neatby and McEown, *Creating Carleton*, 186.
9   Deutsch, as quoted by James Auld, minister of colleges and universities, 26 May 1975, McP, box 86.
10 Monahan, *Collective Autonomy*, 62–70.
11 The term *macro-indicator* was first used officially in 1977, but its origins can be traced back to discussions in the early seventies. See, Sheffield et al., *Systems of Higher Education*, 112.
12 According to "Statistics Canada Reports University Enrolment Figures," *Contact*, 17 January 1975, 3.
13 University Registrar, *Registrar's Report*, 1972–80. McMaster Archives
14 "Mohawk Applications Soaring," *Spectator*, clipping, 7 June 1979, McP, box 75.
15 Minutes of the Senate, 11 September 1974, 4.
16 "5% Increase Hits Schools and Students," *Spectator*, clipping, 8 January 1979, McP, box 75.
17 George Gavrel, "Bourns Says Honeymoon Near End," *Silhouette*, 24 November 1972, 1.
18 Ministry of Colleges and Universities circular, 19 October 1972, and OCUA advisory memorandum, number 74–II, 1975–6, McP, boxes 85 and 86, respectively.
19 University Registrar, *Registrar's Report*, 1969–70, 1980–81. McMaster Archives.
20 McNie to Bourns, 22 January 1973, McP, box 85.
21 Gerstein (CUA chair) to James Auld, 30 April 1974, copy in McP, box 86.
22 A.N. Bourns, interview by Office of Alumni Affairs, transcript, 22 April 2009, 21, McMaster Archives.
23 Levinson, as cited in Jackson, MUFA's *First 50 Years*, 72.
24 Minutes of the Senate, 13 September 1972, 2.
25 Minutes of the PEC, 28 August 1972, McP, box 7.
26 Gavrel, "Honeymoon Near End," *Silhouette*, 24 November 1972, 1.
27 Minutes of the PEC, 30 September 1975, McP, box 8.
28 Minutes of the Senate, 13 September 1972, 1.
29 Ibid, 1–4.
30 Minutes of the PEC, 20 November 1974, McP, box 8.

Notes to pages 242–9   435

31 R.P. Graham to Bourns, 18 October 1972, McP, box 56.

32 "Mac's Energy Saving Program," *Contact*, 4 September 1975, 1.

33 Ontario Ministry of Environment to L. Auger, (MUMC physical plant), 7 March 1975; Helen R. Hobson to H.E. Young (pollution control committee, Hamilton), 24 March 1975, McP, box 43.

34 Bourns to Hedden, 8 April 1975, McP, box 43.

35 Bourns to Hedden, 5 May 1975, McP, box 43.

36 "Energy Conservation Week in Ontario," *Contact*, 29 October 1976, 2.

37 "Conservation Award," *Contact*, 24 February 1978, 1.

38 Minutes of the PEC, 31 October 1974, McP, box 8.

39 "University Must Make 62 Staff Cuts," *Contact*, 30 July 1975, 1–2.

40 "Great Elm Succumbs," *Contact*, 20 September 1974, 3.

41 Minutes of the PEC, 20 November 1974, McP, box 8.

42 King interview.

43 Minutes of the PEC, 20 September 1972, McP, box 7.

44 Bourns to G.W. King, 4 December 1973, McP, box 8.

45 King to Bourns, 20 December 1973, McP, box 8.

46 King to Bourns, 11 February 1974, McP, box 8.

47 Minutes of PEC, 28 August 1974, McP, box 8.

48 Minutes of the Senate, 30 March 1973, 209–17.

49 Ibid., 11 April 1973, 241.

50 Ibid., 25 April 1973, 249.

51 Ibid., 255.

52 Ibid., 18 May 1973, 289–91.

53 University Registrar, *Registrar's Report*, 1 December 1973. McMaster Archives.

54 Lee, *Memoir*, 26 May 2008, 4.

55 Minutes of the Senate, 13 June 1973, 286.

56 Bourns, interview by Alumni, transcript, 24.

57 Minutes of the PEC, 24 January 1975, McP, box 8.

58 Lee, *Memoir*, 23.

59 Lee interview, 14.

60 Bourns interview, 24.

61 Lee, *Memoir*, 23.

62 Bourns interview, 12.

63 University Registrar, *Registrar's Report*, 1973–4. McMaster Archives.

64 Lee interview, 13.

65 "McMaster to Face Deficit," *Silhouette*, 13 October 1972, 1.

66 Bourns, untitled press release, 19 November 1974, McP, box 86.

67 Bourns, presentation to OCUA, 22 November 1974, McP, box 86.

68 Auld to Bourns, 20 February 1975, McP, box 86.

69   Minutes of the Faculty of Social Science, 5 March 1975; Minutes of the Faculty of Humanities, 11 March 1975; Bourns, memorandum to all faculty, 21 April 1975, McP, box 43.

70   Lee, *Memoir*, 22.

71   See, for example, Minutes of the Senate, 12 March 1975, 9 March 1977, and 14 March 1979.

72   Bourns interview, 24.

73   Ibid., 22–3.

74   Cartoon, *Silhouette*, 22 March 1974, 5, clipping, McP, box 72

75   Anonymous, poster copies, March–April 1974, McP, box 72.

76   "French Courses Examined," *Silhouette*, 1 December 1967, 3.

77   "Spoken French Neglected at Mac," *Silhouette*, 16 February 1968, 7.

78   "Committee Pleased: French Reform Continues," *Silhouette*, 23 February 1968, 9.

79   G. Chapple interview with C.B. Mueller, 25 March 1974, in Mueller, *Department of Romance Languages: Final Report*, appendix E, 10 April 1974, McP, box 72.

80   For details of the assistant, exchange, and military arrangements, see Mueller, *Department of Romance Languages: Final Report*, tab B II, 2; Patrick to A. Berland, 3 February 1974, McP, box 72.

81   Patrick to Berland, 3 February 1974, McP, box 72.

82   "Students Seek Reversal of Contract Decision," *Silhouette*, 24 November 1972, 3.

83   "French Student Claims Department Badly Run," *Silhouette*, 9 February 1973, 3.

84   "French Dispute Reaching Climax," *Silhouette*, 9 March 1973, 1.

85   "Tuesday Sit-In Planned," *Silhouette*, 16 March 1973, 1.

86   "Compromise," *Silhouette*, 23 March 1973, 1.

87   Mueller, *Final Report*, tab B III, 2.

88   See, for example, French 1b6 Deserter, "French Problems," *Silhouette*, 25 January 1974, 4.

89   Howard M. Hines to Gravel, editor of the *Silhouette*, 30 January 1974, McP, box 72.

90   Robert Howard, "French Profs Threaten Lawsuit over Criticism," *Silhouette*, 8 February 1974, 1.

91   Warner to Bourns, 31 January 1974, McP, box 72.

92   Bourns to Warner, 5 February 1974, McP, box 72.

93   D. Williams, W.N. Jeeves, A.W. Patrick, B.S. Pocknell, B. Blakey, G.D. West, and P.M Conlon, to Bourns, S. Frankel, A. Berland, and L. King, 24 January 1974, McP, box 72.

94   Pocknell to Berland, 20 January 1974, McP, box 72.

95   Pocknell and Williams to Alessio, chairman of romance languages, 21 January 1974, McP, box 72.

96   Bourns, Statement on romance language appointments, 16 March 1974, McP, box 72.

97   Anonymous, letter to *Radish* editor, clippings, 28 January 1974, McP, box 72.

98   Berland to *Radish* editor and the president of the MSU, clipping, 6 February 1974, McP, box 72.

99   Alessio to FSU, cc. Berland, Bourns, editors of the *Radish*, the *Silhouette*, et al., clippings, 11 February 1974, McP, box 72.

100 Everett Knight, "French Conflict in Wider Perspective," *Radish*, 28 February 1974, 2–3, clipping, McP, box 72.

101 Blakey to Bourns and Berland, 4 March 1974, McP, box 72.

102 King to Bourns, 12 February 1974, McP, box 72.

103 "French Students Plan Strike," *Silhouette*, 1 March 1974, 1.

104 Minutes of the French section, 7 March 1974, in Mueller, *Final Report*, McP, box 72.

105 Ted McMeekin, "Senate Lacks Adequate Representation," *Silhouette*, 21 September 1973, 5.

106 Sociology Students' Association to student senators, 21 February 1974, McP, box 72.

107 Larry Crandall, "French Strike Today Despite Mediation," *Silhouette*, 8 March 1874, 1; Crandall, "Offices Occupied," *Silhouette*, 15 March 1974, 1.

108 Social Work Students' Association to student senators, 25 February 1974, McP, box 72.

109 Minutes of Senate, 14 November 1973, 81.

110 Mueller, "Chronicle of Mediation," in Mueller, *Final Report*, tab C, McP box 72.

111 Crandall, "Offices Occupied," *Silhouette*, 15 March 1974, 1.

112 Ibid.

113 P. Pineo to Berland, Bourns, and the board, 15 March 1974, McP, box 72.

114 "Student Centre Cost Goes Up $10,000," *Silhouette*, 15 March 1974, 3.

115 King to Mueller, 14 March 1974, McP, box 72.

116 Mueller, *Chronicle*, 14 March 1974, McP, box 72.

117 Ibid., 15 March 1974; "Not All Students Agree," *Silhouette*, 15 March 1974, 15.

118 Bourns, statement on appointments, 16 March 1974, McP, box 72.

119 Bourns to Mueller, McP, box 72.

120 Bourns to Paquette, 17 March 1974, McP, box 72.

121 King to Mueller, 18 March 1974, McP, box 72.

122   Mueller, *Chronicle*, 16 March 1974, McP, box 72.

123   Brasch to Mueller, 15 March 1974, McP, box 72.

124   Report by E.B. Heaven, 21 March 1974 on discussions and letters dated 13–18 March 1974, McP, box 72.

125   Bourns, president's statement to the university community, 18 March 1974, McP, box 72.

126   Anonymous, "Berland's Bullshit," poster, 18 March 1974, McP, box 72.

127   Hedden, formal statement, 10 April 1974, McP, box 72.

128   Statements by Zack, 24 April 1974; and Ludlow, 2 April 1974, McP, box 72.

129   "Reaction to Student Arrests is Records Office Sit-In," *Silhouette*, 22 March 1974, 5b.

130   Bourns, memorandum of understanding, 20 March 1974, McP, box 72.

131   "Gym Packed for General Meeting," *Silhouette*, 22 March 1974, 5a.

132   Ibid.

133   David Kidney, et al., letter to the editor, *Silhouette*, 22 March 1974; Steubing noted that an official challenge to the strike vote was registered and that he was seeking legal advice. See MSU circular on general meeting, McP, box 72.

134   Bourns, memorandum to the McMaster community, 22 March 1974, McP, box 72.

135   Jack Stagg, et al., MSU *Special Edition*, 25 March 1974, 1, McP, box 72.

136   Bourns, poster, Senate Academic Policy Committee Acts, 26 March 1974, McP, box 72.

137   MSU Executive, statement to the student body, 27 March 1974, McP, box 72; Robert Howard, "Special Issue' Draws Mixed Student Reaction," *Silhouette*, 29 March 1974, 7.

138   King to Bourns, 26 March 1974, McP, box 72.

139   Bourns' remarks to the open senate, transcript, 28 March 1974, McP, box 72.

140   Minutes of the Special Senate Meeting 28 March 1974, appendix H, McP, box 72.

141   Larry Crandall, "3,000 Hear Issues Aired at Special Senate Meeting," *Silhouette*, 29 March 1974, 1, 7. For a complete transcript of the proceedings see, Minutes of the Senate, 8 March 1974, 189–211.

142   Bourns, Statement, 29 March 1974, McP, box 72.

143   Sackett to Bourns, 1 April 1974, McP, box 72.

144   Jacek and Truman to Bourns, 19 March 1974; Shemilt to Bourns, 3 April 1974, McP, box 72.

145   See, for example, Mary T. Hannon to Bourns, 4 April 1974; Janet Simmons to Bourns, 2 April 1974, McP, box 72.

146   K. Eisenbichler, et al. to Bourns, 26 March 1974, McP, box 72.

147   Winch to Bourns, 19 March 1974, McP, box 72.

148 Oksanen to Bourns, 19 March and 25 March 1974, McP, box 72.
149 French students to Bourns, 11 April 1974, McP, box 72.
150 Letters to high schools, 26 April–6 May 1974, McP, box 72.
151 King to Bourns, 23 April 1974, McP, box 72.
152 Mueller to David Williams (French), 7 May 1974, McP, box 72.
153 Berland to Alessio, 7 May 1974, McP, box 72.
154 Janet Simmons to Dr Harry Parrott, MPP, 2 April 1974, McP, box 72.
155 Simmons, "What is a Farce," draft of a letter to the editor of the *Silhouette*, appended to her letter to Parrott, 2 April 1974, McP, box 72.
156 James Auld to Bourns, 3 May 1974, McP, box 72.
157 L. King to Knight, 16 May 1974; Knight to King, 22 May 1974; King to Bourns, 30 May 1974, McP, box 72.
158 Sgt. Donald Garrett, report #73-1-6-164, 21 June 1974, McP, box 72.
159 Peterson, security reports, 22 May, 9 September; 7 October 1974, McP, box 72.
160 Bourns, interview by Alumni, transcript, 22 April 2009, 19, Office of Alumni Affairs and McMaster Archives.
161 Ibid., 18.
162 "Popular Prof Lapsed," *Silhouette*, 15 November 1974, 1.
163 Lee, *Memoir*, 25.
164 Lee interview, 10.
165 Don Sancton, "Thompson Hearing Exposes Soc. Split," *Silhouette*, 28 March 1975, 1.
166 Ibid.
167 Minutes of the Senate, 12 May 1975, 237–8; 10 December 1975, 59.
168 Ibid., 28 April 1977, 135–50; "New Tenure Document Passes Senate," *Contact*, 24 June 1977, 2; Lee, *Memoir*, 25.
169 Minutes of the Senate, 12 April 1972, 182–90.
170 Ibid., 22 November 1972, 90–3.
171 Ibid., 6 May 1974, 243–5.
172 Ibid., 26 September 1974, 26–31.
173 Ibid., 9 October 1974, 43–7.
174 Ibid., 17 October 1974, 63–9.
175 Ibid., 12 May 1975, 252–8.
176 "Senate Rejects Ombudsman," *Contact*, 20 April 1979, 1.
177 "SRA Vote Unanimous to Fire Security Chief," *Silhouette*, 27 September 1974, 1.
178 Minutes of the Senate, 25 November 1974, 89–103.
179 Dave Thorpe and Don Sancton, "Security Changes Promised after Peterson's Resignation," *Silhouette*, 29 November 1974, 1.

180   Nadeen Latham, "Bomb Found in Toilet: Disarmed Before Exploding," *Silhouette*, 10 January 1975, 1.

181   Minutes of the Senate, 27 February 1975, 163–73.

182   "Security Committee Selected," *Silhouette*, 19 September 1975, 1.

183   Rob Webb, "Don Garrett is Named to Fill Top Security Post," *Silhouette*, 3 October 1975, 1.

184   Tom Hogue, "Combined Force to Patrol Campus," *Silhouette*, 13 December 1979, 1.

185   Minutes of the Senate, 12 March 1975, 176–84.

186   Dan P.H. Parle, "Move for Senate Parity Appears Bogged Down," *Silhouette*, 15 March 1974, 1.

187   David Hitchcock, "Parity," *Silhouette*, 22 March 1974, 4.

188   Minutes of the Senate, 8 October 1975, 13.

189   Ibid., 14 November 1973, 78–86.

190   Ibid., 8 January 1975, 135–6.

191   Ibid., 12 May 1975, 240.

192   Ibid., 21 May 1975, 277–9.

193   Ibid., 14 January 1976, 80.

194   Ibid., 28 April 1977, 145.

195   "Students Removed from Committees," *Silhouette*, 29 September 1977, 1.

196   Ian Thompson, "Tenure Researched by McMaster Ombudsman," *Silhouette*, 27 October 1977, 5; Patricia Moser, "Pressure Promised by Students," *Silhouette*, 3 November 1977, 1.

197   Minutes of the Senate, 9 November 1977, 42–9.

198   Thompson and Anne Forest, "Recommendations for Tenure and Promotions," *Silhouette*, 17 November 1977, 5.

199   Sandra Cruickshanks, "Students Kicked Off Tenure Committees: MSU Plans Retaliation," *Silhouette*, 5 October 1978, 1.

200   June Saunders, "MSU Stays with Open House After Meeting," *Silhouette*, 12 October 1978, 1.

201   Neatby and McEown, *Carleton*, 190.

202   Axelrod, *Scholars*, 31.

203   Horn, *York*, 117, 139; 147.

CHAPTER TEN

1   George Gavrel, "Bourns Says Honeymoon Near End," *Silhouette*, 24 November 1972, 1; Minutes of the PEC, 30 September 1975, McP, box 8; Bourns interview by Alumni, 2008, 24, Office of Alumni Affairs and McMaster Archives.

2 Peter George and James Johnson, interview by author, transcript, February 2010, 2, Office of Alumni Affairs and McMaster Archives.

3 Minutes of the Senate, 9 October 1974, 41–2.

4 Council of Ontario Universities (COU), ACAP *Report 5: Chemistry*, 5 (Toronto: COU, 1973), A-42.

5 Martin Johns to Bourns, September 1974, McP, box 25.

6 King to Bourns, June 1973, McP, box 25.

7 COU, ACAP *Report 6: Solid Earth Science*, 1973, A-34.

8 COU, ACAP *Report 19: Mathematical Sciences*, 19, (Toronto: COU, 1975), A-37, A-58–9.

9 Chairman of Mathematics, *Mathematics: Report to the President*, July, 1975, McP, box 26.

10 For full details, see Minutes of the Senate, 8 June 1978, 213–28.

11 COU, ACAP *Report D: Mechanical Engineering* (Toronto: COU, 1974), A-33–4.

12 COU, ACAP *Report D: Metallurgy and Materials Science* (Toronto: COU, 1974), A-24–6.

13 Younger to Bourns, 15 June 1974, McP, box 25.

14 Frankel to Bourns, 5 July 1973, McP, box 25.

15 Peter George, interview by author, transcript, 10 November 2010, 1–3, Office of Alumni Affairs and McMaster Archives.

16 Winch to Bourns, 17 June 1973, McP, box 25.

17 University Registrar, *Registrar's Report*, 1974–75, 1 December 1974.

18 King, interview by author, 21 August 2012.

19 The precise figures were: sociology 63 and anthropology 25, in 1974, as opposed to sociology 40 and anthropology 35, in 1978. See, Registrar's Reports for the years in question.

20 E.V. Glanville to Bourns, July 1975, McP, box 26.

21 Richard J. Preston to Bourns, spring 1978, McP, box 28.

22 Minutes of the Senate, 29 April 1976, 169.

23 "Sir Peter Medawar Gives Redman Lectures," *Contact*, 17 March 1972, 2.

24 Johns to Bourns, August 1973, McP, box 25.

25 Johns, *Five-Year Plan*, 20 March 1973, 2–6, McP, box 25.

26 Minutes of the Department of Physics, 4 September 1975; 24 October 1975.

27 Malcolm F. Collins, *Report to the President*, 1979–80, 4.

28 Minutes of the Department of Physics, 9 January 1976.

29 Ibid., 24 March 1976.

30 Ibid., 9 April 1976.

31 Collins, *Report to the President*, 1977–78.

32 Ibid., 1979–80.

33 Ibid., 1975–76.

34 Ibid, 1976–77.

35 Ibid, 1978–79.

36 University Registrar, *Registrar's Report: 1978–70.*

37 Ibid, 1969–70; 1979–80.

38 Minutes of the Department of Chemistry, 14 April, 8 November, 17 November 1972.

39 D.B. McLean to Bourns, September 1974, McP, box 25.

40 Ibid., 1 August 1978.

41 Minutes of the Department of Chemistry, 10 October 1980.

42 Douglas Davidson to Bourns, 12 July 1976, McP, box 27.

43 Bayley, *Biology at McMaster University*, 98. On enrolment figures, see appendix A, 143.

44 Bayley to Bourns, 12 June 1973, McP, box 25.

45 Davidson to Bourns, *Annual Report*, 1976–77, McP, box 28.

46 Threlkeld to Bourns, 24 July 1978, McP, box 28.

47 Newbigging, "Psychology at McMaster," 140.

48 University Registrar, *Registrar's Reports*, 1969–70; 1979–80, McMaster Archives.

49 John R. Platt to Bourns, department report, 1977, McP, box 28.

50 "Arm's Length," *Contact*, 14 January 1977, 3.

51 For a handy summary of research in psychology during the period, see Bourns, supplement to *McMaster's Submission to* OCUA, 2 January 1975, McP, box 86.

52 Burghardt, *Geography*, 28.

53 Derek Ford to Bourns, *Annual Report*, July 1974, McP, box 25.

54 Burghardt, *Geography*, 25.

55 Bourns, *McMaster Submission to* OCUA, 2 January 1975, 7–8, McP, box 86.

56 M.J. Webber to Bourns, *Annual Report*, 1978, McP, box 28.

57 Ford to Bourns, *Annual Report*, July 1974, McP, box 25.

58 King to Bourns, July 1973, McP, box 25.

59 "Board Okays Thode Library," *Contact*, 30 June 1975, 4.

60 "Science Library Site," *Contact*, 8 January 1976, 1.

61 Minutes of the Department of Chemistry, 3 November 1975.

62 "Science Library Site," *Contact*, 8 January 1976, 1.

63 Hellmuth to Thode, 1 October 1970, McP, box 3.

64 Bourns to Hellmuth, 5 October 1970, McP, box 3.

65 McCalla to Bourns, 20 August 1973, McP, box 37.

66 Bourns to McCalla, 30 August 1973, McP, box 37.

67 Bourns, remarks to OCUA, 20 June 1975, McP, box 86.

68 Bourns, *Four-Year Financial Forecast: 1978–82*, 3–7, McP, box 5.

69 For a handy summary of Lapp's recommendations, see CODE *Responses to the Lapp Report*, copy, McP, box 35.

70 Shemilt to Bourns, 15 July 1972, McP, box 24.

71 Shemilt and Kirkaldy, confidential draft of "Directions" for Bourns, 8 January 1973, McP, box 37.

72 J.W. Bandler to Shemilt and Kirkaldy, 21 March 1973; Shemilt to Bourns, 22 February 1973, McP, box 37.

73 Purdy, email to author, 24 September 2013.

74 Ibid.

75 For more detail on these research groups, see *Brief History of McMaster*, 1979, 2–9; Morris Milner (Bioengineering) to Shemilt, 18 April 1977, Shemilt Papers, box 1.

76 Kirkaldy to Shemilt, 16 June 1981, Shemilt Papers, box 1.

77 Diane Kolev, "Engineering Draws Largest Enrolment Ever," *Silhouette*, Thursday, 27 September 1979, 2.

78 University Registrar, *Registrar's Reports*, 1969–70, 1980–81.

79 Minutes of the Senate, 23 April 1974, 236–7.

80 Thode, *President's Report*, 1964–5, 106.

81 Dr Dorothy Kergin to Thode, *Annual Report*, 1971–72, McP, box 23.

82 "Employment for Nursing Grads," *Contact*, 19 November 1979, 1.

83 Kergin to Bourns, *Annual Report*, 1975–76, McP, box 27; Spaulding, *Revitalizing Medical Education*, 162.

84 Spaulding, *Revitalizing Medical Education*, 194.

85 List of Health Science Faculty, September 1975, McP, box 43.

86 Spaulding, *Revitalizing Medical Education*, 169–70, 183; 185–93.

87 University Registrar, *Registrar's Report*, 1969–70, McMaster Archives.

88 "2,500 Apply to Health Sciences," *Contact*, 23 February 1979, 3.

89 University Registrar, *Registrar's Report*, 1979–80, McMaster Archives.

90 For example, see departmental reports for 1975–76, McP, box 27.

91 C.A. Moore, Department of Family Medicine, *Annual Report*, 1975–76, McP, box 27.

92 Mueller, *Little Medical School*, 9.

93 Admission Standards: 1967–77, Evans Papers, box 145.8.

94 Spaulding, *Revitalizing Medical Education*, 147–59.

95 *McMaster Faculty of Health Sciences Brief to the Ontario Ministry of Health on Acute Care Beds and Academic Programs*, 5 April 1976, McP, box 43, 8.

96 Ibid., 4–12. Regarding community teaching placements, see John Hay, Department of Family Medicine, *Annual Report*, 16 July 1973, McP, box 25.

97 Evans to Thode, 29 June 1972, McP, box 24.

98 "NOMP Program Evaluated," *Contact*, 3 May 1974, 3.

99 Mustard to Samuel Mitminger (president, Mohawk College), 26 March 1974, McP, box 42.

100 Monahan, *Collective Autonomy*, 22–3.

101 "Senate Approves in Principle McMaster/Mohawk Programs," *Contact*, 21 December 1979, 1.

102 For the earliest minutes of this body, see Mohawk–McMaster file, 1974, McP, box 43.

103 Mustard, *Annual Report*, 1973–74, McP, box 43.

104 "Senate Approves Two New Degrees," *Contact*, 18 April 1980, 1.

105 "Research in the Faculty of Health Sciences," in *McMaster in the 70s*, 1, (copy) in McP, box 43.

106 Mustard, brief to the Ministry of Health, 1976, McP, box 43.

107 Evans to Thode, *Annual Report*, 1970–71, 5, McP, box 23.

108 Ibid.

109 Mustard, *Annual Report*, 1972–73, McP, box 25.

110 "US Funds Medical Education," *Contact*, 18 September 1975, 4.

111 Bienenstock to Bourns, 19 May 1976, McP, box 43.

112 Kirkaldy to Shemilt, 16 June 1981, Shemilt Papers, box 1.

113 Schlatter to Hellmuth, 22 February 1971, McP, box 35. For example, Schlatter noted that enrolment in engineering was roughly the same as business, but the former had sixty-five staff, whereas his faculty had twenty-three. Externally, he pointed to smaller enrolments at Queen's and UBC, each of which boasted forty or more faculty members.

114 J.U. Joseph (supervisor of management development, TD Bank) to Norman White (assistant general manager, TD Bank), 29 January 1969. This letter was passed confidentially to Thode by White, a member of McMaster's board. See also, White to Thode, 4 February 1969; Schlatter to Zack, 10 February 1969; Thode to White, 22 February 1969, McP, box 34.

115 Bourns interview, 26.

116 Schlatter to Bourns, 26 July 1973, McP, box 25.

117 Schlatter to Hellmuth, 22 February 1971, McP, box 35.

118 University Registrar, *Registrar's Report*, 1979–80, McMaster Archives.

119 Len Eckel, et al., *Report to the Faculty of Business from the Subcommittee on the MBA Core*, 31 October 1973, McP, box 35.

120 Schlatter, *Annual Report*, September 1972, McP, box 35.

121 Unsigned, proposal for a PhD program (Business), December 1974, McP, box 35.

122 Minutes of the Senate, 8 February 1978, 127; 12 May 1980, 89; Minutes of Dean's Retreat 8 January, 1979, 2, McP, box, 5.

123   University Registrar, *Registrar's Report*, 1974–5 shows full-time graduate enrolments for economics (76), religious studies (73), and English (63), along with those in chemistry (61), physics (65), and medicine (66). History (43) and philosophy (48) compared favourably with psychology (44), geography (41), mathematics (42), and biology (35).

124   Cassels, *Fascist Italy*; *Fascism*.

125   Owen, *Prose Works of William Wordsworth*.

126   Wood, *Chaucer and the Country of the Stars*.

127   Scammell, *International Monetary Policy*; Winch, *Analytical Welfare Economics*.

128   Minutes of the Humanities Faculty Council, 1 June 1972, v.

129   Ibid., 20 September 1979, ii.

130   University Registrar, *Registrar's Report*, 1969.

131   Ibid., 1980.

132   Minutes, Humanities Faculty Council, 20 September 1979, ii.

133   McKay, *Dean's Report*, July 1970, McP, box 23.

134   Cappadocia to Thode, 16 June 1971, McP, box 23; Cappadocia to Bourns, 28 June 1973, McP, box 24.

135   Cappadocia to Bourns, 17 June 1975, McP, box, 26.

136   Minutes of the Department of History, 21 September 1978.

137   Campbell to Bourns, 23 June 1978, McP, box, 28.

138   Cappadocia to Bourns, 20 June 1974, McP, box 25.

139   Minutes of the Humanities Faculty Council, 20 September 1979, ii; see also comments on trends in University Registrar, *Registrar's Report*, 1980–1, part I, McMaster Archives.

140   University Registrar, *Registrar's Reports*, 1974–80.

141   Chairman S.M. Najm noted a 2 per cent drop in registrations in 1974–5. Najm to Bourns, July 1975, McP, box 26.

142   Questionnaire, David Hitchcock, 28 June 2007.

143   Najm to Bourns, 8 August 1977, McP, box 28.

144   Ibid.

145   Ibid., 18 August 1978.

146   Douglas J.M. Duncan to Bourns, 14 June 1974, McP, box 25.

147   Duncan to Bourns, 20 June 1975, McP, box 26.

148   Duncan to Bourns, 30 June 1976, McP, box 27.

149   Lee, *Developments in Department of English 1960–89*, a brief history, October 2013. Memorandum to author, October 2013. To be donated to McMaster Archives.

150   A sample from the *Registrar's Reports* lists the numbers of graduates registered in English: 1974 (63), 1976 (53), and 1978 (58).

151 César Reuben to Bourns, 7 July 1978, McP, box 28.

152 G. Thomas (Russian) to Bourns 26 July 1978, McP, box 28.

153 Lee interview, 8.

154 Ibid; Minutes of the Senate, 18 May 1977, 180, McMaster Archives.

155 Minutes of the Faculty of Humanities, 2 March 1973.

156 Hellmuth to Bourns, 29 November 1973, McP, box 25.

157 Lee interview, 16.

158 Hilary Turner, "Mills Librarian Retires," *Silhouette*, 2 November 1978, 5.

159 Dan Kislenko, "Mac Joins Library Elite," *Silhouette*, 30 January 1976, 3. The other four were Toronto, McGill, Alberta, and UBC.

160 "SSHRC Grant to Russell Project," *Contact*, 25 April 1980, 1.

161 Frankel to Bourns, September 1974, McP, box 26.

162 Lee interview, 15.

163 Minutes of the Senate, 6 May 1974, 250, McMaster Archives.

164 J.A. Williamson (COU) to members of Graduate Council, 29 August 1974, McP, box 44.

165 Henry Jacek, interview by author, transcript, 18 November 2011. Handwritten notes to be donated to McMaster Archives.

166 Bromke to Bourns, 26 June 1974, McP, box 25.

167 Undated review of political science appended to BSCAP report to the senate, Minutes of the Senate 1986. The date can be approximated by internal references. McMaster Archives.

168 Jacek interview

169 University Registrar, *Registrar's Reports*, 1973–74, 1978–79, McMaster Archives.

170 Bromke, Political Science, *Annual Report*, 20 June 1975, McP, box 26.

171 Novak to Bourns, 26 June 1978, McP, box 28; Minutes of the Senate, 23 February 1978, 146, McMaster Archives.

172 Jacek interview.

173 J.A. Williamson to Graduate Council, 29 August 1974, McP, box 44.

174 Minutes of the Department of Sociology, 14 May 1974.

175 Minutes of the Senate, 6 May 1974, 249.

176 Frankel to Bourns, September 1974, McP, box 26.

177 Minutes of the Department of Sociology, 16 January 1975.

178 F. Jones, et al., proposed plan for the doctoral program, 1976, 3–7, Department of Sociology files.

179 Ibid.

180 D. Shaw to P. Sheriff, 9 March 1979, Department of Sociology files.

181 Shaw to R. Matthews, 20 October 1981, Department of Sociology files.

182 Graduate chairman to all Sociology faculty, 2 April 1979, Department of Sociology files.

183 Ibid., 3; Lee, *Memoir*, 24.

184 Jacek interview.

185 Meyer to Bourns, 6 August 1975, McP, box 26.

186 Meyer to Bourns, June 1976, McP, box 27; Minutes of the Department of Religious Studies, 7 April 1976, 4b.

187 George Grant, untitled, *Spectator*, 11 April 1980, 7; untitled, *Globe and Mail*, 28 April 1980, 7.

188 Younger to Bourns, 18 June 1976, McP, box 87.

189 Minutes of the PEC, 1 May 1975, McP, box 8.

190 Y. Jan to Bourns, 26 January 1978, McP, box 28.

191 Winch to Bourns, 24 June 1976, McP, box 27.

192 Winch to Bourns, 27 June 1976, McP, box 28.

193 Johnson to Bourns, 13 June 1978, McP, box 28.

CHAPTER ELEVEN

1 Bliss, "Founding FIRA," in Spence and Rosenfeld, *Foreign Investment Review* 1–11.

2 Kelley and Trebilcock, *Making of the Mosaic*, 363.

3 Neatby and McEown, *Creating Carleton*, 160–61; Horn, *York University*, 99.

4 Monahan, *Collective Autonomy*, 35.

5 Bourns to Dr Colin Mackay (AUCC), 1 February 1973, McP, box 88.

6 "Foreign Students: New Job Regulations," *Silhouette*, 1 December 1973, 1.

7 "Bourns Gives Support to Foreign Students," *Silhouette*, 9 February 1973, 3; Andras to Colin Mackay, 22 February 1973, McP, box 88.

8 Monahan, *Collective Autonomy*, 101.

9 Minutes of the Senate, 24 January 1973, 143, McMaster Archives.

10 Pierre Maranda to H.G. Thode, 16 January 1973, McP, box 34.

11 "Canadianization Urged for Mac Faculty," *Spectator*, 12 April 1973, 10.

12 Minutes of the Senate, 14 March 1973, 195–200, McMaster Archives.

13 Monahan, *Collective Autonomy*, 101.

14 Minutes of the Senate, 14 April 1973, 153.

15 Parrott, statement to the legislature, 26 April 1976, copy, McP, box 74.

16 "Canada-First Warning Worries Mac," *Spectator*, 27 April 1976, 7; "Hire Canadians, Universities Told," *Globe and Mail*, 27 April 1976, 5.

17 Bourns, "McMaster Encourages Canadian Scholars," *Spectator*, 14 May 1976, 6.

18 Kelley and Trebilcock, *Making of the Mosaic*, 382–3.

19 Bourns, "McMaster Encourages Canadian Scholars," *Spectator*, 14 May, 1976, 6.

20 Bourns to Parrott, 18 November 1976, McP, box 74.

21 Parrott to Bourns, 7 December 1976, McP, box 74.

22 Bourns to D.F. Dawson, University of Guelph president, 2 September 1977, McP, box 74.

23 Parrott to Bourns, 7 December 1976, McP, box 74.

24 Peter Yurksaitis, "McMaster Professor and Wife Champion Cause of Foreign Students," *Silhouette*, 5 January 1973, 1.

25 "Mac to Limit Foreign Student Enrolment," *Contact*, 16 February 1976, 1; "Ontarians to get Preference when Enrolments Limited," *Contact*, 11 March 1976, 1.

26 "Fees for New Foreign Students to Triple," *Globe and Mail*, 5 May 1976, 5.

27 Minutes of the Senate, 19 May 1976, 180–5.

28 Patricia Moser, "Fund Drive to Determine Fee Structure," *Silhouette*, 15 September 1977, 1.

29 "You Pay the Price, Parrott Tells Mac," *Spectator*, 28 January 1977, 7.

30 "Fund Drive a Result of Costly 'Back Door' Loss," *Silhouette*, 22 September 1977, 3.

31 Minutes of the Senate, 11 January 1978, 101–10.

32 Ibid., 12 October 1977, 13; Moser, "Differential Fees Inevitable at Mac," *Silhouette*, 24 November 1977, 1.

33 Minutes of the Senate, 10 November 1976, 39.

34 Ibid., 10 January 1979, 65–8; 14 February 1979, 79.

35 Ibid., 8 September 1976, 1–3.

36 Bourns, pencil note, 2 February 1978, McP, box 5.

37 Parrott to Bourns, 8 May 1978, McP, box 87.

38 Lee to all deans, 17 November 1977, McP, box 87.

39 Bourns, *Four-Year Financial Forecast*, December 1978, McP, box 87.

40 "Governors Predict $745,000 Deficit," *Contact*, 11 May 1979, 1.

41 June Saunders, "Mac to Cut 65 Faculty," *Silhouette*, 29 March 1979, 1.

42 Minutes of the PEC, 7 November 1977, McP, box 8.

43 Minutes of the Senate, 1 November 1977, 28.

44 "Governors Approve Differential Fees," *Silhouette*, 2 February 1978, 1; transcript, Bourns interview, 50.

45 Ian Thompson and Anne Forest, "Recommendations for Tenure and Promotions," *Silhouette*, 17 November 1977, 5; Sandra Cruickshanks, "Students Kicked Off Tenure Committees," *Silhouette*, 5 October 1978, 1.

46 "Late Bus for Queen's Park," *Silhouette*, 9 March 1978, 5; "Protest Resembled Radical 1960s," *Silhouette*, 23 March 1978, 1; Minutes of the Senate, 8 March 1978, 157.

47 Thompson, "The Shape of Things to Come at Mac," *Silhouette*, 9 November 1978, 5.

48 Jackson, MUFA's *First 50 Years*, 72.

49 For confirmation of this homogeneous view, see the reminiscences of MUFA presidents 1972–80 in Jackson, MUFA's *First 50 Years*, 72.

50 Kirkaldy to Thode, 7 March 1969, McP box 74.

51 Jackson, MUFA's *First 50 Years*, 47.

52 MUFA, brief regarding salaries, December 1971, 5–8, McP, box 74.

53 For a particularly raucous debate on these linked issues, see Minutes of the Senate, 8 October 1972, 60–9.

54 Lee, interview, 11, Office of Alumni Affairs and McMaster Archives.

55 King, interview, 17, Office of Alumni Affairs and McMaster Archives.

56 Minutes of the Senate, 13 September 1972, 10.

57 Minutes of the PEC, 10 November 1972, McP, box 7.

58 Hunter to Bourns, 8 November 1972, reprinted in Jackson, MUFA's *First 50 Years*, 59.

59 Minutes of the PEC, 10 and 23 November 1972, McP, box 7.

60 Minutes of the Senate, 8 November 1972, 65–71.

61 Minutes of the PEC, 23 March 1973, McP, box 7.

62 Jackson, MUFA's *First 50 Years*, 57–9.

63 G. Field, in Jackson, MUFA's *First 50 Years*, 68.

64 Jackson, MUFA's *First 50 Years*, 93–9.

65 Ibid., 68; Minutes of the MUFA AGM, 22 April 1976.

66 Minutes of PEC, 7 March 1973, McP, box 7; 4 June 1975, box 8.

67 Ibid., 14 January 1975, McP, box 1.

68 Minutes of MUFA AGM, 1976–78.

69 Ibid., 10 December 1975, 6.

70 Harold Guite, "Letter from the President," *Faculty Association Newsletter*, 2 October 1977, 3, MUFA Office files (hereafter MOF).

71 Ibid., 26 April 1978, 1; Minutes MUFA AGM, 3 March 1978.

72 Bourns, address to the Faculty Association Executive, 27 June 1978, 1–9, McP, box 91.

73 *Faculty Association Newsletter*, Fall 1978, 2–3, copy, McP, box 91.

74 Jackson, MUFA's *First 50 Years*, 81.

75 Ibid., 96.

76 Ibid., 82.

77   Ibid., 85–7; "Faculty Choice Unique in Canada," *Silhouette*, 30 November 1978, 1; "Faculty Choice Not Final," 6 December, 1978, 5.
78   Minutes of the PEC, 12 September 1970, McP, box 7.
79   Minutes of the Senate, 13 September 1972, 1–4.
80   Lee to Bourns, 3 July 1972, McP, box 24.
81   Hedden to Bourns, 29 August 1973, McP, box 25.
82   Minutes of the Senate, 27 September 1974, 42–4.
83   Lee interview, 8.
84   Minutes of the Senate, 10 November 1976, 40–3.
85   Ibid., 18 May 1977, 181–6.
86   Ibid., 189.
87   Ibid., 190.
88   Ibid., 190–1.
89   Ibid., 24 November 1977, 60–74. For precise details, see R. Gillespie, et al., *Plan for McMaster* (PFM), 21–2.
90   Minutes of the Senate, 23 February 1978, 136–8.
91   Ibid., 139–40.
92   Gillespie, PFM, 72.
93   Ibid., 76.
94   Ibid., 77.
95   Minutes of the Senate, 23 November 1978, 145.
96   Gillespie, PFM, 11.
97   Ibid., 14.
98   Ibid., 4, 11.
99   Ibid., 2.
100 Ibid., 3.
101 Ibid, 11–12.
102 Ibid, "Sciences," 79–100.
103 Ibid, 81. The exceptions, here, were those courses that supported more heavily subscribed part-time BA programs.
104 Ibid., 42–3.
105 Ibid., "Business," 30–7.
106 Ibid., "Health Sciences," 51.
107 Ibid., 44–65.
108 Ibid., "Social Sciences," 101–11.
109 "MSU Speaks Out against Research Emphasis," *Spectator*, 27 May 1977, 7.
110 Minutes of the Senate, 14 June 1978, 242–3.
111 Horn, *York University*, 180–6.
112 Lee, *Memoir*, 31.
113 Minutes of the Senate, 24 November 1977, 62–72.

114 Ibid., 27 June 1979, 157–66.
115 The planning council included: Jenkins, J. Carbotte, G. Papageorgiou, D. McCalla, E. Sanders, and W. Wallace.
116 For the decisive debate on the arts and science degree, see the Minutes of the Senate, 21 May 1980, 100–5.
117 Christian, *George Grant*, 324.
118 For a lengthy elucidation of Grant's thought on these matters, see Christian, *George Grant*, 128–368.
119 Peter van Harten, "Professor Unhappy with Mac," *Spectator*, 11 April 1980, 7.
120 Len Sawatsky, "Direction of University Questioned by Resignation of Grant," *Dundas Star Journal*, 9 April 1980, 8.
121 Ann Blackwood, "The Bothersome Students," *Globe and Mail*, 26 April 1980, 7.
122 Grant, "The Battle Between Teaching and Research," *Globe and Mail*, 28 April 1980, 7; Estabrooks, "Letter Backs Grant's Criticism about McMaster Split," *Dundas Star Journal*, 30 April 1980, 6; Harris, "Student Looks at Professor's Comments," *Spectator*, 3 May 1980, 6.
123 Anne E. Yarwood, "Professor's Remarks Called Regrettable and Saddening," *Spectator*, 3 May 1980, 6.
124 Bourns and Kristofferson, "Teaching Doesn't Get Short Shrift, Say Mac Officials," *Globe and Mail*, 22 April 1980, 7.
125 Christian, *George Grant*, 327.
126 Combs, "Shallow"; Robertson, et al, "Unfortunate," *Spectator*, 3 May 1980, 5–6.
127 Bishop, "Dr. Grant's Resignation," *Globe and Mail*, 30 April 1980, 6.
128 Griffin, "Teaching and Research," *Globe and Mail*, 6 May 1980, 6.
129 Lee interview, 19.
130 "McMaster to Receive $25 Million Bequest," *Contact*, 1 February 1980, 1.
131 For a profile of Hooker and background concerning his bequest, see ibid; and "$25 Million for Mac," *Silhouette*, 7 February 1980, 1.
132 Lee interview, 19.
133 Minutes of the Senate, 11 April 1979, 104.

CHAPTER TWELVE

1 For the details of Lee's recruitment as president, see Lee, *Memoir*, 4–5; Lee interview, 11–12.
2 Richard Feenstra, "New President Anticipates His Job," *Silhouette*, 14 February 1980, 3.

3 Lee, "Inaugural Address," Lee Papers, box 2; "Installation Address of Dr. Alvin A. Lee," *Contact*, 21 November 1980, 2–3.

4 "400-Metre Track and Stadium," *Courier*, 29 March 1983, 1, 4.

5 Norrie, Owram, and Emery, *History of the Canadian Economy*, 402–15.

6 Francis, Jones, and Smith, *Destinies*, 533.

7 Paul Wilson, "Our City is Shrinking," *Spectator*, 20 August 1986.

8 "500 Get Good News as Stelco Announces Summer Recalls," *Spectator*, 5 April 1982.

9 Mike Pettapiece, "Layoffs at Stelco May Hit 3,100," *Spectator*, 6 October 1982.

10 John Burman, "Layoffs Urged to Cut Costs in Schools," *Spectator*, 1 June 1982.

11 Lee, "Increased Funding Essential – McMaster President," *Spectator*, 14 November 1981, 6.

12 Monahan, *Collective Autonomy*, 128.

13 "Mac Swamped by Applications," *Spectator*, 12 September 1983.

14 "University Presidents Express Resentment at Threats on Deficits," *Courier*, 23 February 1982, 1; Monahan, *Collective Autonomy*, 129.

15 Darling, "Tensions Increase over Funding Distribution," *Courier*, 15 March 1983, 5.

16 "University Accessibility Key to Ending Ivory Tower Image," *Courier*, 8 November 1983, 4.

17 Darling, "Tensions Increase," *Courier*, 15 March 1983, 5.

18 Monahan, *Collective Autonomy*, 131.

19 "Stephenson Warns Universities," *Toronto Star*, 22 December 1982, 2. Reprinted in *Courier*, 18 January 1983, 3.

20 Monahan, *Collective Autonomy*, 130.

21 "Freeze Removed," *Courier*, 18 January 1983, 2.

22 Minutes of the Senate, 13 October 1982, 14.

23 Sunny Buskermolen, "Visa Fee Hike Hits Students Unaware," *Silhouette*, 17 March 1983, 1.

24 "Closing Doors," *Courier*, 21 October 1986, 5.

25 "COU Submits Brief," *Courier*, 13 September 1983, 5.

26 Bourns interview, 49.

27 Minutes of the PEC, 22 December 1980, McP, box 8.

28 Bourns to J.H. Moore, 20 March 1978, McP, box 60.

29 Mimmo Lostracco, speech to alumni association, 27 May 1978, McP, box 60.

30 Moore to Bourns, 9 March 1977, McP, box 60.

31 Bourns to Moore, 20 March 1978, McP, box 60.

32 Dennis Carson to Bourns, 14 July, 1972, McP, box 60.

33 *Final Report of the Committee of the McMaster University Alumni Association*, October 1971, 34–9, McP, box 60.

34 Ibid., 15.

35 Alumni Council, draft response to COPSE *Report*, 9, McP, box 60.

36 *Final Report*, 45–51, McP, box 60.

37 Ibid., 15.

38 Carson to Bourns, 29 August 1973, McP, box 60.

39 *Report of the Alumni Fund Study Committee*, September 1971, 79–85, McP, box 60.

40 Lostracco, speech, 27 May 1978, McP, box 60.

41 Stuart Winn, Mimmo Lostracco, Jack Moore and Marnie Spears to Charles Jago, chairman of the LRPC, 30 April, 1979, McP, box 60.

42 Bourns to Moore, 5 June 1979, McP, box 60.

43 Moore to Bourns, 1 June 1979, McP, box 60.

44 Bourns to Moore, 5 June 1979, McP, box 60.

45 "Alumni Try to Revive University's School Spirit," *Contact*, 5 September 1980, 1.

46 *Report of the President's Task Force on University-Alumni Relations*, 16 April 1981, 1–2, Lee Papers, box 1. McMaster Archives, uncatalogued.

47 Ibid., 3.

48 Ibid., 3–12; 16.

49 Ibid., 13–15.

50 King to Lee, 15 April 1981, Lee Papers, box 1.

51 Minutes of the Senate, 11 February 1981, 87.

52 "McMaster Alumni Council Approves Recommendations," *Courier*, 8 November 1983, 23.

53 "Limited Membership in Faculty Club Available to Alumni," *Contact*, 4 December 1981, 1.

54 "Alumni Raises Quarter of a Million," *Contact*, 27 February 1981, 3.

55 "Improving on an Impressive record," *Courier*, 20 January 1987, 4.

56 "Alumni Association Forms Fund Raising Commitee," *Courier*, 21 January 1986, 16.

57 Lee Interview, 17; 27.

58 Lee, *Memoir*, 37.

59 Ibid., 41.

60 King interview, 7.

61 For full details of the prolonged sociology affair, see Richard Feenstra, "Students Fight to Retain Tenure Decision Reps," *Silhouette*, 26 February 1981, 1; "Raj Hathiramani, "Sociology Sit-in Seen as Last Hope," 19 March 1981,

1; Willard Lutz, "Sit-ins Staged to Settle Stalemate," 26 March 1981, 1–8; Jeff Andrew, "Fight for Rights Just Beginning Despite Settlement," 2 April 1981, 1; Anne Jarvis, "Graduate Program Threatened: Repeat of 'Nonsense' May Result in Formal Review," 11 March 1982, 1; Jarvis, "Sociology Gets Green Light," 18 March 1982, 1. See also, Minutes of Senate, 8 April 1981, 97–103; 10 February 1982, 151–2.

62   "Students Lose Stake in the Future of Mac," *Silhouette*, 12 November 1981, 2.

63   Minutes of the Senate, 11 November 1981, 48–55.

64   Ibid., 13 January 1982, 100–6.

65   Ibid., 9 December 1981, 63.

66   Steve Worotynec, "Students Speak Out Strongly against King's Actions," *Silhouette*, Thursday, 3 December 1981, 3.

67   Jeff Andrew, "Program Changes Mean Rough Road Ahead for C.A. Hopefuls," *Silhouette*, 3 December, 1981, 1.

68   Minutes of the Senate, 13 January 1982, 87–97.

69   Brian Howlett, "Business Program Changed Despite Student Protest," *Silhouette*, 14 January 1982, 1.

70   Minutes of the Senate, 10 February 1982, 122–9.

71   Editorial, *Silhouette*, 3 December 1981, 1.

72   Brian Howlett, "Residences Outraged Over Proposed Restructuring", *Silhouette*, 3 December 1981, 1.

73   Minutes of the Senate, 8 April 1981, 97–103; 11 May 1981, 136.

74   Ibid., 28 January 1982, 109–18.

75   Ibid., 9 November 1983, 24.

76   Concerning the continuing battle over orientation, see Jim Morreale, "Student Rally Sends Message to Senate," *Silhouette*, 12 March 1987, 1; Minutes of the Senate, 14 December 1983, 41–3; Michael Kukhta, MSU president, to Senate, 9 March 1987, in Minutes of Senate, 25 March 1987.

77   Minutes of Senate, 10 February 1982, 139–46.

78   Jeff Andrew, "Students Band Together to Discuss Problems," *Silhouette*, 25 February 1982, 1.

79   Minutes of the Senate, 10 March 1982, 148–50.

80   Ibid.

81   Krista Foss, "SRA Opposes Residence Policy," *Silhouette*, 9 February 1984, 1.

82   "Senate Accepts Residence Report," *Courier*, 26 November 1985, 1–2.

83   Minutes of the Senate, 14 October 1987, 15.

84   For details on the code of conduct, see Minutes of the Senate, 9 February 1983, 80–7. Concerning part-time scholarships, see Minutes of the Senate, 7 May 1984, 104–7.

85 "Report to Senate of the Planning and Building Committee," 11, Minutes of Senate, 23 May 1986,

86 "MSU Quality of Student Life Report," 1–92, Minutes of the Senate, April 1987.

87 Minutes of Senate, 8 April 1981, 105–8; "New Programs for 1986–87," Courier, 9 September 1986, 3.

88 "Geriatrics Centre Established," Courier, 14 April 1987, 1.

89 Robyn Smith "Cdn. Studies Axed", Silhouette, 15 January 1986, 1.

90 The key debates on the Nice Report can be found in the Minutes of the Senate, 14 October 1981, 20–5; and 29 October 1981, 30–41.

91 Minutes of the Senate, 10 September 1980, 2–4.

92 Ibid., 14 September 1984, 13.

93 "Probe into Admissions Test Urged," Courier, 10 May 1983, 1.

94 Minutes of the Senate, 11 May 1981, 141.

95 For sample BSCAP reviews, see Minutes of the Senate, 12 May 1986 to 8 March 1987.

96 Shona Wynd, "Art Department to Remain Open," Silhouette, Thursday, 22 January 1987, 1.

97 Minutes of the Senate, 29 April 1986, 5. See also the report appended to this session from the undergraduate council, 1–5; and Niall Whelan, "English Test Stress," Silhouette, 28 August 1986, 1.

98 Heidi Hartl, "Error Was Committee's Fault," Silhouette, 9 October 1986, 1.

99 Minutes of the Senate, 8 April 1987, 118.

100 Mark Langton, "Test Mistake Raises Questions," Silhouette, 2 October 1986, 1.

101 Minutes of the Senate, 28 May 1987, 109–15.

102 Report of Meeting of Five University Heads, 17–18 December 1982, Lee Papers, box 1.

103 "Four University Presidents to Hold Talks at McMaster," Contact, 21 March 1980, 1–2.

104 Untitled, press release on the Fisher Report, n.d., Lee Papers, box 1.

105 MQTWW discussion paper, 27 November 1982, Lee Papers, box 1.

106 Monahan, Collective Autonomy, 144.

107 MQTWW discussion paper, 27 November 1982, Lee Papers, box 1.

108 Report of Meeting of the Five University Heads, 17–18 December 1982, Lee Papers, box 1.

109 "Newly Appointed Commission Studies Change to University System," Courier, 17 January 1984, 1–2.

110 Rhoda Metcalf, "Students Protest Bovey," Silhouette, 20 September 1984, 1.

111 "OCUFA Calls for Minister's Resignation," Courier, 17 January 1984, 4–5.

112   Bruce Stewart, "We Need Outcry on Funding: Mac Head," *Spectator*, 27 August 1984.

113   For a concise outline of the main recommendations, see "Higher Fees, Fuel for Bovey Changes," *Courier*, 17 January 1985, 1–2.

114   "Bovey Proposals Draw Praise and Disappointment," *Courier*, 5 February 1985, 1–2.

115   "Won't Support Limits on Accessibility, Miller Says," *Courier*, 2 April 1985, 1.

116   Lee, *Mission Statement*, February 1989, Lee Papers, box 1.

117   Ken Post to Judy Grogan, 22 June 1988, Lee Papers, box 2.

118   Peter George interview by author, transcript, 15, Office of Alumni Affairs and McMaster Archives.

119   Leslie King, "Improved Teaching for Undergraduates to be Encouraged," *Contact*, 16 June 1981, 2–6.

120   David Gagan and Peter George, interview by Alumni, transcript, 6, Office of Alumni Affairs and McMaster Archives.

121   Rowland Smith, BSCAP report on English, 9 March 1988; Chauncey Wood, BSCAP report on Sociology, March 1984; David Gallop, (Trent) BSCAP report on philosophy, April 1984; Arnold Wilson, (University of Cincinnati) BSCAP report on philosophy, 12 August 1984; S. Najm, (chairman of philosophy) General Report and Review, Department of Philosophy, 16 January 1984, 5–6. The material above is available in the files of the respective departments. See also, Bayley, *Biology at McMaster*, 111–17.

122   Wilson, BSCAP philosophy review, department files.

123   Najm, general report, 1984, 6.

124   Lee, *Memoir*, 38.

125   Gagan and George interview, 14.

126   Ibid., 9.

127   Lee, "Teaching and Learning at McMaster," (speech, no location, 4 March 1981); *Knowing McMaster*, brochure, 1987, 69, Lee Papers, box 2.

128   Ibid.

CHAPTER THIRTEEN

1   Douglas Marrs, et al, *Report to Senate from the Committee to Recommend a President*, 14 December 1984, Lee Papers, box 2.

2   "Canadian Universities in Crisis," *Courier*, Special Report, March 1982, 10.

3   "Faculty Association Protests Lack of Budget Information," *Courier*, 24 May 1983, 1; Jackson, MUFA's *First 50 Years*, 97, 100.

4   Minutes of the Special General Meeting of MUFA, 7 May 1982, MOF.

5   MUFA, Minutes of the Annual General Meeting, 22 April 1983, MOF.

6   Lee, *Memoir*, 40.

7   Ibid., 39; Minutes of the Special General Meeting of MUFA, 30 March 1984, 4, MOF.

8   Minutes of the Special General Meeting of MUFA, 30 March 1984, 6, MOF.

9   George interview, 9.

10   Minutes of the Special General Meeting of MUFA, 30 March 1984, 1–8, MOF.

11   Ibid., 12 April 1984, 1–6.

12   Ibid., 25 April 1984, 1–6.

13   Minutes of the General Meeting of MUFA, 12 December 1984, 6, MOF. See also, Jackson, MUFA's *First 50 Years*, 116–18.

14   For details of the tripartite agreement, see Minutes of the General Meeting of MUFA 12 December 1984, 3–6 MOF; "General Approval Given Impasse Solution," *Courier*, 17 January 1985, 6.; and "Agreement Makes Headway for Faculty," *Silhouette*, 10 January 1985, 1.

15   *Report of Committee to Recommend a President*, 14 December 1984, 1–6, Lee Papers, box2.

16   Lee, *Memoir*, 42–4.

17   Jackson, MUFA's *First 50 Years*, 120.

18   Ibid., 120–35. Regarding the revival of concern about collegiality late in Lee's second term, see John Lott in Jackson, MUFA's *First 50 Years,* 127–31. On the other hand, see the upbeat remarks of Henry Schwarcz in MUFA's *Newsletter*, 14 September 1987.

19   Jackson, MUFA's *First 50 Years*, 94.

20   "Health Sciences Grants," *Courier*, 22 October 1985, 10; Krista Foss, "McMaster Research," *Silhouette*, 17 November 1983, 6.

21   "Ceramic Engineering," *Courier*, 20 July 1982, 13.

22   "National Defence Gives $200,000," *Courier*, 4 February 1986, 1.

23   Lee interview, 24.

24   "Half Million NSERC Grant for CRL," *Courier*, 19 March 1985, 1.

25   "McMaster Research: an Overview," *Courier*, 12 April 1983, 10.

26   Concerning the rise and fall of CARED and CIM, see a lengthy retrospective in the *Courier*, 17 February 1987, 1. See also, Minutes of the Senate, 14 October 1987, 12.

27   "$8.4 Million from Province," *Courier*, 26 May 1987, 1.

28   Krista Foss, "McMaster Research," *Silhouette*, 17 November 1983, 6.

29   Richard A. Rempel interviewed by author, handwritten notes, 5 May 2011. (Notes will be deposited in the McMaster Archives.)

30   Lee interview, 9; Lee, *Memoir*, 36–7.

31   "McMaster is Well Poised for its Role in Centres of Excellence," *Courier*, 10 March 1987, 1.

32 "Centres of Excellence Encourage Joint Research and Technology Transfer," *Courier*, 19 August 1987, 1.
33 Minutes of the Senate, 11 June 1986, 22.
34 Ibid., 11 November 1987, 20–6.
35 Gagan and George Interview, 2–3, 6–9.
36 Minutes of the Senate, 14 October 1987, 16.
37 "Centennial Banners Vandalized," *Courier*, 24 March 1987, 4.
38 "Centennial Spotlight," *Courier*, 8 December 1987, 4.
39 Kilbourn, "Making the Grade," *Saturday Night*, September 1988, 50–6. Copy in Lee Papers, box 1.

Bibliography

ARCHIVAL SOURCES

Unless otherwise indicated, these are held in the research and special collections of the William Ready Division of Mills Memorial Library, McMaster University.

MANUSCRIPT SOURCES

Alvin A. Lee Papers.
Department Minutes and Files. Department offices, McMaster University.
Edward Togo Salmon Papers.
Henry G. Thode (personal) Papers.
James Fraser Mustard Papers. McMaster Health Sciences Library special
    collections.
John R. Evans Papers. McMaster Health Sciences Library special collections.
Leslie Shemilt Papers.
McMaster Presidents' Papers, for G.P. Gilmour, H.G. Thode, and A.N. Bourns.
McMaster University Faculty Association Files, MUFA office.
Minutes and Files of Faculties, Decanal offices, McMaster University.
Minutes of the Senate of McMaster University.

NEWSPAPERS AND JOURNALS

Items drawn from clipping files often have either page or day of the week missing.

Clippings, "McMaster University," Hamilton Public Library
Clippings, "McMaster University," Mills Library, special collections.

Contact
Dundas Star
Globe and Mail
Hamilton Spectator
McMaster Courier
McMaster Gazette
McMaster News
Silhouette
Toronto Star
Westdale Reporter

ORAL SOURCES

Transcripts of the various individual and group interviews noted in the endnotes
are on file with the rare books and special collections division of the Mills Memorial Library and with the Office of Alumni Affairs.

PRINTED SOURCES

Axelrod, Paul. *Scholars and Dollars: Politics, Economics, and the Universities of
Ontario 1945–1980*. Toronto: University of Toronto Press, 1982.
Bayley, Stanley T. *Biology at McMaster University: 1890–1990*. Hamilton:
McMaster Innovation Press, 2008.
Bissell, Claude T. *The Strength of a University*. Toronto: University of Toronto
Press, 1968.
Bliss, Michael. "Founding FIRA." In *Foreign Investment Review Law in Canada*.
Edited by James M. Spence and William P. Rosenfeld, 1–11. Toronto: Butter-
worths, 1984.
Bloom, Allan. *The Closing of the American Mind*. New York: Simon & Schuster,
1987.
Cassels, Alan. *Fascist Italy*. London: Routledge & Keegan Paul, 1969.
– *Fascism*, Wheeling, IL: Harlan Davidson, 1975.
Christian, William. *George Grant: a Biography*. Toronto: University of Toronto
Press, 1996.
Clark, Howard C. *Growth and Governance of Canadian Universities: An Insider's
View*. Vancouver: University of British Columbia Press, 2003.
Coward, Harold, Louis Greenspan, Alvin Lee, John Robertson, and Edward
Sanders. "Addresses on the Fortieth Anniversary of the Department of Religious
Studies." Unpublished copies in the files of the Department of Religious Studies,
McMaster University, 6 April 2006.

Crowe, Cameron M., et al. *Chemical Engineering at McMaster University: The Formative Years 1958–1982*. Milton, ON: Global Heritage Press, 2011.

Dear, M.J., J.J. Drake, and L.G. Reeds, eds. *Steel City: Hamilton and Region*. Toronto: University of Toronto Press, 1987.

Duckworth, Henry E. *One Version of the Facts: My Life in the Ivory Tower*. Winnipeg: University of Manitoba Press, 2000.

Duff, James and Robert O. Berdahl. *University Government in Canada*. Toronto: University of Toronto Press, 1966.

Francis, R.D., R. Jones, and D.B. Smith, eds. *Destinies: Canadian History Since Confederation*, 4th ed. Toronto: Harcourt, 2000.

Friedland, Martin. *The University of Toronto: A History*. Toronto: University of Toronto Press, 2002.

Harvey, Edward B. and Joseph Lennards. *Key Issues in Higher Education*. Toronto: OISE, 1973.

Horn, Michiel. *Academic Freedom in Canada: A History*. Toronto: University of Toronto Press, 1999.

– *York University*. Montreal: McGill-Queen's University Press 2009.

Humphries, Jill ed. *McMaster Stratford Shakespearean Seminar Series: 50th Anniversary*. Hamilton: Office of Alumni Advancement McMaster University, 2009.

Jackson, B.W., ed. MUFA's *First 50 Years: The Presidents' Reminiscences 1951–2001*. Hamilton: McMaster Faculty Association, 2001.

Jerkic, Sonia. "The Influence of James E. Anderson on Canadian Physical Anthropology." Accessed 15 December 2011. http://citdpress.utsc.utoronto.ca.

Johnston, Charles M. *McMaster University: Vol. 2, The Early Years in Hamilton 1930–1957*. Toronto: University of Toronto Press 1981.

– and John C. Weaver. *Student Days: Student Life at McMaster University from the 1890s to the 1980s*. Hamilton: D.G. Seldon Printing Ltd., 1986.

Johnston, Hugh. *Radical Campus: Making Simon Fraser University*. Vancouver: Douglas & McIntyre Ltd., 2005.

Jones, Frank E. "Historical Background: A Profile of the Department of Sociology." McMaster University website, Department of Sociology homepage. Accessed 10 January 2010. www. sociology.mcmaster.ca.

Kelley, Ninette and Michael Trebilcock. *The Making of the Mosaic: A History of Canadian Immigration Policy*. Toronto: University of Toronto Press, 2010.

Kerr, Clark. *The Uses of a University*. Cambridge, MA: Harvard University Press, 1964.

Kilbourn, William. "Making the Grade." *Saturday Night*, September 1988, 50–6. Copy in Lee Papers, box 1.

King, Gerald W. *Spectroscopy and Molecular Structure*. Dumfries, NC: Holt, Rinehart, and Winston, 1964.

Kirkaldy, John S., Veronica Morrison, and David Brown. *Howard Petch Compendium*. Hamilton: Department of Metallurgy and Materials Science, unpublished copy in Mills Library special collections, 2007.

– "Knowing McMaster." Unpublished copy in Lee Papers, box 2.

Macleod, Rod. *All True Things: A History of the University of Alberta, 1908–2008*. Edmonton: University of Alberta Press, 2008.

Mathews, Robin and James Steele. *The Struggle for Canadian Universities: A Dossier*. Toronto: New Press, 1969.

McKay, Alexander, G. *Classics at McMaster, 1890–2000*. Hamilton, ON: Department of Classics, McMaster University, 2000.

"McMaster in the 70s." Copy in McP, box 43.

McMaster Reports, 1956–1972. Hamilton, ON: McMaster University.

McPhedran, Norman T. *Canadian Medical Schools: Two Centuries of Medical History, 1822–1992*. Eugene, OR: Harvest House, 1993.

Monahan, Edward J. *Collective Autonomy: A History of the Council of Ontario Universities, 1962–2000*. Waterloo, ON: Wilfrid Laurier Press, 2004.

Muller, C. Barber. *The Little Medical School that Could and Did*. Unpublished typescript. Hamilton, ON: McMaster University Health Sciences Library, special collections.

Neatby, H. Blair and Donald McEown. *Creating Carleton: The Shaping of a University*. Montreal: McGill-Queen's University Press, 2002.

Newbigging, P. Lynn. "Psychology at McMaster." In *The History of Academic Psychology in Canada*. Edited by M.J. Wright and C.R. Myers, 134–41. Toronto: Hogrefe, 1982.

Norrie, Kenneth, Douglas Owram, and J.C. Herbert Emery. *A History of the Canadian Economy*, 3rd ed. Toronto: Nelson, 2002.

Owen, W.J.B. *The Prose Works of William Wordsworth*. Oxford: Clarendon Press, 1974.

Owram, Douglas. *Born at the Right Time: A History of the Baby-Boom Generation*. Toronto: University of Toronto Press, 1996.

Penny, Harry L. *From Dream to Gleam: How Professional Social Work Came to McMaster University*. Hamilton, ON: McMaster Printing Services, 1993.

Preston, Melvin A. and Helen Howard-Lock. "The Emergence of Physics Graduate Work in Canadian Universities: 1945-60." *Physics in Canada* (March–April 2000): 153–63.

Sawchuck, Larry and Susan Pfeiffer, eds. *Out of the Past*, Toronto: CITD Press, 2001. Accessed 10 January 2011, http://citdpress.utsc.utoronto.ca/osteology/pfeiffer.

Scammell, William M. *International Monetary Policy*. New York: John Wiley & Sons, 1975.

Sheffield, Edward, et al. *Systems of Higher Education: Canada*. New York: International Council for Educational Development, 1978.

Shemilt, Leslie. "A Detailed Account of Engineering Education at McMaster University," In *By Design: The Role of the Engineer in the History of the Hamilton Burlington Area*. Edited by J.W. Disher and E.A.W. Smith, 175–83. Hamilton, ON: Hamilton Engineering Interface Inc., 2001.

Spaulding, William. *Revitalizing Medical Education: McMaster Medical School the Early Years, 1965–1974*. Hamilton, ON: McMaster University Faculty of Medicine, 1991.

Wolff, Robert P. *The Ideal of the University*. Boston: Beacon Press, 1969.

Wood, Chauncey. *Chaucer and the Country of the Stars*. Princeton, NJ: Princeton University Press, 1970.

Winch, David. *Analytical Welfare Economics*. London: Harmondsworth, 1971.

Zack, Manuel, Lawrence Martin, and Alvin A. Lee. *Harry Thode: Scientist and Builder at McMaster University*. Hamilton: McMaster University Press, 2003.

Index

cooperation with other departments, 105–6, 119, 122, 303; enrolments and staffing, 89, 122, 218, 230, 327; French strike, 256, 258–62, 266–8; graduate studies, 122–5, 131, 283, 308, 383; growth, 61, 69, 96, 121; internal strife, 218, 283, 306; sit-in, 369–73; student representation, 215–19, 262, 276, 370–1

Spaulding, William, 137, 150, 189, 295–6; medical education committee, 151, 153, 156

Spectator (Hamilton), 7, 118, 161, 167, 349, 356

Spenser, Ian, 45, 159, 168

Spinks Report, 52–3, 73–4, 78, 87, 109, 112; impact of, 124, 131, 172, 174, 239, 279

SQUAL (Subcommittee on the Quality of Academic Life), 362, 364

SRA (Student Representative Assembly), 221, 227, 230, 259, 375; Beaver Food sit-in, 212, 223–5; French strike, 260, 264; Security Service, 272–4; student representation, 204, 207, 213, 275, 370–1

Stagg, Jack, 199, 225

Steele, James, 203, 216, 312

Stelco, 20, 60, 31, 35–6, 106; strikes, 221, 356

Stephenson, Bette, 321, 357–9, 380–1

Steubing, Harley, 260, 262, 264–5, 274

Stone, Ken, 221–2, 228

Stortroen, Charles, 123–4

Student Executive Council (SEC), 274

Symons Report, 313, 315

Theology, Faculty of, 98, 188, 399

Thode, Harry: advisors, relations with, 19–22, 26, 37–8, 45, 48, 147–9;

alumni, relations with, 360, 362, 368; arts, general attitudes toward, 66, 68, 72, 91–2, 94, 97, 180; MBA, misgivings concerning, 299; campus disruptions, approach to, 110–20, 220–1; campus plan, 21, 55, 138–9, 156; criticism of him, 37–8, 57–9, 158–9, 187, 241; differentiation among universities, 15–18, 41, 333, 345, 352; engineering, vision of, 31–2; faculty association, relations with, 182–3, 185, 190, 195, 324; financial squeeze, 52–3, 171–80, 251; formula funding, 18–20, 51–2; leadership manner, 24, 27, 57–64, 98–100, 133, 159, 181–2, 197, 326, 393; medical school, 133–69; nuclear reactor, 27–31, 49; personality, 12–13, 78, 181–2, 240–2, 326, 399; retirement, 237, 285, 399; scientist, status as, 26, 28, 47, 118, 181–2, 237; social sciences, ambivalence regarding, 95–105, 121, 126–8, 131–2; student representation, 207, 210, 214, 217; Thode Library, 290; Thodean ethos/paradigm, 12–23, 31, 46, 49, 54–5, 64, 83–91, 133, 399; university government, 183–93. *See also* chapters 1–8; board of governors; Bourns, Arthur; Gilmour, George; IMR; Kirkaldy, Jack; PBAC; Petch, Harold; Plan for McMaster; Ontario, Province of; senate; Westdale

Thompson, Barry, 270, 274, 276

Thorolfson, Frank, 70

Threlkeld, Stephen, 58, 287, 376

Tiger-Cats, 130, 356

Tomlinson, Richard, 27, 29, 43, 47, 177

Torrance, George, 39